Pine Barrens:
Ecosystem and Landscape

Edited by
Richard T. T. Forman

Department of Botany
Rutgers University
New Brunswick, New Jersey

ACADEMIC PRESS   New York   San Francisco   London   1979

A Subsidiary of Harcourt Brace Jovanovich, Publishers

ACADEMIC PRESS, INC.
111 Fifth Avenue, New York, New York 10003

United Kingdom Edition published by
ACADEMIC PRESS, INC. (LONDON) LTD.
24/28 Oval Road, London NW1   7DX

Library of Congress Cataloging in Publication Data
Main entry under title:

Pine barrens : ecosystem and landscape.

    Includes bibliographies.
    1. Ecology––New Jersey––Pine Barrens. 2. Pine
Barrens. I. Forman, Richard T. T.
QH105.N5P56   574.5'264   79–9849
ISBN 0–12–263450–0

PRINTED IN THE UNITED STATES OF AMERICA

79 80 81 82   9 8 7 6 5 4 3 2 1

Editorial
Steering Committee

Throughout the preparation of this volume an Editorial Steering Committee long experienced in pine barrens research assisted the Editor. Members (listed below) helped select topics and authors, review manuscripts, provide information, and a breadth of perspective.

SILAS LITTLE Principal Silviculturalist, U.S. Forest Service, Northeastern Forest Experiment Station, Pennington, New Jersey 08534

JACK McCORMICK* President, Jack McCormick Associates, WAPORA Inc., 6900 Wisconsin Ave. NW, Washington, D.C. 20015

PAUL G. PEARSON Professor of Zoology and Acting President, Rutgers University, New Brunswick, New Jersey 08903

WILLIAM A. REINERS Professor of Biological Sciences, Dartmouth College, Hanover, New Hampshire 03755

JOHN C. F. TEDROW Professor of Soils and Crops, Rutgers University, New Brunswick, New Jersey 08903

GEORGE M. WOODWELL Director, The Ecosystems Center, Marine Biological Laboratory, Woods Hole, Massachusetts 02543

*Deceased.

Sponsors

New Jersey Academy of Science*: a nonprofit organization of professionals and others interested in science, affiliated with the American Association for the Advancement of Science, with the objective of improving the quality and awareness of science in New Jersey.

OFFICERS OF THE NEW JERSEY ACADEMY OF SCIENCE

President	*Executive Secretary*
Ralph E. Good	M. Lelyn Branin
Past President	*Recording Secretary*
James W. Green	Mary A. Leck
President-Elect	*Treasurer*
Albert F. Eble	James A. Quinn

William L. Hutcheson Memorial Forest†: a research facility under the care of Rutgers University dedicated to the protection of a primeval woods, and the fostering of research in ecology, botany, and related disciplines.

OFFICERS OF THE WILLIAM L. HUTCHESON MEMORIAL FOREST

Director	*Advisory Committee*	
Richard T. T. Forman	James E. Gunckel	Edmund W. Stiles
Honorary Advisors to the Director	Charles F. Leck	Benjamin B. Stout
Helen Foot Buell	James A. Quinn	Herbert T. Streu
John A. Small (Deceased)	Nathan M. Reiss	John C. F. Tedrow

*Hill Center, Rutgers University, New Brunswick, New Jersey 08903.
†Department of Botany, Rutgers University, New Brunswick, New Jersey 08903.

Contents

PART II   GEOLOGY AND SOILS

3 GEOLOGY OF THE PINE BARRENS OF NEW JERSEY

Edward C. Rhodehamel

4 DEVELOPMENT OF PINE BARRENS SOILS

John C. F. Tedrow

5 SOIL SERIES OF THE PINE BARRENS

Marco L. Markley

6 MINERALOGY OF PINE BARRENS SOILS

Lowell A. Douglas and John J. Trela

PART III   CLIMATE, WATER, AND AQUATIC ECOSYSTEMS

7   CLIMATE AND MICROCLIMATE OF THE NEW JERSEY PINE BARRENS

A. Vaughn Havens

8   FLUXES OF WATER AND ENERGY THROUGH THE PINE BARRENS ECOSYSTEMS

John Thomas Ballard

9   HYDROLOGY OF THE NEW JERSEY PINE BARRENS

Edward C. Rhodehamel

10 STREAMS AND LAKES IN THE PINE BARRENS

Ruth Patrick, Barbara Matson, and Lee Anderson

11 NUTRIENT AND HYDROLOGICAL EFFECTS OF THE PINE BARRENS ON NEIGHBORING ESTUARIES

James B. Durand

PART IV   VEGETATION PATTERNS

12 VEGETATIONAL HISTORY OF THE PINE BARRENS

Calvin J. Heusser

13 THE VEGETATION OF THE NEW JERSEY PINE BARRENS

Jack McCormick

14 VEGETATION OF THE NEW JERSEY PINE BARRENS: A PHYTOSOCIOLOGICAL CLASSIFICATION

Hans Olsson

15 VEGETATIONAL GRADIENTS OF THE PINE PLAINS AND BARRENS OF LONG ISLAND, NEW YORK

Linda S. Olsvig, John F. Cryan, and Robert H. Whittaker

16 THE PINE BARREN PLAINS

Ralph E. Good, Norma F. Good, and John W. Andresen

17 FIRE AND PLANT SUCCESSION IN THE NEW JERSEY PINE BARRENS

Silas Little

21   COMMON VASCULAR PLANTS OF THE PINE BARRENS

Wayne R. Ferren, Jr., John W. Braxton, and Louis Hand

22   ENDANGERED, THREATENED, AND RARE VASCULAR PLANTS OF THE PINE BARRENS AND THEIR BIOGEOGRAPHY

David E. Fairbrothers

26   BIRDS OF THE PINE BARRENS

Charles F. Leck

33 **THE PINE BARRENS OF NEW JERSEY: AN ECOLOGICAL MOSAIC**

Richard T. T. Forman

List of Contributors

Numbers in parentheses indicate the pages on which the authors' contributions begin.

LEE ANDERSON (169), Academy of Natural Sciences, Nineteenth and the Parkway, Philadelphia, Pennsylvania 19103

JOHN W. ANDRESEN (283), Faculty of Forestry and Landscape Architecture, University of Toronto, Toronto, Ontario, Canada

JAMES E. APPLEGATE (25), Department of Horticulture and Forestry, Cook College, Rutgers University, New Brunswick, New Jersey 08903

JOHN THOMAS BALLARD* (133), Biology Department, Brookhaven National Laboratory, Upton, New York 11973

HOWARD P. BOYD (505), Oak Shade Road, Tabernacle RD7, Vincentown, New Jersey 08088

JOHN W. BRAXTON (373), Department of Botany, Rutgers University, New Brunswick, New Jersey 08903

HELEN FOOT BUELL (425), Box 234, Middlebush, New Jersey 08873

ROGER CONANT (467), Department of Biology, University of New Mexico, Albuquerque, New Mexico 87131

JOHN F. CRYAN† (265), Department of Entomology, Cornell University, Ithaca, New York 14853

DANIEL L. DINDAL (527), College of Environmental Science and Forestry, State University of New York, Syracuse, New York 13210

LOWELL A. DOUGLAS (95), Department of Soils and Crops, Rutgers University, New Brunswick, New Jersey 08903

JAMES B. DURAND (195), Department of Biology, Rutgers University, Camden, New Jersey 08102

DAVID E. FAIRBROTHERS (395), Department of Botany, Rutgers University, New Brunswick, New Jersey 08903

WAYNE R. FERREN, JR.‡ (373), Botany Department, Academy of Natural Sciences, Philadelphia, Pennsylvania 19103

RICHARD T. T. FORMAN (xxxv, 407, 569), Department of Botany, Rutgers University, New Brunswick, New Jersey 08903

RALPH E. GOOD (283), Department of Biology, Rutgers University, Camden, New Jersey 08102

NORMA F. GOOD (283), Bioscience Department Service, Philadelphia, Pennsylvania 19103

*Present address: R.R. 2, Box 9A, Wading River, New York 11792

†Present address: The Earth and Space Museum, State University of New York, Stony Brook, New York 11794

‡Present address: Department of Biological Sciences, University of California, Santa Barbara, California 93106

LOUIS HAND (373), Department of Botany, Vincentown, New Jersey 08088

ROBERT W. HASTINGS (489), Department of Biology, Rutgers University, Camden, New Jersey 08102

A. VAUGHN HAVENS (113), Department of Meteorology and Physical Oceanography, Cook College, Rutgers University, New Brunswick, New Jersey 08903

CALVIN J. HEUSSER (213), Department of Biology, New York University, New York, New York 10003

CHARLES F. LECK (457), Department of Zoology, Rutgers University, New Brunswick, New Jersey 08903

F. THOMAS LEDIG (347), School of Forestry and Environmental Studies, Yale University, New Haven, Connecticut 06511

SILAS LITTLE (25, 297, 347), Northeastern Forest Experiment Station, U.S.D.A. Forest Service, Pennington, New Jersey 08534

JACK McCORMICK* (xxxv, 229), Jack McCormick Associates, WAPORA, Inc., 6900 Wisconsin Avenue NW, Washington, D.C. 20015

MARCO L. MARKLEY (81), U.S. Soil Conservation Service, 1370 Hamilton Street, Somerset, New Jersey 08873

PHILIP E. MARUCCI (25, 505), Cranberry and Blueberry Research Center, Rutgers University, Chatsworth, New Jersey 08019

BARBARA MATSON (169), Academy of Natural Sciences, Nineteenth and the Parkway, Philadelphia, Pennsylvania 19103

EDWIN T. MOUL (425), 42 F. R. Lillie Road, Woods Hole, Massachusetts 02543

HANS OLSSON (245), Department of Plant Ecology, University of Lund, Ostra Vallgatan 14, S-22361 Lund, Sweden

LINDA S. OLSVIG (265), Ecology and Systematics, Cornell University, Ithaca, New York 14853

RUTH PATRICK (169), Academy of Natural Sciences, Nineteenth and the Parkway, Philadelphia, Pennsylvania 19103

WILLIAM A. REINERS (557), Department of Biological Sciences, Dartmouth College, Hanover, New Hampshire 03755

EDWARD C. RHODEHAMEL (39, 147), U.S. Geological Survey, National Center, Reston, Virginia 22092

EDMUND W. STILES (541), Department of Zoology, Rutgers University, New Brunswick, New Jersey 08903

JOHN C. F. TEDROW (61), Department of Soils and Crops, Cook College, Rutgers University, New Brunswick, New Jersey 08903

JOHN J. TRELA (95), Department of Soils and Crops, Rutgers University, New Brunswick, New Jersey 08903

PETER O. WACKER (3), Department of Geography, Rutgers University, New Brunswick, New Jersey 08903

ROBERT H. WHITTAKER (265, 315), Ecology and Systematics, Cornell University, Ithaca, New York 14853

LEONARD J. WOLGAST (443), Department of Horticulture and Forestry, Cook College, Rutgers University, New Brunswick, New Jersey 08903

GEORGE M. WOODWELL (333), The Ecosystems Center, Marine Biological Laboratory, Woods Hole, Massachusetts 02543

*Deceased.

Preface

Bog iron accumulating in tea-colored streams, a tiny Pine Barrens tree frog announcing its domain, fires sweeping briskly between streams, ships laden with cedar gliding out of rivers, dwarf forests reaching to shoulder height, silent cries of wolves long gone, nutrients flowing out to oysters and fish, spruce forests thriving during colder periods, a gargantuan lake resting in the sands, and a wilderness absorbing quiet recreation in the shadow of American cities—such events have inspired this book. Some we can see and some we can imagine. This volume integrates such phenomena into ecological systems (ecosystems). It describes and explores how a landscape, indeed a mosaic of interrelated ecosystems, such as the Pine Barrens of New Jersey (United States) works. It invites the reader to explore other possible relationships and thus fill the gaps in our knowledge. In short, the book asks questions, answers questions, and raises further questions.

Pine barrens, the ecosystem or vegetation type, has sandy or shallow soil with frequent fire, high acidity and scarce nutrients, and abundant heaths and crooked pines; Pine Barrens, the landscape, adds streams and swamps and other types to form the intertwined mosaic.

People in the landscape provide the initial focus. From Indian activities and initial European perceptions of the land, the reader explores settlement, lumbering, fuelwood and charcoal, iron and glassworks, farming and livestock, and real estate development. Today, hunting for wildlife, blueberry and cranberry agriculture, forestry and forest products continue.

Geology and Soils are portrayed through time and space. Sandy deposits, one on the other, are described sequentially, followed by the geographic distribution of geologic formations and soil types with their ecologically important characteristics. Mechanisms of soil development and dynamic mineralogical patterns provide a penetrating perspective of soil.

Climate, Water, and Aquatic Ecosystems follow, with water movement a common theme. The meteorologic conditions (both climatic and microclimatic), the hydrology of ground and surface water, a regional hydrologic budget, heat energy and evapotranspiration, relationships between uplands and lowlands, stream chemistry and biology, and, finally, variations in water and nutrient flows affecting the surrounding estuary are presented.

Vegetation Patterns traces the history of vegetation starting before the Ice Age. Specialists analyze vegetation using different approaches: community types, community classification according to a European method, and gradient analysis. The dwarf Pine Plains, the dynamic processes of succession and fire, and nutrient relationships of leaky ecosystems are analyzed. Finally, vegetation relationships with similar vegetation elsewhere are explored.

Plants of the Pine Barrens are briefly described or listed to aid the reader when species are mentioned, and when the book is used in the field. Pitch pine, common vascular plants, rare and endangered vascular plants, common bryophytes and lichens, and algae are explored.

Animals and Animal Communities of the Pine Barrens include mammals, common birds, reptiles and amphibians, fish, and common arthropods. Vertebrate communities and soil microcommunities illustrate community relationships.

The special ecological, botanical, and zoological characteristics and the remarkable geologic, hydrologic, and soil phenomena of the Pine Barrens have piqued the curiosity of many, and continue to draw visitors from all continents. By describing these characteristics in the context of ecosystem interrelations, I hope a better understanding of what is really unique and special, and why, will evolve.

Several important books on Pine Barrens provide a solid background. The annual reports of the New Jersey Geological Survey from the late nineteenth and early twentieth centuries contain several major works of ecological significance, including those of the noted botanist Nathaniel Lord Britton cataloguing the plants of New Jersey,[1,2] and America's early foresters and conservationists Gifford Pinchot, John Gifford, and others describing the forests of New Jersey.[3,4] From 1908 through 1911 the naturalist Witmer Stone published treatises on mammals, birds, and plants[5,6,7] which even today remain standard manuals. Shortly thereafter, the plant geographer and perhaps the first of the major ecologists of eastern North America, John W. Harshberger, published an ecological vegetation analysis of the Pine Barrens.[8] In the 1960's H. C. Beck and John McPhee movingly portrayed the people of the Pine Barrens as they interact with one

[1]Britton, N. L. (1881). "A preliminary catalogue of the flora of New Jersey." *N. J. Geol. Surv.* pp. 1–233.

[2]Britton, N. L. (1889). "Catalogue of plants found in New Jersey." *N. J. Geol. Surv., Final Rept. State Geol.* **2**, 25–642.

[3]Pinchot, G. (1899). "A study of forest fires and wood production in southern New Jersey." *N. J. Geol. Surv., Ann. Rept. State Geol. for 1898* (Appendix). pp. 1–102.

[4]Gifford, J. (1900). "State reports on the forestal conditions and silvicultural prospects of the Coastal Plain of New Jersey, with remarks in reference to other regions and kindred subjects." *N. J. Geol. Surv., Ann. Rept. State Geol. for 1899*, Rept. on Forests. pp. 233–318.

[5]Stone, W. (1908). "The mammals of New Jersey." *N. J. State Mus. Ann. Rept. for 1907*. pp. 33–110.

[6]Stone, W. (1909). "The birds of New Jersey." *N. J. State Mus. Ann. Rept. for 1908*. pp. 11–347.

[7]Stone, W. (1911). "The plants of southern New Jersey, with especial reference to the flora of the Pine Barrens and the geographic distribution of the species." *N. J. State Mus. Ann. Rept. for 1910*. pp. 23–828.

[8]Harshberger, J. W. (1916). "The Vegetation of the New Jersey Pine-barrens. An Ecological Investigation." Christopher Sower Co., Philadelphia, Pennsylvania. 329 pp.

another and with their environment.[9,10,11] Jack McCormick then published a useful preliminary ecological inventory of the Pine Barrens, summarizing vegetation characteristics and certain animals and plants of biogeographic interest.[12] Numerous original articles underlie our understanding of the ecology of the Pine Barrens. Together these constitute an exceptionally diverse and scattered literature, written by a remarkable proportion of well-known scientists in ecologically related fields, whose interest was stimulated by the Pine Barrens.

A picture of pine barrens as an ecosystem emerges which complements and enriches the pioneering work on a New York oak-pine forest by George M. Woodwell and colleagues. A further objective here is the portrayal of an ecological mosaic. In this, species, energy, and nutrients are distributed in patches of varying sizes and shapes, and move among the patches. The scale is a landscape, that is, the entire Pine Barrens. Components, such as geologic formations, soil, water, vegetation, and animal communities, also form patches, which are sometimes spatially congruous. Interactions among patches are frequent. Furthermore, the presence and distribution of patches themselves change with forces such as soil development, succession, fire, pest outbreaks, and human activities. The dynamics of the mosaic as a whole integrates the structure, interactions, and change of individual patches. Understanding the principles of ecological mosaics will not be easy as they draw upon theory from ecosystem structure and function, island biogeography, scale, patchiness, and evolution. However, the concept promises to become an important challenge in ecological theory. Too, the focus on patches of species, energy and nutrients in the landscape, and their movement between patches, has important consequences in management of the global landscape.

Time as a perspective recurs through the book. We see the Pine Barrens today in terms of certain animals, plants, vegetation, and stream characteristics as described herein. But when our grandparents were about our age, John Harshberger tells us,[8] "... it is rare to find trees as tall as 15 meters (50 feet). The tree as usually found ranges in height from 6 to 12 meters (20 to 40 feet)." His map also shows extensive cultivated areas and savannas in the Pine Barrens. Today those larger tree sizes might be almost doubled, cultivated areas are very limited in extent, and savannas have largely disappeared. We wonder what the area was like eons ago, or centuries ago. Too, we wonder how much it changes in our lifetime, or simply from year to year. Inevitably we wonder what it will be like in the future. Partial answers are suggested as the book describes several natural processes of change.

Today in the nearly 550 thousand hectare (1.4 million acre) Pine Barrens region we see two large military bases, Fort Dix and Lakehurst Naval Station; five large state

[9]Beck, H. C. (1961). "Forgotten Towns of Southern New Jersey." Rutgers Univ. Press, New Brunswick, New Jersey. 278 pp.

[10]Beck, H. C. (1963). "More Forgotten Towns of Southern New Jersey." Rutgers Univ. Press, New Brunswick, New Jersey. 338 pp.

[11]McPhee, J. (1967). "The Pine Barrens." Ballantine Books, New York. 173 pp.

[12]McCormick, J. (1970). "The Pine Barrens: A preliminary ecological inventory." *N. J. State Mus. Res. Rept. 2*, Trenton, New Jersey. 103 pp.

forests, Wharton, Lebanon, Bass River, Belleplain, and Penn; and eight or more large fish and wildlife management areas. There is a relatively low density of homes and towns and a high density of roads. Current human impacts on the Pine Barrens include sand and gravel extraction, military activities, forestry, collecting plants and animals, hunting, cranberry and blueberry growing, air pollution from the Philadelphia–Camden region and elsewhere, wildfire, fire prevention, prescribed burning, and recreational activities. Past human impacts have included several additional major activities as described herein. Future human impacts, of course, are to be determined by the reader and others. A list of commonly discussed possibilities suggests the magnitude of such impacts: a major jet airport for the New York–Philadelphia metropolitan areas, preservation *in toto,* extensive housing and industrial development, pumping out the fresh water from the sands for surrounding towns and cities, letting wildfires burn as they did before fire prevention techniques were introduced, prescribe burn extensive areas with light surface fires, and widespread on-shore development to support off-shore oil drilling. This volume is thus also a contribution to the future of the specific region, and should permit a better understanding of the environmental impacts of various human activities in the Pine Barrens.

The ancient philosophers' four basic elements, earth, air, fire, and water, seem particularly apropos in the Pine Barrens environment. All are in abundance, and the biological mantle in places seems tenuous indeed. Yet it is there, and should be appreciated and studied for that reason alone.

The landscape though is viewed from many perspectives. To some the Pine Barrens are a series of resources; to others, a barren or waste land, a wilderness in megalopolis, a home and a job, an aesthetic experience, a unique ecological area, or a refreshment of the soul. Viewed from many of these perspectives, the Pine Barrens cry out for preservation—preservation from human misuse. Today preservation will come through legislation, pushed by many with diverse interests. Aldo Leopold, writing from a similar sandy pine area in "A Sand County Almanac,"[13] showed us the need for a land ethic, a self-imposed limitation on the misuse of land and its ecosystems. Preservation in the Pine Barrens will be easier with both the land ethic at work and the carefully documented special ecological characteristics. However time is of essence; tomorrow it may be more difficult. The spreading land ethic is clearly confronting an increasing human density with a highly uncertain outcome.

What should be preserved in the Pine Barrens? Individual authors often briefly express their own conclusions regarding land use. However, the book as a whole, in lieu of proposing land use strategies, presents in as objective a manner as possible known ecological information on the Pine Barrens. It calls on the reader and others to make decisions and take action with as solid an ecological foundation and as broad a perspective as possible.

Whether used for planning and managing purposes, or as a model ecological mosaic for teaching, or to stimulate integrated landscape studies of other regions, the book presents ecological ideas and should stimulate further enquiry. Such enquiry led

---

[13]Leopold, A. (1949). "A Sand County Almanac." Oxford Univ. Press, New York. 226 pp.

Murray F. Buell to love the region and study its botany and ecology. We wrote the book for Murray.

Major historical and other events have occurred in and around the Pine Barrens. Mastodons, mammoths, elephants, horses, reindeer, musk-oxen, and bison roamed New Jersey probably at least as late as the end of the Ice Age some 10,000 years ago.[14,15] Presumably early hunters, Paleo-Indian, having crossed the continent from Asia, were also there at the time. When Europeans landed on the shores and settled the area, Leni-Lenape Indians planted crops and established trails through the Pine Barrens. Native turkeys, bears, and wolves raised young among the pines and cedars, and thrived on a rich diet of fruits and animals.

Henry Hudson, an Englishman, sailed a Dutch ship along the ocean shore and landed just north of the Pine Barrens in 1609. Dutch and, to a lesser extent, Swedish settlers soon arrived and populated areas north and west of the Pine Barrens. In 1664 an English fleet captured New Amsterdam (naming it New York) and New Jersey to the southwest. The Pine Barrens were divided by a line running NNW from Little Egg Harbor, separating East Jersey from West Jersey, though most of the region was in West Jersey. William Penn and several prominent Quakers and associates were able to purchase West Jersey in 1674 for £1000 and East Jersey in 1682 for £34,000[16] to erect a colony based on religious freedom following severe persecution in England and New England. This colony, antedating Pennsylvania by several years, developed a first constitution for West New Jersey 300 years ago (a century before the United States Constitution). "Drafted in March, 1677, the Concessions even today are striking for their liberal humane provisions and deserve to be studied by all who are interested in the roots of American liberty."[16] Settlements through the Pine Barrens began to develop, many of which are pleasant small towns today.[8,9,10,11,17]

In 1702 Queen Anne formally fused the east and west portions of New Jersey into a Royal Colony and, though immigrants from many European nations arrived during the eighteenth century, the area remained overwhelmingly English. In the mid-eighteenth century Princeton and Rutgers universities were founded nearby; slaveholdings were already widely disapproved (a century before the Civil War), particularly through the leadership of John Woolman of nearby Mt. Holly; and iron furnaces in the Pine Barrens were active and were later to play a role in supplying colonial forces during the American Revolution. In the 1770's and 1780's General George Washington spent three winters with his army in New Jersey during its seven years of warfare. Across the Delaware River in Philadelphia the Continental Congress with John Adams, Benjamin

---

[14]Hay, O. P. (1923). "The Pleistocene of North America and Its Vertebrated Animals from the States East of the Mississippi and from the Canadian Provinces East of Longitude 95°." Carnegie Inst. Wash. Publ. No. 322, Washington, D.C. 499 pp.

[15]Jepsen, G. L. (1960). "A New Jersey mastodon." *N. J. State Mus. Bull.* **6,** 1–20.

[16]McCormick, R. P. (1964). "New Jersey from Colony to State 1609–1789." Rutgers Univ. Press, New Brunswick, New Jersey. 191 pp.

[17]McMahon, W. (1973). "South Jersey Towns: History and Legend." Rutgers Univ. Press, New Brunswick, New Jersey. 382 pp.

Franklin, Thomas Jefferson, Richard Stockton, John Witherspoon, and representatives of colonies from New Hampshire to Georgia agreed on a Declaration of Independence. As the third signer of the Constitution in 1787, New Jersey became a state, with one-quarter of its land pine barrens. Today it is the most densely populated American state, and exceeds the density of all European nations.

The idea for this book developed from discussions of Rutgers University botanists and ecologists at the 1975 American Institute of Biological Science meetings, and from interest generated by the 1976 annual New Jersey Academy of Science meeting which focused on the Pine Barrens. The support of the William L. Hutcheson Memorial Forest Advisory Committee was also important. I agreed to spearhead the development of the volume, and first invited and received the support of six leading experts on the Pine Barrens, who served as an Editorial Steering Committee. This group worked with me through successive drafts of an outline, selecting topics and potential authors with established backgrounds and experience. All articles received two or more outside reviews and were revised accordingly. The diversity of approaches and sometimes contrasting results were retained to achieve better perspective. The articles illustrate the rich legacy of areas of ecological theory: biogeography, ecosystems, evolutionary ecology, paleoecology, population ecology, and community ecology. They also cover physical environment, plant and animal groups, and applied or human ecology. To these we might add landscape or ecological mosaic ecology. The concluding summary and synthesis are conceptual rather than informational in tone. I selected ideas which when interrelated and mixed with a bit of solid evidence not only elucidate pine barrens but suggest the richness in ecological frontiers awaiting.

A few unrelated items are introduced here to clarify usages in the text. The term pine barrens is capitalized when referring to the extensive Pine Barrens landscape of southern New Jersey, and lower cased when referring to an ecosystem or vegetation type which is found widely in eastern North America and has analogues in several continents. These two perspectives, ecosystem and landscape, are convergent when the information available is limited. The ecosystem concept focuses not only on the distribution and flows of energy and nutrients, but on controls exerted by the environment and the diverse linkages among species. Though the volume concentrates on the Pine Barrens of New Jersey, the most studied pine barrens, a few articles deal primarily with the pine barrens on the young glacial deposits of Long Island, New York, which differ slightly from the New Jersey Pine Barrens. These articles treat topics not well known in the New Jersey Barrens, and provide an important perspective. Productivity is discussed relatively infrequently in this volume, but considerable published information is available on these oak-pine areas of Long Island. Localities mentioned in the volume are identified in the Introduction following the Preface. In the section on Geology and Soils, in which two major soil nomenclature systems are used, authors have used the system of their preference, but with equivalent names summarized at the outset. Finally, in the sections on Plants and Animals and Animal Communities, different groups of organisms are presented in markedly different ways, depending on our knowledge of the group and the expected use of the information. In most cases, the author introduces the reader to the common species present and provides an ecological perspective.

This volume is for the ecologist, botanist, geologist, soil scientist, zoologist, hydrologist, limnologist, engineer, and scientist dealing with these ideas. It is also for the planner, decision-maker, and manager who may largely determine the future of a region. And it is written for the educated layman, the environmentalist, and the nature club member who, like the authors, can thoroughly enjoy pine barrens. Technical language has been minimized. Few readers will use every term commonly, but all will find the bulk of the book readily understandable, and a goldmine of information and ideas. The book is a reference and a text, but most importantly presents information in a usable form for a wide range of individuals.

No chapter stands alone in the book. Each is enriched by the diverse perspectives of other chapters. The power, and the pleasure, are to explore the perspectives and discover the links.

Richard T. T. Forman

Acknowledgments

I warmly and humbly thank the 43 authors of this book for their manifest scholarship and for their patience as I tried to weave their patterns into a picture; the 78 reviewers of these articles, to whom every reader owes a debt of gratitude; H. Chandlee Forman and the late Caroline Lippincott Forman who introduced me to the variety of southern New Jersey; William C. Denison and John M. Fogg, Jr., who sparked an interest in Pine Barrens ecology; James W. Green and Leland G. Merrill who aided in the realization of this book; the Council of the New Jersey Academy of Science and the William L. Hutcheson Memorial Forest Advisory Committee for sponsorship; the Philadelphia Botanical Club for funds toward publication of the color plate; Michel Godron and the Centre d'Études Phytosociologiques et Écologiques Louis Emberger, Montpellier, France for support, a milieu for writing, and many courtesies; Keith A. Clay and Katherine Semple for bibliographic aid; Kemble Widmer for aid in mapping and for geological information; Ralph E. Good and Norma F. Good for contributing an independent critical review of essentially the entire manuscript; David E. Fairbrothers, Paul G. Pearson, and Benjamin B. Stout for frequent, sage advice during the preparation of the book; Helen F. Buell and the late Murray F. Buell who took me to the Pine Barrens repeatedly and who explained them and had me feel them; Silas Little, Jack McCormick, Paul G. Pearson, William A. Reiners, John C. F. Tedrow, and George M. Woodwell who, as the Editorial Steering Committee, provided fantastic support and a stream of ideas for the book; and Barbara Lee Forman, Sabrina M. Forman, Adrian W. Forman, and Brent C. Forman who for a long time have shared me with the immersion and excitement in this book.

Richard T. T. Forman

Murray Fife Buell (1905-1975)

Born October 6, 1905 in New Haven, Connecticut, Murray Buell received an A.B. from Cornell in 1930, an A.M. in 1934 and a Ph.D. in 1935 from the University of Minnesota. In 1932 he married Helen Foot, who also has a Ph.D. from Minnesota. They had two children, Sally and Peter.

Dr. Buell began his distinguished teaching career at North Carolina State College. He came to Rutgers in 1946, was appointed a full professor in 1956, and during most summers taught at the University of Minnesota Lake Itasca Biology Sessions. Dr. Buell retired from his professorship at Rutgers in 1971, and then spent successive semesters teaching at the University of Minnesota, Yale University, the University of Georgia, the University of Arizona, the University of Montana, Colorado State University, and the University of California at Santa Barbara.

Murray Fife Buell died in the New Jersey Pine Barrens on July 3, 1975 while engaged in a research project to aid land-use policy planning. Murray knew the Pine Barrens well, for during his long association with Rutgers University he and his students made extensive studies of the structure and ecological dynamics of the area's vegetation. While acknowledging the value of this regional research, the authors in dedicating this book to Murray Fife Buell pay further respect to a scholar and a teacher whose influence on ecology was of far-reaching national scope.

Described well as a gentle, warm, and patient man, Murray Buell at the same time was a rigorously disciplined scholar. Through his efforts and those of his wife, Dr. Helen Foot Buell, many promising young students were stimulated to study ecology, urged to achieve academic excellence, and aided in pursuit of careers in this field. Among his scientific peers Dr. Buell strove vigorously and effectively to improve the activities of the professional societies which he served in many capacities, including the presidency of the Ecological Society of America, the Torrey Botanical Club, and the New Jersey Academy of Science. These contributions, his wide-ranging ecological research, and his great influence on ecology as a teacher have received national recognition; the Ecological Society of America named Murray Fife Buell "Eminent Ecologist for 1970."

By their dedication, the authors honor a forward-looking man who, when organizing ecology programs at Rutgers almost three decades ago, recognized that for ecological studies to be of value, they must encompass many scholarly disciplines, a need well illustrated by the collective authorship of this book on the Pine Barrens. They honor as well a scientist, who, from the start of his career to the last day of his life, eagerly contributed his time and energy to public problems in which his special knowledge could help to make the total environment around him a better place for all.

In today's complex world, integrated approaches to problem-solving are desperately needed. Of equal necessity is the establishment of more and stronger interconnections, not only among members of the scientific community, but between them and the decision-makers in public and private institutions as well. To this end, the insight and accomplishments of Murray Fife Buell provide us an outstanding example to follow.

Beryl Robichaud
McGraw-Hill, Inc.
1221 Avenue of the Americas
New York, New York 10020.

Introduction: Location and Boundaries of the New Jersey Pine Barrens

JACK McCORMICK and RICHARD T. T. FORMAN

Vegetation known as pine barrens is scattered throughout northeastern United States and beyond. On a map of vegetation of the United States (Küchler 1970) pine barrens areas are generally depicted as Northeastern oak–pine forests. The largest and most uniform area of such vegetation, however, is the 550,000 hectare (1.4 million acre) region known as the Pine Barrens of New Jersey. This extensive level region appears in Fig. 1 as a relatively undeveloped "wilderness" near the heart of the major Washington-to-Boston metropolitan corridor of North America. Centered at about 39°40′N latutide, 74°40′W longitude, the Pine Barrens lie just south of New York City and east of Philadelphia. The pressures emanating from these major metropolitan areas have had diverse and significant effects on the Pine Barrens.

Eastward, the Pine Barrens generally are bounded by a narrow strip of salt marsh along bays that connect to the Atlantic Ocean. On their other margins, the Pine Barrens are bounded by farmlands and deciduous forests. Two large Pine Barrens outliers are separated by about 15 km (10 miles) from the main body of the region. The Spotswood outlier is found in Middlesex County to the north, and the Alloway outlier in Salem County to the southwest.

The physiographic provinces of New Jersey (Fig. 2), which reflect diverse geological events and times, aid in interpreting the distribution of the Pine Barrens. The hilly to mountainous area of northwestern New Jersey is underlain by very old rocks of pre-Cambrian and Paleozoic age. The Piedmont area, mainly underlain by red shale of Triassic age, runs through central New Jersey. Immediately south of the Piedmont, the relatively narrow Inner Coastal Plain is composed of unconsolidated gravel, sand, and clay, mainly of Cretaceous age. To the south and east of this is the Outer Coastal Plain, which is underlain by more recent unconsolidated gravel and sand; the Pine Barrens are restricted almost entirely to this Outer Coastal Plain. The Pine Barrens area is unglaciated, although the last Pleistocene glacial advance stopped only about 30 km (20 miles) north of the present main Pine Barrens area.

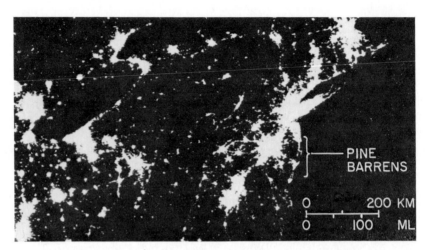

Fig. 1.   Satellite photograph of northeastern United States showing lighted areas at night. Homogeneous black area on right is Atlantic Ocean. Major metropolitan regions are seen as large white areas. Upper left, Toronto (Canada) and Buffalo along shores of two Great Lakes; left edge, Detroit; left bottom corner, Cincinnati; bottom center, Washington–Baltimore as basically a single area; northeastward is Philadelphia; continuing northeastward is New York–northern New Jersey with Long Island projecting eastward and Connecticut–Springfield, Massachusetts projecting northeastward; in upper right the Boston–Providence region. New Jersey Pine Barrens are seen mainly as a black area east of Philadelphia and separated from the ocean by a string of shore communities, the largest of which is Atlantic City. Official U.S. Air Force photograph; the aid of F. H. Bormann and W. A. Reiners is gratefully acknowledged.

Not surprisingly, delimitations of the boundaries of the Pine Barrens have varied over the years. Gordon (1834) recognized a relationship between the geological structure and the distribution of the Pine Barrens when he described "an immense sandy plain, scarce broken by an inequality, and originally covered by a pine and shrub-oak forest" that was bounded by a "strip of loam" (the Inner Coastal Plain) on the west and the coastal marshlands on the east.

The first attempt to map the floristic zones of New Jersey was by Hollick (1899), who recognized a deciduous forest in northern New Jersey, including the Piedmont and Inner Coastal Plain, and a coniferous forest in the Outer Coastal Plain. Delimited between the two was mixed forest, which was relatively narrow along the northern half of the boundary, but which progressively widened to the west and south down to Cumberland County. The Spotswood and Alloway areas were designated as mainly forested, but were within Hollick's deciduous forest zone. On this map, most of the northeastern and southwestern portions of today's Pine Barrens area were shown as only 40–80% forested, with most of the remaining Pine Barrens 80–100% forested. Coniferous forest apparently extended south, nearly reaching the tip of the Cape May peninsula. Hollick, a geologist based in New Brunswick, probably was quite familiar with the northern portion of the Coastal Plain, where the vegetation and geological

Fig. 2. Outline map of the Pine Barrens from W. Stone (1911). Heavy solid line surrounds Pine Barrens of southern New Jersey. Elevations of high points in the Pine Barrens and boundaries of physiographic provinces added: Piedmont northwest of dotted line; Inner Coastal Plain northwest of dashed line; Outer Coastal Plain southeast of dashed line.

boundaries today coincide reasonably well. At the end of the nineteenth century travel in southern New Jersey was difficult, and the vegetation boundaries there probably were not as well known.

Witmer Stone (1911), a Philadelphia zoologist and naturalist, published an outline map of the Pine Barrens in 1911 (Fig. 2). The Spotswood and Alloway outliers were absent, pine barrens were not recognized separately in the Cape May peninsula, and to the southwest the boundary passed near Millville and Malaga. Stone made frequent visits to Medford, Cape May, and other localities in the southern portion of the Pine Barrens, and traveled by train, boat, buggy, and on foot. The boundaries designated by Stone probably are based on the distributions of numerous plant species, because the map accompanied his detailed treatise on the plants of southern New Jersey. His approach may be considered floristic, in contrast with that of Hollick, who apparently used the persistence of leaves of prominent trees as the basis for division. This criterion probably was of particular importance in Cape May and Cumberland counties, where many more southern, often evergreen species grow. In reference to Stone's map, Norman Taylor (1912), a noted botanist of the day, commented: "The true limits of the pine-barrens are perhaps for the first time clearly drawn by Stone. . . ."

John W. Harshberger (1916), an ecologist and plant geographer also of Philadelphia, published a map of the Pine Barrens in 1916 (Fig. 3) that included boundaries as well as several internal features. The size of his map was considerably larger than had been employed previously, and, while the overall outline was nearly identical to that of Stone's map, more boundary details were portrayed. Within the Pine Barrens he also indicated the distribution of deciduous swamps, cedar swamps, savannas, cultivated areas, and plains. Extensive savannas were prominent in the central third of the Pine Barrens, a section which also included large areas of cultivated land which extended into the southern third. In addition to his travels in the Pine Barrens by carriage, wagon, and train, he also traveled widely in North America and Europe. His map was published in a volume on the vegetation of the Pine Barrens, and presumably his criteria for delimiting boundaries also were based on vegetation. Thus, in contrast with the previous scientists, the predominant plant species and their growth forms were primary considerations. Stone's map, which was presumably based on floristic criteria, also was available to Harshberger, who, using vegetational criteria, agreed with his predecessor almost entirely. Thus, the Stone and Harshberger maps probably were accurate representations of the extent of the Pine Barrens in about 1910-1915.

E. B. Moore (1939) published a map of the forested areas of New Jersey that showed forest extending well down the Cape May peninsula, as well as in the Spotswood and Alloway areas, but it did not identify the types of forest. John C. F. Tedrow (1963) published an outline map of the pine-oak forest type in a booklet on New Jersey soils. This was based on general vegetation (with the aid of Murray F. Buell) and soil characteristics, and the area outlined was smaller than the previous maps, especially to the southwest, where pine occurs less frequently.

A map developed by Jack McCormick (McCormick and Andresen, 1963) delineates the boundaries of the Pine Barrens in great detail as they existed during 1957 (Fig. 4). The distribution of oak-pine fringe areas and stands of scrub or Virginia pine (*Pinus virginiana*) also were depicted on the map (McCormick and Andresen, 1963), which was used for the map of United States vegetation (Küchler, 1970).

McCormick compiled his map from ground inspections of the vegetation. He drove every passable road that was suspected to cross an appropriate boundary, and recorded his observations on U.S. Geological Survey topographic maps (scale 1:24,000). The extent of the Pine Barrens was identified by the distribution of upland forest types (McCormick, chapter 13, this volume) which were considered to typify the region. In some areas, the largest of which was near Hammonton, most vegetation had been removed by agricultural activities. In these places, boundaries were established by examining remnant vegetation in small woodlots, hedgerows, and near buildings. Nearly pure oak forests surrounded by forests with abundant pitch pine (*Pinus rigida*)

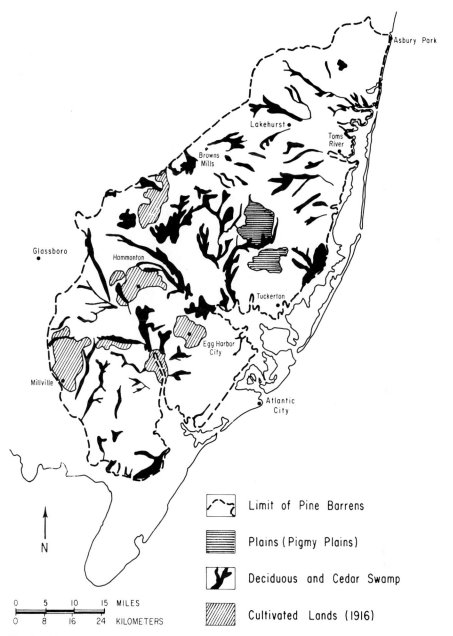

Fig. 3. Map of the Pine Barrens from J. Harshberger (1916). 1 Mile = 0.625 km. Courtesy of J. C. F. Tedrow.

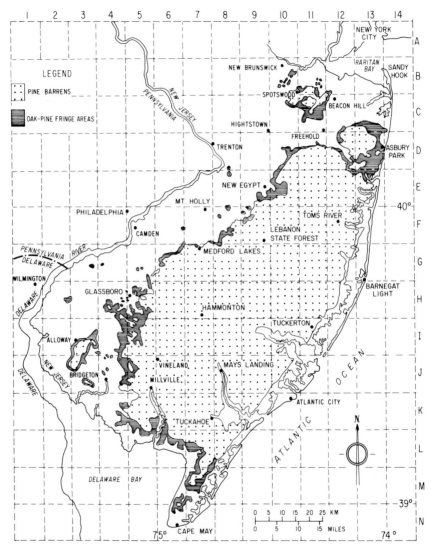

Fig. 4. Outline map of the Pine Barrens by J. McCormick (1957, 1963). Heavy solid line surrounds Pine Barrens of southern New Jersey; shaded areas are oak-pine fringe areas. The units of the grid represent U.S. Geological Survey topographical maps. Place names mentioned in this volume, and letters and numbers referring to grid locations shown on the map, are listed below and on the facing page.

were considered typical of the region. Where nearly pure oak forests occurred on the periphery of the region with scattered pitch pine in the canopy, they were mapped as "oak–pine fringe", if they appeared to contain pitch or shortleaf (*Pinus echinata*) pines at a density of at least 2.5 stems per hectare (1 per acre). Oak–pine fringe areas may have been part of the Pine Barrens region in the past, but due to fire protection for adjacent settlements or from large cultivated fields, the importance of pines decreased in the forest canopy.

Several differences in this 1957 map are evident from the Stone and Harshberger maps of 1911 and 1916. Most notable is the larger area of the Pine Barrens, extending southward on the Cape May peninsula, and southwestward well beyond Millville. McCormick also recognized large outliers around Spotswood and Alloway. The northwest boundary is similar on all three maps. Particularly extensive in the southern and southwestern portions are oak–pine fringe areas, which also are common along the northeastern margin. These suggest transitional areas where the boundaries of the Pine Barrens are the least distinct.

The differences in the available maps of the New Jersey Pine Barrens thus reflect the different criteria that were used to identify the region, differences in the published information available and the accessibility of boundary areas to an author, and perhaps, actual changes in the location of the boundary owing to human exploitation of the region over time.

REFERENCES

Gordon, T. (1834). "A Gazetteer of the State of New Jersey." Daniel Fenton, Trenton, New Jersey.
Harshberger, J. W. (1916). "The Vegetation of the New Jersey Pine-Barrens. An Ecologic Investigation." Christopher Sower Co., Philadelphia, Pennsylvania.
Hollick, A. (1899). The relation between forestry and geology in New Jersey. I. Present conditions. *Am. Nat.* 33, 1–14.
Küchler, A. W. (1970). Potential natural vegetation. *In* The National Atlas of the United States. U.S. Dep. Interior, Washington, D.C. pp. 89–91.
McCormick, J., and Andresen, J. W. (1963). The role of *Pinus virginiana* Mill. in the vegetation of southern New Jersey. *N.J. Nature News* 18, 27–38.
Moore, E. B. (1939). "Forest Management in New Jersey" N.J. Dep. Conserv. Dev., Trenton, New Jersey.
Stone, W. (1911). The plants of southern New Jersey, with especial reference to the flora of the Pine Barrens and the geographic distribution of the species. *N.J. State Mus., Annu. Rep. 1910*, pp. 23–828.
Taylor, N. (1912). On the origin and present distribution of the pine-barrens of New Jersey. *Torreya* 12, 229–242.
Tedrow, J. C. F. (1963). New Jersey soils. *N.J. Agric. Exp. Stn., Circ.* No. 601.

Part I

PEOPLE

1

Human Exploitation of the New Jersey Pine Barrens Before 1900

PETER O. WACKER

The Pine Barrens bear witness to hundreds and possibly thousands of years of human use. Recognition of this human imprint is fundamental to understanding the oft-changing environments within which plant and animal communities likewise have changed dramatically. This brief sketch portrays the more important human activities that have affected the area. The term "Pine Barrens" will be applied very loosely, for, as we shall see, the perceived boundaries of the region, which are still uncertain, have changed with time. These changes emanate from both the changing human perceptions of the Outer Coastal Plain environment and from the impacts of changing uses of the Pine Barrens resources.

INITIAL OCCUPANCY

The earliest human occupation of the region probably occurred at the end of the Pleistocene ice age, when vegetation patterns were quite different and reflected a climate much colder than today's. To date, with one possible exception (Bartlett, 1978, p. 32) no evidence of Paleo-Indian, the big game hunter present elsewhere in New Jersey at the time, has been found in the Pines. However, it is quite possible that these people did hunt extensively in the region.

More is known of the Algonkian speakers, the historic Indians generally known today as the Lenni Lenape or Delaware, who were encountered by the first European explorers and settlers. The Lenape are known to have occupied relatively few sites in the Pine Barrens. When comparing the region with the neighboring Inner Coastal Plain, one finds this to be especially true. There are numerous Indian sites on the rivers and creeks near the bays and lagoons of the coast; however, these locations are peripheral to, rather than entirely within, the Pine Barrens (Cross, 1941).

Indians occupying sites relatively near the Pines almost certainly hunted within the

3

region. A major hunting technique, especially for deer, was the fire drive. In December 1632, the Dutch navigator David DeVries, off Cape May, recorded that he and his crew

> ... smelt the land, which gave a sweet perfume as the wind came from the northwest, which blew off the land, and caused these sweet odors. This comes from the Indians setting fire at this time of the year, to the woods and thickets, in order to hunt; and the land is full of sweet-smelling herbs, as sassafras, which has a sweet smell. When the wind blows out of the northwest, and the smoke is driven to sea, it happens that the land is smelt before it is seen. (Myers, 1912, p. 15)

More than twenty years before, earlier in the fall, Henry Hudson's crew saw a "great fire" before the south Jersey coast itself came into view (Asher, 1860, p. 76). It, too, was most likely of Indian origin. Although the primary purposes of the Indian-set fires probably were to drive deer, improve visibility, and facilitate foot travel, they also encouraged vegetational changes which, in turn, encouraged more game to enter and reproduce in the area (Sauer, 1971, pp. 285–286).

In a sense, the largest recorded Indian settlement in the Barrens was involuntary. A reservation was established for the few remaining Lenape in New Jersey after 1758 at Brotherton, now Indian Mills, north of Atsion. The population of some two hundred Indians was assigned to an area encompassing about 3000 acres (1215 ha), thus forming a population density of about forty persons per square mile (fifteen per square kilometer). Even decades later, such a high density rarely was found in the region, even by white farmers on the fertile soils of the Inner Coastal Plain. The Brotherton settlement was not a success, and by 1801 almost all the Lenape had left New Jersey (Wacker, 1975, pp. 90–91).

EUROPEAN PERCEPTIONS OF THE REGION

In addition to commenting on the Indian-set fires, early Dutch navigators occasionally recorded their impressions of the eastern portion of the Pine Barrens. As early as 1624, a popular Dutch work indicated that the coastal inlets and bays had been explored (Jameson, 1909, pp. 32–35, 52–56, 73). While praise was accorded other areas, the absence by mid-century of any claims for the fertility of soils in the Outer Coastal Plain make it obvious that the Dutch did not perceive the region as favorable for agriculture (O'Callaghan, 1853, pp. 365–367). Such a perception quite evidently was held by the earliest permanent white occupants of the region, the New Englanders who had settled Shrewsbury township, whose original bounds extended from the Navesink River southward to the present Burlington County line (Snyder, 1969, pp. 185, 189, 207). This is implicit in their negotiation of larger than normal individual land grants from Berkeley and Carteret in 1674, "because there is much barren land..." (Whitehead, 1880, p. 171).

During the 1680's, a group of Scottish Proprietors worked hard to encourage settlement in their colony of East New Jersey, and their few promotional pamphlets reveal their assessment of the environment and resources of the colony. One such pamphlet indicated that the Outer Coastal Plain in East Jersey as yet remained unsettled. Navigable Barnegat Bay and its hinterland was said to be "as good land as in all . . . parts of America . . ." and settlement there was encouraged. Admitted, however, was the fact that "some of that Sea-side be Pintree Land, which is the worst sort, though good for the ranging of cattel . . ." (Board of General Proprietors, 1685, p. 5). At about the same time, John Reid, who had been a landscape architect in Scotland, gave a somewhat more accurate assessment of the soils of the area (Whitehead, 1875, pp. 129–130).

> Its a very wholesome, pleasant, and a ferrtill land; there are also some barren land, viz white sandy land, full of Pine trees, it lyes betwixt South River and Barnegate or Neversink [Navesink] (albeit there be much good land in that precinct), yet it is a good place for raising a stock of cattle, providing they have a large room to run in, for cattle finds a good food there in winter. . .

This statement is valuable, for it reveals that, in the contemporary view, some barren, sandy, pine land extended north to South River. This clearly is revealed on Brush's (1976) recent historic map of Middlesex County (largely based on John Reid's map of 1686) as "the barrens of Wickatonk" in South Brunswick township. Today, we would not classify this area as the Pine Barrens, but according to the contemporary view, much of the area very near Perth Amboy was "sandy barren land . . ." (Whitehead, 1875, p. 461).

Another point made by Reid and the Scottish Proprietors was that the pine lands were becoming valued as pasturage, especially during the winter season. The relative mildness of the coastal area and the fact that the area was not cleared for agriculture, long encouraged extensive grazing as a primary land use. The density of stock remained relatively light, however.

The character of the interior of the area currently accepted as the Pine Barrens was known early, a fact that can be seen in the report of George Keith, who surveyed the East–West Jersey line in 1687. Keith began his survey at a point on the north side of the inlet to Little Egg Harbor (Council of Proprietors, 1888, p. 9).

> Through a large marsh or salt meadow about a mile deep to a pine tree on the upland . . . and so through a great tract of barren lands consisting of pine land and sand, crossing rivers small brooks and cedar swamps. . . .

Keith estimated that he traversed 48 km (30 miles) through the tract of pines, whose east–west expanse he guessed to be about 40 km (25 miles). These are very reasonable estimates for our current perception of the extent of the Barrens in this area. After the belt of pines, Keith ran his line "through to the good land but somewhat sandy [Inner Coastal Plain] and having some pines mingled with oaks to Crosswicks Creek . . ." (Council of Proprietors, 1888, p. 9). This line of survey is still clear on modern maps as most of the current boundary between Burlington County and Ocean and Monmouth counties.

Other estimates of the extent of the Pine Barrens in times past occasionally can be derived from later official documents. The first reasonably comprehensive estimate was that of Governor Belcher in 1754. He reported that "the greatest part of Cape May, Gloucester, Cumberland, Burlington and Monmouth counties, as well as a large portion of Middlesex were Pine and barren, sandy lands'' (Whitehead, 1885, p. 79). At present, the counties of Atlantic, Camden, and Ocean, which resulted from the subsequent subdivision of counties listed by Belcher, would be included. Four years after Belcher's report, Thomas Jeffery's map of the Middle Colonies, published in Philadelphia, called the region between the Maurice and the Manasquan Rivers ''Sandy Barren Deserts'' (Jefferys, 1758).

EUROPEAN SETTLEMENT

It is clear from an isochronic map of settlement (Fig. 1) that the Pine Barrens generally were avoided for permanent settlement before the American Revolution (Wacker, 1975, p. 127). This is especially clear when the region is compared with the adjacent Inner Coastal Plain. The area of the Outer Coastal Plain depicted as essentially unsettled by 1765 remarkably resembles in outline the Harshberger (1916) map of the Pine Barrens that is based on vegetation patterns.

Those areas in the Outer Coastal Plain that had been settled by 1765 generally supported activities other than agriculture. Involved were fishing, whaling, lumbering, and hunting and gathering. Not reflecting this generalization were the banks of the Cohansey River and the Cape May peninsula. In the latter case, New England whalers had settled during the late seventeenth century, but by the mid-eighteenth century, agriculture had become an important local activity (Spicer, 1945, pp. 37–50, 82–117, 175–188). On the Cohansey, English Quakers and New Englanders established farms on readily accessible and comparatively fertile soils (Wacker, 1971, p. 48).

Census data (Department of Education, 1778–1822), and hence, estimates of population density, the earliest of which first were recorded in 1784, clearly contrast the area of the Pine Barrens with other regions in New Jersey (Fig. 2). The contrast would be even clearer if the eastern boundaries of townships on the Inner Coastal Plain terminated at the westernmost extension of the Pine Barrens. Where townships of the Inner Coastal Plain adjoin those which are almost entirely in the Outer Coastal Plain, the narrowness of the belt of good soils, supporting relatively dense agricultural settlement, is particularly evident. As can be seen, even by 1784, densities of less than nine people per square mile prevailed in most of the Outer Coastal Plain. The 1784 contrast can be illustrated strikingly: Middletown Township, on Monmouth County's fertile Inner Coastal Plain, had a density of approximately 38 people per square mile, whereas Dover Township, in the same county, but located in the Barrens, had but two people per square mile. Similar contrasts could be found in the other counties. Egg Harbor (fronting Little Egg Harbor), in the Pines of the present Ocean County, had but four people per square mile. Chesterfield Township, on the Inner Coastal Plain, had forty-one.

In many cases, the contrast in landscape and land use between the Barrens and the Inner Coastal Plain was quite clear by 1800. Count Niemcewicz, a particularly keen observer, en route from Batsto to Mount Holly in 1799, recorded the discordance

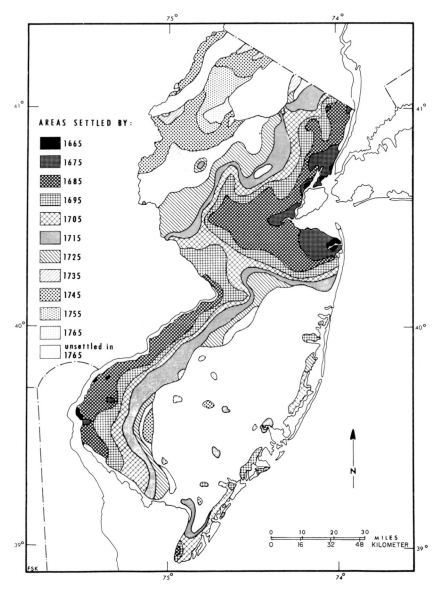

Fig. 1. Settlement of New Jersey, 1665–1765. After E. W. Roberts, as cited in Wacker (1975).

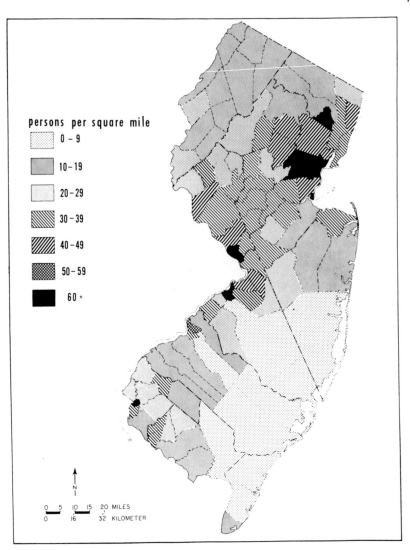

Fig. 2. Population density of New Jersey in 1784. Ten persons per square mile = 3.2 persons per square kilometer.

between the regions (Niemcewicz, 1965, p. 225):

> There are no longer bogs, sand, gloomy cedar and pine forests, but an open and fertile country. My eyes wearied for a long time by the sunken emptiness were cheered by this sight. With the fertility of the land there is much more settlement and the mien of the inhabitants is more prosperous. An abundant tillage is the one bosom at which the inhabitants are fed their needs, their comforts and their affluence. With these gifts their lives are made more comfortable and this makes them both more willing and able for the state of marriage. And that is why the population . . . is large.

By the time of Niemcewicz, the Pines region had experienced at least a century of exploitation of its forest resources. The East Jersey Proprietors had recognized the value of the woodlands early. In 1685, the Deputy Governor of the province had 500 acres laid out to him "amongst the barren pines . . ." (Board of General Proprietors, 1949, p. 69). This probably was for the valuable stand of timber in that locale.

LUMBERING

Records concerning the early lumber industry of the region are few. By 1704, a sawmill existed at Little Egg Harbor (Defebaugh, 1907, p. 497). Especially harvested during the earliest days of the lumber industry was the Atlantic white cedar (*Chamaecyparis thyoides*), which grew in dense stands in swamps. Its decay-resistant but nonresinous and straight-grained character encouraged its wide use for fence rails, cooperage, and house construction. Its primary use in the eighteenth century was for constructing shingles. Houses could be built with lighter beams and thinner walls when the durable and light-weight cedar roofing shingles were used. In addition, these shingles were advantageous in the fire-prone settlements of the day for several reasons. Burnt roofs, being light, did little damage when they collapsed. The shingles absorbed water and could be wetted down to prevent catching fire. At the time, windborne burnt shingles were known as "dead coals" and as such did not start fires easily. Thus, there was quite early a tremendous demand for white cedar shingles. Although some of the cedar swamps were found outside the Pine Barrens (i.e., on Cape May and even in the Hackensack Meadows), the wood was exported primarily from that region. Large quantities were sent to New York City and Philadelphia, both for use in these cities and for redistribution (Harshberger, 1916, pp. 20–21; Muntz, 1959, pp. 155–157). White cedar shingles and staves also were sent to the West Indies directly from landings on the major rivers (Nelson, 1903, p. 149; 1904, pp. 145; 549).

In 1749, Peter Kalm, a student of Linnaeus, and temporarily a resident in southern New Jersey, became quite interested in the white cedar and complained of its overexploitation. His concern was that the lumbermen of his day were "bent only upon their own present advantage, utterly regardless of posterity," and were "not only lessening the number of these trees but are extirpating them entirely." He thought that "the cedar trees will soon be gone in this country . . ." (Benson, 1966, p. 300). In 1765, Samuel Smith claimed that both white and red cedar were "much worked out" in the region (Smith, 1877, p. 487).

Exploitation of white cedar again became important in the early nineteenth century. It is likely that this was largely second growth and not virgin timber, since it took about sixty years for a white cedar to reach a size suitable for lumber (Muntz, 1959, p. 155). The "many swamps . . . already quite destitute of cedars, having only young shoots left" (Benson, 1966, p. 300), which Kalm noted in 1749, should have harbored salable timber by around 1810.

By 1823, hundreds of men again were engaged in cutting white cedar in the swamps near Little Egg Harbor. The same attitudes as were held in Kalm's time again prevailed. Cutting of immature stands, recurring fires, and subsequent incursions of deciduous species in the cedar swamps served virtually to eliminate the industry by the end of the nineteenth century, although some cutting has continued to the present day (Muntz, 1959, pp. 155–157).

A further problem lay with the sparse population of the Pine Barrens. Much like their counterparts elsewhere in eastern North America, these individuals saw little wrong with utilization of unoccupied land not belonging to them. Since the Pines Belt was not attractive to agriculturists, much land remained in vast tracts belonging to individuals or to companies of individuals who were nonresident and who therefore could not supervise their use directly. A large percentage of the early sawmills depended primarily on timber from these lands, which were not in the possession of the owners of the sawmills. It is not surprising that this encouraged a ruinous exploitation of the woodlands.

As early as 1725, the East Jersey Proprietors appointed rangers in order to halt the thievery (Board of Proprietors, 1960a, p. xvii). In 1739, the Board of Proprietors of East Jersey cited "the great destruction of pines" upon land that as yet was undivided in southern Monmouth County. This was because "many persons upon appropriating [buying the right to locate] only a few acres upon a stream do thereon erect sawmills and cut the pines growing upon the lands near to them to supply their mills. . . ." Unfortunately for the Proprietors, and the woodlands, "all means hitherto used to prevent this have proved ineffectual . . ." (Board of Proprietors, 1960a, p. 76). A solution to this was the allocation of dividends of the unappropriated land to individual Proprietors. Given the difficulty of law enforcement in the region and the general attitude of most people toward the Proprietors, the problem continued, and individual Proprietors did not claim all of the undivided land. In 1761, the Board again was informed that, near Barnegat, there continued to be "great destruction made of the timber upon the common [undivided] lands . . . there being several saw mills that are supplied with logs almost entirely from the Proprietors lands . . ." (Board of Proprietors, 1960b, p. 340). Two years later, the Board again was informed of sawmills destroying timber on lands lying between the Manasquan and Metedeconk Rivers, "and that it would be a very difficult matter to prevent it" (Board of Proprietors, 1960b, p. 406).

During the eighteenth century, trees exploited by the sawmills included not only the white cedar but also the oaks and pines of the region. Better soils, especially those in riverine locations, often supported trees of good quality. An important tree for lumber in the early years was the pitch pine (*Pinus rigida*). Originally, it grew 18–30 m (60–100 feet) high, but by the time of Harshberger's (1916) study, its height rarely exceeded 15 m (50 feet). Before the pines of the southeastern U.S. came into general use, the quality of old-growth pitch pines was good enough for widespread use in sills, floors, door and window frames, and beams for buildings (Fig. 3) (Harshberger, 1916, pp. 19–21).

In 1799, Niemcewicz reported that twenty vessels regularly docked at what is now Somers Point. A large part of their cargo was cedar and other lumber from the Great Egg Harbor hinterland. An estimate made by the collector of customs was that each of these vessels made at least sixteen trips per year to Philadelphia or New York loaded with thirty-five thousand board feet (11,200,000 board feet per year or 3,413,760

Fig. 3. Lumber left the Pine Barrens from mills on many rivers, such as this at Bridgeton on the Cohansey River about 1876. From Stewart (1876).

meters) (Niemcewicz, 1965, p. 219). For reasons developed more fully below, this lumber industry declined greatly. One of the major reasons was that stands having trees of saw-log size became uncommon.

FUEL WOOD

In terms of wood leaving the region, the fuel wood industry became much more important than lumbering during the nineteenth century. As woodlands in the vicinity of New York and Philadelphia became depleted, those cities turned to the forests of New Jersey's Outer Coastal Plain, where lack of permanent agricultural clearance allowed regeneration of woodlands to provide trees of fuel wood size. Unlike lumbering, the cutting of cordwood was not selective, and all species were utilized. The greatest impact occurred between the immediate post-Revolutionary period and mid-nineteenth century, during which time depletion of the forests and, more importantly, increasing use of anthracite coal, caused the industry to decline.

A large amount of cordwood also was used during the early era of steam navigation. Writing in 1833, Gordon noted that, while the forests of the Outer Coastal Plain in many cases were almost worthless forty years before, recently they had gained value tremendously due to the fact that the steamboats, "their huge maws ... fed with thousands of shallop loads of [New Jersey] pine wood, were insatiable" (Gordon, 1834, p. 2). Pine wood generally was superior for this purpose, since it burned quickly without seasoning and generated more intense heat than the hardwoods (Muntz, 1959, p. 96).

From around 1815 to 1845, about one hundred vessels of 20–100 tons sailed from the Mullica River carrying cordwood. Fifty operated from Barnegat Bay, and many more sailed from other harbors. Data on the amount of cordwood cut are unavailable except for the census of 1840, which revealed especially heavy cutting in the watersheds of the Great Egg Harbor River and the Mullica (Muntz, 1959, pp. 131–137).

CHARCOAL

As great or greater impact on the forests of the region was made by the production of charcoal for iron and other industries. Charcoal could be made not only from wood suitable for cordwood but also from smaller trees and branches. This meant that second- and third-growth forest could be cut clear again in a very few years in order to produce charcoal. This encouraged repeated cutting of immature forest stands, especially near water transportation, a situation which, in turn, discouraged the lumber industry. Two other affects of charcoaling included an increase in the number of fires, discussed below, and short-term sterilization of small plots where the charcoal actually was produced. Charcoal continued to be exported from the Pines, even after the advent of anthracite, primarily for use as a cooking fuel in New York and Philadelphia.

IRON

The most important and well known of the industries depending on the production of charcoal was the smelting and working of iron. The industry was established several decades after that of the Highlands of New York and New Jersey but before the Revolution. Maximum development and impact occurred shortly after the War of 1812 and then declined markedly after about 1840, when anthracite and then bituminous coal encouraged the iron industry to relocate further west.

Other than as a market for the iron industry, the most significant locational factors were fuel and waterpower. Charcoal was the fuel utilized before anthracite came into wide use. The consumption of charcoal by blast furnaces and forges was huge. Charcoal, being relatively bulky, thus is uneconomical to move great distances to bodies of iron ore. Before the use of steam, waterpower was the motive force required for various industries. Dams were placed across the many streams of the Pine Barrens by iron interests, as well as other industries, providing not only a greater fall of water but also impoundments that could be drawn upon when needed. This, of course, has been a major means of altering both landscape and habitat, as a glance at a modern map of the region will suggest.

The widely occurring iron ore of the Pine Barrens is known as limonite or bog ore. This ore, formed by acidic water percolating through soluble salts of iron and precipitating the same in bodies of water (especially in shallow, sluggish portions of the Mullica and Wading River systems), was a renewable resource but seldom exceeded 40% in iron content. Since such ore was depleted rapidly in the nineteenth century, it became economical to import richer ores to be reduced by locally produced charcoal.

An additional raw material, clam and oyster shells, used as a flux, could be obtained readily from the nearby coast.

It is equally difficult to estimate the area affected by the iron industry, since relatively few data are available and furnaces and forges varied in size and consumption of charcoal. Individual ironworks were established, abandoned, and reopened at various times. A map of the charcoal ironworks established in the Pines at various times (Kury, 1971) suggests that the major impact of the industry occurred between the Mullica and the Manasquan. This was probably due to the availability of fuel (there having been greater lumbering activities farther south) as well as greater deposits of bog ore in this northern area.

The absence of permanent agricultural occupation and clearance in the Pines enabled the iron industry to become established and to flourish for a time. Most iron enterprises, in order to assure fuel and ore supplies and control waterpower, amassed substantial acreages. This was especially true of the iron plantations, which combined smelting and refining with ancillary activities such as commercial lumbering, woodcutting, and even agriculture (for supplying their own workforce). By the 1830's, for example, Atsion, Batsto, and Weymouth each had grown to include from 50,000 to 85,000 acres (20,000 to 34,000 ha).

What were the effects of the iron industry on the Pines? Already mentioned has been the proliferation of impoundments. Additionally, there was the excavation of iron ore and greatly expanded charcoal making. The population of the Pines substantially increased, and new communities were created. Agricultural activities had to be expanded to feed this population, and much food had to be imported to the region. Iron products had to be marketed far afield. This required improvement and expansion of the limited road network and the establishment of many landings on the major rivers (Kury, 1976, pp. 3–11; Pierce, 1957).

GLASS

Contemporaneous with the early iron industry was the development of glass manufacturing. This industry, encouraged by abundant fuel and glass sands, became important in the region shortly after 1800. A pioneer location was Millville (Fig. 4), just within Harshberger's boundary for the Pine Barrens. Almost all of the glassworks in nineteenth-century New Jersey were located from the Mullica south. Over one hundred companies had been established before 1900; however, since many were not successful and disappeared quickly, it is difficult to gauge their total effect. Certainly, the mining of sand and the cutting of wood (especially pitch pine, which provided the high temperatures necessary to fuse the sand) must have had an influence. Even after the 1840's, when anthracite and then bituminous coal came into use, replacing wood, the mining of sand continued. Those glass factories, well located with respect to sand deposits and access to inexpensive transportation to market, continued in operation. Except for Millville, these were located largely outside the Pine Barrens (Johnson, 1971, pp. 18–25, 44–47, 123–128).

Fig. 4. The world-famous glassworks at South Millville in 1890. The Maurice River is in the background. From Pepper (1971), courtesy of Kerr Glass Manufacturing Corp.

THE INDUSTRIAL LEGACY

Nineteenth-century sources such as atlases (Beers, 1872), statewide maps (Cook and Smock, 1878), and Gordon's (1834) "Gazetteer", indicate the wide range of manufacturing activities in the Pines during the nineteenth century. Few of the towns spawned by the industries exploiting the region's resources—relatively inexpensive wood, iron ore, waterpower, sand, clay, and ready access to both the major markets and the internal and external trade of New York and Philadelphia, remain today. There are exceptions, such as Batsto, which was relatively intact when purchased by Joseph Wharton, who amassed an estate of 100,000 acres (Wharton Tract) in the Pine Barrens. Most communities, however, are like Harrisville, located about seven miles northwest of New Gretna. Harrisville Pond is all that remains on most modern road maps. Harrisville was a prosperous, company-owned town that began to decline in the 1860's. The site, part of a 5000-acre holding, had experienced the establishment of sawmills and ironworks during the eighteenth century. Papermaking (a coarse wrapping paper), which depended on the use of marsh grass, waterpower, water for processing, and proximity to New York and Philadelphia, began in the 1830's. Competition by other, better endowed sites was made possible by the expansion of railroads, and doomed this operation in Harrisville, as it did most other Pine Barrens towns. By 1896, when Joseph Wharton acquired the town, the paper factory long had been closed. In 1914, a severe forest fire destroyed most of the buildings. Scavengers and vandals have destroyed much of what remained. Today, the remnants of stone walls, foundations, cellar holes, and the water impoundment characterize the most easily identified human artifacts of Harrisville. Similar histories are repeated for many sites of former industry in the Pine Barrens (Pierce, 1957, pp. 67–83).

AGRICULTURE

Agriculture, conducted on permanently cleared fields, has long had a role in the Pine Barrens, even though most of the region has remained in woodland. Indeed, the early eighteenth century residents, who were engaged in the various extractive industries, often also carried on part-time farming to help support themselves. In 1764, Pastor Wrangel visited individuals who had ''to depend principally on the woods . . . for a livelihood,'' a few miles east of present Hammonton. These woodsmen, largely employed at sawmills, had arrived about twenty years before. Wrangel found them growing ''reasonably good crops of maize and rye'' in soil that consisted ''mainly of drift sand (Anderson, 1969, pp. 11–12).'' In 1799, near Great Egg Harbor, Niemcewicz mentioned traveling through ''sand and pine forests'' until reaching ''oak trees and better land covered with a rather goodlooking stand of rye (Niemcewicz, 1965, p. 219).'' Indeed, the grain lands probably constituted the largest areas permanently cleared for agriculture, and rye and maize seem to have been the major grains, with little or no wheat (Wacker, 1971, pp. 46–50).

As mentioned earlier, from the seventeenth century on the area was perceived to be favorable for stock raising. This was especially true near the coast and to the south, where milder winters prevailed. Pastor Wrangel mentioned that the part-time agriculturists to whom he preached in 1764 made extensive use of the ''good wooded pasturage . . . available for the cattle throughout the summer'' and ''in the winter they bring their herds to the seaside in Egg Harbor,'' where they paid for the privilege of grazing them (Anderson, 1969, pp. 11–12). The few advertisements of farms in the region during the eighteenth century often cite as a distinct advantage the proximity of the location to ''outlets'' for cattle in the woodlands or on barrier islands (Nelson and Honeyman, 1917, pp. 150–151). Tax lists for the late eighteenth century reveal that many sizeable herds of cattle existed in the region, but the actual density of cattle, or horses, per square mile was light. The statistics for Egg Harbor Township, in the Pines and on the coast, and Chesterfield Township on Burlington County's fertile Inner Coastal Plain are typical. In 1784, Chesterfield Township had 0.35 horses and 0.63 cattle per person, while Egg Harbor Township possessed 0.28 horses and 1.15 cattle, respectively. Per square mile, Egg Harbor's woodlands harbored only 1.10 horses and 4.53 cattle, while Chesterfield's cleared pastures supported 14.10 horses and 25.80 cattle, respectively. Even this relatively light density of livestock in the Pines had a great impact, however.

A common practice by the graziers, even if they owned their own land, was to burn woodlands owned by nonresidents. Niemcewicz encountered the practice in 1799 when traveling west of Great Egg Harbor (Niemcewicz, 1965, pp. 217–218).

Again sand and pine forests, the more sad because it was all burnt over. This tremendous damage is caused by indigent inhabitants who, having no meadows in which to feed their cattle, burn the woods. The fire, running along the ground, turns the lower bushes to ashes; with this the earth is enriched and puts forth grass and other plants—in a word excellent pasturage for cattle. This advantage does not compensate for the harm done by the fires which rise from the lower growth to the tops and burn the taller and more useful trees. The largest part of these woods belong to a company of people living in England [probably the West Jersey Society]. With the owners so far distant the harm done their property is given little attention and is not investigated. There has not been a single instance of one of the fire setters being prosecuted.

The traditional agricultural practices still in use among the residents of the present Wharton Tract have been recorded by John W. Sinton (1976, pp. 5–6). Here again, agriculture was and is a part-time practice. Totally cleared acreages were relatively small, averaging just under 1 ha (2.5 acres) per family and rarely larger than 2 ha (5 acres) in a single clearing. The poor soils did not encourage new clearing and the shifting of plots. Rather, once an area was cleared, it was used intensively year after year. Fertilizers such as animal manure, excess herring from the spring runs, night soil, and mussels were used liberally. In the twentieth century, the crops produced generally included maize, rye, potatoes, cabbage, turnips, tomatoes, and sweet potatoes. Except for the tomato, all of these probably also were present in the mid-eighteenth century (Woodward, 1941, pp. 255–262). According to Sinton, much of the diet of many residents still is made up of game. This was certainly true of the earliest settlers of the Pines. Pastor Wrangel recorded that several of the Swedes who had arrived as early as 1700 lived largely by hunting and gathering. He further remarked on the great ease with which fish, fowl, and fruit (grapes) might be obtained during even a casual expedition by the seaside in 1764 (Anderson, 1969, pp. 13–22).

During the second decade of the nineteenth century, farming became more important and commercial rather than remaining only a source of subsistence in some locations within the Pine Belt as well as on its periphery. This was the result of the discovery that glauconite, locally known as greensand marl, was an excellent fertilizer when applied to many soils. Because it was calcareous, glauconite was especially useful for some of the acid soils of the Outer Coastal Plain. The marl, of sedimentary origin, occurs in a 10–21 km-wide belt of the Inner Coastal Plain from an area south of Sandy Hook through Freehold, Mullica Hill, Woodstown, and south of Salem (Schmidt, 1973, p. 129).

The value of this material on poor sandy soils was well understood by 1834, when Gordon remarked that "it has already saved some districts from depopulation, and increased the inhabitants of others; and may, one day, contribute to convert the sandy and pine deserts into regions of agricultural wealth" (Gordon, 1834, p. 5). By 1863, George Cook reported that marl was being widely mined and was being distributed outside the marl belt via the railroads (Cook, 1864, p. 9). By 1868, Cook was praising the marl for making even areas of "bare sand" productive (Cook, 1868, p. 442). Another factor encouraging agriculture was the numerous industrial activities, which provided a larger local market for the agricultural products of the region than had existed before.

Some areas grew in response to promotional efforts. In the 1860's, at least two settlements in the pine lands were growing as agricultural settlements. These were Hammonton and Vineland, both in large part developed by the entrepreneur Charles K. Landis on land previously very sparsely occupied. Land use primarily was devoted to small plots containing orchards, the vine, strawberries, and blackberries. It is probable that promotional efforts by Landis had as much to do with the growth of these areas as did the use of fertilizer, an early beginning of the vegetative growing season for the region, and the proximity of large urban markets (Fry, 1916, pp. 11–14; Cushing and Sheppard, 1883, pp. 703–705; McMahon, 1966, pp. 1–21). By 1890, other commercial fertilizers generally had replaced marl, and agricultural land use in several areas had become well established (Schmidt, 1973, p. 131). Harshberger's 1916 map of the region indicates extensive agricultural clearance in the Pine Barrens from Millville to beyond Vineland, around May's Landing, in the environs of Egg Harbor City, around Hammonton, and a large belt running north and south of Tabernacle. All of these districts lay on railroads.

By the end of the nineteenth century, cranberry cultivation was beginning to be an important local activity. This did not depend on large clearings but rather on the use of flooded fields which required dikes, dams, and sluices to be built. Further major modifications of the environment occurred when bushes and trees were removed and when the soil was removed and fields were graded (Harshberger, 1916, pp. 25–26).

Local residents, who provided labor for the farming enterprises of the late nineteenth century, often augmented their earnings by gathering from the forest. Blueberries especially were sought, but in addition many plants and trees were valued for their real or supposed medicinal value. Wild flowers also found their way to Philadelphia, as did greens such as holly and mistletoe during the Christmas season. Harshberger, among others, called for some "proper control of the ruthless destruction of our most beautiful trees, shrubs, and flowers for purely commercial purposes" (Harshberger, 1916, p. 30).

REAL ESTATE PROMOTION

A major factor, as indicated above, in encouraging settlement in the Pine Barrens, has been promotion by the real estate entrepreneur. The success of Hammonton and Vineland, as well as the common belief that the coming of the railroads would revitalize the region, encouraged many people to buy lots in the Pines. Realtors were able to buy large tracts cheaply from iron, glass, and other interests. In some cases, the promoters developed viable communities based on impoundments and a recreational orientation. In many cases, the land subdivisions did not progress very far beyond sales to gullible urban residents. By 1900, 12,234 small lots on some 11,567 acres had been subdivided in ten "Pine Area" townships in Burlington County alone (Hauck and Lee, 1942, p. 14).

One scheme, Paisley, the "Magic City," has been studied in some detail (Lee,

1939, pp. 5–50). Paisley was located between Chatsworth and Tabernacle on 1400 acres purchased by a Long Island promoter in 1888. The development was advertised extensively between 1888 and 1891. At least 3122 people bought lots in Paisley.

A few streets and buildings were placed on the development by the entrepreneur but they largely had disappeared fifty years later. During Paisley's heyday, when sales were brisk, local people were quoted as saying, "that they never dreamed there were so many suckers in New York" (Lee, 1939, p. 16). Awake to their poor choice, or unable to continue tax payments, many purchasers of the small, and now difficult to locate lots, within Paisley and other developments, simply became tax delinquent. Scattered decaying buildings and disappearing roads remain.

FIRE

Most students of the Pine Barrens would agree that no single other factor in the region has had as much impact as the recurrence of forest fires. Undoubtedly, natural fires do and did occur; but there is abundant evidence that most fires in the region are of human origin.

As we have seen, fires were set deliberately to benefit the local population. Although widespread in New Jersey during the eighteenth century, the practice of burning the woodlands has lasted longest in the Pines (Wacker, 1975, p. 116). The reason for this is that the area, because of its poor soils, did not early attract a sedentary, primarily agricultural population whose main interests would have been to buy individual parcels of land with clear title and certain boundaries for forest clearance and the establishment of permanent fields and pasture. Had this occurred, as it generally did elsewhere, the setting of fires would have been discouraged by the owner-operators of the farms as being destructive of their own crops or remaining woodlands. The latter were very important for the production of fuel, fencing, and construction materials.

Instead, the Pines first attracted individuals who were, at best, only part-time farmers. While many certainly did own land even in the early years, the relative infertility of most soils did not encourage much permanent clearance for agriculture. The population remained sparse. Large land holdings, especially those which had been received by the Proprietors and their descendants, remained undivided, often with very unsure boundaries. Indeed, this also was true of the large acreages amassed by the iron interests, and even small holders were in possession of tracts with unsure bounds and questionable titles. This circumstance has lasted to the present day (Pierce, 1957, p. 8). Where permanent agricultural occupation by owner-operators was the rule, there was great concern for determining proper boundaries and title. Indeed, elsewhere in New Jersey, this process often involved much effort and great expense in lawyer's fees (Wacker, 1975, pp. 221–408).

Large tracts with uncertain boundaries were owned by outsiders who did little to develop them because of the lack of value of the land for agriculture and also because their titles and boundaries were unsure. This situation encouraged the early and longlasting attitude that the land should be exploited by the local population for its own benefit. Thus, wood could be stolen and fires set in the region with little chance of prosecution or local condemnation.

The setting of fires on the lands of others continued to have local short-term benefits for many. It was profitable for charcoal burners to set fires deliberately, in order to kill trees and make them worthless for any purpose other than charcoal making. They thus could purchase the trees cheaply (Muntz, 1959, p. 164).

As late as 1900, the highbush blueberry, which had yet to be domesticated, was stimulated by burning. According to forester John Gifford, writing at the time, "the natives [of the Pine Barrens] know this and accomplish it in a drastic, wholesale fashion by firing the woods. The young shoots which spring up after a fire bear large luscious berries" (Geological Survey, 1900, p. 259). These then could be gathered, often for sale. Gifford Pinchot, writing in the same report, thought that the constant fires in the region had a distinct moral effect. Fires occurred so often that people looked upon them as inevitable (Geological Survey, 1900, pp. 107–108).

> Large tracts of land are owned by non-resident capitalists, and timber-stealing is very common, especially after fires. When the timber is killed many persons consider it better to use the dead trees for cordwood than to allow them to rot on the ground, and they cut such timber on tracts of land to which they have no right. There is no doubt that forest fires encourage a spirit of lawlessness and a disregard of property rights.

While the last sentence is undoubtedly true, abundant evidence from earlier times suggests that the spirit of lawlessness and disregard of property rights was also a cause rather than merely a result of the fires. For example, in 1895 John Gifford claimed that people spitefully set fires when they were angry with landowners, and also that fires were set so that putting them out provided work for jobless individuals (Geological Survey, 1896, p. 166).

Unplanned fires of human origin also occurred widely. Muntz blames the iron industry for "a drastic increase" in the amount of land burned over (Muntz, 1959, p. 164). Sparks from forges and furnaces and improperly attended charcoal pits began conflagrations during dry periods. Woodcutters for cordwood enterprises left slash (unused branches and other debris) which, when dry, encouraged the spread of fires.

After the middle of the nineteenth century, sparks from locomotives started countless fires. By 1900, when the iron industry had disappeared and charcoal making no longer was widespread, it was estimated that about half of all fires were started by trains. Other causes included about ten percent "for evil purposes," ten percent for clearance for pasture and to improve the blueberry crop, and thirty percent were due to general carelessness (Geological Survey, 1900, p. 101).

The amount of widespread burning through time in a 475,000-ha (1,000,000 acre) region is astounding. On June 12, 1755, in a rare reference to the problem in the eighteenth century, a newspaper described a vast fire "which rendered desolate Lands to the Extent of near thirty Miles (forty-eight Kilometers)," from Barnegat to Little Egg Harbor. Not only was a large area of forest destroyed but also cut shingles ready for shipment. Most of the inhabitants of that area were reduced to "meer penury and want" (Nelson, 1897, p. 503).

In the nineteenth century, it was not unusual for 40,000 ha (100,000 acres) to burn in a year. In 1870 and 1871, nearly all of the woodlands lying in Bass River Township, Burlington County, burned. In 1885, approximately two hundred square miles, or 52,000 ha (128,000 acres) burned. Large areas affected included 194 km² (75 mi²) north of Barnegat and 155 km² (60 mi²) near Atsion (Geological Survey, 1900, pp. 39, 100–101).

CONCLUSION

The purpose of this brief sketch has been to set the stage historically for a collection of scientific papers concerning the ecology of the Pine Barrens. A major point made by this writer is that a vast amount of human interference in natural processes has occurred in this region. Few areas have remained relatively undisturbed.

Much of the human activity in the region can be described as *Raubwirtschaft,* that is, a ruinous exploitation of natural resources motivated by thought of immediate gain. Despite such harsh land use, the comparative lack of resources for modern industry and agriculture in the region, when viewed from the perspective of the immense wealth of resources elsewhere in the United States, has left the Pine Barrens relatively unpopulated and a useful scientific and a charming recreational and historical resource. And so it should remain.

A major factor always to be borne in mind is the relationship of the region to the cities of Philadelphia and New York. Through time, these have provided both markets for the products of the Pine Barrens (including land sales) and the entrepreneurs who have exploited the natural resources. More importantly, had the Pine Barrens lay directly between New York and Philadelphia instead of southeast of the most direct route between the two cities, this vast, level, dry land surely would have become as urbanized as the "corridor" between the two cities is today. Had this been the case, the basic nature of this volume would be very different.

SUMMARY

Early human impacts on the Pine Barrens were exerted during prehistoric times and with the seventeenth century settlement. Few, if any, areas within the region have remained free of human interference with natural processes. Especially significant have been recurrent human-caused fires, cutting of the woodlands for lumber, fuel wood, and charcoal, mining for iron ore and glass sands, impoundment of waters, real estate development, agriculture, and the periodic industrial enterprises and communities, dependent on relatively inexpensive local resources. Always sparsely inhabited because of poor soils and a limited supply of industrial raw materials, today the region remains a useful scientific and charming recreational and historic resource, but not an example of an area unaffected by people.

ACKNOWLEDGMENTS

The author would like to gratefully acknowledge the Rutgers University Research Council for financial support. The author also thanks Bertrand P. Boucher, John Brush, and Theodore Kury, who commented on preliminary versions of this manuscript.

REFERENCES

Anderson, C. M. (1969). Pastor Wrangel's trip to the shore. *N.J. Hist.* **87**, 5-31.
Asher, G. M. (1860). "Henry Hudson the Navigator." Hakluyt Soc., London.
Bartlett, M., *et al.* (1978). "A Plan for A Pinelands National Preserve," Center for Coastal and Environmental Studies, Rutgers University, New Brunswick, New Jersey.
Beers, F. W. (1872). "State Atlas of New Jersey." Beers, Comstock & Cline, New York.
Benson, A. B., ed. and trans. (1966). "Peter Kalm's Travels in North America," Vol. 1. Dover, New York.
Board of General Proprietors of the Eastern Division of New Jersey (1685). "An Advertisement Concerning the Province of East New Jersey in America." John Reid, Edinburg.
Board of General Proprietors of the Eastern Division of New Jersey (1949). "The Minutes of the Board of Proprietors of the Eastern Division of New Jersey, 1685-1705," Vol. 1. Board Proprietors East. Div. N.J., Perth Amboy, New Jersey.
Board of Proprietors of the Eastern Division of New Jersey (1960a). "The Minutes of the Board of Proprietors of the Eastern Division of New Jersey, 1725-1744," Vol. 2. Board Proprietors East. Div. N.J., Perth Amboy, New Jersey.
Board of Proprietors of the Eastern Division of New Jersey (1960b). "The Minutes of the Board of Proprietors of the Eastern Division of New Jersey, 1745-1764," Vol. 3. Board Proprietors East. Div. N.J., Perth Amboy, New Jersey.
Brush, J. E. (1976). "The County of Middlesex in the Province of New Jersey During the American Revolution." Middlesex County Cult. Heritage Comm., North Brunswick, New Jersey.
Cook, G. H. (1864). "Report Upon the Geological Survey of New Jersey and its Progress During the Year 1863." David Naar, Trenton, New Jersey.
Cook, G. H. (1878). "Geology of New Jersey." David Naar, Trenton, New Jersey.
Cook, G. H., and Smock, J. C. (1878). "The State of New Jersey: Surface Geology." Geol. Surv. N.J., Trenton, New Jersey.
Council of Proprietors of West New Jersey (1888). "Report of the Committee of the Council of Proprietors of West New Jersey in Relation to the Province Line Between East and West New Jersey." S. Chew, Camden, New Jersey.
Cross, D., ed. (1941). "Archaeology of New Jersey," Vol. 1. Archaeol. Soc. N.J. N.J. State Mus., Trenton, New Jersey.
Cushing, T., and Sheppard, C. E. (1883). "History of the Counties of Gloucester, Salem, and Cumberland, New Jersey." Everts & Peck, Philadelphia, Pennsylvania.
Defebaugh, J. E. (1907). "History of the Lumber Industry of America," Vol. 2. Am. Lumberman, Chicago, Illinois.
Department of Education, Division of State Library, Archives and History, Microfilm and Records Unit (1778-1822). "County Tax Ratables (By Township)." Trenton, New Jersey.
Fry, M. (1916). Owners and residents of the Vineland Tract before its settlement in 1861. *Vineland Hist. Mag.* **1**, 11-14.
Geological Survey of New Jersey (1896). *N.J. Geol. Surv., Annu. Rep. State Geol. 1895.*
Geological Survey of New Jersey (1900). *N.J. Geol. Surv., Annu. Rep. State Geol. 1899.*
Gordon, T. F. (1834). "Gazetteer of the State of New Jersey." Daniel Fenton, Trenton, New Jersey.

Harshberger, J. W. (1916). "The Vegetation of the New Jersey Pine Barrens, an Ecological Investigation." Christopher Sower Co., Philadelphia, Pennsylvania.

Hauck, J. K., and Lee, A. T. M. (1942). Land subdivision in the New Jersey Pines. *N.J. Agric. Exp. Stn., Bull.* No. 701, 1–52.

Jameson, J. F., ed. (1909). "Narratives of New Netherland, 1607–1664." Scribner's, New York.

Jefferys, T. (1758). "A General Map of the Middle British Colonies in America." Lewis Evans, Philadelphia, Pennsylvania.

Johnson, S. (1971). "Millville Glass: The Early Days." Delaware Bay Trading Co., Inc., Millville, New Jersey.

Kury, T. (1971). Iron as a factor in New Jersey settlement. *Proc. Annu. Symp. N.J. Hist. Comm.* **2,** 63–76.

Kury, T. (1975). Iron as a factor in the settlement geography of the New Jersey Pine Barrens. *Pioneer Am. Soc., Annu. Meet., Cape May, N.J., 1975.*

Lee, A. T. M. (1939). A land development scheme in the New Jersey Pine Area. *N.J. Agric. Exp. Stn., Bull.* No. 665, 5–50.

McMahon, W. (1966). "The Story of Hammonton." Hist. Soc. Hammonton, Hammonton, New Jersey.

Muntz, A. P. (1959). "The Changing Geography of the New Jersey Woodlands, 1600–1900." Dep. Geogr., Univ. of Wisconsin, Madison.

Myers, A. C. (1912). "Narratives of Early Pennsylvania, West New Jersey and Delaware, 1630–1707." Scribner's, New York.

Nelson, W., ed. (1897). "Documents Relating to the Colonial History of the State of New Jersey," Vol. 19. Press Print. Publ. Co., Paterson, New Jersey.

Nelson, W., ed. (1903). "Documents Relating to the Colonial Revolutionary, and Post-Revolutionary History of the State of New Jersey," Vol. 25. Call Print. Publ. Co., Paterson, New Jersey.

Nelson, W. (1904). "Documents Relating to the Colonial, Revolutionary, and Post-Revolutionary History of the State of New Jersey," Vol. 26. Call Print. and Publ. Co., Paterson, N.J.

Nelson, W., and Honeyman, A. V. D., eds. (1917). "Documents Relating to the Colonial History of the State of New Jersey," Vol. 29. Call Print. Publ. Co., Paterson, New Jersey.

Niemcewicz, J. U. (1965). "Under Their Vine and Fig Tree: Travels in America in 1797–99, 1805 with Some Further Account of Life in New Jersey." (M.J.E. Budka, ed.) N.J. Hist. Soc., Elizabeth, New Jersey.

O'Callaghan, E. B., ed (1853). "Documents Relative to the Colonial History of the State of New York," Vol. 1, Weed, Parsons, & Co., Albany, New York.

Pepper, A. (1971). "The Glass Gaffers of New Jersey and Their Creations from 1739 to the Present." Scribner's, New York.

Pierce, A. D. (1957). "Iron in the Pines." Rutgers Univ. Press, New Brunswick, New Jersey.

Sauer, C. O. (1971). "Sixteenth Century North America: The Land and the People As Seen by the Europeans." Univ. of California Press, Berkeley.

Schmidt, H. G. (1973). "Agriculture in New Jersey." Rutgers Univ. Press, New Brunswick, New Jersey.

Sinton, J. W. (1976). Agriculture in the Wharton Tract. *Echoes Hist.* **6,** 5–6.

Smith, S. (1877). "The History of the Colony of Nova Caesaria or New Jersey," 2nd Ed. William S. Sharp, Trenton, New Jersey.

Snyder, J. P. (1969). "The Story of New Jersey's Civil Boundaries, 1606–1968." Bureau Geol. Topogr., Trenton, New Jersey.

Spicer, J. (1945). Diary of Jacob Spicer, 1755–56. *Proc. N.J. Hist. Soc.* **63,** 37–50, 82–117, 175–188.

Stewart, D. J. (compiler) (1876). Combination Atlas Map of Cumberland County, New Jersey. Publ. by D. J. Stewart, Philadelphia, Pa.

Thompson, T. (1937). "An Account of Two Missionary Voyages." Soc. Promot. Christian Knowledge, London, (facsimile).

Wacker, P. O. (1971). A preliminary view of the possible associations between cultural background and agriculture in New Jersey during the latter part of the eighteenth century. *Proc. N.Y.-N.J. Div., Assoc. Am. Geographers* **4,** 41–57.

Wacker, P. O. (1975). "Land and People: A Cultural Geography of Preindustrial New Jersey." Rutgers Univ. Press, New Brunswick, New Jersey.

Whitehead, W. A. (1875). "East Jersey Under the Proprietary Governments . . . with An Appendix Containing 'The Model of the Government of East New Jersey in America . . .' Reprinted from the Original Edition of 1685." Martin R. Dennis, Newark, New Jersey.

Whitehead, W. A. (1880). "Documents Relating to the Colonial, Revolutionary, and Post-Revolutionary History of the State of New Jersey." Vol. 1. Daily Journal, Newark, New Jersey.

Whitehead, W. A., ed. (1885). "Documents Relating to the Colonial, Revolutionary, and Post-Revolutionary History of the State of New Jersey," Vol. 8. Daily Advertiser Print. House, Newark, New Jersey.

Woodward, C. R. (1941). "Ploughs and Politics: Charles Read of New Jersey and His Notes on Agriculture, 1715–1774." Rutgers Univ. Press. New Brunswick, New Jersey.

2

Plant and Animal Products of the Pine Barrens

JAMES E. APPLEGATE, SILAS LITTLE, and PHILIP E. MARUCCI

The Pine Barrens seem aptly named. Early settlers from fertile surrounding areas, finding the land unable to support profitable cultivation, pronounced it barren. Yet, over the years the Pine Barrens have provided a livelihood for a relatively limited number of residents. While a few have focused on hunting and gathering or subsistence farming, almost all have benefitted mainly from exports to neighboring metropolitan markets. Iron furnaces and forges, sawmills, glassworks, and similar industries have dotted the landscape. Only in scattered portions of the Barrens having soils heavier than usual did commercial vegetable and fruit farms develop, resulting in communities such as Tabernacle, Nesco, and Hammonton. On typical Pine Barrens soils, however, only native blueberries and cranberries have sustained farming families. Yet throughout the region, wild plants and animals have been harvested and have played important roles in the lives of Pine Barrens residents.

This article describes the plant and animal products of this unique Pine Barrens environment, and in many cases analyzes changes in their use over time. Wood products and wild plants collected for their flowers, fruits, or foliage first are described. We next depict the animals taken from the Pine Barrens for sport and personal consumption. Finally, we examine the growing of crops in the Pine Barrens.

WOOD PRODUCTS

In the seventeenth century, naval stores, mainly tar and pitch needed in shipbuilding, were the first important exports of wood products. But fuel wood and later charcoal soon were needed as the fuel for Pine Barrens industries and all residences. Lumber sawed at countless small mills was used in building southern New Jersey towns or shipped to other cities. Extensive shipbuilding in coastal and river towns

(Cottrell, 1937) consumed the Atlantic white cedar (*Chamaecyparis thyoides*), pine (*Pinus* spp.), and oak (*Quercus* spp.).

Heavy cutting continued in the Pine Barrens for more than a century. Although in 1749 Peter Kalm thought that Atlantic white cedar was being extirpated (Benson, 1937), Cook (1857) could report that many of the swamps in Cape May County had been cut over twice, some three times, until not a single acre of original growth was left. Cutting of white cedar continued, and in the late 1800's logs buried in the swamps (from presettlement windfalls) were raised and split into rails and shingles (Hall and Maxwell, 1911).

Pine sawlogs for lumber also were being cut, but much of the cutting was for fuel wood and charcoal (Fig. 1). Thousands of cords of fuel wood were shipped from coastal towns to supply Philadelphia, New York, Newark, and Wilmington—as many as 16 sloops piled high with wood left a single coastal town on a single tide (Cottrell, 1937). Inland, much of the fuel shipped outside the Barrens was made into charcoal to facilitate hauling in wagons.

About 1860, coal began to replace wood as a fuel, particularly for industries and residences. The decline in the use of fuel wood was much more gradual in rural areas than in cities, and many local residences in the Pine Barrens still were heated by wood

Fig. 1. Charcoal-making about 1926. Charcoal "pits" were not pits, but circular piles of wood about 4 m in diameter. Wood was stacked to a 2-m height, and then the pile was sloped toward a center stake. The surface of the piles was covered with "turf," blocks of shrub roots, and the soil was laid with the soil side up. The pile was fired by pulling out the center stake and dropping burning kindling into the hole. The rate of burning was controlled by closing that hole and any others to produce the proper amount of draft.

through World War II. The use of fuel wood decreased as use of oil fuel increased. Yet over the last five years, the use of wood for domestic heating has increased because of the shortage and increasing cost of fuel oil.

In 1911, Stone noted that portable sawmills were "sounding the doom of the Cedar Swamps, and piles of yellow sawdust now mark many a site where a few years ago stretched one of these dark retreats" (Stone, 1911). However, even today there are still some sawmills cutting cedar, and white cedars are being harvested for posts, rustic furniture, and other round products.

In the last 40 years, much pine has been cut in the Barrens for pulpwood, and occasionally some oak as well. In the 1950's, about 362,450 steres (100,000 cords) were being produced annually (Little *et al.,* 1958). In recent years, about 109,000 to 170,000 steres (30,000 to 47,000 cords) have been cut annually to supply three New Jersey mills (Pierson, 1977).

In spite of the heavy demand over the years, intensive management for wood products, such as recently practiced by the pulp industry in the Coastal Plain of the South, has not been used extensively in the Pine Barrens, largely because of destructive wildfires. These often have negated efforts to establish productive compositions, such as white cedar in the swamps and seedling pine stands on the uplands. However, there are ready markets: stumpage of white cedar stands 60 years old currently sells for about $2300 per hectare; stumpage of seedling pine stands 40 years old for $600 or more per hectare, and oak stands of the same age for about $180. These pines are used chiefly for lumber and pulpwood, while the oaks are used for fuel wood. While Pine Barren sites are not highly productive, they are just as productive as sites in some sections of the South. Hence, the importance of the wood products industry in the local economy could be increased greatly if wildfire losses are reduced substantially and adequate management measures are applied.

OTHER PLANT PRODUCTS

Peat moss (*Sphagnum*) has been collected from Pine Barren swamps, and after drying and baling, had been used for packing nursery stock (Gifford, 1900), surgical dressings, and the cultivation and propagation of various plants (Waksman *et al.,* 1943). The latter authors suggested that moss had been gathered from virtually every bog, and gathering, drying, and baling moss represented a considerable industry in the Barrens. However, the amount of moss gathered in recent years has decreased.

In past years, large quantitites of Christmas greens, including some holly (*Ilex opaca*) and mistletoe (*Phoradendron flavescens*), were harvested for sale in Philadelphia and New York and for use locally (Gifford, 1900; Stone, 1911). Local use has continued, and certain greens, such as mountain laurel (*Kalmia latifolia*), holly when available, white cedars, club mosses (*Lycopodium* spp.), and pines, still are being removed from Pine Barren woodlands.

Wildflowers also have been removed, either for local use or for sale. In 1900, many flowers, especially those of sweetbay (*Magnolia virginiana*), were being collected in large quantities and sold (Gifford, 1900). Pyxie moss (*Pyxidanthera barbulata*) and trailing arbutus (*Epigaea repens*) flowers from the Barrens were sold on the streets of Philadelphia, and during other seasons, mountain laurel and sweetbay flowers, or holly and mistletoe greens (Weygandt, 1940). Plants also have been collected for dried flower arrangements. In recent years, native plants have been suggested for the land-scaping of homes in the Barrens (Woodford, 1975).

Many people also have collected berries, mushrooms, ferns, and other edible plants. Before World War II, blueberries and cranberries were collected in sufficient quantity so that local people sold them at roadside stands.

Pine cones have been collected for the florist trade nearly year round, especially in the Pine Plains. Pine litter has been collected for the bedding of animals and for use on such crops as sweet potatoes, strawberries, and nursery stock (Gifford, 1900).

Some plants have been removed for use in terrariums, both for individuals and florists. Mosses, lichens, teaberry (*Gaultheria procumbens*), partridgeberry (*Mitchella repens*), pixie moss, trailing arbutus, sundews (*Drosera* spp.), and pitcher-plant (*Sarracenia purpurea*) are among the plants so used.

WILDLIFE

Wildlife resources, both food and skins, have been exploited since the earliest settlements, primarily for personal use but occasionally for export. Unregulated hunting and trapping led to the extirpation of black bear (*Ursus americanus*), wolf (*Canis lupus*), and beaver (*Castor canadensis*), and the near extirpation of white-tailed deer (*Odocoileus virginianus*) (Stone, 1908).

In recent decades, the New Jersey Division of Fish, Game, and Shellfisheries has restored populations of most game animals in the Barrens and is attempting to maintain wildlife levels commensurate with habitat conditions. Game animals, including fur-bearers, are taken during restricted seasons and with limited daily bag limits. While a few residents still may harvest wildlife for food at any season, wildlife use has changed over the years in compliance with laws, blending sport with necessity and providing recreation for the nonnative hunter.

Deer

Deer have been and are the principal wildlife resource in the Pine Barrens. During the precolonial period, they were hunted by the Lenni-Lenape Indians and later by colonists. Unrestricted hunting led to an early decline of deer populations, and legislation restricting hunting was passed as early as 1679 (Sweet and Wright, 1954). For two centuries, various restrictions on the hunting of deer were enacted, including total bans on hunting for several years; however, inadequate enforcement rendered the restrictions ineffective. By 1900, the deer population in the Barrens was reduced to a few family groups (Howard, 1972).

The turning point in New Jersey's deer population occurred during the first decade

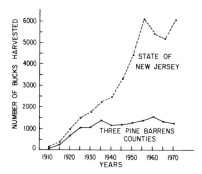

Fig. 2. Number of antlered deer harvested statewide and in Atlantic, Burlington, and Ocean counties. Data are the average annual kill by five-year intervals, beginning with 1910–1914 and ending with 1970–1974.

of this century. The strictest regulations of hunting to date were enacted, and effective enforcement began. Simultaneously, deer from Pennsylvania and Michigan, as well as from several preserves in New Jersey, were released throughout the state.

The first section of New Jersey to reap the benefit of this management was the Pine Barrens. The annual kill of deer in Atlantic, Burlington, and Ocean counties increased from 50 in 1910, the year after a hunting season was reopened under a law restricting kill to bucks, to over 500 in 1920 (unpublished data, New Jersey Division of Fish, Game, and Shellfisheries). The kill in these counties continued to increase to over 1000 bucks in 1931, where it has remained to the present (Fig. 2). Elsewhere in the state, the response of the deer herd was slower. The kill in these three Pine Barrens counties made up more than one-half the statewide harvest through 1940 (Fig. 2). Since then, deer populations of other sections have had the same dramatic increase that occurred earlier in the Barrens. While the Pine Barrens continue to provide a kill of over 1000 bucks a year, the area now contributes only 15–20% of the statewide harvest.

The early increase in deer populations of the Barrens made that section a favorite for hunters. Hunting clubs were formed, and camps were built in "the deer woods." Even today, the culture and traditions that developed during earlier decades persist in the Pine Barrens. Deer camps are filled with hunters during the annual buck season, and the woods reverberate with horns and shouts of the deer drives. However, much of the woods is silent during the single day in New Jersey for harvesting antlerless deer, a season that exists in the rest of the state and in many others to manage deer populations. Buck laws, which were instrumental in building populations in earlier years, are still defended by the hunting culture of the Pine Barrens, and the doe remains a "sacred cow" (Tillett, 1963).

Small Game

Small game is taken legally during a three-month season that begins in early November. Cottontail rabbits (*Sylvilagus floridanus*) and bobwhite quail (*Colinus virginianus*) are the most hunted species, although neither is so abundant nor sought after as in the farmlands of the Inner Coastal Plain. However, both species are favored by the plant communities that develop after fire.

Ruffed grouse (*Bonasa umbellus*), although less common than quail or rabbits, are taken frequently on hunts in or near swamps. The gray squirrel (*Sciurus carolinensis*) is hunted usually in mature hardwood or oak–pine stands. Less commonly hunted are the furbearers, raccoons (*Procyon lotor*), and red and gray foxes (*Vulpes fulva* and *Urocyon cinereoargenteus*). Woodcock (*Philohela minor*) and Wilson snipe (*Capella gallinago*) also are killed legally in the Barrens, but in relatively small numbers.

Waterfowl

Waterfowl long have been hunted by a small number of local residents in the Barrens. In cedar swamps, fresh-water marshes, and cranberry bogs, the species most commonly taken by hunters are wood duck (*Aix sponsa*), black duck (*Anas rubripes*), mallard (*A. platyrhynchos*), and green-winged teal (*A. crecca*). However, other species are shot on occasions, including pintail (*A. acuta*), blue-winged teal (*A. discors*), American widgeon (*A. americana*), ring-necked duck (*Aythya collaris*), hooded merganser (*Lophodytes cucullatus*), and Canada goose (*Branta canadensis*).

Furbearers

Several species of furbearing animals are trapped throughout the Pine Barrens under regulations of the New Jersey Division of Fish, Game, and Shellfisheries. Otters (*Lutra canadensis*) are protected from trapping. Muskrats (*Ondatra zibethica*) commonly are trapped along waterways, although in smaller numbers than in the coastal marshes. Small numbers of mink (*Mustela vison*) and raccoon also are trapped in aquatic habitats, while on the uplands trappers take modest numbers of striped skunk (*Mephitis mephitis*), opossum (*Didelphis marsupialis*), weasels (*Mustela frenata*), and red and gray foxes (Penkala, 1977).

Trapping of beaver is regulated, the number of permits being allocated by counties on the basis of active colonies. While unregulated trapping extirpated beaver in all of southern New Jersey by 1820 (Stone, 1908), beavers were reintroduced in the 1920's, chiefly to northern New Jersey but later in the Pine Barrens, and were repopulating the area successfully by 1934. Sprinks (1976) reported 148 colonies in southern New Jersey, 123 of which were in the Pine Barrens counties of Atlantic, Burlington, Cumberland, Gloucester, and Ocean. Currently, beaver damage is reduced through regulated trapping, and since 1972 20–44 beavers are trapped annually in a three-county (Atlantic, Burlington, Ocean) area.

Reptiles and Amphibians

Snapping turtles (*Chelydra serpentina*) are the only reptiles taken for food or sale by local residents, but various reptiles and amphibians occasionally are removed by local residents or tourists for personal pets. Garter snakes (*Thamnophis sirtalis*) and box turtles (*Terramene carolina*) are the individuals most commonly removed, although many species may be collected by herpetologists. Such collections probably have negligible effects on populations of most Pine Barrens reptiles and amphibians. However, collections for the pet trade already may have adversely affected populations of rare and therefore valuable species such as corn snakes (*Elaphe guttata*), northern pine snakes (*Pituophis melanoleucus*), and timber rattlesnakes (*Crotalus horridus*) (Richard Ryan, personal communication).

CULTIVATION OF CRANBERRIES AND BLUEBERRIES

Cranberries

Indians introduced cranberries (*Vaccinium macrocarpon*) to the Pilgrims more than 350 years ago, and for about 200 years wild berries were collected for home use or sale before culturing began. The first culture was attempted on Cape Cod in 1816 (Peterson *et al.*, 1968), and about 1835 the first bog was planted in the Pine Barrens (Pitt *et al.*, 1933). Nearly all of the New Jersey cranberry bogs have been located within the Pine Barrens.

During the early years, 1857 to 1876, New Jersey produced the largest volume of cranberries. But in 1877, Massachusetts took the leadership, and in 1939 Wisconsin surpassed New Jersey in cranberry production. In 1976 Wisconsin produced 41% of the nation's crop of 2,400,000 barrels, Massachusetts 39%, New Jersey 12%, and Washington and Oregon 4% each.

In New Jersey, the area devoted to cranberry culture increased steadily for 60 years, and then declined (Fig. 3). In 1895, there were about 2000 hectares (5000 acres) in bogs, in 1925 about 4700 ha, but only 2000 in 1945, and currently about 1200 ha.

Much of the decline was due to damage by false blossom, a virus disease which

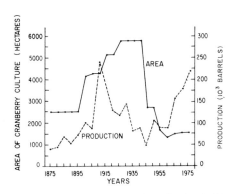

Fig. 3. Five-year averages of cranberry area and production in New Jersey, 1875–1975. 1 hectare = 2.5 acres.

prevents fruiting. This disease, first found in New Jersey in 1915, was in every bog by 1926, and greatly reduced yields to about 37 barrels per hectare (Fig. 3). The only known carrier of this virus is the blunt-nosed leafhopper, *Scleroracus vaccinii,* which breeds on native heath shrubs such as leather leaf (*Chamaedaphne calyculata*), sheep laurel (*Kalmia angustifolia*) and huckleberries (*Gaylussacia* spp.). However, excellent control of this insect through yearly sprays, as well as control of other insect diseases and weeds, has contributed to increased yields, 216 barrels/ha in 1976 (Fig. 3). How-ever, the greatest factor in the sharp increase in yields has been the conversion from hand scooping to the far more efficient mechanical water reel in harvesting.

Several insects are a problem in cranberry culture. Fireworms or leaf rollers such as *Rhopobota vaccinii, Peronea minuta,* and *Sparganothis sulfureana* feed on leaves and fruit, the last insect species sometimes causing losses of more than half the crop. Cranberry fruitworm (a moth), *Acrobasis vaccinii,* also is capable of much damage to the berries. The cranberry girdler, *Crambus hortuellus,* gnaws and girdles stems close to the ground, and several of these insects can kill a large area of vines. However, it may be controlled by heavily sanding infested areas.

Fruit rots caused by fungi are now a problem to the grower and may be controlled by fungicides. But weeds traditionally have been one of the most serious problems. Because bogs cannot be cultivated, competing plants such as switch grass (*Panicum virgatum*), sedge (*Carex bullata*), other sedges, rushes (*Juncus* spp.), redroot (*Lachnanthes tinctoria*), loosestrife (*Lysimachia terrestris*), chain fern (*Woodwardia virginica*), and other ferns (*Osmunda* spp.), which formerly were controlled by hand pulling, today are controlled by herbicides.

Even though the area devoted to cranberries has declined, the crop brings about $3–$3.5 million of gross income to the farmers each year. The processed value of the crop is about $12 million (Brockett and Marucci, 1971).

Blueberries

Cultivation of high-bush blueberries began in the Pine Barrens, and many of the selections, cultural methods, and marketing procedures were made or developed by local residents. Varieties now used come from *Vaccinium australe* Sm. and *V. corymbosum* L., species indigenous to the Pine Barrens. The first crosses of wild plants were made by F. V. Coville of the U.S. Department of Agriculture, using selections of wild plants obtained through Elizabeth White of Whitesbog and her helpers. Plants from New Hampshire also were used in the breeding program (Coville, 1910). The first three varieties, Pioneer, Cabot, and Katherine, were introduced in 1920 (Darrow and Scott, 1966). Since then, 32 additional ones have been developed, mostly through the work of G. M. Darrow, D. H. Scott, R. B. Wilcox, C. A. Doehlert, C. S. Beckwith, and F. L. Hough.

The first planting of cultivated blueberries was made by E. White at Whitesbog in 1916, but additional plantings were delayed because of propagation problems. In 1920, a second planting was begun, and in 1925 the Cranberry and Blueberry Laboratory of the New Jersey Agricultural Experiment Station was established. Its work in cooperation with growers developed methods of propagation, pruning, fertilization, and other needed culture. By 1932, there were 170 ha (419 acres) of cultivated blueberries on 53 farms, in 1963 about 3400 ha (Fig. 4).

During the 1960's, the number of farms having cultivated blueberries dropped from 501 to 383 (Fig. 4). Many owners of small plantings abandoned their fields largely because of the "cost–price squeeze": prices of the picked berries remained relatively stable, while costs and wages for hand pickers climbed. The development of mechanical harvesters enabled the blueberry industry to recover. In 1967, in New Jersey there were nine different harvesting machines, all designed and built by farmers, and two have proved to be economically feasible. As a result, a slight increase in the area of blueberry planting, but not in the number of farms, is occurring.

Insects and fungi have been problems to the growers. The blueberry maggot, *Rhagoletis mendax,* which feeds on native blueberries and huckleberries (especially *Gaylussacia baccata*), is the most important pest to growers. Berries infested by this insect are not acceptable on the market, cannot be removed by any winnowing process, and must be removed by hand. Beetle larvae of cherry fruitworm (*Graptolitha packardi*), cranberry fruitworm (*Acrobasis vaccinii*), and plum cuculio (*Conotrachelus nenuphar*) also infest blueberry fruits, migrating into the fields each year from wild plants. The sharp-nosed leafhopper (*Scaphytopius magdalensis*), which feeds on wild blueberries, huckleberries, and other heath plants, is the only known carrier of blueberry stunt disease. In the 1940's and 1950's, this virus made hundreds of hectares marginal for economic production. The quality and quantity of blueberry crops also can

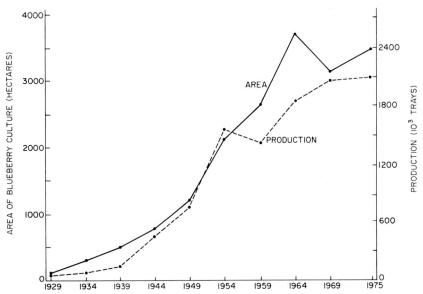

Fig. 4. Five-year averages of blueberry area and production in New Jersey, 1929–1975. 1 hectare = 2.5 acres.

be reduced by another virus, red ring spot, and by three fungi, mummy berry (*Monolinia vaccinii*), gray mold (*Botrytis cinerea*), and anthracnose (*Gloesporium cingulata*). Hence, profitable production of cultivated blueberries utilizes a rigid schedule of fungicide and insecticide sprays.

The gross annual value of the blueberry crop to New Jersey farmers has been $8–$14 million over the past decade, and the crop has provided seasonal employment for several thousand people. If hand picking is used, about 6000 people would be needed to harvest the berries on 3200 ha in a 40-day period, but mechanical harvesters have cut the use of labor by 60%.

OTHER CROPS

In portions of the Pine Barrens, other agricultural crops have been raised on commercial farms, particularly vegetables and fruits on soils with a relatively high clay content. The fruits include peaches, apples, strawberries, raspberries, blackberries, and melons. Vegetables have included a wide variety, with tomatoes, sweet corn, green beans, lima beans, lettuce, broccoli, cabbage, and sweet potatoes forming only a partial list. Such vegetable and fruit farms have been particularly common in the Hammonton, Tabernacle, and Millville areas. In some other sections, as in Ocean County and in the Vineland area, commercial poultry farms have been, and to a lesser extent still are, common. Sod farms and nurseries, as well as such crops as soybeans and field corn, have increased in recent years, particularly in the Tabernacle and Tuckahoe areas. Christmas trees also are grown on some farms.

Preliminary estimates of the New Jersey Department of Agriculture indicate that in recent years farmers have received about $30 million of gross income from these crops and animals annually (E. S. Taylor, personal communication).

FUTURE USE OF THE BARRENS

People use the Pine Barrens in an exceptional variety of ways. Recreational activities such as camping, picnicking, canoeing, hiking, horseback riding, cycling, motoring, photographing rare plants, and observing birds and wildlife attract large numbers of visitors. Hunters desire sufficient areas and wildlife, while landowners and local workers want income and year-round jobs. Supplying pulp mills and local wood-using industries with wood provides some employment, as well as catering to the needs of visitors. Cranberry and blueberry growers desire large tracts that often include unpolluted reservoirs, sanctuaries for wildlife, beautiful fruits, and a picturesque landscape.

To meet future demands on the Pine Barrens, who should own the land, how should the land be allocated according to uses, and how should the land then be managed? About three-quarters of the land is privately owned, and about 112,000 ha (280,000 acres) is under federal and state ownership (excluding road rights-of-way), with some of it designated for education, recreation, and research. Additional public and private areas will be needed, but the total area involved in meeting demands for intensive recreation and for all types of natural areas will require <10% of the Pine Barrens forests. General use of the other Pine Barren forests should include varying degrees of disturbance, as by fire, cutting, or removing "turf," to provide needed habitat diversity.

SUMMARY

Forests repeatedly have been cut over to obtain several wood products. Currently, a small amount of cedar is harvested for boards and round products, and 30,000–47,000 cords of pine are harvested annually for pulp. Many shrubs, herbs and cones are harvested for eating, for use as Christmas greens, for the florist trade, and for nursery use. Past hunting eliminated or reduced certain wildlife species, but management has restored or maintains most wildlife populations. White-tailed deer is the principal wildlife resource. Cottontail rabbits, bobwhite quail, ruffed grouse, and gray squirrel are hunted commonly, and waterfowl, furbearers, reptiles, and amphibians also are removed. Cranberries and blueberries are the major agricultural crops, and their development from native species in the special Pine Barrens environment has resulted in a major portion of the nation's harvest. Insects, fungi, and weeds are major pests requiring management. To meet the wide range of future human demands on the Pine Barrens, specific limited tracts for intensive recreation and natural areas are recommended within the extensive Pine Barrens forests, which in turn are managed for fire control, wood products, and habitat diversity.

REFERENCES

Benson, A. B. (1937). "Peter Kalm's Travels in North America." Wilson–Erickson Inc., New York.

Brockett, J., and Marucci, P. E. (1971). Report of the Small Fruits Task Force of the Governor Cahill Blueprint Commission for the Future of Agriculture in New Jersey. N.J. Dep. Agric., Trenton, New Jersey. (Unpublished manuscript.)

Cook, G. H. (1857). "Geology of the County of Cape May, State of New Jersey." N.J. Geol. Surv., Trenton, New Jersey.

Cottrell, A. T. (1937). Unused South Jersey—its vast latent possibilities. *J. Ind. Finance* **11**(9), 7–12.

Coville, F. V. (1910). Experiments in blueberry culture. *U.S. Dep. Agric., Bureau Plant Ind. Bull.* No. 193.

Darrow, G. M., and Scott, D. H. (1966). Varieties and their characteristics. *In* "Blueberry Culture" (P. Eck and N. F. Childers, eds.), pp. 94–110. Rutgers Univ. Press, New Brunswick, New Jersey.

Gifford, J. (1900). Forestal conditions and silvicultural prospects of the coastal plain of New Jersey. *N.J. Geol. Surv., Annu. Rep. State Geol. 1899* pp. 233–318.

Hall, W. L., and Maxwell, H. (1911). Uses of commercial woods of the United States: I. Cedars, cypresses and sequoias. *U.S. Dep. Agric., For. Serv. Bull.* No. 95, 1–62.

Howard, G. P. (1972). At the crossroads. *N.J. Outdoors* Sept., pp. 3–9.

Little, S., Moorhead, G. R., and Somes, H. A. (1958). Forestry and deer in the pine region of New Jersey. *U.S. For. Serv., Northeast. For. Exp. Stn., Stn. Pap.* No. 109, 1–33.

Penkala, J. (1977). "Trapper Harvest, Recreational and Economic Surveys," Pittman–Robertson Rep. Proj. W-52-R-5. N.J. Dep. Environ. Prot., Div. Fish, Game Shellfish., Trenton, New Jersey.

Peterson, B. S., Cross, C. E., and Tilden, N. (1968). The cranberry industry in Massachusetts. *Mass. Dep. Agric., Bull.* No. 201.

Pierson, G. (1977). New Jersey's renewable resources. *N.J. Outdoors* **4**(1), 6-7, 30-31.

Pitt, D. T., Beckwith, C. S., and Grant, C. J. (1933). A survey of the cranberry and blueberry industries in New Jersey. *N.J. Dep. Agric., Circ.* No. 232.

Spinks, R. (1976). "Beaver-Otter Investigations," Pittman–Robertson Rep. Proj. W-53-R-4. N.J. Dep. Environ. Prot., Div. Fish, Game Shellfish., Trenton, New Jersey.

Stone, W. (1908). The mammals of New Jersey. *N.J. State Mus., Annu. Rep. 1907* pp. 33-110.

Stone, W. (1911). The plants of southern New Jersey with especial reference to the flora of the Pine Barrens and the geographic distribution of the species. *N.J. State Mus., Annu. Rep. 1910* pp. 21-828.

Sweet, J. C., and Wright, C. W. (1954). "A Population Evaluation of White-Tailed Deer," Pittman–Robertson Rep. Proj. W-25-R. N.J. Dep. Conserv. Dev., Div. Fish Game, Trenton, New Jersey.

Tillett, P. (1963). "Doe Day: The Antlerless Deer Controversy in New Jersey." Rutgers Univ. Press, New Brunswick, New Jersey.

Waksman, S. A., Schulhoff, H., Hickman, C. A., Cordon, T. C., and Stevens, S. C. (1943). The peats of New Jersey and their utilization. *N.J. Dept. Conserv. Dev., Geol. Ser. Bull.* No. 55, Part B, 1-278.

Weygandt, C. (1940). "Down Jersey." Appleton, New York.

Woodford, E. M. (1975). "A Home in the Pine Barrens." Medford (N.J.) Township Environ. Comm., Medford, New Jersey.

Part II

GEOLOGY AND SOILS

3

Geology of the Pine Barrens of New Jersey

EDWARD C. RHODEHAMEL

PHYSIOGRAPHY AND GEOGRAPHY

The state of New Jersey has a complex geology made up of about 65 geologic formations ranging from pre-Cambrian age, over 600 MYBP (million years before the present), to those being deposited today. These formations lie in four physiographic provinces (Fig. 1). The youngest, up to about 140 MYBP, is the Atlantic Coastal Plain province occupying the southern half of New Jersey and underlying the Pine Barrens.

The topography of the Pine Barrens region is a gently undulating surface lying mainly between 15–46 m (50–150 ft) above seal level. Upon this predominantly sandy surface, streams flow in shallow, relatively broad valleys. Most streams drain eastward and southeastward on the Atlantic slope to the Atlantic Ocean, although some flow south and west, respectively, into the Delaware Bay and Delaware River. All Pine Barrens streams originate in the region; thus, there are no through-flowing streams. Along a tortuous boundary between easterly and westerly flowing streams lies a gravel-capped narrow belt of uplands with isolated hills, hillocks, and knolls. Altitudes of 107 m (350 ft) or more are found at small, steep-sided, and ironstone-capped outliers in the Clarksburg area of Monmouth County. However, surface gradients are gentle, typical of sandy terrains, and usually range from 0.6–3.8 m/km (0.06–0.38%).

OUTLINE OF GEOLOGICAL HISTORY

Some 50 million years after the North American and African continents began to separate,* the Atlantic Coastal Plain, composed of continental deposits on older metamorphosed rocks, subsided below sea level. Subsequently in New Jersey, mainly marine and (or) marginal marine sediments were deposited. As such, the Atlantic Coastal Plain in New Jersey is composed of a sequence of essentially unconsolidated,

---

*These rock or lithospheric plates separated in Late Triassic or Early Jurassic time, about 200–170 MYBP (National Academy of Sciences, 1973).

ISBN 0-12-263450-0

Fig. 1. Physiographic provinces and terminal moraine in New Jersey. Dotted line is the southernmost limit or terminal moraine of the Pleistocene glaciation (Wisconsin age). Three subprovinces are indicated for the Atlantic Coastal Plain. The Pine Barrens are restricted mainly to the central upland and outer lowland subprovinces. Modified from Minard and Rhodehamel (1969).

highly permeable to relatively impermeable quartzose gravel, sand, silt, glauconitic sand (greensand), and clay strata that dip and thicken southeastward. These extend seaward onto the submerged Continental Shelf. The Coastal Plain deposits are almost entirely of Cretaceous (136–65 MYBP) and Tertiary (65–1.8 MYBP) ages, although a relatively thin wedge of Upper Jurassic strata (roughly 140 MYBP) may be present deep beneath the extreme southeastern part of the Pine Barrens region (Perry *et al.*, 1975). Dips range from about 2.1 to 19 m/km (0.2–1.9%). In general, the lowest (oldest) beds have the steepest dips, and the uppermost (youngest) beds have the gentlest dips. Younger Quaternary deposits overlie these Cretaceous and Tertiary strata.

During either latest Early Cretaceous (about 100 MYBP) or earliest Late Cretaceous, the sea first transgressed over the thick accumulations of continental alluvial sediments deposited in southern New Jersey (Petters, 1976). During Late Cretaceous and Tertiary time, the sea covered all or most of the Atlantic Coastal Plain several times, destroying all terrestrial vegetation.

Having deposited the Cohansey Sand, the sea completed its regress for the last time, and the present topography began to form, perhaps about 5 MYBP. Today, the Cohansey Sand lies at altitudes up to 107 m, indicating that regional uplift as well as possible sea-level lowering followed. Since that time, only the Beacon Hill Gravel of Pliocene (?) and Miocene (?) age (<5 MYBP) has been introduced into the uplands (northern and central part) of the Pine Barrens region. However, the dominant geological activity during the last 5 million years has been dissection, cut and fill, lateral leveling, and redeposition by rivers and streams (fluvial action) aided during the Pleistocene (ice age) Epoch by vigorous aeolian (wind) erosion and deposition. An immense amount of unconsolidated sediments was removed from the Pine Barrens region during this time. This has resulted in a widespread inversion of topography (Salisbury and Knapp, 1917), in which generally older stream deposits now at the higher altitudes are surrounded by younger deposits in present valleys.

Certain plant species that became established at the end of Cohansey time may have held on in a so-called "refugium" throughout the rigorous Pleistocene Glaciation, as suggested by Taylor (1912), Harshberger (1916), and Strock (1929). However, there was no Pine Barrens island refugium created by a "Pensauken Sound" (Salisbury, 1895) as they envisioned. Sea level may have been 12 m higher than it is today during an interglacial time (Sangamon) (Gill, 1962), but there is no evidence (Salisbury and Knapp, 1917; Owens and Minard, 1975) that such a large-scale marine transgression took place during the Pleistocene in the inner lowland area of New Jersey (Fig. 1). Furthermore, during the glacial advances and severe cold, the volume of ice locked up in the world's continental glaciers reduced sea level >100 m below today's level. Thus, during these glacial stages the shoreline was many tens of kilometers east of the present shoreline, producing a wide exposed Coastal Plain.

Accordingly, plants could migrate north and south along the Coastal Plain, as well as westward to higher ground, in response to retreats and advances of the several glaciers entering New Jersey and the rises and falls of sea level (Richards, 1960). Although glacial retreats and sea level rises appear to have been much faster than glacial advances and sea level declines, these events are both measured in thousands of years (Curray, 1965), seemingly ample time for migration of plants along the Coastal Plain corridor. Through-flowing rivers to the west and north of the Pine Barrens would not present migration barriers so that plant migration to and from the west also could occur. If Pine Barrens vegetation were established prior to Pleistocene time, as seems likely, this plant migration (retreat and advance) perhaps may have occurred three times during the Pleistocene and Holocene (post-Pleistocene) epochs.

However, it appears that the Pine Barrens vegetation as we know it today became established after the last glaciation (Wisconsin, 0.01–0.1 MYBP), for at the maximum extent of the several glaciations, the ice front stood for long lengths of time no more than 15–65 km (10–40 mi) north of the northern borders of the Pine Barrens. During Wisconsin Glaciation, the glacial front was only 15 km distant (Fig. 1). Consequently, the climate of the Pine Barrens during this glaciation must have been severe, as evidenced by the (1) many wind-scoured cobbles and boulders (ventifacts), (2) the deep (often >2 m) ice-distorted lateritic soil profiles (congeliturbation) under upland surfaces, (3) the lack of peat deposits within and adjacent to the region older than late Wisconsin age (Buell, 1970; Minard and Rhodehamel, 1969; Sirkin and Minard, 1972; Owens and Minard, 1975), and (4) the present anchored sand dunes and other wind-blown features in many upland surfaces, e.g., in the Middle Branch basin of Lebanon State Forest in Burlington and Ocean counties.

In addition, Minard (1966) described sandblasted ironstone blocks of Beacon Hill Gravel within 5 km of the west border of the Pine Barrens near Perrineville, Monmouth County. The blocks are extensively fluted and faceted with highly polished surfaces, which he believes resulted from wind scour during Wisconsin Glaciation, when strong winds from the ice sheet blew over a sandy surface devoid of vegetation. He characterizes the climate as similar to that now prevailing in northern Greenland.

Thus, the geological evidence (Richards, 1960; Curray, 1965; Minard and Rhodehamel, 1969; Buell, 1970; Owens and Minard, 1975; Minard, 1966) indicates the region has continuously lain above sea level for the last 5 million years, and has been subjected to continuous and vigorous fluvial and aeolian erosion accompanied by local redeposition. It may have lost and regained a Pine Barrens flora on several occasions during the Pleistocene. However, because of the tundra and arctic climate that likely existed in the Pine Barrens during Wisconsin Glaciation, the present Pine Barrens flora apparently entered the region in post-Wisconsin time along either the exposed Coastal Plain corridor prior to the Holocene rise in sea level or by an eastward migration from higher ground to the west, and perhaps by both routes.

STRATIGRAPHY

The Coastal Plain sediments exhibit a rather uniformly increasing range in thickness from a feather edge next to the Piedmont near the Delaware River to as much as 1830 m (6000 ft) in Cape May County. For example, in the Wharton Tract of the central Pine

Barrens the sediments range from about 550–1070 m thick (Spangler and Peterson, 1950). The lowest beds are predominantly continental deposits, the overlying beds mainly marine deposits. An overlying discontinuous veneer of Pliocene (?) age (5 MYBP) and Miocene (?) age (22.5 MYBP) (Owens and Minard, 1975) and Quaternary–Holocene age (0–1.8 MYBP) deposits is composed of fluvial and near-shore marine sand, gravel, silt, and clay.

Formations described here are the Kirkwood Formation and Cohansey Sand of Miocene age (Richards and Harbison, 1942; Rachele, 1976; see also this chapter), plus younger overlying deposits forming discontinuous sedimentary veneers (Table I).

TERTIARY DEPOSITS

Kirkwood Formation

The Kirkwood Formation of middle Miocene age (Table I) is exposed at the surface along the northern and western borders of the Pine Barrens, but underlies the Cohansey Sand throughout the remainder of the Pine Barrens region. The Kirkwood is the oldest and deepest lying deposit believed to influence the nature of the Pine Barrens region by its sandy lithology.* This formation, composed chiefly of sand, silt, clay, and some gravel, was named by Knapp (1904) for its exposure near the village of Kirkwood in Camden County, New Jersey. At least part of the formation (the highly fossiliferous "Shiloh Marl" of Cumberland County) was recognized as of Miocene age by Cook (1868). At its type locality, the Kirkwood Formation is a feldspathic (abundant feldspar), fine-grained, gray- to white-colored, yellow- and red-banded, and thin- to thick-bedded quartz sand.

The Kirkwood, according to Minard and Owens (1963), contains several distinct and mappable lithological units. These include: diatomaceous clay; carbonaceous (lignitic) and micaceous dark silty sand; red, yellow, and gray, somewhat feldspathic sand; and clean fine- to medium-grained gravel and sand. Sandstone, cemented by an opaline and chalcedony† matrix and iron oxide, also is present, especially along the Atlantic coast.

The thickness of the Kirkwood Formation varies from 0–213 m, e.g., about 30 m at Atsion, about 87 m at Harrisburg, 76 m at Island Beach State Park, 90 m about 6.5 km southeast of Oswego Lake, and >213 m at Atlantic City (Richards, 1945). Thickening results from an increase in the number of beds, as well as from a general thickening of individual beds.

The Kirkwood Formation overlaps several formations, representing one of the major unconformities‡ in the New Jersey Coastal Plain. In the subsurface, it overlies the Piney

---

*The physical character of rocks.

†A variety of quartz.

‡Conformity here refers to the contact between strata which have been deposited in uninterrupted sequence under the same general conditions; unconformity refers to the contact representing a gap or interruption in the depositional sequence.

TABLE I Upper Strata of the New Jersey Coastal Plain[a]

Time and age[b]	Formation	Lithology	Thickness (m)
Quaternary			
Holocene (0.01)[c]	Undifferentiated deposits in stream channels, marshes, estuaries, and bays	Clay, silt, sand, bog iron, and peat	0–3
Pleistocene (1.8)[c]	Quartz Sand 2 and Quartz Sand 1 Deposits [Valley-terrace phase of Cape May (?) Formation][a,e,f]	Clay, silt, sand, and gravel	0–37
Tertiary			
Pliocene (?) (5)[g] and	Arkose 1 Deposits [Pensauken (?) Formation][e]	Gravel, sand, and silt; some sand beds	0–6
Miocene (?)[g]	Arkose 2 Deposits [Bridgeton (?) Formation][c]	are hardened with iron oxide	0–21
	Beacon Hill Gravel	Sand and gravel	0–6, usually <3
Miocene (22.5)[g]	Cohansey Sand[h,i]	Sand with gravel, silt, and clay	8–61
	Kirkwood Formation	Clay, silt, sand and gravel	15–137

[a] Modified from Rhodehamel (1973).
[b] Million years before present.
[c] Hopkins (1975).
[d] MacClintock and Richards (1936).
[e] Owens and Minard (1975).
[f] Salisbury and Knapp (1917).
[g] Berggren (1972).
[h] Rachele (1976).
[i] Rhodehamel (this chapter).

Point (?) Formation of late Eocene age (Gill, 1962; Nemickas and Carswell, 1976). In the outcrop area (Fig. 2) several kilometers west of the Wharton Tract, the Kirkwood overlies in ascending order the Hornerstown and Vincentown Formations of Paleocene age and the Manasquan Formation of Eocene age. Farther north, the Kirkwood apparently overlaps the Red Bank Sand of Upper Cretaceous age. This unconformity at the base of the Kirkwood is relatively smooth, perhaps varying no more than 3–4 m locally. Nevertheless, it is highly significant from both a geological and hydrological standpoint, for it indicates an abrupt change from the relatively impervious and predominantly glauconite sand and clay to quartz-rich sand. This quartz predominance

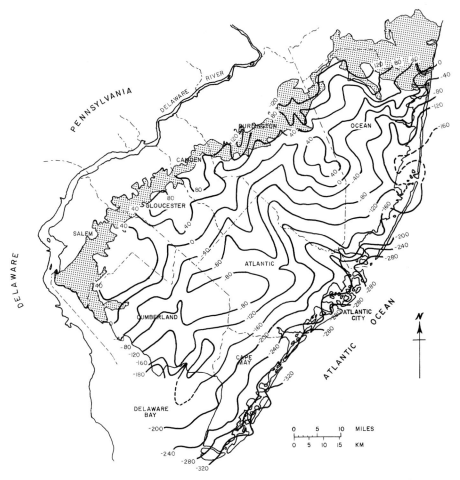

Fig. 2. Contour map of the upper surface of the Kirkwood Formation (Tertiary, Miocene age). Contours are the number of feet above or below sea level; contour intervals are 40 ft (12.1 m). Shaded area is the outcrop area where the Kirkwood Formation reaches the ground surface; southeast of the outcrop area the Kirkwood is covered by younger deposits. See Rhodehamel (1973) for the well-drilling records on which the contours are based.

continues into the younger Cohansey Sand and Beacon Hill Gravel, thus providing general hydrological continuity throughout the sediment column deposited since the beginning of Kirkwood time. According to Carter (1972), the Cohansey Sand lies conformably over the Kirkwood, but Minard (1964) reported an unconformable relationship between these formations. The regional nature of the unconformity is unknown, but it appears widespread.

The different lithologies in the formation represent various nearshore depositional environments. Twenty or more kilometers west of the present coast, coarse sand and gravel, interpreted as beach deposits, have been encountered in well drilling. These deposits are intercalated with nearshore marine and lagoonal sediments. Inland from the present coast, beach deposits are less common and thinner, and lagoonal deposits more common and thicker. Locally, coarse sand and gravel are penetrated by inland wells and may represent lag gravel in tidal inlets. Some of these deposits seem to be aligned with modern drainageways.

Diatom beds in the Kirkwood represent shallow-water sediments, as indicated by the presence of many neritic,* lagoonal, and estuarine fossil animals, and terrestrial plant remains. According to Andrews (1976), the Miocene deposits of the Chesapeake Bay area are associated with very shallow water deposits. Several of the upper diatomaceous clays and their associated water-bearing sands were noted by Woolman (1891, 1892) in wells and outcrops southeast of an irregular line from Shiloh through Bridgeton, Vineland, Hammonton, Herman, and Barnegat. Lower diatomaceous clay beds generally continue for another 8 km northwest of this line. Relatively extensive water-bearing beds may be found southeast of this boundary.

Lack of shell material in places in the formation may be attributed to the dissolving of shells by the saline lagoonal water that had characteristically low pH and oxygen content. Further solution of shell material by subsequent acidic ground water may explain the widespread absence of calcareous fossils in the Kirkwood, especially in the outcrop area.

Toward the end of Kirkwood time, moderate uplift of the land occurred to the west and northwest with accompanying regression of the sea. Channels cut into the Kirkwood are filled with yellow goethite (limonitic) sand, which at most places includes both the upper part of the Kirkwood and the Cohansey Sand. An especially large deep channel beneath the Mullica River basin trending toward Atlantic City is shown in Fig. 2. Rejuvenated streams introduced considerable thicknesses of fine sand and silt to the lagoons. These dark-colored, massive-bedded sands that buried the older diatomaceous sediments were, in part, eroded. Inland, for example, at the Ridgway sand pit at Arneys Mount, the upper Kirkwood sediments probably were subjected to intensive surface weathering before being covered by deposits of Cohansey Sand. Weathering is indicated by the thick, highly oxidized state of Kirkwood beds lying beneath the unoxidized Cohansey Sand. At such places variegated colors of bright orange, yellow, and light gray are common in the Kirkwood.

---

*Oceanic, but generally over the continental shelf.

Cohansey Sand

The name Cohansey first was applied by Knapp (1904) and Kummel and Knapp (1904) to the thick (up to 76 m) and areally extensive wedge of sandy strata lying above deposits of recognized Kirkwood age. The type locality at Cohansey Creek, in Cumberland County, New Jersey, was cited later by Bascom *et al.* (1909). Knapp first considered the Cohansey Sand to be of Pleistocene (?) age but later reported it to be of Miocene (?) or Pliocene (?) age.

For many years, the definition of the formation was uncertain, but beds subsequently called Cohansey were earlier dated as Miocene (?) and Pliocene (?) by Hollick (1892, 1900). In 1968, Rhodehamel (unpublished data) identified Miocene diatoms in the Butler Place (Pine Barrens of Burlington County) well cuttings, tentatively identified as Cohansey Sand. Recently, Rachele (1976), studying pollen in the Cohansey Sand, established a late Miocene or early Pliocene age for the Cohansey. However, the suggested 18 million-year age for the Cohansey materials derived by use of the Barghoorn modernization curve (Barghoorn, 1951) seems to indicate a definite Miocene age.

The Cohansey Sand underlies an area of approximately 6086 km^2 southeast of the Kirkwood outcrop area in the Coastal Plain. The occurrence of Cohansey outliers within the Kirkwood outcrop area indicates that the Cohansey previously was more extensive. Over extensive areas of the Pine Barrens region, this sand is exposed at the surface; at other places it is overlain by thin, more recent deposits. Its sandy nature exerts a major influence on the region, as soils which have developed are generally droughty.

However, the lithology of the Cohansey Sand is variable. It is predominantly a yellow limonitic (mostly goethitic) quartz sand containing minor amounts of pebbly sand, fine to coarse sand, silty and clayey sand, and interbedded clay. It contains small amounts of weathered feldspar; chert, vein quartz, and notable amounts of rounded ironstone pebbles; and lenses or fragments of carbonaceous materials within beds of kaolinitic clay. Fine to medium-sized muscovite flakes are common in some beds, but are found only in trace amounts in other beds. Some beds in the northern part of the outcrop contain detrital lignitic particles, and may contain as much as 2–10% by weight of dark heavy minerals, mainly ilmenite. Markewicz *et al.* (1958) report that the opaque mineral ilmenite and its alteration product leucoxene average 85% by weight of all accessory minerals.

The Cohansey consists of very thick beds (>1 m) to thickly laminated seams (30–61 mm) of sand and clay. Both parallel bedding and cross-stratification occur in the sands. Cross-stratification, where present, may be used to distinguish the Cohansey from the non-cross-stratified Kirkwood. Gravel beds may be 1 m thick but are generally <0.3 m thick. The coarser materials range from very fine-grained sand to well-rounded pebbles of quartz and quartzite up to 13 cm in diameter. Pebbles ranging from subangular to well rounded are predominantly of the milky quartz types, although clear, pink, and smoky-quartz varieties are common. Chert pebbles, in notable amounts (about 2%) in the gravel, are in trace amounts (<1%) in the sand beds. Quartz sand grains are generally clear or slightly opaque smoky, characteristically with a limonitic (goethitic) or, less frequently, a hematitic stain on their surfaces. Some sand grains, however, are clean and light gray to white. Frosted surfaces are common, suggesting that some of the sand has undergone considerable aeolian action. In short, the sand beds of the Cohansey Sand are classified as quartz arenites.

The Cohansey Sand has been identified as stream, fluvial plain, deltaic, estuarine, lagoonal, beach, and other types of nearshore-marine deposits (Richards and Harbison, 1942; Richards, 1960; Markewicz *et al.*, 1958; Markewicz, 1969; Minard and Owens, 1960; Owens and Sohl, 1969; Isphording and Lodding, 1969; Carter, 1972; Rhodehamel, 1973; Rachele, 1976). Gill (1962) interpreted subsurface Cohansey deposits in Cape May County as estuarine in origin. On the other hand, Cohansey materials in an outlier near Arneys Mount (Burlington County) are clean and contain cross laminations and swash-concentrated opaque mineral laminae, indicating a beach and (or) intertidal environment. At Mount Misery (Burlington County), relatively thick sections (>10 m) of long sweeping, steeply dipping beds of clean, white quartzose, very micaceous, fine to very coarse sand, and fine gravel also suggest either a beach environment or perhaps some portion of a marine-deltaic front environment. A few kilometers east of Woodmansie (Burlington County) and at Winslow (Camden County), there are thick sequences of carbonaceous, irregular-shaped, lenticular, and laminated clay layers. These are interpreted to be abandoned fluvial channel slackwater fill and interchannel deposits, characteristic of fluvial environments and alluvial plains. Associated silty sand and less prominent sand and lenticular gravel beds are interpreted as being river channel deposits. Therefore, the Cohansey Sand of the Pine Barrens region is considered to have deposits of all these environments and is interpreted as a mixed or transitional environment deposit which, in overall aspect, is a partly dissected ancient subdelta plain. Examples of modern deltas subjected to destruction by wave and tidal forces are the Nile, Apalachicola, Mississippi, and Mekong. Owens and Sohl (1969) conclude that the Cohansey represents deltaic deposits.

The Cohansey Sand, at least locally, unconformably overlaps the Kirkwood Formation, which, except in the Sandy Hook area (Minard, 1969), is the only formation directly underlying the Cohansey. Bascom *et al.* (1909) and Minard and Owens (1963) report an unconformity between these formations. Isphording (1970a,b), on the other hand, believes the contact is mainly conformable but that local unconformities exist. However, the sharp boundary observed in well samples between the yellowish-orange oxidized Cohansey strata and the light-to-dark-gray oxidized Kirkwood strata (the erosional character of the upper surface shown in Fig. 4) suggests widespread unconformable relations. Other indicators of an unconformity include a hardened (indurated) and sometimes blocky iron oxide zone observed at several locations, the almost total absence of feldspar in the Cohansey relative to the Kirkwood, and a small difference in the dip and the strike* of the two units. In the Mullica River basin, discontinuous deposits of modified Beacon Hill Gravel and Quaternary age sediments unconformably overlie the Cohansey.

---

*The direction the surface of the stratum takes as it intersects the horizontal.

The average strike of the Cohansey Sand according to Minard and Owens (1960) is N. 73°E., and its average dip is about 1.9 m/km (0.19%) to the southeast. It ranges in thickness from a featheredge to >76 m along the southern coastal part of the state, where according to Richards (1945), its base may extend, at least locally, to nearly 122 m below sea level (Fig. 3). Thickness, for example, in the Mullica River basin, ranges from about 7.6 m in the Tabernacle–Indian Mills area to >61 m in the Port Republic area, and the average thickness is about 42.7 m.

Fig. 3. Thickness map of the Cohansey Sand (Tertiary, Miocene age) and overlying deposits. Contours are the number of feet of thickness of the Cohansey Sand with its discontinuous veneer of younger Tertiary and Quaternary age deposits. Contour interval is 50 ft (15.1 m); lines dashed where uncertain. These deposits overlie the Kirkwood Formation (see contours of Fig. 2). The northwestern edge of the Cohansey Sand (thin line north and west of the contours) is the boundary with the Kirkwood at ground surface. The thick dashed line to the south and east is the inland extent of thick Quaternary age deposits. Quaternary deposits generally are very thin north and west of this line and become rather thick to the south and east. See Rhodehamel (1973) for well-drilling records.

The Cohansey contains white, yellow, rêd, and light-gray carbonaceous clay in beds ranging in thickness from thin stringers to as much as 7.3 m. Individual large clay beds may extend over an area of about 100 hectares. Clay and clayey–sand zones, composed of several beds, form thick sections and may be preponderant in the Cohansey throughout several square kilometers. Combined thicknesses are as much as 12.2 m locally, e.g., at Winslow (Camden County) and east of Woodmansie (Burlington and Ocean Counties). Well-drilling records show that some clay beds occur within 6.1 m of the land surface throughout a considerable part of the Pine Barrens.

Three areas of the Cohansey Sand are recognized, based on variations in clay, silt, and sand content (Fig. 4). Area 1 contains thick sand beds, interpreted as fluvial and delta-front deposits containing relatively thin discontinuous sections of laminated clay. Where determined, the clay and silt beds in the upper 30.5 m average 11.3 and 13.3%, respectively, of the deposit. A thicker sequence of more massive-bedded clays generally occurs in area 2. Clay and silt beds here comprise about 24 and 16%, respectively, of the upper 30.5 m of the Cohansey. The more massive-bedded clays are generally gray, blue, and, less frequently, cream in color and contain disseminated plant material. They have a less oxidized appearance than the multicolored laminated clays of area 1. Organic material, including large logs and tree limbs, occurs in distinct beds or layers. Other fossil forms are rare. In area 3 along the coast (Fig. 4), the relative quantities of sand and clay are poorly known. However, evidence from wells in Cape May (Gill, 1962) and Atlantic (Clark *et al.*, 1968) counties indicates a higher proportion of sand than in area 2.

Almost all of the Wharton Tract and most of the Mullica River basin located in the central part of the Pine Barrens (Fig. 4) lie in area 1. Data from 805.5 m of drilled material at 33 well sites, mainly in the upper 30.1 m of sediments, indicate that the Cohansey in the Wharton Tract contains 3.5% clay beds, 3.5% silt beds, and 93% sand beds. Multicolored thin (0.03–1 m thick) laminated clays and silts are widely distributed and are common throughout the upper 30.1 m of the Cohansey. These clays and silts are intercalated with a thick sequence of sand beds which lie above a prominent black, dark-gray, to olive-gray carbonaceous clay. This latter clay zone in the Wharton Tract lies between 9.1 and 27.4 m below sea level.

Shepard (1959) has suggested the use of laminated clay as a valuable criterion for recognizing certain deltaic environments. The occurrence of bluish-colored clay layers containing fine carbonaceous particles is considered to indicate a delta-front environment where the top (topset) beds of marine deltas are formed. The limited areal extent of these clay bodies, which occur in area 1 of the Cohansey Sand (Fig. 4), their large number, and their wide distribution suggest a series of coalescent deltas from small distributary streams.

The boundary line between areas 1 and 2 in Fig. 4 marks the seaward extent of these laminated clays and thus marks roughly the general position of delta-front sedimentation. Northwest of the boundary line (area 1), for example, in Lebanon State Forest (Burlington County), thick fluvial deposits in many places are overlain by beach and (or) delta-front sand. Southeastward (area 2) are sequences of massive-bedded clays,

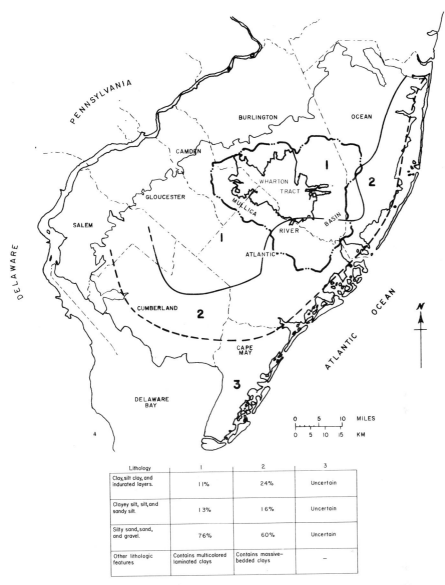

Lithology	1	2	3
Clay, silt clay, and indurated layers.	11%	24%	Uncertain
Clayey silt, silt, and sandy silt.	13%	16%	Uncertain
Silty sand, sand, and gravel.	76%	60%	Uncertain
Other lithologic features	Contains multicolored laminated clays	Contains massive-bedded clays	—

Fig. 4. Distribution of lithological variations in the Cohansey Sand. Thick lines are boundaries between three areas recognized based on selected lithological characteristics; boundaries uncertain where dashed. The northwestern edge of the Cohansey Sand (thin line north and west of the contours) is the boundary with the Kirkwood at ground surface. The Wharton Tract and the surrounding Mullica River basin are indicated in the central region. See Rhodehamel (1973) for well-drilling records.

whose marginal areal position with respect to the laminated clays of area 1 and lenticular shape suggest deposition at the front slope of a delta (distal bar to prodelta). Elongated circular lenses having small thicknesses suggest an interdistributary bay environment. The massive clays persist southeastward toward the coast, where in area 3 (Fig. 4) more sand is present, and marine conditions apparently were predominant throughout much of Cohansey time. This model of the depositional environment of the Cohansey Sand generally agrees with that of Owens and Sohl (1969).

In addition to the clay criteria discussed above, the presence of *Callianassa* borings (marine organism burrows) in many of the Cohansey Sand exposures throughout Salem, Cumberland, Burlington, Ocean, and Atlantic counties (Carter, 1972) indicate at least one, and perhaps more, shallow-water marine transgressions and regressions over the surface of the delta.

As the fluvial Cohansey materials are composed primarily of kaolinitic–illitic clay, quartz sand, and chert, which are typical end-products of multicycled erosion and redeposition, the Cohansey Sand is the product partly of erosion of older Coastal Plain deposits (e.g., the Raritan Formation), and partly from the Adirondack Mountains via the Hudson River, because of the almost exclusive ilmenite character of its heavy minerals. The ilmenite concentrations are especially notable along the Cohansey's present northwestern edge. However, trace amounts of grains with crystal faces, as well as a somewhat larger number of angular-shaped grains suggest that some streams perhaps were eroding areas of weathered crystalline rocks and rocks of the Triassic age Newark group. The cleaner, well-rounded, and well-sorted quartz sands, which contrast sharply with the more angular sand grains, seem to be reworked from older sediments exposed on the shallow submerged continental shelf. This mixing apparently was done by fluvial forces and also by increased wave and current action during marine transgression and regression within the Cohansey.

Waves and currents ultimately removed silt and clay from the delta-front materials and developed gently inclined slopes to the beach sand and gravel. Some of the finer sand, silt, and clay of the Cohansey Sand was deposited in sheltered lagoon and bay environments, but apparently most was transported seaward onto the continental shelf. During periods of marine transgression and regression, quartzose materials were spread out and transported southwestward along the advancing and retreating beaches, and in the nearshore ocean environments along the changing delta periphery (Carter, 1972). Hence, widespread marine sheet sands are intercalated with the distributary–marsh and swamp deposits of Cohansey Sand. At the end of Cohansey time, the sea withdrew, leaving a white sheet-sand as the Cohansey's youngest marine bed. This event seems well preserved in the highest level of exposures at the clay pits east of Woodmansie, where the clean white sand forms the upper bed of the Cohansey Sand and is unconformably overlain by younger, poorly sorted, and very coarse deposits believed to be reworked Beacon Hill Gravel.

In short, the variations both vertically and areally in the Cohansey Sand resulted from the interaction of many depositional processes found in close proximity in a deltaic environment.

Beacon Hill Gravel

Lying unconformably above the Cohansey Sand is the Beacon Hill Gravel of probable Pliocene (?) and Miocene (?) age (Owens and Minard, 1975). The Beacon Hill
Gravel contains coarse-grained quartz sand, pebbles of vein quartz, quartzite, and
fossil-bearing chert derived from the Helderberg Group of Devonian age (395–345
MYBP). The formation is about 6.1 m thick at its type locality just north of the Pine
Barrens at Beacon Hill in Monmouth County, New Jersey. Here and at other sites
where it is less well preserved but clearly recognizable, its predominantly quartzose
gravels contain up to 23% Helderberg age chert from a more northern source (Minard,
1966).

Chert, quartzose gravel, and ilmenite in both the Cohansey Sand and Beacon Hill
Gravel suggest a similar source for the two formations. However, differences in the
coarseness of the material and in the structure of the two formations suggest a change in
both the mechanism and site of deposition. A longer, predominantly marine transport
to a nearshore environment took place during Cohansey time, and a shorter predominantly stream transport to a fluvial environment took place during Beacon Hill time.
The formation appears to result from what once was a more extensive stream channel
deposit, i.e., an ancient Hudson River. Bowman and Lodding (1969) suggest the same
source for the Pensauken Formation, and Owens and Minard (1975) indicate that
post-Beacon Hill deposits (their Arkose 2 and Arkose 1 materials) have a northern
source, perhaps the ancient Hudson River, but these are only in the southern part of the
Pine Barrens. Accordingly, the Beacon Hill Gravel probably represents the last major
introduction of materials into the upland part of the Pine Barrens region from outside
sources. However, the somewhat younger streams (probably from the same ancient,
but younger, Hudson River drainage) that continued to erode, shift westward, and
spread their deposits on the upper delta plain (as defined by LeBlanc, 1972) then being
formed during Arkose 2 and possibly Arkose 1 time [Pliocene (?) and Miocene (?)],
also contributed sediments. These deposits are of a similar nature, and because of the
subsequent weathering and reworking in the Pine Barrens, are not readily distinguishable from the locally reworked deposits of Cohansey Sand and Beacon Hill Gravel.

Prolonged erosion during and since Pliocene time has thinned the Beacon Hill
Gravel in most places and probably has removed the formation from wide areas.
Identifiable Beacon Hill deposits now are restricted to small scattered remnants at the
highest altitudes in the New Jersey Coastal Plain. Inasmuch as they formerly occupied
stream channels and were deposited along the lowest reaches in the topography of that
time, their present location at the highest altitudes indicates the general magnitude of
erosion that has taken place since late Tertiary time.

Many lower prominences in the Pine Barrens possess gravely cappings. Some
contain materials such as cherty and vein-quartz gravels somewhat characteristic of the
Beacon Hill Gravel. These probably are modified Beacon Hill deposits which have
been altered by downslope and fluvial transport since Beacon Hill time. They are
generally <1.2 m in thickness and occupy a total of about 1–2% of the Pine Barrens

region. Weathering has created a notable amount of hardening of the deposit: In places, as much as 6.1 m of impermeable ironstone conglomerate cappings exist.

Arkose 2 (Bridgeton? Formation) and Arkose 1 (Pensauken? Formation) Deposits

More extensive deposits of Pliocene (?) and Miocene (?) age also form a discontinuous veneer, lying unconformably above the Cohansey Sand throughout much of the southern part of the Pine Barrens region. Owens and Minard (1975) named these deposits Arkose 2 of Pliocene (?) and Miocene (?) age, which is approximately equivalent to the earlier, widely used Bridgeton Formation, and Arkose 1, also of Pliocene (?) and Miocene (?) age, which is about equivalent to the earlier term, Pensauken Formation. Arkose 2 and Arkose 1 for these Tertiary deposits replace the earlier names largely because the earlier names are associated extensively with the Pleistocene. Most of the surface veneer in the southern part of the Pine Barrens is Arkose 2, but lesser amounts of Arkose 1 exist. These deposits are differentiated mainly by differences in altitude, degree of weathering, mineral content (e.g., gibbsite and halloysite), and the presence of glauconite in Arkose 2 only.

Before 1975 the Bridgeton and Pensauken Formations were considered Quaternary deposits following Salisbury and Knapp (1917). These formations were considered by MacClintock and Richards (1936) to form a "complex" of deposits resulting from the various episodes of deposition and erosion characteristic of the early Pleistocene in southern New Jersey.

Owens and Minard (1975) report that Arkose 2 and Arkose 1 represent a continuous sequence of fluvial erosion and deposition (cut and fill) cycles that have stripped and reduced the New Jersey Coastal Plain from Miocene and Pliocene time to the beginning of the Pleistocene. Recent investigators noted the deposits have characteristics of fluvial deposition, are cross-stratified in many places, occupy channels, and show rapid vertical and horizontal changes in texture. They are as much as 21.3 m thick (Owens and Minard, 1975). These formations are composed chiefly of a highly weathered mixture ranging from unconsolidated materials to fully iron oxide-cemented beds of red to yellow quartz sand containing large amounts of vein quartz. Pebbles of shale, sandstone, quartzite, chert, and kaolinitic clay are also present. The clay is either in pods and nodular masses or in thin lenses and beds. Owen and Minard indicate that ancient Delaware River valley deposits are largely from northern and western Piedmont sources. However, in the Pine Barrens east of the river, deposits are largely dissected and found on widely scattered hilltops. Consequently, the bulk of the deposits in the tributary valleys is reworked Coastal Plain material from the Cohansey and possibly Beacon Hill.

These deposits, commonly containing lag (residual) gravel at the surface, cap the tops and mantle the upper slopes of most of the pronounced hills and narrow ridges that range in altitude from 15.2–30.5 m. The higher deposits in a Pine Barrens locale generally are less quartzose (i.e., more cherty), coarser, less rounded, more weathered, and more cemented than deposits lying below and along the flanks of the higher deposits.

Hence, it is apparent that the more rounded fragments and fresher-appearing deposits in places are derived from sources similar to those of the Cohansey Sand and Beacon Hill Gravel and are derived from erosion of these older formations. Consequently, it is difficult to distinguish among these deposits accurately. They probably are distributed more widely than shown by Salisbury (1899), Lewis and Kummel (1910–1912), Parker *et al.* (1964), and the U.S. Geological Survey (1967), but less continuous than the general representation given by Owens and Minard (1975).

QUATERNARY DEPOSITS

The Cape May Formation was originally named by Salisbury (1898) for its excellent development in Cape May County, New Jersey. The name was applied to coastal–terrace deposits, considered to be or marine origin, extending from sea level to 9.1 to 15.2 m above sea level. Salisbury believed these deposits to be of Wisconsin age, because the coastal terrace extends up the Delaware River and eventually blends into Wisconsin outwash deposits. Salisbury and Knapp (1917) redefined the Cape May Formation to include valley terrace deposits along many streams of southern New Jersey. These were observed at altitudes as high as 47.5 m and were considered to slope down the valley to merge with the marine terrace deposits bordering the present coast. These deposits, thought to be Cape May stream terrace materials, which exist in the Pine Barrens region, are discussed in this article using the names assigned by Owens and Minard (1975). MacClintock and Richards (1936) demonstrated that the Cape May Formation is of pre-Wisconsin age, probably reaching its present state of deposition and erosional development largely during an interglacial time (Sangamon). Their definition and Kummel's (1940) definition of the Cape May include the stream–terrace deposits of Salisbury and Knapp (1917).

This author believes that the so-called Cape May Formation is a misnomer in the Pine Barrens. All post-Beacon Hill Gravel materials, lying about 12–15 m above sea level within the present stream basins draining either east or west, have been examined in the northern and central parts of the Pine Barrens, which are derived primarily from Cohansey Sand and Beacon Hill formations. It is difficult to distinguish this so-called "Cape May valley–terrace phase" (Salisbury and Knapp, 1917) from these parent materials, except on the basis of its lesser degree of weathering, smaller particle size, and less intense soil development. In the southern area, i.e., that part sloping toward Delaware Bay, the Arkose 2 and probably some Arkose 1 were deposited. However, because of the vast reworking, they now are of a rather similar character.

Significant areas of the Pine Barrens have not been mapped with modern detailed geological techniques. The work of Owens and Minard (1975) extends only a short distance into the Barrens in the Rancocas Creek valley, although they have mapped and described deposits that appear to extend over wide areas of the region. It is probable that somewhat older and less extensive Quaternary deposits exist in some areas >46 m above sea level. Owens and Minard called the Quaternary deposits mapped, the Quartz Sand 2 and Quartz Sand 1, which are described in the following section.

Quartz Sand 2 and Quartz Sand 1 Deposits ("Valley–Terrace Phase" of the Cape May Formation)

Owens and Minard (1975), in mapping the Trenton, New Jersey area, identified and reclassified the so-called valley terrace deposits of the Cape May Formation lying along the Rancocas Creek as Quartz Sand 2 and Quartz Sand 1 deposits. They assigned a Sangamon age (interglacial) to these deposits, correlative in time with the various phases of the Cape May Formation (Gill, 1962). Studies along the upper tributaries of Rancocas Creek in Burlington County (Minard and Rhodehamel, 1969) and along many streams in the Pine Barrens, indicate no significant materials have been introduced into the upland parts of the region since Beacon Hill Gravel time. Cut and fill, lateral stripping, and ephemeral stream–terrace constructional processes by Pine Barrens streams during Quaternary time have produced fluvial deposits in the Pine Barrens that, except for their fresher appearance, diminution of grain size, and certain internal sedimentary structures, are remarkably similar to the parent materials removed and redeposited from the Tertiary Cohansey Sand and Beacon Hill Gravel. The classification and mapping of Owens and Minard account for these phenomena. Such deposits should be differentiated from the marine phase and other fluvial phases of the Cape May Formation deposits which include, among other characteristics, additional sediments from through-flowing streams.

The Quartz Sand 2 especially, and the Quartz Sand 1 deposits form a widespread sheet of sand and pebble alluvium. They underlie broad flats largely within present valley walls and, because of the pervasive erosion of Tertiary deposits, are the most extensive alluvium. They occur at altitudes as high as 58 m above sea level. The deposits are seldom more than 4.6 m thick and usually 0.3 to 2.4 m thick, except in the tidal reaches of the eastward draining streams, where these fluvial–terrace deposits and overlying and thinner alluvium of Holocene age are as much as 6.1 to 12.2 m thick. Quartz Sand 2 and Quartz Sand 1 deposits are differentiated by differences in topographic position within a basin, degree of weathering, and the presence of gravel in the Quartz Sand 2 only.

In Cape May County, Gill (1962) showed that the Cape May Formation contains four sedimentary parts in three depositional environments, namely, estuarine, marine, and deltaic. At least within the tidal reaches of most major eastward and (or) southeastward flowing streams of the Atlantic and Delaware Bay, the estuarine sand and overlying estuarine clay parts extend into the margins of the Pine Barrens region. For example, Rhodehamel (1973) reported that, in the Mullica River basin, estuarine sand and overlying estuarine clay of the Cape May Formation appear to be present in the reaches of an old drainage way below Constables Bridge (about 1.5 km northwest of Batsto in Burlington County). This was based upon the channellike nature of the deposits, their lithology, stratigraphic position, and Quaternary age. The estuarine sand

and overlying estuarine clay fill almost totally bury a Quaternary channel cut into the underlying Cohansey Sand in the vicinity of the Mullica River. The thickness of Cape May estuarine deposits was about 25.9 m along the Mullica River about 4 km northwest of Batsto (Burlington County). The ancient channel was at least 34.1 m deep at Sweetwater and at least 69.8 m at Atlantic City. The slope of the channel base is about 1.3 or 1.5 m/km southeastward to Atlantic City.

Deposits in the major valleys below roughly 12 m above sea level may include the estuarine and (or) fluvial phases of the Cape May Formation (Sangamon age), but these in most cases are no more than small deposits forming a fringe that has produced little or no impact on the dominant Pine Barrens flora.

Holocene Deposits

Alluvial deposits of late Pleistocene–Holocene are closely associated with the Quartz Sand 2 and Quartz Sand 1 deposits (Owens and Minard, 1975). These deposits are the silt, sand, clay, bog-iron ore, and marshland materials (peat) bordering and accumulating in the stream channels, estuaries, and back bays; and the windblown, downslope movement, and sheet-flow alluvium covering the uplands. Most of the riparian deposits are fine-grained, carbonaceous sand, silt, and clay, generally having lower permeabilities than the sandier materials of higher areas.

SUMMARY

Underlying the Pine Barrens of New Jersey is a 200–170 million-year-old Atlantic Coastal Plain ranging in thickness from 400 to 1830 m (1300–6000 ft), with a gentle southeastward dip. Lower Cretaceous age continental deposits are overlain by Upper Cretaceous and Tertiary age strata deposited first in transitional and nearshore–marine environments, followed by open marine shelf, nearshore–marine, transitional (deltaic and interdeltaic), and finally, in fluvial environments. During the middle or late Miocene time 18–5 million years ago, the Coastal Plain emerged >100 m, exposing thick deposits of marine quartzose sand and clay (Kirkwood Formation), overlain by deltaic, beach, and tidal flat quartz–arenite deposits interspersed with carbonaceous silt and clay (Cohansey Sand). Upon this predominantly sandy plain, a quartzose and cherty sand and gravel (Beacon Hill Gravel) was laid down, most probably by an ancient Hudson River. This was the last deposit introduced into the northern and central upland Pine Barrens area and today caps many of the highest hills, attesting to the enormous amount of erosion which followed. Fluvial deposits, Arkose 2 and Arkose 1, were introduced into the southwestern portion of the Pine Barrens in late Tertiary. The so-called "valley-terrace phase" of the Cape May Formation in the Pine Barrens is a misnomer. Quartz Sand 2 and Quartz Sand 1 of a Quaternary interglacial (Sangamonian age) represent redeposition of some of these older deposits.

Because of the tundra and arctic climate that likely existed in the region during the late Pleistocene (Wisconsin Glaciation), the present Pine Barrens flora subsequently entered the region along either a widely exposed Coastal Plain corridor prior to sea level rise, or by an eastern migration from higher ground to the west, and perhaps by both routes. Sand, chiefly from the Cohansey Sand, with patches of younger deposits as a discontinuous veneer on hilltops and elsewhere, suggesting a "reversal of topography," is the primary geological characteristic of the Pine Barrens region.

Thus, eight geologic deposits underpinning the characteristic sandy droughty soil of the Pine Barrens region are the result of many major geologic episodes of deposition and erosion spanning the last 20 or more million years. Of these, the Cohansey Sand is paramount. However, the last 5 million years of continuous erosion and redeposition, i.e., that time since the deposition of the Beacon Hill Gravel, are the most important. This encompasses several critical Pleistocene events in the Pine Barrens and surrounding regions.

REFERENCES

Andrews, G. W. (1976). Miocene marine diatoms from the Choptank Formation, Calvert County, Maryland. *U.S. Geol. Surv., Prof. Pap.* No. 910.

Bascom, F., Clark, W. B., Darton, N. H., Kummel, H. B., Salisbury, R. D., and Knapp, G. N. (1909). Description of the Philadelphia district (Pennsylvania-New Jersey). *U.S. Geol. Surv., Geol. Atlas Folio* No. 3.

Barghoorn, E. S. (1951). Age and environment: A survey of North American Tertiary floras in relation to paleoecology. *J. Paleont.* **25,** (No. 6), 736–744.

Berggren, W. A. (1972). A Cenozoic time-scale . . . some implications for regional geology and paleobiogeography. *Lethaia* **5**(2), 195–215.

Bowman, J. F., and Lodding, W. (1969). The Pensauken Formation—A Pleistocene fluvial deposit in New Jersey. *In* "Geology of Selected Areas in New Jersey and Eastern Pennsylvania and Guidebook of Excursions" (S. Subitzky, ed.), pp. 3–6. Rutgers Univ. Press, New Brunswick, New Jersey.

Buell, M. F. (1970). Time of origin of New Jersey Pine Barrens bogs. *Bull. Torrey Bot. Club* **97**(No. 2), 105–108.

Carter, C. R. (1972). Miocene–Pliocene beach and tidal flat sedimentation, southern New Jersey. Ph.D. Thesis, Johns Hopkins Univ., Baltimore, Maryland.

Clark, G. A., Meisler, H., Rhodehamel, E. C., and Gill, H. E. (1968). Summary of ground-water resources of Atlantic County. *N.J. Div. Water Policy Supply, Water Resour. Circ.* No. 18.

Cook, G. H. (1868). "Geology of New Jersey." N.J. Geol. Surv., Trenton, New Jersey.

Curray, J. R. (1965). Late Quaternary history, continental shelves of the United States. *In* "The Quaternary of the United States" (H. E. Wright, Jr. and D. G. Frey, eds.), pp. 723–735. Princeton Univ. Press, Princeton, New Jersey.

Gill, H. E. (1962). Ground-water resources of Cape May County, New Jersey. *N.J. Div. Water Policy Supply, Spec. Rep.* No. 18.

Harshberger, J. W. (1916). "The Vegetation of the New Jersey Pine Barrens, an Ecologic Investigation." Christopher Sower Co., Philadelphia, Pennsylvania.

Hollick, A. (1892). Paleobotany of the yellow gravel at Bridgeton, New Jersey. *Bull. Torrey Bot. Club* **19,** 330–333.

Hollick, A. (1900). The relation between forestry and geology. *N.J. Geol. Surv., Annu. Rep. State Geol. 1899* pp. 173–201.

Hopkins, D. M. (1975). Time-stratigraphic nomenclature for the Holocene epoch. *Geology* **3**(1), 10.

Isphording, W. C. (1970a). Late Tertiary paleoclimate of eastern United States. *Bull., Am. Assoc. Pet. Geol.* **54,** 334–343.

Isphording, W. C. (1970b). Petrology, stratigraphy and re-definition of the Kirkwood Formation (Miocene) of New Jersey. *J. Sediment Petrol.* **40**, 986–997.

Isphording, W. C., and Lodding, W. (1969). Facies changes in sediments of Miocene age in New Jersey. *In* "Geology of Selected Areas in New Jersey and Eastern Pennsylvania and Guidebook of Excursions" (S. Subitzky, ed.), pp. 7–13. Rutgers Univ. Press, New Brunswick, New Jersey.

Knapp, G. N. (1904). Underground waters of New Jersey; wells drilled in 1903. *N.J. Geol. Surv., Annu. Rep. State Geol. 1903* pp. 75–93.

Kummel, H. B. (1940). The geology of New Jersey. *N.J. Dep. Conserv. Dev., Bull.* No. 50.

Kummel, H. B., and Knapp, G. N. (1904). The stratigraphy of New Jersey clays. *In* "The Clays and Clay Industry of New Jersey" (H. Ries and H. B. Kummel, eds.), Final Rep. State Geologist, Vol. 6, pp. 117–203. N.J. Geol. Surv., Trenton, New Jersey.

LeBlanc, R. J. (1972). Geometry of sandstone reservoir bodies. *In* "Underground Waste, Management and Environmental Implications" (T. E. Cook, ed.), Mem. No. 18, pp. 133–180. *Am. Assoc. Pet. Geol.*, Tulsa, Oklahoma.

Lewis, J. V., and Kummel, H. B. (1910–1912). "Geologic Map of New Jersey" (Revised by M. E. Johnson, 1950). N.J. Geol. Surv., Trenton, New Jersey.

MacClintock, P., and Richards, H. G. (1936). Correlation of late Pleistocene marine and glacial deposits of New Jersey and New York. *Geol. Soc. Am. Bull.* **47**, 289–338.

Markewicz, F. J. (1969). Ilmenite deposits of the New Jersey Coastal Plain. *In* "Geology of Selected Areas in New Jersey and Eastern Pennsylvania and Guidebook of Excursions" (S. Subitzky, ed.), pp. 363–382. Rutgers Univ. Press, New Brunswick, New Jersey.

Markewicz, F. J., Parillo, D. G., and Johnson, M. E. (1958). The titanium sands of southern New Jersey. *Meet. Am. Inst. Min. Eng., New York* Prepr. no. 5818A5.

Minard, J. P. (1964). "Geology of the Roosevelt Quadrangle, New Jersey," Geologic Quadrangle Map GQ-340. U.S. Geol. Surv., Reston, Virginia.

Minard, J. P. (1966). Sandblasted blocks on a hill in the Coastal Plain of New Jersey. *U.S. Geol. Surv., Prof. Pap.* No. 550-B, pp. B87–B90.

Minard, J. P. (1969). Geology of the Sandy Hook Quadrangle in Monmouth County, New Jersey. *U.S. Geol. Surv., Bull.* No. 1276, pp. 1–43.

Minard, J. P., and Owens, J. P. (1960). Differential subsidence of the southern part of the New Jersey Coastal Plain since Early Cretaceous time. *U.S. Geol. Surv., Prof. Pap.* No. 400-B, pp. B184–B186.

Minard, J. P., and Owens, J. P. (1963). Pre-Quaternary geology of the Browns Mills Quadrangle, New Jersey: U.S. Geol. Survey Quad. Map. GQ-264.

Minard, J. P., and Rhodehamel, E. C. (1969). Quaternary geology of part of northern New Jersey and the Trenton area. *In* "Geology of Selected Areas in New Jersey and Eastern Pennsylvania and Guidebook of Excursions" (S. Subitsky, ed.), pp. 279–313. Rutgers Univ. Press, New Brunswick, New Jersey.

National Academy of Sciences (1973). "U.S. Program for the Geodynamics Project—Scope and Objectives." Natl. Acad. Sci., Washington, D.C.

Nemickas, B., and Carswell, L. D. (1976). Stratigraphic and hydrologic relationship of the Piney Point aquifer and the Alloway Clay Member of the Kirkwood Formation in New Jersey. *J. Res. U.S. Geol. Surv.* **4**(1), 1–7.

Owens, J. P., and Minard, J. P. (1975). "Geologic Map of the Surficial Deposits in the Trenton Area, New Jersey and Pennsylvania," Misc. Geol. Invest. Map I-884. U.S. Geol. Surv., Reston, Virginia.

Owens, J. P., and Sohl, N. F. (1969). Shelf and deltaic paleoenvironments in the Cretaceous–Tertiary formations of the New Jersey Coastal Plain. *In* "Geology of Selected Areas in New Jersey and Eastern Pennsylvania and Guidebook of Excursions" (S. Subitzky, ed.), pp. 235–278. Rutgers Univ. Press, New Brunswick, New Jersey.

Parker, G. G., Hely, A. G., Keighton, W. B., Olmsted, F. H., *et al.* (1964). Water resources of the Delaware River basin. *U.S. Geol. Surv., Prof. Pap.* No. 381.

Perry, W. J., Jr., Minard, J. P., Weed, E. G. A., Robbins, E. I., and Rhodehamel, E. C. (1975). Stratigraphy of Atlantic coastal margin of United States north of Cape Hatteras—Brief survey. *Bull., Am. Assoc. Pet. Geol.* **59**, 1529–1548.

Petters, S. W. (1976). Upper Cretaceous subsurface stratigraphy of Atlantic Coastal Plain of New Jersey. *Bull., Am. Assoc. Pet. Geol.* **60,** 87–107.

Rachele, L. D. (1976). Palynology of the Legler lignite: A deposit in the Tertiary Cohansey Formation of New Jersey, USA. *Rev. Palaeobot. Palynol.* **22,** 225–252.

Rhodehamel, E. C. (1973). Geology and water resources of the Wharton Tract and the Mullica River basin in southern New Jersey. *N.J. Div. Water Resour., Spec. Rep.* No. 36.

Richards, H. G. (1945). Subsurface stratigraphy of Atlantic Coastal Plain between New Jersey and Georgia. *Bull., Am. Assoc. Pet. Geol.* **29,** 885–955.

Richards, H. G. (1960). The geological history of the New Jersey Pine Barrens: Trenton, N.J. *N.J. Nat. News* **15,** 146–151.

Richards, H. G., and Harbison, A. (1942). Miocene invertebrate fauna of New Jersey. *Proc. Acad. Nat. Sci. Philadelphia* **94,** 167–250.

Salisbury, R. D. (1895). Surface geology—Report of progress. *N.J. Geol. Surv., Annu. Rep. State Geol. 1894.*

Salisbury, R. D. (1898). Surface geology—Report of Progress. *N.J. Geol. Surv., Annu. Rep. State Geol. 1897* pp. 1–22.

Salisbury, R. D. (1899). *N.J. Geol. Surv., Annu. Rep. State Geol. 1898.*

Salisbury, R. D., and Knapp, G. N. (1917). ''The Quaternary Formations of Southern New Jersey,'' Final Rep., Ser. Vol. 8. N.J. Geol. Surv., Trenton, New Jersey.

Shepard, F. P. (1959). Marine sediments. *Science* **130,** 141–149.

Sirkin, L. A., and Minard, J. P. (1972). Late Pleistocene glaciation and pollen stratigraphy in northwestern New Jersey. *U.S. Geol. Surv., Prof. Pap.* No. 800-D, pp. D51–D56.

Spangler, W. B., and Peterson, J. J. (1950). Geology of the Atlantic Coastal Plain in New Jersey, Delaware, Maryland, and Virginia. *Bull., Am. Assoc. Pet. Geol.* **34,** 1–99.

Strock, L. W. (1929). A study of the Pensauken Formation. *Wagner Free Inst. Sci. Bull.* **4**(1/2), 3–10.

Taylor, N. (1912). On the origin and present distribution of the Pine-Barrens of New Jersey. *Torreya* **12,** 229–242.

U.S. Geological Survey (1967). ''Engineering Geology of the Northeast Corridor, Washington, D.C., to Boston, Massachusetts: Coastal Plain and Surficial Deposits'' (compiled by J. P. Owens), Misc. Geol. Invest. Map I-514-B, Parts 2 and 3. U.S. Geol. Surv., Reston, Virginia.

Woolman, L. (1891). Artesian and other bored wells. *N.J. Geol. Surv., Annu. Rep. State Geol. 1890* pp. 269–273.

Woolman, L. (1892). A review of artesian well horizons in southern New Jersey. *N.J. Geol. Surv., Annu. Rep. State Geol. 1891* pp. 223–226.

4

Development of Pine Barrens Soils

JOHN C. F. TEDROW

The Pine Barrens of New Jersey long have commanded the attention of naturalists, and in recent years interest has been increasing from the standpoint of the region's vegetation, soils, water supply, pollution and, above all, survival as a paranatural area. The forest canopy generally is closed by a pine–oak (*Pinus–Quercus*) mosaic in the uplands, with Atlantic white cedar (*Chamaecyparis thyoides*) and swamp hardwoods (*Acer, Nyssa, Magnolia*) colonizing water courses and other poorly drained locations. Casual examination of the soil features will show the ground to be unusually sandy, xeric, and impoverished (by agricultural standards), but the low-lying areas are universally swampy due to a high water table.

VEGETATION

Harshberger (1916) delineated the Pine Barrens, including isolated areas of deciduous swamps, cedar swamps, savannas, cultivated lands, and pine plains. The northern and northwestern margins of the Pine Barrens are well defined and generally can be established within a distance of 1–2 km. The southern margin, however, is indefinite. Rather than a line, it is a diffuse zone comprising a mosaic of conditions. In some parts of Cape May, Cumberland, Salem, Gloucester, and Camden counties this diffuse zone, which can measure as much as 8 km in width, is exemplified well in the work of McCormick (1970), who designated it as an oak–pine fringe area.

The Pine Plains consist of a pigmy pine–oak forest that may be only head high. Robichaud and Buell (1973) state that, in the Pine Barrens, about 50–80% of the uplands are colonized by pitch pine (*Pinus rigida*). Shortleaf pine (*P. echinata*), black oak (*Quercus velutina*), post oak (*Q. stellata*), scarlet oak (*Q. coccinea*), chestnut oak (*Q. prinus*), and blackjack oak (*Q. marilandica*) also are present.

61

GEOLOGY

The Pine Barrens are formed on unconsolidated, acid, medium-to-coarse-grained sands which range in age from Tertiary to Recent. Kümmel (1940) lists the Quaternary geological formations as follows: (1) Beach sand and gravel; (2) Cape May, 6–12 m of sand and gravel; (3) Pensauken, 39 m of sand and gravel; and (4) Bridgeton, 9 m of sand and gravel (with clay). Tertiary formations are: (1) Beacon Hill, 6 m of sand and gravel (with clay); (2) Cohansey, 30–76 m of quartz sand with a few clay lenses; and

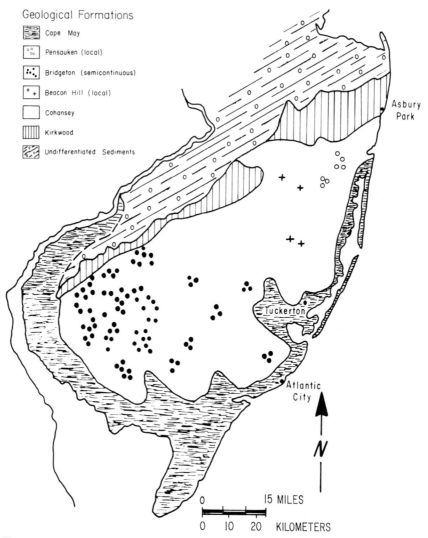

Fig. 1. Geological map of the Pine Barrens of New Jersey. Adapted from Lewis and Kummel (1910–1912) and other sources.

(3) Kirkwood, 30 m of micaceous sand (with clay lenses near the base) which becomes thicker seaward.

Figure 1 shows an abbreviated version of the areal distribution of geological formations of the Pine Barrens (Lewis and Kümmel, 1910-1912). The western margin of the Pine Barrens is formed on the Kirkwood, more definitively, the upper Kirkwood, which is quite sandy and virtually inseparable from the Cohansey insofar as soil composition is concerned (Martens, 1956). Isolated sectors of the Pine Barrens are formed on the Bridgeton formation. The Bridgeton, while primarily made up of coarse sand and small, rounded gravel, also contains considerable quantities of weathered, reddish clay in the matrix. This clay imparts slightly more favorable soil properties insofar as moisture retention is concerned. On a state-wide basis, very productive soils are associated with the Pensauken formation. The main body of the Pensauken, however, lies beyond the Pine Barrens to the west. That which is within the Pine Barrens is somewhat atypical and unusually sandy in character. However, in those sectors of the Pine Barrens where the Bridgeton or Pensauken formation is present, the slight increase in clay is reflected in the soils as well as vegetation. Where there is an increase in clay, there is a blending of xeric-mesic conditions. Within the Pine Barrens, two units of the Cape May formation are present: (1) the marine phase (MacClintock and Richards, 1936), which is primarily sand and gravel; and (2) the stream deposits of the valleys (Salisbury and Knapp, 1917). The Beacon Hill formation occupies a few knobs or topographic highs and consists of a sand–gravel–clay mixture. It is interesting to note that some of the Pine Plains are on the Beacon Hill formation or derived erosional products from the Beacon Hill. The origin, composition, and distribution of these various deposits are discussed by Salisbury (1898), Salisbury and Knapp (1917), Kümmel (1940), MacClintock and Richards (1936), and Martens (1956).

Earlier investigators related the uniqueness of the Pine Barrens to geological conditions. Lutz (1934), however, in reviewing earlier work plus adding his own findings, showed that the distribution of geological formations and vegetative boundaries did not coincide entirely, and that a simple geological answer to the distribution of the Pine Barrens was impossible. If one focuses on the physical and chemical characteristics of the substrate rather than on geological names, however, one obtains a much better correlation.

TOPOGRAPHY

Physiographically, the Pine Barrens lie on a coastal plain with gentle undulations. The seaward slope of southern New Jersey sometimes designated as the "Outer Coastal Plain" includes virtually all of the Pine Barrens.

Most of the Pine Barrens is drained by rather closely spaced, somewhat parallel, southeasterly flowing streams. On the western margin, however, some drainage is to the Delaware River. Relief is low throughout the Pine Barrens, with a few uneroded hills having altitudes of approximately 60 m; in Monmouth County, these levels are slightly higher.

CLIMATE

The Pine Barrens receive about 100–120 cm of precipitation annually, with higher values in the Lakewood–Lakehurst–New Egypt sectors (Biel, 1958). Overall precipitation, however, has a leaching effect in the soil; coupled with a coarse, porous, acid substrate, this results in highly leached conditions. The average summer temperature (June to August) approximates 23°C, and winters, which have an average temperature (December to February) of approximately 1°C, are comparatively mild.

SOIL CONDITIONS

Gray, sandy Lakewood soil,* which is typical of these highly leached, impoverished conditions, is considered by many as synonymous with "Pine Barrens." This depiction is only partly correct, because the Lakewood represents only one of a group of upland soils and does not provide for the high water table found extensively throughout the region.

Soil surveys were conducted in the Pine Barrens during the years 1915–1927, and the results, published by the U.S. Department of Agriculture and the New Jersey Agricultural Experiment Station, were plotted on a scale of 1 inch (2.5 cm) per mile (1.6 km) (Millville Area in 1917, Chatsworth Area in 1919, Trenton Area in 1921, Camden Area in 1926, and Freehold Area in 1927). Examination of the above maps will show that there are two main soil series of the uplands, namely, Lakewood and Sassafras (Fig. 2). The Lakewood is quite xeric and develops a light gray topsoil. Sassafras, on the other hand, while somewhat xeric, usually contains a little more silt and clay and is not so highly bleached as the Lakewood. Interfingering the entire region are extensive areas of poorly drained sands and a few peat deposits of up to about 1 to 2 m in depth.

LAKEWOOD SOIL

Lakewood soil is a podzol, the Sassafras is a podzolic soil, and the St. Johns is a groundwater podzol. At the time when initial soil surveys were being conducted in the Pine Barrens, Russian concepts on pedology had not reached the Western World to any

---

*Soil names used in this report are compared with approximately equivalent terms in U.S. Department of Agriculture mapping as follows: Lakewood = Lakewood† or Lakewood;‡ Lakewood with red clay substratum = Woodmansie;‡ Lakewood with ironstone = Sandy land, ironstone;‡ Sassafras with ironstone = Sandy land, ironstone;‡ Lakehurst = Lakehurst† or Lakehurst;‡ Leon = Leon† or Atsion;‡ St. Johns = St. Johns† or Berryland;‡ Sassafras = Sassafras, Downer;‡ Sassafras incipient podzol = Downer† or Sassafras, Downer;‡ Sassafras Hammonton phase = Downer† or Downer;‡ Woodstown = Woodstown or Woodstown;‡ Muck = Muck† or Muck, shallow.‡

†Camden County Soil Survey Report, 1966.
‡ Burlington County Soil Survey Report, 1971.

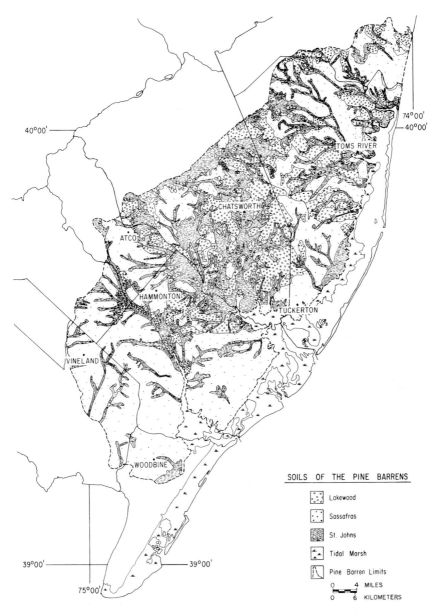

Fig. 2. Generalized soils map of the Pine Barrens. Compiled from various sources.

extent; accordingly, the Pine Barren soils were classed primarily at the series level. Discussion about soil development was very limited and little attention was paid to Great Soil groups. Except for a few outliers such as the Cape May formation in localized areas of Middlesex County, the highly bleached Lakewood soil was recognized in New Jersey only within the Pine Barrens.

If climatic factors alone are used as criteria for projecting Great Soil groups, then the podzol soil of the Pine Barrens is out of place because regional climate theoretically favors formation of a gray brown podzolic soil. Podzol soil formation normally is identified with a cool temperate climate; the New Jersey Pine Barrens, however, are subject to an average summer temperature of about 23°C, a value normally not associated with podzol formation. The compensating factor, of course, is the unusually sandy, quartzose parent material which podzolizes with great ease. The geological material is coarse-grained, siliceous, and highly permeable.

In 1928, C. F. Marbut, who then headed the U.S. Soil Survey Program, gave a series of lectures entitled "Soils, their genesis, classification and development," and on the subject of Pine Barren soils (Marbut, 1928, Lecture 11) stated.

> they [Lakewood series] are developed on the seaward slope of the Coastal Plain in New Jersey from material that is very sandy, in fact, it consists of little else than sand. It is naturally to be expected that soils developed on such material will have reached, in a given time, a more advanced stage of development than the soils derived from heavier material. Since development is partly a matter of eluviation or the transfer of the fine-grained material from the A horizon into the B horizon, it is perfectly evident that where the soil is developing from a material in which there is not much to leach, it will have reached a more advanced state of development, or will have become thoroughly leached out of the A horizon in a short time. This is the case with the Lakewood soils.... On the slopes where soils are younger they have been mapped as Sassafras, although it is well known that they are not fully developed Sassafras soils. They have been mapped as Sassafras because they are slightly browner in color or have a stronger color than the thoroughly leached Lakewood....

Other discussions of podzol soils followed Marbut's description. Joffe (1931) and later Muir (1961) outlined the various European views on the biogeochemical reactions and the morphologies of podzol soils that have evolved since the time of Karl Sprengle's work in Leipzig during the 1830's.

The morphology of the Pine Barren soils and the unusual sandy character of the substrate were demonstrated to be closely correlated (Tedrow, 1952). It was pointed out that Pine Barren soils were extremely sandy and xeric, had an inadequate nutrient supply, were highly acid, and contained toxic levels of soluble aluminum. Some of the earliest chemical investigations on Pine Barren soils were carried out by Joffe and Watson (1933), who provided rather complete chemical analyses of several Lakewood profiles. The data showed the striking impoverished condition of the soil. Chemical analyses of the mineral horizons showed about 95% SiO_2, 3% Al_2O_3, and 1% Fe_2O_3 in the parent material with orderly readjustment of chemical properties according to soil formation. In addition to the total chemical composition, the exchangeable cation data and low pH values indicate a paucity of plant nutrients. The cation exchange capacities of the mineral horizons are of an extremely low order—approximating 1 me per 100 g of soil in the A2 horizon of the Lakewood soil, with a low base saturation (Joffe and Watson, 1933).

Podzol formation nearly always has an appreciable mor (raw humus) accumulation.

In areas such as southeastern Canada, it may be 10 or more cm thick, but progressing southward, the thickness of the mor decreases as temperatures increase. In the Pine Barrens, where in protected sites, the raw humus layer may be 1–2 cm or so thick, in other locations it is much less so. In some places, the gray sand is exposed at the soil surface or colonized with *Cladonia* lichens.

Normally, when humus forms in a soil the C/N ratio approximates a value of 12 or slightly higher. Joffe and Watson reported very high ratios for the Lakewood soil, with some values approximating 50. The organic matter on the surface of the soil has a much higher C/N value. Some of these high values are a reflection of colloid-sized charcoal from forest fires plus the presence of tannins and other resistant organic constituents.

The impoverished condition of the Lakewood and other soils of the Pine Barrens is exemplified further by various reports from the New Jersey Agricultural Experiment Station during the years 1944–1963.* Lakewood was shown to be of an impoverished nature with respect to potential plant nutrients. The soil was shown to be exceedingly deficient in major as well as trace nutrients. Gamble (1963) made a comprehensive study of the Lakewood soil from the standpoint of mineral and chemical composition and further reported the elemental composition of the associated vegetation growing on this soil. His work confirmed earlier reports regarding the deficient nutrient supply of the soil. Elemental composition of the foliage, however, was in line with that from mesic sites beyond the Pine Barrens.

Jordan (1968) made some detailed studies of the Lakewood soil relative to the composition of the soil solution in various horizons. At Pine Barren sites in southern Monmouth County, the cation exchange capacity of the Lakewood A2 horizon was only 0.7 me per 100 g of soil, the B horizon 8.5 (an unusually high value; generally it ranges between 2 and 3), and the C horizon 1.1. The soil was strongly acid and only small quantities of exchangeable bases were present. Jordan designed a lysimeter to collect the drainage water within the various horizons. It was established that the composition of the drainage water varied considerably, depending upon the amount of rainfall during a given time period: The greater the rainfall, the more dilute the soil electrolyte. With regard to the formation of the bleached A2 horizon of podzol soils, the question of what controls its thickness has remained largely unanswered. Using electrodialysis, Mattson (1933) showed that, after the soil colloid largely had been depleted of exchangeable bases and the pH value had dropped to a low level, iron and aluminum were mobilized in much the same manner as during podzolization. It long had been recognized that sandier-textured podzols generally have thicker A2 horizons. In his lecture on podzolization, Marbut quoted a Dr. Albert of Germany who concluded that the B horizon of the podzol marked the average depth of penetration of summer rains (Marbut, 1928, Lecture 6). However, Jordan (1968), testing the Albert hypothesis with lysimeters, was not able to confirm his projection completely. Jordan's studies showed that nutrient composition of the drainage water was greater in the B horizon

*For details, consult the following: *Agric. Food Chem.* **2,** 245 (1954); *N.J. Agric. Exp. Stn., Bull.* No. 709 (1944), No. 721 (1945), No. 744 (1948); *Soil Sci.* **56,** 139 (1944), **63,** 69 (1947), **65,** 297 (1948), **67,** 439 (1949), **75,** 433 (1953), **76,** 115 (1953), **76,** 421 (1953), **96,** 261 (1963), **96,** 337 (1963).

TABLE I Average Chemical Composition of Fresh Surface Waters[a]

County	Conductivity (mmho)	pH	Ca^{2+} (ppm)	Mg^{2+} (ppm)	K^+ (ppm)	$H_2PO_4^-$ (ppm)	$NO_3^-(N)$ (ppm)
Pine Barrens							
Atlantic[b]	83	4.3	1.3	1.7	1.0	0.3	0.9
Ocean[b]	41	4.7	0.8	0.7	0.8	0.1	1.9
Non-Pine Barrens							
Mercer	259	6.9	10.1	7.8	4.7	0.7	0.8
Warren	314	7.8	15.3	12.1	1.1	0.6	0.6

[a] Unpublished data of S. J. Toth. Data are based on >100 samples collected over >10 years.
[b] About 90% of county is in the Pine Barrens.

than in the A1 or C horizons during periods of heavy precipitation. During periods of light precipitation, however, the trend was variable.

If sites are chosen properly, the composition of the drainage waters will give some indication of the degree of eutrophism within the soil. Drainage waters are quite acid, containing only small quantities of plant nutrients (Table I). On the other hand, water samples from Mercer and Warren counties, which are both outside the boundaries of the Pine Barrens, show much higher pH values and a much greater content of plant nutrients than Pine Barren samples.

LAKEWOOD SOIL VARIATIONS

Pedologists have a penchant for depicting a "modal concept" of a particular soil. Depending upon how much detail needs to be recognized, conditions may vary from this modal concept in any number of ways. The modal concept for the Lakewood soil is shown in the tabulation below:

Depth (cm)	Horizon	Morphology
2–0	A0	Dry mor of oak leaves and pine needles
0–20	A2	Gray (10 YR 6/1)[a] sand with loose single-grain structure; pH 4.7
20–23	B1	Dark brown (7.5 YR 4/4) sand, loose with dark brown-stained zones; this horizon sometimes absent; pH 4.6
23–50	B2	Strong brown (7.5 YR 5/8) sand, loose; roots are concentrated in this horizon; pH 4.6
50–100	C	Light yellow (2.5 YR 7/4) sand, loose, with a few iron-enriched nodules at depth; the lower part of the horizon may have some gley formation; pH 5.0

[a] Color chart manufactured by Munsell Color, Baltimore, Maryland.

Fig. 3. Modal Lakewood soil, Archers Corner (left side). The horizon is a loose, gray sand. Beginning at the top of the shovel handle and continuing to the shank of the shovel is the B horizon, which consists of an iron-stained sand. The blade of the shovel rests against the C horizon, which consists of a light yellow sand. Lakewood soil of the Pine Barrens (right side), with the thickness of the A2 horizon controlled largely by aeolian activity. The A2 horizon in this photograph is about 75-cm thick.

Figure 3 shows an example of Lakewood soil with a raw humus surface horizon underlain by a gray sand. The B horizon (shown in the center of the photograph) is a brown sand. The blade of the shovel rests on light yellow sand.

In the uplands, the B horizon of the Lakewood soil normally consists of a yellowish brown to brown sand with very little change in texture among the horizons—a condition commonly referred to as Lakewood soil with a color B. There are other instances in which the B horizon of the Lakewood soil has developed a strong brown to reddish brown color. One such condition is referred to as an iron podzol. A third condition, in which the B horizon of the Lakewood develops a nearly black color with some rust spots in the matrix, is designated as an iron humus podzol. The iron humus podzol generally is associated with those sites in which the B/C horizons are slightly moist. The lower C horizon even may contain the first vestiges of a gley formation. Other sets

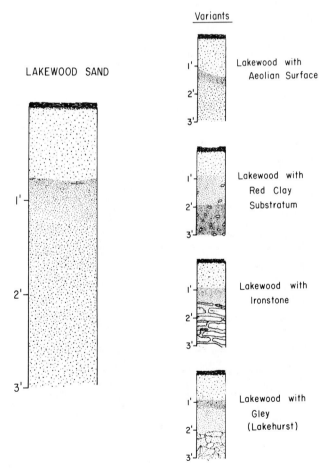

Fig. 4.   Varieties of Lakewood soil in New Jersey. (left) Modal concept for Lakewood; (right) some variants of the Lakewood soil. Soil depths in feet; 1 ft = 30.5 cm.

of conditions can influence the character of the Lakewood soil. Some of these variations can be traced to geological history, while others arise from soil development processes. Figure 4 depicts the central concept for the Lakewood soil. Also shown are a number of para varieties of the Lakewood soil.

AEOLIAN ACTIVITY

There is evidence of considerable aeolian activity (wind deposition) throughout the Pine Barrens and beyond. This condition is striking in the case of the Lakewood soil. While dunes are present in a number of locations, in other situations there is simply a veneer of wind-blown sand at the surface. This added "A2" horizon sometimes attains a thickness of 75 or more cm (Figs. 3 and 4). Aeolian activity has taken place in some of the forested land as well as in abandoned farm sites. Numerous areas give the appearance of having been modified by aeolian sands, and while some dune forms are present, it usually is quite difficult to establish with certainty the degree of past wind action. Particle size distribution patterns of the Cohansey and upper Kirkwood formations do not differ significantly from those of the aeolian mantle, and heavy minerals of the aeolian sands are very similar to those of the underlying material. Most of the heavy minerals of the Pine Barrens consist of ilmenite under various stages of alteration.

WEATHERED TERTIARY HILLTOPS

Podzol soil on the Beacon Hill formation presents one of the most interesting sites within the State. Worldwide, most podzol soils are formed on comparatively unweathered Quaternary age deposits. Podzols on the Beacon Hill formation, however, have a highly weathered red clay–sand matrix in the B/C horizon (Krebs and Tedrow, 1958). Instead of the "clay bulge" in the B horizon typical of conventional podzol, this soil has its greatest clay accumulation in the C (Fig. 4). The weathered C horizon contains up to about 20–25% clay, most of which is formed in place. Clays in the weathered C horizon primarily consist of kaolinite and gibbsite, supplemented with some altered mica, vermiculite, halloysite, mixed-layer minerals, plus a little clay-sized quartz and feldspar. There is considerable reducible iron, up to approximately 4%, in clay from the weathered C horizon. Despite the infusion of clay in the C horizon, the soil matrix is honeycombed with clay flows and clay bridges. In Marbut's (1928) terms, this soil is one of the red soils. I refer to this soil as a red podzol. Genetically, it is similar to many of the red podzolic soils of southeastern United States. The U.S. Department of Agriculture now designates this soil as the Woodmansie. As are other podzolic soils of the Pine Barrens, this soil is extremely impoverished chemically.

Some of the Beacon Hill formation extends into the Pine Plains. Whereas the Beacon Hill formation is not coincident with the Pine Plains, it appears that much of the Pine Plains is formed on erosional products from the Beacon Hill.

The genesis of highly weathered soil on the Beacon Hill formation remains uncertain. The work of Salisbury (1898), while providing a good account of the distribution and properties of the geological formation, did not encompass soil development. Without question, the highly weathered Beacon Hill deposits show lateritic affinities. The formation now occupies topographic highs whose summits dip seaward. Along which evolutionary pathways did the soil develop? We now examine three possibilities: (1) The soil may be a fossil laterite whose highly weathered features having formed during a warmer episode; (2) Because the land form has been subjected to weathering since Tertiary time, the Beacon Hill (which has a high content of weathered feldspar) may develop lateritic affinities under the present type of climate. Indeed, Salisbury and Knapp (1917) state "much of the sand of the Beacon Hill formation is arkose, and the feldspathic material is, as a rule, completely decayed. . . . The clayey element in the sand is not confined to bits of decayed feldspar; films of clay coat the sand grains in many places, increasing the arkose appearance of the whole." (3) The soil may represent a polymorphic condition with a secondary aeolian mantle being present on a previously weathered Tertiary matrix. Even if a polygenic (polymorphic) condition is present, we still must account for the weathering in the reddish clay matrix. That lateritic properties are present in the reddish colored C horizon of the soil cannot be disputed. Marbut (1928) associated laterization with the process of slow, deep-seated weathering whereby minerals underwent thorough decomposition. He considered the weathering attendant to podzolization as deriving from the surface of the soil grains rather than as a decomposition of the feldspathic minerals of the sort which occurs with lateritic weathering. Examining the above possibilities, one finds little evidence to establish the existence of a tropical climate in the vicinity of the Beacon Hill formation during the period of soil evolution. The paleobotanical record is unclear and unconvincing, but the climate at one time may have been several degrees warmer than at present. The weathering that continued unabated in a climate similar to that of the present probably was of sufficient intensity and duration to produce the weathered condition in the soil. The high feldspathic content of the matrix, plus the stable condition of the erosion remnants of the Beacon Hill, provided favorable conditions for a red podzol soil to develop. Evidence suggests that some aeolian-derived quartz sand has been deposited over the weathered red matrix; however, this probability has not been fully established. Particle size distribution curves for the surficial horizons suggest an aeolian influence, but the heavy minerals of the sandy surfaces are virtually identical to those of the highly weathered red clay matrix.

PODZOL FORMATION WITH IRONSTONE, SANDSTONE, AND/OR IRON BANDS

Scattered throughout the Pine Barrens are isolated localities in which ironstone, sandstone, and related hardened zones have formed in the soil (Fig. 4). These localities are generally low hills or cuesta-like forms. The ironstone ranges in character from nodules, platelets, and bands to blocky hardened zones 3 m or more in thickness. The hardened condition generally is present in the B/C horizon.

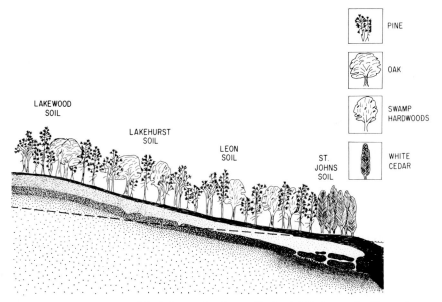

Fig. 5. Drainage catena of the Lakewood soil area. On the left (Lakewood soil) are shown xeric uplands and, as one progresses to the right, the water table is seen to occur at higher levels, with the site becoming more hydric in character. In addition to the Lakewood, the Lakehurst, Leon, St. Johns, and Bog soils are present along this moisture gradient.

PODZOL FORMATION OVER GLEYED SOIL

Extensive parts of the Pine Barrens have Lakewood soil with an incipient gley* formation present in the C horizon (Fig. 4). This condition sometimes is referred to as a gley podzol (Lakehurst), especially by German and Soviet investigators.

PODZOL SOIL WITH A THIN BLEACHED HORIZON

Lakewood soil commonly has a fairly thick A2 horizon of impoverished sand. There are numerous sites—particularly the southern, but to an extent the eastern sectors of the Pine Barrens—in which the bleached horizon is quite thin. This condition generally is more prevalent where clay content is a little higher or in sectors with rolling relief.

LOCAL VARIATIONS IN SOILS—THE DRAINAGE CATENA

When conditions within the Pine Barrens are examined, one of the more striking features that arises is the change in soil characteristics and biotic spectra from the xeric uplands to the low-lying, water-logged cedar swamps (Fig. 5). Most of the wet land-

---

*A pale, dark, or mottled condition resulting from wet conditions.

scape owes its condition to the high water table rather than to low soil permeability. In classifying soils on a catena basis as originally outlined by Milne (1935), one recognizes xeric/shallow soils, deep, well drained soils, and soils with various degrees of impeded drainage. Insofar as the Lakewood group of soils is concerned, the Pine Barrens are somewhat of an anomaly, in that there are few well-drained soils within the drainage catena. Instead, conditions go almost directly from xeric (Lakewood soil) to hydric soils. Wet, swampy soil areas have received relatively little attention in the literature. There are at least three mineral hydromorphic soils common in the main sectors of the Pine Barrens: Lakehurst, Leon and St. Johns.

The St. Johns soil (Fig. 6), referred to widely in the literature, is prominent in the cedar swamp and swamp hardwood areas. The morphology of the St. Johns soil is shown in the tabulation below.

Depth (cm)	Horizon	Morphology
20–0	A0	Dark reddish brown to brownish, black tough, fibrous organic material strongly acid; commonly water saturated
0–18	A1	Black organic–sand mixture
18–75	A2	Brownish-gray (5 YR 6/1) sand with pillow-sized inclusions of brownish-black organic-stained sand that in turn have inclusions of brown sand; this horizon is extremely erratic in composition and appearance
75–100	(B)	Water-saturated, brownish-black to black organic-stained sand
100+	B/C	Dark brown sand, usually becoming lighter in color at depth

Lakehurst is a soil which is similar to the Lakewood, but in which a gley condition is present at a depth of 60 or more cm and there is a general increase in the thickness of the organic mat on the surface. The gley condition is a result of the high water table rather than compaction within the lower horizons.

Leon is a weakly gleyed mineral soil with the water table at a depth of about 30–60 cm. The organic matter on the surface, generally about 5–15 cm thick, is underlain by an A2 horizon of gray, loose sand. At a depth of some 35 cm, one encounters a dark reddish brown B horizon consisting of water-saturated sand. Below the B horizon is a gray, water-saturated sand.

Bog soils are scattered throughout the Pine Barrens region along water courses and in some other broad, flat sectors. The organic material is strongly acid and usually <1 m in thickness, but in some situations thicknesses up to 2 m have been recorded. Composition consists of peat moss (*Sphagnum*), sedge (*Cyperaceae*), and woody components.

Fig. 6. St. Johns soil (left side), a groundwater podzol. The water table is near the surface for extended periods of time each year. Wedge-shaped structure in Lakewood soil (right side) near Woodmansie. The whitish A2 horizon is a sand of probable aeolian origin. Beneath the A2 horizon is the Beacon Hill Formation, consisting of a weathered sand–clay–gravel mixture. Processes producing the complex morphology have not been established. Ruler = 91 cm.

The poorly drained swampy conditions throughout the Pine Barrens commonly contain bog iron ore in the lower soil horizons. Bog iron ore forms in fresh water in association with coarse-grained, acid sediments. Its formation is related to the iron in the soil solution that is chelated with the humic substances. Slow but persistent oxygenation throughout the upper soil layers causes a precipitation of the chelated iron, resulting in a build-up of the bog iron layer.

SASSAFRAS AND RELATED SOILS

Extensive areas of Sassafras soil are scattered throughout the Pine Barrens (Fig. 2). These soils are not to be considered typical or modal Sassafras soils; instead, they are of a very sandy variety, bordering on droughtiness. While the "Pine Barren" Sassafras soils have certain features in common with those Sassafras soils occupying the area between the Pine Barrens and the Delaware River, the former are droughty, highly leached, and do not have the agricultural potential of those of the latter locations. The range of conditions identified with the Sassafras series was outlined by Lyford and Quakenbush (1956), who list 35 soils once included under the name of Sassafras. An idealized description of the Sassafras soil of the pine region follows in the table below.

Depth (cm)	Horizon	Morphology
2–0	A0	Dry mor of deciduous leaves
0–25	A21	Dark grayish brown (10 YR 4/2) sandy loam, loose and friable
25–36	A22	Yellowish brown (10 YR 5/4) sandy loam, loose and friable
36–60	B2	Dark brown (7.5 YR 4/4) sandy loam with a slight increase in clay; sometimes a weak sub-angular blocky structure
60+	C	Yellowish sandy loam; at a depth of 60 cm, a weak gley condition may be present

The Sassafras soil in the Pine Barrens is acid and is highly depleted of the potentially available plant nutrients. Chemically, the Sassafras is not very different from the Lakewood soil, but the pH values and percentage of base saturation may be slightly higher in the former. The soil matrix has a rather stable iron stain which has not reached the threshold of appreciable solubilization. This condition inhibits development of the gray color in the A2 horizon. Hence, some of the differences between Lakewood and Sassafras soils in the Pine Barrens are very narrow insofar as chemical and moisture parameters are concerned.

If earlier attempts at agricultural development in the Pine Barrens are examined (excluding the blueberry–cranberry industry), it will be seen that such endeavors generally were on Sassafras soil. It has been learned, however, that these soils were marginal and questionable for crop cultivation; accordingly, most of the land reverted to forest or remained in an "idle" state.

The central concept of Sassafras soil and deviations from the prototype are shown in Fig. 7. In some of the Sassafras soils, the uppermost portion of the A2 horizon is thin and highly bleached (Fig. 7). It is appropriate to refer to this soil as an incipient podzol. In Scandanavia such genetic soils are referred to as dwarf podzol. Another variety of the Sassafras soil widespread throughout the Pine Barrens consists of a dark grayish-brown, well-drained sand to loamy sand with a yellowish-brown sandy loam B horizon (Fig. 7). This soil is quite similar to that shown as the modal concept, but is sandier throughout and was identified as the Sassafras–Hammonton phase (Tedrow, 1961). Ironstone sometimes is present in the Sassafras soil (Fig. 7), but this condition is not very common. As is the case for almost every well-drained soil, there are associated

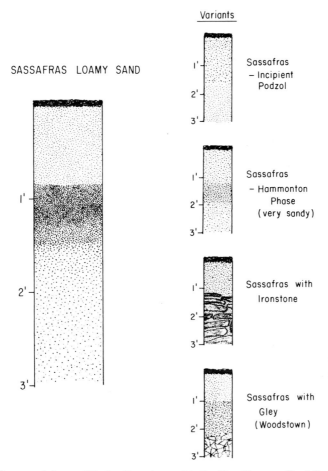

Fig. 7. Some variations within the Sassafras soil in the Pine Barrens. The left side depicts the central concept of Sassafras, with variants shown on the right. 1-ft depth = 30.5 cm.

gley soils, and the Sassafras is no exception. This gley condition is shown in Fig. 7 as Woodstown soil.

DISTURBED SOIL MORPHOLOGY

If the Pine Barren soils are examined in detail, some unusual morphological features are evident. These features vary in form and character from involuted and cuspate-shaped subsoil structures to wedge-shaped features (Fig. 6). On first examination, frost action may be considered the main mechanism causing their development; however, such a depiction cannot be fully established at this time. Many cases of disordered soil morphology may result from uprooted trees, but such a process cannot account for all conditions. The problem of the possible frost structures, climatic record, landscape evolution, soil and vegetative patterns in the Pine Barrens during Cenozoic time demands much additional study.

SUMMARY

Soils of the Pine Barrens are formed on sandy, siliceous, acid materials which are highly leached and strikingly depauperate in plant nutrients. The most highly leached soil is the Lakewood, which is a podzol. Where a little more silt and clay are present in the soil matrix, the Sassafras and other soil series are present. This latter group of soils is not so highly podzolized. On some of the Tertiary hilltops the podzol soils contain lateritic affinities. Very acid mineral gley soils are present in the low positions within the Pine Barrens, and a few bogs are found in cedar swamps and contiguous areas.

REFERENCES

Biel, E. R. (1958). The climate of New Jersey. *In* "The Economy of New Jersey" (S. J. Flink, ed.), pp. 53–98. Rutgers Univ. Press, New Brunswick, New Jersey.

Gamble, J. F. (1963). "A Study of Strontium, Barium, and Calcium Relationships in Soils and Vegetation," AEC Final Rep. NYO-10581. Rutgers Univ., New Brunswick, New Jersey. (Mimeo.)

Harshberger, J. W. (1916). "The Vegetation of the New Jersey Pine-Barrens. An Ecologic Investigation." Christopher Sower Co., Philadelphia, Pennsylvania.

Joffe, J. S. (1931). Soil profile studies: III. The process of podzolization. *Soil Sci.* **32,** 303–323.

Joffe, J. S., and Watson, C. W. (1933). Soil profile studies; V. Mature podzols. *Soil Sci.* **35,** 313–331.

Jordan, C. F. (1968). A simple tension-free lysimeter. *Soil Sci.* **105,** 81–86.

Krebs, R. D., and Tedrow, J. C. F. (1958). Genesis of red-yellow podzolic and related soils in New Jersey. *Soil Sci.* **85,** 28–37.

Kümmel, H. B. (1940). The geology of New Jersey. *N.J. Dep. Conserv. Econ. Dev., Geol. Bull.* No. 50.

Lewis, J. V., and Kümmel, H. B. (1910–1912). "Geologic Map of New Jersey," Atlas sheet No. 40. N.J. Dep. Conserv. Econ. Dev., Trenton, New Jersey.

Lutz, H. J. (1934). Concerning a geological explanation of the origin and present distribution of the New Jersey pine barren vegetation. *Ecology* **15,** 399–406.

Lyford, W. H., and Quakenbush, G. A. (1956). Developments in the classification of the Sassafras soil series. *Soil Sci. Soc. Am., Proc.* **20,** 397–399.

MacClintock, P., and Richards, H. G. (1936). Correlation of Late Pleistocene marine and glacial deposits of New Jersey and New York. *Geol. Soc. Am. Bull.* **47,** 289–338.

McCormick, J. (1970). The pine barrens: A preliminary ecological inventory. *N.J. State Mus., Res. Rep.* No. 2.

Marbut, C. F. (1928). U.S. Department of Agriculture Graduate School Lectures. U.S. Dep. Agric., Washington, D.C. (Unpublished manuscript.)

Martens, J. H. C. (1956). Industrial sands of New Jersey. *Rutgers Univ. Bur. Miner. Res., Bull.* No. 6.

Mattson, S. (1933). The laws of soil colloidal behavior: XI. Electrodialysis in relation to soil processes. *Soil Sci.* **36,** 149–163.

Milne, G. (1935). Some suggested units of classification and mapping, particularly for East African soils. *Soil Res.* **4,** 183–198.

Muir, A. (1961). The podzol and podzolic soil. *Adv. Agron.* **13,** 1–56.

Robichaud, B., and Buell, M. F. (1973). "Vegetation of New Jersey. A Study of Landscape Diversity." Rutgers Univ. Press, New Brunswick, New Jersey.

Salisbury, R. D. (1898). "The Physical Geography of New Jersey," Final Rep. Vol. 4. *N.J. Geol. Surv.,* Trenton, New Jersey.

Salisbury, R. D., and Knapp, G. N. (1917). "The Quaternary Formations of Southern New Jersey," Final Rep., Ser. Vol. 8. N.J. Dep. Conserv. Dev., Trenton, New Jersey.

Tedrow, J. C. F. (1952). Soil conditions in the Pine Barrens of New Jersey. *Bartonia* **26,** 28–35.

Tedrow, J. C. F. (1961). New Jersey soils. *N.J. Agric. Exp. Stn., Circ.* No. 601.

5

Soil Series of the Pine Barrens

MARCO L. MARKLEY

INTRODUCTION

The purpose of this chapter is to describe the soil series of the Pine Barrens in terms of geographic distribution and ecological characteristics. Thirteen soils cover appreciable areas in the region (Fig. 1), and these are described in detail, and general geographic information (Table I) and ecological information (Table II) are summarized. The 13 soils range from excessively drained to very poorly drained: (1) Lakewood; (2) Evesboro; (3) Woodmansie; (4) Downer; (5) Sassafras; (6) Aura; (7) Lakehurst; (8) Klej; (9) Hammonton; (10) Atsion; (11) Berryland; (12) Pocomoke; and (13) Muck. Information on three additional soils of limited distribution, namely, Woodstown, Fallsington, and Fort Mott, is listed in Tables I and II. Most soil series are named for towns in the Pine Barrens.

The soil descriptions below use the popular terms *surface, subsoil,* and *substratum* for the A, B, and C horizons (U.S. Department of Agriculture, 1951). Wooded soils with a sandy surface generally have several thin (3–15 cm or 1–6 in) horizons near the surface, which, when plowed, are mixed with the horizon below to form the plow layer. In sandy soils, this layer frequently is 35 cm (14 in) thick.

Because it shows very little variation among the Pine Barrens soils, acidity is not listed for each soil. For unlimed soils, the surface horizon is extremely acid (pH 3.6–4.0), and the subsoil and substratum either are extremely acid or very strongly acid and range from pH 4.2–5.0, although the average is about 4.6. Liming of cropland in the last 100–150 years has changed the pH of the soils to a depth of >1 m (3.3 ft) (U.S. Department of Agriculture, 1974).

SOILS IN THE PINE BARRENS

Lakewood Series

Lakewood soils are deep, loose, excessively drained sands having a bleached gray surface soil 18 or more centimeters (7 in) thick. Slopes generally are <10% but range to 20%, and altitudes are 6–70 m (20–230 ft).

81

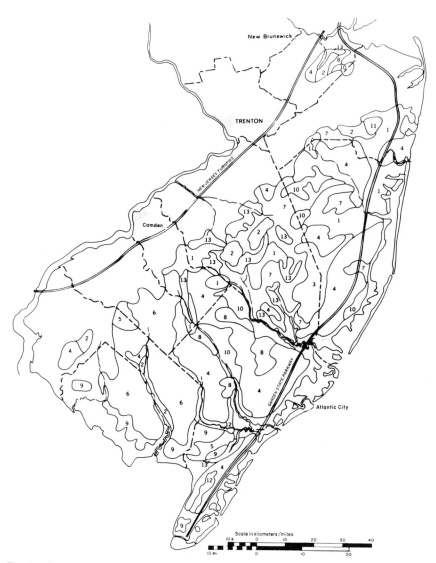

Fig. 1.   General soil map of the New Jersey Pine Barrens. The two long double lines are the New Jersey Turnpike and the Garden State Parkway. Soils: (1) Lakewood; (2) Evesboro; (3) Woodmansie; (4) Downer; (5) Sassafras; (6) Aura; (7) Lakehurst; (8) Klej; (9) Hammonton; (10) Atsion; (11) Berryland; (12) Pocomoke; and (13) Muck. From Soil Surveys of U.S. Department of Agriculture (1951–1978). See Soil Surveys for soil maps of localized areas.

TABLE I   General Distribution and Extent of Soils in the Pine Barrens

Soil series	Former classification[a]	General distribution in Pine Barrens	Area in Pine Barrens and percent of Pine Barrens (hectares)	Position in landscape	Most common trees (in order of abundance)
Lakewood	Lakewood	Rare in southern part	56,000 12%	High	Pitch and shortleaf pines, and few chestnut oaks; dwarf form where fires have been severe
Evesboro	Sassafras	Entire region	40,000 9%	High	Pitch and shortleaf pines and few chestnut oaks
Woodmansie	Lakewood	Burlington and Ocean counties	20,000 4%	High	Dwarf pitch pine
Fort Mott	Sassafras	Mostly in southern part	4,500 < 1%	High	Black, white, and chestnut oaks, hickories, and few pitch and short-leaf pines
Downer	Sassafras	Entire region	80,000 17%	High	Black, white, scarlet, red, and chestnut oaks, hickories, and few pitch and shortleaf pines
Sassafras	Sassafras	Mostly in southern part	12,000 3%	High	Black, red, white, and scarlet oaks, hickories, and few beeches
Aura	Sassafras	Mostly in southern part	24,000 5%	High	Black, white, red, and scarlet oaks, hickories, and few pitch and short-leaf pines
Lakehurst	Lakewood	Mostly in northern part	52,000 11%	Inter-mediate	Pitch pine and few black, white and chestnut oaks
Klej	Sassafras	Entire region	16,000 3%	Inter-mediate	Black and white oaks, blackgum; and few red maples, sweetgums, pitch and shortleaf pines
Hammonton	Woodstown	Entire area	20,000 4%	Inter-mediate	Black, white, red, southern red, and scarlet oaks and few pitch and short-leaf pines
Woodstown	Woodstown	Mostly in southern part	2,000 <5%	Inter-mediate	Red, white, black, southern red oaks, hickories, and few beeches
Atsion	Leon[b]	Entire area except Cape May County	58,000 12%	Low	Pitch pine, red maple, and blackgum
Fallsington	Portsmouth	Southern part	2,000 <5%	Low	Swamp white oak, red maple, blackgum, sweetgum, sweet birch, beech, and few pitch pines
Berryland	St. Johns[b]	Entire area	20,000 4%	Low	Pitch pine, red maple, blackgum, and few Atlantic white cedars
Pocomoke	Portsmouth	Entire area	8,000 2%	Low	Swamp white oak, red maple, blackgum, sweetgum, willow oak, and few pitch pines
Muck	Swamp	Entire area	48,000 10%	Low	Atlantic white cedar and bay magnolia

[a] Bureau of Chemistry and Soils, 1925 to 1929, 1 inch per mile scale.
[b] These soils are similar to Atsion and Berryland, respectively, but now are defined as having higher temperatures.

TABLE II   Some Ecological Characteristics of the Pine Barren Soils.

Soil series	Natural drainage	Depth to water table Winter and Spring (cm)	Summer (cm)	Available water capacity	Permeability (based on least permeable horizons)	Combined litter and humus thickness (cm)	Thickness of bleached surface soil (cm)	Predominant textures Surface soil	Subsoil	Sub-stratum	Organic matter content of surface soil	Fertility (cation exchange capacity in milli-equivalents)
Lakewood	Excessive	>150	>180	Very low	Rapid	0– 5	>18	Sand	Sand	Sand	Low	< 1
Evesboro	Excessive	>150	>180	Very low	Rapid	3–10	3–15	Sand	Sand	Sand	Low	< 4
Woodmansie	Well drained	>150	>180	Low	Moderate	0– 5	>18	Sand	Sandy loam	Sandy loam	Low	< 4
Fort Mott	Well drained	>150	>180	Low	Moderately rapid	5–10	5–15	Loamy sand	Sandy loam	Loamy sand	Low	3– 7
Downer	Well drained	>150	>180	Low or moderate	Moderate or moderately rapid	5–13	2– 5	Loamy sand or sandy loam	Sandy loam	Loamy sand	Low or moderate	4– 7
Sassafras	Well drained	>150	>180	Moderate	Moderate	5–13	2– 5	Sandy loam	Sandy loam or sandy clay loam	Loamy sand	Moderate	4–12
Aura	Well drained	>150	>180	Moderate	Moderate or moderately slow	5–13	5–13	Loamy sand or sandy loam, or gravelly sandy loam	Sandy clay loam	Sandy clay loam	Low or moderate	3– 7
Lakehurst	Moderately well drained or somewhat poorly drained	45–120	>150	Low[a]	Rapid	3– 8	>18	Sand	Sand	Sand	Low	< 1

Klej	Moderately well drained or somewhat poorly drained	45–120	>150	Low[a]	Rapid	5–13	3–10	Loamy sand	Loamy sand	Sand	Low	< 5
Hammonton	Moderately well drained or somewhat poorly drained	45–120	>150	Moderate[a]	Moderately rapid	8–15	5–13	Loamy sand or sandy loam	Sandy loam	Sand	Low or moderate	< 5
Woodstown	Moderately well	45–75	>150	Moderate[a]	Moderate	5–15	2–5	Sandy loam	Sandy loam or sandy clay loam	Loamy sand	Moderate	5–14
Atsion	Poorly drained	0–30	> 75	Excessive[b]	Rapid or moderately rapid	5–15	0	Sand	Loamy sand	Sand	Moderate	< 8
Fallsington	Poorly drained	0–30	> 75	Excessive[b]	Moderate	5–12	0	Sandy loam	Sandy loam or sandy clay loam	Loamy sand	Moderate	5–12
Berryland	Very poorly drained	0	30–60	Excessive[b]	Moderately rapid	8–15	0	Sand	Loamy sand	Sand	High	<10
Pocomoke	Very poorly drained	0	30–60	Excessive[b]	Moderately rapid	8–15	0	Sandy loam	Sandy loam	Loamy sand	High	<10
Muck	Very poorly drained	0	30–60	Excessive[b]	Moderately rapid or rapid	5	0	Muck	Muck	Sand	High	5–10

[a] Additional water is available seasonally from the water table.
[b] Water may not be available to plant roots unable to survive in saturated horizons.

A typical Lakewood soil has a light brownish-gray, loose sand plow layer 25 cm (10 in) thick. The subsoil, from 25 to 91 cm (10–36 in), is yellowish-brown, loose sand. The substratum, from 91 to 152 cm (36–60 in), is brownish-yellow, loose sand. Although it occurs rarely, as much as 15% of the soil is rounded quartzose gravel in some parts of the profile. The predominant size of the sand in most places is medium or coarse, but in Burlington (U.S. Department of Agriculture, 1971), northern Ocean, and southern Monmouth counties, there also are extensive areas of fine sand. The bleached sand ranges in thickness from 18–50 cm (7–20 in). In some places, the upper 3–6 cm (1–2 in) of the subsoil ranges to dark brown, reflecting organic matter and iron leached from the horizon above. In places, the texture of the substratum below 100 cm (39 in) ranges to sandy loam or, rarely, sandy clay loam.

Although extensive areas of Lakewood soils were cleared for farming, nearly all farming has been abandoned, and the areas have reverted to woodland, with some areas in residential use. Lakewood soils were classified as podzols by the 1938 classification system (Baldwin *et al.*, 1938). They are now classified as members of the mesic, coated family of Spodic Quartzipsamments (U.S. Department of Agriculture, 1975).

Evesboro Series

The Evesboro series consists of deep, loose, excessively drained sands that do not have a thickly bleached surface soil. Many areas are broad, with slopes predominantly <10% but ranging to 20%, and altitudes are 3–60 m.

A typical Evesboro soil has a grayish-brown sand plow layer 25 cm thick. The subsurface horizon from 25 to 40 cm is brown loose sand. The subsoil from 40 to 76 cm is yellowish-brown sand. The substratum, from 76 to 152 cm, is light yellowish-brown loose sand. Although occurring rarely, as much as 15% rounded quartzose gravel is found in some parts of the profile. The size of the sand is predominantly medium or coarse, but in certain areas of Burlington, northern Ocean, and southern Monmouth counties, the sand is predominantly fine. In places, the texture of the substratum below 100 cm ranges to sandy loam or sandy clay loam. These horizons are not as permeable as the normal sand texture, and the available water capacity is greater in these textures.

Most Evesboro soils are found in woodland. Extensive areas have been cleared, in which sweet potatoes, peaches, grapes, squash, pumpkins, cantaloupes, and lettuce now are grown, usually with irrigation. Some areas are devoted to residential, commercial, and industrial uses. In Camden County, these soils were called Lakeland. They are the same as Evesboro soils, except they have higher temperatures. By the 1938 classification system, Evesboro soils were classified as regosols. They now are classified as belonging to the mesic, coated family of Typic Quartzipsamments (U.S. Department of Agriculture, 1975).

Woodmansie Series

The Woodmansie series is composed of deep, well-drained soils having a bleached surface horizon 18 or more cm thick and a sandy loam or sandy clay loam subsoil. Slopes generally are in the 0–5% range, but can reach 10%; altitudes are 18–65 m.

The early natural vegetation is believed to have consisted of mostly pitch and shortleaf pines (*Pinus rigida* and *P. echinata*) and a few oaks (*Quercus* spp.). However, because Woodmansie soils occupy high positions in the landscape, wildfires burn up over these positions regardless of wind direction. The vegetation now is dominated by pitch pines, black jack oak (*Q. marilandica*), and scrub oaks (*Q. ilicifolia*), most of which measure less than 180 cm high (Robichaud & Buell 1973). Because of frequent fires, wooded Woodmansie soils generally lack a litter cover.

A typical profile of a Woodmansie soil shows a dark gray 5-cm surface horizon. The upper subsurface horizon, from 5 to 20 cm, consists of gray loose sand. The lower subsurface horizon, from 20 to 43 cm, is light yellowish-brown, loose sand. The subsoil, from 43 to 76 cm, is yellowish-brown, sandy loam. The substratum, from 76 to 114 cm, is yellow, loose, coarse sand. The substratum from 114 to 152 cm, is reddish-yellow, friable, sandy loam. In certain areas, rounded quartzose gravel ranges up to 30% in the subsoil and up to 50% in the substratum in places. The soils are very strongly acid or extremely acid. The texture of the substratum ranges from sand to sandy clay loam (U.S. Department of Agriculture, 1976). In places, the substratum is firm when moist and very hard when dry.

Nearly all of the Woodmansie soils are wooded, and very little has been cleared for farming or urban uses. Some areas have been used for mining gravel. Woodmansie soils now are classified as a member of the coarse-loamy, siliceous, mesic family of Typic Hapludults (U.S. Department of Agriculture, 1975).

Downer Series

The Downer series consists of deep, well-drained soils having a sandy loam subsoil and a loose sandy substratum. Slopes are mostly <5%, but range to 15%; altitudes are 3–60 m.

A typical Downer soil has a dark, grayish-brown, loamy sand surface soil 25 cm thick. The subsurface horizon, from 25 to 46 cm, is yellowish-brown, loose, loamy sand. The subsoil, from 46 to 76 cm, is yellowish-brown, friable, sandy loam. The substratum, from 76 to 152 cm, is yellowish-brown, loose, loamy sand. Rounded quartzose gravel is found to comprise up to 15% of the surface and subsoil and up to 60% of the substratum. Although the substratum texture is loamy sand or gravelly loamy sand in most places, it ranges to sandy loam or sandy clay loam in certain areas.

Most Downer soils are found in woodlands. About 40% is farmed for the cultivation of many vegetables, fruit, corn, wheat, soybeans, hay, pasture, nursery stock, and cultivated sod, generally with irrigation. Some areas are in urban use, while some were utilized for sand mining. Downer soil is the most extensive soil in the Pine Barrens and now is classified as belonging to the coarse-loamy, siliceous, mesic family of Typic Hapludults (U.S. Department of Agriculture, 1975).

Sassafras Series

The Sassafras series consists of deep, well-drained soils which have a sandy clay loam or heavy sandy loam subsoil and a loose loamy sand substratum. Most slopes are <5% but range to 25%; altitudes are 12–60 m.

A typical Sassafras soil has a dark grayish-brown, sandy loam plow layer 20 cm thick. The subsurface, from 20 to 43 cm, is yellowish-brown sandy loam. The subsoil, from 43 to 102 cm, is strong brown or brown sandy clay loam or heavy, sandy loam. The substratum, from 102 to 152 cm, is strong brown, loose, loamy sand. The content of rounded quartzose gravel in the surface and subsoil horizons range up to 20% and up to 30% in the substratum. Unless limed, Sassafras soils are very strongly acid.

Most Sassafras soils are farmed for vegetables, fruit, corn, wheat, soybeans, hay, pasture, nursery stock, and cultivated sod; nearly all high-value crops are irrigated. Extensive areas are in urban use, with some areas for gravel or sand mining.

In the earliest mapping, Sassafras soils were defined rather broadly. Since 1900, many new soils were established, each for a portion of soils formerly mapped as Sassafras (see Table I). Sassafras soils were classified as Gray-Brown Podzolic in the 1938 classification system. It is now classified as a member of the fine-loamy, siliceous, mesic family of Typic Hapludults (U.S. Department of Agriculture, 1975).

Aura Series

The Aura series consists of deep, well-drained soils which have a gravelly sandy clay loam upper subsoil and a firm gravelly sandy clay loam lower subsoil. Most slopes are <5% but range to 15%; altitudes are 12–60 m.

A typical Aura soil has a dark grayish-brown, sandy loam plow layer 25 cm thick. The subsurface horizon, from 25 to 38 cm, is yellowish-brown sandy loam. The upper subsoil, from 38 to 71 cm, is strong brown, friable, gravelly clay loam. The lower subsoil, from 71 to 152 cm, is yellowish-red, firm, sandy clay loam. Quartzose gravel comprises up to 20% of the upper subsoil and up to 50% of the lower subsoil. The surface texture is loamy sand, sandy loam, loam or gravelly equivalents.

About one-half of Aura areas is wooded, with the remainder primarily finding use for the cultivation of vegetables, apples and peaches, corn, wheat, and soybeans. Nearly all vegetables are irrigated. The soil now is classified as a member of the fine-loamy, mixed, mesic family of Typic Hapludults (U.S. Department of Agriculture, 1975).

Lakehurst Series

Lakehurst soils are deep, loose, moderately well or somewhat poorly drained sands having a bleached gray sand surface soil 18 or more cm thick. These soils have a fluctuating water table that rises into the subsoil in late winter. Slopes are nearly level but in rare locations range up to 3%; altitudes are 3–55 m.

A typical Lakehurst soil has a light brownish-gray sand plow layer 25 cm thick. The subsurface is light gray loose sand measuring from 25 to 38 cm. The upper subsoil, from 38 to 46 cm, is dark brown, loose, loamy sand containing some firm nodules. The lower subsoil, from 46 to 91 cm, is loose, yellowish-brown sand. The substratum, from 91 to 152 cm, is loose, pale brown sand. Although rarely the case, rounded quartzose gravel comprises up to 15% in some parts of the profile. The size of the sand is mostly medium and coarse, but in northern Ocean and southern Monmouth counties there are extensive areas of fine sand. The bleached sand ranges in thickness from 18–60 cm. Iron cemented concretions up to 3 cm in diameter are common in the upper 5 cm of the subsoil. In some areas, the substratum texture below 100 cm ranges to sandy loam or, rarely, sandy clay loam.

Although some areas were cleared for farming, most farmland has reverted to woodland. Some areas are in residential use. All Lakehurst soils in the state are in the Pine Barrens. Lakehurst soils now are classified as belonging to the mesic, coated family of Haplaquodic Quartzipsamments (U.S. Department of Agriculture, 1975).

Klej Series

The Klej series consists of deep, moderately well and somewhat poorly drained sands or loamy sands. Most slopes are almost level but range up to 5%; altitudes are 15–45 m.

A typical Klej soil profile has a dark grayish-brown, loamy sand plow layer 25 cm thick. The subsoil, from 25 to 50 cm, is light olive-brown, loose, loamy sand. The substratum, from 50 to 152 cm, is a mottled yellowish-brown, brownish-gray, or light gray loose or loamy sand. Klej soils normally have a very weak structure or lack structure altogether. Sandy loam or sandy clay loam strata normally are found in the substratum below 102 cm. The size of the sand is chiefly medium or coarse, but in Burlington, northern Ocean, and southern Monmouth counties, there are areas in which the sand is predominantly fine.

Most Klej soils are found in woodlands, although some areas are in urban use and about 10% has been cleared for the cultivation of vegetables and fruit. In order to control the water table; the soils generally are drained and then irrigated as needed. The soil currently is classified as belonging to the mesic, coated family of Aquic Quartzipsamments (U.S. Department of Agriculture, 1975).

Hammonton Series

The Hammonton series consists of deep, moderately well, and somewhat poorly drained soils which have a sandy loam subsoil and a loose sandy substratum. Most slopes are almost level but range up to 5%; altitudes are 1.5–50 m.

A typical Hammonton soil profile has a very dark grayish brown plow layer 20 cm thick. The subsurface, from 20 to 46 cm, is a yellowish-brown, loose sand. The subsoil, from 46 to 91 cm, is mottled, yellowish-brown, friable, sandy loam. The substratum, from 91 to 152 cm, is mottled brownish-yellow, loose sand. Rounded quartzose gravel comprises up to 20% in the surface and subsoil horizons and up to

40% in some parts of the substratum. The substratum texture in certain places ranges to sandy loam or sandy clay loam.

Most Hammonton soils are in woodland. Extensive areas are used for the growing of vegetables, fruit, hay, pasture and nursery crops, and almost all vegetable crops are irrigated. Some areas are in urban use, and some are utilized for sand mining. Hammonton now is classified as belonging to the coarse-loamy, siliceous, mesic family of Aquic Hapludults (U.S. Department of Agriculture, 1975).

Atsion Series

Atsion soils are deep, poorly drained sands that have a gray or thin black surface soil and a dark brown subsoil. These soils have a fluctuating water table that is high in late winter and spring. Slopes are nearly level, generally <1%; altitudes are 1.5–52 m.

A typical Atsion soil has a dark gray sand plow layer 20 cm thick. The subsurface, from 20 to 46 cm, is light gray, loose sand. The upper subsoil, from 46 to 60 cm, is very dark brown, loamy sand. The horizon is loose in places and weakly cemented at other places. The lower subsoil, from 60 cm to 91 cm, is very dark gray, loose sand. The substratum, from 91 to 152 cm, is brown, loose sand. Rounded quartzose gravel comprises up to 25%, especially in the lower subsoil or substratum. The size of the sand is mostly medium and coarse, but in northern Ocean County and southern Monmouth County there are extensive areas of fine sand. The consistency of the very dark brown subsoil ranges from loose to very firm. Normally, this horizon becomes firmer if the soil is drained. In certain areas, Atsion soils have several of these very dark horizons separated by loose gray or brown horizons. The substratum texture below 100 cm ranges to sandy loam or, rarely, to sandy clay loam.

Most of the region's Atsion soils are found in woodlands. Extensive areas have been cleared for blueberry and cranberry production, and limited areas are used for vegetable production. All Atsion soils of the state are in the Pine Barrens. The Atsion soil series was established in 1970 for soils, which, except for their lower soil temperatures, were similar to Leon soils. These soils were called Leon in the Gloucester (U.S. Department of Agriculture, 1962) and Camden (U.S. Department of Agriculture, 1966) soil surveys. Leon soils were classified as Groundwater Podzols in the 1938 classification system. Atsion soils now are classified as belonging to the sandy, siliceous, mesic family of Aeric Haplaquods (U.S. Department of Agriculture, 1975).

Berryland Series

The Berryland series includes deep, very poorly drained, sandy soils which have a dark brown subsoil and a thick black surface soil. These soils have a fluctuating water table that is at the surface in late winter. Slopes are almost level, generally <1%; altitudes are 1–50 m.

A typical Berryland soil has a black sand plow layer 25 cm thick. The subsurface, from 25 to 30 cm, is a loose, gray sand. The upper subsoil, from 30 to 50 cm, is dark reddish-brown, loamy sand. The lower subsoil, from 50 cm to 75 cm, is dark gray, loose sand. The substratum, from 75 to 152 cm, is grayish-brown, loose sand. Rounded quartzose gravel comprises up to 20% in the lower subsoil or substratum. The size of the sand is generally medium or coarse, but in northern Ocean and southern Monmouth counties there are areas of fine sand. The consistency of the dark reddish-brown subsoil horizon ranges from loose to very firm, and normally this horizon becomes firmer when the soil is drained. In certain areas, Berryland soils have several of the dark reddish-brown horizons separated by loose gray or brown horizons. In places, the substratum texture ranges to sandy loam or, rarely, sandy clay loam.

Most Berryland soils are found in woodlands. Extensive areas have been cleared for cranberry or blueberry production, and limited areas are used for the growing of vegetables. Small areas are in urban use, but the high water table severely limits the operation of septic tank filter fields. Nearly all Berryland soils in New Jersey are in the Pine Barrens. This soil category was established in 1966 for soils, which, except for their lower temperatures, were similar to St. Johns. Soils mapped St. Johns in Gloucester and Camden counties are the same as Berryland soils. St. Johns soils were classified as Groundwater Podzols by the 1938 classification system. They are now classified as belonging to the sandy, siliceous, mesic family of Typic Haplaquods (U.S. Department of Agriculture, 1975).

Pocomoke Series

The Pocomoke series consists of deep, very poorly drained soils which have a thick very dark surface soil, a gray sandy loam subsoil, and a gray loamy sand substratum. Slopes are <2%; altitudes are 6–30 m.

A typical Pocomoke soil has a black sandy loam surface soil 25 cm thick. The subsurface from 25 to 35 cm is gray sandy loam. The subsoil, from 35 to 71 cm, is mottled, gray, sandy loam. The substratum, from 71 to 152 cm, is mottled, gray, loamy sand. The pH is extremely or very strongly acid. Surface textures are loam, fine sandy loam, or sandy loam. The substratum textures are predominantly sand or loamy sand but range to include sandy loam or sandy clay loam, mostly below 100 cm.

Most Pocomoke soils are found in woodlands. Some areas have been cleared for crop production, most commonly, corn, soybeans, hay, blueberries, and vegetables. The soil is now classified as belonging to the coarse-loamy, siliceous, thermic family of Typic Umbraquults (U.S. Department of Agriculture, 1975). In the Pine Barrens, the temperatures are a few degrees lower than normal for the Pocomoke series.

Muck Soils

The Muck soils are moderately deep, very poorly drained, highly organic soils over a sandy substratum. These soils form in narrow submerged valleys. Slopes are <1%; altitudes are 3–50 m.

A typical Muck soil has a peat moss (*Sphagnum*) cover 5 cm thick. The surface and subsurface horizons are black muck to a depth of 100 cm. The substratum, from 100 to 152 cm, is gray sand. The thickness of the organic material ranges from 40–100 cm. The substratum is sand or gravelly sand.

Nearly all Muck soils are found in woodlands, with only very small areas cleared for the cultivation of cranberries and blueberries. The soil is now classified as a sandy or sandy-skeletal, siliceous, dysic, mesic family of Terric Medisaprists (U.S. Department of Agriculture, 1975).

SUMMARY

A map of the general distribution of soils in the Pine Barrens is presented, along with detailed descriptions of ecologically important characteristics of the 13 major soil series. In order, the most extensive soils are Downer, Atsion, Lakewood, Lakehurst, Muck, and Evesboro. Information on the three additional soils of limited distribution is included. Northern and southern portions of the Pine Barrens generally have different soils, and eastern and western portions differ similarly. Seven soils are well-to-excessively drained, whereas eight soils exhibit impeded drainage, i.e., three moderately well or somewhat poor, and five poor to very poor. Only one uncommon soil is classified as moderately well drained. All unlimed surface soils are extremely acid (pH 3.6–4.0), with subsurface and substratum horizons about pH 4.2–5.0. Except for the upper horizons of Muck soil, all soils range from sandy clay loam to sand and have low fertility (cation exchange capacity generally well under 10). Crops currently are grown on almost all soils.

REFERENCES

Baldwin, M., Kellogg, C. E., and Thorp, J. (1938). Soil classification. *U.S. Dep. Agric. Yearb. Agric.* pp. 979–1001.
Cox, H. R. (1948). Monmouth County soils. *N.J. Agric. Exp. Stn., Bull.* No. 738.
Robichaud, B., and Buell, M. F. (1973). "Vegetation of New Jersey. A Study in Landscape Diversity." Rutgers Univ. Press, New Brunswick, New Jersey.
U.S. Department of Agriculture (1951). Soil survey manual. *U.S. Dep. Agric., Agric. Handb.* No. 18.
U.S. Department of Agriculture (1962). "Soil Survey, Gloucester County (Markley, M.L.)." Soil Conserv. Serv., Somerset, New Jersey.
U.S. Department of Agriculture (1966). "Soil Survey, Camden County (Markley, M.L.)." Soil Conserv. Serv., Somerset, New Jersey.
U.S. Department of Agriculture (1969). "Soil Survey, Salem County (Powley, V.R.)." Soil Conserv. Surv., Somerset, New Jersey.
U.S. Department of Agriculture (1971). "Soil Survey, Burlington County (Markley, M.L.)." Soil Conserv. Surv., Somerset, New Jersey.
U.S. Department of Agriculture (1974). Soil survey laboratory data and descriptions for some soils of New Jersey. *Soil Surv. Invest. Rep.* No. 26.
U.S. Department of Agriculture (1975). Soil taxonomy. *U.S. Dep. Agric., Agric. Handb.* No. 436.

U.S. Department of Agriculture (1976). Soil survey investigations for Lakewood, Lakehurst, and Wood-mansie soils. Soil Conserv. Surv., Somerset, New Jersey (Unpublished report.)

U.S. Department of Agriculture (1977). "Soil Survey, Cape May County (Markley, M.L.)." Soil Conserv. Surv., Somerset, New Jersey.

U.S. Department of Agriculture (1978a). "Soil Survey, Cumberland County (Powley, V.R.)." Soil Conserv. Surv., Somerset, New Jersey.

U.S. Department of Agriculture (1978b). "Soil Survey, Atlantic County (Johnson, J.)." Soil Conserv. Surv., Somerset, New Jersey.

6

Mineralogy of Pine Barrens Soils

LOWELL A. DOUGLAS and JOHN J. TRELA

Those factors that influence the formation of soils—time, topography, parent material, climate, and biological activity (Jenny, 1941)—also influence the formation of minerals in soils. This discussion examines some representative soils of the New Jersey Pine Barrens and the influence of some factors of soil formation on soil mineralogy.

Very sandy soils, as found in the Pine Barrens, extend along the East Coast of the United States south to Florida. The principal soils to be considered in this chapter include the very sandy Lakewood and Lakehurst soils and the more loamy Downer, Sassafras, and Woodstown series (Table I). These soils will be used to illustrate the effect of time (Downer, Sassafras, and Woodmansie) and drainage position (Lakewood and Lakehurst, and Sassafras and Woodstown) on mineralogy. The effect of soil organic matter on some phases of soil mineralogy will be discussed; however, it should be noted that high organic soils (for example, Pocomoke) of the Pine Barrens have not been examined. Typical soil morphologies are described by Markley (in this volume).

AGE OF PARENT MATERIALS

Soils are dynamic and change over time in response to their environments until a stable or climax state is attained. The relative ages of the geologic materials discussed in this chapter are listed in Table II. Although there is significant disagreement in the geologic literature regarding the absolute ages of these formations, there is little controversy over relative ages. A knowledge of the relative age of the parent material of a soil and the associated geomorphic history since the time of deposition of the material may provide some insight into possible soil developmental processes.

These sediments contain clay materials. Hence, the investigator is confronted with the problems of separating sedimentary parent material clay minerals from clay minerals formed *in situ*. This is accomplished by sampling soils by horizons and attributing differences in the type and amount of clay present in the various horizons to soil developmental processes. The degree of change and alteration in the clay minerals is a function of the environmental factors acting upon the soil through time.

95

TABLE I Soil Series Classification, Drainage, and Geologic Formations[a]

Soil series	Great soil group	Soil order	Drainage	Geologic formation
Lakewood	Podzol	Spodosol	Excessively drained	Cohansey, Kirkwood, Cape May
Lakehurst	Podzol	Spodosol	Moderately well drained	Cohansey, Kirkwood, Cape May
Downer	Gray-brown to red-yellow Podzolic intergrade	Ultisol	Well drained	Pensauken, Cape May
Sassafras	Gray-brown to red-yellow Podzolic intergrade	Ultisol	Well drained	Pensauken, Bridgeton
Woodstown	Gray-brown to red-yellow Podzolic intergrade	Ultisol	Moderately well drained	Pensauken, Bridgeton
Woodmansie	Podzol	Ultisol	Well drained	Beacon Hill, Bridgeton

[a] Approximately equivalent terminology is given for great soil groups (Baldwin et al., 1938; Thorp and Smith, 1949) and soil orders (Soil Survey Staff, 1975).

TABLE II   Age of Geologic Formations

Geologic formation	Age	
	Kummel (1940)	Owens and Minard (1975)
Kirkwood	Miocene	—
Cohansey	Miocene–Pliocene	Miocene
Beacon Hill	Pliocene?	Miocene
Bridgeton	Pleistocene	Miocene and Pliocene
Pensauken	Pleistocene	Miocene and Pliocene
Cape May	Pleistocene	Pleistocene

The soils and the geologic formations upon which they develop in the Pine Barrens are listed in Table I. The Downer soil series, as mapped in New Jersey, includes both gray-brown podzolics and gray-brown–red-yellow podzolic intergrades. The gray-brown podzolics are formed on the Cape May formation of Pleistocene (Wisconsin?) age. The gray-brown–red-yellow podzolics are formed on the other deposits that discontinuously mantle the Cohansey formation. Owens and Minard (1975) suggested that these deposits may be as old as Sangamon in the Pleistocene. Platt (1977) studied a Downer soil developed in waterlain sands in this area and suggested that the sediments may be pre-Illinoian (older Pleistocene). Lakehurst soils are found on parent materials varying in age from Miocene to Pleistocene; however, the land surfaces upon which these soils develop probably vary in age from late to pre-Pleistocene. In these sandy materials, the morphology of the podzol forms rather rapidly, but the majority of clay alteration occurs after the characteristic podzol morphology develops.

CONTRIBUTIONS OF SOIL MINERALOGICAL FRACTIONS

The mineral portion of the soil includes the three size fractions, sand (2.0–0.05 mm), silt (0.05–0.002 mm), and clay (<0.002 mm). The reactivity of these separates in the soil is a function of surface area. Clay has thousands of times more surface area than silt and approximately a million times more surface area per unit weight than sand. Hence, the chemical and physical activities of sand and coarse silt are almost nonexistent. Their major function is to serve as a skeleton or framework around which the reactive finer particles aggregate. The fine silt has sufficient surface area to give some slight chemical activity. However, this is significant to the total activity of the soil only when a considerable amount of fine silt is present. The clay fraction has the greatest influence on the nutrient and water-holding capacity of the soil. The ability of the soil to hold nutrients is affected by both the total amount of clay and the type of clay present.

Therefore, the type and amount of clay minerals in the soil are the most significant factors when considering moisture and nutrient availability. The major emphasis in this report will be on the nature of the clay fraction; however, a brief discussion will illustrate the composition of the sand and silt fractions.

MINERALOGY OF THE SAND FRACTIONS

Almost all of the sand fractions of the Pine Barrens soils are dominated (>90%) by quartz (SiO_2). In fact, many of the sands of the Kirkwood, Cohansey, and Cape May formations are composed almost entirely of quartz.

Although feldspars usually are present in the sand fraction in the range of a few hundredths to a few tenths of one percent, in some localities they have been reported in the range of 1–5% (Martens, 1956). The feldspars present in soils are concentrated in the finer sand fractions. Potash feldspars (potassium aluminosilicates) predominate, although some plagioclase feldspars (calcium–sodium aluminosilicates) are found occasionally. The feldspars are susceptible to weathering and form clays and release nutrients during this process. In general, significantly less feldspar is present in the soils and geologic materials in the Pine Barrens region than in most other areas of the state.

The sand in the Pine Barrens usually contains about 1–2% heavy minerals (specific gravity >2.85). Occasionally, there may be a lens or seam of these minerals where the concentration is much higher. The dominant minerals of this fraction are ilmenite (iron-titanium oxides) and leucoxene (a material of indefinite composition dominated by Ti oxides). Other minerals comprising the heavy mineral fraction include, in order of relative abundance, zircon, rutile, anatase, staurolite, tourmaline, and chlorite. Other minerals found, generally in trace amounts, include sillmanite, kyanite, andalusite, sphene, garnet, corundum, epidote, apatite, monazite, and xenotime.

The micas commonly comprise less than 1% of the sand fraction and are concentrated in the finer sands. Muscovite is the only form of mica known to occur in more than trace amounts in the Pine Barrens. It is an important precursor of several of the clay minerals.

The mineralogy of the sand fraction is characterized by the dominance of resistant minerals. It is a major factor conducive to the low nutrient status and low pH of Pine Barrens soils.

MINERALOGY OF THE SILT FRACTIONS

The silt fractions of the soil, like the sands, are dominated by quartz. Quartz is especially abundant in the coarser silts. Some limonite (hydrated iron oxides) almost always is present, which may occur as discrete grains or as coatings on other mineral grains. Some feldspars and micas are present, and these may be altered by weathering to silt-sized kaolinite and vermiculite, respectively. The coarser silt fractions may contain many of the heavy minerals mentioned previously in the discussion of the sands.

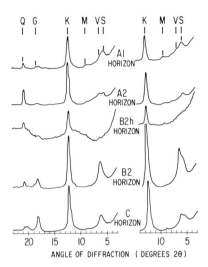

Fig. 1. X-ray diffractograms of clays from major soil horizons of the Lakehurst soil. Clays were Mg-saturated and ethylene glycolated. Samples on right also have had aluminum interlayers removed. The diffraction peaks for the major minerals are identified. The height of the peak is proportional to the amount of the mineral in the sample. Q, quartz; G, gibbsite; K, kaolinite; M, mica; V, vermiculite; and S, smectite.

CLAY IDENTIFICATION

The X-ray diffractograms used for illustration in this chapter were prepared using Ni-filtered Cu radiation on oriented samples from which easily reducible iron previously had been removed. Clays were made homoionic with Mg and were treated with ethylene glycol to expand smectites. The diagnostic diffraction peaks produced by the diffraction of the X-ray beam in the crystal lattice of a mineral will give an indication of the geometric configuration of atoms in that crystalline structure. Since these peaks are associated with the structure and composition of minerals, they may be used to identify minerals. Diagnostic diffraction peaks, for minerals discussed in this chapter, are listed in the caption of Figure 1. These peaks may be described by their diffraction angle ($2\,\theta$) or by crystallographic parameters (Ångstroms) according to the Bragg equation (Bragg, 1913; Brown, 1961).

CLAY MINERALOGY OF PINE BARRENS PODZOLS (SPODOSOLS)

The A horizon of podzols is distinctive. This horizon seldom is found in soils that contain appreciable silt and clay and is recognized readily by its "bleached," very light color (white). The color usually is caused by removal of most of the iron from the horizon by leaching, and the horizon assumes the color of sand-sized quartz. In the

Pine Barrens, well-drained soils that are not podzols often have a very thin (0.6–7.5 cm) A and B horizon (micropodzol) over the A horizon of the soil at the site. This micropodzolic A has the same mineralogy as the A horizon of a podzol. The clay mineralogy of the A horizons of podzols has been studied in several areas: Canada (Kodama and Brydon, 1968), New York (Coen and Arnold, 1972), Michigan (Ross and Mortland, 1966), and Scandinavia (Gjems, 1967). With the added information from our studies, a general theory of mineral clay alteration in podzol A horizons can be developed.

Figure 1 shows X-ray diffractograms of clay fractions of a Lakehurst soil from the Chatsworth vicinity. The major clay minerals of the A horizon are kaolinite, smectite–aluminum-interlayered dioctahedral vermiculite random mixed layer, and small amounts of mica (muscovite).

Dioctahedral vermiculite has been recognized as a clay mineral only recently and has been found only in soils or sediments derived from soils. Dioctahedral vermiculite usually is formed by the alteration of muscovite (Douglas, 1977), although a similar clay mineral might form by precipitation from soil solutions (Barshad and Kishk, 1969). Trioctahedral vermiculite, a more common vermiculite, long has been recognized as a soil clay mineral. Trioctahedral vermiculite is formed by the alteration of biotite. Trioctahedral vermiculite is only typical of environments of low chemical alteration. Although none has been found to date, it is anticipated that trioctahedral vermiculite eventually might be found in some soils developed on the Cape May formation. Henceforth, in this paper, the term vermiculite will indicate only dioctahedral vermiculite.

When treated with ethylene glycol, smectite expands to 17 Å. The smectite in this A1 horizon expands to about 16.6 Å. On the high-angle side, the diffraction line trails off to a weak 14.4 Å line. Higher-order diffraction lines are missing. This pattern in 14–17 Å diffraction lines, with no higher-order diffraction lines, indicates a random-mixed layer of vermiculite-smectite (Platt, 1979). Removal of aluminum interlayers (Tamura, 1958) sharpens the smectite diffraction line, which then expands from 16.7 to 16.8 Å. Aluminum-interlayered smectite had acted as if it were vermiculite, but the removal of the interlayer showed it was a smectite–vermiculite random-mixed layer clay.

The weathering sequence observed is shown below.

illite (muscovite) $\rightarrow$ vermiculite $\rightleftarrows$ aluminum-interlayered vermiculite

$\searrow$

smectite $\rightleftarrows$ aluminum-interlayered smectite

The end product in the A horizon of the Lakehurst soil was a random-mixed layer that included, in order of decreasing amounts, smectite, aluminum-interlayered vermiculite, and aluminum-interlayered smectite. Gjems (1967, 1970) studied this weathering sequence in podzols and found that the amount of smectite compared to aluminum interlayered vermiculite, increased as the organic matter in the A1 horizon increased. He suggested that there was a competition for aluminum between interlayers and chelation by soluble organic matter. When soluble aluminum is chelated by soluble organic matter in the A horizon, the aluminum–organic complex will be translocated to the B horizon. The aluminum is then not available to form interlayers in the A horizon.

Aluminum-interlayered smectite–vermiculite random-mixed-layer clays also are found in the lower portion of the B horizon, and aluminum-interlayered smectite is common in the C horizon of Lakehurst soils (Fig. 1). All of the smectite in these lower horizons has aluminum-interlayers, which must be removed before the smectite will expand when treated with ethylene glycol.

Figure 2 shows diffractograms of clays from soils on several different-aged parent materials in the northeastern United States. The formation of smectite in podzol A horizons is time dependent. It should be noted (Fig. 2, bottom) that, in some cases, the smectite in the soil has been inherited from the parent material. This Lakewood soil contained both smectite and aluminum-interlayered smectite in all of its horizons. A clay "lens" high in smectite was present about 1 m below the B3.

The B2h horizons of Lakewood and Lakehurst soils usually are very thin, only 2.5–5 cm thick. The clays of these horizons contain a very small amount of smectite–aluminum-interlayered vermiculite mixed-layer material. The diffraction pattern is characterized by two broad diffraction humps (7 to 15° and 17 to 32° 2 θ) of the type usually considered to be typical of amorphous materials. The 7 to 15° 2 θ broad peak is

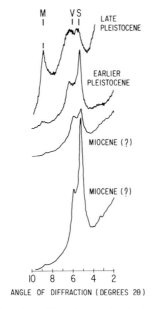

Fig. 2. Diffractograms of clays from A2 horizons of podzols developed on parent materials of different ages. Top, 2nd from top, and bottom have been treated to remove aluminum interlayers. Also see Fig. 1 legend. Parent materials: top, Wisconsin outwash (late Pleistocene), northern New Jersey; 2nd from top, Illinoian outwash (earlier Pleistocene), Martha's Vineyard, Massachusetts; 3rd and 4th from top, Lakewood soils with smectite inherited from the parent material, Burlington County, New Jersey.

removed by the treatment used to remove aluminum interlayers. The B3 was dominated by kaolinite and contained lesser amounts of the aluminum-interlayered vermiculite–aluminum-interlayered smectite random-mixed-layer mineral.

Diffractograms of a Woodmansie soil are shown in Fig. 3. Woodmansie is a highly developed podzol found only on older sediments. Owens and Minard (1975) indicate that the Pensauken and Bridgeton formations are Pliocene or Miocene in age. Woodmansie is found in the older Beacon Hill and highly weathered portions of the Pensauken and Bridgeton. Smectite is found in the A horizon, and aluminum-interlayered smectite in the B3 and C1 of the Woodmansie. Kaolinite from the Woodmansie contrasts with kaolinite from Lakehurst profiles. In both Woodmansie and Lakehurst soils, the amount of kaolinite increases with depth, a property that has been used to indicate intensive weathering processes (Krebs and Tedrow, 1958; Carlisle and Zelazny, 1973) and usually is associated with red-yellow podzolic soils. The half-height width of the 7 Å diffraction line of kaolinite from Woodmansie soils is much less than the half-height width of diffraction lines of kaolinite from Lakehurst soils, indicating a higher degree of crystallinity in the kaolinite in the Woodmansie soils.

The B horizon of the Woodmansie was dominated by kaolinite and aluminum-interlayered vermiculite with only a small amount of the aluminum-interlayered vermiculite–aluminum-interlayered smectite random-mixed-layer mineral in the lower B3 horizon.

While the smectite of A horizons was concentrated in the 0.2–0.8-μm size fraction, the smectite of lower horizons was concentrated in the <0.08-μm fraction (Fig. 4). Little smectite was found in the major zone of clay accumulation. Smectite often was found in horizons with no evidence of clay accumulation by translocation such as the C1 horizons. This same interaction of smectite, particle size, and soil horizons has been observed in all Pine Barrens soils from which we have separated the fine and medium clays.

SMECTITES AND MINERAL ALTERATION
IN PODZOL A HORIZONS

In general, the literature indicates that smectites form in basic soils. The data in this report, in conjunction with the literature previously cited, show that a smectite is the normal clay mineral of podzol A horizons. In Michigan (Ross and Mortland, 1966), a similar smectite has been identified as beidellite. The formation of smectite is time dependent. Appreciable amounts of smectite are found only in older Podzols.

CLAY MINERALOGY OF GRAY-BROWN
PODZOLIC–RED-YELLOW PODZOLIC INTERGRADES
(ULTISOLS)

X-ray diffractograms of a Sassafras soil developed on the Bridgeton formation are shown in Figure 5. This Sassafras profile contains considerable aluminum-interlayered

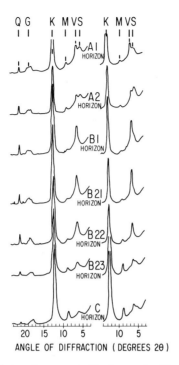

Fig. 3. Diffractograms of clays from several horizons of a Woodmansie soil. Samples on right have had aluminum interlayers removed. Also see Fig. 1 legend.

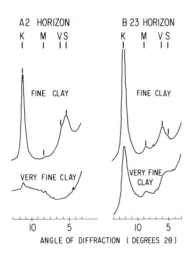

Fig. 4. Diffractograms of fine and very fine clays from the A2 and B23 of a Woodmansie soil. All samples were treated to remove aluminum interlayers. Also see Fig. 1 legend. Fine clay, 0.2–0.08 μm; very fine clay, <0.08 μm. The vermiculite–smectite intergrade was in the fine clay of the A2 and the very fine clay of the B23.

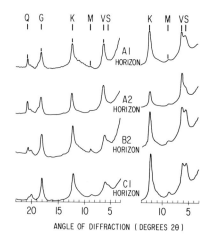

Fig. 5. Diffractograms of clays from major horizons of a Sassafras soil. Samples on right have been treated to remove aluminum interlayers. Also see Fig. 1 legend.

vermiculite–aluminum-interlayered smectite random-mixed-layer material. Large amounts of aluminum-interlayered smectite were found in the A, B3, and C1 horizons, and only a small amount was found in the B2 horizons. A small amount of smectite that was not aluminum-interlayered was found in the B3 and C1 horizons. Large amounts of kaolinite and aluminum-interlayered vermiculite are present in this soil.

In Downer soils on the Cape May formation, the only evidence of *in situ* pedogenic clay mineral alteration was the small amount of smectite–vermiculite mixed-layer mineral found in C1 and A horizons. Downer soils formed on older parent materials have smectite–vermiculite mixed-layer minerals in their A horizons, much as those found in the Lakehurst soil. Kaolinite and vermiculite distribution in Downer soils on older parent materials indicates that the clay minerals are the result of *in situ* pedogenic processes. No aluminum-interlayered smectites have been identified in Downer soils, although the vermiculite is aluminum intelayered (Platt, 1979).

THE EFFECT OF DRAINAGE AND TOPOGRAPHY ON SOIL MINERALOGY

This chapter presents mineralogical data for the moderately well-drained Lakehurst and Woodstown soils. There is very little difference between the clay mineralogy of the well-drained Lakewood soils and the moderately well-drained Lakehurst.

Woodstown soils are found on the same geologic formations as Sassafras soils, but at a slightly lower topographic position. The clay mineralogy of the Woodstown (Fig. 6) is somewhat similar to that of the Sassafras, except for the degree of aluminum-interlayering. In the A and B2 of the Sassafras all of the smectite was aluminum interlayered. In the Woodstown a small amount of the smectite in the A horizon did not

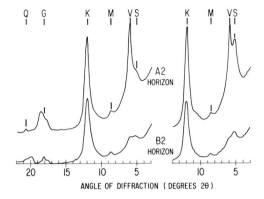

Fig. 6. Diffractograms of clays from two horizons of a Woodstown soil. Samples on right have been treated to remove aluminum interlayers. Also see Fig. 1 legend.

have aluminum interlayers and in the B2 and C horizons most of the smectite was free from aluminum interlayers.

CLAY-SIZED MINOR MINERALS IN PINE BARRENS SOILS

Table III shows the relative amounts and distribution of several clay-sized accessory minerals in Pine Barrens soils. Because of their simplistic semiquantitative nature, these data should be compared only within, and not between, soil series. Figure 5 illustrates a Sassafras soil that has inherited an abnormally large amount of gibbsite from its parent material. The data in Table III illustrate a more typical spectrum of Sassafras characteristics.

Gibbsite [Al (OH)$_3$] tends to accumulate in the lower portions of Pine Barrens soils. Gibbsite probably does not form in the A horizons of those soils, which have a podzol A2. Huang and Keller (1972) showed that in the presence of certain dilute organic acids present in humus, the solubility of aluminum is 75–85 ppm whereas only 0.03 ppm aluminum is dissolved in water extracts. Similarly, lepidocrocite [γ-Fe$_2$O$_3$ · H$_2$O] and goethite [α-Fe$_2$O$_3$ · H$_2$O] are concentrated in the lower horizons of these soils, and little of these minerals are found in the bleached horizons of podzols. These mineral distribution patterns coincide with the concepts of formation of A2 horizons of podzols, that is, these horizons are zones from which aluminum and iron are removed by soil development processes. When gibbsite, lepidocrocite, or geothite is found in the A horizon of these soils, it must be assumed that these minerals have been inherited from the parent material, or that an older soil has been truncated, forming the present profile.

The distribution of clay-sized quartz (SiO$_2$) in these soils in intriguing. It is usually assumed that quartz is very resistant to dissolution. Actually, quartz surfaces often show an etching caused by solution processes (Douglas and Platt, 1977). Partial dissolution of quartz has resulted in an increase in clay-sized quartz in A2 horizons.

TABLE III Clay-Sized Minor Minerals in Horizons of Pine Barrens Soils.[a]

Soil series	Minerals	Soil horizons				
		A1	A2	B2	B3	C1
Downer (Cape May)	Gibbsite	*	*	*	*	*
	Lepidocrocite					
	Goethite					
	Quartz	*	**	*	*	*
Downer (Cohansey)	Gibbsite		*	**	*	*
	Lepidocrocite			*	*	*
	Goethite				*	*
	Quartz	*	***	*	*	*
Lakehurst	Gibbsite			*	**	***
	Lepidocrocite		Tr	Tr	*	**
	Goethite		*	**	***	**
	Quartz	**	***	**	**	*
Sassafras	Gibbsite	*	*	**	***	***
	Lepidocrocite		*	**	**	*
	Goethite	**	**	**	**	*
	Quartz	*	***	**	**	*
Woodstown	Gibbsite	**	**	M	M	*
	Lepidocrocite	*	*	***	***	*
	Goethite	*	*	**	*	Tr
	Quartz	**	**	*	*	*
Woodmansie	Gibbsite	Tr	*	**	M	**
	Lepidocrocite					Tr
	Goethite	Tr	*	*	**	*
	Quartz	**	***	***	**	*

[a] Minerals present are given in increasing amounts: Tr (trace), *, **, ***, M (moderate).

SOIL PROPERTIES INFLUENCED BY MINERALOGY

Typical pH and cation exchange capacity (CEC) values for the soils of the Pine Barrens are shown in Table IV. Although no cause and effect relationship has been established, it is interesting to note that those horizons with appreciable aluminum-interlayered smectite have very low pH values.

The Lakehurst and Woodmansie soils are typical of soils occupying large acreage in the Pine Barrens. These soils are characterized by low CEC, even though the soils contain two minerals that normally have high (90–200 mEq/100 gms) CEC, smectite, and dioctahedral vermiculite. However, all of the vermiculite and much of the smectite of these soils had aluminum interlayers. Such interlayers reduce the effective CEC of the minerals (Jackson, 1963). The small amounts of clay in these soils (Markley, in this volume; Tedrow, in this volume) and the effect of aluminum interlayers on CEC contribute to the low CEC found in these soils. The low pH of these soils indicate that aluminum is the dominant exchangeable cation. When aluminum becomes soluble, it

TABLE IV   pH and Cation Exchange Capacity (CEC) of Pine Barrens Soil Horizons

Soil series	pH and CEC (mEq/100 gm)	Soil horizons				
		A1	A2	B2	B3	C1
Downer (Cape May)	pH	4.3	4.3	4.5	4.6	4.6
	CEC	8	5	6	4	2
Downer (Cohansey)	pH	3.9	4.1	4.3	4.6	4.8
	CEC	7	6	6	4	2
Lakehurst	pH	3.9	3.9	3.8	4.1	4.1
	CEC	3	2	3	2	1
Sassafras	pH	4.0	3.9	4.1	4.1	4.3
	CEC	15	9	11	6	3
Woodstown	pH	4.2	4.2	4.4	4.5	4.5
	CEC	17	8	8	9	4
Woodmansie	pH	3.8	3.9	3.9	4.1	4.1
	CEC	5	2	6	6	4

causes hydrolysis and liberates hydrogen ions to the solution. The combination of small amounts of clay, low CEC, and low pH results in soils with low native fertility.

Native fertility is not the only factor contributing to potential productivity of soils. Lakewood and Lakehurst soils are major soils for both citrus and vegetable production in Florida. In New Jersey, Purvis (1964) showed that Lakehurst and the more poorly drained Atsion and Berryland soils respond to proper fertilization and liming practices if soil moisture is adequate and could be used for either field crop or vegetable production.

CONCLUSION

The clay mineralogy of most Pine Barrens soils (highly developed podzols) is partially the result of the alteration sequences:

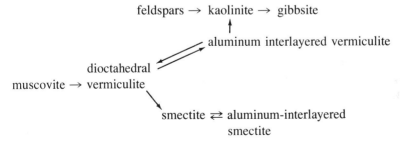

The end product is present as a mixed-layer mineral. Soil kaolinite and gibbsite are assumed to be the result of the weathering of feldspars, although kaolinite can be formed by the decomposition of aluminum-interlayered vermiculite.

The soil mineral alteration evident in younger soils is the production of a small amount of aluminum-interlayered vermiculite–smectite mixed-layer material in A and C1 horizons. On older parent materials (mid- to early Quaternary) the amount of smectite increases, and in early Quaternary materials some smectite has aluminum interlayers. Kaolinite is dominant in older B3 and C1 horizons. In soils developed on Pliocene–Miocene (?) sediments, an aluminum-interlayered smectite–aluminum-interlayered vermiculite often is present. Kaolinite, which exhibits a high degree of crystallinity, and gibbsite may be major components in B and C1 horizons. It is thought that some of the characteristics of the aluminum interlayers are related to the very low pH of these soils.

SUMMARY

Quartz dominates the sand and silt fractions of Pine Barrens soils, most of which have bleached A2 horizons typical of highly developed podzols. Clay minerals were examined in horizons of soils which varied in age of parent material from Miocene to late Quaternary. The clay mineralogy is dependent upon mineral inheritance and the time of soil formation. A clay mineral alteration sequence from muscovite (mica) through dioctahedral vermiculite to either aluminum-interlayered vermiculite or aluminum-interlayered smectite has been recognized as being time dependent. Hence, smectite is a normal end product of the weathering of muscovite in acid soils with very low pH. Similarly, the amount and crystallinity of kaolinite and the amount of gibbsite, both of which probably result from the weathering of feldspars, change over time. Kaolinite predominates in soils on the oldest land surfaces. Pine Barrens soils generally contain small amounts of fine materials, and have low cation exchange capacity and low pH, resulting in low fertility.

REFERENCES

Baldwin, M., Kellogg, C. E., and Thorp, J. (1938). Soil classification. *In* ''Soils and Men,'' pp. 979–1001. U.S. Dep. Agric. Yearb., Washington, D.C.

Barshad, I., and Kishk, F. M. (1969). Chemical composition of soil vermiculite clays as related to their genesis. *Contrib. Mineral. Petrol.* **24**, 136–155.

Bragg, W. L. (1913). The diffraction of short electromagnetic waves by a crystal. *Proc. Cambridge Philos. Soc.* **17**, 43–57.

Brown, G., ed. (1961). ''The X-Ray Identification and Crystal Structures of Clay Minerals.'' Mineral. Soc., London.

Carlisle, V. M., and Zelazny, L. W. (1973). Mineralogy of selected Florida paleudults. *Soil Crop Sci. Soc. Fla., Proc.* **33**, 136–139.

Coen, G. M., and Arnold, R. W. (1972). Clay mineral genesis of some New York spodosols. *Soil Sci. Soc. Am., Proc.* **36**, 342–350.

Douglas, L. A. (1977). Vermiculite. *In* ''Minerals in the Soil Environment'' (J. B. Dixon and S. B. Weed, eds.), pp. 259–292. Soil Sci. Soc. Am., Madison, Wisconsin.

Douglas, L. A., and Platt, D. W. (1977). Surface morphology of quartz and age of soils. *Soil Sci. Soc. Am., J.* **41**, 641–645.

Gjems, O. (1967). Studies on clay minerals and clay-mineral formation in soil profiles in Scandinavia. *Medd. Nor. Skogforsoeksves.* **81**, 303-415.

Gjems, O. (1970). Mineralogical composition and pedologic weathering of the clay fraction in podzol soil profiles in Zalesine, Yugoslavia. *Soil Sci.* **110**, 237-243.

Huag, W. H., and Keller, W. D. (1972). Geochemical mechanics for the dissolution, transport, and deposition of aluminum in the zone of weathering. *Clays Clay Miner.* **20**, 69-74.

Jackson, M. L. (1963). Interlayering of expansible layer silicates in soils by chemical weathering. *Clays Clay Miner.* **11**, 29-46.

Jenny, H. (1941). "Factors of Soil Formation." McGraw-Hill, New York.

Kodama, H., and Brydon, J. E. (1968). A study of clay minerals in podzol soils in New Brunswick, Eastern Canada. *Clay Miner.* **7**, 295-309.

Krebs, R. D., and Tedrow, J. C. F. (1958). Genesis of red-yellow podzolic and related soils in New Jersey. *Soil Sci.* **85**, 41-53.

Kummel, H. B. (1940). The geology of New Jersey. *N.J. Dep. Conserv. Econ. Dev., Bull.* No. 50.

Martens, J. H. C. (1956). Industrial sands of New Jersey. *Rutgers Univ. Bur. Miner. Res., Bull.* No. 6.

Owens, J. P., and Minard, J. P. (1975). "Geological Map of the Surficial Deposits in the Trenton Area, New Jersey and Pennsylvania." U.S. Dep. Inter., Geol. Surv., Trenton, New Jersey.

Platt, D. W. (1979). Mineralogy as an indicator of weathering in the Downer soil series. M.S. Thesis, Rutgers Univ., New Brunswick, New Jersey.

Purvis, E. R. (1964). Crop production on high water table soils on the New Jersey Pine Barrens. *N.J. Agric. Exp. Stn., Bull.* No. 806.

Ross, G. J., and Mortland, M. M. (1966). A soil beidellite. *Soil Sci. Soc. Am., Proc.* **30**, 337-343.

Soil Survey Staff (1975). "Soil Taxonomy." *U.S. Dep. Agric. Soil Conserv. Serv., Handb.* No. 436.

Tamura, T. (1958). Identification of clay minerals from acid soils. *J. Soil Sci.* **9**, 141-147.

Thorp, J., and Smith, G. D. (1949). Higher categories of soil classification: Order, Suborder, and Great Soil Groups. *Soil Sci.* **67**, 117-126.

Part III

CLIMATE, WATER, AND AQUATIC ECOSYSTEMS

7

Climate and Microclimate of the New Jersey Pine Barrens

A. VAUGHN HAVENS

MAJOR FACTORS CONTROLLING THE MACROCLIMATE OF THE SOUTHERN INTERIOR OF NEW JERSEY

Large-scale features of the circulation of the atmosphere, with its great seasonal variation, control the climate of the Pine Barrens (Biel, 1958). In winter, a strong semipermanent high-pressure area with very cold air masses forms over central Canada and the northern Great Plains of the United States. From time to time during most winters and to a lesser extent in spring, strong surges of cold air accompanied by strong northwesterly winds will push southeastward from Canada across the eastern half of the country, including the Pine Barrens, following the passage of a storm center across the eastern United States. Occasionally in winter, southwesterly winds may bring unusually mild, humid, maritime, tropical air masses from the Gulf of Mexico as far northward as New Jersey.

As spring progresses, the cold high-pressure area over Canada gradually weakens, and by June it usually is about gone. As a result, the surges of cold air gradually diminish in frequency and intensity during the spring transitional season.

By summer, the cool polar air masses are infrequent and usually last only a day or two. The principal large-scale feature of atmospheric circulation that dominates the summer Pine Barrens climate is the large, semipermanent, high-pressure area centered near Bermuda in the Atlantic Ocean referred to as the Bermuda high. Its clockwise circulation causes southwest winds to bring warm, humid, maritime, tropical air masses into southern New Jersey from the Caribbean Sea and the Gulf of Mexico. Such air masses have a high moisture content, which, when combined with moderately high afternoon temperatures is responsible for the well-known summer discomfort suffered by residents of much of the mid-Atlantic region, including the Pine Barrens, with the exception of a narrow strip (usually <15 km or 9 mi wide) near the coast that is affected by sea breezes. However, this high moisture content of the dominant summer

113

air mass also is responsible for the frequent afternoon and evening thundershowers that are a major source of summer precipitation in the Pine Barrens.

The autumn transitional season is characterized by the gradual weakening of the Bermuda high and its retreat southward until early December, when the occurrence of maritime, tropical air masses over the Pine Barrens is usually nil. By mid-December, the winter circulation pattern usually has been restored completely.

Autumn frequently brings extended periods of tranquil weather associated with stationary or very slow-moving high-pressure areas which originated as cold, shallow highs over Canada, but which then stagnated over the eastern United States while undergoing transition to warm highs. This anticyclonic stagnation is rare in winter and spring, while 76% of such cases occur during autumn (Donley, 1963). It usually is associated with periods of mild, dry "Indian summer"-type weather or "hazy sunshine," since a gradual build-up of dust and haze is a common occurrence. This autumn anticyclonic stagnation has been responsible for most major air pollution episodes over the nearby densely populated, heavily industrialized areas (Havens, 1964).

SOURCES OF CLIMATIC DATA IN THE PINE BARRENS

In at least 12 locations in the Pine Barrens, official Weather Service observations have been recorded over a substantial number of years: Atlantic City Airport (elevation 19.5 m), Belleplain State Forest (9.1 m), Chatsworth (30.5 m), Hammonton (25.9 m), Indian Mills (30.5 m), Lakehurst Naval Air Station (39.0 m), Mays Landing (6.1 m), McGuire Air Force Base (43.6 m), Pemberton (24.4 m), Toms River (3.0 m), plus Berlin and Bass River State Forest, which have been closed. Atlantic City Airport at Pomona is the only First-Order Station of the National Weather Service that records complete data 24 hours a day, with data available since 1943.

Hourly weather observations have been made continuously since the mid-1920's at Lakehurst Naval Air Station. Except for a lapse of several months between 1946 and 1948, observations have been continuous since the early 1940's at McGuire Air Force Base near Wrightstown.

All other locations are Class C Cooperative Climatological Stations of the National Weather Service that normally record the daily high and low temperature and the 24-hour total precipitation. These rain gauge measurements and thermometer readings at a height of 1.2–1.5 m (4–5 ft) in a standard National Weather Service Instrument Shelter are adequate to obtain a good picture of the macroclimate of the Pine Barrens (U.S. Department of Commerce, 1956, 1976).

However, measurement of the microclimate of the Pine Barrens has been very limited. Probably the most extensive measurements of the microclimate of the Pine Barrens are the bog minimum temperatures recorded at Whitesbog since 1944 by the Cranberry and Blueberry Research Center of Rutgers University (Marucci, personal communication). These bog minimum temperatures were recorded during April through October on nights when frost either occurred or was expected.

TEMPERATURES IN THE PINE BARRENS

As in most of the northeastern United States, the high degree of variability probably is the most striking aspect of winter temperatures in the Pine Barrens. In most winters, January is slightly colder than December and February. January 1977 is the coldest January on record, with a temperature of −6.1°C (21°F) at Pemberton, as compared with the January normal of 0.2°C (32°F) (Table I). However, during February 1934, the coldest month ever recorded, a temperature of −7.7°C, 8.7 degrees below the February normal of 1.0°C was recorded at Pemberton.

Although March usually is considered the beginning of the spring transition, in occasional years, e.g., 1960, March has been the coldest month of the entire winter. On the other hand, March can be surprisingly mild, as in 1945, when the average temperature at Pemberton was 6.1°C above the normal of 5.3°C, and when an all-time high temperature for March of 31.7°C (89°F) was recorded (Table I).

The timing of the beginning of real winter weather also is highly variable. In the severe winter of 1976–1977, persistently subnormal temperatures began in mid-October, and temperatures were distinctly wintry before Thanksgiving (even though the first significant snowfall did not occur until Christmas). However, some Decembers at Pemberton have averaged more than 4°C above the normal of 1.5°C. In such years, it may be well into January or even February before the Pine Barrens experiences any real winter.

The coldest temperatures ever recorded in the Pine Barrens occurred during February 1934, when an all-time low of −27.2°C (−17°F) was observed at Pemberton. However, all of the winter months, even March, have brought below −18°C (0°F) temperatures to the region. Temperatures in the mid- to upper 20's also have been observed in all of the winter months, again illustrating the highly variable nature of winter temperatures in the Pine Barrens (U.S. Department of Commerce, 1973; Marucci, 1976a).

As the spring transition season progresses, average temperatures climb quite rapidly, at a rate of about 5°C each month, from near 0°C in winter to the low or middle 20's in summer. Since the circulation of the atmosphere still is very active through May, large day-to-day fluctuations in temperature occur in association with frequent frontal passages and air-mass changes. This causes the spring period of frost danger to be an especially critical period for the vegetation of the Pine Barrens. The spring period of frost danger is the period between the beginning of the vegetative season and the last spring occurrence of killing frost. Of course, this period will vary considerably among the various plant species. Accordingly, if we define the beginning of the vegetative growing season as the date when the average temperature reaches 6.1°C and the last spring killing frost as the date of the last spring occurrence of a shelter minimum temperature of 0°C or less (Table II), we find that the spring period of frost danger averages 39 days at Indian Mills, and that in years with an unusually late frost it may be much longer.

In the summer months of June, July, and August, daily maximum temperatures average in the mid-20's and daily minimum temperatures average in the 10°–15°C

TABLE I Temperature Patterns (°C) for Pemberton in the Pine Barrens

	Jan.	Feb.	Mar.	Apr.	May	June	July	Aug.	Sep.	Oct.	Nov.	Dec.	Annual
Extreme maximum (1929–1971)	23.9	25.6	31.7	33.9	36.7	37.8	41.7	38.9	36.7	35.0	28.9	23.3	41.7
Average daily maximum (1941–1970)[a]	4.9	5.7	10.3	17.2	22.4	27.6	29.6	28.2	25.0	19.2	13.1	5.9	17.4
Average (1941–1970)[a]	0.2	1.0	5.3	11.1	16.6	21.4	23.8	22.9	19.4	13.7	7.8	1.5	12.1
Average (1929–1971)	0.7	1.1	5.4	10.9	16.8	21.6	24.0	22.9	19.6	13.5	7.8	1.7	12.2
Average daily minimum (1941–1970)[a]	−4.6	−3.7	0.3	5.6	10.8	15.3	17.9	17.6	13.9	8.1	2.6	−2.9	6.7
Extreme minimum (1929–1971)	−26.7	−27.2	−18.3	−9.4	−3.3	2.2	7.8	5.0	−2.2	−5.6	−15.6	−20.6	−27.2

[a] 1941–1970 is the standard 30-year period currently in use by the Environmental Data Service of NOAA and by the World Meteorological Organization.

TABLE II   Spring Threshold Temperature Probability for Indian Mills, 1926–1955[a]

Temperature (°C)	Date when chance of last occurrence of indicated temperature (or lower) in spring decreases to						
	90%	75%	67%	50%	33%	25%	10%
0	Apr. 16	Apr. 23	Apr. 25	Apr. 30	May 5	May 8	May 14
−2.2	Apr. 4	Apr. 11	Apr. 14	Apr. 19	Apr. 24	Apr. 27	May 4
−4.4	Mar. 16	Mar. 24	Mar. 27	Apr. 2	Apr. 8	Apr. 11	Apr. 18
−6.7	Mar. 5	Mar. 12	Mar. 15	Mar. 21	Mar. 27	Mar. 30	Apr. 7
−8.9	Feb. 25	Mar. 3	Mar. 5	Mar. 10	Mar. 14	Mar. 17	Mar. 22

[a] From Havens and McGuire (1961)

range (Table I). However, extreme maximum temperatures have exceeded 37.8°C (100°F) in each of the summer months.

The eastern sections of the Pine Barrens often experience afternoon temperatures lower than those farther inland as a result of sea breezes. The sea breeze most frequently occurs in spring and summer, when the land is much warmer than the ocean. The sea breeze often begins to blow at about midday and will penetrate only a few kilometers inland. For example, on many days in spring and summer, the Atlantic City Marina on the coast experiences a sea breeze from the southeast, with afternoon temperatures as much as 5–8°C cooler than the airport at Pomona about 16 km inland. Infrequently, in spring and summer the sea breeze may complement a large-scale easterly wind, causing Atlantic air to penetrate much farther inland and influence all or most of the Pine Barrens.

The autumn transition season usually is more tranquil than spring, since the large-scale circulation of the atmosphere does not return to its winter intensity until December. As the day length decreases, and as cold air outbreaks become more frequent, average temperatures drop about 6°C each month, from the low 20's in summer to near 0°C in winter. Excluding cranberries, the autumn period of frost danger may not be as significant as the spring period, for many crops already are harvested before the autumn frost threatens. At Indian Mills (Table III), while the autumn period of frost

TABLE III   Autumn Threshold Temperature Probability for Indian Mills, 1926–1955[a]

Temperature (°C)	Date when chance of first occurrence of indicated temperature (or lower) in autumn increases to						
	10%	25%	33%	50%	67%	75%	90%
0	Sept. 28	Oct. 4	Oct. 6	Oct. 11	Oct. 15	Oct. 18	Oct. 23
−2.2	Oct. 6	Oct. 13	Oct. 16	Oct. 21	Oct. 26	Oct. 29	Nov. 5
−4.4	Oct. 14	Oct. 21	Oct. 24	Oct. 29	Nov. 3	Nov. 6	Nov. 13
−6.7	Nov. 2	Nov. 9	Nov. 12	Nov. 17	Nov. 22	Nov. 25	Dec. 2
−8.9	Nov. 18	Nov. 24	Nov. 26	Dec. 2	Dec. 6	Dec. 9	Dec. 16

[a] From Havens and McGuire (1961).

danger is the same as in spring, averaging 39 days in length, in years with an unusually early autumn frost, it may be much longer.

MICROCLIMATIC TEMPERATURES IN THE PINE BARRENS

At Whitesbog, minimum temperatures in a cranberry bog have been measured for many years using a toluol-in-glass minimum thermometer mounted on a metal backing and exposed just above the cranberry vines. Such an exposure undoubtedly causes the thermometer to experience a larger negative radiation balance at night than the thermometer that is mounted in an instrument shelter. However, the vines and other vegetation also experience a large negative radiation balance at night, and the bog minimum temperatures therefore are probably more representative of bog conditions than minimum temperatures recorded in an instrument shelter. Bog minimum temperatures usually were recorded during the growing season on nights only when frost was expected, in general, clear nights with little or no wind.

During 1976, the most recent year for which data are available, there were 29 nights with bog minimum temperatures of 0°C (32°F) or less between April 29 and October 27; in contrast, instrument shelter minimum temperatures were 0°C or less on only ten occasions. Of these 29 frost nights, three were in June and one was in August. The bog minimum temperature averaged 4.8°C colder than the shelter minima, with 7.2°C the largest difference. Since 1944, when these measurements first were taken, there has been one year, 1965, when a frost occurred at Whitesbog in July (Marucci, 1976b). This observation tends to support the report by Harshberger (1916) of his discovery of ice in a bog of peat moss (*Sphagnum*) in the Pine Barrens in July. The natural bog areas of the Pine Barrens may have an even more extreme microclimate than the cranberry bogs, since the latter have been modified to a certain extent by cultural and management practices.

On generally fair days with light winds, the maximum temperatures at the level of the vegetation can be expected to be several degrees warmer than the maxima in the instrument shelter. In general, at times of strong winds, especially when accompanied by overcast skies and rain or snow, very little microclimatic temperature differences can be found in the Pine Barrens, except in the most densely forested regions where strong winds seldom penetrate.

In the Pine Plains sections of the Pine Barrens, microclimatic temperatures at night generally should be somewhat warmer than in the bogs, and frost should be less frequent and less severe. On clear days with light winds, it is quite likely that afternoon temperatures in the Pine Plains will be higher than anywhere else in the Pine Barrens, especially during dry spells when less solar energy is consumed by evapotranspiration in the Pine Plains, as compared with bogs and forested sections.

In forested sections of the Pine Barrens, daytime temperatures will be highest at the top of the crown. Thus, during generally fair days a persistent temperature inversion (crown temperatures higher than in trunk space) extending from the forest floor to the crown can be found, and in densely forested sections this may be true even on days with considerable wind, especially when it is sunny (Geiger, 1965).

At night in forested areas, the crown is the principal emitter of terrestrial radiation. The resulting cooling may produce a slight and usually brief minimum of air temperature at crown height. However, the cooler air at crown height is slightly heavier and tends to settle into the trunk space (Geiger, 1965). The result is a nearly isothermal temperature profile in the forested areas during most of the nighttime hours.

PRECIPITATION IN THE PINE BARRENS

Long-term annual precipitation totals in the Pine Barrens average between 1067 mm and 1168 mm (42–46 in), which shows remarkable spatial uniformity for an area of this size. In years when precipitation is near or above normal, 50% or more may run off into the many streams which drain the Pine Barrens, a large proportion during early spring when soils are moist and evapotranspiration rates low. However, precipitation shows a notorious yearly variation, and the Pine Barrens have been affected seriously by extended droughts and by heavy rains and storms.

Precipitation data for Pemberton in the northwestern portion of the Pine Barrens (Table IV) are typical and agree very closely with those for Atlantic City Airport at Pomona near the southeastern edge of the Pine Barrens (U.S. Department of Commerce, 1973; Marucci, 1976a). Annual totals of precipitation at Pomona range from 642 mm in the drought year of 1965 to 1706 mm in 1958 (U.S. Department of Commerce, 1975a). The effect of drought on the survival of tree seedlings in the Pine Barrens has been described by Little *et al.* (1958).

A northeastern regional research project on agricultural climatology utilized the Palmer Drought Index (Palmer, 1965) to evaluate the frequency and severity of drought in the northeastern United States, including southern New Jersey (Dickerson and Dethier, 1970). The index assigns positive values to wet periods and negative values to dry periods. There are five classes of dry periods. Incipient drought includes values from -0.50 to -0.99. Mild drought, from -1.00 to -1.99, is a period during which the growth of native vegetation almost ceases. Moderate drought, from -2.00 to -2.99, is a condition in which the least drought-resistant plant species may die. In a severe drought, from -3.00 to -3.99, only the most drought-resistant plants should be able to survive, and the general cover of vegetation decreases. During an extreme drought, when the index reaches -4.00 or lower, many woody plants are expected to die.

In the Pine Barrens, the following drought severities and return periods (see tabulation) are expected (a two-year return period indicates a 50% probability of having a drought of that severity during a year; a 25-year return period, a 4% probability; etc.):

	Return period (years)				
	2	5	10	25	50
Palmer drought index:	-1.42	-2.80	-3.85	-5.23	-6.28

The longest and most extreme drought ever recorded in the Pine Barrens lasted five years, from late summer 1961 to September 1966. The Palmer Drought Index value in

TABLE IV   Precipitation (mm) at Pemberton

	Jan.	Feb.	Mar.	Apr.	May	June	July	Aug.	Sep.	Oct.	Nov.	Dec.	Annual
Average (1941–1970)	75.2	74.7	102.1	86.9	89.2	86.9	130.0	115.1	83.8	71.9	91.4	92.5	1099.7
Average (1929–1971)	80.5	73.7	97.8	85.6	90.2	94.5	113.0	123.4	96.3	78.2	85.6	78.2	1097.0
Driest (1929–1971)	15.2	34.5	29.2	17.0	9.1	3.6	4.6	16.3	5.3	6.6	19.3	7.6	756.2(1965)
Wettest (1929–1971)	163.6	147.6	169.9	159.8	209.3	252.0	297.4	324.4	263.9	173.7	171.5	222.5	1524.3(1958)

southern New Jersey reached -6.47 in December 1965. Along the Atlantic coast of New Jersey, where the drought was only slightly less extreme, the lowest index reached was -5.09.

Most heavy rains in the Pine Barrens result from three distinctly different weather situations. Extratropical cyclones that form as waves along the polar front are responsible for most winter and spring precipitation. These storms follow a variety of tracks, and the weather is equally varied. If the storm center is off the coast and the temperatures low enough, northerly winds and widespread snow may cover all of the Pine Barrens. If the storm center passes to the west of New Jersey, southerly winds, mild temperatures, and precipitation in the form of showers and even thunderstorms may result. The precipitation from these so-called winter storms usually is distributed rather uniformly and flooding is usually not serious. However, it should be noted that these storms can occur at any time of year and occasionally can be severe. For example, in November 1950, a storm formed over North Carolina and brought winds close to 160 km/hour, well in excess of the lower limit for hurricanes, i.e., 120 km/hour. This led to the widespread belief that this 1950 Thanksgiving storm was a hurricane, even though it was not of tropical origin.

A more frequent cause of heavy rains and flooding in the Pine Barrens is tropical cyclones, which in their most intense stage are called hurricanes, and which generally occur from August through October. These storms have high winds and usually, but not always, high precipitation, which causes flooding. For example, the September 1938 hurricane, most noted for the heavy damage it caused in New England, produced 231.9 mm of rain in three days at Pemberton, New Jersey; tropical cyclone Doria in August 1971 produced 239.5 mm of rain in two days at Pemberton and widespread flooding in the region. Cry (1966, 1967) showed that a substantial portion of the rainfall over the Atlantic and Gulf Coastal Plains regions in late summer and autumn, particularly in September, is associated with tropical cyclones. In years when no tropical cyclones affect southern New Jersey, the autumn can be quite dry. It is probable a number of droughts have been relieved substantially by heavy rains associated with tropical cyclones.

The third weather situation capable of producing heavy rains over the Pine Barrens also is primarily a warm-season weather pattern. From late spring into mid-autumn, much of New Jersey's rainfall results from scattered shower and thunderstorm activity. Unlike extratropical cyclones and tropical cyclones, which are long-lived macroscale features of the atmospheric circulation having diameters of hundreds of kilometers, thunderstorms are mesoscale phenomena with a duration of one to four hours and averaging only about two to a maximum of about 30 km in diameter. In their most severe stage, thunderstorms may produce tornados with funnels averaging only 0.5 km or less in diameter. Most commonly, however, the cumulonimbus clouds produce thundershowers over the Pine Barrens, often as air-mass thunderstorms involving no frontal or cyclonic activity. The shower activity will be scattered over the area almost at random. Some locations receive locally heavy showers while nearby locations receive only very light showers or none at all; flooding usually will be strictly local and minor.

There is some indication from radar reports (Beitel, 1976) and personal observations of experienced meteorologists that at times a sea breeze convergence line forms a short distance inland from the coast at Barnegat Bay. Such convergence between the south-easterly sea breeze and the prevailing southwesterly wind from the interior would tend to enhance thundershower activity over the eastern portions of the Pine Barrens. Although too few weather stations are available to test this hypothesis, a slight difference is noted between the Atlantic City Marina by the coast, having an average 23 thunderstorms per year and the Atlantic City Airport 16 km inland, receiving 25 thunderstorms annually.

Another factor which could enhance thunderstorm activity over the Pine Barrens is its location downwind from the Philadelphia–Camden metropolitan complex. A study of the effects of the St. Louis, Missouri metropolitan area on weather conditions over the surrounding area has presented strong evidence that the addition of heat and condensation and ice nuclei to the atmosphere by the city can influence thunderstorm activity and other weather conditions over and downwind from the city (Changnon *et al.*, 1974). It seems likely that similar effects occur over southern New Jersey.

SNOWFALL IN THE PINE BARRENS

Heavy snowfall in the Pine Barrens is limited to the months of November through March. Snow has been known to fall during October and April; however, when this does occur, it usually melts very rapidly, and accumulations have been very small.

Although the data (Table V) at three locations do not cover the same period of years, there is considerable overlapping of the records. There is no significant difference in average monthly and seasonal snowfall between Pemberton and Atlantic City Airport; these data can be considered representative of the Pine Barrens in general. At the city office in Atlantic City, on the other hand, average snowfall is nearly 200 mm (8 in) lower than at the airport and Pemberton. Thus, the effect of the Atlantic Ocean on aver-

TABLE V   Snowfall (mm) at Pemberton, Atlantic City Airport, and Atlantic City[a]

		Nov.	Dec.	Jan.	Feb.	Mar.	Season
Pemberton	Average	16	100	133	140	88	477
(1929–1971)	Maximum	254	279	362	620	457	1156
Atlantic City Airport	Average	12	73	143	166	72	466
(1958–1975)	Maximum	198	218	404	894	447	1191
Atlantic City (City	Average	11	43	96	93	52	295
Office 1936–1958)	Maximum	150	315	351	363	259	851

[a] Atlantic City data are from the pre1958 city office about one block from the ocean (Marucci, 1976a; U.S. Department of Commerce, 1975a).[a]

age snowfall is confined to a very narrow coastal strip and probably is negligible insofar as the Pine Barrens are concerned.

Since maximum amounts can be highly dependent upon a single heavy snow storm, the differences between the city office and the two Pine Barrens stations are less significant. These data indicate that, when conditions are appropriate, heavy snow can and does occur over all sections of the Pine Barrens. The record snowfall in a single storm for New Jersey occurred at Cape May during February 11–14, 1899, when nearly 1270 mm (50 in) was measured. Dunlap (1970) found the maximum 24-hour snowfall to be expected is slightly greater at Indian Mills than at Atlantic City Airport at Pomona.

The depth and duration of snow cover in the Pine Barrens are influenced strongly by the forest microclimate, in particular, by its effect upon wind, solar radiation, and temperature. Wales (1966, 1967), in comparing the microclimate of the northern and southern boundaries of a hardwood forest in central New Jersey, found large differences between the depth and duration of snow cover. Most heavy snows in New Jersey occur with winds from the north or northeast. As a result, the windward sides of the forest receive heavier snowfalls initially, and these same locations receive more shading and thus lower temperatures following the snowfall. These effects produce a snow cover that is much deeper and of much longer duration on the northern boundaries of forested areas, as compared with other locations where microclimatic conditions are less favorable for the retention of snow. It is quite likely that these effects would be even more pronounced in the pine forests of the Pine Barrens than in the mature hardwood forest, Hutcheson Memorial Forest, studied by Wales.

The occurrence of freezing rain of significance over southern New Jersey is limited to the months of December through March. Addess and Shulman (1966) studied the frequency of such storms during 1950–1965 and found an average of four cases of freezing rain per year in the Pine Barrens. In many of these storms, the accumulation of ice is small; if the wind is not strong, damage usually is minor. However, a combination of strong winds and a heavy accumulation of ice (10–15 mm) occasionally may produce severe damage, especially to trees. Low-growing vegetation usually will not be damaged so severely, since winds near the ground are not as strong as at tree-top height, and since many shrubs and bushes can be bent all the way to the ground by the weight of ice without breaking. No data on the frequency of severe ice storms are available.

WIND IN THE PINE BARRENS

There are only two official National Weather Service wind-recording stations in or near the Pine Barrens. Atlantic City Airport near Pomona, about 16 km (10 mi) WNW of Atlantic City, is near the southeastern edge of the Pine Barrens. Philadelphia International Airport is about 9.6 km (6 mi) southwest of the center of Philadelphia and about 21 km NW of the western edge of the Pine Barrens. The wind sensors at these stations have been moved from time to time, and they have not always been at their present height above ground, namely, 6.1 meters (20 ft). Thus, a detailed comparison of wind at these two locations is difficult. However, the major features of the general wind flow are quite similar at these two stations and therefore also should be quite representative of wind conditions in the Pine Barrens (U.S. Department of Commerce, 1975a and b).

At both stations, the average wind speed is strongest in March; however, the other cold-season months of November through April have average wind speeds only slightly weaker than those of March. The months of June through October have the lowest average wind speeds, with July and August being only slightly weaker than September.

Wind direction is highly variable throughout New Jersey, and the direction listed as prevailing for a particular month (Table VI) may occur with a frequency only one or two percentage points higher than some other directions. Winds from the northwesterly quadrant dominate in the Pine Barrens during the months of December through March. In late spring and summer, however, the sea breeze influence causes Atlantic City Airport on the eastern side of the Pine Barrens to experience southerly onshore winds more frequently than those from any other direction. At Philadelphia, which is farther inland and on the western side of the Pine Barrens, the sea breeze influence is absent, and winds from the southwesterly quadrant predominate from April through October.

Of ecological significance is the fact that destructive winds, while infrequent, can occur at any time of the year in the Pine Barrens (Table VI). Thom (1963) estimated that the Pine Barrens will experience wind speeds between 96 and 112 km/hr at least once every ten years, and that once every 25 years wind speeds between 112 and 128 km/hr will occur.

TABLE VI   Wind Speed and Direction at Atlantic

	Jan.	Feb.	Mar.	Apr.	May
Average wind speed (km/hr)					
Atlantic City (1960–1972)	19.4	19.7	20.0	19.4	17.3
Philadelphia (1940–1975)	16.5	17.8	18.4	17.8	15.5
Prevailing wind direction					
Atlantic City (1959–1963)					
Direction	WNW	WNW	WNW	WNW/S	S
Observations (%)	18	14	14	13/13	10
Philadelphia (1951–1960)					
Direction	N	NW	NW/WNW	WSW	WSW
Observations (%)	12	12	11/11	10	12
Maximum recorded wind speed					
Atlantic City (1960–1975)					
Speed	75	69	74	74	56
Direction	WNW	W	WSW	ENE	NW
Philadelphia (1940–1975)					
Speed	98	94	90	94	90
Direction	NE	NW	NW	SW	SW

[a] Maximum wind speed values (km/hr) are maximum sustained winds ("fastest mile"); peak gusts

There are five weather situations capable of producing destructive winds in the Pine Barrens. During the colder half of the year, intense extratropical cyclones are one of the principal causes. The destructive winds often blow from an easterly quadrant and may be accompanied by heavy precipitation, rain, snow, or freezing rain, depending upon the temperature at the time of the storm.

Perhaps of greater ecological significance are the strong northwesterly winds which often persist for several days following the passage of a strong cold front or an intense extratropical cyclone. In these situations, the wind damage may be limited to killing twigs and small branches. These cyclones, however, may coincide with an outbreak of forest fires such as that which occurred on March 30 through April 1, 1977, when fire burned over many thousands of hectares of the Pine Barrens and destroyed a number of buildings. Such widespread fires, which have occurred periodically in the Pine Barrens, usually occur in spring when the forest litter has been dried by sun and wind.

In summer and early autumn, strong winds can be produced locally by severe thunderstorms or tornados. Damage from the gusty winds associated with severe thunderstorms usually is neither extensive nor widespread; tornado damage may be extensive, but the area affected is small. Since 1916, 41 tornados have been observed in New Jersey. Of these, 25 (61%) occurred in southern New Jersey. Thom (1963) estimated that the probability of a tornado occurring over southern New Jersey in any year is much less than 1%.

Tropical cyclones, which occur primarily in late summer and early autumn, are capable of producing damaging winds over all of southern New Jersey. Since 1891, 62 tropical cyclones have affected New Jersey, with 48 (77%) occurring from August through October.

City Airport and Philadelphia International Airport[a]

June	July	Aug.	Sep.	Oct.	Nov.	Dec.
15.7	14.7	14.2	15.0	15.8	18.2	18.4
14.1	13.0	12.6	13.3	14.2	15.5	16.2
S	S	S	S	S/N	WNW	WNW
17	16	12	8	9/9	13	16
WSW	WSW	WSW	SW/WSW	WSW	WSW/WNW	WSW/WNW
14	15	11	10/10	11	11/11	12/12
59	59	56	96	66	64	88
WNW	W	ESE	NW	WNW	W	N
117	107	107	78	106	96	75
NW	W	E	NE	SW	SW	NW

may exceed the "fastest mile" by as much as 50%.

Climate, Water, and Aquatic Ecosystems

TABLE VII   Number of Occurrences of Atmospheric Stagnation (Wind Speed <13 km/hr) Persisting for Four Days or Longer over Southern New Jersey, 1936–1965

Jan.	Feb.	Mar.	Apr.	May	June	July	Aug.	Sep.	Oct.	Nov.	Dec.	Total
0	0	0	0	1	1	1	5	10	9	3	1	31

During wind storms which influence all or most of the Pine Barrens, the strongest surface winds most likely will be found over the Pine Plains sections where wind resistance by vegetation is minimal. In forested sections, the strongest winds occur above the canopy. Wind speed in the trunk space decreases sharply with distance into the forest. In the interior of very dense forested sections, wind speed near the forest floor in the trunk space may be very slight, even when strong winds are blowing above the canopy. The microclimatic aspects of wind in the Pine Barrens may be described as highly variable as a result of stand density, characteristics of the understory, distance from the forest boundary, and orientation of the boundary with respect to the wind direction.

Stationary or slow-moving anticyclones can produce extended periods of atmospheric stagnation over the Pine Barrens, usually in late summer or autumn. In the Pine Barrens, these stagnant periods generally are characterized by fair, mild, "hazy sunshine," but if development and air pollution sources become extensive, these periods of atmospheric stagnation could contain pollutant concentrations toxic to vegetation and wildlife in the Pine Barrens. Korshover (1967) showed that, during the period 1936–1965, of the 31 cases of atmospheric stagnation (surface winds <13 km/hr) persisting for four days or longer and affecting southern New Jersey, 27 (87%) occurred during the months of August through November (Table VII). No such cases of stagnation were recorded during the months of January through April.

HUMIDITY IN THE PINE BARRENS

Relative humidity normally has a pronounced diurnal variation, ranging from a maximum in the early morning hours near the time of minimum temperature to a minimum in the early afternoon at the time of maximum temperature. The average relative humidity at Atlantic City Airport is consistently higher than at Philadelphia International Airport, both at 7 AM and at 1 PM (Table VIII) and probably is more representative of the Pine Barrens in general. Average monthly 7 AM relative humidity is 75–88% and at 1 PM, 51–60%.

The above data are consistent with the fact that Atlantic City Airport experiences more frequent occurrences of dense fog (visibility equal to or less than 0.4 km) than Philadelphia International Airport (Table IX). The frequency of dense fog in the Pine Barrens probably is at least as high, or possibly even higher, than at Atlantic City Airport, a frequency which is constant throughout the year. This would be explained by the Pine Barrens' more numerous local sources of moisture and greater vegetation,

TABLE VIII Average Relative Humidity (%) at 7 AM and 1 PM at Atlantic City Airport (1965–1975) and Philadelphia International Airport (1960–1975)

	Jan.	Feb.	Mar.	Apr.	May	June	July	Aug.	Sep.	Oct.	Nov.	Dec.
7 AM												
Atlantic City	75	77	77	76	79	85	85	87	88	87	82	77
Philadelphia	74	71	71	69	75	78	79	81	83	82	77	74
1 PM												
Atlantic City	57	57	55	51	57	60	59	57	58	56	57	59
Philadelphia	60	57	53	49	53	55	54	54	56	53	55	61

TABLE IX Average Number of Days with Dense Fog (Visibility ≤ 0.4 km) at Atlantic City Airport (1959–1975) and Philadelphia International Airport (1940–1975)

	Jan.	Feb.	Mar.	Apr.	May	June	July	Aug.	Sep.	Oct.	Nov.	Dec.
Atlantic City	4	4	4	3	4	5	4	4	4	5	3	4
Philadelphia	3	3	2	1	1	1	1	1	2	4	3	3

especially trees, than are found in the immediate vicinity of the Airport. These local environmental factors tend to increase the humidity and enhance the occurrence of radiation fog in many sections of the Pine Barrens.

Occasional periods of unusually low relative humidity can occur in the Pine Barrens. This situation occurs most often with northwesterly winds in spring and can be an important contributing factor in the outbreak and spread of forest fires.

SOLAR RADIATION IN THE PINE BARRENS

There are no solar radiation observation stations in the Pine Barrens; however, Sakamoto and Dunlap (1974) have carried out a detailed analysis of solar radiation measurements at New Brunswick, New Jersey (Table X). These data should be adequate for indicating the seasonal variation of solar radiation in the Pine Barrens, although the actual levels of solar radiation should be slightly higher in the Pine Barrens compared with New Brunswick.

These data show that, on very clear days with clean air, the maximum daily values can exceed the average by amounts which range from 65–75% in summer to more than 100% in winter. The coefficient of variation exceeds 45% during the months of November through April, when the day-to-day variability of solar radiation is considerably higher than during the months of May through October, when the coefficient of variation is 40% or less. Minimum values are not presented in the table, since they can be less than 25 langleys/day (calories received per cm^2 per day) on days with a heavy overcast during October through March and less than 50 langleys/day on similar days during April through September.

In the forested sections of the Pine Barrens, the intensity of solar radiation decreases

TABLE X Solar Radiation (langleys/day) at New Brunswick, New Jersey (1948–1965)[a]

	Jan.	Feb.	Mar.	Apr.	May	June	July	Aug.	Sep.	Oct.	Nov.	Dec.
Maximum[b]	375	475	700	775	825	875	850	800	675	525	400	325
Average	173.1	248.1	348.1	416.5	496.1	540.6	516.3	458.6	396.1	303.0	200.3	158.9
Standard deviation	88.8	115.3	170.9	190.9	200.6	189.0	165.2	164.2	149.6	121.9	90.7	75.1
Coefficient of variation (%)	50.3	46.4	49.0	45.8	40.4	34.9	31.9	35.8	37.7	40.2	45.2	47.2

[a] One langley/day equals one calorie received per square centimeter per day.
[b] Lower limit of 25 langley class interval.

rapidly from the top of the canopy downward toward the forest floor. Geiger (1965) has shown that the percentage of solar radiation reaching the forest floor is a function of stand density. In a very dense stand of Atlantic white cedar (*Chamaecyparis thyoides*) in the Pine Barrens, Buell (1956 personal communication) found that light intensity at the forest floor was only 2% of that in the open. On the other hand, Knoerr (1976), who recently reported on measurements in a loblolly pine (*Pinus taeda*) forest in North Carolina, indicated that solar radiation reaching the forest floor averaged 25% of the intensity above the canopy. In this case, numerous gaps in the canopy resulted in many sun flecks on the forest floor.

Geiger (1965) also has indicated that the quality of solar radiation reaching the trunk space and the forest floor is changed by the canopy. In a hardwood forest in Europe, light intensity at a wavelength of 0.71 micrometers (red light) on the forest floor was 14% of that above the canopy. At wavelengths ranging from 0.36 to 0.65 μm (violet, blue, green, yellow, orange), only 3–5% of the solar radiation above the canopy was transmitted to the forest floor. For details of radiation measurements in Lebanon State Forest during the period April 1964 to April 1965, see Lull and Reigner (1967).

POTENTIAL HUMAN IMPACT ON THE MICROCLIMATE OF THE PINE BARRENS

The continuing fluctuation of the climate of the Pine Barrens gives one every reason to expect similar changeability in the future. The extreme and prolonged drought of 1961–1966 preceded several very wet years in the following decade, including the wettest year on record in 1975. While a great deal of study is being devoted to possible climatic trends and their causes, no definite trends of climate have been delineated for this region. Although it is conceivable that people may have an impact on global climate as a result of factors such as the increasing CO_2 in the atmosphere or reduction of the ozone layer in the stratosphere, what happens in the Pine Barrens will not change this significantly one way or another.

However, human use of the land most definitely does have an impact on the microclimate. Frequently, planning and designing are carried out in ignorance or disregard of this fact, and the results most often undesirably alter the microclimate. This alteration usually results from modification of the radiation balance and the water balance, although modification of the wind flow also can be important.

The most undesirable modification of the radiation balance and water balance takes place when natural vegetation and soil are replaced by a large area of asphalt paving. This results in locally higher air and soil temperatures, especially during the growing season, and the movement of this heat into surrounding areas. The loss of evapotranspiration, combined with higher air temperatures, causes locally lower relative humidity. Runoff of precipitation is speeded up drastically, so that flooding and silting of streams become much more serious. If further development of the Pine Barrens is permitted, then very careful planning and designing will be necessary in order to minimize undesirable effects on the microclimate.

SUMMARY

In winter, a strong northwesterly flow of cold, dry air masses from Canada predominates in the Pine Barrens, and temperatures average 0°–2°C (32°–36°F). In summer, a southwesterly flow of warm, humid air around the Bermuda high-pressure area dominates the Pine Barrens, with temperatures averaging 22°–24°C (72°–75°F). From year to year, however, both summer and winter temperatures are highly variable. A coastal sea breeze in spring and summer lowers afternoon temperatures and increases relative humidity over the extreme eastern portions of the Pine Barrens. Average annual precipitation throughout the Pine Barrens is 1067–1168 mm (42–46 in), but again annual variability is high, e.g., 642–1706 mm (25–67 in) at Atlantic City Airport. Drought occurs relatively frequently and influences the entire region; flooding is occasional and of localized importance. Temperature, humidity, wind, solar radiation and precipitation before and during fire outbreaks, particularly in spring, are important in determining the spread of major forest fires. At least five weather situations produce strong winds and heavy precipitation in different seasons. Stationary or slow-moving high-pressure areas, 87% of which occur during August through November, cause extended periods of atmospheric stagnation with haze and pollution buildup. Although the climate of the Pine Barrens generally is similar to that of surrounding regions, the microclimate is unique in several respects. Since human use of the land often has profound effects upon the microclimate, any further development in the Pine Barrens must be evaluated carefully for potential microclimatic changes.

ACKNOWLEDGMENTS

The author acknowledges, first and foremost, the inspiration that comes from having known and worked with Murray Fife Buell. Thanks are expressed to James A. Carr and Donald V. Dunlap, who were very helpful in locating data. Special thanks are extended to Philip E. Marucci, who very kindly provided the data on Whitesbog and most of the data for Pemberton and to Valeria Bowers for her invaluable help in assembling and typing the manuscript.

REFERENCES

Addess, S. R., and Shulman, M. D. (1966). A synoptic analysis of freezing precipitation in New Jersey. *Bull., N.J. Acad. Sci.* **11**, 2–7.

Beitel, T. C. (1976). A radar climatological study of convective precipitation over southern New Jersey and adjacent areas. M.S. Thesis, Rutgers Univ., New Brunswick, New Jersey.

Biel, E. R. (1958). The climate of New Jersey. *In* "The Economy of New Jersey" (S. J. Flink, ed.), pp. 53–89. Rutgers Univ. Press, New Brunswick, New Jersey.

Changnon, S. A., *et al.* (1974). Metromex: An overview of Illinois state water survey projects. *Bull. Am. Meteorol. Soc.* **55**(2), 89–100.

Cry, G. W. (1966). Effects of tropical cyclone rainfall on the distribution of precipitation over the eastern and southern United States. M.S. Thesis, Rutgers Univ., New Brunswick, New Jersey.

Cry, G. W. (1967). Effects of tropical cyclone rainfall on the distribution of precipitation over the eastern and southern United States. *U.S. Dep. Commer., ESSA Prof. Pap.* No. 1.

Dickerson, W. H., and Dethier, B. E. (1970). Drought frequency in the northeastern United States. A northeast regional research publication. *W.Va. Agric. Exp. Stn., Bull.* No. 595.

Donley, D. L. (1963). Air pollution potential in New Jersey as affected by anticyclonic stagnation. M.S. Thesis, Rutgers Univ., New Brunswick, New Jersey.

Dunlap, D. V. (1970). Probabilities of extreme snowfalls and snow depths. A northeast regional research publication. *N.J. Agric. Exp. Stn., Bull.* No. 821.

Geiger, R. (1965). "The Climate Near the Ground." Harvard Univ. Press, Cambridge Massachusetts.

Harshberger, J. W. (1916). "The Vegetation of the New Jersey Pine Barrens. An Ecologic Investigation." Christopher Sower Co., Philadelphia, Pennsylvania.

Havens, A. V. (1964). Weather increasingly significant in control of air pollution. *N.J. Public Health News* **45**(1), 20–22.

Havens, A. V., and McGuire, J. K. (1961). The climate of the northeast—spring and fall low temperature probabilities. A northeast regional research publication. *N.J. Agric. Exp. Stn., Bull.* No. 801.

Knoerr, K. R. (1976). The comparison between measured fluxes and profiles in a forest canopy. *Bull. Am. Meteorol. Soc.* **57**, 1401.

Korshover, J. (1967). "Climatology of Stagnating Anticyclones East of the Rocky Mountains, 1936–65." Natl. Cent. Air Pollut. Control, Cincinnati, Ohio.

Little, S., Crammer, C. B., and Somes, H. A. (1958). Direct seeding of pitch pine in southern New Jersey. *U.S. For. Serv., Northeast. For. Exp. Stn., Stn. Pap.* No. 111.

Lull, H. W., and Reigner, I. C. (1967). Radiation measurements by various instruments in the open and in the forest. *U.S. For. Serv., Northeast. For. Exp. Stn., Res. Pap.* NE-84.

Marucci, P. E. (1976a). Summary of climatological data for Pemberton, New Jersey, 1929–71. (Unpublished data compiled by the official observer for Pemberton, New Jersey.)

Marucci, P. E. (1976b). Summary of bog minimum temperatures at Whitesbog, New Jersey for 1976. (Unpublished data compiled by the official observer for Pemberton, New Jersey.)

Palmer, W. C. (1965). Meteorological drought. *U.S. Dep. Commer., Weather Bur. Res. Pap.* No. 45.

Sakamoto, C. M., and Dunlap, D. V. (1974). Solar radiation at New Brunswick, New Jersey. *N.J. Agric. Exp. Stn., Bull.* No. 833.

Thom, H. C. (1963). Tornado probabilities. *Mon. Weather Rev.* **91**(10–12), 730–748.

U.S. Department of Commerce (1956). "Substation History—New Jersey, Key to Meteorological Records Documentation 1.1." Washington, D.C.

U.S. Department of Commerce (1973). "Monthly Normals of Temperature, Precipitation, and Heating and Cooling Degree Days, 1941–70." Climatography of the United States, No. 81—New Jersey. Asheville, North Carolina.

U.S. Department of Commerce (1975a). "Local Climatological Data—Annual Summary with Comparative Data for Atlantic City, New Jersey." Asheville, North Carolina.

U.S. Department of Commerce (1975b). "Local Climatological Data—Annual Summary with Comparative Data for Philadelphia, Pennsylvania." Asheville, North Carolina.

U.S. Department of Commerce (1976). "Climatological Data—New Jersey," Vol. 81, No. 11. Asheville, North Carolina.

Wales, B. A. (1966). Some relationships between climate, microclimate, and vegetation on north and south forest boundaries in New Jersey. M.S. Thesis, Rutgers Univ., New Brunswick, New Jersey.

Wales, B. A. (1967). Climate, microclimate, and vegetation relationships on north and south forest boundaries in New Jersey. *William L. Hutcheson Mem. For. Bull.* **2**(3), 1–60.

8

Fluxes of Water and Energy through the Pine Barrens Ecosystems

JOHN THOMAS BALLARD

INTRODUCTION

Although upland and lowland ecosystems differ markedly in the manner in which they partition water and energy resources, the single conceptual model described may be used to investigate the fluxes of water and energy through these systems. Evapotranspiration is the connecting link between water and energy dynamics. This may be measured in several ways by capitalizing on important upland–lowland hydrological differences. During summer, the highest evapotranspiration rates are from lowland tree communities. Lowland shrub communities and upland forest communities have progressively lower rates. Sensible heat energy carried by wind from relatively dry uplands to lowland swamps increases an already high evapotranspiration rate in the lowlands and the removal of water from the groundwater aquifer. Such interactions between ecosystems emphasize the importance of spatial configuration of ecosystems and have implications in a landscape in which human activities dissect ecosystems. The homogeneity of large tracts thus is destroyed, and an increasingly fine-grained mosaic is produced.

"Flying" over the New Jersey Pine Barrens by consulting aerial photographs, one is presented with an overall impression of a light-colored matrix, with bands of darker color forming dendritic patterns eastward toward the coastal bays, and the Delaware River westward. The different intensities of color are caused by the different reflectivities of two main types of vegetation. Superposition of a topographic map upon the aerial photographs shows the darker-colored vegetation occupying the low-lying areas of the Pine Barrens, while the lighter-colored vegetation mantles the upland areas, leading to a convenient classification of the two broad vegetation types as lowland and upland. The variations in vegetation recorded on the photographic emulsion largely result from the water and energy fluxes that occur through and within the thin biotic membrane lying atop the Tertiary and Quaternary sands of New Jersey's Outer Coastal Plain. Yet

133

the vegetation is not a passive response to externally applied conditions. It exerts a large degree of control upon the various fluxes of water and energy that pass through the ecosystem.

The objectives of this chapter are (a) to describe a general model of energy and water fluxes through an ecosystem, with a focus on evapotranspiration, the flux overlap component, (b) to estimate the levels of energy and water flows in certain Pine Barrens ecosystems, and (c) to evaluate the interaction between Pine Barrens ecosystems in terms of energy and water.

By definition, a flux of matter or energy must occur across a boundary surface; accordingly we shall enclose a section of the Pine Barrens ecosystem in an imaginary boundary across which fluxes will be determined. The vertical limits of our imaginary boundary are designated arbitrarily as the bottom of the root zone and the top of the tree canopy, but the problem of determining the horizontal extent of the boundary cannot be solved arbitrarily.

Traditionally, hydrological ecosystem analysis has been done for watersheds. Two aspects of the Pine Barrens energy and water relationships, however, make this approach less than entirely satisfactory. First, the distinct difference between upland and lowland communities in terms of the partitioning of water and energy suggests the value of considering each vegetational community as an independent unit and as an interacting part of an entire hydrological unit. Watershed analyses treat the watershed as a homogeneous unit with a single water yield. Second, small watersheds which are located near the coast and in which a considerable amount of groundwater moves to coastal bays by subsurface flow rather than surface drainage require a substantially different approach than that of a guaged watershed. Knowledge of water table contours, transmissivity of water through the aquifer, and water input rates from soil water percolation is needed to evaluate and model groundwater dynamics.

ENERGY FLOW THROUGH AN ECOSYSTEM

The conceptual model of Fig. 1, allows us to trace the paths of energy flow through the ecosystem. The vast majority of energy input to the ecosystem arrives as insolation from the sun. Almost half of this energy occurs in the visible range of the electromagnetic spectrum 400–700 nm (Reifsnyder and Lull, 1965). On days when visible solar radiation is low due to cloud cover, the importance of the longer-wave infrared radiation may be enhanced; however, on cloudless days, energy distribution in insolation is about 45, 45, and 10% for infrared, visible, and shorter wavelengths, respectively (Reifsnyder and Lull, 1965). Daily insolation is measured at relatively few National Weather Service stations, generally with pyrheliometers, that are sensitive in the visible and near-infrared wavelengths.

A fraction of insolation energy, generally 10–45% (Reifsnyder and Lull, 1965), is reflected by the ecosystem. This fraction is known as the albedo. The albedo of an ecosystem depends upon the reflectivities of the components of the ecosystem, such as

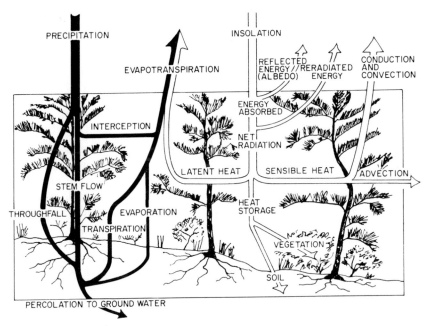

Fig. 1. Flows of water and energy through an ecosystem. The evapotranspiration flux is the common link between the water and energy dynamics.

vegetation, litter, and soil. Spatial variations in albedo are due to different proportions of these components, while temporal variations are due mainly to the phenological state of the vegetation and the water status of the soil. Albedo measurements are made by using upward- and downward-facing pyrheliometers.

The balance of the insolation energy that is not reflected is absorbed in the ecosystem and distributed in several ways. First, a tiny fraction of the light may be captured in the photosynthetic process, but while this is a pathway for some energy, the relative amount is so small that it generally is neglected when energy balances are investigated. A portion of the absorbed radiation may be reradiated to the sky as infrared radiation. The amount of reradiation largely depends upon the temperature and the emission characteristics of the radiating surface. Net radiation instruments measure insolation energy and subtract from it radiation energy coming up from the surface, thereby yielding the net amount of radiation that is absorbed by the ecosystem. Net radiation is of great importance to energy studies, since it may be partitioned by the ecosystem into three pathways, whose magnitudes play a large role in determining what vegetation may exist at a site.

Since net radiation is absorbed by vegetation and soil, a process which causes them to warm, energy may be stored in the ecosystem at least temporarily. The time span under consideration is important for determining whether this energy storage term is significant in the balance equation. For instance, during the daytime these components heat up and store energy; however, energy is released during the nighttime cooling period, leaving very little net storage of heat energy in the ecosystem for a 24-hour period. Seasonally, there may be small changes in net storage of energy in the system, but these amounts are slight, compared to the total energy passing through the ecosystem. The net amount of heat storage generally is taken to be zero during long-term energy studies.

There are two pathways for the distribution of energy absorbed within an ecosystem: sensible heat flux to the air and latent heat flux used in the evaporation of water. Taken together, these two energy fluxes may comprise 90% of the total daily energy incident upon an ecosystem such as the Pine Barrens (Slatyer, 1967). The partitioning of energy between sensible and latent heat depends largely upon the water status of the ecosystem, with the latent heat pathway dominating in systems with abundant water and the sensible heat flux dominating in xeric systems. Under most conditions, some energy follows both pathways.

Sensible heat, as the name implies, is energy that can be detected directly. It increases the temperature of the air within the ecosystem and may be carried upward across the hypothetical boundary by conduction or convection (Hicks *et al.*, 1975). Some sensible heat may be transported laterally by wind, a transfer of energy known as advection. When the portion of an ecosystem under consideration is surrounded by a large area of similar terrain and vegetation, positive advection toward the area may equal negative advection away from the area. When the area adjacent to the experimental ecosystem is not of the same conditions, net advection may play an important role in the energy balance of one system by supplying energy exceeding that which is available from net radiation. This situation is illustrated particularly well by the so-called "oasis" effect, whereby an area of well-watered vegetation is surrounded by a dry area from which it receives advected energy. This is important in the Pine Barrens, where lowland communities are surrounded by relatively dry oak–pine uplands. The horizontal advection of energy is difficult to measure, since it depends upon accurate temperature profiles and a description of the wind pattern.

The last energy pathway, that is, the flux of latent heat used in evaporating water, is of primary concern in ecosystem analysis. Evaporation of water from soil, vegetation surfaces, and from the intercellular spaces below stomatal openings in leaves requires latent heat energy for liquid water to be transformed to the vapor phase. The collective term *evapotranspiration* is applied to this vaporization process, whether it occurs as transpiration from surfaces of organisms or as evaporation. The flux of latent heat used in the evaporative process is not measurable directly, but is calculated from measurement of evapotranspiration rates multiplied by a constant, the latent heat of vaporization of water. This flow of latent heat in evapotranspiration forms the connecting link between studies of energy and hydrology in ecosystems. While a certain portion of the energy dynamics can be studied without a complete investigation of the hydrological dynamics of the system, and hydrological studies need not consider all aspects of the energy balance, energy and water dynamics are linked inseparably through the process of evapotranspiration.

WATER FLOW THROUGH AN ECOSYSTEM

Annual precipitation for the Pine Barrens area is about 110 cm and occurs relatively evenly throughout the year (U.S. Department of Agriculture, 1941). Spatial variations in rainfall are especially notable during the summer months, when thunderstorms sweep across the area and create locally intense precipitation. A pit or standard National Weather Service rain guage fitted with a wind shield may be placed in a large opening in the forest canopy to measure precipitation input, including snow, in the Pine Barrens (Fig. 1).

Not all of the precipitation falling on an ecosystem reaches the ground; a certain amount is retained on vegetation surfaces, wetting them until their absorptive capacity is exceeded, and water falls from canopy surfaces or flows down the stems of vegetation. The water retained in this manner by vegetation is called interception, and its determination is important in hydrological studies, since spatial and temporal variations in interception patterns have a great impact on the water yield of an ecosystem. Once precipitation enters the canopy, its trajectory follows one of three pathways. It may be intercepted by the vegetation, fall through the canopy (either directly through open spaces or after being detained temporarily by vegetation surfaces), or reach the ground as stemflow down the trunks of trees and the stems of shrubs.

Interception can be determined directly by harvesting the vegetation and measuring weight loss as water on the surfaces evaporates. Stem flow may be measured using collars around the stems that are connected to large collection containers. Throughfall may be measured with containers distributed through the ecosystem, although the variability associated with throughfall usually is reduced by using linear trough collectors (Helvey and Patrick, 1965; Kimmins, 1973). Throughfall measurements made in an ecosystem are site specific and usually do not lead to general principles of throughfall mechanisms that can be utilized for other sites. Models for interception (Rutter *et al.*, 1975), based upon easily obtainable site characteristics such as the leaf area index, probably are adequate for most hydrological work on the ecosystem level.

Although a small amount of interception does occur in the litter layer (Bernard, 1963), the Pine Barrens communities have dense root systems in the A_{00} soil horizon, and the water reaching the forest floor is available to roots. Throughout the root zone, water is removed from the soil and subsequently returned to the atmosphere by transpiration, completing a segment of the hydrological cycle. However, a quantity of water is not captured by the roots and percolates below the root zone. This water, which in effect has left the ecosystem, drains through soil pores to the water table, where it enters the groundwater aquifer. This percolation flux is of utmost importance to the hydrologist, since it provides recharge to the groundwater and determines the quantity of water that may be removed from the aquifer without causing adverse effects, e.g., local regional lowering of the water table, causing lower streamflow, drying of wetlands, and salt water intrusion. In lowland ecosystems, where the water table occurs within or only slightly below the root zone, the concept of water percolating from the root zone through an unsaturated layer of soil to the groundwater is not applicable;

subsequent discussion of soilwater percolate applies only to the uplands. Soilwater percolate may be measured by gravity lysimeters (Jordan, 1968) or by newer tension-plate lysimeters (Cole and Gessel, 1968; Cochran *et al.*, 1970). As an alternative to the direct measurement of soilwater percolate, field measurements of the soilwater potential at various depths can be combined with laboratory measurements of the hydraulic conductivity of the soil over a range of moisture, so that waterflow down potential gradients can be calculated (Rose and Stern, 1965).

The mathematics of the theory of waterflow in porous soils such as the Pine Barrens sands are understood well, but their application is limited by the difficulties of obtaining routine soilwater potential measurements. Although quantifying the amount of percolation from the root zone and recharge to the aquifer is the main reason for the hydrological study of ecosystem water dynamics, this quantity usually is obtained by difference, namely, the unknown quantity in the water balance equation (where Δ is net change):

$$\text{precipitation} = \text{evapotranspiration} + \Delta \text{ soil moisture} + \text{percolation} \qquad (1)$$

Change in soil moisture in the root zone may be determined by use of: (1) gravimetric analysis, removing soil samples, and determining their water content, at best a tedious and destructive form of sampling; (2) a neutron probe, which determines *in situ* water content by back-scattering and detection of neutrons (Gardner, 1965); (3) starting and ending times for hydrological analysis such that the net change in soil moisture is zero. Periods of heavy rainfall, during which the soil is saturated, make convenient end points.

MEASUREMENT OF EVAPOTRANSPIRATION

Evapotranspiration is the key remaining term in the water balance equation, and can be determined from vegetational communities by means of three basic methods (Federer, 1970). The first utilizes lysimeters, which enclose blocks of soil and determine weight changes or measure volumes of water draining from the soil. In the second technique, measurements of soil moisture changes under some conditions, can yield evapotranspiration rates. Third, water vapor flux from the system can be determined from meteorological measurements above the canopy.

In lysimetric investigations, the water balance of Eq. (1) is applied to small units of the ecosystem that are isolated physically from, but contiguous with, the adjacent vegetation. Weighing lysimeters usually involve complicated apparatus and have been used mainly in agricultural experimentation. Volumetric lysimeters have been used in the lowland shrub communities of the Pine Barrens, as will be described later in the estimation of actual water budgets (Ballard, 1971).

During certain dry periods, it is safe to assume that water is not percolating to the groundwater. The water consequently lost from the soil column must be removed entirely by evapotranspiration; the measurement of this water loss by sequential determinations of soil water content will yield evapotranspiration rates. Two such studies have been done in coastal plain forests of New Jersey and Long Island, New York (Lull and Axley, 1958; Reiners and Woodwell, 1966). Studies of this type are limited to and are applicable mainly to selected dry periods when there is no recharge to the groundwater. A radioactive labeling technique, usually involving tritiated water, has been developed to determine evapotranspiration even during periods of recharge (Woodwell *et al.*, 1974). A layer of soilwater is labeled, the radioactivity followed, and soilwater content above the radioactive layer measured to estimate evapotranspiration.

The idea of determining evapotranspiration from the measurement of soilwater changes is stretched to the limit in the lowland communities where the soil is saturated. Changes in soil moisture thus are reflected in changes in water table level. During rainfall, the water table in the lowland areas rises rapidly and then subsides exponentially in a few days. When the water table has receded to about 20 cm below the ground surface, oscillations with wavelengths of 24 hr begin to occur in a graph of water table level versus time. The amplitude of these oscillations increases as the water table falls, until the water table trace is essentially a horizontal sine wave with a 24-hour wavelength. This oscillation of the water table is caused by the withdrawal of water by transpiration during the daylight period and by the recharge of water to the area at night. Analysis of water table fluctuations of this type has been used under hydraulically simpler conditions (White, 1932; Heikurainen, 1963; Bay, 1967), but the drainage of water to the streams in the Pine Barrens area necessitates a more complex analysis of the water table trace. Development of a theoretical model for the interaction of vegetation with the groundwater in the lowlands and a simulation using this model have shown promise for the determination of evapotranspiration rates (Ballard, 1971; Buell and Ballard, 1972).

Measuring evapotranspiration with meteorological techniques over the canopy usually has involved determining energy budgets of systems which yield evapotranspiration rates, since the latent heat flux is an integral part of the energy balance. Meteorological conditions resulting in logarithmic wind profiles are necessary for an adequate mathematical analysis. Recent advances in anemometer and water vapor detection equipment also have enabled the evaporative flux from surfaces to be investigated by an eddy correlation technique (Dyer and Maher, 1965; Businges and Miyake, 1967; Hicks *et al.*, 1975).

Computer models of the evapotranspiration process based on meteorological theory, field data on meteorological inputs, and measured vegetational and soil parameters have been developed and provide a tool for the rapid exploration of the questions concerning the hydrology of ecosystems (Goldstein *et al.*, 1974). These models yield daily values for the components of the hydrological flow processes through an ecosystem and have proved quite successful when applied to experimental watersheds for which corroborative data on water yield are available (Swift *et al.*, 1975). Evapotranspiration data are not available with which to check the validity of these computer models when applied to Pine Barrens ecosystems. However, using accurate site parameter and meteorological input data, models based on correct principles should be very useful when investigating water fluxes through Pine Barrens ecosystems. When sufficient empirical data have been collected, the coupling of these ecosystem models to models of groundwater flow (Pinder and Bredehoeft, 1968) will provide a powerful tool with which to investigate and predict the consequences of human activities on the precious groundwater reservoir of southern New Jersey.

ESTIMATED ENERGY AND WATER FLUXES IN THE PINE BARRENS

A paucity of data marks our understanding of water and energy dynamics in Pine Barrens ecosystems. Scattered investigations concerned with the distribution of vegetation have yielded a few data on soil water content (Buell and Cantlon, 1950; Stephenson, 1965), and the groundwater investigations of the U.S. Geological Survey have provided watershed evapotranspiration measurements (Rhodehamel, in this volume). Only two studies, however, have measured long-term evapotranspiration from different vegetational units of the Pine Barrens (Lull and Axley, 1958; Ballard, 1971). Hydrological studies of the oak–pine ecosystem of central Long Island, New York (Woodwell *et al.*, 1974) can be applied to the New Jersey Pine Barrens upland ecosystems, but since the three studies were conducted at different times and under different meteorological conditions, the results are not strictly comparable.

Although we previously have grouped all lowland vegetational communities into one category, it now is expedient to recognize three subcommunities within the lowlands. The hardwood swamps dominated by red maple (*Acer rubrum*), the cedar swamps dominated by Atlantic white cedar (*Chamaecyparis thyoides*), and the shrub communities, a mixture of sheep laurel (*Kalmia angustifolia*) and leather leaf (*Chamaedaphnae calyculata*), are three vegetational communities for which evapotranspiration data are available. No differences in evapotranspiration rates of the hardwood swamp communities and the cedar swamp communities could be detected by water table fluctuation analysis during the summer of 1970 (Ballard, 1971; Buell and Ballard, 1972); therefore, these two communities are referred to as the lowland tree community. Even though the shrub communities that often border lowland tree communities form a part of the lowland vegetation type, the partitioning of water and energy resources in the shrub communities appears to be quite different than in the tree communities. During the six-month experimental period of May–October for which evapotranspiration rates were calculated, the most striking difference between these two lowland communities was in their evapotranspiration rates. The tree communities returned water to the atmosphere at a rate approximately 2.5 times the evapotranspiration rate of the shrub community, resulting in a net water removal of 25 cm from the groundwater. Whereas the shrub communities yielded a net input of 18 cm to the groundwater. The microclimatic differences between these two communities appeared to be the major cause of this water use difference. The tree communities were 15 m tall, with evaporative surface held high into the airflow, in which energy advected from the uplands could accelerate the evaporative process readily. The microclimate of the 0.6-m-tall shrub community was very different, since the shrubs were sheltered on the west by tall dense cedars, resulting in lower wind speeds and less mixing of the air above the shrub community with the general atmospheric flow of the region.

Low evapotranspiration rates of upland communities are due to low water-holding capacity of the coarse, sandy soil, which allows rapid percolation to groundwater beyond the reach of roots. Figure 2 shows typical water and energy fluxes through three Pine Barrens ecosystem types for the six-month summer period May–October. The values are from data taken during different experimental periods in widely separated ecosystems and should not be considered actual measurements obtained during concurrent experimentation in contiguous ecosystems. To provide a common denominator for the comparison of energy and water fluxes, energy fluxes in langleys (calories/cm^2) have been converted to the equivalent centimeters of water by dividing by the latent heat of vaporization of water (585 cal/cm^3). Thus, all values are in centimeters of water per unit area (Fig. 2).

Pyrheliometer measurements of solar radiation taken during three summers (1968–1970) in the Pine Barrens yielded an average value equivalent to about 90 cm for the six-month period, and this value was used as input to all three ecosystems (Fig. 2). Relative reflectivities of the three ecosystem types were determined with aerial photographs, which, in conjunction with albedo measurements of different vegetation surfaces reported by Reifsnyder and Lull (1965), were used to assign albedo values to the

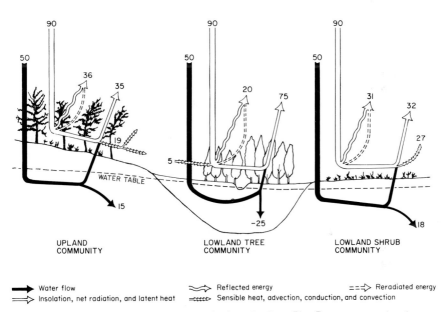

Fig. 2. Typical summer water and energy budgets for three Pine Barrens ecosystem types. Values are expressed in centimeters of water per unit area. Energy fluxes were converted to equivalent depths of water by dividing by the latent heat of vaporization. The amount of evapotranspiration equals the output of latent heat. See Fig. 1 and text.

three ecosystems. No site-specific data were available on the albedos of the three communities; however, net radiation in the shrub community was measured concurrently with solar radiation, and the albedos used to estimate reflected energy fluxes in Fig. 2 yield net radiation values consistent with the field measurements. This net radiation sets the upper limit on the amount of locally available energy that may be used in the evaporative process.

Evapotranspiration was measured by water table fluctuation analysis in the swamps during the summer of 1970 and yielded a value of 75 cm for both the cedar and hardwood communities. During three summers, from 1968–1970, measurements obtained using replicated volumetric lysimeters in the shrub community yielded remarkably consistent evapotranspiration rates for the shrub community, with an average value of 32 cm.

Evapotranspiration rates for both nonirrigated and heavily irrigated forest systems at Brookhaven National Laboratory during the 1973–1974 summers were determined from computer simulation of the hydrological process in the ecosystem. While solar energy input for these summer periods on Long Island was similar to the 90 cm measured in the Pine Barrens, precipitation input for both summers was far lower in the case of the nonirrigated system in 1973 and in all other cases was far higher than the 50 cm measured in the Pine Barrens during 1968–1970. No simple normalization of the Long Island and Pine Barrens conditions can be used, but the evapotranspiration rate of 35 cm for the upland ecosystem (Fig. 2) is the best estimation of the rate that would occur with a precipitation input of 50 cm. Ideally, site measurements from the Pine Barrens and meteorological data from 1968–1970 should be used as inputs to the computer simulation model in order to calculate the evapotranspiration rate for the Pine Barrens uplands, but this has not been possible.

Evapotranspiration rates were subtracted from the amounts of net radiation to yield the sensible heat fluxes from the three systems. One result of these calculations is that the sensible heat flux from the lowland tree communities had a negative value, that is, the amount of energy utilized as latent heat of vaporization was greater than the energy locally available from net radiation. Thus, the difference, 5 cm, must have been supplied from energy advected from the uplands. This heat carried by wind into the lowland forest represents about 5.3% of the total energy input, a significant portion. This then completes the energy balance of the ecosystems, since no net storage of energy in soil or vegetation is considered to be present.

The water budgets depicted in Figure 2 are simply graphic representations of the solution of Eq. (1). The measured, or in the case of the uplands, the calculated evapotranspiration rate is subtracted from the precipitation input to calculate the quantity of soilwater percolate recharging the groundwater. The soil moisture change in Eq. (1) is taken to be zero, since soil moisture quantities on May 1 and November 1 are likely to be similar. Calculation of these recharge quantities indicates that the major source of recharge to the groundwater per unit area is the upland ecosystem, followed by the lowland shrub communities. The very high evapotranspiration rate of the lowland tree communities, which are fueled by the advected energy and by the extreme availability of soilwater, results in a net discharge or loss of water from the groundwater of 25 cm.

Although data on evapotranspiration from the Pine Barrens ecosystems are available only for the summer period, the differences between the upland and lowland hydrological patterns are likely to be accentuated during the winter months. The deciduous nature of a large fraction of the upland vegetation, the lowland shrub communities, and the hardwood swamp communities of course would lower the evapotranspiration from these communities during the winter, coincident with sharply reduced interception of precipitation. With lower evapotranspiration and interception, more recharge to the groundwater would occur, and although evapotranspiration in the cedar communities would continue at a much reduced rate due to lower solar insolation, there would be a net input of water to the groundwater by these communities. The quantities shown in Fig. 2 are for water and energy fluxes on a per unit area basis. To apply these data to a regional analysis of water and energy budgets, the percentage distribution of these vegetational communities within a region could be applied to the water and energy fluxes per unit area. This provides estimates of the percent of total evapotranspiration and recharge attributable to the different communities (Ballard and Buell, 1975). This procedure is a second-generation approach to the analysis of water use in the Pine Barrens. The first-generation approach to evapotranspiration investigations is by the use of empirical models based upon climatic data (Thornthwaite and Mather, 1957). With the advent of successful computer modeling of evapotranspiration processes on the ecosystem level, it appears timely to apply this third-generation technique to water management problems in the Pine Barrens.

In this modeling, the spatial distribution of the various functional units, a parameter which is neglected by simply listing the percent coverage of the various communities, would become an important and investigatable consideration when predicting the future water resources of the Pine Barrens. As a subject for hydrological modeling, of both the groundwater and the ecosystem processes, the Pine Barrens has several positive characteristics. Human impact, although increasing, has not yet interrupted the natural processes of water- and energy flows to a great extent and should pose few problems in developing a basic model for the Pine Barrens. The unconsolidated porous sands of the area, although not conducive to traditional watershed work, provide a manageable system for computer modeling of groundwater flow. The relatively abundant information on vegetation and soils in the Pine Barrens will assist in the determination of the site characteristics that can be used to formulate parameters in ecosystem models of waterflows.

INTERACTIONS BETWEEN ECOSYSTEMS: EFFECTS OF UPLANDS ON LOWLANDS

The Pine Barrens does not exist as an isolated unit. Rather, the system is impacted upon by processes that originate in the surrounding ecosystems, and in turn it is connected to and affects other surrounding ecosystems. Likewise, functional units within the Pine Barrens form an interconnected network of ecosystems, with the interconnections between the subunits of the Pine Barrens mainly being flows of energy and water. The flow of water and energy in the Pine Barrens is largely unidirectional proceeding from the uplands, which act as sources for water and energy, to the lowlands, which act as sinks. The groundwater flows from the uplands to the lowlands, moving down potential gradients resulting from the elevational differences of the water table. This abundant flow of water to the lowland vegetational communities is used to maintain a high evapotranspiration rate when the locally available net radiation energy is supplemented by the advection of heat energy from the uplands to the lowlands. In a sense, water that is not evapotranspired from the uplands as it passes rapidly through the porous sands to the groundwater has another chance to interact with energy that is incident upon the upland areas. A portion of this energy is transformed to sensible heat and is advected to the lowlands, where it is used in the evapotranspiration of water that has flowed from the uplands. This integration of the upland and lowland ecosystems into a single hydrological unit results, of course, in a larger evapotranspiration rate for the entire Pine Barrens than would occur if these interconnections of water and energy did not exist.

CONCLUSIONS

We are becoming increasingly aware that the surface of the earth is a mosaic of interacting ecosystems, and that this mosaic is becoming more fine grained as human activities dissect ecosystems and destroy the homogeneity of large tracts. The encroachment of human activities upon the Pine Barrens serves to illustrate how the destruction of an ecosystem's homogeneity may force us to adopt new investigative tactics when dealing with energy- and water-related questions. It is not adequate to speak of watershed yield of a certain number of gallons per day—not when the salient problems are caused by salt water intrusion due to excessive pumping of the groundwater in a certain locality, or by contaminants introduced into the groundwater aquifer that force us to determine the future trajectory of these pollutants in the aquifer. Data for a watershed or even a region may be pertinent for certain managerial purposes. But different approaches are needed to answer questions and develop policies pertaining to the water and energy of increasingly prevalent smaller units of landscape.

Toward this goal, namely, of providing a rationale for the management of the water resources of the Pine Barrens, research was directed by Dr. Murray Buell. This volume is a testament to his impact, on both the body of knowledge about the Pine Barrens and the philosophy serving to guide students toward research in areas that are relevent to the maintenance and improvement of the quality of life for this and future generations.

REFERENCES

Ballard, J. (1971). Evapotranspiration from lowland vegetation communities of the New Jersey Pine Barrens. Ph.D. Thesis, Rutgers Univ., New Brunswick, New Jersey.

Ballard, J., and Buell, M. F. (1975). The role of lowland vegetation communities in the evapotranspiration budget of the New Jersey Pine Barrens. *Bull. N.J. Acad. Sci.* **20,** 26–28.

Bay, R. (1967). Factors affecting soil moisture relationships in undrained forest bogs. *In* "Forest Hydrology," (W. E. Sopper and H. W. Lull, eds.), pp. 335–343. Pergamon, New York.

Bernard, J. M. (1963). Forest floor moisture capacity of the New Jersey Pine Barrens. *Ecology* **44,** 574–576.

Buell, M. F., and Ballard, J. T. (1972). "Evapotranspiration from Lowland Vegetation in the New Jersey Pine Barrens." N.J. Water Resourc. Res. Inst., Rutgers Univ., New Brunswick, New Jersey.

Buell, M. F., and Cantlon, J. E. (1950). A study of two communities of the New Jersey Pine Barrens and a comparison of methods. *Ecology* **31,** 567–586.

Businges, F., and Miyake, M. (1967). On the direct determination of the turbulent heat flux near the ground. *J. Appl. Meteorol.* **6,** 1025–1032.

Cochran, P., Marion, G. M., and Leaf, A. L. (1970). Variation in tension lysimeter leachate volumes. *Soil Sci. Soc. Am., Proc.* **34,** 309–311.

Cole, D. W., and Gessel, S. (1968). Cedar River research: A program for studying the pathways, rates and processes of elemental cycling in a forest ecosystem. *In* "Forest Resources Monograph," Coll. For. Resour., Univ. of Washington, Seattle.

Dyer, Z., and Maher, F. (1965). Automatic eddy flux measurement with the evapotron. *J. Appl. Meteorol.* **4,** 622–625.

Federer, A. (1970). Measuring forest evapotranspiration: Theory and problems, *U.S. For. Serv., Northeast. For. Exp. Stn., Stn. Pap.* No. 165.

Gardner, W. (1965). Water content. *In* "Methods of Soil Analysis," Part I (C. A. Black, D. D. Evans, J. L. White, L. E. Ensminger, and F. E. Clark, eds.), pp. 82–125. Am. Soc. Agron., Madison, Wisconsin.

Goldstein, R., Mankin, J., and Luxmoore, R. (1974). "Documentation of PROSPER: A Model of Atmosphere, Soil, Plant Water Flow." Publ. No. 579. Oak Ridge Natl. Lab., Oak Ridge, Tennessee.

Heikurainen, L. (1963). On using ground water table fluctuations for measuring evapotranspiration. *Acta For. Fenn.* **76,** 5–16.

Helvey, J. D., and Patrick, J. H. (1965). Canopy and letter interception of rainfall by the hardwoods of eastern United States. Water Resources Research **1,** pp. 193–205.

Hicks, B. B., Hyson, P., and Moore, C. J. (1975). A study of eddy fluxes over a forest. *J. Appl. Meteorol.* **14,** 109–113.

Jordan, C. F. (1968). A simple tension-free lysimeter. *Soil Sci.* **105,** 81–86.

Kimmins, J. P. (1973). Some statistical aspects of sampling throughfall precipitation in nutrient cycling studies in British Columbia coastal forests. *Ecology* **54,** 1008–1019.

Lull, J. W., and Axley, J. H. (1958). Forest soil moisture relations in Coastal Plains sands of southern New Jersey. *For. Sci.* **4,** 3–19.

Pinder, G. F., and Bredehoeft, J. D. (1968). Application of the digital computer for aquifer evaluation. *Water Resour. Res.* **4,** 1069–1093.

Reifsnyder, W. E., and Lull, J. W. (1965). Radient energy in relation to forests. *U.S. Dep. Agric., Tech. Bull.* No. 1344.

Reiners, W. A., and Woodwell, G. M. (1966). Water budget of a forest damaged by ionizing radiation. *Ecology* **47,** 303–306.

Rose, C. and Stern, W. (1965). The drainage component of the water balance equation. *Aust. J. Soil Res.* **3,** 95–100.

Rutter, A. J., Morton, A. J., and Robins, P. C. (1975). A predictive model of rainfall interception in forests. II. Generalization of the model and comparison with observations in some coniferous and hardwood stands. *J. Appl. Ecol.* **12,** 367–380.

Slatyer, R. O. (1967). "Plant–Water Relationships." Academic Press, New York.

Climate, Water, and Aquatic Ecosystems

Stephenson, S. N. (1965). Vegetation change in the Pine Barrens of New Jersey. *Bull. Torrey Bot. Club* **92,** 102–114.

Swift, L. W., Luxmoore, R. J., Mankin, J. B., Swank, W. T., and Goldstein, R. A. (1975). Simulation of evapotranspiration and drainage from mature and clear cut deciduous forests and young pine plantations. *Water Resour. Res.* **11,** 667–673.

Thornthwaite, E. C., and Mather, J. R. (1957). "Instructions and Tables for Computing Potential Evapotranspiration and the Water Balance," Publications in Climatology, Vol. X, No. 3. Drexel Inst. Technol., Centerton, New Jersey.

U.S. Department of Agriculture (1941). "Climate and Man." U.S. Dep. Agric. Yearb., Washington, D.C.

White, W. N. (1932). A method of estimating ground water supplies based on discharge by plants and evaporation from soil. *U.S. Geol. Surv., Water Supply Pap.* No. 659-A.

Woodwell, G. M., Ballard, J., Small, M., Pecan, E. V., Clinton, J., Wetzler, R., German, F., and Hennessy, J. (1974). "Experimental Eutrophication of Terrestrial and Aquatic Ecosystems," Rep. No. 50420. Brookhaven Natl. Lab., Upton, New York.

9

Hydrology of the New Jersey Pine Barrens

EDWARD C. RHODEHAMEL

INTRODUCTION

Since the earliest days of the European settlers, the forested interior region of southern New Jersey was known to provide large quantities of water. During the 18th and early 19th century, bog-iron furnaces, grist, lumber, and paper mills, as well as glassmaking factories, were built in the approximately 5828 km² (2250 square miles) Pine Barrens. These locations were chosen at least partly because of the dependable water supply and the water power generated from stable streamflows. Potable water has been and presently is one of the principal resources of the Pine Barrens.

Continuous stream gauging of all major streams by the U.S. Geological Survey, begun in the 1920's, continues today. Early important studies (Vermeule, 1892; Coman, 1892) included brief discussions of the flow characteristics of several southern New Jersey streams. Vermeule (1893, 1894a,b, 1899) provided calculations of monthly and annual evaporation for the region and daily water use supply estimates for important southern New Jersey streams. He proposed that these streams be conserved for future use for similar reasons and in much the same manner as proposed today. Vermeule (1900) also introduced a general formula for annual evaporation applicable to all New Jersey.

However, with the exception of many reports on wells (Woolman, 1889–1902), studies of ground-water hydrology in the Pine Barrens lagged and were begun by Monroe and Pentz (1936) in the early 1930's. Since 1950, studies by the state and U.S. Geological Survey on cooperative water resources have provided county reports including all the New Jersey Pine Barrens region. Barksdale (1952) reported on the magnitude of the Pine Barrens ground-water resource and suggested both conservation and development techniques. Rhodehamel (1970, 1973) reported on the water resources of the Pine Barrens region, and Durand *et al.* (1974) indicated the magnitude of water yield to be expected from the Mullica River basin by conjunctive use of streamflow and ground water.

147

ISBN 0-12-263450-0

The Pine Barrens region experiences a temperate, humid, and predominantly continental climate, modified by intrusions of oceanic air masses, particularly during the summer and early fall. The annual precipitation is approximately 114.3 cm, ranging from about 76.2 to 167.6 cm, and is distributed rather evenly throughout the year and over the area. Four seasons of roughly equal length prevail, and monthly average temperatures range from 0°C (32°F) in January to about 24°C (76°F) in July. The average annual temperature is about 12.2°C (54°F), with a vegetative growing season of about 245 days. The duration of sunshine in New Jersey in percent of astronomical possible sunshine hours is approximately 60% for all of New Jersey (Biel, 1958), or 56.2% for the Pine Barrens as calculated from available sunshine data (U.S. Geological Survey, 1967).

The source of all water in the Pine Barrens is precipitation. Much of the precipitation either is transpired by plants or is evaporated from the litter, soil, water, and vegetation surfaces on which it falls and thus is returned to the atmosphere as water vapor. These phenomena collectively are termed evapotranspiration. Except during unusually intense rainfall, when there is some overland flow, the precipitation on upland areas that either is not evaporated or transpired infiltrates the permeable sandy soil of the region and percolates to the ground-water reservoir. As ground water, it gravitates more or less laterally to nearby streams or continues greater distances to move to deeper horizons from which it eventually is discharged to major streams.

SURFACE WATER

Surface water runoff is divided conveniently into (1) direct runoff, either that from precipitation falling directly on the stream or that reaching stream channels by overland flow soon after rain or snowmelt, and (2) base runoff, predominantly ground-water runoff which has been discharged into a stream channel. Pine Barrens streams differ in their capacity for surface runoff (U.S. Geological Survey, 1976; Rhodehamel, 1970), in part due to variation in amount, intensity, and frequency of precipitation, vegetational uptake, and the variation in geological conditions within and adjacent to the region. Long-term streamflow records of the U.S. Geological Survey (1976) for southern New Jersey streams show an average annual runoff of 57.2 cm (22.5 in) (Rhodehamel, 1970). However, the range is 35.6 cm in McDonalds Branch, an upland stream of 6.0 km² drainage area, to 121.6 cm (exceeding precipitation input) in Oyster Creek, which is near the coast, and which has a surface drainage area of 19.2 km². Other basins having high average annual runoff are the Mullica River, with a surface drainage area of 119.4 km² and 83.8 cm runoff, and Batsto River, with a drainage area of 182.6 km² and 61.2 cm runoff. Additional low average annual runoff basins are the West Branch Cohansey River (modified by agriculture), with a drainage area of 6.6 km² and 24.5 cm runoff (fair data record), and the Oswego River, with a drainage area of 102 km² and 46.4 cm runoff.

Published streamflow characteristics (Miller and McCall, 1961; Thomas, 1964; Miller, 1966; Laskowski, 1970) are illustrated by three major Pine Barrens streams, with gauging stations on the Mullica River 4 km north of Batsto, the Batsto River at Batsto, and the Oswego River at Harrisville (Rhodehamel, 1973). Highest mean monthly streamflow of these streams occurred in March, and lowest was measured in either September or October (Fig. 1). Streamflow per unit area of drainage differed greatly in the three gauged basins: Oswego River had the lowest unit stream discharge,

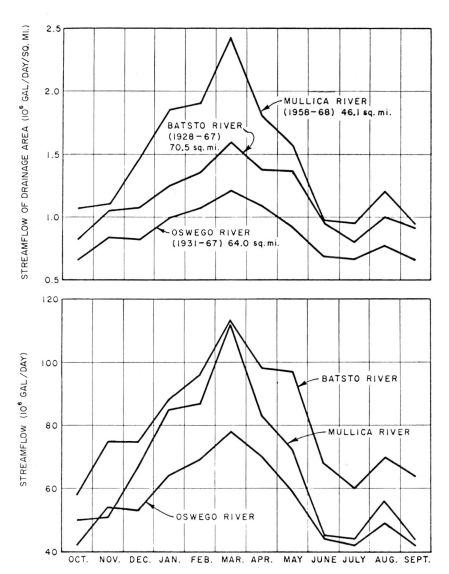

Fig. 1. Average monthly streamflow for three streams in the Mullica River basin, New Jersey. The lower graph is for each stream basin, and the upper graph is for a square mile within a stream basin (1 mi² = 2.59 km²). (From Rhodehamel, 1973.)

and the Mullica River had the highest unit stream discharge. Inasmuch as annual precipitation, temperature, and vegetation conditions do not differ greatly among these basins, deep subsurface percolation of ground water from uplands is probably the major hydrological factor causing variation in the per-unit-area discharge shown at the top of Fig. 1. The gauged Oswego River area, although significantly larger than the gauged Mullica River area, has the lowest annual discharge because of the smaller per-unit-area streamflow, probably due to deep subsurface percolation.

Large damaging floods occur infrequently. A flood that would be expected to occur on the average about once every 50 years probably will be no larger than three or four times the size of the annual flood, except in the southern one-fifth of the state, where it may be five times the annual flood size (Thomas, 1964). The curves shown in Fig. 2 indicate the percentage of time during which specified discharges of three streams either were equaled or exceeded in a given period and may be considered probability curves to estimate future floods (Searcy, 1959). For example, during the period October 1927 to September 1967, the average daily discharge of the Batsto River at Batsto was at least 38 mgd (143,845 m³/day) for 90% of the days.

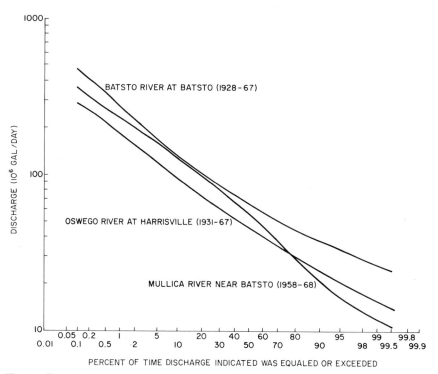

Fig. 2. Flow-duration curves for three streams in the Mullica River basin, New Jersey. These cumulative frequency curves show the percent of time during which specified discharges are equaled or exceeded (Searcy, 1959). 1 mgd (million gallons per day) = 3,785.0 m³/day water. (From Rhodehamel, 1973.)

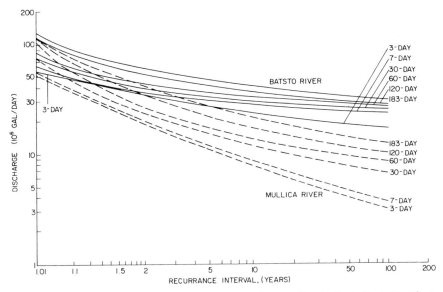

Fig. 3. Frequency and magnitude of minimum annual streamflow for the indicated number of consecutive days in the Batsto and Mullica Rivers, New Jersey. Batsto River data at Batsto, New Jersey for climatic years 1923–1966; Mullica River data near Batsto, New Jersey for climatic years 1958–1967. Curves for the Oswego River generally are parallel to those for the Batsto River but lower (i.e., between 37 and 82 mgd at 1.01 year and between 9 and 19 mgd at 100 years). 1 mgd (million gallons per day) = 3,785.0 m³/day water. (Modified from Laskowski, 1970; see also Rhodehamel, 1973.)

The low-flow characteristics of the Mullica, Batsto, and Oswego Rivers at the gauging stations were analyzed by curves (Fig. 3) from a log-Pearson Type III analysis (Laskowski, 1970) indicating the magnitude and frequency of the lowest flow each year for the indicated number of consecutive days. For example, the minimum average flow of the Mullica River for 30 consecutive days, to be expected once in an average time interval of five years, is 15 mgd (56,781 m³/day). Such values obtained from these curves assist in planning, designing, and operating surface-water supply systems by estimating the frequency of given water-supply stresses.

The upper left-hand portions of the curves in Fig. 2 represent wet periods with direct storm runoff and high ground-water discharge. The lower right-hand side of the curves indicates the expected flow during drought periods, when sustained flow is composed entirely of ground-water discharge. Duration curves like those for the Pine Barrens (Fig. 2), with gentle and rather uniform slopes, indicate stream discharge supported by a large and permeable aquifer. The Batsto River has the largest and the best sustained (gentlest slope) flow characteristics, and the Mullica River has the poorest sustained flow, as seen in the downward curvature in the duration plot at about the 60% flow duration point (Fig. 2). This reduced discharge rate may be related to more swampland vegetation in the Mullica basin compared with the Oswego River basin, where the aquifer is deeper and unavailable to most plant roots.

GROUND WATER

The water table is that surface in an unconfined ground-water body at which the pressure is atmospheric. It fluctuates with recharge and discharge of ground water. Water level fluctuations (Rhodehamel, 1973) are as much as 4.0 m (13 ft) between extreme recorded wet and dry periods and as much as 3.0 m (10 ft) from spring to fall in one year (Fig. 4). However, an average annual fluctuation of about 1.5–2.1 m (5–7 ft) may be considered normal for upland areas (Fig. 4).

Coastal Plain formations in the Pine Barrens region contain water, yet not all contain important aquifers. An aquifer is a layer of rocks that acts as a hydrological unit and that is sufficiently permeable to yield water in a usable quantity to a well or spring. Clayey strata may form part of the boundary of an aquifer and establish whether the aquifer is confined or unconfined. If the ground-water reservoir is unconfined, it is classified as a water-table aquifer. However, if the ground-water reservoir is bounded by overlying and underlying clayey strata and possesses a hydrostatic pressure head by virtue of its being full, the aquifer is classified as an artesian aquifer, and a well penetrating the aquifer is an artesian well. In the Pine Barrens, an aquifer may be confined in one area and unconfined in an adjacent area.

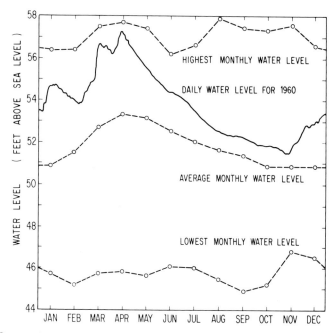

Fig. 4. Seasonal and daily variations in ground-water level at the Mount well in the central Pine Barrens area. Monthly averages are from 1956–1963 data and daily values from 1960. The Mount well is in the Wharton Tract, New Jersey, 5.8 km NNE of Batsto, Burlington County, New Jersey. 1 ft = 0.305 m. (From Rhodehamel 1973.)

Ground water is moving constantly under the force of gravity from positions of high head to those of lower head. In unconsolidated Coastal Plain sediments, this movement is through connected pores in the reservoir materials. Because of friction along the irregular walls of the pores and various other impeding forces, ground water flow is slow, often measured in several tens to hundreds of meters per year. Average velocity of movement for a more permeable part of the near-surface Pine Barrens aquifer was estimated in the northwestern part of the Wharton Tract as ranging from 36.6 to 48.8 m/year (120–160 ft/year), based on an average of 1.3 m/km and an average effective porosity of 40%.

The general configuration of the water table in a basin may be inferred from surface topography and from altitudes of streams, swamps, and lakes shown on U.S. Geological Survey 7½ minute topographic quadrangle maps, plus scattered data on groundwater levels. For example, in the Mullica River basin, highest water table levels (55 m above sea level) are found in the highest part of the Mullica River basin, 3 km east of Woodmansie in Burlington County. The lowest water levels approach sea level along the lower reaches of the Mullica River. The water table slopes generally toward the major rivers and streams of the region, such as the Mullica, Batsto, Tulpehocken, Oswego, Wading, and Bass rivers. Water-table conditions like these prevail throughout the Pine Barrens.

HYDROLOGICAL CHARACTERISTICS OF GEOLOGIC FORMATIONS

Kirkwood Formation

Several aquifers have been identified along the coast (Clark *et al.*, 1968) in the Kirkwood Formation of Miocene age (Owens and Sohl, 1969). In addition, there are several indirectly connected Kirkwood aquifers in the Pine Barrens, generally at depths of 61 to 122 m. Correlation of the Pine Barrens aquifers with higher-yielding aquifers along the coast in general is poorly understood. Westward from the coast, the Kirkwood Formation thins; water-bearing sands, prominent along the coast, become attenuated, and in many locations the materials change from medium-to-coarse sand to clayey and silty fine sand. Accordingly, in the interior areas the formation contains fewer and less permeable water-bearing sands. However, higher than usual yields from wells (up to 3815 m³/day or 700 gpm) have been obtained in an ill-defined southeast trending zone perhaps several kilometers wide lying between Blue Anchor in Camden County and Pomona in Atlantic County adjacent to the coast (Clark *et al.*, 1968; Farlekas *et al.*, 1976; Donsky, 1963; Rhodehamel, 1973). A possible explanation for this unusual high-permeability zone may be that it contains a large buried drainage way of Kirkwood or post-Kirkwood age. The cities of Hammonton and Egg Harbor, located along this trend, are the principal users of water from the Kirkwood in the central Pine Barrens area. Throughout most of the Pine Barrens, the number of identifiable and areally extensive Kirkwood water-bearing horizons is probably no more than two or three.

Most of the Kirkwood aquifers in the Pine Barrens probably are those lying stratigraphically above diatomaceous clays, and are aquifers which, in general, are less permeable and probably less extensive than the aquifers along the coast (Clark *et al.*, 1968; Rhodehamel, 1973). Most of the water-bearing strata are connected hydraulically to the overlying Cohansey Sand and consequently are a part of a large upper Kirkwood–Cohansey aquifer system underlying all the Pine Barrens region.

Cohansey Sand

Based upon its storage capacity, hydraulic conductivity, and accessibility for direct recharge, the Cohansey Sand of Miocene age (Rhodehamel, in this volume; Rachele, 1976) is the most important fresh water aquifer in the New Jersey Coastal Plain (Barksdale *et al.*, 1958; Rhodehamel, 1970, 1973). The Cohansey is essentially a water-table aquifer, but low-pressure confined conditions exist over relatively large areas, especially in the lower parts of the aquifer. The Mullica River basin, and more specifically the central parts of the Wharton Tract, contain some of the more permeable water-bearing materials in the Cohansey Sand (Rhodehamel, 1973).

Calculated values for hydraulic conductivity* range from 27.5 to 76.2 m/day at nine sites in southern New Jersey (Table I). More common values throughout much of the aquifer range between 40 and 46 m/day.

The reported general range of the transmissivity† in much of southern New Jersey (Rhodehamel, 1973) is about 372–1858 m²/day. Within the Wharton Tract, typical values range from 929 to 1858 m²/day. Transmissivity values increase as the aquifer thickens to the southeast and within the buried drainage ways that perhaps were established in post-Kirkwood time.

Low storage coefficients‡ at test sites 1, 4, and 9 (Table I) are indicative of confined aquifer conditions, whereas higher values such as are obtained at test site 5 are indicative of unconfined conditions. During aquifer tests, calculated coefficients of storage that initially are representative of moderately confined artesian aquifers (for example, 1.0×10^{-3} to 1.0×10^{-2}) may change with continued pumping to coefficients representative of unconfined conditions, ranging from about 1.0×10^{-1} to as much as 2.6×10^{-1}.

An aquifer test described by Lang (1961), Lang and Rhodehamel (1962), Rhodehamel and Lang (1962), and Rhodehamel (1973) was conducted in June 1960 on a six-

---

*Hydraulic conductivity is the volume of water at the existing kinematic viscosity that will move through an isotropic medium in unit time under a unit hydraulic gradient through a unit area measured at right angles to the direction of flow.

†Transmissivity is the rate at which water of the prevailing kinematic viscosity is transmitted through a unit width of the aquifer under a unit hydraulic gradient.

‡Storage coefficient is the volume of water an aquifer releases from or takes into storage per unit surface area of the aquifer per unit change in head.

TABLE I Hydraulic Characteristics of the Cohansey-Upper Kirkwood Aquifer System in New Jersey[a]

Well no.	Aquifer test location	Date of test[b]	Hydraulic conductivity		Transmissivity		Storage coefficient[b]
			(m/day)	(gpd/ft²)[c]	(m²/day)	(gdp/ft)[c]	
1	Clayton City well, Gloucester County	Nov. 9, 1956 [1]	39.6	1000	371.6	30,000	Estimated initially at about 1.0×10^{-3}
1	Clayton City well, Gloucester County	Aug. 7, 1957 [1]	76.2	1885	696.8	56,500	Not determined
2	Williamstown well no. 1, Gloucester County	Nov. 12, 1951 [1]	27.4	660	771.1	62,000	Not determined
3	Well 18-V, Lebanon State Forest, Burlington County	Aug. 4, 1958 [2]	36.6[d]	880[d]	1114.8[d]	88,000[d]	Not determined; unconfined
4	Paulaitis Farm, (4.5 km NE of Centerton) Salem County	Nov. 1959 [3,4]	45.8	1100	399.5	32,000	3×10^{-4} (initial value)
5	Wharton Tract 4 km NW of Batsto, Atlantic and Burlington counties	June 1961 [5]	39.6	1000	1858	150,000	0.16 [6]
6	1.5 km N of Brotmanville, Salem County	1966 [3]	45.8	1130	1858	150,000	4.4×10^{-2}
7	Toms River Chem. Co., Toms River, Ocean County	Jan. 1956 [3]	42.7	1050	353.0	28,400	Not determined; unconfined
8	Vineland, Cumberland County	1963–1964 [2]	51.8	1300	929.0	77,000	Not determined
9	Linwood Country Club, Linwood, Atlantic County	April 22, 1953 [3,1]	39.6[e]	1000[e]	929.0[e]	122,000[e]	4.2×10^{-4e}

[a] Revised from Rhodehamel (1973). [b] Methods used for evaluating well drillings are indicated by numbers in parentheses: [1] Jacob (1950) semilog; [2] Theim (1906) equilibrium; [3] Theis (1935) nonequilibrium; [4] Hantush and Jacob (1955) nonsteady leaky; [5] Theis (1935) equilibrium; [6] Ramsahoye and Lang (1961). [c] gpd, gallons per day. [d] Average of 20 values. [e] Average value.

hectare (hectometer) area adjacent to the Mullica River, 4 km northwest of Batsto, to determine the hydraulic characteristics of the water-bearing materials along the lower reaches of the major streams, and to determine the degree of hydraulic continuity between the Mullica River and the bounding aquifer. The pumped well, with a well screen installed 21.6–24.7 m below the land surface and surrounded by observation wells, was pumped at 5451 m^3/day for 12 days. The Theis (1935) nonequilibrium formula indicated transmissivities of 3066–3716 m^3/day, which are considered too great because drawdown was affected by recharge boundaries. An equilibrium formula (Theim, 1906) indicated that average transmissivity was 1858 m^3/day, probably indicative of the transmissivity of the full thickness of the water-bearing sands beneath the test site. The coefficient of storage using an equilibrium formula developed by Ramsahoye and Lang (1961) was computed to be 0.16.

During the test, ground water that normally would move downgradient toward the stream was diverted toward the pumping well. Poor hydraulic connection between the aquifer and the Mullica River was shown by a water-level contour map, which indicated that little water moved from the river into the aquifer under pumping conditions. This poor connection was probably caused by a thin deposit of relatively impermeable bog iron in the bed of the Mullica River, a condition to be expected in the downstream (gaining) segments of Pine Barrens streams. Good hydraulic connection of the aquifer and water in the swamps was indicated by the drying up of the swamps on both sides of the river after about six days of pumping.

Post-Cohansey Formations

Because the Beacon Hill Gravel of Miocene (?) and Pliocene (?) age (Owens and Minard, 1975) occurs only at the higher altitudes, is of small areal extent, has reduced hydraulic conductivity by deposition of clay and iron oxide, and is only a meter or two thick, it does not constitute an important aquifer. The major hydrological function of the formation is to transmit precipitation laterally and (or) downward to recharge the aquifer in the Cohansey Sand.

The Arkose 2 deposits (roughly the Bridgeton ? Formation) and the Arkose 1 deposits (roughly the Pensauken ? Formation) of Miocene (?) and Pliocene (?) ages (Owens and Minard, 1975) have a large amount of impermeable iron oxide in the thicker sections due to deep weathering. Although their hydraulic connection to the underlying Cohansey Sand is imperfect, their main hydrological function is transmitting precipitation to local streams and to the upper Kirkwood–Cohansey aquifer.

The Quartz Sand 2 and Quartz Sand 1 deposits of Pleistocene age (Owens and Minard, 1975) absorb precipitation and, with excellent hydraulic continuity, transmit water directly to the underlying main upper Kirkwood–Cohansey Sand aquifer system. On the other hand, the Cape May estuarine clay (Pleistocene age) acts as a hydraulic barrier to downward or upward percolation to and from the main Cohansey aquifer, and where present is restricted to the periphery of the region beneath the tidal reaches of streams.

HYDROLOGICAL BUDGET

A hydrological budget is a statement accounting for water gains and losses for selected periods in an area. Under present hydrological conditions in which pumpage is negligible, the long-term annual hydrological budget for the Pine Barrens can be stated as follows: water input (precipitation) equals water yield (runoff) plus water loss (evapotranspiration), i.e., $P = R + ET$. P is average annual precipitation in centimeters depth over the area (here measured as 114.3 cm), R is average annual stream runoff in centimeters depth over the area (here measured as 57.2 cm) and ET is the average annual evapotranspiration in centimeters depth over the area.

If significant amounts of water are removed from the region for water supply purposes in the future, the amount of pumpage, Q, not returned to the aquifer must be counted as a loss and added to the right-hand side of the equation (Hardt and Hilton, 1969). Another term X_{oc}, could be inserted on the right-hand side of the equation to account for direct ground-water discharge to the ocean. However, because the Pine Barrens region does not extend to the coastline, there can be little direct leakage to the sea that is not accounted for in the later discussion of streamflow variation. Nevertheless, a very small amount may discharge directly seaward through the aquifer underlying the coast and bay areas. On the bases of existing low hydraulic gradients extending seaward and on the conclusions of Nace (1969, 1970), this is estimated to be <1% of the runoff R.

In the equation shown, the observable seasonal and the more or less cyclic changes in water storage are considered negligible, because the surface and ground-water reservoirs are considered to be filled to capacity. Disparities between volumes of annual storage from year to year are small when compared to the total flux of water passing through the system over many years. Inserting the known quantities of water input and output into the equation gives an estimate of 57.2 cm (22.5 in) average annual water loss. This is equivalent to 1564 m³/day/km² or to a total evapotranspiration loss of 9.12 million m³/day for the Pine Barrens region. Independent checks on the validity of the ET value derived from the hydrological equation follow.

Assuming insignificant variation in vegetative cover and precipitation, evapotranspiration is dependent principally upon the amount of incident radiative energy and air temperature. Estimated values of monthly and annual evapotranspiration for the New Jersey Pine Barrens were computed using the nomogram prepared by van Bavel (1957) for a modified Penman (1956) energy balance method. Daily values of percent sunshine were estimated for the 1931–1960 normal period records at Washington, D.C. and New York City (U.S. Geological Survey, 1967) and standard daily temperatures used for the same period for the Southern Division U.S. weather stations in New Jersey. This gave an annual evapotranspiration estimate of 61.2 cm, or, if monthly evapotranspiration values are summed, >66 cm. Although these evapotranspiration values exceed the 57.2 cm estimated by the long-term hydrological budget equation, they are the maximum values obtainable under maximum vegetation cover and minimum soil–moisture stress (van Bavel, 1957).

In Lebanon State Forest, Lull and Axley (1958) studied evapotranspiration losses throughout 1.5-m soil columns during the growing season (April–November) of 1955, when precipitation was 16% below normal. Evapotranspiration losses from five common vegetation conditions were measured, and values ranged from 43.8 cm on a bare ground plot to 58.9 cm under a tree reproduction plot. The average *ET* loss from the five plots was 55.1 cm during this relatively dry growing season. A. V. Havens computed evapotranspiration to be 49.8 cm by the Thornthwaite method during the year 1955 for field crops at New Brunswick just north of the Pine Barrens (Biel, 1958). Hardt and Hilton (1969) made a water budget study for the years 1946–1955 in Gloucester County, part of which lies in the Pine Barrens. Their reported loss of about 50% of the precipitation to evapotranspiration agrees with the present 50% estimated loss for the entire Pine Barrens. Thus the evapotranspiration value of 57.2 cm (50% of precipitation) computed from the long-term hydrological budget is in reasonable agreement with the *ET* values of Lull and Axley, Havens, Hardt, and Hilton and those calculated here from sunshine and temperature records. The 50% estimated evapotranspiration for the Pine Barrens is 20% less than the national average of about 70%, as computed from the data of Leopold and Langbein (1960).

Precipitation

Long-term records (1931–1964) show that the average annual precipitation in southern New Jersey is about 114.3 cm (45 in). This amounts to an average 3127 m³/day of water for each square kilometer, or 18.24 million m³/day for the approximately 5828 km² of contiguous Pine Barrens. During the period 1931–1964, annual precipitation has ranged from 75–125% of this average.

When precipitation rates or amounts falling on a basin exceed the infiltration capacities of the soil, the excess water either is detained temporarily and stored at the surface to eventually infiltrate or evaporate, or runs overland as sheetflow to nearby drainage ways. In the Pine Barrens, infiltration is the predominant hydrological phenomenon. Temporary surface detention and surface runoff seldom are important outside of swamp areas, because most of the loose sandy soil, with or without a forest litter cover, can absorb 5 cm of precipitation per hour. Data assembled by the author show that in fact much of the region is covered with soils capable of accepting >16 cm of water per hour. Such capacities for infiltration of water seldom are exceeded by precipitation in the Pine Barrens.

Evapotranspiration

Here evapotranspiration losses in the Pine Barrens region are divided into: (1) interception, (2) evapotranspiration from undrained depressions, and (3) evapotranspiration from soil and ground water.

Interception

The part of precipitation retained on the leaves, twigs, limbs, and trunk bark that never reaches the mineral soil is intercepted water. Interception may be considered a water loss factor, because it soon is evaporated to the atmosphere and transported out of the area by wind. Part of precipitation is intercepted by and evaporated from the forest litter, so that total interception loss is the sum of tree canopy, understory vegetation, and forest litter interception.

Although the presence and nature of forest vegetation obviously are important in interception losses, the manner of precipitation input also has a direct influence on total interception losses. Precipitation studies by the author in Lebanon State Forest continued for an eight-year period (1956–1963) indicated that at least 46% of the time the total weekly precipitation averaged 1.27 cm or less. Much of the water is intercepted and fails to have a measurable hydrological effect upon the ground water resources.

The amounts of precipitation intercepted by forest vegetation, including its litter component, are exceedingly variable, because these losses are dependent on diverse and complex variables (Knoerr, 1967; Rutter, 1967; Hewlett, 1967). Studies in the Pine Barrens and elsewhere suggest that, on the average, about 13% of rainfall is intercepted. Wood (1937) estimated 13% interception in the Pine Barrens and Zinke (1967) concurred with the estimate. Rhodehamel and Reiners (unpublished data) analyzed eight summer and fall storms in the Pine Barrens in 1961 and found that interception ranged from 2–60%, with an average of about 20%. Part of this interception was by the forest litter. Moul and Buell (1955) measured 22% interception by mosses and lichens. On the average, well-developed moss mats had the capacity to intercept about 1.52 cm of water. The average interception by lichens was about 0.5 cm of water. Bernard (1963) studied the soil moisture changes on the Pine Barrens of Burlington County and reported losses up to 5.1 cm per year. Another study of individual storms (Cantlon, 1951) indicated that pine stands and oak with understory vegetation may intercept as much as 23 and 28%, respectively, of the total rainfall. Helvey and Patric (1965) report 13% interception for eastern hardwoods. These studies suggest that total interception capacity for a particular storm >1.27 cm generally may be expected to amount to as much as 1.27 cm of water for nonriparian forests of oak and pine, and perhaps 0.75 cm for saturated riparian (low swampy) areas where litter interception is not included.

Elsewhere, Leonard (1961) found that 13% of the annual precipitation over northern hardwood forests was intercepted. U.S. Department of Agriculture (1955) summary reports and an evaluation of Baumgartner's data (1967) indicate that interception by forest stands generally equals about 15% of total annual precipitation. Other studies throughout the country and elsewhere show that interception in forested areas generally accounts for about 10–25% of the perennial supply (American Society of Civil Engineers, 1956; Houk, 1951; Horton, 1923; Kittredge, 1937; Butler, 1957), although many of these studies do not include interception by the forest litter. Thus, the roughly

13% interception value estimated for the Pine Barrens is in general agreement with data from other forested areas.

The 13% interception value represents an average annual water loss of about 15.0 cm (5.9 in). On each square kilometer of the Pine Barrens region, it amounts to a loss of about 409 m³/day or about 2.38 million m³/day for the 5828 km² Pine Barrens.

Evapotranspiration from Undrained Depressions

Approximately 2% of the Pine Barrens region is covered by relatively small, shallow, undrained depressions that have highly impermeable clayey (gley) layers beneath them. Here, precipitation is virtually trapped and held at the surface or in the root zone, where all of it eventually is evapotranspired. This undrained depression evapotranspiration loss, estimated to be 2% of the average annual precipitation or 2.3 cm (0.9 in), is 340,686 m³/day for the Pine Barrens region, an average of about 58.5 m³/day/km².

Evapotranspiration from Soil and Ground Water

The greatest single transfer of water as vapor from the Pine Barrens probably is by plant transpiration. Porous and mainly litter-covered sandy surfaces prevent large soil evaporation losses. The general lack of lakes, ponds, and nonvegetated wetlands indicates low total evaporation from open-water surfaces.

When average annual interception losses of 409 m³/day/km² and evapotranspiration losses of 58.5 m³/day/km² from undrained depressions are subtracted from the 1564 m³/day/km² overall evapotranspiration loss, there remains about 1096 m³/day/km² of evapotranspiration resulting from (a) soil and open-water evaporation and (b) plant transpiration taking water from the soil column and main ground-water body. Because the soil is sandy and open textured, and because the water table usually lies deeper than 0.6 m below the surface, direct evaporation losses from the main ground-water body are relatively small (Buckingham, 1907; Houk, 1951; Remson, 1962; Davis and DeWiest, 1966). Thus, plant transpiration most likely accounts for practically all of the 1096 m³/day/km² loss. The combined interception and undrained depression loss of 17.3 cm, when subtracted from the 57.2 cm of total long-term evapotranspiration losses, provides 39.9 cm (15.7 in) of water loss (about 6.4 million m³/day for the region) from soil moisture and ground water, an approximation of actual transpiration for the New Jersey Pine Barrens. It would seem to compare well with the average of 55.1 cm of *ET* observed by Lull and Axley (1958). The value is in good agreement with humid region values (American Society of Civil Engineers, 1957) and with the work by Wilm (1948), who reports that annual transpiration from a hardwood forest with dense shrub understory in western North Carolina was 48.3 cm. There, the annual precipitation is about 152–158 cm, compared with 114 cm in southern New Jersey; this may in part account for the larger transpiration value observed by Wilm.

Stream Runoff

As noted previously, water yield or stream runoff has two major components, direct runoff and base runoff (predominantly ground-water runoff). Precipitation falling directly on riparian lands creates direct runoff, particularly during the colder months of the nongrowing season, when both infiltration into saturated wetlands and evapotranspiration rates are low.

Most direct runoff from riparian areas occurs from December through April, when the Pine Barrens region normally receives about 43.8 cm (17.25 in) of precipitation. Because the riparian area occupies about 15% of the region, direct runoff is approximately 6.4 cm (2.5 in) or, on the average, about 175.4 m^3/day/km^2 or 1.02 million m^3/day for the 5828 km^2 contiguous Pine Barrens region.

Thus, an estimate of 50.8 cm (20.0 in) for the annual ground-water contribution to runoff can be arrived at by subtracting the computed 6.4 cm of annual direct runoff from the 57.2 cm of measured average annual runoff. Ground-water runoff is equal to about 1388 m^3/day/km^2 or 8.1 million m^3/day for the 5828 km^2 contiguous Pine Barrens region.

Since Pine Barrens streams carry only about 6% (6.4 cm) of the average annual precipitation as direct runoff, disastrous floods are uncommon events and usually occur during early spring months. Thus, ground-water discharge, which on the average constitutes 89% (50.8 cm) of the total annual discharge, gives streams a remarkably uniform flow (Hardison and Martin, 1963; Miller, 1966).

Water yields as determined from stream gauging are not uniform throughout the Pine Barrens region. Some small part of these differences is accounted for by variations in precipitation distribution and evapotranspiration. However, variations in water yield among streams with respect to time, amount, and areal distribution probably are the result of some ground-water bypassing certain local streams and discharging into more distant, lower-lying streams. An idealized flow pattern for ground water in the Pine Barrens region (Fig. 5) is based on models utilized by Back (1960) and Toth (1962a,b) and accounts for the variations in water yield in the Pine Barrens. Some recharge enters shallow local flow systems in the Cohansey Sand and the underlying upper sediments of the Kirkwood Formation and discharges to more distant streams at lower altitudes.

Most recharge to the deeper regional flow system probably is from precipitation on the upland areas lying above roughly 25 m elevation that occupy about 25% of the Pine

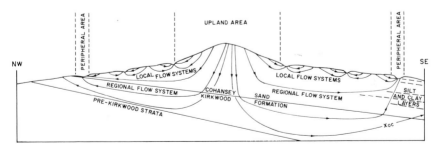

Fig. 5. Idealized section showing pattern of ground-water flow in the Pine Barrens region. Inner Coastal Plain lowlands are to the northwest and Atlantic coast to the southeast. The flow X_{oc} represents a small water volume discharged oceanward. (Modified from Rhodehamel, 1970.)

Barrens region. Discharge from this deep regional flow system, under topographic control (pressure head), generally appears to be to portions of streams intersecting the peripheral areas of the region. These discharges are enhanced by geological conditions at the perimeter of the Pine Barrens region. To the east, there is an increase in silt and clay content in the Cohansey Sand; to the south, the Kirkwood Formation (largely the Alloway Clay Member of Isphording and Lodding, 1969) becomes silty and clayey in the upper part; and to the north and west, the Cohansey Sand thins to a feather edge. These characteristics of the perimeter areas impede downward movement of aquifer water and force ground-water flow to the surface and the lower reaches of streams.

The quantity of water in the regional flow system within the Cohansey Sand and Kirkwood formations that recharges in the upland areas and discharges in the peripheral areas is unknown. The magnitude of that part of it that flows in the more permeable Cohansey Sand, however, can be estimated by use of the simplified form of the Darcy equation (Darcy, 1856), where the flow of ground water into the peripheral area equals the transmissivity of the aquifer times the hydraulic gradient times the circumference of the peripheral area.

The transmissivity of the Cohansey Sand in the peripheral area is estimated conservatively to be about 697 m^3/day based on an average thickness of saturated aquifer of 23 m and a hydraulic conductivity of about 30.5 m/day (Lang and Rhodehamel, 1963). An average hydraulic gradient is estimated to be about 0.93 m/km and a smooth line around the periphery of the Pine Barrens about 402 km.

The flow of water in the deep regional flow system in the Cohansey Sand discharging to streams in the peripheral area of the Pine Barrens region therefore is of the magnitude of 264,978 m^3/day. This is equivalent to about 1.8 cm of water per year from the entire Pine Barrens region, or 7.1 cm of water per year from the upland areas occupying 25% of the total Pine Barrens region. This constant water loss from many small upland area drainage basins to be gained later by the major and lower-lying drainage areas partly explains the often determined fact that small upland drainages have annual water yields several centimeters less than the large streams having the same general geological, vegetative, and climatic conditions.

Summary of Hydrological Budget

A long-term hydrological budget for the Pine Barrens relating water input (precipitation) to water yield (stream runoff) plus water loss (evapotranspiration) is shown in Table II and in the following equation: precipitation (114.3 cm) = interception (15.0 cm) + evapotranspiration from undrained depressions (2.3 cm) + evapotranspiration from soil and ground water (39.9 cm) + direct runoff (6.3 cm) + ground-water contribution to runoff (50.8 cm).

QUALITY OF GROUND WATER

Ground-water comes from precipitation that percolates through forest litter and enters a porous ground-water reservoir which is remarkably inert to chemical solution. As

TABLE II   Annual Hydrological Budget for the New Jersey Pine Barrens Region 1931–1964[a]

		Centimeters of water	Water $(m^3/day/km^2)$	Water $(m^3/day/5828\ km^2)$
Water input	Precipitation	114.3	3127	18,224,000
Water loss	Interception	15.0	409	2,384,000
	Evapotranspiration from undrained depressions	2.3	58.5	341,000
	Evapotranspiration from soil and ground water	39.9	1096	6,387,000
	Total water loss	57.2	1563.5	9,112,000
Water yield	Direct runoff	6.4	175.5	1,023,000
	Ground water contribution to runoff	50.8	1388	8,089,000
	Total water yield	57.2	1563.5	9,112,000

[a] Water input − water loss = water yield, or Precipitation = evapotranspiration + runoff. Pine Barrens region is approximately 5828 km².

ground water moves through the aquifer, it loses its dissolved oxygen and incorporates soluble ferrous iron ions; carbon dioxide is expended, the carbon dioxide–bicarbonate buffering system is altered, and the pH of the water eventually may be shifted to a slightly alkaline state.

When discharging from the principal aquifer to the lower reaches of the major river basins, the ground water may be classified broadly as a sodium–bicarbonate–chloride–sulfate type (U.S. Geological Survey, 1964–1966). When not contaminated by human activities, it contains high concentrations of iron, manganese (>0.3 mg/liter), dissolved carbon dioxide, and carbonic acid. The pH is low, ranging from 4.2–7.3, but most often <6.0. Iron concentrations generally range from 1–11 mg/liter, although concentrations as high as 49 mg/liter have been measured in areas where bog-iron deposits are forming owing to iron-fixing bacteria (Crerar *et al.*, 1979). Uncontaminated water is low in dissolved solids, ranging from 13–50 mg/liter, and hardness, mainly noncarbonate, is low, generally <40 mg/liter. The water has a rather uniform temperature (that approximates southern New Jersey's average annual air temperature) of about 12.2°C (54°F).

After aeration for iron removal and small additions of alkali for pH adjustment, water from the ground-water reservoir is of excellent quality, suitable for agriculture, domestic use, and most industrial uses. However, contaminants and pollutants will enter readily and move long distances in the ground-water reservoir.

Surface water is derived chiefly from ground-water contribution to discharge most of the time and hence is similar in chemical quality. The predominant ions in nontidal streams are sodium, chloride, and sulfate (U.S. Geological Survey, 1964–1966), although the amount of these and other dissolved substances is quite low. The water is clear throughout most of the nongrowing season, but during the growing season the characteristic tea color is formed by the complexing of iron compounds with organic exudates of riparian vegetation such as tannins. The iron in suspension, either as ferric hydroxide or complexed with the organic exudates, appears to increase with increased streamflow, perhaps because iron compounds entrapped in the large swamplands bordering the streams are flushed out into the streams during periods of precipitation. The influx of ground water having a temperature of about 12.2°C (54°F) generally prevents the streams from freezing bank to bank, even though winter air temperatures drop well below freezing. The salt water–freshwater interface in Pine Barrens streams, as defined by a sharp change in chloride concentrations, generally lies within 8–16 km upstream from the coast, although tidal effects extend farther upstream. Seasonal movement of salinity concentrations within the tidal reaches of Pine Barrens streams appears strongly and inversely related to the volume of streamflow, as shown by Durand *et al.* (1974) for the Mullica River. Hence, the salinity front moves upstream during the summer and fall low-flow periods and migrates downstream during the nongrowing season high-flow periods.

Relative to surface water, ground water is (a) higher in carbon dioxide, iron, and aluminum; (b) lower in sulfate and phosphate; and (c) less variable in pH, sodium, chloride, silica (SiO_2), color, and temperature. Substantial quantities of surface water may be developed for water supply from Pine Barrens streams, as suggested by Durand *et al.* (1974), but a number of water quality factors must be considered (Rhodehamel, 1970, 1973).

SUMMARY

The source of all water in the Pine Barrens is 114 cm (45 in) of average annual precipitation (3128 m^3/day/km^2). One-half of this water is lost by evapotranspiration. The remaining half enters the ground-water reservoir and may discharge directly to local streams or may move long distances at average rates as great as 40 to 50 m/year (130–160 ft/yr) to discharge many years later into the lower reaches of major Pine Barrens drainages. Thus, Pine Barrens streams vary widely in average annual runoff, from 36 to 84 cm of water (depth per unit area), and averaging about 57 cm. The water-table configuration is a subdued image of the land surface and slopes toward major rivers, varying in upland areas from 18.3 m (60 ft) deep to within centimeters of the surface. At a given site, it may fluctuate between extreme wet and dry periods by as much as 4 m (13 ft), or 3 m from spring to fall; average annual fluctuation in upland areas is 1.5 m (5 ft). The principal aquifer in the Pine Barrens is essentially a water-table reservoir lying in the upper Kirkwood–Cohansey Sand strata of Miocene age, with younger overlying deposits generally hydraulically connected. Lesser, poorly defined, deeper aquifers extend a few kilometers inland from the present coast. Because there is practically no overland flow, most streamflow is ground-water discharge from the principal aquifer. A long term hydrological budget for the Pine Barrens relating water input to water yield plus water loss is: precipitation (114.3 cm) = interception (15.0 cm) + evapotranspiration from undrained depressions (2.3 cm) + evapotranspiration from soil and ground water (39.9 cm) + direct runoff (6.3 cm) + ground-water runoff (50.8 cm).

REFERENCES

American Society of Civil Engineers (1957). Hydrology handbook. *ASCE Man. Rep. Eng. Pract.* No. 28.

Back, W. (1960). Origin of hydrochemical facies of ground water in the Atlantic Coastal Plain. *Internat. Geol. Congr., 21st, Rep. Sess. Norden,* Part 1, Copenhagen pp. 87–95.

Barksdale, H. C. (1952). Ground water in the New Jersey Pine Barrens area. *Bartonia* **26,** 36–38.

Barksdale, H. C., Greenman, D. W., Lang, S. M., Hilton, G. S., and Outlaw, D. E. (1958). Ground-water resources of the Tri-State region adjacent to the lower Delaware River. *N.J. Div. Water Policy Supply, Spec. Rep.* No. 13.

Baumgartner, A. (1967). Energetic bases for differential vaporization from forest and agricultural lands. *In* "Forest Hydrology" (W.E. Soper and H.W. Lull, eds.), pp. 381–389. Pergamon, New York.

Bernard, J. M. (1963). Forest floor moisture capacity of the New Jersey Pine Barrens. *Ecology* **44,** 574–576.

Biel, E. R. (1958). The climate of New Jersey. *In* "The Economy of New Jersey" (S. J. Flink, ed.), Rep., pp. 53–98. N.J. Dep. Conserv. Econ. Dev. Trenton, New Jersey.

Buckingham, E. (1907). Studies on movement of soil moisture. *U.S. Dep. Agric., Bur. Chem. Soil Bull.* No. 38.

Butler, S. E. (1957). "Engineering Hydrology." Prentice-Hall, Englewood Cliffs, New Jersey.

Cantlon, J. (1951). A preliminary investigation of the influence of prescribed burning on soil water supplies in south Jersey. *Proc. Am. Cranberry Grow. Assoc.* pp. 18–26.

Clark, G. A., Meisler, H., Rhodehamel, E. C., and Gill, H. E. (1968). Summary of ground-water resources of Atlantic County, New Jersey. *N.J. Div. Water Policy Supply, Water Resour. Circ.* No. 18, pp. 1–53.

Coman, C. W. (1892). Oak-land and pine-land belts and their relation to agriculture. *N.J. Geol. Surv., Annu. Rep. State Geol. 1891* pp. 111–140.

Crerar, D. A., Knox, G. W., and Means, J. L. (1979). Biogeochemistry of bog iron in the New Jersey Pine Barrens. *Chem. Geol.* **24,** 111–135.

Darcy, H. (1856). "Les Fontaines Publiques de la Ville de Dijon." V. Dalmont, Paris.

Davis, S. N., and DeWiest, R. J. M. (1966). "Hydrogeology." Wiley, New York.

Donsky, E. (1963). Records of wells and ground-water quality in Camden County, N.J. with special reference to public water supplies. *N.J. Div. Water Policy Supply, Water Resourc. Circ.* No. 10, pp. 1–70.

Durand, J. B., Grandstrom, N. L., and Nieswand, G. H. (1974). Water resources development in the Mullica River basin. *Water Resour. Bull.* **10**(2), 272–282.

Farlekas, G. M., Nemickas, B., and Gill, H. E. (1976). "Geology and Ground-Water Resources of Camden County, New Jersey," Water Resour. Invest. 76-76, 1–146. U.S. Geol. Surv., Reston, Virginia.

Hantush, M. S., and Jacob, C. E. (1955). Non-steady radial flow in an infinite leaky aquifer. *Trans., Am. Geophys. Union* **36**(1), 95–100.

Hardison, C. H., and Martin, R. O. R. (1963). Water-supply characteristics of streams in the Delaware River Basin and in Southern New Jersey. *U.S. Geol. Surv., Water-Supply Pap.* No. 1669-N, pp. 1–45.

Hardt, W. F., and Hilton, G. S. (1969). Water resources and geology of Gloucester County, New Jersey. *N.J. Div. Water Policy Supply, Spec. Rep.* No. 30, 130 pp.

Helvey, J. D., and Patric, J. H. (1965). Canopy and litter interception of rainfall by hardwoods of eastern United States. *Water Resourc. Res.* **1**(2), 193–206.

Hewlett, J. D. (1967). Summary of forests and precipitation session. *In* "Forest Hydrology" (W. E. Sopper and H. W. Lull, eds.), pp. 241–243. Pergamon, New York.

Horton, R. E. (1923). Transpiration of forest trees. *Mon. Weather Rev.* **51**, 571–581.

Houk, I. E. (1951). "Irrigation Engineering," Vol. 1. Wiley, New York.

Isphording, W. C., and Lodding, W. (1969). Facies changes in sediments of Miocene age in New Jersey. *In* "Geology of Selected Areas in New Jersey and Eastern Pennsylvania and Guidebook of Excursions" (S. Subitzky, ed.), pp. 7–13. Rutgers Univ. Press, New Brunswick, New Jersey.

Jacob, C. E. (1950). Flow of groundwater. *In* "Engineering Hydraulics" (H. Rouse, ed.), pp. 321–386. Wiley, New York.

Kittredge, J., Jr. (1937). Natural vegetation as a factor in the losses and yields of waters. *J. For.* **35**, 1011–1115.

Knoerr, K. R. (1967). Contrasts in energy balances between individual leaves and vegetated surfaces. *In* "Forest Hydrology" (W. E. Sopper and H.W. Lull, eds.), pp. 391–401. Pergamon, New York.

Lang, S. M. (1961). Natural movement of ground water at a site on the Mullica River in the Wharton Tract, southern New Jersey. *U.S. Geol. Surv., Prof. Pap.* No. 424-D, pp. D52–D54.

Lang, S. M., and Rhodehamel, E. C. (1962). Movement of ground water beneath the bed of the Mullica River in the Wharton Tract, southern New Jersey. *U.S. Geol. Surv., Prof. Pap.* No. 450-B, pp. B90–B91.

Lang, S. M., and Rhodehamel, E. C. (1963). Aquifer test at a site on the Mullica River in the Wharton Tract, Southern New Jersey. *Internat. Assoc. Sci. Hydrol. Bull.* **8**(2), 31–38.

Laskowski, S. L. (1970). Statistical summaries of New Jersey streamflow records. *N.J. Div. Water Policy Supply, Water Resour. Circ.* No. 23, pp. 1–264.

Leonard, R. E. (1961). Interception of precipitation by northern hardwoods. *U.S. For. Serv., Northeast. For. Exp. Stn., Stn. Pap.* No. 159, pp. 1–16.

Leopold, L. B., and Langbein, W. D. (1960). A primer on water. *U.S. Geol. Surv., Spec. Circ.*, pp. 1–50.

Lull, H. W., and Axley, J. H. (1958). Forest soil-moisture relations in the Coastal Plain sands of southern New Jersey. *For. Sci.* **4**, 2–19.

Miller, E. G. (1966). Flow probability of New Jersey Streams. *N.J. Div. Water Policy Supply, Water Resourc. Circ.* No. 15, pp. 1–61.

Miller, E. G., and McCall, J. E. (1961). New Jersey streamflow records analyzed with electronic computer. *N.J. Div. Water Policy Supply, Water Resourc. Circ.* No. 6, pp. 1–89.

Monroe, W. H., and Pentz, M. A. (1936). Availability of shallow ground-water supplies in parts of the Atlantic Coastal Plain, with special reference to their use in forest fires. U.S. Geol. Surv., Reston, Virginia. (Unpublished manuscript.)

Moul, E. T., and Buell, M. F. (1955). Moss cover and rainfall interception in frequently burned sites in the New Jersey Pine Barrens. *Bull. Torrey Bot. Club* **82**, 155–162.

Nace, R. L. (1969). Ground water: Perspectives and prospects. *Water Well J.* **23**, 28–29.

Nace, R. L. (1970). World hydrology: Status and prospects. *Internat. Assoc. Sci. Hydrol. Symp. Proc., Reading, Eng.* World Water Balance, Pap. No. 92, pp. 1–10.

Owens, J. P., and Minard, J. P. (1975). "Geologic Map of the Surficial Deposits in the Trenton Area, New Jersey and Pennsylvania," Misc. Invest. Map Ser. I, 1–884. U.S. Geol. Surv., Reston, Virginia.

Owens, J. P., and Sohl, N. F. (1969). Shelf and deltaic paleoenvironments in the Cretaceous–Tertiary formations of the New Jersey Coastal Plain. *In* "Geology of Selected Areas in New Jersey and Eastern Pennsylvania and Guidebook of Excursions" (S. Subitsky, ed.), pp. 235–278. Rutgers Univ. Press, New Brunswick, New Jersey.

Penman, H. L. (1956). Estimating evaporation. *Trans., Am. Geophys. Union* **37**, 43–46.

Rachele, L. D. (1976). Palynology of the Ledger lignite: A deposit in the Tertiary Cohansey formation of New Jersey, U.S.A. *Rev. Paleobot. Palynol.* **22**, 225–252.

Ramsahoye, L. E., and Lang, S. M. (1961). A simple method for determining specific yield from pumping tests. *U.S. Geol. Surv. Water-Supply Pap.* No. 1472, pp. 83–92.

Remson, I. (1962). Review of some elements of soil-moisture theory. *U.S. Geol. Surv., Prof. Pap.* No. 411-D, pp. D1–D38.

Rhodehamel, E. C. (1970). A hydrologic analysis of the New Jersey Pine Barrens region. *N.J. Div. Water Policy Supply, Water Resour. Circ.* No. 22, pp. 1–35.

Rhodehamel, E. C. (1973). Geology and water resources of the Wharton Tract and the Mullica River basin in southern New Jersey. *N.J. Div. Water Resour., Spec. Rep.* No. 36, pp. 1–58.

Rhodehamel, E. C., and Lang, S. M. (1962). Winter ground-water temperatures along the Mullica River, Wharton Tract, New Jersey. *U.S. Geol. Surv., Prof. Pap.* No. 450-D, pp. D165–D168.

Rutter, A. J. (1967). An analysis of evaporation from a stand of Scots pine. *In* "Forest Hydrology" (W. E. Sopper and H. W. Lull, eds.), pp. 403–417. Pergamon, New York.

Searcy, J. K. (1959). Flow-duration curves. *U.S. Geol. Surv., Water Supply Pap.* No. 1542-A, pp. 1–33.

Theim, G. (1906). "Hydrologische Methoden." J. M. Gebhardt, Leipzig.

Theis, C. V. (1935). The relation between the lowering of the piezometric surface and the rate and duration of discharge of a well using ground-water storage. *Trans., Am. Geophys. Union 16th Annu. Mtg.,* Part 2, 519–524.

Thomas, D. M. (1964). Floods in New Jersey magnitude and frequency. *N.J. Div. Water Policy Supply, Water Resour. Circ.* No. 13, pp. 1–145.

Toth J. (1962a). A theory of groundwater motion in small drainage basins in central Alberta, Canada. *J. Geophys. Res.* **67**, 4375–4387.

Toth, J. (1962b). A theoretical analysis of groundwater flow in small drainage basins. *Proc. Hydrol. Symp., No. 3, Ground-Water, Univ. Alberta* pp. 75–96.

U.S. Department of Agriculture (1955). "Water." U.S. Dep. Agric. Yearb., Washington, D.C.

U.S. Geological Survey (1964–1966). "Water Resources Data for New Jersey. Part 2. Water Quality Records" (Issued annually). N.J. Water Resour. Div., Trenton, New Jersey.

U.S. Geological Survey (1967). National Atlas—"Monthly Sunshine Chart I-67," pp. 94–95. U.S. Geol. Surv., Reston, Virginia.

U.S. Geological Survey (1976). Surface water supply of the United States, 1966–70. Part I. North Atlantic Slope basins. Vol. 2. Basins from New York to Delaware. *U.S. Geol. Surv., Water Supply Pap.* No. 2102, pp. 1–985.

van Bavel, C. H. M. (1957). Estimating soil moisture conditions and time for irrigation with the evapotranspiration method. *U.S. Dep. Agric. Soil Conserv. Serv., Misc. Publ.* ARS 41-11, pp. 1–16.

Vermeule, C. C. (1892). Water-supply and water-power. *N.J. Geol. Surv., Annu. Rep. State Geol. 1891* pp. 141–215.

Vermeule, C. C. (1893). Water-supply and water-power. *N.J. Geol. Surv., Annu. Rep., State Geol. 1892* pp. 247–272.

Vermeule, C. C. (1894a). Water-supply and water-power. *N.J. Geol. Surv., Annu. Rep. State Geol. 1893* pp. 371–385.

Vermeule, C. C. (1894b). "Report on Water-Supply, Water-Power, the Flow of Streams and Attendant Phenomena," Final Rep. Ser., Vol. 3, pp. 1–352 and appendix 1–96. N.J. State Geol., Trenton New Jersey.

Vermeule, C. C. (1899). The pine belt of southern New Jersey and water-supply. *N.J. Geol. Surv., Annu. Rep. State Geol. 1898* pp. 183–193.

Vermeule, C. C. (1900). The forests of New Jersey. *N.J. Geol. Surv., Annu. Rep. State Geol. 1899* pp. 13–166.

Wilm, H. G. (1948). Report of the committee on evaporation and transpiration 1946–1947. *Trans., Am. Geophys. Union,* **29**, 258–262.

Wood, O. M. (1937). The interception of precipitation in an oak–pine forest. *Ecology* **18**, 251–254.

Woolman, L. (1889–1902). (Consecutive reports dealing with artesian wells and water-bearing horizons of New Jersey, presented annually.) *N.J. Geol. Surv., Annu. Rep. State Geol. 1889–1902.*

Zinke, P. J. (1967). Forest interception studies in the United States. *In* "Forest Hydrology" (W. E. Sopper and H. W. Lull, eds.), pp. 137–161. Pergamon, New York.

10

Streams and Lakes in the Pine Barrens

RUTH PATRICK, BARBARA MATSON, AND LEE ANDERSON

INTRODUCTION

Streams, lakes, and bogs are the main surface waters of the Pine Barrens (Fig. 1). The streams are of two types, namely, those which form the headwaters of larger systems that lie mostly outside the Pine Barrens and those streams whose complete river basins are within the Pine Barrens.

Since the Pine Barrens have a very low topographic gradient, the streams are usually slow flowing. They flow through sand and gravel, which constitute an unconsolidated substrate. For the most part, the large Cohansey Formation underlies these streams. This formation covers an area of about 475,000 hectares (1.2 million acres), and in many places this aquifer is estimated to be 11 m (37 ft) deep (U.S. Department of Interior, 1976). This formation is seldom more than 6 m (20 ft) below the surface. As a result, it influences the surface waters greatly, so that in summer the temperatures are relatively cool, generally 25°C, and in winter waters rarely freeze.

These river basin systems include white cedar swamps (*Chamaecyparis thyoides*) and *Sphagnum* and cranberry bogs that drain into the stream channels. Scattered throughout many of the river systems are man-made lakes, formed by the damming of streams. McCormick (1970), Thomas (1967), Conant (1962), and Fairbrothers and Moul (1955) provide recent useful perspectives of the Pine Barrens.

The literature on the fauna and flora and on the chemical composition of surface water of the Pine Barrens is very scattered and varies considerably in technical detail. In this chapter, we have attempted to bring together much of this literature and to summarize the known data.

The biological data summarized are for fish (Table I), insects (Table II), and diatoms and other algae (Table III). In some papers, such as Stokes' work on protozoa (Stokes, 1884, 1885a,b, 1886a,b), no specific collection locations in New Jersey were given for a species; therefore, these are excluded. The records included pertain to those areas definitely within the New Jersey Pine Barrens (Fig. 1). Some watersheds lie partially within and partially outside the New Jersey Pine Barrens (Fig. 1); records for these watersheds are only for the Pine Barrens portion. The biological data that are in-

169

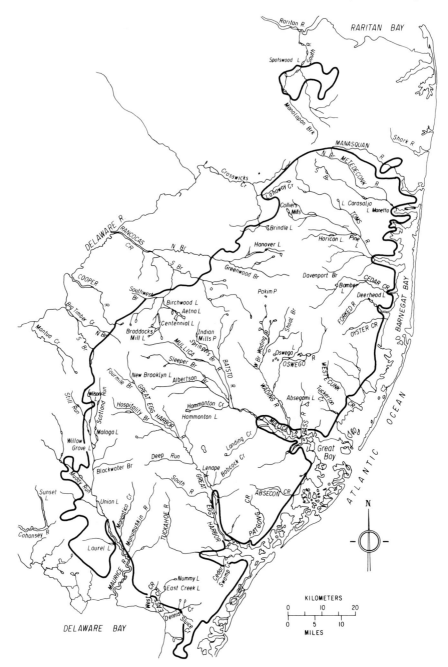

Fig. 1. Major rivers, streams, lakes, and ponds of the New Jersey Pine Barrens. R, river; Cr, creek; Br, branch; Brk, brook; L, lake; P, pond.

TABLE I Fish of the Pine Barrens River Basins.[a]

Anguilliformes
  Anguilla chrisypa (American eel)—A*, C*, D, D*, F, F*, I, I*, L, L*, M, O, O*, P*, Q, Q*, S
Atheriniformes
  Fundulus diaphanus (freshwater killifish)— D*, N, P*, Q*
  Fundulus heteroclitus macrolepidotus (saltwater killifish)—P*, Q*
  Tylosorus marinus (green gar)—N
Culperformes
  Alosa sapidissima (shad)—B, C, P
  Anchovia mitchelli (common anchovy)—M*
  Pomolobus pseudoharengus (alewife)—L, M*, Q*
Cypriniformes
  Catostomus commersonnii (common sucker)—A*, B, C*, I, M, N, O, P*, Q*, S
  Cyprinus carpio (carp)—Q*
  Erimyzon sucetta oblongus (chub sucker)—A*, C*, D, D*, I, I*, K, L, L*, M, O*, P, P*, Q*, S, S*
  Lucania parva (rainwater fish)—E
  Notropis chalybaeus (iron-colored shiner)—I, L*, P, P*, Q*, S
  N. hudsonius amarus (spot-tailed shiner)—Q*
  Schilbeodes gyrinus (tadpole madtom)—C*, L, P*, Q*, S*
  Semotilus atromaculatus (creek chub)—N
  S. bullaris (fallfish)—L, M, N, S
Gasterosteiformes
  Apeltes quadracus (three-spined stickleback)—F, K, N
  Gasterosteus aculeatus (two-spined stickleback)—F
Perciformes
  Acantharchus pomotis (mud sunfish)—A*, C*, D*, F, F*, I*, L, L*, M, N, O, O*, P, P*, S, S*, T*
  Ambloplites rupestris (red-eyed bass)—I
  Aphredoderus sayanus (pirate perch)—C*, D*, F*, I, I*, L, L*, N, O*, P*, S, S*, T*
  Bairdiella chrysura (silver perch)—F
  Boleichthys fusiformis (fusiform darter)—A*, C*, D*, F*, I, I*, L, L*, O*, P*, Q*, S, S*, T*
  Boleosoma nigrum olmstedi (tessellated darter)—M, S
  Brama crysoleucas (roach)—A*, C*, D*, I*, L, L*, M, O, O*, Q*, S, S*
  Cynoscion regalis (weakfish)—F
  Enneacanthus gloriosus (blue-spotted sunfish)—A*, D*, F, I, I*, L, L*, M, O, P, P*, Q*, S, S*,
  E. obesus (sphagnum sunfish)—A*, C*, D*, F*, I, I*, L*, N, O*, P*, S*, T*
  Lepomis auritus (red-breasted sunfish)—I*, N, P*, Q*, S
  L. gibbosus (pumpkinseed sunfish)—A*, C*, D*, I*, M, N, O, O*, P*, Q*, R, S, S*
  L. macrochirus (bluegill sunfish)—C*, I*, P*, Q*, S*
  Menticirrhus saxatilis (kingfish)—M
  Mesogonistius chaetodon (banded sunfish)—D*, I, I*, L, L*, M, N, O, O*, P*, S, S*, T*
  Micropogon undulatus (croaker)—I
  Micropterus dolomieu (smallmouth bass)—O
  M. salmoides (largemouth bass)—A*, C*, D*, M, O*, P*, Q, Q*, S*
  Morone americana (white perch)—B, D, I, L, M, N, O, P*
  Perca flavescens (yellow perch)—A*, C*, D*, I*, L, M, O, O*, P*, Q, Q*, S*
  Pomoxis sparoides (calico bass)—A*, C*, I*, P*, Q, Q*, S*
  Roccus lineatus (striped bass)—C, D, I, P*
Petromyzontiformes
  Entosphenus aepypterus (brook lamprey)—Q
Salmoniformes
  Esox americanus (banded pickerel)—A*, D*, I, L, L*, M, O*, P, Q
  E. lucius (great northern pike)—P*
  E. reticulatus (chain pickerel)—A*, C, C*, D, D*, F, F*, I, I*, L, L*, M, N, O, O*, P, P*, Q*, S, S*, T
  Salmo fario (brown trout)—I*
  S. gairdneri (rainbow trout)—I*
  Salvelinus fontinalis (brook trout)—I, I*, P, R, S
  Umbra pygmaea (mud minnow)—A*, D*, E, F, F*, I, I*, L, L*, N, O, O*, P, P*, Q, S, S*
Siluriformes
  Ameiurus catus (white catfish)—M, N, O, O*, P*
  A. natalis prosthistius (northern yellow bullhead)—D*, F*, I, I*, L, L*, M, N, O*, P*, Q, Q*, S, S*, T*
  A. nebulosus (northern brown bullhead)—A*, B, C*, D*, I*, L, L*, M, N, O, O*, P*, Q*, S*

---

[a] Key to major river basins: A, Raritan River (N); B, Manasquan River (E); C, Metedeconk River (E); D, Toms River (E+); E, Cedar Creek (E); F, Forked River (E); G, Oyster Creek (E); H, Westecunk Creek (E); I, Mullica River (E+); J, Absecon Creek (E); K, Patgong Creek (E); L, Great Egg Harbor River (E+); M, Tuckahoe River (E); N, Cedar Swamp Creek (E); O, Dennis Creek (S); P, Maurice River (S+); Q, Big Timber Creek (W); R, Cooper River (W); S, Rancocas Creek (W+); T, Crosswicks Creek (W). N, E, S, and W in parentheses are general directions rivers flow; + indicates a major river basin in terms of area in the Pine Barrens. All records refer to rivers or streams except those marked with an asterisk (*) which are from lakes or ponds.

171

TABLE II Insects of the Pine Barrens River Basins.[a]

Odonata
Aeschna umbrosa—Q
Amphagrion saucium—A, P, Q, T
Anax longipes—E, Q
Argia apicalis—Q
A. bipunctulata—D, L, P, Q, S
A. tibialis—E, L, S
Basiaeschna janata—D, S
Boyeria vinosa—D, E, Q
Calopteryx apicalis—D, E, L, P, S
Celithemis fasciata—L, P, Q
C. ornata—D, I, L, Q
Chromagrion conditum—C, P, S
Cordulegaster masculatus—D, E
Dorocordulia lepida—A, D, P, S
Enallagma aspersum—I, L, P, Q
E. divagans—P
E. doubledayi—L
E. durum—D, K, N
E. exsulsans—A, P
E. geminatum—A, L, P, Q
E. traviatum—Q
Geranomyia rostrata—Q
Gomphaeschna furcillata—D, L, P, S
G. furcillata var. antilope—Q
Gomphus albistylus—Q
G. brevis—S
G. plagiatus—P
G. sordidus—Q
Hagenius brevistylus—E, L, S
Helocordulia uhleri—P, S
Hetaerina americana—E
Ischnura kellotti—I*, K, O, P, Q
Lestes unguicalatus—I, L, Q
Leucorrhinia intacta—Q
Libellula axillena—Q
L. axillena var. vibrans—Q
L. cyanea—A, M, P
L. flavida—D, S
L. quadrimaculata—A, L
Macromia illinoisensis—E, S
Nannothemis bella—D, L, P, Q
Nehalennia gracilis—I, P
N. integricollis—P
N. irene—C, L, S
Pantala flavescens—Q
Progomphus obscurus—D, E, S
Sympetrum albifrons—M, P
Telagrion daeckii—P
Tetragoneuria cynosura—D, Q
T. semiaquea—D, P, Q
T. spinosa—P, Q

Ephemeroptera
Leptophlebia cupida—A, T
Plecoptera
Leuctra ferruginea—T
Coleoptera
Creniphilus despectus—D
C. digestus—D
Cryptopleurum minutum—L
Cymbiodyta rotundata—D
Dineutes carolinus—I
D. emarginatus—A, L, Q
D. nigrior—A, D, Q, T
Gyrinus analis—I, L, Q
G. aquiris—A
G. borealis—A, I, T
G. dichorus—D
G. fraternus—A
G. gibber—A
G. limbatus—A, I, L
G. lugens—A, L
G. minutus—L
G. opacus—A
G. pernitidus—D
G. picipes—A, D, L
G. rockinghamensis—C, D, L
G. ventralis—A
Helochares consors—D
H. maculicollis—A
H. ochraceus—D, T
Helocombus bifidus—D
Helophorus lineatus—D
H. tuberculatus—A
Hydraena pennsylvanica—N
Hydrobius fuscipes—D
H. tessellatus—A, D, Q
Hydrochus scabratus—A, D
H. squamifer—L
Hydrous ovatus—C
Laccobius agilis—A, D
Limnebius piceus—A
Lepidoptera
Cercyonis analis—T
Trichoptera
Beraea nigritta—Q
Chilostigma difficilis—T
Hydropsyche analis—T
Limnephilus submonifer—T
Limnophila contemota—D
Neuronia angustipennis—A
N. ocellifera—A
N. postica—T
Platycentropus maculipennis—A

Plectronemia confusus—A, T
Pycnopsyche scabripennis—D
Diptera
Bittacomorpha clavipes—A, L, T
B. jonesi—Q
Ceratopogon piceus—Q
Chironomus cristatus—Q
C. dispar—Q
C. fascipennis—Q
C. ornata—Q
C. pedellus—Q
C. tendens—Q
C. zonopterus—Q
Dicranomyia haeretica—A
D. immodesta—Q
D. liberata—A
D. liberta—Q
Epiphragma fascipennis—Q
Geranomyia distincta—P
Goniomyia cognatella—Q
Limnobia triocellata—Q
Megarhina (Rhamphidia) flavipes—Q
Molophilus ursinus—Q
Oropeza (Dolichopeza) subalpipes—Q
Pachyrhina collaris—Q
P. eucera—L
P. tenuis—P
Palpomyia rufus—L, Q
P. trivalis—Q, S
Procladius (Protenthes) culiciformis—T
Ptychoptera rufocincta—Q
Rhipidia domestica—Q
Simulium bracteatum—Q
S. invenustum—P, Q
S. venustum—Q
Tanypus dyari—Q
T. melanops—Q
Tipula bella—Q
T. caloptera—P
T. cincta—P
T. costalis—Q
T. dejecta—Q
T. fasciata—A, Q
T. flavicans—P
T. longiventris—P, Q
T. tricolor—A, Q
Tricyphona (Amalopis) inconstans—Q
T. vernalis—Q

[a] Letters refer to river basins of Table I. All records, except as indicated with an asterisk (*) for a lake, refer to streams and rivers.

TABLE III   Diatoms and Other Algae of the Pine Barrens River Basins.[a]

A. DIATOMS
  Fragilariaceae
  Asterionella bleakeleyi—L
  A. formosa—S*
  A. inflata—L
  A. ralfsii—I, S*
  A. ralfsii var. *americana*—S*
  Diatoma vulgare—S*
  Fragilaria bicapitata—S*
  F. brevistriata—S*
  F. constricta—S*
  F. construens—S*
  F. vaucheriae—S*
  F. virescens—S*
  Licmorpha abbreviata—S*
  Semiorbis hemicyclus—I*
  Synedra famelica—S*
  S. fasciculata—S*
  S. fasciculata var. *parva*—S*
  S. fasciculata var. *truncata*—S*
  S. radians—S*
  S. rumpens—S*
  S. rumpens var. *meneghiniana*—S*
  S. ulva—R
  S. ulva var. *subaequalis*—R
  Tabellaria fenestrata—S*
  T. flocculosa—S*
  Thalassionema nitzschioides—S*
  Eunotiaceae
  Actinella punctata—D, I*, L, S*
  Desmogonium rabenhorstianum var. *elongatum*—S*
  Eunotia arcus—S*
  E. biceps—L
  E. bidentula—L
  E. curvata—S*
  E. diodon—I*
  E. elegans—S*
  E. fallax—S*
  E. flexuosa—S*
  E. gibbosa—S*
  E. glacialis—I*
  E. incisa—S*
  E. major—D
  E. monodon—S*
  E. naegellii—I*, S*
  E. obesa var. *wardii*—S*
  E. pectinalis—I
  E. pectinalis var. *minor*—S*
  E. pectinalis var. *undulata*—I
  E. pectinalis var. *ventricosa*—L, S*
  E. perpusilla—S*
  E. praerupta—S*
  E. robusta—I*
  E. serra—S*
  E. sudetica—S*
  E. tenella—S*
  E. vanheurckii var. *intermedia*—S*
  Achnanthaceae
  Achnanthes clevei var. *rostrata*—S*
  A. exigua var. *heterovalvata*—S*
  A. flexella—S*

A. hauckiana—S*
A. lanceolata—S*
A. lanceolata var. *dubia*—S*
A. minutissima—S*
A. wellsiae—S*
Cocconeis pediculus—S*
C. placentula var. *euglypta*—S*
C. placentula var. *lineata*—S*
Rhoicosphenia curvata—S*
R. curvata forma *minor*—S*
  Naviculaceae
Amphipleura rutilans var. 1CB—S*
Anomoeoneis serians—S*
A. serians var. *brachysira*—S*
A. vitrea—S*
Caloneis hyalina—S*
Capartogramma crucicula—S*
Diploneis ovalis—S*
Frustulia rhomboides—I*, J, S*
Gyrosigma nodiferum—S*
Navicula aikenensis—S*
N. bacillum—S*
N. biconica—S*
N. capitata—S*
N. cocconeiformis—S*
N. confervacea—S
N. contenta forma *biceps*—S*
N. cryptocephala—S*
N. cuspidata—L
N. decussis—S*
N. dicephala—S*
N. diserta—S*
N. erythraea—L
N. exigua—S*
N. expansa—S*
N. gastrum—R*
N. humerosa—B, J
N. luzonensis—S*
N. minima—S*
N. mutica—S*
N. mutica var. *cohnii*—S*
N. mutica var. *stigma*—S*
N. oculata—B
N. palpebralis—B
N. peregrina—J
N. punctata—J
N. pupula—S*
N. pygmaea—S*
N. radiosa—S*
N. radiosa var. *parva*—S*
N. radiosa var. *tenella*—S*
N. rhombica—I*
N. salinicola—S*
N. schultzei—L
N. scopulorum—S*
N. secreta var. *apiculata*—S*
N. seminulum—S*
N. tenelloides—S*
N. tripunctata var. *schizonemoides*—S*
N. tumida—J
N. viridula—S*

(continued)

TABLE III   (*continued*)

N. vulpina—J	G. intricatum—S*
Neidium affine—S*	G. parvulum—S*
N. apiculatum—S*	Bacillariaceae
N. dilatum—I*	Bacillaria paradoxa—S*
N. dubium forma constrictum—S*	Nitzschia acicularis—S*
N. hitchcockii—R*	N. amphibia—S*
N. iridis var. amphigomphus—I	N. angusta—S*
N. productum—R*	N. clausii—S*
Pinnularia abaujensis—S*	N. filiformis—S*
P. abaujensis var. rostrata—S*	N. fonticola—S*
P. abaujensis var. subundulata—S*	N. frustulum—S*
P. biceps—S*	N. frustulum var. perminuta—S*
P. bihastata—R*	N. gracilis—S*
P. borealis—S*	N. kutzingiana—S*
P. dactylus var. dariana—J	N. linearis—S*
P. gibba—I*	N. obtusa—S*
P. interrupta—S*	N. palea—S*
P. major—I*, S	N. parvula—S*
P. major var. pulchella—I*	N. sigma—S*
P. microstauron—S*	Surirellaceae
P. nodosa—R*	Surirella delicatissima—S*
P. parvula—I	S. ovalis—S*
P. stauroptera—I	S. ovata—S*
P. subcapitata—S*	S. tenera—S*
P. substomatophora—S*	Coscinodiscaceae
P. viridis—J	Coscinodiscus lineatus—S*
P. viridis var. commutata—I	C. marginatus—S*
Stauroneis anceps—I*	C. pygmaea var. micropunctata—S*
S. anceps forma gracilis—S*	Cyclotella atomus—S*
S. phoenicenteron—S*	C. caspia—S*
Amphiphoraceae	C. comta—S*
Amphiphora alata—S*	C. kutzingiana—S*
A. ornata—S*	C. meneghiniana—S*
Cymbellaceae	C. pseudostelligera—S*
Amphora coffeiformis—S*	C. stelligera—S*
A. delicatula—S*	C. striata—S*
A. ovalis—S*	Melosira ambigua—S*
A. submontana—S*	M. distans var. lacustris forma lirata—S*
A. tenuissima—S*	M. granulata—S*
A. tumida—S*	M. granulata var. angustissima—S*
Cymbella gracile—S*	M. sulcata forma coronata—S*
C. naviculiformis—S*	M. sulcata forma radiata—S*
C. sinuata—S*	M. varians—S*
C. tumida—S*	Stephanodiscus astraea var. minutula—S*
C. ventricosa—S*	S. invisitatus—S*
Gomphonemaceae	Thalassiosira nitzschioides—S*
Gomphonema constrictum var. capitata—S*	Biddulphiaceae
G. gracile—S*	Biddulphia laevis—S*

(*continued*)

TABLE III *(continued)*

B. OTHER ALGAE	*Euastrum attenuatum*—P*
Cyanophyta	*E. binale* var. *majus*—P*
Anabaena flos-aquae var. *aestuarii*—O	*E. crassum* var. *depressum*—P*
Hapalsiphon brebissonii—O	*E. cuspidatum*—J*
H. tenuissimus—O	*E. inerme* var. *depressum* (var. *scrobiculatum*?)—P*
Lyngbya aestuarii—J*, O	*E. intermedium*—O
Microcoleus anguiformis—I*	*E. formosum*—D*
M. lacustris—I, I*	*E. magnificum*—P*
M. pulvinatus—E, I	*E. purum*—S
Sirosiphon coralloides—E*	*Hyalotheca undulata*—S
Chlorophyta (Chlorococcales)	*Micrasterias dichotma*—P*
Arthrodesmus fragilis—I	*M. fimbriata* var. *apiculata*—I
A. rauii—P*	*M. papillifera*—I
Chlorophyta (Oedogoniales)	*Penium clevei*—S
Bulbochaete brebissonii—I*	*Phymatodocis nordstetianum*—S
B. setigera—I, I*	*Sphaerozosma secedens*—S
Oedogonium ciliatum—I, I*	*Spirogyra punctata*—I
O. flavescens—I	*Staurastrum ankyroides*—P*
O. polymorphum—S	*S. aspinosum*—S
Chlorophyta (Zygnematales)	*S. divarticum*—I*
Bambusina delicatissima—I*	*S. elongatum* var. *tetragonium*—S
Closterium decorum—I*	*S. forficulatum* forma *tetragona*—S
C. ralfsii—I*	*S. inconspicuum*—S, I*
Cosmarium kitchelli—I*	*S. iotomum*—P*
C. pseudotoxichondrum—S	*S. leptacanthum* var. *tetractocerum*—P*
C. sejinctum—P*	*S. pulchrum*—S
C. sportella—P*	*S. quaternium*—P*
Desmidium elongatum—S	*Xanthidium torreyi*—D*
D. quadratum—S	Rhodophyta
Docidium dilatum—I*, S	*Batrachosperum vagum*—I*
D. spinulosum—O	*B.* sp.—I
D. tridentulum—I*, S	*Chantransia macrospora*—I*

a Letters refer to stream basins shown in Table I. All records refer to rivers or streams except those marked with an asterisk (*) which are from lakes and ponds.

cluded concern organisms that spend most of their life in water, and as far as we know, pertain to the under-water stages of the organisms.

Chemical and bacteriological data are summarized for the rivers and streams (Table IV) and the lakes and ponds (Tables V and VI) of the Pine Barrens. These data are derived mostly from the 1975 water year (U.S. Geological Survey, 1976) and from studies made by the Limnology Department of the Academy of Natural Sciences (1973). It would be beyond the scope of this chapter to summarize the chemistry for all water years. Since the biological data usually are not taken at the same times as the chemical analyses, only general relationships between the two can be drawn.

Following the data presentation of Tables I–VI, each of the twenty river basins for which there are data is reviewed briefly. Some general biological and chemical characteristics of streams and lakes in the Pine Barrens are discussed subsequently.

TABLE IV Chemical and bacteriological data for the Water Year 1975 for rivers and streams of the Pine Barrens.[a]

River or Stream[b]	Instantaneous discharge (cfs)	Temperature (°C)	Specific conductance (micromhos)	pH (units)	Dissolved oxygen (mg/l)	Biochemical oxygen demand 5-day (mg/l)	Immediate coliform (col./100 ml)	Fecal coliform (EC broth mpn)	Fecal coliform (col. per 100 ml)	Streptococci (colonies/100 ml)	Turbidity (Jackson turbidity units)	Color (platinum-cobalt units)
(A) Manalapan Brk[c]	31-180	8.0-23.2	86-129	4.8-9.1	6.3-11.5	0.8-2.6	200-1020	<2->2400	0-816	4-270	4-30	4-30
(B) Manasquan R[d]	45-93	5.8-19.2	177-249	6.7-8.8	6.3-10.8	2.3-16	605-3300	330-2400	80-680	120-680	2-20	7-23
(D) Toms R[e]	110-435	1.2-23.2	57-72	3.9-6.4	6.7-12.4	0.7-8.0	4-14700	5-540	0-700	10-784	1-5	20-230
(G) Oyster Cr[f]	20-80	5.1-18.5	37-61	3.9-4.7	7.6-10.0	0.0-1.2	110-268	2-920	0-302	92-184	1-2	3-40
(L) GEHR Berlin[g]	—	18.0-24.4	161-214	5.7-6.3	3.0-10.0	0.8-8.2	—	20->2400	420-3800	—	5-25	2-35
(L) GEHR Sicklerville[h]	—	1.0-23.0	49-130	4.4-6.7	3.0-9.8	0.7-7.1	256-6700	4-230	2-170	10-560	—	—
(L) GEHR Tributary #1[i]	.30-6.9	2.0-30.0	42-156	5.9-8.2	6.0-13.4	1.5-8.6	188-1320	<20-920	10-876	20-2080	—	—
(L) GEHR Winslow Crosg	—	1.0-14.5	76-88	4.9-7.4	7.8-12.9	0.5-5.1	75-1100	—	4-50	40-85	—	—
(L) New Brooklyn Lake[j]	—	9.0-26.0	41-82	4.5-6.1	3.2-13.7	1.5-5.8	520	<20-490	16-640	24-1520	—	—
(L) East Storm Drain[k]	—	25.5	196	6.5	4.4	2.4	—	790	600	940	—	—
(L) GEHR Tributary #2[l]	—	1.0-26.1	140-681	5.8-8.1	6.8-13.0	0.2-8.4	60-1600	5-920	0-450	12-600	—	—
(L) Fourmile Branch[m]	—	4.4-21.0	45-143	3.0-5.8	6.2-11.4	0.1-4.8	480-1560	9-540	0-720	20-2100	—	—
(L) Fourmile Branch[n]	6.8-34	3.8-22.0	48-104	3.7-5.9	5.0-12.4	0.1-5.4	36-1680	<5-220	<5-220	24-1100	—	—
(L) GEHR Blue Anchor[o]	—	1.3-22.5	50-90	3.4-6.6	4.8-12.0	0.2-5.0	88-1020	8->2400	0-300	16-772	—	—
(L) Squankum Branch[p]	32-312	17.5-20.7	188-432	5.7-7.0	.8-5.8	6.3-16	—	27->2400	90-7800	—	5-27	10-60
(L) GEHR Folsom[q]	48-338	5.4-23.0	71-116	4.2-6.9	5.8-10.8	0.0-2.9	175-1240	23->2400	0-800	0-104	5-10	1-270
(L) Hospitality Branch[r]	—	20.5-23.1	46-46	4.8-6.0	6.7-8.7	0.8-2.0	—	240-920	54-540	—	2-12	25-75
(L) Hospitality Branch[s]	—	18.0-24.3	40-40	4.7-6.6	5.9-7.9	0.2-1.1	—	350-920	4-240	—	3-12	35-70
(L) GEHR Weymouth[t]	—	17.0-22.8	57-101	4.8-6.4	6.7-9.0	0.0-2.0	—	540-920	12-430	—	3-10	3-140
(L) Deep Run, Weymouth[u]	—	13.0-21.0	51-53	3.9-7.0	5.9-9.4	1.0-1.7	—	49-130	42-140	—	1-6	15-130
(L) GEHR Mays Landing[v]	—	21.0-25.8	47-73	4.9-6.4	7.4-8.4	0.0-3.0	—	33-240	28-200	—	4-5	35-160
(L) Babcock Cr[w]	—	19.0-21.3	38-53	5.2-6.4	6.4-8.6	0.2-1.3	—	130-240	22-40	—	1-10	20-200
(M) Tuckahoe R Estell[x]	—	19.0-27.5	26-53	4.6-6.4	5.6-9.6	0.7-2.0	—	23-49	12-70	—	1-2	30-110
(M) Tuckahoe R Head[y]	—	15.5-24.0	17-37	4.7-7.2	5.4-8.8	0.1-2.2	—	17-79	8-72	—	1-5	20-120
(P) Scotland Run[z]	—	21.0-24.4	46-61	4.1-6.1	5.0-8.1	0.6-2.0	500	<20-80	8-54	—	1-2	45-190
(P) Maurice R Norma[aa]	85-1170	5.4-23.0	41-91	4.3-6.8	4.7-11.4	0.8-3.1	—	<2-1300	5-3080	190-2330	2-6	10-150
(P) Muddy Run Norma[bb]	—	19.5-25.0	77-114	6.0-6.9	6.3-8.0	1.6-2.5	—	20->2400	56-510	—	2-43	19-110
(P) Maurice R Milly[cc]	—	18.1-22.0	93-99	5.9-6.7	5.0-7.7	1.1-2.4	—	140-540	80-268	—	3-8	50-190
(P) Maurice R Milly[dd]	—	19.0-25.0	74-111	5.8-6.4	6.6-8.6	0.6-2.1	—	13-920	14-360	—	4-28	50-150
(P) Manantico Cr[ee]	—	19.5-25.7	41-67	5.1-6.7	5.1-9.4	0.3-2.8	—	23-330	8-120	—	3-7	2-70
(P) Manumuskin Cr[ff]	—	16.0-22.6	35-83	4.5-6.0	5.9-8.2	0.0-1.5	—	11-240	2-98	—	1-3	15-110
(S) S Brh Rancocas Cr[gg]	—	19.0-24.1	60-128	3.8-5.8	5.4-8.2	0.3-2.3	—	79-130	90-430	—	2-16	4-450
(S) N Brh Rancocas Cr[hh]	—	21.2-29.5	44-49	6.2-6.4	5.2-8.6	0.8-1.9	—	<20-33	8-30	—	5-9	80-160
(S) McDonalds Branch[ii]	1.1-3.3	2.1-17.8	33-61	3.7-4.8	2.2-8.6	0.2-0.9	0-920	<2-23	0-4	0-36	1-2	20-100
(S) Greenwood Branch[jj]	—	17.0-22.0	40-44	5.3-6.4	5.6-8.8	0.6-2.0	—	49-1600	4-1470	—	3-4	90-220
(S) N Brh Rancocas Cr[kk]	74-106	18.5-22.6	42-51	5.3-6.4	5.8-8.0	0.7-1.6	—	170-239	8-116	—	4-7	100-300

River or Stream[b]	Total organic nitrogen (N) (mg/l)	Ammonia nitrogen (N) (mg/l)	Total nitrite nitrogen (N) (mg/l)	Total nitrate nitrogen (N) (mg/l)	Total kjeldahl nitrogen (N) (mg/l)	Total nitrogen (N) (mg/l)	Total phosphorus (P) (mg/l)	Total ortho phosphorus (P) (mg/l)	Total organic carbon (C) (mg/l)	Total acidity as H$^+$ (mg/l)	Alkalinity as CaCO$_3$ (mg/l)	Carbonate (CO$_3$) (mg/l)
(A) Manalapan Brk[c]	.00–1.1	.12–.34	.00–.01	.66–1.2	.20–1.4	1.1–2.4	.01–.13	.00–.05	3.3–7.4	—	0–6	0–0
(B) Manasquan R[d]	.00–.59	.61–2.5	.01–.13	.42–1.9	1.2–2.5	1.6–3.5	.19–.36	.00–.18	5.0–8.3	—	16–54	0–0
(D) Toms R[e]	.00–.65	.03–.26	.00–.01	.12–.51	.18–.76	.33–1.1	.02–.09	.01–.05	4.7–19	.1–.5	0–1	0–0
(G) Oyster Cr[f]	.00–.20	.00–.08	.00–.03	.00–.03	.03–.21	.06–.22	.00–.05	.00–.05	2.0–26	.0–.4	0–0	0–0
(L) GEHR Berlin[g]	.29–1.1	.08–.36	.01–.04	.13–.98	.37–1.5	.66–2.5	.04–.18	.01–.04	7.1–17	—	9–20	0–0
(L) GEHR Sicklerville[h]	.00–1.3	.00–1.5	.01–.03	.00–1.7	.45–1.5	1.0–2.6	.22–1.2	.16–.95	9.6–45	—	—	—
(L) GEHR Tributary #1[i]	.00–1.9	.00–.73	.00–.06	.28–.85	.20–1.9	.91–2.3	.03–.15	.00–.12	4.6–20	—	—	—
(L) GEHR Winslow Cros[g]	.00–.32	.23–.34	.00–.02	.58–1.4	.24–.55	1.1–1.2	.17–.42	.17–.37	8.2–12	—	—	—
(L) New Brooklyn Lake[j]	.24–.81	.03–.39	.00–.02	.04–1.1	.38–1.0	.92–1.7	.09–.24	.04–.18	14–45	—	—	—
(L) East Storm Drain[k]	.26	.32	.02	.98	.58	1.6	.05	.02	22	—	—	—
(L) GEHR Tributary #2[l]	.02–2.1	.02–.13	.01–.04	1.2–3.6	.13–2.2	1.5–5.5	.01–.08	.00–.08	2.0–6.5	—	—	—
(L) Fourmile Branch[m]	.06–1.9	.00–.21	.00–.01	.53–1.9	.14–1.0	1.2–3.2	.00–.14	.00–.06	4.5–29	—	—	—
(L) Fourmile Branch[n]	.07–1.1	.01–.18	.00–.02	.29–1.8	.09–1.1	.82–2.2	.05–.13	.02–.11	4.4–28	—	—	—
(L) GEHR Blue Anchor[o]	.00–.95	.00–.32	.00–.03	.07–1.3	.13–1.1	.85–1.8	.10–.31	.06–.20	4.7–22	—	11–129	0–0
(L) Squankum Branch[p]	.82–4.0	.78–14	.01–.10	.02–2.5	1.6–18	3.4–18	.45–4.2	.33–3.7	17–24	—	0–2	0–0
(L) GEHR Folsom[v]	.07–.84	.01–.18	.00–.02	.04–1.4	.25–.85	.77–1.9	.06–.37	.01–.17	5.5–24	1.0	2	0–0
(L) Hospitality Branch[r]	.22–.49	.01–.04	.00–.01	.09–15	.23–50	.37–6	.01–.04	.01–.01	5.9–13	.3	1–2	0–0
(L) Hospitality Branch[s]	.36–.59	.00–.03	.00–.01	.06–14	.37–59	.51–67	.01–.03	.01–.01	5.3–11	—	0–2	0–0
(L) GEHR Weymouth[t]	.22–.62	.01–.08	.00–.01	.10–.71	.24–63	.73–1.0	.05–.12	.02–.08	5.8–15	.3–.5	0–2	0–0
(L) Deep Run, Weymouth[u]	.13–.61	.00–.01	.00–.01	.05–33	.13–61	.41–67	.06–.08	.04–.08	3.5–19	.5	0–2	0–0
(L) GEHR Mays Landing[v]	.26–.77	.01–.05	.01–.01	.04–49	.27–81	.72–92	.01–.11	.01–.08	14–28	.4	0–0	0–0
(L) Babcock Cr[w]	.22–.61	.01–.08	.00–.01	.06–20	.23–69	.43–76	.03–.05	.02–.03	3.3–22	1.3	0–1	0
(M) Tuckahoe R Estell[x]	.22–.84	.01–.05	.01–.05	.02–04	.23–85	.26–89	.01–.19	.01–.01	5.8–14	.2	0–2	0–0
(M) Tuckahoe R Head[y]	.16–.81	.00–.06	.00–.01	.01–08	.17–83	.18–92	.01–.05	.01–.01	5.2–17	.2–1.1	0–10	0–0
(P) Scotland Run[z]	.25–.60	.01–.09	.01–.01	.06–55	.27–69	.76–83	.01–.03	.01–.01	11–16	.5	0–6	0–0
(P) Maurice R Norma[aa]	.00–.58	.01–.26	.00–.03	.25–1.7	.23–59	.85–2.1	.04–.11	.01–.08	7.7–21	.5	3–13	0–0
(P) Muddy Run Norma[bb]	.42–1.4	.02–.08	.01–.03	.29–1.3	.45–1.5	.87–2.5	.03–.25	.01–.07	6.4–15	—	7–11	0–0
(P) Maurice R Millv[cc]	.36–.49	.17–.73	.01–.02	.48–2.0	.56–1.1	1.6–2.6	.03–.13	.01–.06	6.7–24	—	2–31	0–0
(P) Maurice R Millv[dd]	.46–3.2	.08–.71	.01–.03	.30–3.4	.54–3.9	.99–7.3	.04–.18	.01–.10	8.2–14	—	0–8	0–0
(P) Manantico Cr[ee]	.25–.57	.01–.08	.01–.01	.98–1.2	.27–65	1.1–1.6	.03–.09	.01–.04	5.0–14	—	0–0	0–0
(P) Manumuskin R[ff]	.11–.37	.00–.04	.01–.01	.01–06	.12–41	.17–42	.01–.03	.01–.01	4.5–16	—	0–0	0–0
(S) S Brh Rancocas Cr[gg]	.56–.90	.10–.14	.00–.01	.09–16	.66–1.0	.76–1.2	.01–.14	.01–.15	16–35	—	0–0	0–0
(S) N Brh Rancocas Cr[hh]	.35–1.2	.02–.17	.01–.07	.01–07	.38–1.2	.46–1.2	.01–.08	.01–.04	8.6–15	—	1–2	0–0
(S) McDonalds Branch[ii]	.07–.44	.00–.07	.00–.01	.00–06	.09–45	.09–46	.00–.02	.00–.03	6.0–17	.1–5.5	0–0	0–0
(S) Greenwood Branch[jj]	.01–.85	.06–.09	.01–.01	.03–07	.07–94	.11–99	.01–.05	.01–.04	9.5–23	—	0–0	0–0
(S) N Brh Rancocas Cr[kk]	.22–.39	.03–.15	.01–.01	.10–12	.32–51	.43–64	.03–.09	.01–.06	9.7–32	—	0–2	0–0

(continued)

177

TABLE IV (continued)

River or Stream[b]	Bicarbonate (HCO₃) (mg/l)	Carbon dioxide (CO₂) (mg/l)	Hardness (Ca, Mg) (mg/l)	Non-carbonate hardness (mg/l)	Dissolved calcium (Ca) (mg/l)	Dissolved magnesium (Mg) (mg/l)	Dissolved sodium (Na) (mg/l)	Dissolved potassium (K) (mg/l)	Dissolved chloride (Cl) (mg/l)	Dissolved sulfate (SO₄) (mg/l)	Dissolved solids (residue at 180° C) (mg/l)	Total Non-filtrable residue (mg/l)
(A) Manalapan Brk[c]	0–7	.0–20	25–34	2–34	6.0–8.2	2.5–3.4	4.1–6.3	2.0–3.2	4.5–12	14–28	32–90	11–38
(B) Manasquan R[d]	20–66	5.1–12	44–70	15–27	11–21	1.6–7.2	7.3–12	1.2–3.7	12–22	12–35	107–145	8–29
(D) Toms R[e]	0–1	.0–5.1	8–25	10–25	2.3–7.8	.5–1.5	3.5–5.8	.8–1.5	3.4–8.9	5.7–24	17–68	2–13
(G) Oyster C[f]	0–0	.0–0	4–10	4–10	.9–3.0	.4–8	2.3–4.5	.3–8	3.7–7.8	2.8–6.5	18–41	0–12
(L) GEHR Berlin[g]	11–24	14–34	13–49	4–20	3.7–14	.8–3.4	.8–3.4	5.2–14	1.3–3.7	8.3–20	47–108	17–26
(L) GEHR Sicklerville[h]	—	—	—	—	—	—	—	—	—	—	—	—
(L) GEHR Tributary #1[i]	—	—	—	—	—	—	—	—	—	—	—	—
(L) GEHR Winslow Crosg	—	—	—	—	—	—	—	—	—	—	—	—
(L) New Brooklyn Lake[j]	—	—	—	—	—	—	—	—	—	—	—	—
(L) East Storm Drain[k]	—	—	—	—	—	—	—	—	—	—	—	—
(L) GEHR Tributary #2[l]	—	—	—	—	—	—	—	—	—	—	—	—
(L) Fourmile Branch[m]	—	—	—	—	—	—	—	—	—	—	—	—
(L) Fourmile Branch[n]	—	—	—	—	—	—	—	—	—	—	—	—
(L) GEHR Blue Anchor[o]	—	—	—	—	—	—	—	—	—	—	—	—
(L) Squankum Branch[p]	13–157	23–29	33–39	0–0	7.3–8.8	3.5–4.1	3.4–39	1.8–11	5.3–29	11–17	121–179	6–22
(L) GEHR Folsom[v]	0–3	.0–19	8–22	6–20	1.5–5.8	.8–1.9	3.3–11	.9–1.9	4.8–18	6.3–9.2	64–93	3–19
(L) Hospitality Branch[r]	3	4.8	7–13	10	1.4–3.5	.8–1.0	1.9–2.5	.9–1.2	3.5–4.4	4.5–5.4	37–65	2–9
(L) Hospitality Branch[q]	1–2	.4–1.0	6–10	5–9	1.3–3.0	.5–9	2.1–2.3	.8–1.0	3.2–3.5	3.0–5.2	31–48	3–10
(L) GEHR Weymouth[t]	0–2	.0–1.3	7–11	6–10	1.5–3.2	.6–1.0	3.1–6.4	1.1–1.4	4.8–11	5.6–6.8	46–81	3–18

Location										
(L) Deep Run, Weymouth[u]	0–2	6–11	1.3–3.5	.5–6	2.7–4.0	.7–1.4	4.5–6.7	6.7–7.8	42–74	1–5
(L) GEHR Mays Landing[c]	0–3	10–10	2.4–3.0	.6–1.0	2.5–5.6	.8–1.2	5.3–10	6.0–7.6	29–63	2–14
(L) Babcock Cr[e]	0–0	6–8	1.6–1.8	4–8	2.7–3.0	.8–9	4.6–7.6	3.4–8.2	30–43	1–6
(M) Tuckahoe R Estell[v]	0–1	4–10	.9–2.3	.1–1.2	1.7–2.1	.2–4	2.5–5.0	1.8–4.1	17–78	0–6
(M) Tuckahoe R Head[w]	0–3	4–8	.9–2.0	.1–1.1	1.6–2.2	.2–4	2.9–4.9	2.9–4.8	19–52	0–61
(P) Scotland Run[z]	0–12	2–15	2.0–4.7	.9–1.6	1.5–2.4	1.1–1.3	4.1–4.5	6.0–11	41–76	0–2
(P) Maurice R Norma[aa]	0–7	10–19	3.0–4.1	.7–2.1	4.3–8.4	1.3–3.6	4.0–9.3	8.2–14	14–84	0–26
(P) Muddy Run Norma[bb]	4–16	16–33	3.9–7.0	1.6–3.8	1.4–3.9	2.4–2.7	5.0–9.6	6.0–11	32–73	2–33
(P) Maurice R Milv[cc]	8–13	12–23	2.8–5.4	1.1–2.5	6.3–8.5	1.6–2.5	9.2–12	5.6–12	67–96	5–26
(P) Maurice R Milv[dd]	3–38	13–26	2.7–7.0	1.4–2.2	3.3–6.4	1.9–2.1	5.7–8.6	6.8–11	60–78	2–32
(P) Manantico Cr[ee]	0–10	15–23	4.0–5.8	.5–2.0	2.2–3.1	1.9–2.4	4.6–7.5	6.5–12	46–74	4–15
(P) Manumuskin R[ff]	0–0	10–50	1.0–4.0	-1–1.3	1.4–2.0	.2–6	2.4–5.0	4.1–7.0	24–58	0–5
(P) S Brh Rancocas Cr[gg]	0–0	12–19	3.0–5.5	1.0–1.2	2.6–2.8	1.3–1.3	3.0–5.0	13–26	34–63	26–46
(S) N Brh Rancocas Cr[hh]	1–3	11–15	2.9–4.5	.4–9	2.1–3.5	.8–1.1	3.3–5.7	6.2–8.3	32–48	2–15
(S) McDonalds Branch[ii]	0–0	2–7	.5–2.5	.1–1.2	1.1–2.3	.0–1.0	2.5–5.7	3.4–9.5	15–42	0–2
(S) Greenwood Branch[jj]	0–0	5–11	1.3–3.1	.2–7	2.0–2.0	.5–7	3.3–6.0	5.6–8.9	29–58	2–22
(S) N Brh Rancocas Cr[kk]	0–2	11–15	2.9–4.7	.6–8	2.4–5.0	.8–1.8	3.4–3.9	7.0–9.1	34–56	7–38

[a] From the U.S. Geological Survey (1976).

[b] Letters (in parentheses) to the left of names of rivers refer to river basins listed in Table I.

[c] At Spotswood; total acidity as CaCO₃ = 10.   [d] At Squankum.   [e] Near Toms River; dissolved solids (sum of constituents) (mg/l) = 27–45; dissolved fluoride (F) (mg/l) = 0.0–0.3; dissolved silica (SiO₂) (mg/l) = 1.4–5.8; total acidity = 5.0–25; total iron (Fe) (μg/l) = 400–1500; dissolved iron (Fe) (μg/l) = 340–1200; total manganese (Mn) (μg/l) = 30–60; dissolved manganese (Mn) (μg/l) = 20–60; suspended manganese (Mn) (μg/l) = 0–10; total arsenic (As) (μg/l) = 0–1.   [f] Near Brookville, dissolved solids = 28; dissolved F = 0.1; dissolved Si = 6.0; tot. acidity = 0.0–20; dissolved Fe = 170; dissolved Mn = 20.   [g] Great Egg Harbor R = GEHR.   [h] Chemical oxygen demand (low level) (mg/l) = 23–87.   [i] At Sicklerville; chem. oxyg. demand = 13–42.   [j] West outlet, at Winslow Crossing; chem. oxyg. demand = 19–82.   [k] Winslow Crossing near Sicklerville; chem. oxyg. demand = 14.   [l] At Winslow Crossing; chem. oxyg. demand = 5–22.   [m] At Winslow Crossing; chem. oxyg. demand = 8–99.   [n] Chem. oxyg. demand = 15–91.   [o] At Malaga Rd. near Williamstown.   [p] Chem. oxyg. demand = 28; total acidity = 50.   [q] At New Brooklyn.   [r] At Penny Pot.   [s] Tot. acidity = 15–25.   [t] Tot. acidity = 25.   [u] Near Mays Landing; tot. acidity = 65.   [v] Near Estell Manor; tot. acidity = 10.   [w] Head of river; tot. acidity = 15.   [x] Near Franklinville; tot. acidity = 25.   [y] Tot. acidity = 25.   [z] Tot. acidity = 20.   [aa] Tot. acidity = 25.   [bb] Near Norma.   [cc] Near Millville.   [dd] At Sharp St. at Millville.   [ee] Near Port Elizabeth.   [ff] Near Manumuskin; tot. acidity = 10–50.   [gg] At Retreat; tot. acidity = 25–65.   [hh] At Browns Mills.   [ii] Dissolved solids = 15–24; dissolved F = 0.0–0.3; dissolved Si = 1.6–5.0; tot. acidity = 5.0–273; tot. Fe = 210–2100; tot. Mn = 10–70; tot. As = 0–1; in Lebanon State Forest 1 km east of Pakim Pond.   [jj] At New Lisbon: tot. acidity = 5.0–35.   [kk] At Pemberton; tot. acidity = 30.

179

TABLE V   Chemical Data for Lakes and Ponds throughout the Pine Barrens.

Lake or pond[b]	Depth (m)	Water color[h]	Visibility (Secchi) (m)	Temp. (°C)	Oxygen (ppm)	CO_2 (ppm)	Alkalinity ph-th (ppm)	Alkalinity M.O. (ppm)	Total Alkalinity	pH
(A) Spotswood[e]	0	brn–yell	0.98	20.8	6.8	8	0	8	—	6.3
	2.4	—	—	19.4	6.8	—	—	—	—	—
	3.0	—	—	19.2	1.2	12	0	12	—	6.3
(C) Carasaljo[e]	0	brn–yell	0.91	30.3	9.6	3.8	0	15	—	6.9
	0.9	—	—	29.4	8.9	—	—	—	—	—
	1.2	—	—	27.5	—	—	—	—	—	—
	1.5	—	—	25.9	6.7	—	—	—	—	—
	3.0	—	—	19.2	0.24	—	—	—	—	—
(C) Manetta[e]	0	brn–yell	0.91	27.1	9.8	16	0	16	—	6.3
	1.5	—	—	24.7	8.4	—	—	—	—	—
	2.7	—	—	20.8	4.6	—	0	15	—	5.7
(D) Collier's Mills[c,g]	S[a]	brn–brn	1.14	—	—	—	0	4	4	5.7
	B[a]	—	—	—	—	—	—	18	18	5.3
(D) Upper Shannock[c,f]	S	brn–yell	1.64	—	—	—	0	6	6	4.5
	B	—	—	—	—	—	—	9	9	4.7
(D) Middle Shannock[c,f]	S	brn–yell	1.40	—	—	—	0	3	3	4.7
	B	—	—	—	—	—	—	19	19	5.8
(D) Lower Shannock[c,f]	S	brn–yell	1.51	—	—	—	0	9.5	9.5	5.1
	B	—	—	—	—	—	0	20	20	5.7
(D) Turn Mill[c,g]	S	brn–yell	1.64	—	—	—	0	13	13	6.0
	B	—	—	—	—	—	—	7	7	5.8
(D) Horicon[e]	0	brn–yell	1.51	27.8	8.1	9	0	5	—	4.3
	0.6	—	—	21.7	7.6	—	—	—	—	—
	2.7	—	—	16.4	5.5	13	0	5	—	4.3
(F) Barnegat Pine[d]	0	brn–clear	B	27.2	7.2	5.5	0	5	—	4.6
	2.7	—	—	25.0	7.6	5.0	0	5	—	4.9
(F) Deerhead[d]	0	brn–clear	B	27.8	6.4	4.5	0	5	—	5.0
	2.4	—	—	22.2	8.4	5.5	0	5	—	5.0
(I) Absegami[c,g]	S	brn–brn	1.03	—	—	—	0	7	3	4.4
	B	—	—	—	—	—	—	—	7	5.0
(I) Hammonton[d]	0	brn–yell	1.52	27.2	6.4	3	0	10	—	6.7
	1.5	—	—	26.4	6.4	—	—	—	—	—
	2.7	—	—	23.3	2.0	21	0	18	—	5.9
(I) Oswego[e]	0	brn–brn	1.21	26.9	5.7	10	0	6	—	4.3
	1.2	—	—	26.7	5.7	—	—	—	—	—
	2.1	—	—	23.1	6.2	—	0	0	—	4.3

(continued)

TABLE V (*continued*)

Lake or pond[a]	Depth (m)	Water color[h]	Visibility (Secchi) (m)	Temp. (°C)	Oxygen (ppm)	CO_2 (ppm)	Alkalinity ph-th (ppm)	Alkalinity M.O. (ppm)	Total Alkalinity	pH
(L) Lenape[d]	0	brn–yell	1.36	27.2	6.7	5.5	0	7	—	4.2
	3.6	—	—	27.8	5.1	—	—	—	—	—
	4.3	—	—	22.8	4.6	10.5	0	10	—	4.9
(L) New Brooklyn[e]	0	brn–yell–brn	1.21	23.1	4.7	—	0	7	—	5.3
	1.8	—	—	20.8	5.2	—	0	10	—	5.3
(O) East Creek[e]	0	brn–brn	0.70	27.5	3.6	24	0	14	—	4.7
	0.9	—	—	23.3	2.7	—	0	13	—	4.1
	2.1	—	—	22.5	2.2	—	0	12	—	4.1
(O) Nummy[e]	0	brn–brn	0.61	28.4	4.2	23	0	10	—	4.1
	1.8	—	—	23.9	3.2	24	0	12.3	—	4.5
(P) Laurel[d]	0	brn–brn	0.73	31.9	6.9	6	0	5.5	—	4.9
	1.5	—	—	25.0	3.7	—	—	—	—	—
	2.7	—	—	23.9	2.3	18	0	0	—	4.9
(P) Malaga[e]	0	brn–yell	0.76	18.6	5.6	10	0	6	—	5.1
	1.8	—	—	17.1	5.4	—	—	—	—	—
	2.4	—	—	17.1	2.8	—	0	7	—	5.1
(P) Union[c,f]	S	brn–brn	1.43	—	—	—	0	14	14	6.0
	B	—	—	—	—	—	—	15	15	6.0
(P) Willow Grove[e]	0	brn–brn	0.76	21.5	7.0	11	0	8	—	5.3
	1.8	—	—	17.8	3.2	15	0	10	—	5.3
(P) Wilson[e]	0	brn–yell	1.06	27.8	6.2	—	0	11	—	5.9
	1.5	—	—	21.9	5.7	—	—	—	—	—
	2.1	—	—	20.8	3.6	—	0	15	—	5.9
(Q) Blackwood[c,g]	S	brn–brn	1.21	—	—	—	0	22	22	6.9
	B	—	—	—	—	—	—	25	25	6.6
(Q) Laurel Springs[d]	0	green–yell	0.53	26.9	8.7	1	0	18	—	6.8
	2.1	—	—	23.6	4.8	—	—	—	—	—
	2.7	—	—	23.3	0.5	14.5	0	22	—	6.3
(T) Brindle[c,f]	S	brn–brn	0.70	—	—	—	0	6	6	4.3
	B	—	—	—	—	—	—	68	68	5.8

[a] Sampling locations within a lake are: S = surface, B = bottom.
[b] Letters (in parentheses) to left of names of lakes refer to river basins listed in Table I.
[c] New Jersey Division of Fish and Game (1950).
[d] New Jersey Division of Fish and Game (1951).
[e] New Jersey Division of Fish and Game (1957).
[f] Thermal stratification present. [g] Thermal stratification absent.
[h] Brn, brown; Yell, yellow.

TABLE VI Chemical Data for Lakes and Ponds in the Rancocas Creek Basin.[a]

Lake or pond[b]	Temp. (°C)	Oxygen (ppm)	pH	Chloride (ppm)	Nitrate as N (ppm)	Nitrite as N (ppm)	Tot. Kjel. N (ppm)	Ammonia as N (ppm)	Phosphate PO_4 (ppm)	Phosphate PO_4–P (ppm)	Total phosphorus	Tot. hard. $CaCO_3$ (ppm)	Ca hard. $CaCO_3$ (ppm)	Mg hard. $CaCO_3$ (ppm)
Lower Aetna O	19.8	8.31	4.89	7.13	0.114	0.005	—	0.025	0.023	0.006	0.02	15.38	6.88	8.50
Upper Aetna O	19.3	8.41	4.66	6.88	0.089	0.004	—	—	0.026	0.009	0.01	11.75	5.63	6.13
Lower Birchwood'O	19.2	8.06	6.30	9.88	0.175	0.023	1.234	1.054	1.550	0.505	0.31	19.38	11.13	8.25
Upper Birchwood'O	19.3	8.03	6.17	10.25	0.395	0.033	1.286	0.985	1.796	0.586	0.46	21.38	12.00	9.38
Upper Birchwood'I	19.5	8.54	6.21	9.63	0.255	0.019	1.744	—	1.373	0.448	0.50	20.63	11.3	9.25
Braddocks Mill O	18.2	8.89	4.89	7.25	0.705	0.003	0.336	0.084	0.026	0.009	0.02	15.25	4.63	—
Braddocks Mill I	18.0	8.88	4.77	7.63	0.755	0.004	—	0.149	0.033	0.010	0.02	10.38	5.38	5.50
Browns Mills[d,i]	25.9	6.6	4.9	—	—	—	—	—	—	—	—	—	—	—
Browns Mills 2.7m[d]	21.4	2.0	—	—	—	—	—	—	—	—	—	—	—	—
Camp Hilltop O	18.4	9.14	4.61	6.50	0.130	0.005	—	0.060	0.026	0.008	0.02	10.88	5.38	5.50
Camp Hilltop U	18.4	7.71	4.44	6.38	0.035	0.004	0.282	0.055	0.020	0.006	0.03	12.00	6.63	5.38
Centennial O	19.0	8.11	4.57	6.63	0.604	0.004	0.594	0.070	0.060	0.020	0.02	13.50	5.13	8.38
Centennial M	18.7	8.30	4.53	7.00	0.360	0.003	0.502	0.070	0.026	0.009	0.01	9.75	4.75	—
Centennial I	17.8	8.04	4.63	7.38	0.060	0.004	0.502	0.084	0.030	0.009	0.02	10.50	5.25	—
Hanover[c,j]	—	—	5.0	—	—	—	—	—	—	—	—	—	—	—
Hanover[c,k]	—	—	6.3	—	—	—	—	—	—	—	—	—	—	—
Mishe-Mokwa[l]	19.9	9.37	6.59	7.75	0.150	0.005	0.552	0.030	0.043	0.014	0.04	17.88	9.75	—
Pakim[d,m]	26.7	4.8	4.1	—	—	—	—	—	—	—	—	—	—	—
Pakim 0.9m[d]	24.4	2.8	—	—	—	—	—	—	—	—	—	—	—	—
Pakim 1.2m[d]	23.3	2.0	—	—	—	—	—	—	—	—	—	—	—	—
Pine	18.3	8.56	4.54	7.38	0.445	0.006	0.432	0.060	0.033	0.011	0.03	20.63	5.6	6.00
Squaw O	18.1	8.91	4.41	7.75	0.100	0.004	0.601	0.030	0.026	0.008	0.03	12.63	5.63	7.00
Squaw I	15.1	8.33	4.17	7.57	0.155	0.005	—	0.060	0.026	0.008	0.02	10.88	5.38	5.50
Taunton	17.9	8.27	4.34	7.00	0.010	0.003	—	0.060	0.046	0.015	0.02	7.86	5.14	2.71

[a] Except as indicated, data from Academy of Natural Sciences (1973).
[b] Sampling locations within a lake are: O, outfall; M, midway up; U, upper end; I, inflow; S, surface; B, bottom; or, depth given in meters.
[c] New Jersey Division of Fish and Game (1950). [f] Alkalinity M.O. (ppm) = 8.86.
[d] New Jersey Division of Fish and Game (1951). [g] Alkalinity M.O. (ppm) = 8.00.
[e] New Jersey Division of Fish and Game (1957). [h] Alkalinity M.O. (ppm) = 12.14.
[i] Visibility (Secchi disc) (m) = 0.73; water color = brown-yellow; CO_2 (ppm) = 8.0; alkalinity ph-th (ppm) = 0; alkalinity M.O. (ppm) = 0.
[j] Thermal stratification present; visibility (Secchi disc) (m) = 1.44; water color, brown-yellow; alkalinity ph-th (ppm) = 0; alkalinity M.O. (ppm) = 65; total alkalinity = 65.
[k] Alkalinity M.O. (ppm) = 101; total alkalinity = 101.
[l] Alkalinity M.O. (ppm) = 6.14.
[m] Visibility (Secchi disc) (m) = 0.30; water color = brown-brown; CO_2 (ppm) = 14; alkalinity ph-th (ppm) = 0; alkalinity M.O. (ppm) = 8.5.

THE RIVER BASINS

Raritan River Basin

Manalapan Brook is the only tributary of the Raritan River Basin in the Pine Barrens for which data are available. The chemical data indicate that the water of this stream, while typically acid, has been affected by an increased organic load in the area where the chemical samples were taken. This was evidenced by a fluctuation in pH from 4.8–9.1, a shift which correlated with a range of oxygen levels from 6.3–11.5 mg/liter, thus indicating that photosynthesis was fairly high at certain times. The BOD (biochemical oxygen demand) of 6.3 mg/liter, which is high, also indicates an organic load. This is further evidenced by the variation in the level of nitrates from 0.66–1.2 mg/liter, phosphates at a level of 0.05 mg/liter, and ammonia varying from 0.12–0.34 mg/liter. The sulfates also are high for a stream of this type.

The fish list indicates that this typically is an acid-water stream. We find such acid-water fish as the sphagnum sunfish, mud sunfish, and creek chub sucker, although these records were mainly from nearby lakes and ponds. The insect fauna mainly consisted of Odonata, the dragonfly and damselfly order. However, quite a few species of gyrinids (whirligig beetles) were present, and two tipulids (craneflies) were found. The most characteristic aspects of the fauna were the large number of Odonata and the absence of Ephemeroptera (mayflies).

Manasquan River Basin

The basin is very small, and the only chemical information we have was obtained from Squankum, near its mouth. The relatively high conductivity at Squankum indicates that it is under marine influence, and the pH is circumneutral, ranging from 6.7–8.8. The bacterial count and the biochemical oxygen demand were quite high. However, nitrates, ammonia, and phosphates were not unusually high. This would indicate that complex sewage components had not been mineralized were entering the river at this point. The stream is of intermediate hardness, harder than most streams of the Pine Barrens. It would appear that water use in this area by human habitation is causing the shift in BOD and bacterial load.

Only a few records of fish and diatoms are available. These do not particularly indicate the characteristic acid water condition of Pine Barrens streams.

Metedeconk River Basin

River collections are very scarce and were taken mainly from Lakewood. The lake collections, particularly of fish, from Carasaljo and Manetta Lakes are more extensive and are indicative of acid waters, as evidenced by the presence of the eastern creek chub sucker, sphagnum sunfish, mud sunfish, fusiform darter, and pirate perch.

Toms River Basin

This basin is the northernmost of the three large river systems confined to the Pine Barrens. However, the only chemical records we have are from the town of Toms River at the mouth, where the river receives some organic pollution and may be influenced slightly by tidal action. The organic load is indicated by the BOD, which varies from 0.7 to 8 mg/liter, and by the levels of fecal coliform bacteria, varying from 5 to 540 mpn (most probable number), and of ammonia, ranging from 0.03 to 0.26 ppm. All indicate that some sewage is present at times. Dissolved oxygen ranges from 6.7 to 12.4 mg/liter. This large amount of dissolved oxygen indicates the presence of algal blooms, undoubtedly associated with the organic enrichment of the stream at Toms River. Alkaline metals are very low. Thus, at Toms River the river is a typically acid Pine Barrens water drainage subjected to moderate pollution.

The algal flora collected from Toms River is composed of typical acid-water species. Among these are *Actinella punctata, Eunotia major,* and *Eunotia zygodon.*

The insect fauna is rich in species of Odonata and in addition contains quite a few species of gyrinids. As in other New Jersey acid streams, it is very poor in mayflies, and few midge species or other groups of insects are present.

The chub sucker and chain pickerel are the characteristic acid-water species of the streams, while ponds contained several acid-water species, such as banded sunfish, mud sunfish, sphagnum sunfish, northern yellow bullhead, fusiform darter, and creek chub sucker.

Cedar Creek Basin

This is a small river basin, and the species listed are not particularly indicative of acid water conditions. This may be due to the paucity of collections.

Forked River Basin

Located in this small river basin are one river station at Waretown and two lake stations. In the river, only the mud sunfish and mud minnow are characteristic of acid waters, whereas in the lakes were found the northern yellow bullhead, the mud sunfish, the pirate perch, the fusiform darter, the sphagnum sunfish, and the mud minnow, all characteristic of acid water.

Oyster Creek Basin

The single series of chemical data from near Brookville indicates that, although this is typically an acid-water stream, it probably is affected by some organic pollution, particularly sanitary wastes. The BOD is not very high, varying from 0.0 to 1.2 mg/liter. The fecal coliform bacteria count (BC broth NBM) of 920 is high for these streams. However, the levels of nitrate-nitrogen, ammonia, and phosphates are very low, so it is hard to explain this fecal coliform bacteria count. Possibly it is an error or due to animal waste.

Westecunk Creek Basin

No data on chemistry, fish, insects, or algae are available. However, the rare frog *Hyla andersonii* is reported from Staffords Forge on the creek (Fowler, 1907b).

Mullica River Basin

This large basin is confined to the Pine Barrens and in its upper headwaters contains many white cedar swamps, *Sphagnum* bogs, and cranberry bogs. Some cranberry bogs have been used extensively in the cultivation of cranberries.

The diatom flora of lakes and bogs contains many species of *Eunotia*, *Actinella punctata*, *Semiorbis hemicyclus*, and *Frustulia rhomboides*. Several species of *Pinnularia* also are present, those which are characteristic of very low conductivity or acid waters.

Lakes and ponds contain several fish characteristic of acid waters. These include the sphagnum sunfish, banded sunfish, chub sucker, northern yellow bullhead, and fusiform darter.

In the river, we again see that the algae are typical of acid or low-conductivity waters, e.g., diatom species of *Pinnularia* and *Eunotia*. Also quite common was the freshwater red alga *Batrachospermum*, which is typical of acid waters in New Jersey. In this river basin, we also find many desmids characteristic of low conductivity in acid waters.

The insects are characterized by several species of Odonata and gyrinids. Fish characteristic of the acid river waters include the sphagnum sunfish, chub sucker, pirate perch, banded sunfish, and chain pickerel.

Absecon Creek Basin

Typical acid-water diatoms are *Frustulia rhomboides* and two *Pinnularias* that also may be found in waters of low conductivity. The acid-water desmid, *Euastrum cuspidatum*, is found here.

Patgong Creek Basin

Chemical data are absent. Biological data are very sparse and are not particularly indicative of stream conditions.

Great Egg Harbor River Basin

This third large river basin is confined to the Pine Barrens. Typically, the stream, like others flowing through sand and gravel, is very low in alkaline metals and in hardness. The pH is relatively low, usually <6, although in areas polluted by human habitation or agriculture, it often is much higher. The temperature of the river usually is <25°C (U.S. Geological Survey, 1976), although in areas of human habitation or agricultural activities or where the tree cover has been removed, the temperature may be higher. The BOD, coliform bacteria count, nitrates, phosphates, and ammonia all are low. There are areas where the iron content is high, as evidenced by the growth of *Leptothrix ochracea,* an iron bacterium. A considerable iron content exists in some headwater tributaries of the Great Egg Harbor River, but overall little is known of the iron content of the waters in this river system. The area of Batsto had active bog iron furnaces, typical of those common in New Jersey at one time. There are a few instances of high sulfur, with the highest concentrations to be found where pollution evidently is entering the stream.

The effects of pollution are evidenced by higher than usual dissolved oxygen, generally the result of algal growth, pH, BOD, nitrate, ammonia, and phosphates. The areas of greatest pollution include the following: the Great Egg Harbor River at Sicklerville; a tributary at Sicklerville; Winslow Crossing near Sicklerville; tributary No. 2, four-mile branch at New Brooklyn; the river near Blue Anchor; Squankum Branch at Malaga Road near Williamstown; and the river at Folsom.

In the upper part of the basin, the diatoms *Actinella punctata, Eunotia pectinalis* var. *ventricosa, Eunotia biceps,* and *Eunotia bidentula* were found. All are characteristic of acid-water streams.

The fish include some of the typical acid-water species, although other, more tolerant species also are present. The typical acid-water fish are the chub sucker, chain pickerel, mud sunfish, banded sunfish, sphagnum sunfish, and northern yellow bullhead.

The insect fauna largely consists of genera belonging to the Odonata, although some midge species also are present. The mayflies and caddisflies are absent or rare. Several species of gyrinids were found. Thus, the Great Egg Harbor River fauna reflects the acid characteristics of the watershed, but includes some species commonly found under moderately polluted water. The slight invasion of salt water near the bay also is evident in some of the algal species.

Tuckahoe River Basin

Chemistry data from two areas, one near Estell Manor and one at the head of the river, indicate the river varies in pH from 4.6–7.2. There appears to be very little pollution on this river, and it seems to be typically an acid-water stream. There is no evidence that pollution is present from either the biochemical oxygen demand, the levels of nitrates, ammonia, phosphates, or from the fecal coliform bacteria count.

The fish fauna is a typical acid-water fauna. Species include the yellow bullhead, chain pickerel, chub sucker, banded sunfish, and mud sunfish.

Cedar Swamp Creek Basin

The most extensive collections are of fish. Some species are indicative of the acid water conditions of the river system, e.g., sphagnum sunfish, banded sunfish, pirate perch, mud sunfish, and mud minnow.

Dennis Creek Basin

The basin mostly lies south of the Pine Barrens. However, one small headwater stream, Sluice Creek, is in the Pine Barrens.

The algae mainly consist of blue-green algae and desmids. Four species of frogs were found in this creek, including the acid-water species *Rana virgatipes* (Fowler, 1907b). Only one insect species is recorded, an odonate larva. The fish most clearly indicate the acid water characteristics of Sluice Creek, i.e., the mud minnow, chain pickerel, banded sunfish, and mud sunfish. Fish collected from East Creek Lake, Nummy Lake, and a few small ponds indicate that these lakes and ponds are typically acid surface waters: yellow bullhead, pirate perch, chain pickerel, chub sucker, banded sunfish, mud sunfish, and sphagnum sunfish.

Maurice River Basin

This is a relatively large basin, part of which is within the Pine Barrens. There are significant chemical and biological differences between streams within and outside the Pine Barrens. Two streams, the Manantico and the Manumuskin, are confined mainly to the Pine Barrens, although Scotland Run near Franklinville also seems to be a Pine Barrens-type stream. The watershed includes many lakes.

In the typically Pine Barrens portion of this watershed, the pH varied from 4.1–6.7. The higher pH values probably were due to photosynthesis in the stream. The temperature of the waters varied, with maxima of 22.6° to 25.7°C and minima of 16° to 21°C. Fecal bacteria counts and levels of nitrates, ammonia, and phosphates were very low in the streams. However, phosphorus does not seem to be limiting nor does nitrate-nitrogen, whose maximal levels vary from 0.06 to 1.2 ppm $N-NO_3$ and the lows from 0.01 to 0.98 ppm $N-NO_3$. At Scotland Run, the ammonia was 0.01 ppm ammonia-N and the nitrate-N varied between 0.06 and 0.55 ppm. The P-orthophosphates were 0.01 ppm. These levels are sufficient to support a fair amount of algal growth. The fecal coliform bacteria were very low at Scotland Run and moderately high in the Manantico and the Manumuskin, the highest records being 240 to 330 fecal coliform bacteria (on EC broth).

The algae, which are mainly from the ponds in Newfield and Malaga, are mostly desmids, to be expected in acid waters. The insects, as in other acid water streams, are rich in Odonata.

The fish of the streams that demonstrate the acid waters characteristic of this part of the basin are the mud sunfish, banded sunfish, and chub sucker. The following acid-water species were found in lakes and ponds: banded sunfish, chub sucker, chain pickerel, mud sunfish, sphagnum sunfish, northern yellow bullhead, pirate perch, and fusiform darter. Many other species characteristic of the more neutral waters of non-Pine Barrens tributaries and near the mouth of the Maurice River also were found in the Pine Barrens streams. Scotland Run near Franklinville appears very clean, whereas based on coliform bacteria counts, a small amount of pollution enters the other two streams in the areas studied.

Big Timber Creek Basin

The headwaters of Big Timber Creek Basin lie within the Pine Barrens, although it is a tributary to the Delaware River and much of the lower part of the basin is outside the Pine Barrens. The localities of Clementon and Turnersville lie within the Pine Barrens area.

The insect fauna is fairly diverse, but as in other Pine Barrens streams, the Odonata is the dominant order of insects. However, it should be noted that this stream basin is characterized by many more Diptera (flies) than other Pine Barrens streams. As in typical Pine Barrens streams, the Ephemeroptera are absent, and there are very few Trichoptera (caddisflies).

Characteristic of acid rivers are such fish as the eastern creek chub sucker and the mud minnow. In lakes and ponds, we again find characteristic acid-water species, such as the fusiform darter and eastern creek chub sucker. However, these streams do not support some of the typical acid-water forms found in other basins. The rare frog *Hyla andersonii* is recorded from here (Fowler, 1907b).

Cooper River Basin

A collection of algae at Kirkwood on Cooper's Creek is not particularly indicative of acid waters. In Kirkwood Pond, we note certain species of *Pinnularia*, whose presence would indicate low conductivity of the water. Only two species of fish are recorded.

Rancocas Creek Basin

Most of the large Rancocas Creek arises in the Pine Barrens. However, the larger part of the stream flows in the area between the Pine Barrens and the Delaware River into which it empties. In the headwater areas are a great many lakes, the most important of these being the Medford Lakes group.

Chemical analyses of the Pine Barrens streams indicate that these are typical acid-water streams, with the pH varying from 3.7 to 6.4. The temperature was typically <25°C, except at Browns Mills, where a high temperature of 29.5°C was recorded. Alkaline metals were very low in this stream basin. Dissolved oxygen varied considerably, with lows from 2.2 to 5.8 ppm and the highs ranging from 8.0 to 8.8 ppm. Very low oxygen at 2.2 ppm was found in McDonalds Branch in Lebanon State Forest.

There were some slight signs of organic enrichment in this river basin at New Lisbon on the Greenwood Branch, at Pemberton on the North Branch of the Rancocas, and at Retreat on the South Branch of the Rancocas. At New Lisbon, this was evidenced by a BOD of 2 mg/liter, fecal coliform bacteria (in EC broth) of 1600, and phosphorus as orthophosphate of 1.04 mg/liter. At Pemberton on the North Branch of the Rancocas the only evidence of organic enrichment was the phosphorus, which was 0.05 mg/liter. At Retreat on the South Branch of the Rancocas, the BOD was 2.3 mg/liter, which was the highest BOD found in the Rancocas streams, and the phosphorus as orthophosphate was 0.5 mg/liter. The bacterial count had a most probable number (mpn) of 130, which was relatively low. This would indicate that something other than sanitary wastes possibly was increasing the phosphorus and BOD.

There are a great many records concerning the chemical characteristics of the lakes, the most important being the studies of the Academy of Natural Sciences (1973). The chemistry of the lakes indicates that, with a few exceptions, they are typical brownwater, acid lakes. These exceptions are the Upper and Lower Birchwood Lakes, where the pH ranged from 6.17 to 6.3, the bottom of Hanover Lake, where the pH was 6.3, and Mishe-Mokwa Lake, with a pH of 6.58.

The dissolved oxygen at the time of the analyses generally was about 8 mg/liter or above, with, however, two exceptions. One was at Browns Mills, where the oxygen content was 6.6 mg/liter at the surface and 2 mg/liter at a depth of 2.7 m. At Pakim Lake, the oxygen content was 4.8 mg/liter at the surface and 2 mg/liter at a depth of 1.2 m.

The lakes showing the most evident effects of sanitary wastes or organic enrichment were the Upper and Lower Birchwood Lakes and Braddock Mill Pond. In the Lower Birchwood Lake at the outfall and in Upper Birchwood Lake at both the inflow and outfall, ammonia and phosphates indicate this condition. In both lakes, a higher pH accompanied this evidence of sanitary wastes, as usually happens in these acid waters. At Braddock Mill Pond, there was evidence of increased nutrient levels as indicated by nitrate and ammonia levels. Although in many cases the lakes were surrounded by human habitation, the chemical analyses indicated that they were not adversely affected.

The biological collections from these lakes indicate a very diverse diatom flora and, as one would expect of acid waters, a large number of species of *Eunotia* and certain species that are typically found in acid waters such as *Actinella punctata, Frustulia rhomboides, Surirella delicatissima,* and *Tabellaria flocculosa.* Several species of *Pinnularia* were found in these lakes, species characteristic of water of low conductivity that may be of acid pH. Many other species that have much wider pH ranges also were found. This is particularly true in the lakes with higher pH.

The fish collections from the lakes contained several species that are characteristic of acid waters, such as the northern yellow bullhead, fusiform darter, mud minnow, pirate perch, chain pickerel, chub sucker, banded sunfish, mud sunfish, and sphagnum sunfish. Although these lakes are surrounded by human habitation and have suffered from urbanization, for the most part, they nevertheless maintain the characteristics of the acid waters which are natural for this area.

The biological collections from the streams of the Pine Barrens that form the headwaters of the Rancocas Creek indicate their acid conditions. For example, most of the algae are desmids, which are characteristic of acid waters; of the diatoms, *Pinnularia major* is a species often found under these conditions, as is *Navicula confervacea.* As is characteristic of other Pine Barrens streams, the insects consist mainly of genera of Odonata. The fish that are characteristic of acid waters include the yellow catfish, fusiform darter, mud minnow, pirate perch, chain pickerel, chub sucker, banded sunfish, and mud sunfish. The lower part of the Rancocas, which has more circumneutral waters, has a very different fauna and flora.

Crosswicks Creek Basin

The only portion of this basin in the Pine Barrens is Lahaway Creek and Brindle Lake in the Fort Dix Military Reservation.

The insect fauna of Lahaway Creek is more diverse than that which typically is found in the Pine Barrens, in that many more orders of insects are present than are typical of acid-water streams.

Our only biological records from Brindle Lake are of fish, which include some typical acid-water forms such as the mud sunfish, sphagnum sunfish, fusiform darter, banded sunfish, and northern yellow bullhead.

SOME GENERAL CHARACTERISTICS OF PINE BARRENS SURFACE WATERS

The waters of Pine Barrens streams typically are rich in humates and have a brown color. The pH naturally varies from about pH 3.6–5.2, with an average around 4.4. However, we often find this pH is altered considerably due to fertilizers from cranberry bogs and other agricultural drainage entering the streams and from sanitary or farming wastes. The effect of these wastes typically is reflected in elevated levels of pH, BOD (biochemical oxygen demand), nitrates, and phosphates.

Because these surface waters naturally have a pH below that of the carbonate-bicarbonate buffering system, they for the most part have a unique fauna and flora. These species are supplemented by more tolerant species which have invaded the area.

These acid waters with low levels of alkaline metals are inhospitable to many species. For example, snails and molluscs generally cannot deposit calcium in their shells if the pH is <5.8. Thus, we find very few unionids or gastropods in these waters. Crustacea typically are scarce in waters with a pH <6. Many common species of fish are inhibited from reproducing at a low pH. For example, bass, bluegills, and yellow perch typically do not reproduce at pH <4.9, and the golden shiner and the calico bass generally do not reproduce at pH <6. Stocking often is not very successful in these acid-water lakes and streams. Pickerel is one fish that seems able to reproduce and to be very successful under such conditions. The algal flora is unique, and many species are only known from these kinds of acid streams and lakes. Of course, any algal flora contains widely tolerant species, as well as those with narrow tolerance limits. Many desmids are found in these waters as they frequently occur in water which has low conductivity and is low in alkaline metals. One of the most common algae in these Pine Barrens streams, particularly in the spring of the year, is the freshwater red alga *Batrachospermum*. The productivity of these streams normally is very low. Typically, one finds very few blue-green algae in these acid waters.

The effect of eutrophication (addition of fertilizers and farm and sanitary wastes) is to greatly increase diatoms. For example, in the Great Egg Harbor River, below the entrance of sanitary wastes where the levels of nitrates and phosphates are fairly high, the senior author has found huge populations of the diatoms *Eunotia pectinalis* and *E.*

pectinalis var. *ventricosa*. As much as a pint of diatoms has been collected with relatively little effort. The senior author also has noted large masses of the red alga *Batrachospermum* under such conditions. Species that are characteristic or confined to the Pine Barrens are noted under the various watersheds.

It is difficult to draw conclusions concerning the ecosystems of Pine Barrens streams or to make comparisons between these and other streams because very few data have been published about them.

SUMMARY

Most river basins are confined to the Pine Barrens, although a few originate there and flow into adjacent terrain. Records of fish, insects, diatoms, and other algae, plus chemical and bacteriological data, are summarized for each river basin. Chemical data indicate that the streams and lakes are low in hardness, alkalinity, and pH, and that most are high in humic compounds. Typical acid water conditions are indicated by nine fish species widespread throughout the Pine Barrens, and by an insect fauna with abundant dragonflies and damselflies (Odonata) and abundant whirligig beetles (Gyrinidae), but with no mayflies (Ephemeroptera), indicating an acid condition, and few caddisflies (Trichoptera) and other insect groups. Algae are characteristic of acid water streams, as witnessed by the prevalence of genera such as *Eunotia, Actinella, Anomoeoneis, Pinnularia,* and *Batrachospermum.* Stream temperatures are relatively cool and constant. Changes in stream chemistry and/or biology indicate scattered sources of pollution (fertilizers, farm, and sanitary wastes) in the Pine Barrens.

REFERENCES

Academy of Natural Sciences of Philadelphia (1973). "Chemical and Biological Studies of the Surface Waters of Medford Township, New Jersey, 1971–1972." Cent. Ecol. Res. Plann. Des., Dep. Landscape Archit. Reg. Plann., Univ. of Pennsylvania, Philadelphia.

Conant, R. (1962). Reptiles and amphibians of the New Jersey Pine Barrens. *N.J. Nat. News* **17**(1), 16–21.

Cope, E. D. (1883). The fishes of the Batsto River, New Jersey. *Proc. Acad. Nat. Sci. Philadelphia* **35**, 132–133.

Cope, E. D. (1896). Fishes in isolated pools. *Am. Nat.* **30**, 943–944.

Fairbrothers, D. E., and Moul, E. T. (1955). Aquatic vegetation of New Jersey. Part I. Ecology and identification. *N.J. Coll. Agric., Ext. Bull.* No. 382.

Fikslin, T. J., and Montgomery, J. D. (1971). An ecological survey of a stream in the New Jersey Pine Barrens. *Bull. N.J. Acad. Sci.* **16**, 8–12.

Fowler, H. W. (1906). The fishes of New Jersey. *N.J. State Mus., Annu. Rep. 1905* Part 2, pp. 35–477.

Fowler, H. W. (1907a). A supplementary account of the fishes of New Jersey. *N.J. State Mus., Annu. Rep. 1906* Part 3, pp. 251–350.

Fowler, H. W. (1907b). The amphibians and reptiles of New Jersey. *N.J. State Mus., Annu. Rep. 1906* pp. 23–250.

Fowler, H. W. (1908a). Further notes on New Jersey fishes. *N.J. State Mus., Annu. Rep. 1907* pp. 120–189.

Fowler, H. W. (1908b). A supplementary account of New Jersey amphibians and reptiles. *N.J. State Mus., Annu. Rep. 1907* pp. 190–202.

Fowler, H. W. (1909a). Notes on New Jersey fishes. *N.J. State Mus., Annu. Rep. 1908* pp. 351–392.

Fowler, H. W. (1909b). Notes on New Jersey amphibians and reptiles. *N.J. State Mus., Annu. Rep. 1908* pp. 393–408.

Fowler, H. W. (1920). A list of the fishes of New Jersey. *Proc. Biol. Soc. Wash.* **33,** 139–170.

Fowler, H. W. (1952). A list of the fishes of New Jersey, with off-shore species. *Proc. Acad. Nat. Sci. Philadelphia* **104,** 89–151.

Juneja, N. (1974). "Medford: Performance Requirements for the Maintenance of Social Values Represented by the Natural Environment of Medford Township, N.J." Cent. Ecol. Res. Plann. Des., Dep. Landscape Archit. Reg. Plann., Univ. of Pennsylvania, Philadelphia.

McCormick, J. (1970). The Pine Barrens: A preliminary ecological inventory. *N.J. State Mus., Res. Rep.* No. 2.

New Jersey Division of Fish and Game (1950). "New Jersey Fisheries Survey Report: Lakes and Ponds," No. 1. Trenton, New Jersey.

New Jersey Division of Fish and Game (1951). "New Jersey Fisheries Survey Report: Lakes and Ponds," No. 2. Trenton, New Jersey.

New Jersey Division of Fish and Game (1957). "New Jersey Fisheries Survey Report: Lakes and Ponds," No. 3. Trenton, New Jersey.

Smith, J. B. (1910). The insects of New Jersey. *N.J. State Mus., Rep. 1909* pp. 15–888.

Stokes, A. C. (1884). Notes on some apparently undescribed forms of fresh-water Infusoria. *Am. J. Sci.* **28,** 38–49.

Stokes, A. C. (1885a). Notes on some apparently undescribed forms of fresh-water Infusoria. *Am. J. Sci.* **29,** 313–328.

Stokes, A. C. (1885b). Some new Infusoria from American fresh waters. *Ann. Mag. Nat. Hist.* **15,** 437–449.

Stokes, A. C. (1886a). Some new Infusoria from American fresh waters, No. 2 *Ann. Mag. Nat. Hist.* **17,** 98–112.

Stokes, A. C. (1886b). Notices of new fresh-water Infusoria. *Proc. Am. Philos. Soc.* **23,** 562–568.

Thomas, L. (1967). "The Pine Barrens of New Jersey." N.J. Dep. Conserv. Econ. Dev., Div. Parks, For. Recreat., Nat. Areas Sect., Trenton, New Jersey.

U.S. Department of Interior Task Force Report (1976). The Pine Barrens resource. *N.J. Audubon* **2**(6), 3–10.

U.S. Geological Survey, Water Resources Division (1976). "Water Resources Data for New Jersey, 1975," Rep. No. USGS/WRD/HD-76/020. Washington, D.C.

Wolle, F. (1880). Fresh-water algae, IV. *Bull. Torrey Bot. Club* **7,** 43–48.

Wolle, F. (1881a). Fresh-water algae, V. *Bull. Torrey Bot. Club* **8,** 37–40.

Wolle, F. (1881b). American fresh-water algae: Species and varieties of desmids new to science. *Bull. Torrey Bot. Club* **8,** 1–4.

Wolle, F. (1882). Fresh-water algae, VI. *Bull. Torrey Bot. Club* **9,** 25–30.

Wolle, F. (1883). Fresh-water algae, VII. *Bull. Torrey Bot. Club* **10,** 13–21.

Wolle, F. (1884). Fresh-water algae, VIII. *Bull. Torrey Bot. Club* **11,** 13–17.

Wolle, F. (1885). Fresh-water algae, IX. *Bull. Torrey Bot. Club* **12,** 1–6.

Wolle, F. (1887). "Fresh-Water Algae of the United States (Exclusive of the Diatomaceae)." Comenius Press, Bethlehem, Pennsylvania.

APPENDIX

All insect records are from Smith (1910). The fishes are reported in the following river basins: Raritan River (Fowler, 1920; New Jersey Division of Fish and Game, 1957); Manasquan River (Fowler, 1920); Metedeconk River (Fowler, 1920; New Jersey Division of Fish and Game, 1957); Toms River (Fowler, 1920; New Jersey Division of Fish and Game, 1950, 1957); Cedar Creek (Fowler, 1920, 1952); Forked

River (Fowler, 1920, 1952; New Jersey Division of Fish and Game, 1951); Mullica River (Fowler, 1906, 1920, 1952; New Jersey Division of Fish and Game, 1950, 1951, 1957; Cope, 1883); Patgong Creek (Fowler, 1952); Great Egg Harbor River (Fowler, 1906, 1908a, 1920, 1952; Cope 1896; New Jersey Division of Fish and Game, 1951, 1957); Tuckahoe River (Fowler, 1907a, 1908a, 1920, 1952; New Jersey Division of Fish and Game, 1950); Cedar Swamp Creek (Fowler, 1906, 1907a, 1908a, 1920); Dennis Creek (Fowler, 1907a, 1908a, 1909a, 1920; New Jersey Division of Fish and Game, 1957); Maurice River (Fowler, 1909a, 1920, 1952; New Jersey Division of Fish and Game, 1950, 1951, 1957); Big Timber Creek (Fowler, 1908a, 1909a, 1920, 1952; New Jersey Division of Fish and Game, 1950, 1951); Cooper River (Fowler, 1908a, 1920); Rancocas Creek (Fowler, 1906, 1907a, 1908a, 1920, 1952; New Jersey Division of Fish and Game, 1950, 1951); and Crosswicks Creek (New Jersey Division of Fish and Game, 1950).

Amphibians and reptiles in streams and lakes are not discussed here, but are reported in Fowler (1907b, 1908b, 1909b), as well as in additional records for the Mullica River basin found in Fikslin and Montgomery (1971) and Juneja (1974), and for the Great Egg Harbor River basin discussed by Cope (1896).

Diatom records for Rancocas Creek are from the Academy of Natural Sciences (1973), and all other diatom records are from the Diatom Herbarium Files, Academy of Natural Sciences. Records of other algae are as follows: Toms River (Wolle, 1880, 1887); Cedar Creek (Wolle, 1887); Mullica River (Fikslin and Montgomery, 1971; Fowler, 1952; Wolle, 1880, 1881a,b, 1882, 1883, 1887); Absecon River (Wolle, 1883, 1887); Dennis Creek (Wolle, 1881a,b, 1887); Maurice River (Wolle, 1883, 1884, 1885, 1887); and Rancocas Creek (Wolle, 1880, 1884, 1885). Specific collection localities are given in the references.

11

Nutrient and Hydrological Effects of the Pine Barrens on Neighboring Estuaries

JAMES B. DURAND

INTRODUCTION

The studies reported in this chapter are part of a series of studies on the primary productivity and nutrients in the Mullica River of the Pine Barrens and the Great Bay estuary into which it drains. Several studies of estuarine productivity are available for comparison (Aurand and Daiber, 1973; Jeffries, 1962; Mandelli *et al.,* 1970; Williams, 1966; Williams and Murdoch, 1966). In general, these studies involve a low frequency of sampling and are not concerned primarily with the relationship between primary productivity and nitrogen. The research in New Jersey reported here has utilized a high frequency of sampling for primary productivity and nitrogen measurements and has been concerned primarily with evaluating the relationship between the phytoplankton productivity of the estuary and the nitrogen supply from the river drainage basin. This research illustrates the sensitivity of the phytoplankton community in the bay to the delivery of minute quantities of nitrogen from the drainage in the Pine Barrens, suggesting an intimate relationship between an estuary and the drainage system that supplies it.

METHODS

Locations of principal sampling stations are given in Fig. 1. Dissolved oxygen in the water was measured by the azide modification of the Winkler method. Salinity was measured according to the method described in Harvey (1955). Water transparency was estimated using Secchi discs. The amount of chlorophyll *a* in the water was measured and calculated according to Strickland and Parsons (1968), after filtration on 0.8 μm-pore-sized Millipore filters. The results presented here are taken from several studies between 1961 and 1977.

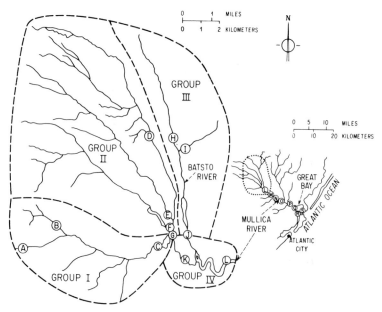

Fig. 1. Sampling locations in the Mullica River basin and Great Bay. Dotted area of map on right is expanded on left to show the four groups of locations sampled. Group I includes urban and agricultural drainage; Group II, swampland drainage below agricultural areas; Group III, drainage from undisturbed areas; Group IV, combination drainage areas. Sampling locations other than those listed in Table 1 are: L, Crowley Landing (CL); M, Station R17 (27 km upriver from station Q); N, Station R14 (22 km upriver from station Q); O, Station R11 (18 km upriver from station Q); P, French Point, the lower river station (FP); Q, Turtle Island, the upper bay station (TI); R, Mid Bay (MB) and; S, Cape Horn (CH).

Nitrogen

In 1961–1963, ammonium-nitrogen and nitrate-nitrogen concentrations were measured at eight stations (shown later in Figs. 4–6) along the Mullica River and in Great Bay. Measurements were taken approximately once a week during September–May and twice a week during June–August.

In the summer of 1976 and in January 1977, ammonium-N and nitrate-N were measured in the uppermost part of the Mullica River drainage basin (Fig. 1). As shown in Figure 1, stations were classified on the basis of the degree to which the drainage of each was subject to agricultural or urban influence. Sandy Lakewood soils and St. Johns soils characterize the area (Tedrow, 1963).

Group I—Urban and agricultural drainage. Station A received drainage from the town of Hammonton and from the Hammonton sewage treatment plant. Station B received drainage from an agricultural area. Station C was located downstream from Stations A and B and therefore received drainage from areas of both types.

Group II—Swampland drainage below agricultural areas. Stations D, E, and F all drained agricultural areas. However, large areas of swampland were located between the agricultural area and the sampling station. Station G was located downstream from the above three stations and represents a mix of those stations.

Group III—Drainage from undisturbed areas. Stations H, I, and J were located on the Batsto River and its tributaries, all of which drain relatively undisturbed forest and swampland.

Group IV—Combination drainage areas. Station K was located downstream from the junction of drainage from Groups I and II. Station L was located downstream from the junction of Groups I, II, and III.

Samples for nitrogen measurements were collected in glass or polyethylene bottles that had been cleaned with concentrated H_2SO_4 and thoroughly rinsed with deionized water. Samples were stored in the dark prior to processing a few hours later. During the early 1960's, nitrate-N was measured on Millipore-filtered samples by the hydrazine reduction method of Mullin and Riley (1955) within 24 hours of collection. Nitrate-N was measured in the upper Mullica in 1976–1977 by the brucine method (Jenkins and Medsker, 1964) on samples that had been Millipore-filtered and frozen within hours of collection. In both the hydrazine reduction method and the brucine method, standards were run with each sample. Standards were run with each series in the cadmium reduction method. Ammonium-N was measured in the early 1960's on unfiltered samples on the day of collection by the method of Riley and Sinhaseni (1957). The upper Mullica River samples of 1976–1977 were Millipore-filtered and frozen on the day of collection. Ammonium-N was measured subsequently by the Solorzano (1969) procedure. Quantities are expressed as milligrams of N and concentrations as ppm.

Primary Productivity

Primary productivity measurements were made at French Point, Turtle Island, and Cape Horn (Fig. 1) four to five times each week during the summer of 1963. These stations represent river, upper bay, and lower bay, respectively. Oxygen production and chlorophyll production were measured in dark–light bottle experiments. Surface water was siphoned from a polyethylene bucket into 300-ml BOD bottles. In addition to unenriched control bottles in each experiment, separate nutrient enrichments were made to three bottles by: (1) 0.21 ppm nitrate-N; (2) 0.10 ppm ammonium-N; and (3) a mixture of nutrients. The mixture was a modification of that used by Ryther and Guillard (1959) and contained nitrate-N, phosphate-P, sodium thiosulfate, sodium silicate, and salts of copper, cobalt, manganese, and molybdenum. Light bottles were suspended from a spar buoy at 0.3 m, and dark bottles were positioned immediately below the light bottles. At this depth, the bottles were exposed to approximately 50% surface illumination. Wave action generally was sufficient to keep the bottle contents suspended. All experiments were begun between 8 and 9 AM and were terminated 24 hours later. Vertical mixing, especially in the river area, was complete. Because experiments were conducted at the same time each day, the local stage of the tide of sampling changed by approximately one hour per day. Thus, within about two weeks all tidal stages had been sampled. Production rates were expressed as ml O_2 produced or as mg C/mg chlorophyll *a*/hour. One milliliter oxygen produced was taken as equivalent to 0.209 mg carbon fixed (Ryther, 1956). Chlorophyll production was taken as the difference in chlorophyll *a* concentration between the light and dark bottles.

Compensation depth experiments were carried out on eight dates at river and bay stations during the summer of 1963. In these experiments, bottles containing surface water were suspended at 0.3-m intervals to 1.5 m. Experiments were begun between 8 and 9 AM and were terminated 24 hours later. Gross production at 0.3-m depth intervals was plotted, and the graphs were measured with a planimeter to provide production/m^2 values. Nitrogen (ammonium-N plus nitrate-N) was taken according to the closest nitrogen sampling date, in general either one day before or one day after the productivity measurements. According to Strickland (1960), roughly 0.035 mg N is required on the average for every milliliter of oxygen produced by the phytoplankton. Using this estimate, the amount of nitrogen required for the measured production was calculated and compared with that available at a given station.

In the next section, test results will be presented in the following order: salinity and transparency; sources of nitrogen in the Mullica River–Great Bay estuary; and primary productivity in relation to nitrogen supply.

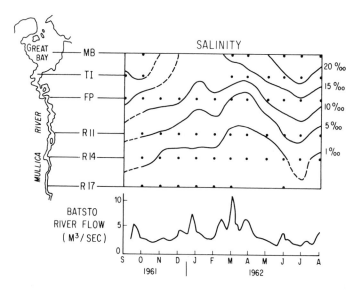

Fig. 2. Salinity of the Mullica River–Great Bay system throughout the year. Dots indicate locations and months during 1961–1962 for which average salinity measurements are available. Contour lines are plotted for 1, 5, 10, 15, and 20 parts per thousand (‰) salinity. See Fig. 1 for sampling.

RESULTS

Salinity

The salinity distribution in the Mullica River–Great Bay system (Fig. 2) varies upriver to downriver and seasonally according to variations in precipitation and evapotranspiration, as indicated by riverflow records observed at the Batso River gauging station located at station J in Fig. 2. The upper end of the estuary, where sea water is diluted measurably with freshwater from land drainage (Pritchard, 1967), was in the vicinity of station R14 (Fig. 1). This station also marked the uppermost distribution of typical salt marsh vegetation. Salinities at French Point, the downriver station, ranged essentially between 10 and 15‰ throughout the year. High flows in the winter resulted in a downstream shift in salinity values, while low flows in the summer resulted in an upstream shift in salinity values.

Transparency

Seasonal and spatial variations in transparency were pronounced (Fig. 3). Upriver, the water was rather clear in the winter, but in summer upriver water was characterized by deep (tea-colored) cedar stain and large amounts of particulate material. Both the stain and the particulate material were reduced considerably in winter, such that after filtering only a light yellow color remained in upriver water. During the summer, filters became plugged with only 100 ml of water. In contrast, at downriver and bay stations

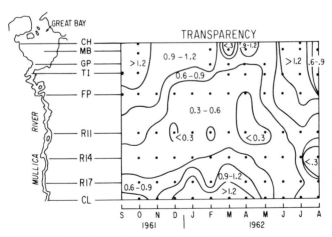

Fig. 3. Transparency of the Mullica River–Great Bay system throughout the year. Dots indicate locations and months during 1961–1962 for which average Secchi disc measurements are available. Contour lines are plotted for 0.3-m intervals. GP, Graveling Point; see Fig. 1 legend for other location names.

water transparency was minimal in the winter, and maximal in the summer. Here, turbidity was caused by a grayish-colored material not typical of the "humus" river particles and lacking the cedar stain.

Nitrogen

River–Bay Gradients

A marked upriver–downriver gradient in nitrate-N concentrations existed throughout the year (Fig. 4), with lower concentrations downriver. Concentrations usually decreased to very low levels, <0.028 mg nitrate-N/liter in the summer in the bay.

In addition, a marked seasonal pattern in nitrate-N concentrations was observed. The late spring through summer period was characterized by the lowest upriver concentrations. In October, when the leaves had turned color and when most of the farm crops had been harvested, concentrations rose sharply. Nitrate-N concentrations were maximal in January and February and decreased through the early spring.

In contrast to the nitrate-N concentrations, ammonium-N concentrations (Fig. 5) did not show an upriver–downriver gradient. Ammonium-N concentrations frequently varied considerably between successive measurements. Again, a well-defined seasonal pattern occurred. Maximal ammonium-N concentrations occurred in January and February, and minimal were recorded in July and August. It is probable that little ammonium-N was leached from the land into the river.

Sources

The data in Table I show the highest nitrogen concentrations, particularly nitrate-N concentrations, at the Group I stations (Fig. 1), those stations draining urban and agricultural areas. The highest concentrations occurred at station A in association with

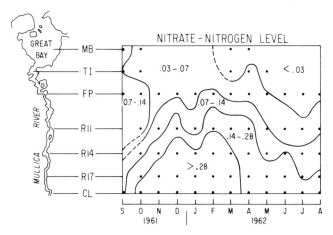

Fig. 4. Nitrate–nitrogen (mg N/liter) in the Mullica River–Great Bay system throughout the year. See legends to Figs. 1 and 2.

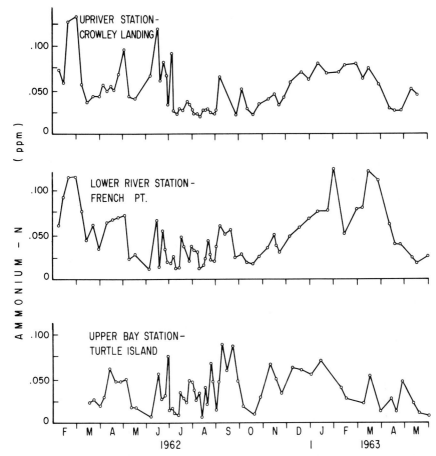

Fig. 5. Ammonium-nitrogen concentrations at three locations in the Mullica River–Great Bay system.

the sewage treatment plant. Although lower nitrogen concentrations occurred at stations B and C, the concentrations were greater than those found elsewhere in the Mullica River basin.

Group II, III, and IV stations were characterized by generally low ammonium-N concentrations. Nitrate-N concentrations, however, were higher in the summer from swampland drainage below agricultural areas at Group II station F. In January, nitrate-N concentrations increased in the Group II drainage, reflecting nitrogen uptake by farmland and swamps. Therefore, excess nitrate-N in the soil was leached into the streams. To a lesser degree, the Group III stations also showed elevated nitrate-N concentrations in January. Ammonium-N concentrations, however, remained low. Group IV stations generally reflected the expected averaging of concentrations since they were located downstream from the Group I, II, and III drainages.

TABLE I   Nitrogen Concentrations at Selected Stations in the Upper Mullica River Drainage Basin in Summer and Winter.[a]

	June, July, August 1976		January 1977	
	NH$_4$-N	NO$_3$-N	NH$_4$-N	NO$_3$-N
Group I. Urban and agricultural drainage				
A. Hammonton Creek	4.42	3.77	5.12	1.25
B. Hammonton Branch	0.07	0.38	0.12	2.55
C. Hammonton Creek				
at Nescochaque Lake	0.07	0.31	0.81	0.56
Group II. Swampland drain- age below agricultural areas				
D. Mullica River at Wilderness Well	0.06	0.08	0.06	0.47
E. Sleeper Branch	0.04	0.06	0.05	0.18
F. Nescochaque Creek, N. Branch	0.01	0.25	0.05	1.04
G. Mullica River at Rt. 542	0.04	0.16	0.05	0.52
Group III. Drainage from undisturbed areas				
H. Batsto River at Wilderness Well	0.02	0.04	0.04	0.13
I. Penn Swamp Branch	0.04	0.01	0.04	0.07
J. Batsto River at Rt. 542	0.02	0.02	0.02	0.07
Group IV. Combination drainage areas				
K. Mullica River at Thurston Ave.	0.04	0.26	0.17	0.47
L. Crowley Landing	0.03	0.12	0.08	0.32

[a] Concentration as mg N/liter. 1976 = average 77–15 measurements; 1977 = average of 2–3 measurements.

Nitrogen Limitation

In primary productivity measurements, enrichment with nitrate-N often resulted in increased gross production rates, often as much as a doubling of the rate (Fig. 6). Although no information is available concerning which organisms of the phytoplankton community responded to the enrichment, gross production patterns for both control and enriched samples were similar to the Turtle Island and Cape Horn stations. These stations were located about 6 km apart, at the upper and lower ends of Great Bay. The similarity of patterns suggests relative uniformity of performance throughout the bay.

Enrichment with ammonium-N was as effective as enrichment with nitrate-N, indicating that the phytoplankton community made equally effective use of either form of nitrogen enrichment. The regression equation relating oxygen production in ammonium-N-enriched experiments (y) to oxygen production in nitrate-N-enriched experiments (x) was $y = 0.275 + 0.718\,x$; $r = 0.944$. Thus, phytoplankton production increases with added nitrogen in either the nitrate or ammonium form.

Enrichment with a mixture of nutrients containing ammonium-N, nitrate-N, phosphate-P, sodium thiosulfate, sodium silicate, and various trace metals rarely caused greater oxygen production than enrichment with nitrate-N alone. The regression

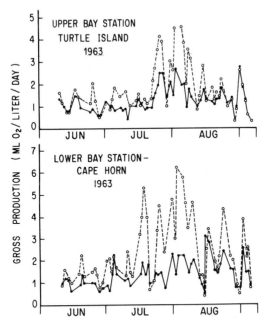

Fig. 6. Effect of nitrate enrichment on gross production in the Great Bay estuary. Solid line, production in unenriched control; dashed line, enriched with 0.21 ppm nitrate–nitrogen.

equation relating oxygen production in experiments enriched with the nutrient mixture (y) to oxygen production in nitrate-N-enriched experiments (x) was $y = 0.09 + 0.93 x$; $r = 0.919$. Thus, production with the enriched nutrient mixture was about the same as with the enriched nitrate-N, and the added elements had very little effect. At least with ample nitrate-N present, these other elements apparently were not limiting to phytoplankton productivity.

Often, as pulses of increasing production occurred in the daily control experiments, the response to nitrate-N enrichment increased. After a few days, maximal response to enrichment occurred, control production rates dropped off, and a period followed during which nitrate-N enrichment was ineffective in increasing production. The mixture of other nutrients also was ineffective at these times.

Chlorophyll Production

The results of chlorophyll production experiments for summer 1963 are shown in Fig. 7. The chlorophyll produced is plotted against the sum of the field concentrations of ammonium-N plus nitrate-N present at the beginning of the experiment. The results are from stream samples (unenriched) incubated under field conditions for 24-hour periods. During the sampling schedule, samples were collected and run under practically all tidal and weather conditions. The phytoplankton communities probably differed at different times over the course of these experiments. The regression equation

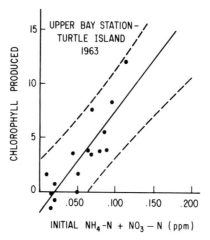

Fig. 7. Chlorophyll *a* production related to nitrogen concentration in the Great Bay estuary. Initial field ammonium–nitrogen and nitrate–nitrogen concentrations are summed. Dashed lines indicate 95% confidence limits.

relating chlorophyll production (y) to initial ammonium-N plus nitrate-N concentrations (x) was $y = -2.015 + 1.338\ x$; $r = 0.850$. Data (not given here) from years other than 1963 show similar results, although correlation coefficients for those years were lower. One factor probably contributing to the high correlation in 1963 was that the riverflow monitored at the Batsto River gauging station was extremely uniform.

Nitrogen Demand versus Nitrogen Supply

The depth in the water at the point where photosynthesis and respiration are equal, i.e., the compensation point, for both the lower part of the river and bay was 1.5–1.6 m (Table II). For the lower river, average low water depths were 6 m and for the bay 1.7–3.2 m. Thus, the main photosynthetic or euphotic zone constituted only 25% of the water column in the river but 50–100% in the bay.

For each station, the excess nitrogen was the difference between the standing stock of ammonium-N plus nitrate-N/m² and the nitrogen required/m² as calculated from productivity measures. Regeneration of ammonium-N in the water column was not considered in the calculations.

Nitrogen was present in the river in excess of production demands, but present in insufficient quantities in the lower bay. The relationship between nitrogen supply and demand at the upper bay station tended toward an intermediate condition. Excess nitrogen ranged from 2.8 to over 336 mg of nitrogen in the river. Comparison of excess nitrogen with the stage of the tide of sampling (Table II) shows that the least excess of nitrogen occurred in experiments run with flood tide water that had been located in the bay for some time prior to sampling. Ebb tide water showed larger excess nitrogen quantities. This water had been located in the river in the hours prior to sampling.

TABLE II Relationship between Primary Productivity and Nitrogen Supply in the Mullica River–Great Bay System, 1963[a]

Date	French Point—Lower River					Turtle Island—Upper River					Cape Horn—Lower Bay				
	GP mgC	mg N required	mg N available	Excess mg N	Tide ±hr[b]	GP mgC	mg N required	mg N available	Excess Mg N	Tide ±hr[b]	GP mgC	mg N required	mg N available	Excess mg N	Tide ±hr[b]
6/25	344	57.4	—	—	H−2¼	302	50.4	—	—	H−2½	308	51.8	—	—	H−3
6/24	198	—	260.4	203.0	H−¾	—	—	53.2	2.8	H−1	—	—	35.0	−16.8	H−1¾
7/4	—	33.6	—	—	H+2¾	312	51.8	—	—	H+2½	386	64.4	—	—	H+1¾
7/5	—	—	512.4	478.8	H+2¼	—	—	100.8	49.0	H+2	—	—	15.4	−49.0	H+1
7/12	—	—	—	—	—	270	44.8	—	—	L−2¾	226	37.8	—	—	L+1¼
7/11	—	—	—	—	—	—	—	57.4	12.6	H+2½	—	—	25.2	−12.6	H+1¾
7/18	321	53.2	—	—	L−2½	196	32.2	—	—	H+3	367	61.6	—	—	H+2½
7/18	—	—	148.4	95.2	L−2½	—	—	173.6	141.4	H+3	—	—	47.6	−14.0	H+2½
7/24	297	50.4	—	—	H−2	428	75.6	—	—	H−2	—	—	—	—	—
7/25	—	—	436.8	386.4	H+1	—	—	173.6	98.0	H−½	—	—	—	—	—
8/7	258	43.4	—	—	H−1	228	37.8	—	—	H−1	382	64.4	—	—	H−1¼
8/8	—	—	344.4	301.0	H−1	—	—	72.8	35.0	H−1	—	—	63.0	−1.4	H−1½
8/11	209	35.0	—	—	L−1½	227	37.8	—	—	L−2	—	—	—	—	—
8/15	—	—	352.8	317.8	L−2	—	—	380.8	343.0	L−2¼	—	—	—	—	—
8/23	287	47.6	—	—	H−1¼	373	63.0	—	—	H−2¼	638	106.4	—	—	H−2¾
8/22	—	—	690.2	642.6	H−1	—	—	154.0	91.0	H−1¼	—	—	71.4	−35.0	H−2
8/28	507	85.4	—	—	L−¾	246	40.6	—	—	L−1	270	44.8	—	—	L−1
8/29	—	—	344.4	259.0	L−½	—	—	294.0	253.4	L−1	—	—	68.6	23.8	L−1
Average depth of compensation point		1.5 m					1.5 m					1.6 m			
Average low tide depth		6.0 m					3.2 m					1.7 m			

[a] Primary productivity (GP) expressed as mgC/m²/day. Nitrogen required calculated as mgN/m²/day. Nitrogen available equals sum of ammonium−N and nitrate−N/m² on day of sampling indicated. Excess nitrogen is the difference between nitrogen required/m²/day and nitrogen available/m²/day.

[b] H, high tide; L, low tide.

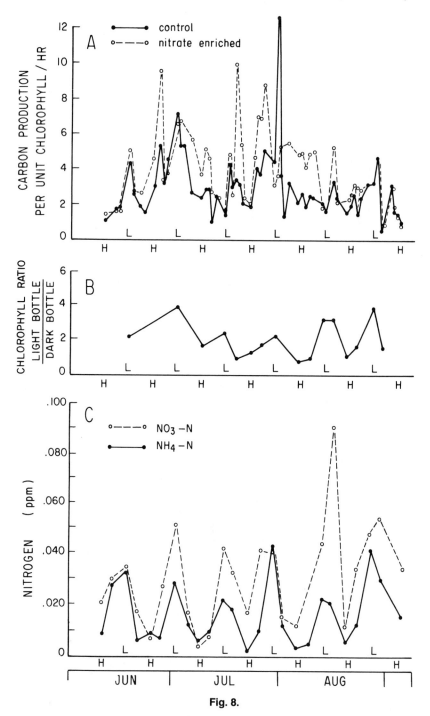

Fig. 8.

Thus, phytoplankton production placed a demand upon nitrogen stocks that was greater in the bay than in the river. Water at the lower bay station at any stage of tide was mostly bay water, while water at the river station was almost entirely river water. Water between the river station and the bay station was composed of varying proportions of river and bay water, with the proportion of river water increasing during ebb tide.

These experiments show that phytoplankton demands for nitrogen in the bay were in excess of local standing stocks of inorganic-N. Phytoplankton demands for nitrogen in the river were less than local standing stocks. Therefore, nitrogen usually was not exhausted in the river but was transported into the bay.

Measurements of (a) primary productivity at 0.3 m, (b) the ratio of chlorophyll concentration after 24 hours in light bottles to that in dark bottles, and (c) ammonium-N concentrations and nitrate-N concentrations for June–August, 1963, including sampling at both high and low water levels (Fig. 8), indicated that pulses in all three characteristics occurred in association with low water sampling times. Low values were associated with high water sampling times. Therefore, nitrogen limitation, as indicated by high enriched values of C/chl/hr, occurred at times of high water level.

DISCUSSION

The purpose of this chapter is to evaluate the influence of Pine Barrens drainage on neighboring estuaries and to consider in more general terms other important aspects of riverflow and the New Jersey estuaries. Clearly, nutrient load and riverflow are two parameters of interest.

Nutrient Load

Although regeneration of nutrients in river nutrient cycles undoubtedly occurred and probably accounted for a considerable amount of the ammonium-N in the system, an input of nitrate-N in the upper reaches of the river system accounted for an appreciable addition to the aquatic nutrient stocks. The gradient of nitrate-N concentrations from upriver to downriver stations indicates the upriver regions as the source of nitrate-N. The high concentrations associated with drainage, under urban or agricultural influence, suggests that the input was primarily nitrogen being leached from agricultural areas plus some from the Hammonton sewage plant. Large quantities of nitrate-N were leached in the winter months when nitrogen uptake by terrestrial metabolic processes was minimal. The possible regeneration of ammonium-N *in situ* and the entrance of

Fig. 8. Summer nitrogen supply, chlorophyll and carbon production in Great Bay estuary. Measurements at upper bay station, Turtle Island, 1963. H, high water; L, low water. (A) Carbon produced per unit chlorophyll per hour. Solid line, control samples; dashed line, samples enriched with 0.21 mg nitrate-N/liter. (B) Ratio of chlorophyll concentration in control light bottles to that in control dark bottles after 24-hour field exposure to light. (C) Nitrogen concentrations, mg N/liter, plotted against time. Solid line, nitrate-N; dashed line, ammonium-N.

large quantities of nitrate-N at the upper end agree with the findings of Hobbie *et al.* (1975) for the Pamlico River estuary in North Carolina. Uttormark *et al.* (1974) reported that transport by streams draining agricultural watersheds was the most important source of nutrient enrichment of lakes in agricultural areas. Data presented here from undisturbed Pine Barrens areas are in agreement with those of Toth and Smith (1960) and indicate that little nitrogen was available from undisturbed areas.

The data presented here suggest that nitrogen was the nutrient most often present in limiting concentrations when other conditions, such as light, were adequate for phytoplankton photosynthesis. Rarely did enrichment with other nutrients result in increased production. Limitation by nitrogen occurred in the bay because of the penetration of light to or near the bottom. Depths of the compensation point sometimes exceeded the average low water depth in the bay. Because of the large nitrogen uptake by phytoplankton in the bay, very low nutrient levels were present in the water. On the other hand, less light penetration and greater depth of the river, exceeding the depth of the compensation point, were conditions that provided a large volume of water whose nutrient stocks were not limiting. Excess nutrient, therefore, was transported to the bay. Because of the tidal circulation, the nutrient additions were made in pulses at the head of the bay during low water.

Thomas (1970) showed increases in chlorophyll concentrations in natural phytoplankton populations in proportion to nitrogen enrichment. Variations of as much as 1–10 in C/chl/hr values have been reported (Ryther and Yentsch, 1957). Curl and Small (1965) obtained low C/chl/hr rates in natural phytoplankton communities from nutrient-depleted water and high values in communities from nutrient-rich waters. In our experiments, the light-bottle chlorophyll/dark-bottle chlorophyll ratios show that chlorophyll concentrations increased during experiments with low water samples but not with high water samples. Increases in C/chl/hr occurred because in calculating the value, the oxygen produced was divided by the initial chlorophyll concentration rather than by the final light-bottle chlorophyll concentration. Therefore, C/chl/hr did not increase in the high water samples. Chlorophyll production has been shown to be proportional to the initial nitrogen concentration. Therefore, as the river contributed nitrogen to the bay, chlorophyll production, or C/chl/hr, increased accordingly.

It is stressed that the regularity of the nutrient pulsations shown here probably stems from the extremely uniform riverflow conditions of the summer of 1963. In the event of irregular riverflow (e.g., frequent thunderstorms), variations in upriver nitrogen input would occur. Since we have described a system that represents an equilibrium between nutrient supply and nutrient uptake, the regular pulsing observed in the upper bay in 1963 might not occur there. Instead, it might occur slightly upriver or further down in the bay, depending upon those factors governing the activities of a phytoplankton community.

Riverflow

Maintenance of riverflow is important to river–estuarine systems in ways other than through nutrient supply. Removal of water from the system will cause lowering of the water table. Because circulation in the Mullica River–Great Bay system is largely tidal, lowered riverflow will cause an upriver extension of saline water. Salinity gradients will be maintained, but they will be displaced further upriver.

While it would be possible to remove water from the drainage basin so as to delay the effect upon riverflow, efforts should be made to ensure that such effects be minimal. Since human needs for water and demands upon the water table usually are independent of the rate of resupply of groundwater, limitations on water use should be exercised in order to avoid a situation of conflicting needs that could have ecological repercussions on estuarine ecology. Clearly, removal of water to regions outside a drainage system should be prohibited.

Shifts in gradients, particularly in salinity gradients, normally occur on a seasonal basis and in response to local storm conditions. Maintenance of such variations may be important to organisms inhabiting the estuary.

Some planktonic organisms probably require particular salinity regimes. For example, the association of salinity gradients and presence of bordering vegetation, e.g., salt marshes, may be important to the feeding and reproduction of certain species of copepods. The restriction of copepods such as *Eurytemora affinis* to lower saline parts of estuaries occurs in the Mullica River (Durand and Nadeau, 1972), and lower salinities remove such forms from competition with others, e.g., *Acartia tonsa*. The existence of salt marsh and associated creeks may play a variety of important roles in the estuarine ecosystem.

Salinity gradients are necessary for the development of nursery areas for various species (Van Engel and Joseph, 1968). Thus, some fish require low-salinity water in their early stages. Low-salinity regions may keep larval stages separated from predators until such time as the young are large enough to escape. Ctenophores for example, are excluded from very low salinity water in which larval fish may be developing.

Bottom organisms, of course, bear most directly the brunt of changes in salinity regime because they usually cannot move out when conditions change. Shifts in distribution of many bottom organisms are dependent largely upon distribution of larvae or relatively slow locomotion of the individuals. Some predators of commercially important shellfish are prevented from occupying nursery and growing grounds by salinity barriers. Thus, oyster drills are not found over most of the oyster seed beds in the lower region of the Mullica River, but are present in large numbers in the bay on the planted oyster grounds (Haskin, unpublished data). Seasonal salinity patterns are important in this instance, because young oyster drills hatch out at about the time of setting of oyster spat and begin feeding upon small newly attached oysters. Other predators, such as starfish, are present well down the estuary in the inlet. Echinoderms are kept out of these estuaries by salinities less than those of sea water. Decreased riverflow would permit invasion of oyster grounds by such echinoderms.

The output of estuarine water to the ocean immediately along the shore undoubtedly is of ecological significance. Bays and inlets are favorite gathering places for many organisms. Some are attracted because of the availability of food, while others in response to clues leading them upstream for spawning. The output of nutrient material, both inorganic and organic, may be of importance to immediately nearshore phytoplankton production. Some of our recent data show that the entrance of the Little Egg Inlet is particularly productive of phytoplankton. The primary production occurring at the junctions of bays and the ocean has not been studied adequately. Production in these locations is probably very susceptible to variations in riverflow and nutrient load of that flow.

Statement

In the midst of a developing megalopolis extending from Boston to Washington, D.C. lies one of the most populated states in the nation. In it is located the Pine Barrens. Because such a system cannot serve a large number of functions, priorities of use must be established. Disturbance of the Pine Barrens will result in changes in the water quality, depending upon the nature of the disturbance. It is clear that even minute changes in water quality can cause significant changes in other communities of the estuaries downstream.

SUMMARY

Primary production by the phytoplankton community in the Great Bay estuary was controlled by the supply of nitrogen derived from the Mullica River drainage basin in the Pine Barrens. Low nitrate-nitrogen concentrations were found in streams of relatively undisturbed areas of the drainage basin, while high nitrate-nitrogen concentrations were characteristic of streams draining the agricultural and urban areas of the Pine Barrens. Low nitrogen levels often limited primary production, especially in the well-lighted bay. Primary production in the bay increased in response to nitrogen supplied by the river, even when the nitrogen was supplied in minute quantities. Salinity gradients in the estuary, maintained by the volume of river water flow, are critical to many estuarine animals. Thus, the relatively low nutrient levels and the amount and relative constancy of water flow in Pine Barrens streams have a major controlling and stabilizing effect on the ecosystems of the coastal estuaries.

ACKNOWLEDGMENTS

This work was supported by the New Jersey Department of Conservation and Economic Development through the New Jersey Oyster Research Laboratory, Rutgers University, by the National Science Foundation, NSFG 17827 and GB2650, by the Center for Coastal and Environmental Studies, Rutgers University, and by the National Science Foundation Program RANN through the Water Resources Research Institute, Rutgers University.

REFERENCES

Aurand, D., and Diaber, F. C. (1973). Nitrate and nitrite in the surface waters of two Delaware salt marshes. *Chesapeake Sci.* **14,** 105–111.

Curl, H. J., and Small, L. F. (1965). Variations in photosynthetic assimilation ratios in natural, marine phytoplankton communities. *Limnol. Oceanogr.* **10**, Suppl., R67–R73.

Durand, J. B., and Nadeau, R. J. (1972). ''Water Resources Development in the Mullica River Basin. Part I. Biological Evaluation of the Mullica River–Great Bay Estuary.'' Water Resour. Inst., Rutgers Univ., New Brunswick, New Jersey.

Harvey, H. W. (1955). ''The Chemistry and Fertility of Sea Waters.'' Cambridge Univ. Press, London and New York.

Hobbie, J. E., Copeland, B. J., and Harrison, W. G. (1975). Sources and fates of nutrients of the Pamlico River estuary, North Carolina. *In* ''Chemistry, Biology, and the Estuarine System'' (L. E. Cronin, ed.), Estuarine Research, Vol. 1, pp. 287–302. Academic Press, New York.

Jeffries, H. P. (1962). Environmental characteristics of Raritan Bay, a polluted estuary. *Limnol. Oceanogr.* **7**, 21–31.

Jenkins, D., and Medsker, L. L. (1964). Brucine method for determination of nitrate in ocean, estuarine, and fresh waters. *Anal. Chem.* **36**, 610–612.

Mandelli, E. F., Burkholder, P. R., Doheny, T. E., and Brody, R. (1970). Studies of primary productivity in coastal waters of southern Long Island, New York. *Mar. Biol.* **7**, 153–160.

Mullin, J. B., and Riley, J. P. (1955). The colorimetric determination of nitrate in natural waters with particular reference to sea water. *Anal. Chim. Acta* **12**, 464–480.

Pritchard, D. W. (1967). What is an estuary: Physical viewpoint. *In* ''Estuaries'' (G. H. Lauff, ed.), Publ. No. 83, pp. 3–6. Am. Assoc. Adv. Sci., Washington, D.C.

Riley, J. P., and Sinhaseni, P. (1957). The determination of ammonia and total inorganic nitrogen in sea water. *J. Mar. Biol. Assoc. U.K.* **36**, 161–168.

Ryther, J. H. (1956). The measurement of primary production. *Limnol. Oceanogr.* **1**, 72–84.

Ryther, J. H., and Guillard, R. R. L. (1959). Enrichment experiments as a means of studying nutrients limiting to phytoplankton production. *Deep Sea Res.* **6**, 65–69.

Ryther, J. H., and Yentsch, C. S. (1957). The estimation of phytoplankton production in the ocean from chlorophyll and light data. *Limnol. Oceanogr.* **2**, 281–286.

Solorzano, L. (1969). Determination of ammonia in natural waters by the phenolhypochlorite method. *Limnol. Oceanogr.* **14**, 799–801.

Strickland, J. D. H. (1960). Measuring the production of marine phytoplankton. *Bull., Fish. Res. Board Can.* **122**, 1–172.

Strickland, J. D. H., and Parsons, T. R. (1968). ''A Practical Handbook of Seawater Analysis.'' Fish. Res. Board Can., Ottawa.

Tedrow, J. C. F. (1963). New Jersey soils. *N.J. Coll. Agric., Circ.* No. 601.

Thomas, W. H. (1970). Effect of ammonium and nitrate concentration on chlorophyll increases in natural tropical Pacific phytoplankton populations. *Limnol. Oceanogr.* **15**, 386–394.

Toth, S.J., and Smith, R.F. (1960). Soil over which water flows affects ability to grow fish. *N.J. Agric.* **42**, 5–11.

Uttormark, P. D., Chapin, J. D., and Green, K. M. (1974). ''Estimating Nutrient Loadings of Lakes from Non-Point Sources,'' Program Element 1BA031, Roap/Task 21AJ828. Water Resour. Cent. Univ. of Wisconsin, Madison.

Van Engel, W. A., and Joseph, E. J. (1968). Characterization of coastal and estuarine fish nursery grounds as natural communities. U.S. Bur. Commer. Fish., Washington, D.C. (Unpublished report.)

Williams, R. B. (1966). Annual phytoplanktonic production in a system of shallow temperate estuaries. *In* ''Some Contemporary Studies in Marine Sciences'' (H. Barnes, ed.), pp. 699–716. Allen & Unwin, London.

Williams, R. B., and Murdoch, M. B. (1966). Phytoplankton production and chlorophyll concentration in the Beaufort Channel, North Carolina. *Limnol. Oceanogr.* **11**, 73–82.

Part IV

VEGETATION
PATTERNS

12

Vegetational History of the Pine Barrens

CALVIN J. HEUSSER

PERSPECTIVE

The Coastal Plain of New Jersey has undergone a lengthy and varied development beginning as early as the Cretaceous period. The plant communities that ultimately gave rise to the modern Pine Barrens took shape as part of this evolving physical scene. In response to the changing geological and climatic environment, community makeup was shuffled and reshuffled throughout the Tertiary and Quaternary periods. Certain taxa occurring today appear to have endured from ancient times, while others have become established only since the Pleistocene. Ice-age climates caused species to die out in the region or to migrate toward the equator; as a result, many plants of the Late Tertiary Coastal Plain in New Jersey now range south in the southeastern states, Caribbean, or Central America. The temperate species of today's Pine Barrens invaded the region during the Late Pleistocene or Holocene, as the ice age climate ameliorated.

Botanists long have speculated on the origin of the flora and vegetation of both the Pine Barrens and the Atlantic Coastal Plain (Stone, 1911; Fernald, 1911, 1931; Taylor, 1912; Harshberger, 1916; Lutz, 1934; Braun, 1950). A scattering of evidence, both direct and indirect, permits the major events affecting past plant distribution to be outlined, but details are lacking. Plant-bearing deposits are scarce because of the low-lying, flat terrain that is deficient in basins of sedimentation. Unlike northern New Jersey, where lakes resulted from glacial scour during the Pleistocene, the lacustrine history of the unglaciated Coastal Plain has few natural lakes. Plant remains have been preserved almost entirely in fluvial or estuarine environments.

The perspective presented here derives for the most part from palynological work (analysis of pollen in cores from sediments) emphasizing the Late Tertiary (Neogene) and Quaternary. Reports on megafossils are few, because of the scarcity of stratigraphic exposures and well samples, and these are mostly of uncertain relevance. Palynological findings, although they also are few and limited in value, offer a broader base on which to reconstruct the past vegetation of the Pine Barrens. Several sources of evidence come from elsewhere on the Coastal Plain and from marine deposits.

215

PINE BARRENS

Copyright © 1979 by Academic Press, Inc.
All rights of reproduction in any form reserved.
ISBN 0-12-263450-0

DEVELOPMENT OF THE COASTAL PLAIN DURING
TERTIARY AND QUATERNARY TIME

The Coastal Plain in the region of the Pine Barrens is formed largely of an upland that slopes east and south toward an outer lowland facing the Atlantic Ocean and

Age			Stratigraphic Unit
Quaternary	Holocene		
	Pleistocene	Wisconsin	
		Sangamon	Cape May
		Illinoian	Pensauken
		Yarmouth	
		Kansan	Bridgeton
		Aftonian	
		Nebraskan	Beacon Hill
Tertiary	Pliocene (?)	Neogene	Cohansey
	Miocene (?)		
	Middle Miocene		Kirkwood
	Early Miocene		
	Oligocene		
	Early-Middle Eocene		Manasquan
	Paleocene		Vincentown
			Hornerstown
Mesozoic	Late Cretaceous		9 units"
			Magothy
			Raritan

Fig. 1. Sequence of stratigraphic units and corresponding ages of the New Jersey Coastal Plain. " In order of increasing age: Tinton and Red Bank, Navesink, Mount Laurel, Wenonah, Marshalltown, Englishtown, Woodbury, Merchantville. (From MacClintock and Richards, 1936; Owens and Sohl, 1969; Minard and Rhodehamel, 1969.)

Delaware Bay, and westward toward an inner lowland bordering the Delaware River and the Piedmont (Owens and Sohl, 1969). Elevations on the upland reach some 120 m but are mostly less than 60 m (Kümmel, 1940).

Deposits of the Coastal Plain (Fig. 1), including those with plant remains, are both marine and nonmarine. In the past, the ocean transgressed and regressed, at times drowning river mouths and low-lying border areas and at other times exposing extensive portions of the continental shelf. Possibly ten or more cycles occurred during the Cretaceous and Tertiary (Owens and Sohl, 1969). The last major transgression affected the upland area during the Middle Miocene. It gave rise to the sands and other fine-grained sediments of the Kirkwood Formation.

Overlying much of the Kirkwood is the Cohansey Sand, which is of Miocene-Pliocene (?) age and which is exposed over most of the Pine Barrens area. Although the Cohansey is predominantly a fluvial deposit laid down by streams crossing the Coastal Plain from the Appalachians, it is in part a marginal marine deposit formed in an estuarine setting (Isphording and Lodding, 1969). Locally exposed in the region of the Pine Barrens are erosional remnants of Pliocene (?) Beacon Hill Gravel, a stream deposit probably extensive at one time (Richards, 1960; Minard and Rhodehamel, 1969).

The Coastal Plain never was glaciated, but, rather, was influenced indirectly by changes in Pleistocene sea level and by the proximity of ice sheets and their associated glacial environments. Pre-Illinoian gravels, believed to be interglacial, of the Bridgeton Formation occur in the southwestern part of the Pine Barrens (MacClintock and Richards, 1936). The Bridgeton and the younger Pensauken Formation, fringing the Barrens in the Delaware River Valley and to the northeast, are considered to be fluvial in origin (Minard and Rhodehamel, 1969). The Pensauken, which contains ice-rafted boulders near its base, also is interpreted as interglacial (Bowman and Lodding, 1969). The youngest Quaternary formation, the Cape May, is found along portions of the outer lowland of the Coastal Plain, particularly where embayments are located. It consists of estuarine, marine, and deltaic deposits provisionally ascribed to a Sangamon interglacial age (MacClintock and Richards, 1936). During Wisconsin Glaciation, lowering of the sea level by an estimated 100 m exposed the continental shelf for almost 150 km off the present New Jersey shore (Antevs, 1928; Richards, 1960).

Considerable evidence in the way of ice wedge casts, congeliturbate structures, freeze–thaw depressions, ventifacts, and loess attest to environments in proximity to a glacier during glaciation (Wolfe, 1953; Tedrow and MacClintock, 1953; Judson, 1965; Minard and Rhodehamel, 1969; Walters, 1978). Low temperature and strong abrasive wind evidently were in effect on the Coastal Plain during Quaternary ice ages.

PRE-QUATERNARY VEGETATION

Evidence from the Cretaceous

The plant record of the early Coastal Plain consists of pollen and megafossils in deposits (Raritan and Magothy Formations) of Upper Cretaceous age (Dorf, 1952;

Groot *et al.*, 1961). Assemblages are represented by pine (*Pinus*), cedar family (Cupressaceae), magnolia (*Magnolia*), tulip poplar (*Liriodendron*), sassafras (*Sassafras*), oak (*Quercus*), bayberry family (Myricaceae), and heath family (Ericaceae), all of which are included among a number of other taxa. Of significance is the fact that both pine and oak, dominants of the modern Pine Barrens communities, were present on the Coastal Plain at this ancient time.

Tertiary Evidence Particularly with Regard to the Neogene

A gap in the plant record following the Cretaceous extends through the Paleocene, Eocene, Oligocene, and Early Miocene epochs. Paleocene and Eocene formations (Hornerstown, Vincentown, and Manasquan) thus far reveal no data, while the Oligocene and Early Miocene are unrepresented in the geological sequence (Richards, 1960). Exploratory studies of pollen in the Middle Miocene marine Kirkwood Formation suggest that the major assemblage consisted of oak and hickory (*Carya*) (Goldstein and Cousminer, 1973). The source of the pollen presumably is the Appalachians.

The palynology of the Legler lignite of probable Late Miocene or Early Pliocene age is a key source of data on Neogene vegetation (Rachele, 1976). The lignite is contained in ilmenite-bearing sand of the Cohansey Formation exposed in a pit near Lakehurst in the northern sector of the Pine Barrens (Markewicz, 1969). Source vegetation for the pollen assemblages appears to have been principally oak and pine. Additional arboreal genera include spruce (*Picea*), podocarp (*Podocarpus*), willow (*Salix*), poplar (*Populus*), alder (*Alnus*), beech (*Fagus*), chestnut (*Castanea*), hickory, sweet gum (*Liquidambar*), basswood (*Tilia*), black gum (*Nyssa*), and ash (*Fraxinus*); nonarboreal taxa are holly (*Ilex*), sweet pepperbush (*Clethra*), heath family, parsley family (Umbelliferae), plantain (*Plantago*), composite family (Compositae), cattail (*Typha*), and the grass family (Gramineae). The assemblages are mixed with genera which at present are warm temperate to tropical in distribution, for example, *Cyrilla, Jussiaea, Engelhardia, Gordonia,* and tree fern (*Cyathea*), and with the juglandaceous *Pterocarya,* now extinct in North America. The lignite and associated sediments appear to have been deposited in a wooded swamp that for a time was estuarine, as shown by the appearance of dinoflagellates (Hystrichospheridae) and by *Ophiomorpha* (a wormlike amphibian) burrows (Carter, 1975; Rachele, 1976).

QUATERNARY VEGETATION

Pre-Wisconsin

Sirkin *et al.* (1970) describe a pollen spectrum of a silt-clay peat more than 38,000 radiocarbon years old from south of Millville off Delaware Bay. The leading components, pine and birch (*Betula*), occur with some spruce and with minor amounts of willow, hickory, alder, chestnut, and oak. The deposit is assigned to the Sangamon Interglaciation or a warm interval (interstade) during the Mid-Wisconsin glaciation.

Assignment to the Sangamon seems less likely, because Sangamon deposits located on the Coastal Plain to the south in Delaware, District of Columbia, and the Carolinas contain pollen of broadleaf trees such as oak, hickory, and sweet gum in proportions greater than at Millville (Frey, 1952; Knox, 1966, 1969; Whitehead and Davis, 1969; Sirkin, 1974). At the moment, the nature of the Pine Barrens area vegetation immediately preceding the Wisconsin Glaciation remains speculative, but under climatic and edaphic conditions allegedly comparable to those of today, communities of pine and oak probably were extant during the Sangamon in much the same manner as at present.

Wisconsin Glacial Age

Sirkin *et al.* (1970) further describe pollen spectra in deposits radiocarbon-dated at $26,800 \pm 1000$, $16,700 \pm 420$, $13,200 \pm 400$, $13,680 \pm 300$, $12,330 \pm 300$, and $10,770 \pm 330$ years BP (Before Present = 1950 AD) from sites just west of the Pine Barrens principally in the Delaware River Valley. Throughout the time intervals spanned by these ages, pine, spruce, and birch were major types, with pine predominant during the latest interval. Species are not identified, but are believed to be those found in the modern boreal forest. Up until the end of the Wisconsin, pine and spruce were noteworthy on the Coastal Plain south to the Carolinas (Buell, 1945; Frey, 1953). Lacking direct evidence, Sirkin *et al.* (1970) and Whitehead (1973) interpret the vegetation in New Jersey, to have been tundra and taiga during full-glacial conditions some 20,000 years ago.

Sirkin and Stuckenrath (1975) find pine, spruce, fir *(Abies),* and birch in a deposit radiocarbon-dated between 37,700 and >40,000 BP on western Long Island. Between 36,400 and 26,000 BP, pine became associated with oak, hickory, and black gum during a warmer interval. Because of the proximity to New Jersey of the Long Island deposit, the genera described are suggestive of the community makeup in the Pine Barrens during time spans prior to full glacial time.

Holocene

In the first pollen analyses of Holocene peats in the Pine Barrens, Potzger (1945) showed that pine, oak, chestnut, and birch were the leading types over the interval of his cores. Pine by far was the dominant in most spectra in the eight sections studied. No major trends were discernible in the diagrams, and the percentage differences between sections appear to reflect merely local variations in source communities. These diagrams unfortunately are of limited utility, because only the arboreal component of the pollen rain was measured, and because time relations in the sections were not ascertained. A later study by Potzger (1952) included a pollen diagram of a bog section at Helmetta, situated about 20 km south of New Brunswick in an outlier of the Pine Barrens. The diagram, unlike others from the Pine Barrens, shows assemblages consisting of pine, spruce, and fir in the lower part and of oak and pine in the upper. This early record is presumed to be of late glacial boreal forest. A comparable early assemblage radiocarbon-dated between 12,330 and 13,680 BP in a deposit near Middletown, about 28 km east of Helmetta (Sirkin *et al.,* 1970), appears correlative.

Buell (1970) discusses the radiocarbon ages of 9125 ± 195 and 10,485 ± 240 BP for basal peat in two bogs in the Pine Barrens. He concludes that the bogs originated in river courses following an interval during which discharge "must have been larger and environmental conditions in the area much different. . ." In a palynological study of a section taken from the older of the two bogs situated in a meander scar of the Oswego River, Florer (1972) recognizes three pollen assemblage zones: pine–oak–hemlock (*Tsuga*) in the lower part; pine–oak over most of the section; and pine–oak composites (Tubuliflorae) in the upper part. Mesic conditions suggested by hemlock appear to have been greater before about 10,000 years ago, and the recent influx of Tubuliflorae (largely ragweed, *Ambrosia*) may result from settlement in the area by Europeans or

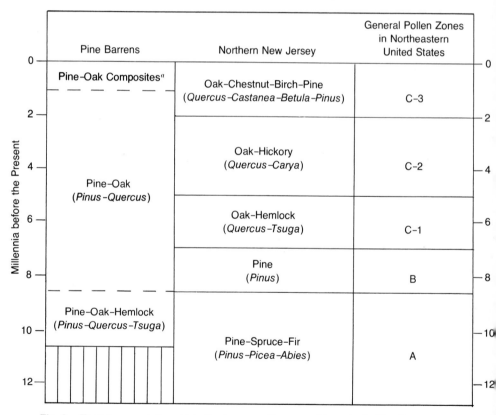

Fig. 2. Tentative correlation of late Quaternary pollen assemblages in the Pine Barrens and northern New Jersey. Time scale (thousands of years) is based on ¹⁴C (radiocarbon) ages. *ᵃPinus, Quercus,* and *Tubuliflorae* (largely ragweed, *Ambrosia*). Pine Barrens data from Florer (1972); northern New Jersey data from Niering (1953) and Sirkin and Minard (1972); data on general pollen zones in northeastern United States from Deevey (1939, 1943, 1958).

presettlement burning by Indians. In addition, Atlantic white cedar (*Chamaecyparis thyoides*) is recorded only in the upper half of the diagram, especially at and near the surface. This species represents a late arrival in the area, possibly in response to the increased humidity and lower temperatures of Late Holocene millennia. Pollen studies by Belling (1977) show the development of Atlantic white cedar in the Belleplain area near Delaware Bay beginning about 4000 BP. Figure 2 illustrates the dominance of pine and the relative stability of the vegetation throughout the Holocene in the Pine Barrens, in contrast with the vegetational development in northern New Jersey.

ORIGIN OF MODERN COMMUNITIES

Pine and oak were found to be leading pollen producers on the New Jersey Coastal Plain during the Late Neogene (Rachele, 1976). These genera are assumed to have formed vegetation analagous to the present-day Pine Barrens on the sandy soil of the Cohansey Formation, in place at the time. Under the warmer climate, as compared with today's, taxa more thermophilous than those currently established grew in the region. Species are not known, but it seems unlikely that pitch pine (*P. rigida*), the leading pine at present, was a major community component, if it occurred at all. A temperate species, pitch pine does not grow south along the Coastal Plain beyond Delaware and Maryland (Fowells, 1965). In its place, more southerly Coastal Plain species, for example, loblolly pine (*P. taeda*) and longleaf pine (*P australis*), proba-bly ranged to higher latitudes and occupied the region. Species oɪ oak, on the other hand, perhaps were not unlike those growing today in the Pine Barrens, for example, black oak (*Q. velutina*), scarlet oak (*Q. coccinea*), post oak (*Q. stellata*), and blackjack oak (*Q. marilandica*), all of which are wide-ranging along the southern Coastal Plain.

The widespread evidence of cold, inhospitable environments during the Pleistocene glaciations makes it virtually certain that tundra and(or) boreal forest covered what is now the Pine Barrens. The region was a thoroughfare for migration following each glacial age. Communities in the region were reconstituted and restructured as climatic and soil conditions dictated. The portion of the Coastal Plain that emerged during the glacial phase of each glacial–interglacial cycle supported a changing plant cover, as well as mastodons, mammoths, and other large mammals (Richards, 1959; Daddario, 1961; Stuiver and Daddario, 1963; Emery *et al.*, 1967; Whitmore *et al.*, 1967).

The conifers, pine, spruce, and fir, along with birch and herbaceous species, are noteworthy during the Late Pleistocene (Sirkin *et al.*, 1970) and are interpreted to be representative of open boreal forest. Species of pine are believed to have included "northern" jack pine (*P. banksiana*) and/or red pine (*P. resinosa*). Whitehead (1973) is of the opinion that either or both of these trees formed part of the Pleistocene forests in the Carolinas, and Watts (1970) shows macrofossil evidence for jack pine as far south as Georgia.

When the modern pine–oak communities in the Pine Barrens developed is conjectural. They could have developed close to 10,500 years ago with the demise of boreal forest species. Florer (1972) shows these genera to be dominant at this time, while Sirkin *et al.* (1970) find pine and some spruce, but only a trace of oak, on the northwest border of the Barrens at 10,770 BP. The species of pine, and of oak as well, were not determinable, and the replacement of boreal vegetation by modern communities might have occurred later. Species unlike those dominant at present, for example, white pine *(P. strobus)* and red oak *(Q. rubra)*, also may have constituted transitional communities. If so, the modern arboreal species on the upland in the Pine Barrens became manifest at a subsequent time under the comparatively warm climate of the Holocene. The time of development for Atlantic white cedar in the "cedar swamps" appears to have been Holocene.

LOSS OF SUBTROPICAL TAXA AND INFLUX OF TEMPERATE SPECIES IN THE VEGETATION DURING THE LATE TERTIARY AND QUATERNARY

The elimination of "warmer" species from high latitudes during this period was extensive in the Northern Hemisphere (Graham, 1972). The loss of *Podocarpus, Pterocarya, Engelhardia, Cyrilla, Gordonia, Jussiaea,* and *Cyathea* from the New Jersey Coastal Plain (Rachele, 1976) is a case in point. As atmospheric cooling proceeded, species shifted their ranges southward or to lower elevations in the mountains. Evidence from various sources in North America and Europe indicates a net temperature depression of 8°–10°C for the middle lower latitudes over the course of the Tertiary (Emiliani and Geiss, 1957). Studies of $^{18}O/^{16}O$ (oxygen isotope) ratios in tests of foraminifers in tropical deep-sea sediments (see Flint, 1971, for theoretical aspects) show that the temperature of ocean-bottom water has decreased by about 5°C since the Lower–Middle Miocene (Emiliani, 1954). Rachele (1976) estimates that, since the Late Neogene, average January temperature on the Coastal Plain has dropped approximately 6°C, whereas average July temperature has remained more or less unchanged, and annual precipitation is about 100 mm lower.

Boreal forest conifers and cool–temperate, broadleaf trees migrated into New Jersey during the Quaternary. Available evidence points toward migratory movement of taxa equatorward during times of glaciation but also poleward during interglaciations. Leopold (1957) concluded that, during the late glacial interval, when boreal forest dominated by spruce occupied southern New England, average July temperature was 4°–5°C lower than today's.

The 10,000 years of Holocene climatic fluctuations in the Pine Barrens constitute a time of floristic adjustments. When, where, and how taxa became part of the Barrens for the most part remain to be determined. Climatic change during the transition from the Hypsithermal (a relatively warm episode in the Holocene) to the Late Holocene several millennia ago no doubt affected the floristic makeup of the region. Today, the Pine Barrens is occupied by plants of local distribution, as well as by species ranging widely to the Canadian provinces and to Florida (Stone, 1911).

THE PINE BARRENS AS A HYPOTHESIZED REFUGIUM DURING THE PLEISTOCENE

Potzger's (1945, 1952) concept of the Pine Barrens as a refugium during glacial times is no longer tenable. Potzger had conceived "that unglaciated New Jersey was during Wisconsin times a refugium for southern broad-leaved trees." Pollen diagrams of the bog sections he studied in the Barrens consistently show pine, oak, chestnut, and birch in leading proportions. These trees were thought to "represent the leading genera in the Pleistocene forests crouching south of the ice lobe." Potzger's concept was set forth before the advent of radioisotope chronology, and had he known that his sections were of Holocene age, his interpretation would have been different. Botanical evidence discussed by Sirkin *et al.* (1970) and Whitehead (1973) consistent with the geomorphic evidence summarized by Judson (1965) makes it clear that southern New Jersey supported boreal forest and perhaps tundra during the last Wisconsin ice maximum.

DISJUNCT TAXA IN THE PINE BARRENS

The Barrens is a meeting ground of species at both their southern and northern limits. Many of the plants are disjuncts, their ranges discontinuous over extensive segments. McCormick (1970) lists 14 species of higher latitudes that range no farther south than the region and at least 109 reaching the Pine Barrens from southern distribution centers. Among the former are curly grass fern (*Schizaea pusilla*) and broom crowberry (*Corema conradii*), as well as the aquatics, Oakes' pondweed (*Potamogeton oakesianus*) and water milfoil (*Myriophyllum tenellum*). In the latter group are turkey beard (*Xerophyllum asphodeloides*), pyxie moss (*Pyxidanthera barbulata*), Pine Barrens gentian (*Gentiana autumnalis*), and resinous boneset (*Eupatorium resinosum*).

Disjunct distributions of species with stations in the Pine Barrens have been recognized by phytogeographers for some time (Fernald, 1911, 1931). Disjuncts of the Atlantic Coastal Plain are explained in the context of the continental shelf, which was emergent for a time following the maximum of the Wisconsin ice sheet and is believed to have served as a migratory pathway. The wealth of plant remains found on the shelf is impressive, but few studies (Livingstone, 1964; Groot and Groot, 1964; Harrison *et al.*, 1965) have dealt with the botanical composition of the material. The more extensive, Late Pleistocene Coastal Plain undeniably supported a vegetation cover, but evidence from the shelf of former continuous ranges of species now disjunct has not been demonstrated.

Significant is the occurrence of curly grass fern as part of the Pleistocene flora of the Carolinas (Whitehead and Barghoorn, 1963; Whitehead, 1963, 1973). It is found in deposits of both the Coastal Plain and the Piedmont during the full glacial and late glacial, along with trailing clubmoss (*Lycopodium clavatum*), shining clubmoss (*L. lucidulum*), ground pine (*L. obscurum*), and burnet (*Sanguisorba canadensis*), all of which are found in the present flora of the Pine Barrens. With the exception of curly grass fern, these species occur in the southern Appalachians, and all range northward to Canada (Fernald, 1950). Their migration route northward onto deglaciated terrain could have followed the continental shelf, and if so, their disseminules probably were carried by subtropical air masses as the Late Quaternary pattern of northeast-moving, low-pressure storms became established with the wastage of the last ice sheet.

PROBLEMS FOR FUTURE RESEARCH

The discontinuity and the lack of botanical and chronological detail in the vegetation record are areas in need of attention by future workers on the Coastal Plain. Gaps are wide, as shown by the above data, and until these are bridged our understanding of the Pine Barrens in a developmental sense will remain sketchy at best. The botanical record of the Quaternary, might be considered of first-order importance, because it offers the greatest opportunity to develop an uninterrupted sequence of events. In this regard, there is need for intensified reconnaissance of Quaternary deposits and the collection of sections for study. The speed with which the Pine Barrens is undergoing commercial exploitation is reason for a measure of urgency in stockpiling and preserving material for future research.

A problem foremost among those for consideration is the plant record of the New Jersey Coastal Plain during the last glaciation. Although Sirkin *et al.* (1970) provide insight for this interval, data are lacking for ten millennia between approximately 26,000 and 16,000 BP. This is the critical time on which is centered the last maximum of the continental ice sheet. Another problem concerns the chronology and vegetation of the Holocene and earlier interglaciations. Although the pollen stratigraphy for more than the past 10,000 years is known in the Barrens (Florer, 1972), only the behavior of genera or larger taxa is accounted for, and nothing is known about either the macroremains of modern species of the pine–oak communities or the timing of events. Here lies an opportunity to investigate the plant fossils other than pollen and spores in the deposits. The identification of fruits, seeds, leaf cuticles, and wood would enlarge the picture provided by palynology alone. These studies are applicable as well to the Sangamon and earlier interglacial remains in New Jersey that are virtually unknown botanically.

Deposits from both the Coastal Plain and the continental shelf are sources of pertinent data. Those from the shelf exposed above the limit of Late Wisconsin marine regression span only part of the sequence. Grab samples of bottom sediments or cores penetrating bog and lake remains now submerged are potential sources of valuable information. Below the minimum level reached by the Atlantic Ocean during the Late Wisconsin, marine sediments offer records unusually valuable for both antiquity and continuity. Using pollen stratigraphy, Balsam and Heusser (1976) were able to trace the succession of vegetation changes since the full glacial in two cores from the continental rise off North Carolina in what was presumed to be the Chesapeake drainage basin. The palynology of marine sediments farther north offers a means for reconstructing New Jersey vegetation during intervals when the land record may not be complete.

SUMMARY

Some taxa in the vegetation of the Pine Barrens occupied the Coastal Plain during Cretaceous time, while the remainder are Tertiary or younger in age. The development of the Coastal Plain by marine and fluvial processes during and since the Cretaceous has influenced the past vegetation greatly. The major changes influencing the plant communities occurred during Quaternary time. Boreal forest species appear to have been prevalent in the region in late glacial time. Oaks and pines reinvaded subsequently, although the time of establishment of the present species is speculative. Atlantic white cedar appears to be a relatively recent arrival. The plant record shows many gaps in time, and future investigations should include Quaternary fossils of continental plants in marine sediments.

REFERENCES

Antevs, E. (1928). "The Last Glaciation," Res. Ser. No. 17. Am. Geogr. Soc., New York, pp. 1–292.

Balsam, W. L., and Heusser, L. E. (1976). Direct correlation of sea surface paleotemperatures, deep circulation, and terrestrial paleoclimates: Foraminiferal and palynological evidence from two cores off Chesapeake Bay. *Mar. Geol.* 21, 121–147.

Belling, A. J. (1977). Postglacial migration of *Chamaecyparis thyoides* (L.) B.S.P. (southern white cedar) in the northeastern United States. Ph.D. Thesis, New York Univ., New York.

Bowman, J. F., and Lodding, W. (1969). The Pensauken Formation—a Pleistocene fluvial deposit in New Jersey. *In* "Geology of Selected Areas in New Jersey and Eastern Pennsylvania and Guidebook of Excursions" (S. Subitzky, ed.), pp. 3–6. Rutgers Univ. Press, New Brunswick, New Jersey.

Braun, E. L. (1950). "Deciduous Forests of Eastern North America." Blakiston, Philadelphia, Pennsylvania.

Buell, M. F. (1945). Late Pleistocene forests of southeastern North Carolina. *Torreya* 45, 117–118.

Buell, M. F. (1970). Time of origin of New Jersey Pine Barrens bogs. *Bull. Torrey Bot. Club* 97, 105–108.

Carter, C. H. (1975). Miocene–Pliocene beach and tidal deposits, southern New Jersey. *In* "Tidal Deposits—A Casebook of Recent Examples and Fossil Counterparts" (R. N. Ginsburg, ed.), pp. 109–116. Springer-Verlag, Berlin and New York.

Daddario, J. J. (1961). A lagoon deposit profile near Atlantic City, New Jersey. *Bull., N.J. Acad. Sci.* 6, 7–14.

Deevey, E. S., Jr. (1939). Studies on Connecticut lake sediments. I. A postglacial climatic chronology for southern New England. *Am. J. Sci.* 237, 691–724.

Deevey, E. S., Jr. (1943). Additional pollen analyses from southern New England. *Am. J. Sci.* 241, 717–752.

Deevey, E. S., Jr. (1958). Radiocarbon-dated pollen sequences in eastern North America. *Veroeff. Geobot. Inst. Eidg. Tech. Hochsch. Stift. Ruebel Zuerich* 34, 30–37.

Dorf, E. (1952). Critical analysis of Cretaceous stratigraphy and paleobotany of Atlantic Coastal Plain. *Bull., Am. Assoc. Pet. Geol.* 36, 2161–2184.

Emery, K. O., Wigley, R. L., Bartlett, A. S., Rubin, M., and Barghoorn, E. S. (1967). Freshwater peat on the continental shelf. *Science* 158, 1301–1307.

Emiliani, C. (1954). Temperatures of Pacific bottom waters and polar superficial waters during the Tertiary. *Science* 119, 853–855.

Emiliani, C., and Geiss, J. (1957). On glaciations and their causes. *Geol. Rundsch.* 46, 576–601.

Fernald, M. L. (1911). A botanical expedition to Newfoundland and southern Labrador. *Rhodora* 13, 109–162.

Fernald, M. L. (1931). Specific segregations and identities in some floras of eastern North America and the Old World. *Rhodora* **33**, 25–63.

Fernald, M. L. (1950). "Gray's Manual of Botany," 8th ed. American Book Co., New York.

Flint, R. F. (1971). "Glacial and Quaternary Geology." Wiley, New York.

Florer, L. E. (1972). Palynology of a postglacial bog in the New Jersey Pine Barrens. *Bull. Torrey Bot. Club* **99**, 135–138.

Fowells, H. A., compiler (1965). Silvics of forest trees of the United States. *U.S. Dep. Agric., Agric. Handb.* No. 271.

Frey, D. G. (1952). Pollen analysis of the Horry clay and a seaside peat deposit near Myrtle Beach, South Carolina. *Am. J. Sci.* **250**, 212–225.

Frey, D. G. (1953). Regional aspects of the late-glacial and postglacial pollen succession of southeastern North Carolina. *Ecol. Monogr.* **23**, 289–313.

Goldstein, F. R., and Cousminer, H. L. (1973). The palynology of the Kirkwood Formation in New Jersey. *Prog. Geol. Soc. Am.* **5**, 168. (Abstr.)

Graham, A. (1972). Outline of the origin and historical recognition of floristic affinities between Asia and eastern North America. *In* "Floristics and Paleofloristics of Asia and Eastern North America" (A. Graham, ed.), pp. 1–16. Elsevier, Amsterdam.

Groot, C. R., and Groot, J. J. (1964). The pollen flora of Quaternary sediments beneath Nantucket Shoals. *Am. J. Sci.* **262**, 488–493.

Groot, J. J., Penny, J. S., and Groot, C. R. (1961). Plant microfossils and age of the Raritan, Tuscaloosa, and Magothy Formations of eastern North America. *Paleontographica* **108**, 121–140.

Harrison, W., Malloy, R. J., Rusnak, G. E., and Terasmae, J. (1965). Possible Late Pleistocene uplift: Chesapeake Bay entrance. *J. Geol.* **73**, 201–229.

Harshberger, J. W. (1916). "The Vegetation of the New Jersey Pine Barrens, an Ecologic Investigation." Christopher Sower Co., Philadelphia, Pennsylvania.

Isphording, W. C., and Lodding, W. (1969). Facies changes in sediments of Miocene age in New Jersey. *In* "Geology of Selected Areas in New Jersey and Eastern Pennsylvania and Guidebook of Excursions" (S. Subitzky, ed.), pp. 7–13. Rutgers Univ. Press, New Brunswick, New Jersey.

Judson, S. (1965). Quaternary processes in the Atlantic Coastal Plain and Appalachian Highlands. *In* "The Quaternary of the United States" (H. E. Wright, Jr. and D. G. Frey, eds.), pp. 133–136. Princeton Univ. Press, Princeton, New Jersey.

Knox, A. S. (1966). The Walker interglacial swamp, Washington, D.C. *J. Wash. Acad. Sci.* **56**, 1–8.

Knox, A. S. (1969). Glacial age marsh, Lafayette Park, Washington, D.C. *Science* **146**, 795–797.

Kümmel, H. B. (1940). The geology of New Jersey. *Bull. N.J. Dep. Conserv. Econ. Dev.* **50**, 1–203.

Leopold, E. B. (1957). Some aspects of late-glacial climate in eastern United States. *Veroeff. Geobot. Inst. Eidg. Tech. Hochsch. Stift. Ruebel Zuerich* **34**, 80–85.

Livingstone, D. A. (1964). The pollen flora of submarine sediments from Nantucket Shoals. *Am. J. Sci.* **262**, 479–487.

Lutz, H. J. (1934). Concerning a geologic explanation of the origin and present distribution of the New Jersey Pine Barren vegetation. *Ecology* **15**, 399–406.

MacClintock, P., and Richards, H. G. (1936). Correlation of late Pleistocene marine and glacial geology of New Jersey and New York. *Geol. Soc. Am. Bull.* **47**, 289–338.

McCormick, J. (1970). The Pine Barrens: A preliminary ecological inventory. *N.J. State Mus., Res. Rep.* No. 2.

Markewicz, F. J. (1969). Ilmenite deposits of the New Jersey Coastal Plain. *In* "Geology of Selected Areas in New Jersey and Eastern Pennsylvania and Guidebook of Excursions" (S. Subitzky, ed.), pp. 363–382. Rutgers Univ. Press, New Brunswick, New Jersey.

Minard, J. P., and Rhodehamel, E. C. (1969). Quaternary geology of part of northern New Jersey and the Trenton area. *In* "Geology of Selected Areas in New Jersey and Eastern Pennsylvania and Guidebook of Excursions" (S. Subitzky, ed.), pp. 279–313. Rutgers Univ. Press, New Brunswick, New Jersey.

Niering, W. A. (1953). The past and present vegetation of High Point State Park, New Jersey. *Ecol. Monogr.* **23**, 127–148.

Owens, J. P., and Sohl, N. F. (1969). Shelf and deltaic paleoenvironments in the Cretaceous–Tertiary formations of the New Jersey Coastal Plain. *In* "Geology of Selected Areas in New Jersey and Eastern Pennsylvania and Guidebook of Excursions" (S. Subitzky, ed.), pp. 235–278. Rutgers Univ. Press, New Brunswick, New Jersey.

Potzger, J. E. (1945). The Pine Barrens of New Jersey, a refugium during Pleistocene times. *Butler Univ. Bot. Stud.* **7**, 1–15.

Potzger, J. E. (1952). What can be inferred from pollen profiles of bogs in the New Jersey Pine Barrens. *Bartonia* **26**, 20–27.

Rachele, L. D. (1976). Palynology of the Legler lignite: A deposit in the Tertiary Cohansey Formation of New Jersey, U.S.A. *Rev. Palaeobot. Palynol.* **22**, 225–252.

Richards, H. G. (1959). Pleistocene mammals dredged off the coast of New Jersey. *Geol. Soc. Am. Bull.* **70**, 1769.

Richards, H. G. (1960). The geological history of the New Jersey Pine Barrens. *N.J. Nat. News* **15**, 146–151.

Sirkin, L. A. (1974). Microflora in the Sangamon and younger beds of the Delmarva Peninsula, Delaware, Maryland and Virginia. *Prog. Geol. Soc. Am.* **5**, 74. (Abstr.)

Sirkin, L. A., and Minard, J. P. (1972). Late Pleistocene glaciation and pollen stratigraphy in northwestern New Jersey. *U.S. Geol. Surv., Prof. Pap.* No. 800–D, pp. 51–56.

Sirkin, L. A., and Stuckenrath, R. (1975). The mid-Wisconsin (Farmdalian) interstadial in the northern Atlantic Coastal Plain. *Prog. Geol. Soc. Am.* **7**, 118–119. (Abstr.)

Sirkin, L. A., Owens, J. P., Minard, J. P., and Rubin, M. (1970). Palynology of some Upper Quaternary peat samples from the New Jersey Coastal Plain. *U.S. Geol. Surv., Prof. Pap.* No. 700–D, pp. D77–D87.

Stone, W. (1911). The plants of southern New Jersey with especial reference to the flora of the Pine Barrens and the geographic distribution of the species. *N.J. State Mus., Annu. Rep. State Geol. 1910* pp. 23–828.

Stuiver, M., and Daddario, J. J. (1963). Submergence of the New Jersey coast. *Science* **142**, 951.

Taylor, N. (1912). On the origin and present distribution of the Pine Barrens of New Jersey. *Torreya* **12**, 229–242.

Tedrow, J. C. F., and MacClintock, P. (1953). Loess in New Jersey soil materials. *Soil Sci.* **75**, 19–29.

Walters, J. C. (1978). Polygonal patterned ground in central New Jersey. *Quat. Res. (N.Y.)* **10**, 42–54.

Watts, W. A. (1970). The full-glacial vegetation of northwestern Georgia. *Ecology* **51**, 17–33.

Whitehead, D. R. (1963). "Northern" elements in the Pleistocene flora of the Southeast. *Ecology* **44**, 403–406.

Whitehead, D. R. (1973). Late-Wisconsin vegetational changes in unglaciated eastern North America. *Quat. Res. (N.Y.)* **3**, 621–631.

Whitehead, D. R., and Barghoorn, E. S. (1962). Pollen analytical investigations of Pleistocene deposits from western North Carolina and South Carolina. *Ecol. Monogr.* **32**, 347–369.

Whitehead, D. R., and Davis, J. T. (1969). Pollen analysis of an organic clay from the interglacial Flanner Beach Formation, Craven County, North Carolina. *Southeast. Geol.* **10**, 1–16.

Whitmore, F. C., Jr., Emery, K. O., Cooke, H. B. S., and Swift, D. J. P. (1967). Elephant teeth from the Atlantic continental shelf. *Science* **156**, 1477–1481.

Wolfe, P. E. (1953). Periglacial frost-thaw basins in New Jersey. *J. Geol.* **61**, 133–141.

13

The Vegetation of the New Jersey Pine Barrens

JACK McCORMICK

INTRODUCTION

Two relatively distinct floristic complexes are present in the Pine Barrens, namely, a lowland complex and an upland complex. Plants of the lowlands occupy about 15–20% of the region and grow on sites in which the water table is near or above the surface during some part of the year. The presence of abundant water within the root zone acts as a selective agent and inhibits the growth of many species. This water supports dense stands of vegetation and reduces the flammability of the vegetation, thereby lessening the frequency of fires in lowland stands.

Plants of the upland floristic complex grow in the remainder of the region. In upland sites, the level of the water seldom is nearer to the surface than 0.7–0.9 m (2–3 ft), and its depth is as great as 18–21 m (60–70 ft) in a few places.

In some localities, upland vegetation and lowland vegetation merge with no abrupt boundary. Nearly imperceptible irregularities in the surface of the mineral soil also may support enclaves of upland plants on minute ridges within the lowland complex, or enclaves of lowland plants in swales or depressions within the upland complex. Elsewhere, particularly at places where a stream is entrenched a meter or more (a few feet) below the general surface of the area or where fires have destroyed accumulations of organic matter, the boundary between the upland and lowland vegetation complexes may be delimited sharply.

Throughout the Pine Barrens, repeated cutting and frequent and severe fires have been of paramount importance in shaping the vegetation. No large area in the region has escaped cutting and/or burning within the past century. Most areas have been burned repeatedly, at intervals of 10–30 years. At least until the end of the first quarter of this century, most stands were clear-cut on a rotation of about 25–50 years. Regardless of the inordinate cutting, and largely because of the frequent fires, the modern vegetation of the Pine Barrens is unique in the world. Much of the area now is settled sparsely; as a natural open space and recreation resource, the region also is of overwhelming significance to the state, to the megapolitan region, and to the nation.

This chapter is based on the author's field observations throughout the Pine Barrens from 1951 to the present. The distribution of vegetation types in the central Pine Barrens is detailed by McCormick (1955, 1970). The vegetation types of the entire region were mapped by McCormick and Jones (1973), although in less detail. Quantitative data in regard to plant heights, density, basal area and cover, except as credited otherwise, are from McCormick (1955) and a reevaluation of the same information can be found in McCormick (1979). These data were obtained from stands on two experimental watersheds in Lebanon State Forest, Burlington and Ocean Counties. The work, conducted under the direction of Murray F. Buell from 1951–1955, focused on upland vegetation types and the pitch pine lowland type. References to the position of the water table are based on personal observations, especially while the author served as Field Hydrologist for the U.S. Geological Survey, and on personal communications from Edward C. Rhodehamel and Marco Markley (see Fernald, 1950, for plant nomenclature).

VEGETATION OF THE LOWLANDS (WETLANDS)

Wetland vegetation ranges from sites of continuous inundation to those in which water covers the surface or saturates the soil only a few days or weeks during most years. With regard both to floristic diversity and to physiognomic diversity or appearance, the greatest variety of vegetation in the Pine Barrens occurs in these wetland habitats. By virtue of regulations under the Federal Water Pollutional Control Act Amendments of 1972, all or most of these areas currently are under the jurisdiction of the U.S. Army Corps of Engineers and the U.S. Environmental Protection Agency. With stringent regulation, continuous scrutiny, minimal alteration, and informed husbandry, these immensely valuable, but terribly fragile, habitats will survive into the 21st century and beyond.

The wetland forests of the Pine Barrens are composed principally of southern white cedar, trident red maple, black gum (*Chamaecyparis thyoides, Acer rubrum, Nyssa sylvatica*). In many stands, pitch pine, gray birch, and sassafras (*Pinus rigida, Betula populifolia, Sassafras albidum*) are present, with the latter sometimes of relatively large size. The lowland forests, particularly the broadleaf swamp type, extend well beyond the limits of the Pine Barrens. Within the region, but principally near its perimeter and beyond, sweetgum, pin oak, willow oak, basket oak, water oak (*Liquidambar styraciflua, Quercus palustris, Q. phellos, Q. michauxii, Q. nigra*), and several other types of trees also are members of the lowland forest grouping.

Herbaceous Wetland Communities

Several types of treeless communities commonly occur in ponds and streams, in concentric bands around depressions, and in parallel bands along the margins of streams in the Pine Barrens (Rigg, 1940). Deeper sections of ponds may be colonized by various algae. Near the margins of ponds, and in stream coves, white waterlilies (*Nymphaea odorata*), spatterdocks (*Nuphar variegatum*), bladderworts (*Utricularia* spp.), and other submerged or floating leaf plants may cover the bottom as well as the surface. *Sphagnum* mosses, sedges (*Carex* spp.), rushes (*Juncus* spp.), pipeworts (*Eriocaulon* spp.), chain ferns (*Woodwardia* spp.), and other emergent plants occur along the shores and in water that is no more than a few centimeters deep (Fables, 1960).

In a few places, particularly in the channels of intermittent streams and in off-channel areas which are inundated seasonally, lowland broomsedge (*Andropogon virginicus* var. *abbreviatus*), bullsedge (*Carex bullata*), and other grasses and grasslike plants form marshes known locally as savannas (Rose and Price, 1878). About 1900, savannas apparently covered thousands of hectares (several thousand acres) in the Pine Barrens (Stone, 1911; Harshberger, 1916). Today, individual savannas are small, and collectively they probably cover no more than 400 ha (a thousand acres) (McCormick and Jones, 1973). Thickets of leatherleaf (*Chamaedaphne calyculata*) or highbush blueberry (*Vaccinium corymbosum*) and swamp forests of red maple, blackgum, sweetbay (*Magnolia virginiana*), and southern white cedar have replaced most of the former savannas (McCormick, 1955; Fables, 1960).

Shrubby Wetland Communities

Leatherleaf or, less commonly, highbush blueberry grows in the channels of intermittent streams, on the margins of ponds (Fig. 1), and over the central sections of many of the nearly circular depressions that are scattered through the region. These thickets are known locally as spungs, but the term also is applied to broadleaf swamp forests. Peat mosses (*Sphagnum*) form nearly complete ground covers in the spungs, and chain ferns project from the *Sphagnum* at intervals of a few meters. Sheep laurel (*Kalmia angustifolia*) and staggerbush (*Lyonia mariana*) are scattered throughout most stands of highbush blueberry. In stands of leatherleaf, the highbush blueberry may be a minor associate, and small trees of pitch pine and red maple may be spaced widely.

Southern White Cedar Swamp Forests

Mature southern white cedar trees (Fig. 2) typically have straight stems which are devoid of branches and foliage except in their topmost sections (Little, 1950). The trees usually begin to grow after an existing forest has been destroyed by fire or cutting. As many as 521,000 seedlings per hectare (211,000 per acre) may germinate during the first year after disturbance (Little and Somes, 1965). By the twentieth year, 95% of the stems may have died, and the forest is formed by about 26,200 trees per hectare (Pinchot, 1899). During the 35th through 50th years, the density averages about 7900 stems per hectare (Pinchot, 1899; Baker, 1922; Moore and Waldron, 1940). Surveys of New Jersey white cedar forests 70–80 years old indicate about 2350 mature trees per hectare (Pinchot, 1899; Bamford and Little, 1960). Although this process of natural thinning is general, the densities of trees in different stands of the same age and in different parts of a single stand may vary considerably. Mature forests of white cedar still are relatively dense. The basal area of 50-year-old stands in New Jersey has been

Fig. 1. Vegetation distribution near a small pond. The pond is less than a meter deep (1-2 ft), has a sandy bottom, and has patches of white waterlily on the surface. The low shrub layer seen on the right and left is leatherleaf, and the higher shrubs in center and right are highbush blueberry scattered throughout the leatherleaf. Low, dense pines beyond the shrubs form a narrow band of pitch pine lowland forest, and the tall pines are mostly of a pine transition forest. Tall deciduous oak trees in the background indicate the proximity of upland oak-pine forest.

observed to be 56.2-57.4 m²/ha (300 ft²/acre). In contrast, the basal areas of mature upland forests in the Pine Barrens region seldom exceed 23 m²/ha (100 ft²/acre).

Many streams in the Pine Barrens flow through white cedar swamp forests from their sources to tidewater. The canopies of the mature forests generally are about 15-18 m (50-60 ft) above the ground. The stands range from a few meters to 1600 m or more in width (a few yards to a mile or more), but few exceed 300 m (1000 ft) (McCormick and Jones, 1973).

Tall pitch pines may be scattered throughout the canopies of white cedar forests, and red maple, blackgum, and sweetbay may form a more or less continuous understory, or they may be sparse and relatively inconspicuous. The crowns of highbush blueberry, dangleberry (*Gaylussacia frondosa*), clammy azalea (*Rhododendron viscosum*), sweet pepperbush (*Clethra alnifolia*), fetterbush (*Leucothoe racemosa*), bayberry (*Myrica pensylvanica*), and various other shrubs mingle with the crowns of the broadleaf trees in the understory. The herbaceous vegetation is rather sparse in most stands, but it is composed of many species (Harshberger, 1916; Little, 1951). Chain ferns, bladder-worts, sundew (*Drosera* spp.), pitcherplants (*Sarracenia purpurea*), swamp pink (*Helonias bullata*), and partridgeberry (*Mitchella repens*) are rather common. Curly

Fig. 2. Southern white cedar swamp forest. A high density of tall, straight trees and an almost closed canopy producing very low light levels beneath are characteristic. The canopy is mainly a single species, while several species of shrubs and peat moss are abundant.

grass fern (*Schizaea pusilla*), a grasslike boreal fern which is at the southern limit of its range in the Pine Barrens, is rather rare, but is widely distributed throughout the white cedar forests. Hummocks around the bases of the trees and much of the surface between the trees are blanketed with *Sphagnum* mosses.

Broadleaf Swamp Forests

Trident red maple, a variety of red maple, is the principal tree in the broadleaf forests of the lowlands (Fig. 3). Blackgum and sweetbay are the principal associates, but gray birch and sassafras are abundant from place to place. Pitch pines are scattered

Fig. 3. Broadleaf swamp forest. The trident red maple seen here, in addition to the blackgum and sweetbay in the canopy and a variety of tall shrubs, characterizes this forest. The forest commonly consists of a narrow band along stream channels and the upland borders of white cedar swamp forests.

throughout the canopy and, locally, pines may be nearly as abundant as the broadleaf trees. Southern white cedar also is a part of the canopy in many places.

In most stands, the crowns of the broadleaf trees extend about 9–12 m (30–40 ft) from the ground. The tops of the taller shrubs, which are 1.5–3 m (5–10 ft) in height, mingle with the lower limbs of the trees. Highbush blueberry and sweet pepperbush form the bulk of the shrub layer. Clammy azalea, leatherleaf, fetterbush, black huckleberry (*Gaylussacia baccata*), dangleberry, and sheep laurel are less abundant, but are distributed throughout the shrub layer in most stands. The herbaceous plants, mosses, and lichens in the broadleaf swamp forests generally are of the same species as those of the cedar swamp forests. Although no quantitative data are available, shrubs generally are more abundant and form a more continuous undergrowth in broadleaf swamp forests than in cedar swamp forests. Herbaceous plants, in contrast, appear to be more abundant in cedar swamp forests than in broadleaf swamp forests.

Pine Transition Forests

Pitch pines, which generally are about 12 m (40 ft) tall, form a distinct canopy above an understory of smaller red maples, blackgums, and gray birches in stands of the pine transition forest (Fig. 1). Most stands of this type are narrow and elongate and occupy a position between the white cedar swamp forests or broadleaf swamp forests and forests characteristic of upland sites. At places where the slopes are gentle, the canopy is composed almost exclusively of pitch pine, and the stands may be relatively broad. In contrast, this type may be pinched out in areas with steep slopes between the lowlands and the uplands.

The bulk of the well-developed low shrub layer of the pine transition type is formed by sheep laurel and dangleberry (Moore and Waldron, 1940). Black huckleberry, grouseberry (*Gaylussacia dumosa*), bayberry, winterberry (*Ilex verticillata*), and staggerbush also are present in this stratum. A less continuous layer, 1.5–2.4 m (5–8 ft) tall, is composed of highbush blueberry, sweet pepperbush, clammy azalea, maleberry (*Lyonia ligustrina*), and fetterbush. Catbrier (*Smilax glauca*) or bullbrier vines (*S. rotundifolia*) are draped over the shrubs and in many places present a nearly impenetrable barrier to pedestrians. Scrub oak (*Quercus ilicifolia*) is prominent in the taller shrub layer in most areas in which pines form a nearly pure canopy.

Herbs and small shrubs cover only about 1% of the ground in pine transition forests. Wintergreen (*Gaultheria procumbens*) and bracken fern (*Pteridium aquilinum*) are the most common of these plants, but cinnamon fern (*Osmunda cinamomea*) and turkeybeard (*Xerophyllum asphodeloides*) are conspicuous owing to their size. *Sphagnum* moss, haircap moss (*Polytrichum* spp.), and other bryophytes also cover about 1% of the surface.

Pitch Pine Lowland Forest

Pitch pine forms 90% or more of the canopy of this type (Fig. 1). Red maple and blackgum are present in most of these forests, and gray birch may be a very minor component. The stands are dense, and the crooked trees, many of which have two or more stems from a single root crown, seldom are taller than 4.6–7.6 m (15–25 ft). Forests of this type cover many of the circular depressions within the Pine Barrens, level sites adjacent to white cedar and broadleaf swamp forests, and other poorly drained soils in the region (Moore, 1939; Moore and Waldron, 1940; Little and Moore, 1953; McCormick and Jones, 1973).

At least 20 species of shrubs and woody vines form the undergrowth of pitch pine lowland forests, and more than one-half of the cover is formed by black huckleberry, sheep laurel, and dangleberry. Leatherleaf, however, is predominant on sites that are inundated most frequently. Nearly 30% of the ground in these forests is covered by turkeybeard, wintergreen, bracken fern, and various associated herbs, including several orchids. About 10% of the surface is covered by spongy mats of *Sphagnum* mosses.

VEGETATION OF THE UPLANDS

Except for areas in which human activities have destroyed the cover, the uplands of the Pine Barrens region are forested continuously. Truck farms utilize thousands of hectares (several thousand acres), particularly along the western boundary and in areas near Hammonton and Vineland (McCormick and Jones, 1973). The fallow fields that are scattered throughout the region are revegetated rapidly by pitch pine and, less commonly, by shortleaf pine (*Pinus echinata*). Along the western margin, Virginia pine (*P. virginiana*) is an important old-field tree (McCormick and Andresen, 1963) and, particularly near the coast, red cedar (*Juniperus virginiana*) may be abundant. The common shrubs of the Pine Barrens, especially lowbush blueberry (*Vaccinium vacillans*) and black huckleberry, apparently do not reproduce from seeds on these disturbed sites, and the ground beneath the pines is covered by firesedge or, less frequently, orange broomsedge (*Andropogon virginicus*), switchgrass (*Panicum virgatum*), or other grasses (McCormick and Buell, 1957).

Pitch pine, shortleaf pine, black oak (*Quercus velutina*), white oak (*Q. alba*), chestnut oak (*Q. prinus*), post oak (*Q. stellata*), and blackjack oak (*Q. marilandica*), which virtually are absent from the lowland forests, are prominent in the canopies of the upland types. Scarlet oak (*Q. coccinea*) and southern red oak (*Q. falcata*) also are common in the upland forests in the northeastern and southern sections of the Pine Barrens, respectively, but they appear in lowland forests near the perimeter of the region.

The oaks generally are of sprout origin after fires or cutting, and many of the trees have two or more trunks that develop from a single large root crown, or stool. The trunks of the oaks are very susceptible to heart rots. These fungi and the excavations of carpenter ants weaken the trunk and larger branches. As a result, larger oak trees may be "stagheaded" from wind breakage.

Several shrubs prominent in the lowland sites are absent from upland forests, and others are much less abundant. Two heaths, black huckleberry and lowbush blueberry, form the bulk of the shrub cover (Buell and Cantlon, 1950, 1953). These plants grow about 30–60 cm (1–2 ft) high, with their cover nearly uniform over hundreds of hectares (thousands of acres), regardless of the overshadowing tree canopy. In many places, scrub oak (or bear oak), a shrub 1–5 m (3–15 ft) tall, emerges above the heaths, but appears to have no significant effect on the lower shrubs. Thus, two shrub synusia, or communities, a heath type and a scrub oak type, are recognized in the uplands of the Pine Barrens. The cover of huckleberry and blueberry is essentially the same in both shrub types, but in the scrub oak type scrub oak covers 20% or more of the ground.

The herbaceous components of upland forests are sparse. Bracken fern and wintergreen are the most constant species, but cowwheat (*Melampyrum lineare*), goatsrue (*Tephrosia virginiana*), and several other herbs occur sporadically. The cover of mosses and lichens is related inversely to the proportion of ground blanketed by litter. In most upland forests, litter forms a continuous cover, and lichens and mosses are limited to 1–2% of the surface.

The canopy trees (tree synusia) and the undergrowth types (shrub synusia) of the central Pine Barrens occur together in nine combinations, or community types, in the uplands: pine-blackjack oak-heath, pine-blackjack oak-scrub oak, pine-post oak-scrub oak, pine-black oak-heath, pine-black oak-scrub oak, oak-pine-heath, oak-pine–scrub oak, scarlet oak–shortleaf pine–heath, and chestnut oak with a unique undergrowth. These combinations reflect the irregular distribution of scrub oak and the various tree species.

PINE–OAK FORESTS

Forests chiefly composed of pines give the Pine Barrens its typical aspect. In these forests (Fig. 4), pitch pine covers 30% or more of the ground, contributes 50% or more of the tree stems 2.5 cm (1 in) or greater in diameter, and forms 50% or more of the basal area. Large broadleaf trees, including black oak, chestnut oak, scarlet oak and white oak, cover no more than 25% of the ground, contribute no more than 25% of the stems, and form no more than 25% of the basal area in stands of pine–oak forest.

Pine–Blackjack Oak Forest

A large part of the central Pine Barrens is covered by open forests of pitch pines averaging about 7.5 m (25 ft) in height and by blackjack oaks mostly <6 m (<20 ft) high (McCormick and Jones, 1973). Post oaks, which are similar to the blackjack oaks

Fig. 4. Pine–oak forest with pitch pine and black oak in canopy. Most small crooked trees are blackjack oak, with scattered post oaks. The taller shrubs on the left are scrub oak, and the shorter shrubs in the center are black huckleberry and lowbush blueberry.

in size, range from widely scattered to relatively abundant in these stands. Black oaks and scarlet oaks are distributed sporadically throughout the pine–blackjack oak forests, but seldom exceed 12 trees/ha (5 trees/acre).

This forest type apparently represents a dramatic example of the selective action of frequent, severe fire. Shortleaf pines and most treeform oaks are rare or absent in the pine–blackjack oak forest and probably were eliminated by fires hundreds, or even thousands, of years ago. The forests of the East and West Pine Plains near Warren Grove are the extreme expression of this type (Fig. 5). They consist of dense stands of 1.2–1.8-m (4–6 ft)-tall pitch pines, blackjack oaks, and in places, scrub oaks. There are 7200–16,000 individuals (clumps of shoots from a single stool) per hectare (2900–6500/acre) in the West Plains (Little and Somes, 1964; Gill, 1975; McCormick and Andresen, 1978). Of these, 18–68% are pitch pine, and almost all the rest are blackjack oak, with relatively few scrub oaks present. McCormick and Andresen (1979) found 83,800 stems/ha (39,900 stems/acre) in a stand burned seven years previously. Little and Somes (1964) found 39,500 stems/ha (16,000 stems/acre) in a stand 27 years after burning. The difference in densities may reflect natural thinning during the fire free period and a substantially greater proportion of oaks in the older stand. In the younger stand (McCormick and Andresen, 1979), there were 6.74 stems per pine clump but only 1.85 stems per oak clump.

Fig. 5. Pine Plains, a 1–3 m (2–10 ft)-high pine–oak stand. Dominant species, which are seen in right and left foreground, are pitch pine and blackjack oak. These have multistemmed sprouts from a large root crown called a stool. Scrub oak and heath shrubs also are common. The Pine Plains vegetation is considered an extreme form of the pine–blackjack oak forest.

The pine–blackjack oak canopy type occurs with both the heath and scrub oak undergrowth types. In the Pine Plains and in several nearby areas, mountain laurel (*Kalmia latifolia*), sheep laurel, sweetfern (*Comptonia peregrina* var. *asplenifolia*), broom crowberry (*Corema conradii*), and bearberry (*Arcostaphylos uva-ursi*) are occasional to frequent members of the woody undergrowth. Pyxie moss (*Pyxidanthera barbulata*) and false heather (*Hudsonia ericoides*) are unusually abundant in the Pine Plains.

Pine–Post Oak Forest

Two types of this forest occur in the central Pine Barrens, but neither is widespread. Pitch pine is the principal tree. Post oak contributes about 20% of the cover, and black oak is a minor, but widely distributed, associate. In one type, the canopy is about 6 m (20 ft) tall, and the bulk of the woody undergrowth is scrub oak and sheep laurel. In the other type, the trees are larger and more widely spaced, and scrub oak and black huckleberry are the most abundant shrubs.

Pine–Black Oak Forest

Pitch pine is predominant in the canopy, but 10–20% of the trees are black oak, scarlet oak or southern red oak (Fig. 4). White oak or chestnut oak is present in a few small areas, and the smaller blackjack oak may vary from absent to nearly as abundant as is the case in the pine–blackjack oak forest types. The average height of the canopy is about 10.5 m (35 ft).

OAK–PINE FORESTS

In oak–pine forests (Fig. 6), larger treeform oaks, including black oak, chestnut oak, scarlet oak, and white oak, cover 40% or more of the ground, contribute 50% or more of the stems, and form 35% or more of the basal area. Pitch pine is present in nearly all stands but is less common than the broadleaf trees. In many areas, shortleaf pines outnumber pitch pines. In most stands, there are 1500–2200 stems/ha (600–900 stems/acre), whereas in most pine–oak forests there are 2700–3000 stems/ha (1100–1200 stems/acre). The canopy generally is 11–15 m (35–50 ft) high, but in stands without a crown fire for a century or more, the trees may be 23–31 m (75–100 ft) tall. Overall, these forests are less dense than the pine–oak forests.

Oak–Pine Forest

Several treeform oaks may be prominent in the canopy, with black oak the most common species north of the Mullica River (Fig. 6) and southern red oak prominent to the south. Chestnut oak, scarlet oak, and white oak vary in abundance from stand to stand. Of the two smaller treeform oaks, post oak generally is more abundant than

Fig. 6. Oak–pine forest dominated by unusually large black oaks, chestnut oaks, and pitch pines. Pitch pine trunk is on left, black oak with prominent basal fire scar in center, and chestnut oak on right. Shrubs in the foreground include the taller deciduous scrub oak and a lower heath layer. A relatively open canopy is indicated by small pines in background center.

blackjack oak. In a few places, post oak attains relatively large size and is in the canopy.

The average height of stands of the oak–pine forest type is about 12 m (40 ft). The canopy covers over 70% of the ground, and at least 60% of its cover is contributed by oaks. Pines form about 50% of the basal area. This probably reflects the fact that pines commonly sprout from the branches after a fire, and a new crown develops on the old trunk. Oaks, in contrast, seldom develop new crowns after a fire. The old trunk dies, and new sprouts develop from the root crown. Therefore, in oak–pine forests, the root systems of the pines and oaks may be of the same age, but the trunks of pines may be many years older and larger in diameter than those of oaks.

Chestnut Oak Forest

Forests with chestnut oak and black oak forming 90% or more of the canopy occur on many small hilltops and on a few larger areas in the Pine Barrens. The canopy is relatively low, averaging about 11 m (35 ft) in height. Fifty or more sprouts may originate from a single stump of chestnut oak after fire or cutting. Two or three commonly survive as a multiple-trunk tree. Thus, chestnut oak is represented by about 40% of the individuals in the forest, but by about 51% of the stems in the forest.

The woody undergrowth is sparse in chestnut oak stands. Shrubs occur in scattered islandlike clumps and in rows, covering only about 25% of the ground. Whereas lowbush blueberry and black huckleberry are greatly reduced in abundance compared with other upland forests, dangleberry and scrub oak appear to be equally or more abundant.

Mosses and lichens cover 30% or more of the soil surface in chestnut oak stands. This unusual development of the ground layer reflects the sparse litter layer, and indeed much ground is bare. Because shrubs are sparse, the wind apparently concentrates the dead leaves in patches.

Scarlet Oak–Shortleaf Pine Forest

These forests occur most commonly in the eastern half of the Pine Barrens and north of the Mullica River. In mature stands, the canopy may be 15 m (50 ft) or more high, but in most stands it is 9–12 m (30–40 ft) in height. Scarlet oak and black oak form about 60% of the canopy and shortleaf pine nearly 20%. Chestnut oak, white oak, post oak, and pitch pine are minor components. The density of pitch pine stems, 37/ha (15/acre), is less than that in any other upland type for which measurements are available. In contrast, shortleaf pine, with 561 stems/ha (227/acre), is more abundant than in any other forest type.

SUMMARY

The vegetation of the Pine Barrens is composed of two relatively distinct floristic complexes, namely, lowlands on soil saturated for prolonged periods, and uplands with a water table generally >0.7 m (2 ft) below the soil surface. Lowland vegetation includes swamp forests and relatively small freshwater marshes. Although southern white cedar swamp forests are considered characteristic of the region, broadleaf swamp forests of trident red maple, blackgum, and sweetbay now are more widespread than white cedar forest.

Upland vegetation includes two shrub types, i.e., the heath type, in which lowbush blueberry and black huckleberry are predominant, form a nearly continuous cover throughout the uplands, and the scrub oak type, in which scrub oak projects above the heaths. The upland canopy layer is divided into two broad groupings, depending on the relative abundance of pitch pine and several oak species (particularly chestnut, scarlet, white, black to the north, and southern red oak to the south). The (a) *pine–oak* forest types are pine–blackjack oak, pine–post oak and pine–black oak; (b) the *oak–pine* forest types are oak–pine, chestnut oak, and scarlet oak–shortleaf pine. Except for the chestnut oak forest with a depauperate heath undergrowth, the shrub and canopy layers appear to be distributed independently, producing at least eight combinations in the changing mosaic of the upland Pine Barrens vegetation.

REFERENCES

Baker, W. M. (1922). "Forestry for Profit." N.J. Dep. Conserv. Dev., Trenton, New Jersey.

Bamford, G. T., and Little, S. (1960). Effects of thinning in Atlantic white-cedar stands. *U.S. For. Serv., Northeast. For. Exp. Stn., Res. Note* No. 104.

Buell, M. F., and Cantlon, J. E. (1950). A study of two communities of the New Jersey Pine Barrens and a comparison of methods. *Ecology* **31,** 567–586.

Buell, M. F., and Cantlon, J. E. (1953). Effects of prescribed burning on ground cover in the New Jersey pine region. *Ecology* **34,** 520–528.

Fables, D. (1960). Plant succession in the New Jersey Pine Barren wetlands. *Bull. N.J. Acad. Sci.,* **5**(1), 9.

Fernald, M. (1950). "Gray's Manual of Botany," 8th ed. American Book Co., New York.

Gill, D. E. (1975). Spatial patterning of pines and oaks in the New Jersey Pine Barrens. *J. Ecol.* **63,** 291–298.

Harshberger, J. W. (1916). "The Vegetation of the New Jersey Pine Barrens, an Ecologic Investigation." Christopher Sower Co., Philadelphia, Pennsylvania.

Little, S. (1950). Ecology and silviculture of whitecedar and associated hardwoods in southern New Jersey. *Yale Univ. Sch. For. Bull.* **56,** 1–103.

Little, S. (1951). Observations on the minor vegetation of the Pine Barren swamps in southern New Jersey. *Bull. Torrey Bot. Club* **78,** 153–160.

Little, S., and Moore, E. B. (1953). Severe burning treatment tested on lowland pine sites. *U.S. For. Serv., Northeast. For. Exp. Stn., Stn. Pap.* No. 64.

Little, S., and Somes, H. A. (1964). Releasing pitch pine sprouts from old stools ineffective. *J. For.* **62,** 23–26.

Little, S., and Somes, H. A. (1965). Atlantic white-cedar being eliminated by excessive animal damage in South Jersey. *U.S. For. Serv., Res. Note* NE-33.

McCormick, J. (1955). A vegetation inventory of two watersheds in the New Jersey Pine Barrens. Ph.D. Thesis, Rutgers Univ., New Brunswick, New Jersey.

McCormick, J. (1970). The Pine Barrens: A preliminary ecological inventory. *N.J. State Mus., Res. Rep.* No. 2.

McCormick, J. (1979). Water, vegetation, fire, and man in the Pine Barrens: Vegetation of two watersheds in Lebanon State Forest, New Jersey, and a consideration of the origin and nature of the Pine Barrens. *U.S. Geol. Surv., Prof. Pap.* No. 563-B (in press).

McCormick, J., and Andresen, J. W. (1963). The role of *Pinus virginiana* Mill. in the vegetation of southern New Jersey. *N.J. Nat. News* **18,** 27–38.

McCormick, J., and Andresen, J. W. (1979). Vegetation of the West Plains, New Jersey. *Bull., N.J. Acad. Sci.* (in press).

McCormick, J., and Buell, M. F. (1957). Natural revegetation of a plowed field in the New Jersey Pine Barrens. *Bot. Gaz.* **118,** 261–264.

McCormick, J., and Jones, L. (1973). The Pine Barrens: Vegetation geography. *N.J. State Mus., Res. Rep.* No. 3.

Moore, E. B. (1939). "Forest Management in New Jersey." N.J. Dep. Conserv. Dev., Div. For. Parks, Trenton, New Jersey.

Moore, E. B., and Waldron, A. F. (1940). Growth studies of southern white cedar in New Jersey. *J. For.* **38,** 568–572.

Pinchot, G. (1899). A study of forest fires and wood production in southern New Jersey. *N.J. Geol. Surv., Annu. Rep. State Geol. 1898* appendix, pp. 1–102.

Rigg, G. B. (1940). Comparisons of the development of some sphagnum bogs of the Atlantic Coast, the interior, and the Pacific Coast. *Am. J. Bot.* **27,** 1–14.

Rose, T. F., and Price, T. T. (1878). "Historical and Biographical Atlas of the New Jersey Coast." Woolman & Rose, Philadelphia, Pennsylvania.

Stone, W. (1911). The plants of southern New Jersey with especial reference to the flora of the Pine Barrens and the geographic distribution of the species. *N.J. State Mus., Annu. Rep. 1910* pp. 23–828.

14

Vegetation of the New Jersey Pine Barrens: A Phytosociological Classification

HANS OLSSON

INTRODUCTION

Although its first impression is of a monotonous extensive pine plain, on closer examination the vegetation of the New Jersey Pine Barrens emerges as a rich and intriguing diversity of types. The history of human activities in the area is known to be long and diverse, and the degree of coupling of the vegetation diversity with human activity commanded this investigation. Accordingly, the information and analysis reported here represent a study of the vegetation in the central fifth of the New Jersey Pine Barrens, an area bounded by New Lisbon, Browns Mills, Whiting, East Plains, and the Oswego River. The objective of this chapter is to describe the types of vegetation present and to show their relationships in a phytosociological classification, that is, a hierarchical concept based on plant distributions. Such a classification utilizes the presence and abundance of all species to indicate the relative similarity of vegetation types. This approach, developed from the European ecological traditions of Raunkiaer (1913), Du Rietz (1921), and Braun-Blanquet (1928), utilizes relevés (vegetation samples) in each vegetation type, and permits correlation with such environmental factors as disturbance.

Many human impacts on the environment are evident today. The development of sandy podzolic soils from parent material has been influenced by extensive wild fires and heavy cutting, e.g., the effects of fire may be seen at Upton. The use of timber for wood pulp, and for the charcoal, iron, and glasswork industries drastically changed the structure of the woodland, as, for example, around Whiting, where the landscape is reminiscent of a stressed boreal forest. Many swamps have been influenced by the mining of bog ore, logging, peat digging, and *Sphagnum* moss gathering.

Major wetlands have been utilized for the cultivation of cranberries. Today, com-

245

Copyright © 1979 by Academic Press, Inc.
All rights of reproduction in any form reserved.
ISBN 0-12-263450-0

mercial cranberry bogs are dependent upon water reservoirs, canals, ditches, sluices, gates, and, indirectly, on cedar logging. Unprofitable blueberry and cranberry fields today are recognized as abandoned sods with scattered bushes. Weeds and ruderal species are spreading in many new developments, construction of roads, and sand excavation projects. Housing projects threaten such unique localities as Webbs Mills. Increased camping, picnicking, littering, dumping, and the traffic of off-road vehicles influence the floristic composition.

Introduced species occur in and around abandoned villages. Many nonnative trees are used in silviculture, and tall shrubs such as dogwood (*Cornus florida*) are planted ornamentally along some roads. Stone (1911) pointed out that, "... all these influences are bound to make changes in the flora of the region in the near future, and it is none too soon to make a serious effort to record its characteristic features and its component species before it is too late."

METHODS

Various methods for vegetation analysis were developed in Europe by Raunkiaer (1913), Du Rietz (1921), Braun-Blanquet (1928), and in North America by Gleason (1917). Segments of similar vegetation may be recognized readily in a landscape. These are sampled to determine relationships among segments based on floristic composition (Mueller-Dombois and Ellenberg, 1974).

Representative stands were selected, and a representative spot within each stand was selected for sampling (a relevé) in as environmentally uniform an area as possible (Dahl, 1960). In a releve the abundance of tree, shrub, herb, bryophyte, and lichen species was estimated. The size and shape of samples varied with the type of stand: 100–400 m² for forests and 1–4 m² for smaller specific locations, such as certain bogs and haul roads. The size of the samples essentially agrees with the quadrats for various synusiae suggested by Cain and de O. Castro (1959). Relevés in a community type vary in their combinations of species, but together should contain essentially all of the species belonging to a vegetation type. The abundance of a species is estimated by the logarithmic Hult–Sernander–Du Rietz scale (Trass and Malmer, 1973) which has been modified by the author in the following way: $5+ = > 75\%$; $5 = 50\text{--}75\%$; $4 = 25\text{--}50\%$; $3 = 12.5\text{--}25\%$; $2 = 6.25\text{--}12.5\%$; $1 = 1\text{--}6.25\%$; $1- = < 1\%$; $+ = $ few or scattered. This scale permits a finer breakdown in the lower values. Instead of frequency studies (Raunkiaer, 1913; Gleason, 1920; Buell and Cantlon, 1950), the variation among the different stands, i.e., the constancy of species, has been emphasized.

My classification of the vegetation into 19 entities only partially agrees with the Du Rietz concept (Trass and Malmer, 1973) and the Braun-Blanquet interpretation (Westhoff and van der Maarel, 1973), because of the necessity of considering site criteria. All disturbance factors, such as fire and drainage, control the establishment of plant communities. Thus, total diversity is influenced by human activity, and the releves within a community type consequently show deviations from one another. The investigation approaches a classification of vegetation pattern based on causality as was suggested by Kershaw (1963) and by niche requirements (Little, 1974b). The pattern changes trace environmental gradients between plant communities (Whittaker, 1973) and various secondary successions, such as on fallow fields (McCormick, 1968) and burned areas (Little and Moore, 1949). In short, the classification demonstrates relationships among vegetation types based on species composition. In addition, by reflecting variations in natural and human disturbance factors, the classification is a useful ecological tool. The nomenclature mainly follows Fernald (1950) for vascular plants, Crum (1973) for mosses, and Thomson (1967) for the lichen genus *Cladonia*.

VEGETATION TYPES

The field work was done from the beginning of July 1975 to the end of July 1976. The utmost objectivity was exercised in choosing the sites, and as high a sampling intensity as possible was used. The 247 releves obtained then were arranged into 19 tables corresponding to distinguishable vegetational entities (Table I). The first level of the phytosociological classification is characterized by the following six major vegetation types, somewhat related to formations but different from Harshberger's (1916) and Conard's (1935) formations.

Pine–oak forest vegetation is divided into three entities (A1, A2, A3); *white cedar–red maple swamp* vegetation into four entities (B1, B2, B3, B4); *thicket–bog* vegetation into four entities (C1, C2, C3, C4); *marsh–sod* vegetation into four entities (D1, D2, D3, D4); *stream–pond* vegetation is one entity (E1); and *old-field* vegetation includes three entities (F1, F2, F3). With this separation, it is possible to proceed with a Braun-Blanquet analysis (Conard, 1935; Tüxen, 1937). McCormick (1970) and Robichaud and Buell (1973) emphasized the lowland–upland concept, grading conditions from wet to moist to dry, while Stone (1911) and Wherry (1920) emphasized geographical differences in the Pine Barrens.

Wherry (1920) indicated that soil acidity differentiates the vegetation. Throughout the study area, my measurements indicated that the pH of surface water ranges from 3.9–4.3. The nutrients calcium and potassium were present in 1.0–1.7 ppm and 0.3–0.5 ppm, respectively, agreeing with the results of Givnish (1971). Soil pH was about 4.0. Late summer daily maximum temperatures in the vegetation averaged about 25°C at moister sites, about 30°C at drier sites, and still higher at exposed lichen-covered spots. Light showed a similar increasing trend, but the reverse was true for relative humidity (average daily minima), i.e., 70, 60, and 40% respectively, for the three environments. The variation in temperature is important in determining the length of the growing season and the duration of the frost-free period (Robichaud and Buell, 1973).

TABLE I Synopsis of the Floristics of the Pine Barrens in 19 Vegetation Entities of the six Major Vegetation Types.[a]

	Pine-oak			Cedar–maple swamp				Thicket–bog				Marsh–sod				Stream–pond	Old-field		
	A 1	A 2	A 3	B 1	B 2	B 3	B 4	C 1	C 2	C 3	C 4	D 1	D 2	D 3	D 4	E 1	F 1	F 2	F 3
Polytrichum juniperinum B	×	○	○	○	—	○	—	○	—	—	—	—	○	×	○	—	○	×	×
Gaylussacia baccata S	●	●	●	●	—	○	—	×	×	—	—	—	—	○	—	—	○	—	○
Quercus ilicifolia S	●	×	○	○	—	○	—	○	○	—	—	—	—	—	—	—	○	—	○
Vaccinium vacillans S	×	×	×	○	—	—	○	○	—	—	—	—	—	○	○	—	○	—	—
Pinus rigida T	×	●	×	×	—	—	—	○	—	—	—	—	—	○	—	—	—	—	○
Quercus marilandica T	×	●	○	○	—	—	—	○	○	—	—	—	○	○	○	—	○	—	○
Cladonia cristatella L	○	○	○	○	—	—	—	○	—	—	—	—	—	—	—	—	—	—	—
Gaultheria procumbens S	○	○	○	○	—	—	—	—	—	—	—	—	—	—	—	—	—	—	—
Corema conradii S		×	—	—	—	—	—	—	—	—	—	—	—	—	—	—	—	—	—
Quercus prinus T	—		●	—	—	●	—	—	×	—	—	×	—	×	—	—	—	—	—
Quercus alba T	—	●	●	—	—	●	—	—	○	—	—	●	—	—	—	—	—	—	—
Quercus velutina T	○		×	—	—	×	—	○		—	—	○	—	—	—	—	—	○	—
Cladonia squamosa L	○	○	○	—	—	—	—	○	—	—	—	○	—	—	—	—	—	—	—
Leucobryum glaucum B	○	—	○	—	—	—	—	×	×	—	—	—	—	○	—	—	—	—	—
Gaylussacia frondosa S	○	○	×	○	○	○	○	×	○	×	○	○	—	○	—	—	—	—	—
Kalmia angustifolia S	—	○	○	●	●	●	●	●	×	×	—	×	—	×	○	—	—	—	—
Clethra alnifolia S	—	—	—	×	×	●	×	×	×	×	—	○	—	—	—	—	—	—	○
Leucothoe racemosa S	—	—	—	×	○	×	○	×	○	○	—	○	—	○	○	—	○	○	○
Rhododendron viscosum S	—	—	—	×	×	×	×	×	×	—	—	○	—	×	—	—	—	×	—
Chamaecyparis thyoides T	—	—	—	—	●	●	○	×		×	—	×	—	—	—	—	—	—	—
Sphagnum pulchrum B	—	—	—	—	●	●	●	●		—	—	●	—	—	—	○	—	—	—
Sphagnum palustre B	—	—	—	—	●	×	×	×	×	×	○	○	—	—	—	—	—	—	—
Acer rubrum T	—	—	—	○	×	●	×	×	×	○	—	○	○	○	○	—	○	—	○
Vaccinium corymbosum S	—	—	—	○	×	●	○	×	×	×	—	○	○	×	○	—	○	×	—
Nyssa sylvatica T	○	—	○	○	○	×	×	×		×	—	—	—	—	—	—	—	—	○
Smilax rotundifolia V	○	○	○	○	—	×	●	×	×	—	—	—	—	—	—	—	—	—	—
Liquidambar styraciflua T	—	—	—	—	—	—	×			—	—	—	—	—	—	—	—	—	○
Rhus radicans V	—	—	—	—	—	—	—	×	×	—	—	—	—	—	—	—	—	—	—
Lyonia ligustrina S	○	—	○	○	○	○	○	○	○	○	○	○	○	○	—	—	—	—	—
Smilax glauca V	○	○	○	○	—	—	—	●	●	—	—	—	—	—	—	—	—	—	—
Pyrus melanocarpa S	—	—	—	—	—	—	—	×	×	○	—	○	—	○	—	—	—	—	○
Rhus copallina S	—	○	—	○	—	—	—	○	×	○	—	○	—	○	—	—	—	○	—
Amelanchier canadensis T	—	—	—	—	—	—	—		×		—	—	—	○	—	—	—	×	—

Panicum virgatum H
Andropogon virginicus H
Chamaedaphne calyculata S
Sphagnum cuspidatum B
Sphagnum subnitens B
Woodwardia virginica H
Vaccinium macrocarpon S
Carex bullata H
Rhynchospora alba H
Sphagnum magellanicum B
Carex exilis H
Drosera intermedia H
Sphagnum tenellum B
Rhexia virginica H
Lachnanthes tinctoria H
Dulichium arundinaceum H
Sphagnum capillaceum B
Leiophyllum buxifolium S
Aster spectabilis H
Habenaria
  blephariglottis H
Polygala lutea H
Juncus dichotomus H
Hypericum canadense H
Nymphaea odorata H
Scirpus subterminalis H
Cladonia caroliniana L
Hudsonia ericoides S
Breweria pickeringii H
Arenaria caroliniana H
Solidago odora H
Erigeron canadensis H
Ambrosia artemisiifolia H
Cladonia strepsilis L
Triodia flava H
Diodia teres H
Bromus tectorum H

a The symbols mainly stress the average abundance, and to a certain degree the constancy, of species: o = <6.25%; × = 6.25-25%; ● = >25%. B, bryophyte; L, lichen; H, herb; S, shrub; T, tree; V, vine. See text.

249

PINE–OAK VEGETATION TYPE

Entity A1—*Pinus rigida-Quercus ilicifolia* (29 relevés)

This pine forest chiefly consists of trilayered, open to dense, dry stands. The arborescent layer is composed of eight to ten pitch pine (*Pinus rigida*) trees per 100 m², with a height of about 10 m. The understory is characterized by scrub oaks grading into a conspicuous heath of black huckleberry (*Gaylussacia baccata*). Reiners (1967) found higher coverage of scrub oak in pine stands and less in oak stands. Prominent on the forest floor are the haircap moss *Polytrichum juniperinum* and the lichens *Cladonia* spp.

A separation of the vegetation into three facies or types is evident: stands with (a) bearberry (*Arctostaphylos uva-ursi*), oak seedlings, and oak sprouts following severe fire damage; (b) dense coppice (sprout) oak woods including the shrub, chinquapin oak (*Quercus prinoides*), which is favored by repeated burning; and (c) blackjack oak (*Q. marilandica*) and scrub oak (*Q. ilicifolia*) in the undergrowth. The last two types comprise the *Quercetum ilicifoliae* and the *Pinetum rigidae* communities described by Conard (1935) and the pitch pine–scrub oak forest on ridge tops in northern New Jersey (Niering, 1953).

Pinus rigida is one of the most fire-adapted species, occurring from dry sandy plains to poorly drained sands and swamps. Repeated wildfires explain the near absence of *P. echinata* and tall oaks (Little, 1974a) and the depauperization of the floristic composition. Sweet fern (*Comptonia peregrina*) and wild indigo (*Baptisia tinctoria*) seem to be favored, however. Removal of much of the forest floor is significant for both the germination and the establishment of pine seedlings (Little and Moore, 1949) and for the notable change in *Cladonia* composition. Thus, cushion-forming *C. arbuscula* and *C. subtenuis* occur in the less burned spots, while the upright, nearly unbranched lichens *C. cristatella, C. atlantica,* and *C. squamosa* are more striking in the repeatedly burned areas. Disturbances in the plant cover influence the soil profile, the thickness of the mor (organic) layer, the mottling of leached sand, and the root penetration of 15–60 cm.

On both old fields and clear-cut stands is a trend toward a hardwood climax forest, with the pine forest a subclimax or fire climax. Little (1973) documented succession over 18 years from an old field.

Entity A2—Pygmy Forest (7 relevés)

This pine forest is a single- to trilayered, dense to very closed, dry coppice woodland approximately 1–5 m (3–15 ft) high. Today, the stunted trees dominated by blackjack oak and pitch pine (*Quercus marilandica, Pinus rigida*) seem to be in balance. Lutz (1934) reported the greater prevalence of the main fire indicators, scrub oak and sweet fern (*Quercus ilicifolia, Comptonia peregrina*), than was tallied by this author. Apparently, the floristic composition has changed over the last 50 years with herbs, lichens, and bryophytes all diminishing. Certain heath shrubs are ubiquitous. This vegetation is an extreme expression of the more widespread pitch pine–blackjack oak forest (McCormick and Buell, 1968) or pine–scrub oak forest, which in some areas forms a transitional woods with a height of 3–4 m (10–13 ft).

Two types of vegetation are recognized. (a) A low-growing broom crowberry (*Corema conradii*) stand with bearberry (*Arctostaphylos uva-ursi*) is present in open, denuded sites. According to Stone (1911), *C. conradii* was more abundant earlier, in patches confluent to large masses, although in certain spots it was exterminated by severe fire. This dwarf shrub heath now is maintained chiefly by other disturbances, such as bulldozing and sand excavation. In the (b) typical stands containing broom crowberry (*Corema*), the stunted growth depends partly upon the competition between and within sprout clumps of the coppice wood (Little, 1974a). *Cladonia caroliniana* and *C. strepsilis* sparsely cover the ground.

This pygmy forest entity is limited mainly to the west Pine Plains and east Pine Plains. The west Pine Plains contain more mountain laurel (*Kalmia latifolia*) and are somewhat richer in species, suggesting more available moisture (Pinelands, 1974), in contrast to the drier east Pine Plains, which have a more closed plant cover.

Entity A3—*Quercus alba–Q. prinus–Q. velutina* (28 relevés)

This oak forest consists of tri- to quadrilayered, dense to closed, moist to dry stands. The arborescent layer reaches 10–20 m in height, and the canopy covers 50% or more of the ground. The tree composition depends on the site and the type of disturbance. Within the study area, chestnut oak (*Quercus prinus*) seems to be the most abundant, with 10–15 trees per 400 m², normally accompanied by two to three pitch pine (*Pinus rigida*) trees and one to two shortleaf pine (*P. echinata*) trees, plus other oaks. Black oak (*Quercus velutina*) is more frequent than white oak (*Q. alba*), although both are present in some stands. The understory (1–4 m high) is irregular, with post oak (*Quercus stellata*) and sassafras (*Sassafras albidum*) sparsely overtopping scattered scrub oaks, above a distinct *Gaylussacia baccata* layer that includes dangleberry (*G. frondosa*) and lowbush blueberry (*Vaccinium vacillans*). The herbaceous species are scattered, but the ground cover of mosses and lichens is often well developed, with *Dicranum scoparium, Leucobryum glaucum, Polytrichum juniperinum, Cladonia grayi,* and *C. squamosa* predominant, and *C. coniocraea* and *Parmelia rudecta* on tree bases. The stratification is similar to a rather homogeneous community of oaks with a small amount of pine studied by Buell and Cantlon (1950).

Vegetation is separated as follows. (a) Scarlet oak (*Quercus coccinea*) stands occur in the eastern and central Pine Barrens (McCormick, 1970), with wintergreen (*Gaultheria procumbens*) on the ground and the moss *Thelia hirtella* on tree bases, affiliated with the *Quercetum velutinae* community of Conard (1935). (b) Mountain laurel (*Kalmia latifolia*) stands, i.e., a *Quercetum kalmietosum* community (Conard, 1935), occur on sandy loam soil and in less burned areas, e.g., locations at Fort Dix. (c) Many typical recently burned stands, equivalent to a *Quercetum prini* (Conard, 1935), or if compared with European oak forests, are very similar to the *Querceto-Betuletum* (Tüxen, 1937) or *Melampyro-Quercetum roboris* community (see Olsson, 1974b).

Increased rainfall interception and stemflow seem to favor the spreading of *Dicranum* spp. and *Cladonia* spp., e.g., *Dicranum scoparium* and *Cladonia apodocarpa* may be found near the base of trees. Where they occur, mosses may intercept as much as 50% of the throughfall (Moul and Buell, 1955).

Normally, most of the herb species are restricted to road edges exposed to sufficient light (Little, 1974b). In openings on better soils, however, lichens are favored (Buell and Cantlon, 1953), as well as such showy herbs as *Gerardia pedicularia* and *Scleria triglomerata*. Woods with black cherry (*Prunus serotina*) around clearings are particularly rich in herbs and vines growing on tree trunks. At Mount Misery, tall chestnut oak (*Quercus prinus*) trees solely are dominant, with an even understory including black locust (*Robinia pseudo-acacia*) on hard, sandy loam soil with a thin dark brown mor. I regard this as a final stage in vegetational succession. According to Little (1974a), the climax forest on upland sites in the Pine Barrens is a mixture of oaks and hickories.

WHITE CEDAR-RED MAPLE SWAMP VEGETATION TYPE

Entity B1—*Pinus rigida–Leucothoe racemosa* (13 relevés)

This pine forest consists of bi- to trilayered, dense, wet to moist, homogeneous stands. The tree canopy is almost solely pitch pine (*Pinus rigida*), and is 7–10 m in height. The relatively small dense trees, 15–20 per 100 m², have multiple stems from a single root crown (McCormick, 1970), and the crooked trunks often are branched. Sweet pepperbush (*Clethra alnifolia*), fetterbush (*Leucothoe racemosa*), and *Gaylussacia frondosa* are very striking in the conspicuous understory (2–3 m high). With a more open, broadleaf, tall shrub layer, a secondary shrub layer, including *Kalmia angustifolia,* staggerbush (*Lyonia mariana*), and *Gaylussacia baccata,* is found. *Smilax glauca, Gaultheria procumbens,* bracken fern (*Pteridium aquilinum*), and the widespread cowwheat (*Melampyrum lineare*) are among the herbaceous plants. The bottom layer is almost absent. These pine stands correspond to Harshberger's (1916) wet Pine Barrens along meandering streams and disturbed wetlands near cranberry bogs. *Pinus rigida* seems to be rather stable in such habitats, although it may be encroached upon by adjoining hardwoods.

The soil has a rather distinct organic mat with intertwined roots sometimes containing charcoal relicts of a former fire. The subsoil is distinctly reddish, largely due to fluctuations in the water table. On imperfectly to very poorly drained soils between uplands and swamps, 18 shrub species were recorded (Little, 1974b). *Leiophyllum buxifolium* is particularly favored by human disturbance of drainage, *Xerophyllum asphodeloides* by fire, and the ferns *Pteridium aquilinum* and *Osmunda cinnamomea* by clearing and burning. After the death of *Osmunda,* pitch pines may become established on tussocks and thus invade wet cedar swamps (Harshberger, 1916). Within the pine lowlands, the shrub leatherleaf (*Chamaedaphne calyculata*), often dominates the sites having the poorest drainage.

Entity B2—*Chamaecyparis thyoides* (13 relevés)

This swamp forest consists of trilayered, dense to closed, wet stands. The arborescent layer typically is an upper canopy of Atlantic white cedar (*Chamaecyparis thyoides*) 15–20 m high (20–30 trees per 100 m²) sometimes having a weakly developed lower stratum of *Acer rubrum* and *Nyssa sylvatica*. Tree cover exceeds 60%. The 4–5-m-high undergrowth is sparse and mainly composed of tall shrubs such as *Clethra alnifolia*, *Rhododendron viscosum*, and *Vaccinium corymbosum*. *Osmunda cinnamomea*, chain ferns (*Woodwardia* spp.), and sedge (*Carex collinsii*) are striking among the herbaceous plants, in agreement with a list compiled by Little (1951). The ground is covered mainly with a *Sphagnum* mat containing *S. fallax*, *S. magellanicum*, *S. palustre*, and *S. pulchrum*. Logs and tree bases are colonized by liverworts and *Cladonia incrassata*.

Vegetation is separated into two types. (a) Shaded sweet pepperbush (*Clethra alnifolia*) stands are present, in which deciduous trees are common, and in which there is less hummock development except around white cedar trunks. The soil, which is similar to a carr (Givnish, 1971), has developed from coniferous debris. Clearcutting usually occurs when the trees are about 60 years old, resulting in considerable resistant slash. (b) A second type present in rather open sites, often having a mosaic of hummocks and interlocking pools containing New Jersey rush (*Juncus caesariensis*), has more plant species.

At Webbs Mills, this transitional type contains dwarf huckleberry (*Gaylussacia dumosa*) and along with *Sphagnum pulchrum*, a smooth ground layer of *S. flavicomans*. As in glaciated areas, a peat layer is present, but is very thin and contains small hummocks. Excluding the mounds of *Sphagnum flavicomans* (Osvald, 1940), zonation occurs on the hummocks (Givnish, 1971), with liverworts at the summit, *S. magellanicum* on the slope, often with cedar seedlings (Little, 1950, and *S. pulchrum* at the rims of the pools or floating. A very open example of this vegetation with cedar saplings approaches the beak rush (*Rynchospora alba*) vegetation to be described later. At Mount Misery, an opening in the swamp has been created (probably by fire) where *Aralia nudicaulis* and *Sphagnum subnitens* can be found.

The white cedar swamp is a subclimax to the hardwoods. These, in turn, gradually replace the overstory to form a deciduous swamp (Little, 1950).

Entity B3—*Acer rubrum–Nyssa sylvatica* (8 relevés)

This swamp consists of trilayered, dense to closed, wet to moist stands. The tree layer, with a canopy cover of 75% and 15 m in height, is estimated to be composed of roughly 20 red maple (*Acer rubrum*) trees, five black gum (*Nyssa sylvatica*) trees, and one or two gray birch (*Betula populifolia*) trees per 100 m², although in some stands *Nyssa sylvatica* is more prominent. Sweet bay (*Magnolia virginiana*) forms an irregular understory over a shrub layer of >50% cover, chiefly highbush blueberry (*Vaccinium corymbosum*) and *Clethra alnifolia*. The greenbrier vine (*Smilax rotundifolia*) makes some areas difficult to penetrate. Apart from *Osmunda cinnamomea*, the herbaceous plants are less numerous, in contrast to open cedar swamps. On the forest floor, patches of *Sphagnum fallax* and *S. palustre* occur together with scattered *Leucobryum glaucum* and *Dicranum* spp.; although *Calypogeia trichomanis* occurs on the tree hummocks, most liverworts are more characteristic of cedar swamps (Little, 1951).

Vegetation is separated into two types: (a) rarely found pin oak (*Quercus palustris*) stands, e.g., at Whitesbog, and (b) typical deciduous swamps, the *Aceretum osmundaceum* of Conard (1935), in moist sites adjacent to dense thickets, often in the border between cedar swamps and upland forests or along stream courses and intermittent drainages. A very closed red maple (*Acer rubrum*) forest is the final successional stage.

Entity B4—*Liquidambar styraciflua–Liriodendron tulipifera* (4 relevés)

This deciduous forest consists of trilayered, closed, moist stands near the edge of the Pine Barrens and on richer soils in the Pine Barrens, as is evident at Browns Mills and New Lisbon. In some upland stands, (a) tulip poplar (*Liriodendron tulipifera*) is characteristic with Japanese honeysuckle (*Lonicera japonica*) covering the ground. (b) Stands of sweet gum (*Liquidambar styraciflua*) with abundant poison ivy (*Rhus radicans*) are strongly human influenced. Many species not native to the Pine Barrens, such as *Ailanthus altissima* and *Asarum canadense,* are present.

THICKET-BOG VEGETATION TYPE

Entity C1—*Shrub thicket* (11 relevés)

The shrub thicket consists of single-, bi- or trilayered, wet to dry stands, 1–4 m in height. Dangleberry, staggerbush, highbush blueberry (*Gaylussacia frondosa, Lyonia mariana, Vaccinium corymbosum*), and in certain stands chokeberry (*Pyrus* spp.) are among the tall shrubs. Various herbaceous species are sparse, with *Smilax glauca* and *Pteridium aquilinum* being the most frequent. *Polytrichum juniperinum, Sphagnum capillaceum,* and *Cladonia squamosa* occur on the ground.

Vegetation is separated into three types. (a) Possum haw (*Viburnum nudum*) stands with maleberry (*Lyonia ligustrina*) and swamp azalea (*Rhododendron viscosum*) are present, overtopped by scattered *Nyssa sylvatica* and *Magnolia virginiana*. Under-shrubs of *Leucothoe racemosa,* tufts of *Carex hovei,* and *Sphagnum* spp. may be striking. (b) Typical, and sometimes pure, blueberry stands, the *Vaccinietum corymbosi* of Conard (1935), border lakes, swamps, and neglected cranberry bogs. In somewhat drier sites, clumps of oak are mixed with *Myrica pensylvanica*. Related shrub complexes are reported by Wright (1941) and Buell (1946). Of special interest is (c) the abandoned cranberry bog with scattered cedar saplings or, e.g., at Whitesbog, sweet gum (*Liquidambar styraciflua*), which is usually associated with the Inner

Coastal Plain (Hanks, 1971). The mesic conditions favor tall herbs such as *Eupatorium* and *Solidago*. Most thickets are transformed gradually into red maple swamps.

Entity C2—*Dike bush* (7 relevés)

The dike bush consists of single- to bilayered, closed, moist to dry stands. The shrub layer is composed mainly of serviceberry (*Amelanchier canadensis*), *Clethra alnifolia*, *Leucothoe racemosa*, *Lyonia mariana*, black chokeberry (*Pyrus melanocarpa*), *Vaccinium corymbosum*, and scattered *Pyrus arbutifolia*, *Rhus copallina*, and *Cephalanthus occidentalis*. Saplings of *Acer rubrum* often are adjacent. Common herbaceous plants include *Aster spectabilis*, *Smilax glauca*, *Rumex acetosella*, *Andropogon virginicus*, *Paspalum setaceum*, and *Panicum clandestinum*. Dodder, *Cuscuta gronowii*, may infest certain shrubs.

The dikes, often used as small roads, are constructed to allow flooding of the cranberry bogs, and are built up partly by "turfing" and drainage of surrounding fields. Dike vegetation is influenced by both road-scraping and regular cutting of the plant cover.

Entity C3—*Chamaedaphnae calyculata* (11 relevés)

This spongy thicket consists of bilayered, closed, wet stands covered by leatherleaf (*Chamaedaphne calyculata*), with sheep laurel (*Kalmia angustifolia*) as a subdominant. *Woodwardia virginica* and *Carex bullata* often are intermixed. A bog mat is composed mainly of *Sphagnum cuspidatum, S. fallax, S. magellanicum,* and *S. subnitens*, similar to the *Chamaedaphnetum calyculatae* community of Conard (1935), but differing from the *Chamaedaphe–Sphagnum flavicomans-sociation* (Osvald, 1940). The European counterpart is classified as *Erico–Sphagnion* (Moore, 1968).

Vegetation is separated into: (a) rather open arrowhead (*Sagittaria latifolia*) stands along streams and canals; and (b) typical stands in depressions encircled by highbush blueberry (*Vaccinium corymbosum*), overgrown ponds, and stream margins and dammed streams, where swamp loosestrife (*Decodon verticillatus*) is prominent. In these sites, including many flat bogs, the peat layer is 30–40 cm thick and mixed with muck (Rigg, 1940).

Entity C4—*Vaccinium macrocarpon–Carex bullata–Glyceria obtusa* (13 relevés)

This vegetation complex consists of single or sometimes bilayered, dense to closed, wet stands in bog and stream habitats. Vegetation is separated into three types. (a) Cranberry (*Vaccinium macrocarpon*) stands are present in neglected cranberry fields, accompanied by sparse *Cladium mariscoides* and, with increased time since abandonment, *Rubus hispidus* and *Acer rubrum* saplings. (b) Sedge (*Carex bullata*) stands in spongy and stream sites normally develop a *Sphagnum* mat. *Carex bullata*, conspicuous on abandoned bogs, is regarded as a serious weed, along with *Woodwardia virginica* in the cranberry culture, and may be eradicated by lowering the water table (Beckwith and Fiske, 1925). (c) Blunt mannagrass (*Glyceria obtusa*) is luxuriant in stands along ditches and meandering streams.

MARSH-SOD VEGETATION TYPE

Entity D1—*Rhynchospora alba–Sphagnum* spp. (18 relevés)

This marsh vegetation complex chiefly consists of bilayered, open to dense, wet stands associated with scattered and stunted cedar growth, many herbaceous plants such as sundews, shortleaf milkwort, beakrush, slender yellow-eyed grass (*Drosera* spp., *Polygala brevifolia, Rhynchospora* spp., *Xyris torta*), and a ground cover of *Sphagnum magellanicum, S. pulchrum,* and *S. papillosum.* Lichens grow on the summits of hummocks.

The vegetation is separated into four types. (a) Bog asphodel (*Narthecium americanum*) stands include pitcher plants (*Sarracenia purpurea*) and other carnivorous plants, *Eriocaulon* spp., *Danthonia epilis,* and *Sphagnum portoricense.* The yellow *Narthecium* patches develop on wet savannas and quaking bogs near rivers. The quaking bog has a *Sphagnum* mat floating atop water and muck of considerable depth (Wright, 1941; Givnish, 1971). (b) Tussocky and spongy coast sedge (*Carex exilis*) stands include numerous mounds of *Sphagnum* spp., including *S. flavicomans* and, although rarely, also *S. quinquefarium.* Larger hummocks have *Rhynchospora gracilenta* encircling clumps of cedar and pools of water and are fringed by *Aster nemoralis.* The floristic composition resembles that of a *Carex exilis–Sphagnum magellanicum–S. pulchrum sociation,* reminiscent of the *Eriophorum vaginatum–S. magellanicum sociation* of European bogs (Osvald, 1940). (c) Curly grass fern (*Schizaea pusilla*) stands occur in open, leached sand, where large dry hummocks inhabited by *Gaylussacia dumosa, Cladonia calycantha,* and *C. santensis* are scattered with *Sphagnum tenellum,* a species favored by inundation. Interhummock patches resemble savannas, with *Lophiola americana* and bladderwort (*Utricularia cornuta*) present. (d) Finally, *Sphagnum*-covered seepage areas and turfed flats (the organic turf removed), with broomsedge (*Andropogon virginicus* var. *abbreviatus*) and slender yellow-eyed grass (*Xyris torta*) form microzonations on certain slopes and neglected bogs.

Entity D2—*Lachnanthes tinctoria–Rhexia virginica– Dulichium arundinaceum* (24 relevés)

This marsh or sod vegetation consists of single- to bilayered, open to dense, wet, low-growing herbaceous stands associated with herbs such as sundew (*Drosera inter-*

media), *Hypericum virginicum, Cyperus dentatus,* and *Juncus pelocarpus.* Also present are *Sphagnum cuspidatum* and *S. tenellum* in sites with fluctuating inundation.

Vegetation is separated into three types. (a) Redroot (*Lachnanthes tinctoria*) stands commonly exhibit profuse flowering on neglected cranberry bogs (Beckwith and Fiske, 1925) and are fringed by *Leersia oryzoides* at wetter sites. (b) Meadow beauty (*Rhexia virginica*) stands including *Sphagnum pylaesii* have a homogeneous structure in neglected bogs and turfed spots. (c) *Dulichium arundinaceum* stands accompanied by *Utricularia geminiscapa* occur along meandering streams.

Entity D3—*Polygala lutea*–*Habenaria blephariglottis* (12 relevés)

This sod and meadowy vegetation consists of bilayered, open to dense, moist stands often rich in species, such as occur at Warren Grove. Low shrubs such as sand myrtle (*Leiophyllum buxifolium*) and *Kalmia angustifolia* dominate, along with such herbs as *Aster spectabilis, Habenaria blephariglottis, Lobelia nuttallii, Polygala lutea, Juncus dichotomus,* and *Rhynchospora capitellata.* Common bryophytes are *Aulacomnium palustre, Sphagnum capillaceum,* and *S. compactum,* and the lichens *Cladonia floridana* and *C. squamosa.*

Vegetation is separated into (a) drier stands with abundant *Cladonia* lichens and (b) moister *Sphagnum*-characterized stands including *S. strictum.* In certain sites, pyxie moss (*Pyxidanthera barbulata*) and *Cladonia subtenuis* form transitions to roadsides. In some neglected bogs, Virginia cottongrass (*Eriophorum virginicum*) is striking.

Entity D4—*Haul road* (11 relevés)

This vegetation consists of single- to bilayered, open, moist stands in the narrow, sharp gradient habitats of many abandoned haul roads once used for removing cedar (Little, 1974b). Rush (*Juncus dichotomus*) and clustered beakrush (*Rhynchospora capitellata*) are the most frequent species. Vegetation is separated into (a) drier St. John's wort (*Hypericum gentianoides*) stands with *H. canadense* and (b) moister stands characterized by the presence of *Sphagnum capillaceum* and *S. compactum* and in certain spots also scattered Torrey's beakrush (*Rhynchospora torreyana*). Many species grow in the middle of the sandy roads and along the small strips bordering shrub thickets. Human littering may favor seed box (*Ludwigia alternifolia*).

STREAM–POND VEGETATION TYPE

Entity E1—Aquatic vegetation (10 relevés)

The stream–pond vegetation complex consists of single-layered, open to dense, wet stands. Vegetation is separated into (a) water club rush (*Scirpus subterminalis*) stands in meandering streams; (b) Condon's yellow-eyed grass (*Xyris congdoni*) stands with *Eleocharis robbinsii* on river banks that overflow periodically; (c) water lily (*Nymphaea odorata*) stands in shallow intermittent ponds and deeper artificial lakes; (d) free-floating bladderwort (*Utricularia*) stands including *Sphagnum torreyanum;* (e) water shield (*Brassenia schreberi*) stands with *Sphagnum teres* between hummocks of low cedar growth, such as at Webbs Mills; and (f) golden club (*Orontium aquaticum*) stands accompanied by purple bladderwort (*Utricularia purpurea*) in sluggish water.

OLD-FIELD VEGETATION TYPE

Entity F1—*Breweria pickeringii–Hudsonia ericoides* (5 relevés)

This pioneer vegetation consists of single- to bilayered, open, dry stands in disturbed sites on leached sand that undergo secondary succession (Levin, 1966). Vegetation is separated into (a) Pickering's morning glory (*Breweria pickeringii*) stands characterized by the presence of *Cladonia caroliniana* and *Pyonothelia papillaria,* and (b) stands with false heather (*Hudsonia ericoides*) forming cushions on dry outwash sandy bogs, also colonized by *Panicum virgatum*. In contrast to *Hudsonia tomentosa,* which is found along abandoned railroads, *H. ericoides* grows on various sandy upland spots and is characteristic of burned patches on the Pine Plains.

Entity F2—*Solidago* spp.–*Ambrosia artemisiifolia–Prunus maritima* (10 relevés)

This old-field vegetation consists of single- to bilayered, open to closed, moist to dry stands in upland sites and neglected bogs. Vegetation is separated into four types (a) Ragweed (*Ambrosia artemisiifolia*) stands are found on fallow fields, such as at Upton, with luxuriantly growing horseweed (*Erigeron canadensis*) and relics of corn (*Zea mays*) adjacent to more open spots containing *Oenothera laciniata* and patches of mosses. About one year after abandonment of a cultivated field at Mount Misery, McCormick and Buell (1957) reported > 100 species, but no bryophytes. (b) The irregular beach plum (*Prunus maritima*) stands originating from orchards, reveal a diverse flora including *Pyrus malus, Solidago altissima, Carex muhlenbergii,* and *Cladonia subcariosa*. (c) Rare pickly pear (*Opuntia compressa*) stands occur in open disturbed habitats of flat and southern exposure (Hanks and Fairbrothers, 1969).

Depending on the length of time a bog has been fallow, (d) fragrant goldenrod (*Solidago odora*) stands gradually change in floristic composition, with an invasion of herbs such as *Andropogon* spp., *Juncus dichotomus,* and *J. effusus* among clumps of abandoned blueberry shrubs and increasing *Lyonia mariana* shrubs. The vine *Rubus hispidus* and *Solidago fistulosa* inhabit somewhat moister places, while *Eupatorium hyssopifolium* and *Solidago tenuifolia* are present in drier spots.

Entity F3—Asphalt road edge (16 relevés)

This vegetation, rich in species, consists of single- to bilayered, open to closed, moist to dry stands in disturbed and unstable habitats. There is an encroachment of introduced European plants such as Queen Anne's lace and bromegrass (*Daucus carota, Bromus* spp.), naturalized species including *Achillea millefolium* and *Rudbeckia hirta,* as well as rare colonists such as *Froelichia gracilis* and *Solidago sempervirens,* which apparently are favored by vehicular traffic. Native plants such as *Monarda punctata* and *Triodia flava* also are common. Various disturbances, including the municipal cutting of road edges and the application of herbicides in narrow strips along the roads, have increased the number of herbaceous species (Little, 1974b). Many species of *Panicum* and other grass and grasslike plants are common to fallow fields (McCormick and Buell, 1957) and cleared habitats (Levin, 1966).

Vegetation is separated into four types. (a) Low-growing buttonweed (*Diodia teres*) stands contain pioneers such as *Aster spectabilis, Plantago aristata, Aristida* spp., *Panicum* spp., and the moss *Ceratodon purpureus.* (b) St. Andrew's cross (*Ascyrum hypericoides*) stands with *Chrysopsis mariana* and *Carex pensylvanica* characterize more closed vegetation. (c) Most roadside species are in the tick trefoil (*Desmodium* spp.) stands of medium height, including *Eupatorium* spp., *Lespedeza* spp., *Solidago* spp., and encroaching *Leucothoe racemosa* shrubs mingled with *Oenothera biennis* and *Asclepias syriaca.* The floristic composition is rather similar to that of old fields in other parts of the United States (Evans and Dahl, 1955). (d) Sumac (*Rhus* spp.) stands are the most irregularly shaped.

Thus, commencing from the asphalt road edge, *Xanthium* spp. and *Euphorbia* spp. distinguish the sparse growth on smooth sand. These are followed by a higher fringe of *Cassia fasciculata* and *Ambrosia artemisiifolia* in front of taller shrubs of *Rhus* spp. and saplings of *Acer rubrum,* producing a pattern suggestive of a secondary succession on the Inner Coastal Plain (Hanks, 1971).

DISCUSSION

Two of the six major vegetation types are related in large part or entirely to human activities in the landscape, and six of the 19 vegetation entities and 20 of the 51 finer vegetation separations are chiefly or entirely human caused. The human activities responsible for these patterns are bulldozing and sand excavation, the abandonment of cranberry bogs, dikes and the construction of ditches, the removal of organic turf, the traffic of haul roads, the asphalting of road edges, the damming of lakes and ponds, the deterioration of old orchards and the increasing area of fallow fields. The loss of any one of these would eliminate a type of present Pine Barrens vegetation. In addition, several types of vegetation are related to human-caused fires, fire control, and cutting. The presence of individual species also is found to be related to these and other human activities in the Pine Barrens landscape.

The New Jersey Pine Barrens, situated on sand south of the terminal moraine, and the glaciated sandland of southern Sweden (Olsson, 1974a) have points of similarity. Both areas are vegetation outliers, of the eastern North American deciduous region and of the European Nemoral hardwood zone, respectively. The development of the Pine Barrens has been determined by its fire history, with attempts to control large wildfires being made since as early as 1750 (Little, 1974a). Heavy cutting for wood pulp and charcoal also has influenced the area and the forest structure. In this century, the flooding of cranberry bogs has been detrimental to the native flora, as have clearing and plowing of the forest land (Stone, 1911). In southern Sweden, the landscape with deciduous trees has been transformed largely into coniferous forests since 1800 (Olsson, 1974b), through afforestation to stop the moving of sand. From the beginning of the 16th century, documents record the widespread shifting of sand.

Due to changes in agriculture, silviculture, and intensity of grazing, the seminatural dwarf shrub heath in northwestern Europe drastically decreased in area. In southern Sweden in particular, the heaths developed into various forests more rapidly than in any other European country. Regular burning in the winter, every six to 12 years is necessary to regenerate the *Calluna* heath. The New Jersey pine forest is favored by a fire frequency of about 20 years, and the Pine Plains by a frequency of about ten years (Robichaud and Buell, 1973). The northwestern European heathland developed in a region with an oceanic climate. To the east, which has a more continental climate, pine trees may form an arborescent layer above the dwarf shrubs. Accordingly, Harshberger (1916) concluded that with a more continental climate in New Jersey, oak will be subordinate to the pine. Today, pitch pine stands are the fire climax of a deciduous forest dominated by oak.

In contrast to the Pine Barrens, the acid oak forests on the quartz sand of the northwestern European plain are composed of dwarf shrubs, herbaceous plants, prostrate branching (pleurocarpous) mosses, and few tree species. The soil is podzolized more clearly than that of the Pine Barrens, whose soil is influenced by fire and drainage. In southern Sweden the semistable state of the planted Scotch pine (*Pinus sylvestris*), encroached upon by few oak trees, is in sharp contrast to the New Jersey pitch pine forest, which has a pronounced scrub oak understory maintained by fire. However, light winter surface fires over a long period probably would favor the pine overstory such that its shade might reduce the scrub oak cover.

Through succession, a potential final climax, the *Melampyro-Quercetum roboris,* is obtained on the southern Swedish sandland (Olsson, 1974a). A similar vegetational succession toward a dense oak wood, and the development of the immature soil to podzol is not present in the New Jersey Pine Barrens. However, certain coppice oak stands show similarities in vegetation appearance. Mature Swedish stands, with birch as a subdominant, have a rather homogeneous structure. This is in contrast to the *Quercus prinus* forest containing *Pinus echinata,* an irregular understory of heath shrubs, and a bottom layer of scattered lichens and upright little-branched (acrocarpous) mosses.

The Pine Barrens wetland, characterized by the white cedar swamp, has developed several vegetation types unlike those in Europe as a consequence of specific water conditions, cultivation, and the abandonment of bogs. In addition, the fallow fields show divergence in floristic composition, depending on previous crops and human activity.

Both the Pine Barrens and the sandland of southern Sweden are phytogeographically very interesting, with many uncommon plant distributions. In southern Sweden, the number of species has been fairly constant for 200 years. In New Jersey, various unstable habitats, such as cleared sites and roadsides, are colonized by a continually increasing number of species, including European immigrants. Drainage has contributed new habitats, e.g., for *Lachnanthes tinctoria*. Elimination of the disturbances may lead to impoverishment of the flora. The diversity of habitats and the distribution and pattern of vegetation types thus are highly affected by human disturbance in the New Jersey Pine Barrens.

SUMMARY

The vegetation of the New Jersey Pine Barrens was analyzed using European phytosociological methods to show the floristic diversity of, and the relationships within, the vegetational pattern. Trees, shrubs, herbs, bryophytes, and lichens sampled in 247 relevés formed the basis of a hierarchical classification. Six major vegetation types, (1) pine–oak forest, (2) white cedar–red maple swamp, (3) thicket–bog, (4) marsh–sod, (5) stream–pond, and (6) old field (including roadsides), comprised 19 distinct vegetational entities. Fifty-one finer subdivisions of the vegetational entities were delineated. Human activities, including drainage and the development of lakes, roads, sand, and turf removal, abandoned agriculture, and cranberry bog development, are responsible mainly or entirely for a third of the types of vegetation at all three levels of classification. Human-caused fires, fire control, and cutting are significant in several additional types. The number of plant species in most open unstable environments exceeds that in closed shady sites.

ACKNOWLEDGMENTS

I am grateful to A. Damman for introducing me to the New Jersey Pine Barrens. Thanks are due to E. Vivian, W. Michalsky, and D. Zollinhofer for facilities during my stay at Whitesbog, New Jersey. To T. Gordon I am indebted for help with the Pine Barrens flora.

REFERENCES

Beckwith, C. S., and Fiske, J. G. (1925). Weeds of cranberry bogs. *N.J. Agric. Exp. Stn., Circ.* **171**, 1–22.
Braun-Blanquet, J. (1964). "Pflanzensoziologie," 3rd Ed. Springer-Verlag, Berlin and New York. (Orig. Ed., 1928.)
Buell, M. F. (1946). Jerome bog, a peat filled "Carolina bay." *Bull. Torrey Bot. Club* **73**, 24–33.
Buell, M. F., and Cantlon, J. E. (1950). A study of two communities of the New Jersey Pine Barrens and a comparison of methods. *Ecology* **31**, 567–586.

Buell, M. F., and Cantlon, J. E. (1953). Effects of prescribed burning on ground cover in the New Jersey pine region. *Ecology* **34**, 520–528.

Cain, S. A., and de O. Castro, G. M. (1959). "Manual of Vegetation Analysis." Harper, New York.

Conard, H. S. (1935). The plant associations of central Long Island. *Am. Midl. Nat.* **16**, 433–516.

Crum, H. (1973). "Mosses of the Great Lakes Forests." Publ. Univ. Michigan Herbarium, Ann Arbor.

Dahl, E. (1960). Some measures of uniformity in vegetation analysis. *Ecology* **41**, 805–808.

Du Rietz, G. E. (1921). "Zur metodologischen Grundlage der modernen Pflanzensoziologie." Holzhausen, Vienna.

Evans, F. C., and Dahl, E. (1955). The vegetational structure of an abandoned field in southeastern Michigan and its relation to environmental factors. *Ecology* **36**, 685–706.

Fernald, M. L. (1950). "Gray's Manual of Botany." Amer. Book Co., New York.

Givnish, T., ed. (1971). "A Study of New Jersey Pine Barrens Cedar Swamps." Rep. Princeton–N.S.F. Cedar Swamp Study Group, Princeton, New Jersey.

Gleason, H. A. (1917). The structure and development of the plant association. *Bull. Torrey Bot. Club* **44**, 463–481.

Gleason, H. A. (1920). Some applications of the quadrat method. *Bull. Torrey Bot. Club* **47**, 21–33.

Hanks, J. P. (1971). Secondary succession on the inner coastal plain of New Jersey. *Bull. Torrey Bot. Club* **98**, 315–321.

Hanks, S. L., and Fairbrothers, D. E. (1969). Habitats and associations of *Opuntia compressa* (Salisb.) Macbr. in New Jersey. *Bull. Torrey Bot. Club* **96**, 592–596.

Harshberger, J. W. (1916). "The Vegetation of the New Jersey Pine Barrens, an Ecologic Investigation." Christopher Sower Co., Philadelphia, Pennsylvania.

Kershaw, K. A. (1963). Pattern in vegetation and its causality. *Ecology* **44**, 377–388.

Levin, M. H. (1966). Early stages of secondary succession on the coastal plain, New Jersey. *Am. Midl. Nat.* **75**, 101–131.

Little, S. (1950). Ecology and silviculture of white cedar and associated hardwoods in southern New Jersey. *Yale Univ. Sch. For. Bull.* **56**, 1–103.

Little, S. (1951). Observations on the minor vegetation of the Pine Barrens swamps in southern New Jersey. *Bull. Torrey Bot. Club* **78**, 153–160.

Little, S. (1973). Eighteen-year changes in the composition of a stand of *Pinus echinata* and *P. rigida* in southern New Jersey. *Bull. Torrey Bot. Club* **100**, 94–102.

Little, S. (1974a). Effects of fire on temperate forests: Northeastern United States. *In* "Fire and Ecosystems" (T. T. Kozlowski and C. E. Ahlgren, eds.), pp. 225–250. Academic Press, New York.

Little, S. (1974b). Wildflowers of the Pine Barrens and their niche requirements. *N.J. Outdoors* **1**(3), 16–18.

Little, S., and Moore, E. B. (1949). The ecological role of prescribed burns in the pine–oak forests of southern New Jersey. *Ecology* **30**, 223–233.

Lutz, H. J. (1934). Ecological relations in the pitch pine plains of southern New Jersey. *Yale Univ. Sch. For. Bull.* **38**, 1–80.

McCormick, J. (1968). Succession. Student Publication of the Graduate School of Fine Arts, University of Pennsylvania. *VIA* **1**, 22–35, 131–132.

McCormick, J. (1970). The Pine Barrens: A Preliminary Ecological Inventory," Rep. No. 2. N.J. State Mus., Trenton, New Jersey.

McCormick, J., and Buell, M. F. (1957). Natural revegetation of a plowed field in the New Jersey Pine Barrens. *Bot. Gaz.* **118**, 261–264.

McCormick, J., and Buell, M. F. (1968). The plains: Pygmy forests of the New Jersey Pine Barrens, a review and annotated bibliography. *Bull. N.J. Acad. Sci.* **13**, 20–34.

Moore, J. J. (1968). A classification of the bogs and wet heaths of northern Europe (Oxycocco-Sphagnetea Br.-Bl. et Tx. 1943). *In* "Pflanzensoziologische Systematik" (R. Tüxen, ed.), pp. 306–320. Junk, The Hague.

Moul, E. T., and Buell, M. F. (1955). Moss cover and rainfall interception in frequently burned sites in the New Jersey Pine Barrens. *Bull. Torrey Bot. Club* **82**, 155–162.

parent materials. On moraines, topography is rolling, and soils tend to be medium or coarse textured and moderately well to excessively drained. The soils of the southern outwash plain generally are infertile, nearly level, coarse textured, and excessively drained; these include the Riverhead–Plymouth–Carver and Plymouth Carver associations (Warner *et al.*, 1975). The study area is on moraine soils of the Plymouth Carver association, as well as these two outwash soil associations.

The climate of Long Island is mild and uniform due to the influence of the Atlantic Ocean and the Long Island Sound. Annual precipitation is about 100–115 cm, but periods of drought, especially in the interior of the island during summer months, are not uncommon. Average annual temperatures are between 10° and 18°C, increasing westward due in part to the presence of New York City in western Long Island (Brodo, 1968). The frost-free season is 175–215 days. The island is usually breezy; winds of 15–35 km/year are common most of the year. The relative humidity exceeds 50% most of the year and is much higher near the shores (Brodo, 1968; Taylor, 1927).

The original vegetation of Long Island was remarkably diverse. Most of the island was covered by forest (Svenson, 1936), with oak-chestnut forest in the west (Cain, 1936; Harper, 1917a,b) merging with oak–pine forest and pine barrens in Suffolk County (Conard, 1935). Near Hempstead, Long Island, and possibly extending into western Suffolk County (Fig. 1), an anomolous natural (grass-dominated) prairie known as the Hempstead Plains occurred (Cline, 1957; Cain *et al.*, 1937; Harper, 1911, 1912; Hicks, 1892). This gradually merged with the pine-dominated forests to the east through an area in southwestern Suffolk County known as the Oak-Brush Plains (Peters, 1949). The two shrub oaks, *Q. ilicifolia* (scrub oak) and *Q. prinoides* (chinquapin oak), formed scattered "shrub islands" in the Hempstead Plains, gradually occupying more area eastward until they grew together in a dense canopy 1–2 m in height. The only trees were widely scattered *Pinus rigida;* toward the east, this species became more abundant and *Q. prinoides* decreased in cover. Heath species such as blueberry, lowbush blueberry, bearberry, black huckleberry, and sheep laurel (*Vaccinium angustifolium, V. vacillans, Arctostaphylos uva-ursi, Gaylussacia baccata, Kalmia angustifolia*) also increased along the gradient from Hempstead Plains to Brushy Plains, and the grassy vegetation of the Hempstead Plains was reduced to small open spaces among the shrub oaks.

The "pine barrens" vegetation, with which the Brushy Plains intergrade, consists of *Pinus rigida* 10–25 m (33–83 ft) tall, in varying densities over a tall shrub layer composed almost entirely of *Q. ilicifolia* and a low heath shrub layer mainly of *Gaylussacia baccata, Vaccinium angustifolium, V. vacillans, Kalmia angustifolia,* and *Arctostaphylos uva-ursi* (Harper, 1908a,b; Reiners, 1965, 1967). To the north, pitch pine-dominated forests blend into pine–oak forest dominated by pitch pine, white oak, scarlet oak, northern red oak, and black oak (*P. rigida, Quercus alba, Q. coccinea, Q. rubra, Q. velutina*), and these in turn grade to oak-dominated forest of *Q. rubra* or *Q. velutina,* with scattered pitch pine. A 1–2-km-wide belt of oak-dominated forest runs between the south shore of Long Island and the pine-dominated vegetation.

Around the edges of a small elliptical area of about 3.5 km² (875 acres) between Riverhead and Westhampton, the pines abruptly decline in height until they average

1.5 m (5 ft). With the shrub oak *Q. ilicifolia,* the dwarf pines form a dense sprout growth very similar in appearance and physiognomy to the pitch pine "plains" or pygmy forests found in the New Jersey Pine Barrens. The transition zone of increasing pine height from pine plains to pine barrens generally is less than 800 m wide, and this zone contains a narrower belt of decreased pine and increased *Q. ilicifolia* cover (somewhat resembling the Oak-Brush Plains) along its interface with the 3.5-km² pine plains. Occasional, open disturbed areas within the pine plains contain heaths with scattered dwarf pines and *Q. ilicifolia.* Plant nomenclature follows Fernald (1950).

METHODS

During January 1976, 25 stands selected to represent the upland forest vegetation of the Long Island pine barrens region were sampled; these were revisited in June and July 1976. In addition to the gradient from oak–pine forest to pine plains, areas of open heathland were sampled. An additional 17 stands were sampled during January 1977, concentrating on the pine plains and the transition belt of stunted pitch pine surrounding them. At this time three stands in the Pine Plains of southern New Jersey also were sampled.

Within each stand, a representative area was selected for sampling, varying from about 500 m² in oak–pine and pine barrens to 300–350 m² in the pine plains and transitional zone to 800 m² in the heaths. Vegetation sampling of a stand included determining all of the canopy species in the representative area and estimating cover on 25 (0.5 × 2 m) plots per stand. A point-frequency method was used for trees and shrubs: At 1-m intervals along a 50-m transect (30 m for pine plains and transitional zone), two points 0.5 m from either side of the central axis were determined. At each point, tree and shrub species were recorded, for a total 100 points per stand. Because this sampling technique included all species, these data were used for ordination.

All 45 stands are included in gradient analyses of vegetation, and location of stands sampled is presented in Fig. 1. At present, soil nutrient analyses have been made only for the original 25 stands; therefore, all statements relating vegetation to soil factors are based on these 25 stands only.

Soil profiles were observed in two pits per stand, and materials from both pits were combined for nutrient analyses. Since preliminary samples showed that most nutrients were concentrated in the organic horizon, extractions of O horizon samples were used to determine phosphorus, potassium, calcium, and magnesium levels. All analyses were done by the Cornell Agronomy Extension Service using colorimetry for P analyses, flame photometric emission for K, and flame photometric absorption for Mg and Ca. During late summer, 1976, six stands previously sampled for vegetation and soil were resampled for quantitative estimates of litter biomass per unit area. Twenty 30 × 20 cm plots per stand were harvested for litter biomass, oven-dried, and weighed. Mechanical analysis of soil B horizon samples to determine percentages of three sand size classes and percentage of fine particles (silt and clay) was done by sieving. The U.S. Department of Agriculture system of classification (Brady, 1974) was used, dividing sand into coarse (>0.5 mm), medium (0.25–0.5 mm), and fine (0.1–0.25 mm) categories.

In order to clarify the relationships among the plant communities and with environmental factors, we submitted the samples to ordination. Ordination is basically the arrangement of stands or species along continuous gradients of environmental change or of similarity in species composition (Noy-Meir and Whittaker, 1977). Different types of ordination have been developed for different purposes and tend to be more effective at presenting different kinds of information. Therefore, several ordination techniques were used, with the expectation that the information obtained from each would complement the results of the others (Gauch *et al.*, 1977). Of the three techniques used in this study, weighted averages, WA (Whittaker, 1967), and reciprocal averaging, RA (Hill, 1973), are more effective for expressing a vegetational gradient in response to a single environmental factor or complex gradient. Polar ordination, PO (Bray and Curtis, 1957; Cottam *et al.*, 1973), is better for detecting more than one gradient and as a tool for identifying major and minor gradients. PO presents samples and species in relation to the gradients, although the ordering of samples in relation to a single gradient may not be as accurate as in the previous two techniques.

For WA, the average heights of five randomly selected pines per stand were determined, first, to arrange the samples on a height axis, and second, to calculate indices for relative positions of species along the axis. (This procedure is the converse of the more common use of species weights to calculate sample indices.) RA is an indirect ordination, producing species and sample ordinations solely on the basis of the vegetational data (Hill, 1973). PO uses a pair of end-point samples and arranges the others by relative similarity to these; end points were chosen by the automatic method of Bray and Curtis (1957), and samples were compared by percentage similarity.

RESULTS

Community Types

Long Island pine barrens communities characteristically are dominated by five to eight very common species (Table I), most of which are ubiquitous in the pine barrens. Differences among communities or along gradients are typically in relative abundance of species, rather than in species composition. Although winter sampling precluded studying herbaceous flora, examination of the area in summer indicates that, except in the most mesic oak–pine forest, herbaceous cover is negligible in biomass. The pine barrens communities characteristically have heath species mixed with scrub oak as the understory, with herbaceous species appearing briefly in spring and early summer and setting seed before a summer drought begins.

Oak–pine forest generally has a rather open canopy of oaks (mainly *Q. coccinea* and *Q. alba* on the outwash soils; *Q. rubra* and *Q. velutina* on moraines) and scattered pines, which often are emergent above the canopy. In most stands at Brookhaven National Laboratory, where our oak–pine samples were taken, the oaks are young and

TABLE I   Woody Plants in Each Vegetational Type[a]

	Vegetation types [Number of stands sampled]					
	Oak–pine [5(OP)]	Barrens [11(B)]	Transition [11(T)]	Plains [10(P)]	Heath [5(H)]	New Jersey Plains [3(NJP)]
A. Species in study plots						
Acer rubrum	5.17	—	—	—	—	—
Arctostaphylos uva-ursi	0.17	0.9	17.9	36.5	61.4	1.3
Corema conradii	—	—	—	—	—	1.3
Gaultheria procumbens	5.0	11.6	9.4	8.0	0.8	0.3
Gaylussacia baccata	28.6	36.0	48.3	35.3	6.8	16.3
Hudsonia ericoides	—	—	—	0.2	4.4	1.3
Kalmia angustifolia	—	3.2	0.18	—	—	3.3
K. polifolia	—	3.4	—	—	—	—
Lonicera japonica	0.5	—	—	—	—	—
Lyonia ligustrina	0.3	—	0.09	—	—	—
Myrica pensylvanica	—	0.2	0.09	—	—	—
Pinus rigida	23.6	55.0	46.0	39.8	10.4	58.3
Prunus virginiana	3.5	—	—	—	—	—
Quercus alba	31.3	5.8	5.5	—	—	—
Q. coccinea	13.1	9.3	—	—	—	—
Q. ilicifolia	9.6	48.2	29.9	29.7	11.4	5.0
Q. marilandica	—	—	—	—	—	21.6
Q. velutina	4.6	—	—	—	—	—
Rhamnus sp. (*cathartica?*)	2.5	—	—	—	—	—
Smilax glauca	—	0.1	—	—	—	—
S. rotundifolia	0.5	—	—	—	—	—
Vaccinium angustifolium[b]	0.6	—	1.7	—	5.2	—
V. corymbosum	13.1	0.7	—	—	0.8	—
V. sp. (*myrtilloides?*)	—	1.3	0.09	—	—	0.3
V. vacillans	12.1	2.9	7.6	5.5	0.4	19.0

(continued)

small, mostly <20 cm dbh (diameter at breast height), 12 m high, and 60 years old above ground), although some pines are larger (to 30 cm, 16 m, and 80–100+ years). A high shrub layer coverage (40–80%) usually includes scattered clumps of *Q. ilicifolia* 1–3 m tall and a denser heath layer with patches of *Gaylussacia baccata, Vaccinium vacillans,* and *V. angustifolium* 0.2–0.8 m tall. Total herb cover is usually 1–3%, with bracken fern, Pennsylvania sedge, and wintergreen (*Pteridium aquilinum, Carex pensylvanica,* and *Gaultheria procumbens*) present as major species. Of the stands sampled, oak–pine has the greatest species richness in both tree and shrub layers. Species reaching their maximum abundance in this relatively moist forest type include the trees *Acer rubrum, Quercus alba,* and *Q. coccinea,* and the shrub *Vaccinium corymbosum.* (For further discussion, see Whittaker and Woodwell, 1968, 1969.)

The samples termed ''pine barrens'' in this study represent the prevailing vegetation of the area, namely, stands of pure or nearly pure pitch pine with scattered oaks (mostly

TABLE I   *(continued)*

B. Species outside plots

Amelanchier arborea R(OP, B)	*P. canadensis* R(B)
Ascyrum hypericoides C(B, T,P); R(OP, H)	*Rhus copallina* R(OP, B)
A. stans C(B, T, P); R(OP, H)	*R. toxicodendron* R(OP)
Betula populifolia R(OP)	*Robinia pseudo-acacia* R (OP, B)
Chimaphila maculata R(OP)	*P. fruiticosa* R(OP, B)
Clematis virginiana R(OP)	*P. recta* R(B)
Comptonia peregrina C(OP, B); R(T, P, H)	*Prunus maritima* R(B)
Cornus florida R(OP)	*P. pensylvanica* R(OP, B, T)
Epigaea repens C(OP); R(B, P, H)	*P. virginiana* R(OP)
Gaylussacia frondosa C (OP); R(B)	*Quercus prinoides* R(B)
Hudsonia tomentosa C(B); R(OP, T, P, H)	*Q. prinus* R(OP, B)
Hypericum gentianoides R (B, T, P, H)	*Q. rubra*[c] A(OP); C(B); R(T)
H. majus R(B)	*Q. stellata* R(B)
H. perforatum A(P); C(B, T, H); R(OP)	*Rhododendron maximum* R(OP)
Ilex opaca R(OP, B)	*Rosa blanda* R(OP)
Juniperus virginiana R(OP)	*R. carolina* R(OP, B)
Kalmia latifolia R(OP, B)	*R. multiflora* R(OP, B)
Parthenocissus quinquefolia R(OP)	*Rubus hispidus* R(OP)
Pinus strobus R(OP)	*R. idaeus* R(OP)
Populus tremuloides R(OP, B)	*Salix tristis* R(B)
Potentilla anserina R(B)	*Sassafras albidum* R(OP, B, T)
P. argentea R(OP, B)	*Vaccinium stamineum* C (OP); R(B)
	Vitis aestivalus R(OP)

[a] Section A gives average percent cover for species recorded in study plots. Section B gives additional species observed in the representative areas of Long Island vegetation surrounding the plots; abundance estimates are scaled to species, not site maximum: A, abundant; C, common; R, rare.

[b] Sometimes common in Pine Barrens where canopy exceeds 50% in areas east of the pine plains, where *V. vacillans* may not yet have reached.

[c] Common in the oak–pine forests on glacial moraine, but not at Brookhaven National Laboratory, which is mostly on glacial outwash. In this respect, the oak–pine forest at Brookhaven is atypical.

Q. alba and *Q. coccinea*), dense *Q. ilicifolia* at 1–2 m as an upper shrub layer, a scattered low heath shrub layer at 0.2–0.5 m, and *Arctostaphylos uva-ursi* and *Gaultheria procumbens* forming a lower ground layer. Pitch pine reaches maximum cover in such pine barrens, although its maximum basal area is in the following transition zone to pine plains.

The transition from pine barrens to plains is fairly abrupt. The outer part of the transition is essentially pine barrens with shorter, more contorted pitch pine. The inner part of the transition adjacent to the pine plains is a narrow oak belt, with vigorous scrub oak growth and less pitch pine cover. *Quercus ilicifolia* reaches its maximum cover at this point. Beneath the dense cover of this shrub, heaths form a second well-developed shrub layer, and *Arctostaphylos uva-ursi* and *Gaultheria procumbens* dominate the ground stratum as in the barrens and plains.

Most samples of Long Island pine plains (Fig. 2) contain only seven woody species,

Fig. 2. Pine plains near Westhampton, New York. This community, seen covered with snow, is dominated by dwarf pitch pine and scrub oak. Unlike the New Jersey Plains, only one oak species is present.

i.e., dwarf *Pinus rigida* and *Quercus ilicifolia* in a single "tree" or tall shrub stratum, *Gaylussacia baccata*, *Vaccinium vacillans*, and *V. angustifolium* as a low shrub layer, and *Arctostaphylos uva-ursi* and *Gaultheria procumbens* with numerous upright, much-branched (fruticose) lichen species as ground cover. In less extreme stands, the pitch pine and scrub oak form a rather open canopy, 60–80%, cover and 1–2 m in height; in extreme stands the canopy is no higher than 1 m. *Hudsonia ericoides* is present locally in open disturbed areas.

Large areas of heath (Fig. 3), up to 15 ha (38 acres), occur abruptly within the pine plains and contain the same species in different proportions. In the heaths, *Gaylussacia baccata* is dominant, forming a sparse canopy at 0.4–0.5 m. The two *Vaccinium* species are present, and the low shrubs *Arctostaphylos uva-ursi* and *Hudsonia ericoides* are more common than in the plains. In the same way that the plains are "reduced" barrens (lacking oak and pine as trees), the heaths are suggestive of reduced plains (lacking the shrubby pine and oak). The heaths thus are the end point of the progressive shift of foliage downward into the lower strata that is characteristic of the gradient from oak–pine forest to pine plains.

Fig. 3. Heath near Westhampton, New York. Black huckleberry and other heath species dominate patches measuring several hectares in area within the pine plains. Disturbance appears to have caused these heaths.

Ordination of Samples

Initially, samples were classified loosely as oak–pine forest, barrens or pine forest, transition, pine plains, and heath, as described previously. WA and RA ordinations of the 42 stands sampled both placed the Long Island pine plains samples together with heaths at one end of a major gradient, with oak–pine forest at the other end. In ordinations RA, WA, and one axis of PO, samples followed the assumed order from oak–pine to barrens to transition to pine plains.

Heaths were not separated from plains in WA or RA. However they were displaced along a second axis in PO.

Curves of species distributions provided by RA (Fig. 4) were smoother and more unimodal than distributions provided by WA ordinations, using average pine height as a sample weight. It was hypothesized that two or more unrelated factors, such as stand age and soil conditions, significantly affected pine height, such that distributions of samples along an unknown secondary axis were superimposed upon and distorted the primary gradient. RA, with samples weighted on the basis of total vegetational composition, was less vulnerable to the influence of a secondary axis.

PO ordination also suggested an important secondary axis (Fig. 5). Samples plotted with the first polar axis horizontal and the second polar axis vertical fell into three groups: (1) in the upper left, the heaths and some plains samples; (2) in the upper right, plains and barrens samples, including the New Jersey Pine Plains at the right end point; and (3) in the lower right, oak–pine forest and some barrens samples.

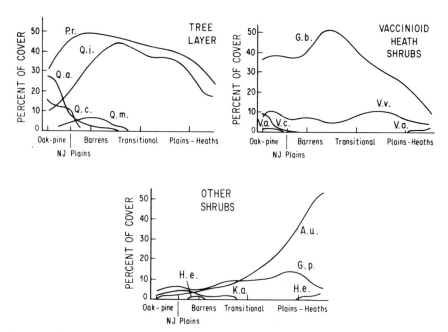

Fig. 4. Species distributions along a vegetational gradient as determined by reciprocal averaging (RA) ordination. Curves are based on running averages for values along the RA axis. P.r., *Pinus rigida;* Q.i., *Quercus ilicifolia;* Q.a., *Q. alba;* Q.c., *Q. cocinea;* Q.m., *Q. marilandica;* G.b., *Gaylussacia baccata;* V.v., *Vaccinium vacillans;* V.c., *V. corymbosum;* V.a., *V. angustifolium;* A.u., *Arctostaphylos uva-ursi;* G.p., *Gaultheria procumbens;* K.a., *Kalmia angustifolia;* H.e., *Hudsonia ericoides.*

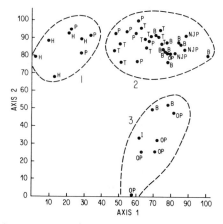

Fig. 5. Distribution of 45 stands along two axes as determined by polar ordination (PO). Axes represent presumed environmental gradients. H, heath; P, pine plains; T, transition; B, pine barrens; OP, oak-pine; NJP, New Jersey Pine Plains. Samples fall into three major groups; see text.

It was hypothesized that the primary axis presented in WA and RA ordinations and axis 2 of the PO represented a soil texture–moisture gradient. This could be tested by soil data.

We suspected that heaths resulted from disturbance of the pine plains, on the basis of aerial photographs taken in the 1950's that represented these areas as rectangular clearings with little or no vegetation and from statements by local residents that the area had been partly bulldozed by the nearby air base during and after World War II. Because polar ordination placed the heaths at one end of the first PO axis and the New Jersey Pine Plains, which were believed to be less disturbed than most Long Island vegetation on similar soils, at the other end, we interpreted axis 1 of PO as a distur-bance gradient. Significantly, most of the Long Island oak–pine forests and barrens were near the "undisturbed" end of the gradient, and most Long Island pine plains samples were nearer the "disturbed" end (Fig. 5).

Hence, the three groups in the PO appeared to represent (1) a xeric, highly disturbed group, (2) a xeric, fairly undisturbed group, and (3) a mesic fairly undisturbed group. The New Jersey Pine Plains resembled the Long Island pine plains in growth form, but differed in species composition and position on the axes of RA and WA. *Quercus marilandica,* which is rare in Suffolk County, is the dominant scrub oak in the New Jersey Pine Plains. *Kalmia angustifolia,* a mesic pine barrens species on Long Island, is abundant in the pine plains samples collected in New Jersey. RA ordination placed the three samples collected in the New Jersey Pine Plains toward the more "mesic" end of the gradient and the Long Island pine plains on the "xeric" end. This marked difference between the two pine plains was quite unexpected and warrants more exten-sive study.

Soil Relationships

Soil texture analysis (Table II and Fig. 6) indicates that slight but consistent dif-ferences in particle distribution occur among soils of the different vegetation types on Long Island. These differences appear mainly due to the percentage of coarse sand, silt, and clay in the B horizon; medium and fine sand percentages do not change noticeably among the community types. The soil measurements are from widely dis-persed stands, but averages of the coarse sand and of total fine materials (silt and clay) along the gradient produced by RA (Fig. 6), show a linear increase in the percentage of coarse sand and a decrease in the percentage of fine particles from oak–pine forest through barrens to heath and plains. Since the moisture-holding capac-ity of the soil decreases with the increasing percentage of sand, this trend supports the belief that a moisture gradient from more mesic in the oak–pine to more xeric in the pine plains relates these communities.

Since our preliminary samples indicated that most of the nutrient content of the soil was in the organic material, it became important to know the organic content of the soil. Measurements of O and A horizon depths (Table II) showed a decrease in the depth of the O horizon, accompanied by an increase in the A horizon depth (podzolization), although little difference in percentage of organic material in the O horizon was

TABLE II   Average Canopy and Soil Characteristics for the Long Island Communities

	Oak–pine	Barrens	Transition	Plains	Heath
No. of stands sampled	4[a]	6	5	4	5
Total canopy basal area (m²/ha)	9.88	8.90	12.22	3.06	0.53
Pine basal area (m²/ha)	4.56	6.54	6.88	1.98	0.39
Percent pine (%)	46	73	56	65	74
Pine height (n)	13.9	12.7	3.9	1.8	2.0
Soil texture of the B horizon					
Coarse sand (%)	40.4	38.8	48.8	53.6	50.8
Medium sand (%)	31.2	31.6	30.6	34.0	33.6
Fine sand (%)	9.2	11.8	7.2	5.6	6.4
Silt and clay (%)	18.8	17.6	13.2	6.4	9.0
Soil profile depth (cm)					
O horizon	5.25	4.17	2.20	1.75	1.60
A horizon	7.50	5.83	8.90	13.00	12.40
B horizon	37.60	43.33	55.80	35.50	58.75
Litter biomass (g dry wt/900 cm²)	852.5	—	615.0	299.0	272.0
Soil nutrients (ppm in the O horizon)					
Phosphorus	207.5	70.0	103.4	117.0	24.0
Potassium	757.5	138.3	514.0	456.0	176.0
Calcium	1850.0	1191.5	1460.0	1737.5	440.0
Magnesium	525.0	323.0	360.0	415.0	172.0
Percent organic matter (O horizon)	40.0	37.7	28.0	42.0	23.0

[a] One very mesic stand with extremely different litter biomass and soil nutrient contents was omitted from the averages.

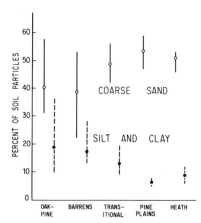

Fig. 6. Soil texture of the B horizon in each vegetation type. Circles are average values, and ends of vertical lines are extreme values. Coarse sand has particles >0.5 mm diameter. Percent medium sand and percent fine sand do not appear to change along the gradient (Table II), and are not plotted.

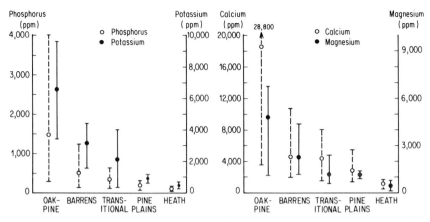

Fig. 7. Total nutrients in organic horizon of soil in each vegetation type. Values are nutrient concentrations (in ppm) multiplied by depth of the organic horizon for each soil sample. Circles are average values and ends of vertical lines are extreme values.

discernible among community types. Average litter cover showed a clear decline from oak–pine forest to heath.

Concentrations of P, Ca, K, and Mg expressed as ppm varied widely among the stands (Table II), although the organic horizon of the oak–pine forest was richer in nutrients than the other community types. However, when the concentrations were multiplied by the depth of the organic horizon to reflect the total nutrient availability in the organic horizon of each stand, a marked and consistent decrease in all nutrients from the oak–pine forest to the heaths was evident (Fig. 7). Since this reflected the nutrient pools for these communities, the differences were significant. This need not imply, however, that lower nutrient availability was the simple cause of pine plains vegetation.

Disturbance Factors

Throughout the period for which records are available, fires have swept the vegetation of the Long Island outwash plains at frequencies ranging from a few years to a few decades. These communities are fire adapted and maintain themselves in successional cycles with a normal pattern of repeated fires. The pine plains may burn more frequently than most pine barrens communities, perhaps with a major fire occurring somewhere in the area about once every seven years (Southampton town fire inspector's office, personal communication). The structure and the composition of the oak–pine and pine barrens vegetation are affected by fire frequency (mostly in terms of decades). Fire suppression tends to shift the vegetation of an area toward the more mesic oak forest end of the gradient, as observed in RA ordination.

We believe the heaths to be more clearly a product of disturbance, that is, bulldozing in order to clear areas of pine plains for military use. With the long-lived root systems of the canopy dominants (*P. rigida* and *Q. ilicifolia*) thus destroyed, the heath species that spread more rapidly and that are part of the succession to forest in this area became dominant. Succession, where the soil has been disturbed by bulldozing, may be very slow. We saw little evidence of return of pine and scrub oak to the heath areas; the stands appear to be relatively stable.

Increased urbanization has resulted in heavier demands on the water supply in this region within recent years, with a consequent lowering of the water table in the pine plains region. Lowered water tables tend to shift community composition in the direction opposite to the effects of fire control—toward more xeric composition. The Long Island pine plains might have been more like the New Jersey Pine Plains prior to the drop in water table and drying of streams.

Species Distributions

The behavior of individual species along the moisture–nutrient gradient is examined best within four groups: (a) pitch pine–dwarf pitch pine; (b), *Quercus* species; (c) Vaccinioideae heaths; and (d) the remaining shrubs.

It is beyond the scope of this chapter to discuss fully the relationship between *Pinus rigida* of normal height and dwarf *P. rigida,* a relationship which has concerned biologists since the 1800's (cf. Andresen, 1959; McCormick and Buell, 1968; Little, 1972; Good and Good, 1975). We note, however, that the pines in the Long Island plains differ from normal *P. rigida* in their percentage of serotinous cones and contorted stems with (in the more extreme stands) many prostrate branches, and short annual stem internodes. Field observations indicate that, unlike *P. rigida* in the barrens and oak–pine forest, our plains pines have massive root crowns that survive fires and send up new shoots following each fire. It seems probable that the plains pines are an ecotype adapted to frequent fire, genetically different from the oak–pine and barrens pines, which also are adapted to fire, but to less frequent ones.

In the transition between barrens and plains, the above-ground characters of the pines, at least, are mixed, with less contorted growth and varying proportions of nonserotinous cones. Overall, *P. rigida* reaches maximum height in the older oak–pine forests, maximum cover in the pine barrens, maximum basal area in the transitional vegetation, and maximum percent of canopy coverage in the pine plains. The species appears limited by competition with oaks on the mesic end of its distribution, and by disturbance, low nutrients, and/or drought stress on the xeric end (Fig. 5).

Among the oaks (Fig. 4), *Quercus ilicifolia* has a distribution similar to *P. rigida* but reaches its maximum cover in the "oak belt" portion of the transitional zone. *Quercus alba* and *Q. coccinea* have similar distributions, but *Q. alba* reaches its peak in cover in more mesic sites than *Q. coccinea. Q. marilandica,* found in the New Jersey Pine Plains, appears to be centered somewhere between the peaks for *Q. coccinea* and *Q. ilicifolia,* but the few samples from New Jersey do not show the distribution of this species clearly. Tentatively, the distribution of these oak species along a gradient from mesic to xeric habitats in the Pine Barrens would be *Q. alba, Q. coccinea, Q. marilandica,* and *Q. ilicifolia.*

The Vaccinioideae heaths (Fig. 4) show interesting relationships along the gradient. *Vaccinium corymbosum* is a mesic species here, but *Gaylussacia baccata* and *V. vacillans* are important throughout, with *G. baccata* apparently centered in somewhat more mesic sites than *V. vacillans*. One peak of *V. angustifolium* is in sites still more xeric than those in which *V. vacillans* peaks. Reiners (1965, 1967) examined *V. vacillans, V. angustifolium,* and *G. baccata* as a synusium in the oak–pine forests at Brookhaven National Laboratory and observed that these species may form a fire-successional sequence in the order just given. Woodwell (1967), Woodwell and Whittaker (1968), and Whittaker and Woodwell (1969) noted that these and other species form a sequence of increasing plant heights and increasing vulnerability to irradiation (*Carex pensylvanica, V. angustifolium, V. vacillans, G. baccata, Q. ilicifolia*). To these sequences, our data add a vaccinioid sequence of increasing plant height, mesophytism, and apparent vulnerability to nutrient limitations, that is, from the xeric population of *V. angustifolium* through *V. vacillans* and *G. baccata* to *V. corymbosum*. *V. angustifolium,* however, has a bimodal distribution, occurring in the most mesic and most xeric samples. Reiners (1967) has suggested that *V. vacillans* may be invading the range of *V. angustifolium* in this area, with concurrent hybridization. If so, we may be seeing *V. vacillans* dominating the optimal habitats for both species within our transect, forcing *V. angustifolium* into the marginal habitats of shady deciduous forests on the one hand, and the edapically stressed pine plains and heaths on the other. These populations deserve further study.

Among the other species (Fig. 4), *Hudsonia ericoides* grows best in the open vegetation of the pine plains of both Long Island and New Jersey. Its distribution appears to be affected more by competition with other species than by soil factors. *Arctostaphylos uva-ursi* and *Gaultheria procumbens* both peak in cover at the xeric end of the gradient, with *G. procumbens* at a maximum in the pine plains and *A. uva-ursi* rising steadily to reach a peak at the xeric end point of the gradient. Toward the opposite extreme of the gradient, *G. procumbens* extends into more mesic oak–pine forests (Whittaker and Woodwell, 1969), but *A. uva-ursi* does not.

DISCUSSION

In summary, the Long Island pine barrens vegetational pattern seems determined by the interaction of two sets of factors. Disturbance, both human and natural, creates a mosaic of successional communities that is superimposed upon an underlying soil complex of moisture and nutrient changes. The use of indirect ordination to study the interrelationships between these two sets of factors, together with direct ordination to examine each gradient separately, appears to be a useful way of gaining insights about vegetational patterns resulting from complicated interactions.

This study is incomplete as a treatment of the Long Island vegetational pattern; we have not dealt with the gradations into oak and beech–maple forest on the morainal soil of the north shore, nor with the poorly drained forests and swamps of the Long Island vegetation. Because of the destruction of natural areas in the western part of the island, the relationship with the unique Hempstead Plains might never be known. However, the key problem for our study is the "cause" of the dwarf pine plains. We reject the suggestion that these are simply young successional stands following a recent fire. Estimations of stand age we have made on the basis of growth rings indicate ages of 20–30 years are typical. Higher fire frequency than in the surrounding pine barrens and oak–pine forests seems to be a contributing factor but not a sufficient explanation. In this region of formerly wide-ranging fires, it is unclear why fires should be more frequent in the pine plains than in the pine barrens with which they are continuous. The genetically distinctive dwarf pines seem to imply either a continuing long-term selective process, or long-term survival of this population, or both.

We suggest a possible hypothesis on the origin of the pine plains. (a) The coarser sandy soils of the pine plains have a lower moisture- and nutrient-retaining capacity than soils of the other communities. (b) Because of poor moisture retention, pine plains soils have a drier and longer drought season than soils of surrounding communities. (c) The pine plains vegetation therefore is subject to greater drought stress and to somewhat more frequent and sometimes more severe fires than other communities. (d) The pine plains are also subject to more severe loss of nutrients by leaching in the soils following fire and therefore become even more severely nutrient limited than the surrounding pine barrens soils. (e) In adaptation to the combined influences of soil structure, nutrients, drought, and fire, the fire-susceptible communities on this soil differ from the remainder of the vegetation in structure, composition, and in the genetics of at least the dominant pitch pine. (f) These communities are not successional; they are part of a different ecosystem having a different adaptive design in relation to more severe soil limitations than the other Long Island forests.

Many comparisons between the pine barrens of Long Island and New Jersey might prove informative. The Long Island area is highly disturbed, whereas the New Jersey Pine Barrens appear less so and are much more extensive. Gradient analysis techniques could provide insight into species distributions in the New Jersey region. Were the pine barrens of Long Island and New Jersey once connected (Britton, 1880)? What factors do these areas have in common which have caused the pine plains and maintain the dwarf pine?

Unlike the Pine Plains of New Jersey, the Long Island pine plains exist in an area of rapidly increasing urbanization. Although some portions still are government-owned, there are few plans for preservation. Most of the Long Island pine plains now are owned by real estate speculators with intentions for development related to a proposed free trade center in Suffolk County. As this is being written, bulldozing of the pine plains has already (illegally) begun, despite the protests of citizens and environmentalists. It will be tragic indeed if, like the Hempstead Plains, this unique and interesting region were to be destroyed by industrialization and suburban sprawl.

SUMMARY

The relationship of the Long Island pine plains, a forest of dwarf pitch pine (*Pinus rigida*), to surrounding pine barrens communities and to the New Jersey Pine Plains is examined. Three ordination techniques were applied to vegetation samples from 42 Long Island and three New Jersey stands. Soil texture and nutrients were measured, and degree of disturbance was estimated. The sample Long Island communities relate to one another along a primary vegetational gradient from oak–pine forests through pine barrens (pine forests with shrub oak and heath undergrowth) and transitional scrub (dominated by scrub oak *Quercus ilicifolia*) to pine plains. Along this primary gradient, soil nutrient content and the percentage of silt and clay decrease. A secondary vegetational gradient leads from the pine plains to heaths (dominated by vaccinioid heath shrubs about 0.5 m tall) and is correlated with increasing disturbance. The New Jersey Pine Plains appear more mesic and less disturbed than the Long Island Pine Plains. The Long Island pine plains are interpreted as a distinctive plant community adapted to a combination of interrelated environmental factors, including soil texture, drought stress, low soil fertility, and frequent fire.

ACKNOWLEDGMENTS

We thank Frederick C. Schlauch for his help and guidance in the field; Carl Helms at Quogue Wildlife Refuge and the Biology Department staff at Brookhaven National Laboratory for their help in permitting us to sample in these areas; and Silas Little for permission to base at the Northeastern Forest Experiment Station, Lebanon State Forest while sampling in New Jersey. Deepest thanks go to Helen Buell for her hospitality, advice, and encouragement and to Hugh G. Gauch, David Pimentel, and Earl Stone for discussion and support.

REFERENCES

Andresen, J. W. (1959). A study of pseudonanism in *Pinus rigida,* Mill., *Ecol. Monogr.* **29,** 309–332.

Bailey, P. (1959). "Physical Long Island; Its Glacial Origin, Historical Storms, Beaches, Prairies, and Archaeology." Long Island Forum, Amityville, New York.

Brady, N. C. (1974). "The Nature and Properties of Soils," 8th Ed. Macmillan, New York.

Bray, J. R., and Curtis, J. T. (1957). An ordination of the upland forest communities of southern Wisconsin. *Ecol. Monogr.* **27,** 325–349.

Britton, N. L. (1880). On the northward extension of the pine-barren flora on Long and Staten Islands. *Bull. Torrey Bot. Club* **7,** 81–83.

Brodo, I. M. (1968). "The lichens of Long Island, New York: A vegetational and floristic analysis". *N.Y. State Mus. Sci. Serv., Bull.* No. 410.

Cain, S. A. (1936). The composition and structure of an oak woods, Cold Spring Harbor, Long Island, with special attention to sampling methods. *Am. Midl. Nat.* **17,** 725–740.

Cain, S. A., Nelson, N., and McLean, W. (1937). Andropogonetum Hempsteadi: A Long Island grassland vegetation type. *Am. Midl. Nat.* **18,** 334–350.

Cline, M. G. (1957). Soils and soil associations of New York. *Cornell Ext. Bull.* No. 930, 1–72.

Conard, H. S. (1935). The plant associations of central Long Island. *Am. Midl. Nat.* **16,** 433–516.

Cottam, G., Goff, F. G., and Whittaker, R. H. (1973). Wisconsin comparative ordination (Ger. sum.). *In* "Ordination and Classification of Communities" (R. H. Whittaker, ed.), Handbook of Vegetation Science, Vol. 5, pp. 193–221. Junk, The Hague.

Fernald, M. L. (1950). "Gray's Manual of Botany," 8th Ed. Van Nostrand, New York.

Flint, R. F. (1953). Probable Wisconsin substages and late-Wisconsin events in northeastern United States and southern Canada. *Geol. Soc. Am. Bull.* **64,** 897–919.

Fuller, M. L. (1914). Geology of Long Island. *U.S. Geol. Surv., Prof. Pap.* No. 82.

Gauch, H. G., Jr., Whittaker, R. H., and Wentworth, T. R. (1977). A comparative study of reciprocal averaging and other ordination techniques. *J. Ecol.* **65**(1), 157–174.

Good, R. E., and Good, N. F. (1975). Growth characteristics of two populations of *Pinus rigida* from the Pine Barrens of New Jersey. *Ecology* **56**, 1215–1220.

Harper, R. M. (1908a). The pine-barrens of Babylon and Islip, Long Island. *Torreya* **8**, 1–9.

Harper, R. M. (1908b). Notes on the pine-barrens of Long Island. *Torreya* **8**, 33–34.

Harper, R. M. (1911). The Hempstead Plains: A natural prairie on Long Island. *Bull. Am. Geogr. Soc.* **43**, 351–360.

Harper, R. M. (1912). The Hempstead Plains of Long Island. *Torreya* **12**, 277–287.

Harper, R. M. (1917a). The natural vegetation of western Long Island south of the terminal moraine. *Torreya* **17**, 1–13.

Harper, R. M. (1917b). The native plant population of northern Queens County. *Torreya* **17**, 131–143.

Hicks, H. (1892). The flora of the Hempstead Plains. B.S. Thesis, Cornell Univ., Ithaca, New York.

Hill, M. O. (1973). Reciprocal averaging: An eigenvector method of ordination. *J. Ecol.* **61**, 237–249.

Little, S. (1972). Growth of planted white pines and pitch seedlings in a south Jersey Plains area. *Bull. N.J. Acad. Sci.* **17**(2), 18–23.

MacClintock, P., and Richards, H. G. (1936). Correlation of late Pleistocene marine and glacial deposits of New Jersey and New York. *Geol. Soc. Am. Bull.* **47**, 289–338.

McCormick, J. and Buell, M. F. (1968). The Plains: Pygmy forests of the New Jersey Pine Barrens, a review and annotated bibliography. *Bull. N.J. Acad. Sci.* **13**(1), 20–34.

Muller, E. H. (1965). Quaternary geology of New York. *In* "The Quaternary of the United States" (H. E., Wright, Jr. and D. G. Frey, eds.), pp. 99–112. Princeton Univ. Press, Princeton, New Jersey.

Noy-Meir, I., and Whittaker, R. H. (1977). Continuous multivariate methods in community analysis: Some problems and developments. *Vegetatio* **33**(2/3), 79–98.

Peters, G. H. (1949). The flora of Long Island. *In* "Long Island" (P. Baileys, ed.), Vol. 2, No. 27, pp. 137–150. Lewis Hist. Publ. Co., New York.

Reiners, W. A. (1965). Ecology of a heath-shrub synusia in the pine barrens of Long Island, New York. *Bull. Torrey Bot. Club* **92**, 448–464.

Reiners, W. A. (1967). Relationships between vegetational strata in the pine barrens of central Long Island, New York. *Bull. Torrey Bot. Club* **94**, 87–99.

Svenson, H. K. (1936). The early vegetation of Long Island. *Brooklyn Bot. Gard. Rec.* **25**, 207–227.

Taylor. N. (1927). The climate of Long Island: Its relation to forests, crops, and man. *Cornell Univ. Agric. Exp. Stn., Bull.* No. 458.

Warner, J. W., Jr., Hanna, W. E., Landry, R. J., Wulforst, J. P., Neely, J. A., Holmes, R. L., and Rice, C. E. (1975). "Soil Survey of Suffolk County, New York." U.S. Dep. Agric. Soil Conserv. Serv., Washington, D.C.

Whittaker, R. H. (1967). Gradient analysis of vegetation. *Biol. Rev. Cambridge Philos. Soc.* **42**, 207–264.

Whittaker, R. H., and Woodwell, G. M. (1968). Dimension and production relations of trees and shrubs in the Brookhaven Forest, New York. *J. Ecol.* **56**, 1–25.

Whittaker, R. H., and Woodwell, G. M. (1969). Structure, production, and diversity of the oak-pine forest at Brookhaven, New York. *J. Ecol.* **57**, 155–174.

Woodwell, G. M. (1967). Radiation and the patterns of nature. *Science* **156**, 461–470.

Woodwell, G. M., and Whittaker, R. H. (1968). Effects of chronic gamma irradiation on plant communities. *Q. Rev. Biol.* **43**(1), 42–55.

16

The Pine Barren Plains

RALPH E. GOOD, NORMA F. GOOD,
AND JOHN W. ANDRESEN

INTRODUCTION

Within the Pine Barrens are several areas of dwarf pitch pine (*Pinus rigida*) forest known as the Pine Plains or Plains (Fig. 1). The two largest areas are the East Plains, measuring about 2368 ha (5920 acres), and the West Plains, covering about 2467 ha (6168 acres), both located along the Ocean–Burlington County line near Warren Grove (Fig. 2). The Spring Hill Plains, a smaller tract covering about 108 ha (270 acres) on the northern border of Penn State Forest, sometimes is recognized (McCormick and Buell, 1968). Estimates of the size of the Plains have varied considerably, with a maximum estimate of about 9000 ha (Harshberger, 1916) and a minimum of 4888 ha (Lloyd, 1955). Estimates vary primarily because of differences in the definition of Plains, and because of the presence of types intermediate between Plains and Barrens.

Several criteria usually are accepted in defining the Plains: (a) low stature of the pines [usually less than 3.0 or 3.3 m (10 or 11 ft)]; (b) absence of some tree species of the Barrens, such as shortleaf pine, black oak, scarlet oak, white oak, and chestnut oak (*Pinus echinata, Quercus velutina, Q. coccinea, Q. alba, Q. prinus*); (c) increased importance of scrub-form oaks, blackjack oak, and scrub oak (*Q. marilandica, Q. ilicifolia*); (d) predominance of stump (root crown) sprouts in the vegetation and the scarcity of seedling regeneration; (e) serotinous habit (fire opens the cones) of the pines; and (f) increased occurrence of low shrub species such as pyxie moss (*Pyxidanthera barbulata*) and broom crowberry (*Corema conradii*).

The general boundaries of the major Plains are thought to have remained fairly stable since the time of European settlement, and the areas were mentioned in the earliest land surveys, taken in about 1832–1833 (Lutz, 1934). The "Grouse Plains" were mentioned in a 1823 advertisement for a stagecoach trip. The grouse alluded to was the heath hen (*Tympanuchus cupido cupido*), which was very common and much hunted on the Plains in the early 1800's (Stone, 1937), but which is extinct now.

The objectives of this chapter are (a) to describe the Plains vegetation, including a detailed examination of two characteristic species, and (b) to review the possible causes of the Plains, examining particularly the evidence for an adaptive cause of this pygmy forest.

Copyright © 1979 by Academic Press, Inc.
All rights of reproduction in any form reserved.
ISBN 0-12-263450-0

Fig. 1. The Pine Plains of New Jersey. This extensive pygmy forest is dominated by pitch pine, seen in right and left foreground, and scrub and blackjack oaks, the deciduous woody plants visible. The matted shrub is mainly bearberry, and in this open sandy spot clumps of golden heather, seen in right foreground, are common. The taller vegetation seen in left background occurs along a stream and consists of red maple, black gum, pitch pine, and white cedar.

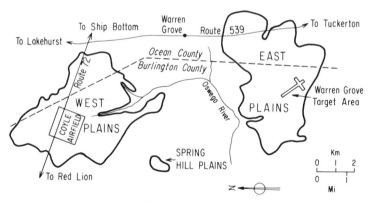

Fig. 2. Locations of the three Pine Plains near the center of the New Jersey Pine Barrens.

PLANTS AND COMMUNITY STRUCTURE

Although the Plains are distinct visually from typical Barrens vegetation, no species are present which are not found elsewhere in the Barrens. Plains vegetation has been regarded as an extreme expression of the pitch pine-blackjack oak type of the Barrens (McCormick and Buell, 1968). While distinct canopy, subcanopy, shrub, and herb layers are not as discrete as in taller forest types, pitch pine typically forms a "canopy" only slightly overtopping the oaks. The taller shrubs often include mountain laurel (*Kalmia latifolia*), sheep laurel (*K. angustifolia*), inkberry (*Ilex glabra*), sweetfern (*Comptonia peregrina*), black huckleberry (*Gaylussacia baccata*), and dangleberry (*G. frondosa*). Sand myrtle (*Leiophyllum buxifolium*) and broom crowberry are two low shrubs often associated with the Plains, while low herbs and subshrubs include pyxie moss, false heather (*Hudsonia ericoides*), and bearberry (*Arctostaphylos uva-ursi*).

Plains vegetation is by no means uniform. Broom crowberry, bearberry, pyxie moss, and sand myrtle are scarce or absent over fairly large areas while very abundant in others. Lutz (1934) listed *Andropogon scoparius, Panicum tsugetorum, Cracca virginiana, Euphorbia ipecacuanhae, Helianthemum canadense,* and *Epigaea repens* as among the common herbs. Lichens are more conspicuous in the Plains than Barrens. Lutz (1934) recorded 21 species in the Plains and only nine in the Barrens, with *Cladonia* spp. predominating. He found the same mosses (two *Dicranum* spp. and *Polytrichum juniperinum*) in both the Plains and Barrens, but more abundant in the Plains.

Pyxie moss, the conspicuous small shrub, and pitch pine, the dominant tree, are discussed in detail to provide insight on the distributions and dynamics of two characteristic species.

Pyxie Moss

Pyxie moss is a low prostrate shrub of the primarily arctic–alpine family Diapensiaceae that occurs in small clumps (clones) in open areas (Fig. 3). Abundant white, bee-pollinated, and self-incompatible flowers make the prostrate clones conspicuous in early–mid-April. Although the species occurs in pine areas as far south as South Carolina, it generally is more abundant in the Plains.

The species was studied in the field and laboratory from 1969–1971 (R. E. Good, unpublished observations). Growth of 49 collections of pyxie moss in the greenhouse over a three-year period indicates that this species dies quickly under, and thus is extremely sensitive to, both very wet or moderately dry conditions. Seeds are small, averaging only 1.08×10^{-4} g, and the number of seeds per capsule averages 11, but ranges up to 18. Although seed capsules invariably are empty several days after opening, careful observation in the field and laboratory did not detect any active dispersal mechanism. Wind and water are the most likely natural dispersal agents. Seedlings and young plants in the field usually were close to an older clone, providing further evidence of limited dispersal. For the first few years, initial growth in the field appears to be very slow, probably as a result of an early extensive root development, a pattern observed in laboratory studies. Mature clumps have roots extending to a depth of about 50 cm under natural conditions, although most roots are concentrated in the upper 20 cm.

The increase in the density of pyxie moss in open areas as well as an increase in flower density in open-grown clones suggest the importance of high light intensity for this species, although a rather poor competitive ability of the species also may be a

Fig. 3. Pyxie moss in flower. *Pyxidanthera barbulata,* a characteristic plant of the Pine Plains, forms patches, here among sedge (*Carex pensylvanica*), pine litter, and pebbles of the coarse sandy soil. Measuring tape marked in centimeters.

factor. Greenhouse specimens grew poorly in containers with *Epigaea, Hudsonia,* or the heath shrubs that are common field associates.

Seed in the laboratory germinates erratically and over a long period, producing seedlings with bright red cotyledons. Regardless of length of storage or treatments, germination never began sooner than four weeks after exposure to suitable moisture and temperature conditions and often did not start for eight weeks. After initiation, germination usually continued over a four- to six-week period. Germination was not altered appreciably by acid treatments, nor by refrigeration or freezing for up to 20 weeks, but was somewhat promoted by heat treatments (49° and 60°C). Tetrazolium tests indicated about 90% seed viability, although germination averaged only 50%. Considerable germination still was possible after two years' storage in vials at room temperature. Primack and Wyatt (1975), working with pyxie moss in North and South Carolina, found no germination in the laboratory nor seedlings in their study sites.

If germination in the field is similar to that in the laboratory, the species probably rarely has a large seedling population which could be lost to drought or fire. Seed longevity and uneven germination ensure a reserve of propagules to repopulate areas after fire or take advantage of favorable conditions for establishment. The high frequency of disturbance in the Plains continues to provide open sites suitable for local dispersal and colonization by pyxie moss.

Pitch Pine

Community structure in the Plains is influenced strongly by the predominance of root crown sprouting and the relative scarcity of seedling pines. Both pitch pine and scrub oaks sprout readily after fire (Fig. 4). After repeated burning, pitch pine forms stools (root crowns) that commonly give rise to a variable number of spindly sprouts, exceeding 200 in extreme cases (Lutz, 1934). The vigor of these stools apparently declines with age and repeated burning (Little and Somes, 1964). Old pine stools were found to have dead taproots (McCormick and Buell, 1968) and to exhibit poor sprout growth. Pinchot (1899) found that such root crowns commonly were 40-60 years old, and recorded a maximum of 100 years, while the oldest sprouts were 22 years old.

Gill (1975), comparing spatial patterning in Plains and Barrens sites, found the Plains pines to have a strong tendency toward uniform spacing of individuals (stools

Fig. 4. Pitch pine sprouts one season after fire. The few dozen shoots here, about 20 cm (8 in) high, sprouted from a large root crown. Note the bare sand and upright dead mature pine stems, which contain cones opened by fire.

with sprouts) in contrast to the clumping of individuals in the Barrens. Gill suggested that uniform spacing might be due to exploitative competition, allelopathy, or seed and seedling predation. Since no evidence for the first two possibilities was found, Gill favored the idea of predation. Pitch pine density was about three times greater in the Plains: 2437 individuals/ha for the Plains and 650 individuals/ha for the Barrens. Pitch pine comprised about 34% of the tree vegetation in both cases.

Little (1954) and Little and Somes (1964) reported densities of 13,342 sprout clumps/ha, of which 3706 were pitch pine, while Andresen and McCormick, investigating a stand with older sprouts (in McCormick and Buell, 1968), reported 3484 sprout clumps/ha, of which 2199 were pitch pine. Little and Somes reported approximately 82 pitch pine seedlings/ha, while Gill found no pitch pine seedlings. Andresen (1959) found pitch pine densities of 2500–10,000 stools per hectare for 11 Plains sites and, like Gill, found no seedlings. In an effort to favor better-growing pitch pine sprouts or to convert the area to seedlings, Little and Somes (1964) tried treatments of burning, poisoning of some or all existing sprouts, and combinations of the two treatments. Burning or poisoning alone yielded 103 and 141 seedlings/acre, respectively, while combined treatments yielded 1449 and 1256 pine seedlings/acre.

Thus, the dominant tree species has few seedlings and abundant, relatively uniformly distributed old root crowns with many younger shoots. However, based on three responses of pitch pine, i.e., that burning increases seedling density, the density of pine stools decreases during the years following fire, and the vigor of sprouts decreases over decades, it seems likely that the few pine seedlings play a role in community dynamics.

POSSIBLE CAUSES OF THE PLAINS

The striking appearance of the Plains has prompted many explanations based on careful research, observation, or conjecture. The earliest suggestions for causes centered on soil factors. Cook (1868) analyzed top and subsoils from three Plains areas and found low lime and alkali contents. Low soil fertility was thought by Redfield (1889), Smock (1892), and Clute (1914) to be a major factor. Gifford (1895) pointed out that Plains soils were not poorer than Barrens soils according to N.J. Geological Survey analyses and suggested that fire together with a hard subsoil were important. Pinchot (1899) stated that hardpan or ironstone was present or forming in much of the Plains. Harshberger (1916) considered the Plains to be "due primarily to the stiff, impervious subsoil; and the light, easily dried-out, sandy surface soil which may freeze to a depth of a meter in winter and dry out in midsummer until the subsoil is hard and stiff and the surface soil almost devoid of moisture." He also cited strong winds and the elevated nature of the land. Harshberger ascribed a secondary role to the influence of fire, because he assumed that fire in non-Plains areas burned with the same frequency and severity.

Aluminum toxicity is another soil factor that more recently has been suggested as important (Joffe and Watson, 1933). Tedrow (1952) noted that the low pH of Pine

Barrens soil could cause aluminum to dissolve, thereby creating toxic quantities in the soil. Lutz (1934) and Andresen (1959) both presented data which discount soil factors as determining Plains–Barrens differences. Lutz found soils in both areas to be much the same, i.e., sandy, acid, low water-holding capacity, and low nutrient content. Growth of experimental plants (oats, rye) did not indicate any important soil differences. Andresen's findings were similar to Lutz's with respect to soil fertility. In addition, Andresen found little evidence of hardpan or ortstein. Some soil samples were found to be high in aluminum content, but the highest amount (500+ ppm) was recorded from a Barrens soil supporting normal growth. Little (1972) found that a planting of white pine (*Pinus strobus*) in the Plains indicated the sites were potentially as productive as Barrens sites.

Lutz recorded evaporation rates in the Plains to be nearly double that of the Barrens, but attributed the difference to the low resistance to air movement of the low Plains vegetation. This was judged to be a result rather than a cause of the vegetation.

Lutz found that the frequency of fire in the Plains prior to 1923 was about once every eight years, while that of the Barrens about once every 16 years. He also noted that fires in the Plains have tended to be more severe (i.e., crown fires), because of the smaller number of streams and the low tree stature. Lutz felt that if fire frequency were reduced, one stem from the stool would assume dominance and attain normal pine stature in time. He also felt that a stand composed of a greater proportion of seedlings would become essentially the same as Pine Barrens stands. Andresen generally concurred with these views, suggesting that the dwarf size is an example of pseudonanism, rather than a genetically transmitted trait. However, Little (1972) cast considerable doubt on the growth potential of Plains seedlings. Although initial growth was high, as the trees aged height growth slowed and many stems became crooked or flat topped, without a well-defined terminal shoot. Because of this poor growth and the early onset of maturity, Little suggested the possibility of a genetically different race of pitch pine in the Plains with its different fire history. Thus, fires of the scope and frequency of those encountered in the Plains could be a powerful selective force.

THE ADAPTIVE HYPOTHESIS

Recent work has supported the existence of genetic and physiological differences in Plains pitch pine, which are adaptive to frequent fires. These differences also may tend to perpetuate the pygmy nature of the Plains. Ledig and Fryer (1972) discussed and analyzed the occurrence of serotiny in pitch pine, a phenomenon which also was noted by earlier writers. Serotiny varied from 100% in Plains samples to almost zero in distant Barrens areas, a variation which could reflect a difference in selective factors, probably fire. If serotiny is related directly to fire, the degree of serotiny reflects the past frequency of fire.

Serotinous cones remain closed in the absence of high heat. Thus, seeds are released only after a fire, enabling colonization of favorable sites. However, in areas of infrequent fire, serotiny results in only sporadic contribution to seedling populations. The observed geographical pattern of decline in sprouting, i.e., rapid initial decline proceeding away from the edge of a pocket of serotinous pines followed by slow decline, suggests relatively sharp boundaries between zones of high and low fitness. The cline in frequency of sprouting does not seem to reflect a gradual pattern of variation in selective factors. Areas with sharply contrasting fitness, resulting in a pocket of variability, are implied.

Using seeds from several consecutive years, Andresen (1963) found some loss in germinating ability and a delay in time of germination by older seeds. The resulting pattern of staggered germination would increase the probability of successful regeneration. Frasco and Good (1976) compared Plains serotinous cones with open cones from the Barrens and with cones from "intermediate" trees containing both serotinous and open cones. On the average, Plains closed cones required more heat to achieve complete opening than Barrens closed cones, although in both cases 55°C was required to open all cones. At 40°C, about 43% of the Barrens closed cones opened, while only 12% of the Plains closed cones opened. Seed germination was greatest from Barrens open cones (96.9%) and was lower (59%) and somewhat slower in the Plains closed cone seeds. Good and Good (1975) found germination of Plains seed (86%) to be almost as high as Barrens seed (96%). In the latter study, seeds were obtained from cones opened with shorter periods of higher heat than those tested by Frasco and Good (1976). Differences could be due to different seed years or differences in opening techniques.

Pitch pine is an extremely variable species, as a result of phenotypic plasticity, genetic variation, or both (Ledig and Fryer, 1974). Good and Good (1975) reported significant differences in the growth characteristics of pitch pine seedlings derived from Plains and Barrens stock. In one experiment utilizing an ordinary greenhouse for three years and a commercial nursery for two and one-half years, the biomass of Plains young plants was approximately 67% that of the Barrens. Cone production in the experiment also was strikingly different; 22 of 35 Plains pines had female cones, and 13 of these had mature seeds, while only five of 33 Barrens pines had female cones, and only one with mature seeds. Growth form, while variable in both populations, also was different. About 75% of the Barrens plants were classified as tree form (single, dominant leader) while only 25% of the Plains plants were so classified. Shrubby forms (no leader, usually several branches of equal size) were unimportant in Barrens pines (2.5%) but constituted a significant portion (30%) of the Plains plants. Basal sprouting was variable in both groups and did not indicate better sprouting for Plains plants. Another group of seedlings, grown from 1.5–14.5 months of age under the controlled conditions of the Duke University phytotron, indicated height differences, with the Plains seedlings consistently shorter. Height differences did not exist in seedlings of these ages grown in the ordinary greenhouse experiment but did appear later. One Plains seedling initiated a female cone at only 14 months. [Precociousness in *Pinus rigida* also was noted by Andresen (1957) and Namkoog (1960).] Early cone production presumably would be a greater advantage in the Plains than in the Barrens due to the greater frequency of fire in the Plains. The poorer growth rate and form of Plains seedlings, if common under field conditions, could contribute to increased fire severity and perpetuation of the pygmy form. Any selective advantage of slow growth is difficult to explain unless it is coupled with other factors of selective value, such as precociousness. Heybrock and Visser (1976), in their discussion of juvenility in fruit-growing and forestry, indicate that early flowering may be correlated with low growth potential in trees. They also state that, because the length of the juvenile period within a species is quite variable and responds quickly to selection, for most forest trees the length of the period is in balance with environmental conditions. Long juvenile periods are regarded as an adaptation to tall forest conditions, in which survival is linked closely with height growth. Species growing under open and pioneer conditions tend to have shorter juvenile periods. The Plains environment seems to provide conditions conducive to a short juvenile period. The absence of the taller oaks of the Barrens lessens the competitive advantage of rapid height growth, while the frequent fires eliminate most plants with long juvenile periods and later reproductive maturity. In view of the great distances pine pollen and seed may travel, some individuals capable of more vigorous growth always would be present, especially near the borders of the Plains. If the Plains plants are sufficiently distinct genetically, the conversion of Plains to Barrens vegetation would be a more lengthy and complex process than that envisioned by Lutz (1934) and Andresen (1959) and would involve a shift in population structure.

Other possible lines of evidence with regard to genetic divergence remain to be explored. Isoenzyme and terpene studies have been useful in detecting genetic differences in other conifer populations and might be applied usefully to pitch pine populations. Terpene differences have been used in taxonomic studies of Douglas fir (*Pseudotsuga*) (von Rudloff, 1972, 1973), spruce (*Picea*) (von Rudloff, 1967a,b), juniper (*Juniperus*) (Flake *et al.*, 1969), and pine (*Pinus*) (Pauly and von Rudloff, 1971). Provenance samples in Douglas fir indicated genetic control with a lack of environmental influences (von Rudloff, 1972). Preliminary terpene investigations with gas chromatography (Good and Good, unpublished observations) indicate that the total terpene content of the Plains mature trees is less than half that of Barrens trees. However, periodic testing of developing seedlings up to two years old gave very variable and overlapping data. Although the quantitative chemical characteristics of mature trees from the Plains and Barrens differed, qualitatively they were similar at all ages.

THE PLAINS AS A PYGMY FOREST

Viewed in a broader sense, the Plains can be regarded as an example of a pygmy conifer forest. Pitch pine forms at least two other pygmy forest areas outside New Jersey, near Albany, New York and near the Suffolk County Air Force Base on Long Island, New York. The latter area consists largely of pitch pine and scrub oak, *Quercus ilicifolia*, with bearberry abundant where the ground is open. Other conifers form pygmy forests elsewhere. For example, the pinyon–juniper vegetation of the western United States commonly occurs between sagebrush and ponderosa pine communities (Woodbury, 1947). Beaman and Andresen (1966) described a krummholz-like *Pinus culminicola* association between subalpine forest and alpine meadow from the summit of Cerro Potosi, northeastern Mexico. The spreading, widely branched habit here was judged to be genetically, rather than environmentally, controlled since it was retained in well-protected locations. Due to wind and winter desiccation, krummholz occurs fairly frequently at subalpine forest–alpine tundra boundaries and may be formed by pine, spruce, larch (Arno and Habeck, 1972), fir, and hemlock.

The pygmy forests of Mendocino, California analyzed by Westman (1971, 1975) and Westman and Whittaker (1975) show several features in common with the Plains, such as a podzol soil, scarce nutrients, abundant heath shrubs, and dominance of serotinous conifer species (*Cupressus pygmaea* and *Pinus contorta* ssp. *bolanderi*, both endemic). In the Mendocino pygmy forest, the role of nutrient deficiency appears to be of prime importance, and the dominants lack sprouting ability. Aluminum toxicity was suggested as possibly significant in limiting nutrient uptake. Rapid nutrient cycling, with a relatively low percentage stored in vegetation, was believed to be an important adaptive character of the ecosystem. Although fire is present in the system, its role was not assessed.

The Plains and perhaps other pygmy forests which have been in existence for long periods must be regarded as more than dwarf versions of normal-sized forests. Their evolution has been determined by selection for characters enhancing survival under often harsh conditions, such as frequent fire and/or unfavorable soil conditions, which prevent both the successful establishment of normal-sized forests and the development of other vegetation types, such as grassland. The major contribution of conifers to pygmy forests is striking. Evergreens may be better adapted to nutrient-poor substrates than deciduous species (Monk, 1966; Jordan, 1971). Apparently, the tree niche in a pygmy forest is somewhat different from the tree niche in a normal-sized forest; consequently the population structure best suited to the pygmy habitat would differ significantly. Pygmy forests, then, may represent a collection of genotypes generally unsuited for more optimal growth conditions but better suited for survival under severely limiting conditions.

FUTURE OF THE PLAINS

The Plains today are sparsely inhabited and largely undeveloped. Portions of the West Plains however, particularly in the vicinity of the Coyle Airfield (Fig. 2) and Coyle VORTAC station, areas which are used as practice bombing target and airdrop sites, have been extensively disturbed. About 147 ha (363 acres) were bulldozed for the latter use in 1968 and still are used. The East Plains include the 325-ha (800 acre) Warren Grove target area established in 1942 and used for practice-bombing and strafing (McCormick and Buell, 1968). A runway occupies about 28 ha (70 acres), and small target areas also have been cleared of vegetation.

The Plains must be regarded as threatened from a conservation standpoint. They are limited in extent, forming only a small portion of the Pine Barrens, with only tiny areas included in a state forest or other type of reservation. The West Plains include considerable frontage along Route 72 that could be attractive for future development. The Plains are largely devoid of natural features with recreation potential such as ponds, lakes, or large streams. These probably are also the factors which to date have limited home site and other development. These factors may not be adequate in the future as the population expands and disperses more widely from urban areas. Serious thought must be directed at including a major portion of this remarkable vegetation type in a protected area.

The Plains as a unique type of Pine Barrens vegetation seems to be maintained successfully by the frequency and severity of present wildfires, much as it has been in the past. Unless a concentrated effort is made to eradicate Plains vegetation through replanting and the maintenance of extended fire-free periods, these patches of fascinating pygmy forest probably will remain as a distinct type.

SUMMARY

Three areas totaling approximately 4950 hectares (12,400 acres) of pygmy pine forest or "Plains" occur within the Pine Barrens of New Jersey and are dominated by pitch pine (*Pinus rigida*) <3 m (10 ft) high and shrubby oaks (*Quercus marilandica, Q. ilicifolia*). No plants are endemic to the Plains, but several species, such as pyxie moss (*Pyxidanthera barbulata*), broom crowberry (*Corema conradii*), and bearberry (*Arctostaphylos uva-ursi*), are more abundant than in the Barrens. Lengthy seed viability, asynchronous germination, and frequent habitat disturbance are suggested as important in the success of pyxie moss. Pitch pine has few seedlings but has many old root crowns, producing numerous young stems; sprouting from root crowns is important in recovery following fire. High fire frequency is considered the most significant factor in the development of the Plains vegetation. However, the roles of genetic and physiological factors also are considered important in its perpetuation. Plains pitch pine has almost only serotinous cones, appears to be slower growing, and is more precocious in seed production than typical Barrens pitch pine. The Plains, along with other pygmy conifer forests, are regarded as a product of selection for characters enhancing survival under severely limiting environmental conditions, such as frequent fires and (or) unfavorable soil. These conditions prevent the successful establishment of both normal-sized forests and other vegetation types such as low shrubland or grassland. Thus, the Plains trees will remain dwarf even if fire is eliminated.

REFERENCES

Andresen, J. W. (1957). Precocity of *Pinus rigida* Mill. *Castanea* **22**, 130–134.
Andresen, J. W. (1959). A study of pseudo-nanism in *Pinus rigida* Mill. *Ecol. Monogr.* **29**, 309–332.
Andresen, J. W. (1963). Germination characteristics of *Pinus rigida* seed borne in serotinous cones. *Broteria, Ser. Cienc. Nat.* **32**, 151–178.
Arno, S. F., and Habeck, J. R. (1972). Ecology of alpine larch (*Larix lyallii* Parl.) in the Pacific Northwest. *Ecol. Monogr.* **42**, 417–450.

Beaman, J. H., and Andresen, J. W. (1966). The vegetation, floristics and phytogeography of the summit of Cerro Potosi, Mexico. *Am. Midl. Nat.* **75**, 1–33.

Clute, W. N. (1914). An elfin wood. *Am. Bot.* **20**, 14–15.

Cook, G. H. (1868). "Geology of New Jersey." Daily Advertiser, Newark, New Jersey.

Flake, R. H., von Rudloff, E., and Turner, B. L. (1969). Quantitative study of clinal variation in *Juniperus virginiana* using terpenoid data. *Proc. Natl. Acad. Sci. U.S.A.* **64**(2), 487–494.

Frasco, B. R., and Good, R. E. (1976). Cone, seed and germination characteristics of pitch pine (*Pinus rigida* Mill.). *Bartonia* **44**, 50–57.

Gifford, J. (1895). A preliminary report on the forest conditions of South Jersey. *N.J. Geol. Surv., Annu. Rep. State Geol.* 1894, pp. 245–286.

Gill, D. E. (1975). Spatial patterning of pines and oaks in the New Jersey Pine Barrens. *J. Ecol.* **63**, 291–298.

Good, R. E., and Good, N. F. (1975). Growth characteristics of two populations of *Pinus rigida* Mill. from the Pine Barrens of New Jersey. *Ecology* **56**, 1215–1220.

Harshberger, J. W. (1916). "The Vegetation of the New Jersey Pine-Barrens, an Ecologic Investigation." Christopher Sower Co., Philadelphia, Pennsylvania. (Reprint, Dover, New York, 1970. Original ed. 1916).

Heybroek, H. M., and Visser, T. (1976). Juvenility in fruit growing and forestry. *Acta Hortic.* No. 56.

Joffe, J. S., and Watson, C. W. (1933). Soil profile studies: V. Mature podzols. *Soil Sci.* **5**, 313–329.

Jordan, C. F. (1971). A world pattern in plant energetics. *Am. Sci.* **59**, 425–433.

Ledig, F. T., and Fryer, J. H. (1972). A pocket of variability in *Pinus rigida*. *Evolution* **26**, 259–266.

Ledig, F. T., and Fryer, J. H. (1974). Genetics of pitch pine. *U.S. For. Serv., Northeast. For. Exp. Stn., Res. Pap.* WO-27.

Little, S. (1954). "Coastal Oak-Pine Research Center, Quarterly Report, October–December, 1953," pp. 1–4. Northeast. For. Exp. Stn., Lebanon Exp. For., New Lisbon.

Little, S. (1972). Growth of planted white pine and pitch pine seedlings in a South Jersey Plains area. *Bull. N.J. Acad. Sci.* **17**, 18–23.

Little, S., and Somes, H. A. (1964). Releasing pitch pine sprouts from old stools ineffective. *J. For.* **62**, 23–26.

Lloyd, H. C. (1955). A preliminary report, the New Jersey Plains. Div. Parks, For. Recreat., N.J. Dep. Conserv. Econ. Dev., Trenton, New Jersey. (Unpublished manuscript.)

Lutz, H. J. (1934). Ecological relations in the pitch pine Plains of southern New Jersey. *Yale Univ. Sch. For. Bull.* **38**, 1–80.

McCormick, J., and Buell, M. F. (1968). The Plains: Pigmy forests of the New Jersey Pine Barrens, a review. *Bull. N.J. Acad. Sci.* **13**, 20–34.

Monk, C. D. (1966). An ecological significance of evergreenness. *Ecology* **47**, 504–505.

Namkoog, G. (1960). Female flowers on one-year-old pitch pine. *For. Sci.* **6**, 163.

Pauly, G., and von Rudloff, E. (1971). Chemosystematic studies in the genus *Pinus:* The leaf oil of *Pinus contorta* var. *latifolia*. *Can. J. Bot.* **49**, 1201–1210.

Pinchot, G. (1899). A study of forest fires and wood production in southern New Jersey. *N.J. Geol. Surv., Annu. Rep. State Geol.* 1898, pp. 1–102.

Primack, R. B., and Wyatt, R. (1975). Variation and taxonomy of *Pyxidanthera* (Diapensiaceae). *Brittonia* **27**, 115–118.

Redfield, J. H. (1889). *Corema* in New Jersey. *Bull. Torrey Bot. Club* **16**, 193–195.

Smock, J. C. (1892). Geological work in the southern part of the state. *N.J. Geol. Surv., Annu. Rep. State Geol.* 1891, pp. 4–10.

Stone, W. (1965). "Bird Studies at Old Cape May, an Ornithology of Coastal New Jersey." Dover, New York. (Orig. Ed., 1937.)

Tedrow, J. C. F. (1952). Soil conditions in the Pine Barrens of New Jersey. *Bartonia* **26**, 28–35.

von Rudloff, E. (1967a). Chemosystematic studies in the genus *Picea* (Pinaceae). I. Introduction. *Can. J. Bot.* **45**, 891–901.

von Rudloff, E. (1967b). Chemosystematic studies in the genus *Picea* (Pinaceae). II. The leaf oil of *Picea glauca* and *P. mariana*. *Can. J. Bot.* **45**, 1703–1714.

von Rudloff, E. (1972). Chemosystematic studies in the genus *Pseudotsuga*. I. Leaf oil analysis of the coastal and Rocky Mountain varieties of Douglas fir. *Can. J. Bot.* **50,** 1025–1040.

von Rudloff, E. (1973). Chemosystematic studies in the genus *Pseudotsuga*. III. Population differences in British Columbia as determined by volatile leaf oil analysis. *Can. J. For. Res.* **3,** 443–452.

Westman, W. E. (1971). Production, nutrient circulation, and vegetation-soil relations of the pygmy forest region of northern California. Ph.D. Thesis. Cornell Univ., Ithaca, New York.

Westman, W. E. (1975). Edaphic climax pattern of the pygmy forest region of California. *Ecol. Monogr.* **45,** 109–135.

Westman, W. E., and Whittaker, R. H. (1975). The pygmy forest region of northern California: Studies on biomass and primary productivity. *J. Ecol.* **63,** 493–520.

Woodbury, A. M. (1947). Distribution of pigmy conifers in Utah and Northeastern Arizona. *Ecology* **28,** 113–126.

17

Fire and Plant Succession in the New Jersey Pine Barrens

SILAS LITTLE

The present-day forests of the Pine Barrens have been shaped by myriad factors. Forest composition and productivity mirror major soil differences, e.g., moisture. Yet fires, especially large wildfires, have been a major factor in the development of the present differences among forest stands on similar sites in the Pine Barrens. Cutting, especially clear-cuttings, also have exerted great effects on the present-day composition of the forests; many areas in the Barrens apparently have been clear-cut four or five times since 1600. Land-clearing and abandonment, and the natural succession of plants that differ in site and seedbed requirements and in their tolerance to shade also play an important role. Deer browsing, beaver-caused flooding, and human activities, such as road building and abandonment, removal of sand or gravel, and planting of native or nonnative species, have important but less widespread effects. This chapter will focus on analyzing the inherent patterns of succession, and on how fires modify these patterns to produce both sharp and subtle variations in the Pine Barrens landscape.

FIRE HISTORY

The Indian inhabitants apparently already had modified and shaped the composition of the Pine Barrens forests found by the settlers in the 1600's. Smith (1765) wrote that, before European settlements, Indians regularly burned the woods to facilitate their hunting. Thus, forests of many upland sites may have been dominated by relatively large pines with little undergrowth (Day, 1953); small scattered pines and oaks, low shrubs such as blueberries and huckleberries, and some sedges, legumes, and other herbaceous plants.

Such a composition could have been created and maintained only by frequent and relatively light fires (Little, 1946, 1973). The intensity of fires may have been low because of their frequency, which permitted only small accumulations of fuel, and because of the seasons in which most fires occurred. There is some evidence that the Indians set fires primarily during the fall and winter (Pritts, 1841; Hawes, 1923), when fires would be less severe than in spring or summer.

Fire use between 1700 and 1930 in the Pine Barrens was limited largely to reduction of fuels around cranberry bogs, some villages, and homesteads. Certain areas were burned annually for more than 30 years (Little, 1946) to provide firebreaks against large wildfires. Because of the relatively low fire intensity, pitch pines in these areas were often larger than those in nearby areas that remained unburned except for periodic wildfires.

In much of the Barrens, however, fires occurred by chance. Common to the Barrens are droughty soils, periodic droughts sometimes coupled with high winds, and fuel conditions that favor fire occurrence. The leaves of some evergreen shrubs, e.g., sheep laurel (*Kalmia angustifolia*), mountain laurel (*K. latifolia*), and leatherleaf (*Chamaedaphne calyculata*), burn intensely, apparently because of their oil or wax content. Forest floors are mats of dead organic matter, decomposing by fungi without incorporation into the soil by earthworms and millipedes. Consequently, extensive wildfires, which started soon after settlement, have been common. In 1755, one fire burned for 48 km (30 mi) (Beck, 1945), and in 1894 a single fire burned 50,587 ha (125,000 acres) (Gifford, 1895). Vermeule (1900) estimated that 51,800 ha burned in 1885, and in May 1930 eight large wildfires burned 69,142 ha (Banks and Little, 1964). Even in moist years, fires usually have burned thousands of hectares in the Barrens.

State participation in the organization of fire-suppression forces began early in this century, but only since the 1940's has motorized fire-fighting equipment been used extensively. About 1928, prescribed or controlled burning (Fig. 1) was begun in the state forests to provide firebreaks, first by treating strips 8–61 m wide along roads and later by treating certain forest tracts (Little *et al.*, 1948). Research on prescribed burning began in 1936 and helped to prompt the State Division of Parks and Forestry to adopt in 1947 a policy of using prescribed fires on state forests and private lands (Little *et al.*, 1948). The area prescribe-burned has tended to increase over time, although it has varied according to available crews and suitable weather conditions.

The reductions of fuels to decrease the start and spread of wildfires and to reduce mortality* and basal wounding of trees are the primary reasons for prescribed burning (Little *et al.*, 1948; Moore *et al.*, 1955). Other effects of prescribed burning include the following: (a) pines are favored over the more susceptible oaks; (b) herbaceous plants are favored over shrubs; and (c) both larger and more nutritious amounts of suitable and succulent browse apparently are provided for some wildlife (Little *et al.*, 1958; Menzer, 1977; Hallisey and Wood, 1976).

The fire picture today is not constant. Restrictions on debris-burning plus an appreciable decrease in railroad usage have reduced the number of fires so caused, which comprised about 30% of all fires from 1931–1940. Concurrently, the increasing use of the Barrens for recreation has acted to increase the total number of fires, averaging

---

*Mortality or killing as used in this chapter refers to the killing of aerial portions or stems. Whether the plants subsequently sprout or die depends on several factors.

Fig. 1. A light winter fire in an oak-pine stand. Sometimes these prescribed fires burn more intensely, but flames are commonly <1 m high. A light fire as pictured here has little effect on these trees, despite their relatively small size and thin bark. (Lebanon State Forest.)

1700 annually since 1970, as compared to 1300 before 1960. In 1975–1976, about 1% of the Pine Barrens, i.e., 5600 ha (14,000 acres), was prescribe-burned on state, federal, and private lands. The area burned by wildfires since 1970 often has been less than 6000 ha and has been as low as 800 ha in certain years. Yet large fires occur under extreme weather conditions, such as in 1963 when six wildfires burned 65,393 ha (161,585 acres) over one April weekend.

SUCCESSION

Upland Sites

On upland sites, succession proceeds through several stages and results in an oak–hickory forest. Herbaceous plants dominate recently abandoned fields. McCormick and Buell (1957) studied a 0.4-hectare field that had been an orchard and that was plowed without further cultivation. At five months after plowing, they found 25 species of grasses and sedges, 30 species of broad-leaf herbs, and five woody species. Although species of panic grass (*Panicum*) and sedge (*Cyperus*) were the most important components in that field, personal observations and those of Stone (1911) indicate that other grasses, usually *Andropogon* spp., often are the dominant plants in old fields before woody plants come to dominate.

Seedlings of pitch pine (*Pinus rigida*) or shortleaf pine (*P. echinata*) become established in old fields near good seed sources, and herbaceous plants may dominate fields for only a few years. On the other hand, if seed supplies are low because of a poor seed source or a period of poor cone crops, the invasion by pines may be slow, especially if a dense cover of herbaceous plants and such woody plants as dwarf sumac (*Rhus copallina*) and blackberries (*Rubus* spp.) become established. In a 0.2-hectare field cleared in Lebanon State Forest and bordered by large shortleaf pines, such a cover still prevailed at 11 years. Yet in a nearby field cleared, only a few months earlier than the first, but before a good crop of pine seed was dispersed, a dense stand of shortleaf pine 3–5 m tall had developed.

Hardwoods, especially oaks, soon invade the pine stands. One shortleaf–pitch pine stand 22 years old in 1953 in Green Bank State Forest contained 7530 hardwoods per hectare, 4265 oaks (mostly *Quercus velutina* and *Q. falcata*), and 3265 other hardwoods, but only 30 were 1.4 cm or larger in diameter (at breast height) (Fig. 2). In contrast, 18 years later there were 16,223 hardwoods in the same area, 1930 of which were 1.4 cm or larger (Fig. 3). Similar changes were observed in plots in the Wharton and Lebanon State Forests (Little, 1973). By the time old-field stands of pine have reached 50–55 years of age, the second story of oaks and other hardwoods usually is very conspicuous (Little and Moore, 1949).

Concurrently, the pines are becoming larger and less numerous. In the Green Bank stand during the 18-year period, the number of pines ≥ 1.4 cm fell from 1745 to 885 per hectare. No pines were >24.2 cm in diameter in 1953, but 130 per hectare were this size in 1971. In the absence of fire or other disturbances that favor the pines, pines are

Fig. 2.   An old-field stand of shortleaf and pitch pines 22 years old. Note the large number of overstory pines, the scattered stems of small hardwoods, and the pine litter.

Fig. 3. The same stand as in Figure 2 but 18 years later. View is the same 0.1-ha plot. Note the larger and fewer overstory pines, the much larger number and size of oaks, the scarcity of shrubs, and the change in the litter. (Green Bank State Forest.)

replaced by hardwoods, chiefly oaks (mostly *Q. velutina, Q. alba, Q. prinus,* and *Q. coccinea,* with *Q. stellata* and *Q. falcata* being less common) and hickories (*Carya* spp.). In some stands, particularly on moist sites, other hardwoods, such as red maple (*Acer rubrum*), holly (*Ilex opaca*), and blackgum (*Nyssa sylvatica*), may be a part of the mixture (Little and Moore, 1949; Little, 1973).

The invasion of old-field pine stands by shrubs usually is slower than the invasion by hardwood trees. After the pines have developed a closed canopy and thereby eliminated most of the old-field herbaceous plants, herbs and shrubs are relatively sparse for several years (Figs. 2 and 3) (Little and Moore, 1949). One old-field shrub, sweetfern (*Comptonia peregrina*), may persist for some time in the pine stands, especially in openings. Shrub oaks, such as bear or scrub oak (*Q. ilicifolia*), often invade along with the tree oaks (Little and Moore, 1949 and unpublished observations), but usually in small numbers.

Invasion by huckleberries and blueberries is slow. For example, in 1930 old-field plantations near Ongs Hat and Four Mile, both in Lebanon State forest, composed respectively of loblolly (*Pinus taeda*), and of pitch, shortleaf, and loblolly pine, the clumps of lowbush blueberry (*Vaccinium vacillans*) and other invading shrub species such as huckleberries (*Gaylussacia* spp.) on the average still are scattered. The clumps vary from about 25 m apart to intermingling to form a fairly complete cover.

The development of a relatively complete cover of lowbush blueberries and huckleberries probably depends on the establishment of scattered seedlings and subsequent spread by rhizomes (Laycock, 1967). Near Atsion in an area last used as a field about 90 years ago, the blueberry–huckleberry cover has few gaps >5 m in diameter. By the time the dominant cover can be classed as oak–pine, shrub understories apparently resemble those of climax hardwoods.

Lowland Sites

On lowland sites, the successional trend is also from conifers to more shade-tolerant hardwoods. On the imperfectly to very poorly drained sites, pitch pine is the prevailing conifer (Fig. 4), and occasional stems grow on swamp sites. Atlantic white cedar (*Chamaecyparis thyoides*) is the dominant conifer in the swamps, but also may occur on very poorly drained soils. The climax hardwoods on the driest sites in the lowlands apparently are the same as on the uplands, chiefly oaks; while on other sites they are red maple, blackgum, sweet bay (*Magnolia virginiana*), and holly (Little, 1946, 1950, 1964).

Pitch pine often is the principal invader of abandoned clearings on the imperfectly to very poorly drained soils, and white cedar in the swamps (Little, 1950). However, red maple and gray birch (*Betula populifolia*) also may occur in varying numbers. White cedar apparently forms a more stable stand than pine, being more shade tolerant and long lived.

More than 20 species of shrubs and woody vines occur on the pine lowlands (McCormick, 1970), and in one study 25 species of shrubs and 11 of vines and

Fig. 4.   A pine lowland stand on poorly drained soil. Overstory trees are pitch pine, probably of sprout origin. Note the dense tall shrub layer and scattered understory hardwoods.

subshrubs were found on swamp sites (Little, 1951). On the imperfectly drained soils, the drier spots may have a cover consisting chiefly of bear oak, golden heather (*Hudsonia ericoides*), bracken fern (*Pteridium aquilinum*), turkeybeard (*Xerophyllum asphodeloides*), and certain grasses and sedges. However, this changes rapidly to a dense cover (Fig. 4) of shrubs such as sheep laurel, staggerbush (*Lyonia mariana*), and leatherleaf, along with several other species.

Scattered tall shrubs, such as sweet pepperbush (*Clethra alnifolia*), azalea (*Rhododendron viscosum*), and highbush blueberries (*Vaccinium* spp.), occur on the poorly drained sands, but the same species develop dense understories on the very poorly drained sites (Fig. 4) and in swamps, unless they are well shaded (Little, 1950; Little and Moore, 1953; McCormick, 1970). For example, shrubs under dense pole or mature stands of white cedar are scattered and form a relatively light and inconspicuous layer. Under similar stands that have been partially cut and in many climax hardwood stands, the layer is dense and very conspicuous (Little, 1950).

Where standing water is not a limiting factor, shrub species associated with the hardwood climax apparently invade cleared areas on the poorly drained to swamp sites much more rapidly than they do the dry uplands. On formerly cultivated swamp sites, leatherleaf, sheep laurel, sweet pepperbush, staggerbush, maleberry (*Lyonia ligustrina*), highbush blueberries, azalea, black huckleberry (*Gaylussacia baccata*), chokeberry (*Pyrus arbutifolia*), and fetterbush (*Leucothoe racemosa*) were among the shrubs found in stands with most future dominant trees <5 m tall (Little, 1947, 1951).

Fire, as a significant modifier of these successional patterns described, will be considered next. The discussion will concern fire as related to the uplands, pine lowlands, and swamps.

FIRE EFFECTS ON COMPOSITION

Upland Sites

Existing Trees

Fire effects vary greatly, depending upon size and species of trees, intensity and frequency of fires, site, and season of year. On poorly drained or swamp sites, many dormant buds and some roots occur in the organic mat, where they are killed if fire consumes the mat. In contrast, on upland sites, direct damage to trees usually is limited to the crown and trunk, because most roots are in mineral soil, which is not heated appreciably by forest fire (Little, 1946). Increases in temperature, even under severe surface or surface–crown fires, are confined largely to the uppermost centimeter of mineral soil (Heyward, 1938).

Season of year is somewhat important, largely because of differences in air temperature. On days when air temperatures are low, more heat is needed to raise temperatures of bark or foliage to a lethal level than is required on hotter days. Consequently, low-intensity fires cause less damage at 0°C than those at 20°C, resulting, for example, in less scorching of the foliage of sapling pines.

Trees that survive a fire may be wounded, that is, the cambium on a portion of the trunk is killed. Large trees with relatively thick bark are, of course, more resistant than smaller trees with thin bark, and pitch or shortleaf pines are much more resistant than oaks to both wounding and killing (Little, 1946; Little and Moore, 1945; Little *et al.*, 1948; Cumming, 1964). However, basal wounding by fire may not reduce growth if crowns survive undamaged (Jemison, 1944).

Since more fuel, drier fuel, and higher winds all increase fire intensity, intensity varies not only between fires but also within the same burn. Cumming (1964) found that a wildfire killed 97% of the oaks and 70% of the pines 3.9–9.0 cm in diameter in areas not previously prescribe-burned with light winter fires; in contrast, 42 and 0%, respectively, of similar trees in areas previously burned with light winter fires, and hence with less fuel, were killed. Little (1946), studying large wildfires, found that even though strong headfires pushed by wind killed all oak stems, 35% of the pines 22–34 cm in diameter survived by developing crown sprouts. Weak headfires and strong sidefires permitted 10% of the oaks and all of the pines of that size to survive. Weak sidefires were even less damaging, enabling many oaks and all pines only 4–11 cm in diameter to survive.

Consequently, existing trees, especially pitch and shortleaf pines, can survive and grow if fire intensity is low. Once pitch and shortleaf pines exceed 6 cm in diameter, they may not even be wounded. In stands near Green Bank and in the Salem County Barrens, diameter growth of overstory pines in areas burned three times with light winter fires was slightly increased over that in unburned areas (Somes and Moorhead, 1954; Little, 1973).

Subsequent Reproduction

After a killing fire, oaks on upland sites reproduce predominantly by sprouting from dormant buds, which are located sufficiently far beneath the soil surface to be protected from damage. Of course, old trees and stems of low vigor may not sprout. Seedlings seldom occur because fire usually damages or consumes any acorns.

The period preceding seed production and potential new seedlings after a killing fire is different for "tree oaks" than for "shrub oaks." Tree oaks, such as black and white oaks, generally do not begin producing seeds until stems are 20 years old. Indeed, prolific crops are borne, usually periodically, only by dominant or open-grown trees that are 40 years old or older (Little *et al.*, 1958; Fowells, 1965). In contrast, shrub oaks bear seed at an early age: some of the bear and dwarf chinquapin (*Q. prinoides*) oak sprouts when only three or four years old (Little *et al.*, 1958).

Acorns produce stems and taproots roughly three to six times longer than those which develop from pitch and shortleaf pine seeds. Consequently, oak seedlings may start and survive in relatively thick mats of dead leaves. For example, Fowells (1965) noted that litter 3–5 cm deep forms the best seedbed for chestnut oak. Even light fires may kill acorns, completely kill seedlings <45 cm tall, and kill back, usually with subsequent sprouting, most other seedlings <1.4 cm in diameter (Little and Moore, 1949).

Like the oaks, pitch and shortleaf pines sprout from dormant buds at the base, but pitch to a greater age than shortleaf pine. In the Pine Barrens, shortleaf pine loses its basal-sprouting ability when trees reach diameters of 5-10 cm at breast height, and at a maximum age of about 30 years. In contrast, pitch pine stems up to about 80 years old may produce basal sprouts (Little and Somes, 1956), although on single stems over 40 years old all sprouts may die (Andresen, 1959), especially if shaded. Pitch pine, however, seems more capable than shortleaf pine of producing several crops of sprouts from the same stool; age counts of some sections of Pine Plains stools indicated that many were 40-60 years old when the last crop of pitch pine sprouts started (Little and Somes, 1964). In sapling stands burned by wildfire, pitch pine is favored over shortleaf; most stems of pitch pine and fewer of shortleaf (probably none where stems are $\geq$ 10 cm in diameter) develop basal sprouts.

In contrast to the oaks, pitch and shortleaf pines require relatively high light conditions and mineral soil or a filmlike cover of dead debris for good seedbeds and the establishment of seedlings. Most seedlings of both species develop basal crooks within a few years (Little and Mergen, 1966), and their basal dormant buds thereby are forced into mineral soil and protected from killing by fire. Suitable light conditions commonly occur along roads or under open canopies, and suitable seedbeds are present in prescribe-burned areas (Fig. 5) (Little and Moore, 1950).

Of course, if only pitch pines having serotinous cones occur, the pattern differs. In such areas, a relatively severe fire may be required to open the cones. For example, wildfires in stands of large pitch pines west of Chatsworth in 1954, and near routes 72 and 539 in 1946, completely killed most of the trees, but their serotinous cones were opened so that many pitch pine seedlings restocked the burns.

Shrubs and Herbs

Severe fires on upland sites reduce the shrub cover, but usually only for a few years. Many of the killed shrubs sprout, and as a result cover rebuilds rapidly. However, huckleberries recover much more slowly than lowbush blueberries, apparently because the roots and rhizomes of the former are shallower and more damaged by fire (Laycock, 1967).

Light winter fires also reduce shrub cover. When such fires occur frequently over a long period, they cause a great reduction in huckleberries, while favoring herbaceous plants, mosses, and lichens (Buell and Cantlon, 1953). Especially on Evesboro or heavier soils and under favorable light conditions, as are found in open stands or along roads, herbaceous plants greatly increase under frequent light winter fires. There the cover may be dominated by sedges (*Carex* spp.) or in many spots by herbs such as goldenrod (*Solidago* spp.), butterfly weed (*Asclepias tuberosa*), false foxgloves or gerardias (*Gerardia* spp.), button snakeroot (*Liatris graminifolia*), and several legumes (Little, 1974).

Composition in General

The most common composition on upland sites is a mixture of pitch or shortleaf pines and tree oaks (Figs. 1 and 5). The oaks usually are more numerous and often are much smaller and younger than the pines as a result of the oaks starting as sprouts after

Fig. 5. Changes in the composition of an upland site. Left: an old oak–pine stand. The well developed shrub layer indicates it has not burned for several years. Center: the same area after 10 annual light winter fires. Note the sparse shrub and litter layers. Right: the same area again, 11 years after most of the oak–pine stand was cut, leaving some pines as seed trees (12 years after the last burn). Note the density and height of pitch and shortleaf pines. Near Mt. Misery, Lebanon State Forest.

the last wildfire and the pines living through that, and frequently earlier, fires (Little, 1946).

Such a composition appears to be the logical result of both natural succession to an oak–hickory forest and periodic interruptions by heavy cuttings and wildfires, with the fires that killed back the oaks possibly having occurred at intervals of 40 years or longer. These disturbances favor the establishment and dominance of some pines in the mixture, but usually not enough so that they outnumber oaks.

Another common mixture is that of pitch pine and "shrub" oaks, especially bear and blackjack (*Q. marilandica*) oaks. In some areas, the pitch pines are much taller than the shrub oaks, while at the other extreme are areas, like much of the Pine Plains, where their heights are similar. This general composition seems to be due to frequent killing fires over a long period, with the end result that the fires eliminated the tree oaks and shortleaf pine, precisely the species that bear viable seed only on stems 20 or more years old. Where fires have been infrequent or sufficiently light to allow the continued development of pines, the pitch pines form an overstory over the shrub oaks. Where a heavy cutting or killing fire occurred recently, pines and shrub oaks may be of similar size. Where killing fires have been frequent over a long period, sprouts from old and relatively large stools form the cover known as Plains (Little, 1946; Little and Somes, 1964).

Both Lutz (1934) and Andresen (1959) estimated the past frequency of fires in Plains areas as once every eight years, while Lutz also estimated fire frequency in areas having relatively tall pitch pines over shrub oaks as once every 16 years. Probably, however, the actual frequency varies appreciably, and stand compositions have been shaped by the combined effects of varying wildfire frequencies, intensities of these fires, and heavy cuttings. The heavy cuttings sometimes create young stands more susceptible to fires than nearby older stands.

Pine Lowlands

The fire history of the pine lowlands differs in two ways from that of uplands. First, fires occur on fewer days during the year, because the poor drainage and a high water table typical of the pine lowlands mean that fuels in these areas dry less readily. Second, because of a dense understory (Fig. 4) of intensely burning shrubs, especially sheep laurel and leatherleaf, fires more easily "crown," that is, burn the foliage of overstory pines (Little, 1946).

Although varying fire intensity, different sizes of trees, and variability in soil moisture content produce variations in fire effects, in general the intensely burning fuels of the pine lowlands produce fewer gradations in damage than occur on the uplands. Typical wildfires on the lowlands advance as a wall of flame, consuming the foliage of overstory pines and most understory shrubs, especially those <1 m tall. These fires typically leave a stubble only a few centimeters tall that consists of such shrubs, although in drought periods when fires burn deep in the organic mat, little or no stubble is left. Usually many, if not all, pine stems are killed by wildfires, and survivors are damaged, although basal wounds rarely occur. Heat injury or scorching of the foliage is common in light winter fires. On pines surviving wildfires, the branches often are killed, and new branches develop from dormant buds on the trunk. Common in trees that survive severe fires are (1) crooks resulting from the killing of terminal shoots and subsequent development of new terminals from dormant buds, or (2) "flat tops" in trees that do not form new terminal shoots (Little, 1946).

After typical wildfires, most trees reproduce via sprouting, although if fires occur during extended droughts, they may burn deep enough in the organic mat to prevent sprouting of most shrubs and trees. Under such conditions, large numbers of pine seedlings may originate the next stand (Little and Moore, 1953).

Although killed by almost all fires, shrubs commonly replace the cover in a few years, since most fires do not consume all of the organic mat, and since many shrubs sprout. However, if fires consume most of the organic mat, replacement of shrub cover will take several years where a few shrubs survive, and still longer where shrubs have to reinvade the site.

As on upland sites, fires apparently favor herbaceous plants over the shrubs. Turkeybeard on drier portions, and, on moister sites, Pine Barren gentian (*Gentiana*) *autumnalis*), sundews (*Drosera* spp.), milkworts (*Polygala* spp.), and certain orchids seem to be favored by the reduction of shrubs. In areas of frequent light fires or in some areas after wildfires, bracken fern may dominate during the first year.

Fires have perpetuated pine stands on lowland sites and have prevented succession to hardwoods, and because most present stands have been shaped by repeated severe fires, relatively young, short (3–7 m), crooked, pitch pine sprouts predominate (Little, 1946). However, pitch pines of 23–31 m in height and 60–100 years of age from four lowland sites were selected for a breeding study. Variation in the amount of cementation in the soil B horizon exists, but its effect on the vegetation is unknown. Much of the slow growth and poor appearance of many pitch pine stands is believed to be due either to their origin as sprouts from relatively old stools, or to wildfire damage to existing trees.

Swamps

Existing Trees

Fire history on swamp sites (Fig. 6) differs from that on the uplands or pine lowlands in four respects. First, wildfires seldom start and spread on wet swamp sites containing white cedars or swamp hardwoods. Second, white cedars and swamp hardwoods have relatively thin bark, so trees are killed or wounded easily by light fires. Third, unlike pitch and shortleaf pines, white cedar does not sprout after stems are killed by fire. Fourth, because of the usually organic soil, groundfires may occur during severe droughts and burn much of the root systems of trees (Little, 1946).

Swamp stands frequently have served as firebreaks. Damage to existing stands has been chiefly the result of large wildfires that started on uplands or pine lowlands. Trees on the edges of stands, particularly if white cedar, often were killed. Occasionally, the heat of a large wildfire driven by a steady wind will so dry or sear the foliage of white cedars that the fire will run through the crowns (Fig. 6) and cross the swamp, especially

Fig. 6. A white cedar stand with trees killed by wildfire. If large enough for posts or other products, such trees are usually cut. Shrubs and understory hardwoods were sparse. With few hardwood sprouts and little organic soil consumed, cedar should become reestablished.

if it is <60 m wide. Some of these crown fires have occurred when the organic debris on the swamp surface was too wet to burn. At the other extreme, during unusually dry periods, the organic soil may also be consumed down to the water table or the underlying mineral soil (Little, 1946, 1950).

Subsequent Reproduction

The composition of swamp stands which follow killing fires varies greatly, depending on the depth of organic soil consumed relative to the normal water table level, the presence or near-absence of hardwood trees and shrubs in the killed stands, and the available seed sources (Little, 1950). If the level of organic soil is lowered such that water normally stands on the surface, invasion of trees is delayed until the *Sphagnum* mosses build up a suitable seedbed. At this point, available seed sources may shape the composition to white cedar, to hardwoods (especially red maple and gray birch), or to a mixture. If the level of organic soil remains essentially unchanged and many shrubs and hardwoods were present in the previous stand, their sprouts can be expected to dominate the next stand.

However, if the level of organic soil remains about the same after fire kills a dense white cedar stand, cedar seedlings usually occur in profusion and may form another relatively pure stand. However, deer browsing, especially in narrow swamps, may have a significant effect on the pattern (Little, 1950; Little and Somes, 1965). A single crop of white cedar seed may deposit 19–22 million seeds per hectare under mature stands, and the seed remains viable in the forest floor for a year or more. Because shrubs and hardwood trees usually are scattered widely under dense white cedar stands (Fig. 6), such a profusion of seed favors the establishment of another white cedar stand. Of course, mixed stands of cedar and hardwoods follow white cedar stands wherever partial cuttings have increased the amount of shrubs and hardwoods sufficiently in the killed stands, or where white cedar reproduction is inhibited by browsing deer or other factors (Little, 1950).

Shrubs and Herbs

In swamps and sometimes in depressions of pine lowlands, deep-burning fires may lower the surface such that water normally stands on the area. If the water usually is more than several centimeters deep, a quaking bog develops. However, if the water normally is <5 cm or so deep, and in wet periods up to 15 cm deep, leatherleaf may develop a thick cover (Little, 1946, 1950).

Where fires do not burn deep enough to produce conditions for quaking bogs or leatherleaf, they may burn deep enough to eliminate shrubs and favor a temporary meadow (Little, 1946). Probably some of the meadows or savannas described by Stone (1911) in his discussion of *Lophiola* were so created and contained a wide variety of herbaceous plants adapted to open wet sites.

General Composition

While certain fires have favored the perpetuation of white cedar stands, the general fire history since settlement, coupled with the effect of cuttings that left hardwoods, apparently has favored an increase in the area occupied by swamp hardwoods. Quaking bogs, meadows, and especially leatherleaf areas also have been favored, but to a lesser extent.

OTHER FIRE AND SUCCESSIONAL EFFECTS

Soil

Varying fire histories on upland sites apparently have had no appreciable effects on soil productivity, although only two studies are available (Lutz, 1934; Burns, 1952). Lutz, comparing soils in Plains and other areas with mostly pitch pine–shrub oak stands, concluded that, over a long period, stand conditions, resulting from fires at 8-, 12-, and 16-year intervals, had no significant differences among them in the physical and chemical properties of the soils. Burns (1952) investigated plots of two prescribe-burning studies and concluded that burning at about four-year intervals might benefit the soil chemically and have little effect on physical properties. In contrast, annual burning over a long period benefited the soil chemically but resulted in compaction of the surface soil, primarily from precipitation. However, reduced infiltration of water in these sandy soils is unimportant.

Many factors influence the effects of fire on soils (Lutz, 1956; Ahlgren and Ahlgren, 1960; Metz *et al.*, 1961). It is believed that, in the Barrens, the fires on uplands and most of the fires in the lowlands and swamps have not reduced the nutrient contents of the soils appreciably. Regrowth of vegetation is rapid, a pattern which would tend to recapture nutrients before they are leached to the groundwater or streams. While much of the nitrogen in organic matter consumed by fire apparently is volatilized and lost to the site, nitrogen-fixing bacteria should be favored; this possibly would account for the increased nitrogen Burns (1952) found in A horizons of Evesboro soil after 15 annual burns.

Lowland or swamp sites, where fires burn deep in the organic mat or soil, and subsequent vegetation is delayed for a long time or composed mostly of invading species, should be examined for possible nutrient losses. Although Waksman *et al.* (1943), in analyzing the organic soils of Pine Barren swamps, found nitrogen contents of about 1.5% and ash contents of 5–33% of dry samples, no estimates of nutrient losses due to wildfires have been made.

Wood Production

On upland sites, the most productive composition is the relatively pure stand of pitch or shortleaf pine, which, when developed on old fields and undamaged by wildfires (Fig. 2), produces about 200 m^3/ha or more of merchantable wood at 40 years (Fig. 3). Predominantly oak stands of similar age on similar sites yield about 90 m^3, and sometimes less. Possibly because of past wildfire damage, most oak–pine stands grow about a third as much merchantable wood as do pine seedling stands. Because of sprouting from old stools or too short intervals between crown fires, pitch pine–scrub oak mixtures may never produce merchantable stands, or at best may produce about one-tenth as much merchantable wood as old-field stands (Moore, 1939; Moore and Waldron, 1940; Little, 1964).

On typical swamp sites in the Barrens where the dominant white cedars are 15–17 m tall at 60 years, relatively pure stands may contain 373–497 m^3/ha in total stem volume, or 185–328 m^3 of merchantable wood (to a 10-cm top diameter) (Korstian and Brush, 1931). Basal areas of such stands may be 58–66 m^2/ha, compared to 17–26 in two hardwood stands with the oldest trees >100 years old (Little, 1947; Bamford and Little, 1960).

Thinnings or partial cuttings of the forest overstory tend to hasten the succession toward a hardwood climax in both uplands and in white cedar swamps (Little, 1950, 1973; Bamford and Little, 1960). In the uplands, commercial seed-tree cutting and clear-cutting commonly may be followed by seedling pines if additional forest treatments are included (Little and Moore, 1950, 1952); otherwise, slower growing, often more crooked trees or new stands of oak sprouts may develop. In the white cedar swamps, clear-cutting favors new stands of white cedar if additional treatments are included (Little, 1950).

Roads and the Removal of Sand, Gravel, or Turf

Roads provide openings and, hence, increased light under the edges of adjoining stands, which commonly favor herbaceous and shrub species. On Lakewood and Lakehurst soils, such low-growing plants as bearberry (*Arctostaphylos uva-ursi*), golden heather, sand myrtle (*Leiophyllum buxifolium*), and lowbush blueberry may dominate road edges; milkworts can dominate on haul roads in the pine lowlands. Eventually, the shrub layer usually will build up and crowd out most herbs.

Pits from which sand or gravel has been removed may form ponds where excavated below the usual water table. Where there is no standing water, a slow reinvasion by plants follows, and for many years such pits may bear scattered plants of golden heather, sweetfern, pitch pine seedlings, and possibly some sedges. A pine stand eventually develops.

In the lowlands, the removal of "turf" (shrubs, roots, and some soil), used to stabilize road cuts and fills or dam slopes, has a long-lasting effect, possibly because water often stands on the turfed spots. Until *Sphagnum* mosses re-cover these spots and provide favorable conditions for shrubs and trees, sundews may form much of the sparse cover. Some such spots created 40 years ago gradually are being invaded by woody plants, although in large spots such invasion is limited mostly to the edges (Little, 1974).

SUMMARY

The present Pine Barrens vegetation has been shaped in large part by extensive wildfires and heavy cuttings, and locally by other disturbances. Abandoned upland fields progress, in order of dominance, from grass to pine to oak, but the shrub layer develops slowly. Abandoned swamp sites, invaded by shrubs, Atlantic white cedar, or hardwoods, also tend toward hardwoods. Cutting may hasten succession toward hardwoods in both uplands and lowlands. Successional rates vary enormously: whereas an upland field may become a thicket of pine saplings in 15 years, leatherleaf shrubs may dominate a lowland spot for 50 years before trees begin to dominate.

Different fire frequencies and intensities interrupt succession, thus accounting for most of the current variations in forest composition, and largely obscuring the effects of soil differences. In swamps, fire may favor the reproduction of white cedar or hardwoods; if fire consumes enough of the organic soil, quaking bogs, meadows, or leatherleaf areas may be favored. On uplands and lowlands, many pines are sprouts from old root crowns, or have recovered from the last fire by trunk sprouts. Fire kills oak stems more readily than pines, but most oaks sprout. Periodic wildfires at possibly forty-year intervals have produced oak–pine mixtures over extensive areas of upland, while more frequent fires have created mixtures of pitch pine and shrub oaks, and the most frequent fires created the Pine Plains.

REFERENCES

Ahlgren, I. F., and Ahlgren, C. E. (1960). Ecological effects of forest fires. *Bot. Rev.* **26,** 483–533.

Andresen, J. W. (1959). A study of pseudo-nanism in *Pinus rigida* Mill. *Ecol. Monogr.* **29,** 309–332.

Bamford, G. T., and Little, S. (1960). Effects of low thinning in Atlantic white-cedar stands. *U.S. For. Serv., Northeast. For. Exp. Stn., Res. Note* No. 104, 1–4.

Banks, W. G., and Little, S. (1964). The forest fires of April 1963 in New Jersey can point the way to better protection and management. *Soc. Am. For. Proc.* 1963, 140–144.

Beck, H. C. (1945). "Jersey Genesis; the Story of the Mullica River." Rutgers Univ. Press, New Brunswick, New Jersey.

Buell, M. F., and Cantlon, J. E. (1953). Effects of prescribed burning on ground cover in the New Jersey pine region. *Ecology* **34,** 520–528.

Burns, P. Y. (1952). Effect of fire on forest soils in the Pine Barren region of New Jersey. *Yale Univ. Sch. For. Bull.* **57,** 1–50.

Cumming, J. A. (1964). Effectiveness of prescribed burning in reducing wildfire damage during periods of abnormally high fire danger. *J. For.* **62,** 535–537.

Day, G. M. (1953). The Indian as an ecological factor in the Northeastern forest. *Ecology* **34,** 329–346.

Fowells, H. A. (1965). Silvics of forest trees of the United States. *U.S. Dep. Agric., Agric. Handb.* No. 271, 1–762.

Gifford, J. (1895). A preliminary report on the forest conditions of South Jersey. *N.J. Geol. Surv., Annu. Rep. State Geol.* 1894, pp. 245–286.

Hallisey, D. M., and Wood, G. W. (1976). Prescribed fire in scrub oak habitat in central Pennsylvania. *J. Wildl. Manage.* **40,** 507–516.

Hawes, A. F. (1923). New England forests in retrospect. *J. For.* **21,** 209–224.

Heyward, F. (1938). Soil temperatures during forest fires in the longleaf pine region. *J. For.* **36,** 478–491.

Jemison, G. M. (1944). The effect of basal wounding by forest fires on the diameter growth of some southern Appalachian hardwoods. *Duke Univ. Sch. For. Bull.* **9,** 1–63.

Korstian, C. F., and Brush, W. D. (1931). Southern white cedar. *U.S. Dep. Agric., Tech. Bull.* No. 251, 1–75.

Laycock, W. A. (1967). Distribution of roots and rhizomes in different soil types in the Pine Barrens of New Jersey. *U.S. Geol. Surv., Prof. Pap.* No. 563-C, 1–29.

Little, S. (1946). The effects of forest fires on the stand history of New Jersey's pine region. *U.S. For. Serv., Northeast. For. Exp. Stn., For. Manage. Pap.* No. 2, 1–43.

Little, S. (1947). Ecology and silviculture of whitecedar and associated hardwoods in southern New Jersey. Ph.D. Thesis, Yale Univ., New Haven, Connecticut.

Little, S. (1950). Ecology and silviculture of whitecedar and associated hardwoods in southern New Jersey. *Yale Univ. Sch. For. Bull.* **56,** 1–103.

Little, S. (1951). Observations on the minor vegetation of the Pine Barren swamps in southern New Jersey. *Bull. Torrey Bot. Club* **78,** 153–160.

Little, S. (1964). Fire ecology and forest management in the New Jersey pine region. *Proc. Annu. Tall Timbers Fire Ecol. Conf.* **3,** 34–59.

Little, S. (1973). Eighteen-year changes in the composition of a stand of *Pinus echinata* and *P. rigida* in southern New Jersey. *Bull. Torrey Bot. Club* **100,** 94–102.

Little, S. (1974). Wildflowers of the Pine Barrens and their niche requirements. *N.J. Outdoors* **1**(3), 16–18.

Little, S., and Mergen, F. (1966). External and internal changes associated with basal-crook formation in pitch and shortleaf pines. *For. Sci.* **12,** 268–275.

Little, S., and Moore, E. B. (1945). Controlled burning in South Jersey's oak-pine stands. *J. For.* **43**, 499–506.

Little, S., and Moore, E. B. (1949). The ecological role of prescribed burns in the pine-oak forests of southern New Jersey. *Ecology* **30**, 223–233.

Little, S., and Moore, E. B. (1950). Effect of prescribed burns and shelterwood cutting on reproduction of shortleaf and pitch pine. *U.S. For. Serv., Northeast. For. Exp. Stn., Stn. Pap.* No. 35, 1–11.

Little, S., and Moore, E. B. (1952). Mechanical preparation of seedbeds for converting oak-pine stands to pine. *J. For.* **50**, 840–844.

Little, S., and Moore, E. B. (1953). Severe burning treatment tested on lowland pine sites. *U.S. For. Serv., Northeast. For. Exp. Stn., Stn. Pap.* No. 64, 1–11.

Little, S., and Somes, H. A. (1956). Buds enable pitch and shortleaf pines to recover from injury. *U.S. For. Serv., Northeast. For. Exp. Stn., Stn. Pap.* No. 81, 1–14.

Little, S., and Somes, H. A. (1964). Releasing pitch pine sprouts from old stools ineffective. *J. For.* **62**, 23–26.

Little, S., and Somes, H. A. (1965). Atlantic white-cedar being eliminated by excessive animal damage in South Jersey. *U.S. For. Serv., Res. Note* NE-33, 1–3.

Little, S., Allen, J. P., and Moore, E. B. (1948). Controlled burning as a dual-purpose tool of forest management in New Jersey's pine region. *J. For.* **46**, 810–819.

Little, S., Moorhead, G. R., and Somes, H. A. (1958). Forestry and deer in the pine region of New Jersey. *U.S. For. Serv., Northeast. For. Exp. Stn., Stn. Pap.* No. 109, 1–33.

Lutz, H. J. (1934). Ecological relations in the pitch pine plains of southern New Jersey. *Yale Univ. Sch. For. Bull.* **38**, 1–80.

Lutz, H. J. (1956). Ecological effects of forest fires in the interior of Alaska. *U.S. Dep. Agric., Tech. Bull.* No. 1133, 1–121.

McCormick, J. (1970). The Pine Barrens: A preliminary ecological inventory. *N.J. State Mus. Res. Rep.* **2**, 1–100.

McCormick, J., and Buell, M. F. (1957). Natural revegetation of a plowed field in the New Jersey Pine Barrens. *Bot. Gaz.* **118**, 261–264.

Menzer, C. H. (1977). Prescribed burning for wildlife. *N.J. Outdoors* **4**(1), 2–3.

Metz, L. J., Lotti, T., and Klawitter, R. A. (1961). Some effects of prescribed burning on Coastal Plain forest soil. *U.S. For. Serv., Southeast. For. Exp. Stn., Stn. Pap.* No. 133, 1–10.

Moore, E. B. (1939). "Forest Management in New Jersey," pp. 1–55. N.J. Dep. Conserv. Dev., Trenton, New Jersey.

Moore, E. B., and Waldron, A. F. (1940). A comparison of the growth of oak and pine in southern New Jersey. *N.J. Dep. Conserv. Dev., Div. For. Parks, Tech. Note* No. 10, 1–6.

Moore, E. B., Smith, G. E., and Little, S. (1955). Wildfire damage reduced on prescribe-burned areas in New Jersey. *J. For.* **53**, 339–341.

Pritts, J. (1841). "Incidents of Border Life, Illustrative of the Times and Conditions of the First Settlements in Parts of the Middle and Western States. . . ." G. Mills, Lancaster, Pennsylvania.

Smith, S. (1765). "The History of the Colony of Nova-Caesaria, or New-Jersey. . . ." James Parker, Burlington, New Jersey.

Somes, H. A., and Moorhead, G. R. (1954). Do thinning and prescribed burning affect the growth of shortleaf pine? *U.S. For. Serv., Northeast. For. Exp. Stn., For. Res. Note* No. 34, 1–2.

Stone, W. (1911). The plants of southern New Jersey with especial reference to the flora of the Pine Barrens and the geographic distribution of the species. *N.J. State Mus. Annu. Rep.* 1910, pp. 21–828.

Vermeule, C. C. (1900). The forests of New Jersey. *N.J. Geol. Surv., Annu. Rep. State Geol.* 1899, pp. 13–101.

Waksman, S. A., Schulhoff, H., Hickman, C. A., Cordon, T. C., and Stevens, S. C. (1943). The peats of New Jersey and their utilization. *N.J. Dep. Conserv. Dev. Geol. Ser., Bull.* No. 55, Part B, 1–278.

18

Vegetational Relationships of the Pine Barrens

INTRODUCTION

In a region of deciduous forest climaxes, the extensive pine forests of the New Jersey Pine Barrens are an anomaly that aroused the interest of early American botanists (Harshberger, 1911, 1916; Stone, 1911). As a landscape, the Pine Barrens are distinguished not only by their low relief and for the prevalence of pines and of drought-adapted pine–oak forests, but also for the occurrence of swamps and bogs and of rare and narrowly endemic species. These features, the relation northward to the vegetation of Long Island and southward to coastal plain pine forests, and the affinity with the heathlands of northwestern Europe all were discussed and illustrated in the book on the Barrens by Harshberger (1916). Pine Barrens vegetation is described by Harshberger (1916), Little (1979), McCormick (1970, Chapter 13, this volume and maps, McCormick and Jones 1973), Robichaud and Buell (1973), and Olsson (chapter 14, this volume); related communities on Long Island are described by Conard (1935) and Olsvig *et al.* (Chapter 15, this volume). My purpose here is not to describe the Pine Barrens communities, but rather to suggest how they may be related to one another and to communities of other areas. A few themes may be mentioned in advance: a coastal plain of low relief, a humid, forest climate, predominantly sandy and infertile soils, the importance of fire, and the prevalence of pines and heaths in the vegetation.

THE PINE BARRENS PATTERN

Despite the many studies of plant communities in the New Jersey Pine Barrens, these communities scarcely have been treated as a coherent landscape pattern. Although it is difficult to do justice to that complex pattern, some major features can be

315

Copyright © 1979 by Academic Press, Inc.
All rights of reproduction in any form reserved.
ISBN 0-12-263450-0

inferred from Harshberger (1916), who provided the most detailed and effective treatment of Pine Barrens vegetation, and from the recent accounts of McCormick (1970, Chapter 13, this volume) and Robichaud and Buell (1973). I suggest interpretations of the Pine Barrens in terms of three groups of influences on plant communities, that is, a soil moisture gradient, soil texture (and fertility) gradients, and effects of disturbance.

Soil Moisture Gradient

In regions of high relief, the soil moisture gradient is defined clearly by topographical relationships, i.e., from the moist or mesic sites of canyons or ravines with flowing streams, through lower and north-facing slopes and intermediate (east- and west-facing) slopes, to the open south- and southwest-facing slopes that (in the northern hemisphere) form the dry or xeric end of the gradient along with exposed ridges. In areas of low relief, soil moisture is determined by the more subtle effects of topography or height of the soil surface above the soil water table, or in wetter sites, by the fraction of the year with water standing above the soil surface. For such effects, topographical heights may be measured in terms of meters and even centimeters. In general, it seems that landscapes of low relief have as striking a differentiation of plant communities along the moisture gradient as those of high relief, as if in either case evolution can produce a comparable specialization of species and communities for different parts of the gradient. For the Pine Barrens, the "moisture gradient" is considered a complex gradient, in which the depth to the water table and the duration (if any) of standing water on the soil surface are major factors. The response to the moisture gradient in the Barrens may be characterized broadly by a sequence of types of communities (although these types may be continuous with one another).

Aquatic Communities

These communities consist of the open water of flowing streams, ponds, and bogs. They are described by Harshberger (1916) and by Patrick *et al.* and McCormick in this volume.

Swamp Forests

In swamps containing standing water throughout much of the year, white cedar (*Chamaecyparis thyoides*) typically is dominant. Broadleaf trees, such as *Acer rubrum, Nyssa sylvatica,* and *Magnolia virginiana,* may be present and are dominant in some stands. These are the cedar swamp formation of Harshberger (1916), the southern white cedar swamp forests of McCormick (1970, Chapter 13, this volume; see also Little, 1950, 1951). Shrubs of the heath family (Ericaceae) are prominent in both the upper shrub layer (*Rhododendron viscosum, Clethra alnifolia, Kalmia latifolia, Gaylussacia frondosa, Chamaedaphne calyculata, Leucothoë racemosa, Vaccinium* spp.) and the lower shrub layer (*Gaylussacia dumosa, Kalmia angustifolia*) along with nonheath species (*Myrica pensylvanica, Ilex glabra,* and *I. verticillata, Rhus vernix, Smilax rotundifolia,* etc.). The swamps characteristically are dense stands of small, young trees, which, despite their wetness, are subject to fires, as are other Pine Barrens communities.

Transition Wet Forests

These are forests of seasonally wet soils that link the swamp forests with other, drier types. Pitch pine (*Pinus rigida*) usually is dominant with *Acer rubrum* and *Nyssa sylvatica*. While many of the species of the swamp forests are present, these are joined, particularly where soils are less wet, by *P. rigida, Quercus ilicifolia,* and other species of the pine–oak forests. The type includes the pine transition forests and pitch pine lowland forest of McCormick (1970, Chapter 13, this volume). Broadleaf swamp forests dominated by *Acer rubrum* often occur in the transition between cedar swamp forest and drier pine forest. However, since the wet pine forests also are often in contact with the cedar swamp forest, the broadleaf swamp forests probably are produced from the latter by disturbance, rather than representing a separate type along the moisture gradient.

Mesic Pine–Oak Forests

In these less xeric pine–oak forests, that is, the Flat Pine Barren Facies of Harshberger (1916), the soil surface is dry throughout most of the year. *Pinus rigida* is dominant, with a well-developed lower tree stratum of post oak (*Quercus stellata*), blackjack oak (*Q. marilandica*), *Sassafras albidum,* and other species. The upper shrub stratum is dominated by a mixture of shrubby oaks (*Q. ilicifolia, Q. prinoides*) and heaths (*Kalmia latifolia, Gaylussacia frondosa, Clethra alnifolia, Myrica pensylvanica*); the lower shrub stratum includes *Gaylussacia baccata* and *G. dumosa, Kalmia angustifolia, Comptonia peregrina, Ilex glabra, Leiophyllum buxifolium,* and *Vaccinium vacillans.* A grass and fern (*Andropogon scoparius* and *Pteridium aquilinum*) are important in the herb stratum along with *Arctostaphylos uva-ursi* and *Xerophyllum asphodeloides.*

Xeric Pine–Oak Forests

In more xeric pine–oak forests, i.e., the High Pine Barrens Facies of Harshberger (1916), *Pinus rigida* is dominant either alone or in combination with shortleaf pine (*P. echinata*). *Quercus marilandica* and *Q. stellata* are less abundant than in forests of the preceding type, while the shrub oaks (*Q. ilicifolia, Q. prinoides*) and heaths (*Kalmia latifolia, Gaylussacia frondosa*) are denser and may form a well-defined and sometimes almost continuous shrub cover at about 1 m. Most of the shrubs and herbs of the mesic pine–oak forest occur, and dry, sandy areas have patches of low shrubs (*Vaccinium vacillans, Arctostaphylos uva-ursi, Comptonia peregrina, Hudsonia ericoides*) and lichens (*Cladonia* spp.).

Soil Texture Gradient

It is harder to characterize a gradient of soil texture and related effects on fertility because of the many, partly independent properties of the soils involved. If, however, we limit ourselves to well-drained soils of the Pine Barrens, then we may define a textural gradient along which average soil particle size increases and the proportions of fine particles (silt and clay) decrease. As the soil becomes increasingly coarse, its capacity to retain both water and nutrients decreases, and the soil becomes both increasingly subject to drought and low in nutrients. Along the gradient, the organic matter content of the soil also decreases, and the soil may be increasingly subject to podzolization, i.e., the downward leaching of nutrients and other soil materials that leaves a predominantly siliceous or sandy upper layer 20–50 cm thick, that may be underlain by a hardened zone of deposit of the leached materials. The gradient occurs in a well-defined form (without strong podzolization) in the Long Island soil catena and vegetation continuum described by Olsvig *et al.* (chapter 15, this volume). I assume here that the soil texture and vertical structure affecting drainage also are significant (in interaction with fire effects) in the New Jersey Pine Barrens. The relationships are more complex, however, in the more extensive and more diverse soils of the New Jersey Barrens (Markley, Chapter 5, this volume; Tedrow, Chapter 4, this volume), and research there has not demonstrated effects of soil texture on vegetation (Lutz, 1934; Andresen, 1959). The soil texture gradient more strongly affects the drier part of the soil moisture gradient just described, i.e., the pine–oak communities. Along the texture gradient, the mesic and xeric pine–oak types as previously described become the intermediate members of a second vegetation gradient, linked with oak forests on finer soils and with the dwarf Pine Plains on the coarsest (or otherwise most limiting) soils.

Oak Forests

Oak species often present in the less xeric pine–oak forests (*Q. prinus, Q. coccinea, Q. alba, Q. velutina*) are dominant in closed-canopy oak forests, with undergrowth related to that of the widespread oak forests and oak heaths (dominated by *Q. prinus*, and formerly by *Castanea dentata*) of acid soils of the highlands around and inland from the Pine Barrens. Closed oak forests thus seem marginal to the Pine Barrens vegetation; but, because of combinations of soil properties with fire protection, they occur within the region (Buell and Cantlon, 1950; McCormick, Chapter 13, this volume).

Oak–Pine Forests

These fire-susceptible forests generally are composed of young stands of oaks (*Q. coccinea, Q. alba, Q. velutina, Q. prinus*, etc.) forming a lower canopy above which scattered, larger individuals of *Pinus rigida* emerge. *Quercus velutina* is more common in the northern, while *Q. falcata* becomes prominent in the southern Pine Barrens (McCormick, Chapter 13, this volume). Scattered shrub oaks (*Q. ilicifolia, Q. prinoides*) and heaths (*Kalmia latifolia, Gaylussacia frondosa*, and *Myrica pensylvanica*) form an upper shrub layer, with other heaths (*Gaylussacia baccata, Vaccinium vacillans, V. angustifolium, Kalmia angustifolia Comptonia peregrina*) forming moderately dense lower shrub layers. Species in an herb stratum of very low coverage include the ground heath *Gaultheria procumbens*, the sedge *Carex pensylvanica*, and the bracken fern, *Pteridium aquilinum*. Such forests have been studied intensively on Long Island by Woodwell and others (Woodwell and Rebuck, 1967; Whittaker and Woodwell, 1968, 1969; Woodwell, Chapter 19, this volume) and are described also by Olsvig *et al.* (Chapter 15, this volume).

Pine–Oak Forests

In the pine-oak forests, pine dominates more strongly, while the tree oaks of the preceding type are reduced in cover or are absent. *Q. stellata* and *Q. marilandica* are the principal species. Cover of both shrub oaks and heaths is usually denser than in the oak-pine forests, and low heaths (*Arctostaphylos uva-ursi, Vaccinium angustifolium,* and the prostrate *Gaultheria procumbens* and *Epigaea repens*) often are conspicuous. Mesic and xeric phases of the pine-oak forests have been distinguished separate in the soil moisture series.

Pine–Shrub Oak Transition

Toward more extreme soils, the pines are reduced in density and exhibit stunted growth; in the transition they are still primarily erect and single stemmed, but some bear serotinous cones. The tree oaks are much reduced or absent (except for the rather shrubby *Q. marilandica*), and the shrub oaks (*Q. ilicifolia* and/or *Q. prinoides*) are strongly dominant along with the heaths (Olsvig *et al.,* Chapter 15, this volume).

Dwarf Pine Plains

On the most extreme soils, a different, shrubby ecotype of *Pinus rigida* becomes dominant and, together with shrubby oaks, forms a canopy only 1–2 m tall. Among these, *Q. ilicifolia* occurs on eastern Long Island and is joined in New Jersey by other species, principally *Q. prinoides* and dwarfed forms of *Q. marilandica* and *Q. stellata*. Apart from the miniature pine-oak canopy, heaths with high coverages, i.e., *Gaylussacia baccata* and *Vaccinium vacillans* prevail on Long Island, often joined in New Jersey by *Leiophyllum buxifolium* and *Ilex glabra* mainly reaching 0.5 m or more. *Arctostaphylos uva-ursi, Vaccinium angustifolium* (Long Island), *Corema conradii* (New Jersey), *Leiophyllum buxifolium* (New Jersey), and dwarfed *Kalmia latifolia* (New Jersey) occur as low shrubs mainly below 0.3 m, with *Gaultheria procumbens* and *Epigaea repens* as prostrate ground heaths. The pine plains are discussed further by Harshberger (1916), Lutz (1934), Andresen (1959), McCormick and Buell (1968), McCormick (Chapter 13, this volume), Good *et al.* (Chapter 16, this volume), and Olsvig *et al.* (Chapter 15, this volume). Comparing the New Jersey and Long Island dwarf pine plains, the former apparently are a mesic and the latter a xeric phase (Olsvig *et al.,* Chapter 15, this volume).

Disturbance

As the two gradients, soil moisture and texture, interact with each other, more and less xeric vegetation types can be expected within each step of the soil texture gradient from oak forest to pine plains. These relationships are complicated further by fires and differences in fire frequency. Increasing fire frequency may produce type displacements along both gradients, extending a more xeric type of vegetation along the moisture or soil texture gradient into sites that would be occupied by a less xeric type with lower fire frequency; prolonged fire protection can produce type extensions in the opposite direction. Other replacements occur because of disturbances. Destruction of the white cedars (*Chamaecyparis thyoides*) can convert a cedar swamp into one dominated by broadleaf trees (Harshberger, 1916). Disturbance of the pine and oak canopy can convert Long Island pine plains into a heath community with a relatively dense cover of *Gaylussacia baccata, Vaccinium vacillans,* and *V. angustifolium* (Olsvig *et al.,* Chapter 15, this volume); and stands with one or more low heaths (*G. baccata, V. vacillans, Arctostaphylos uva-ursi, Hudsonia ericoides*) are observed on disturbed sites in New Jersey. Destruction of tree oaks and the tree ecotype of *Pinus rigida* by frequent fire may have converted some pine–oak forests into stands resembling pine plains (Andresen, 1959). Destruction of pines by frequent fire may have converted transition pine plains into the oak thickets described for Long Island by Conard (1935) and Olsvig *et al.* (Chapter 15). Along the Wading River and elsewhere in the Pine Barrens, dry-season fires, together with soil factors, may have controlled the formation of marsh and savanna-like communities (Harshberger, 1916), communities which do not fit into the scheme of soil gradients just described and which now are much reduced in area (McCormick, 1970). Local clearing, cultivation of cranberries, and other disturbances have complicated the present pattern of Pine Barrens vegetation.

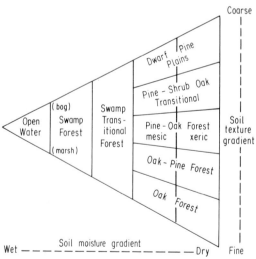

Fig. 1. A suggested interpretation of the pattern of Pine Barrens vegetation. Major community types are related to a topographical soil moisture gradient on the horizontal and to a gradient of soil texture relating to nutrient conditions and fire susceptibility on the vertical. Soil drought and fire frequency increase to the right and upward, and increased fire frequency can extend a given type into the range of one less xeric. Fire frequency alone (without soil relationships affecting fire frequency), however, is not considered capable of providing a sufficient interpretation of the pattern or of the extensive occurrence of contrasting communities in contact without fire barriers.

Vegetational Pattern

Apart from disturbance, the major features of the vegetational pattern of the Pine Barrens in response to soil gradients are suggested in Fig. 1. The figure by necessity is a simplification, if not an oversimplification; however, the major relationships of the communities described by Harshberger (1916) and others seem accounted for in terms of the major gradients of soil moisture and texture. Neither one is a simple gradient of linearly related variables; both are "complex-gradients" summing the effects of numerous, partly independent environmental factors as expressed in gradients of natural communities. The discussion of soil and community gradients implies that these are continuous, and that the pattern of Fig. 1 consequently is a two-dimensional continuum. This is probably so in the sense that the communities of the Barrens continuously intergrade with one another when neither disturbance nor abrupt change in soil properties interrupts that continuity. Disturbance and soil contrasts, however, are extensive. Consequently, the actual vegetation in the field often appears as a complex discontinuum, that is, a mosaic of elements that probably are related to one another continuously in the overall pattern, but that form on the ground a sometimes bewildering array of patches and tracts of vegetation often contacting one another through relatively sharp transitions.

DISTINCTIVENESS OF BARRENS VEGETATION

Climate

These observations permit some discussion of the distinctive characteristics of the Pine Barrens vegetation related to the themes already mentioned. The climate of the area is humid, with a mean annual precipitation of 105–120 cm, i.e., as much as, or slightly more than, that of nearby uplands supporting oak forests with closed canopies. From this and from the fact that, with suppression of fires in the less extreme barrens, plant succession will proceed from pine–oak or oak–pine to oak forest, the climate is demonstrated to be appropriate for temperate deciduous forest. The maritime influence of the Atlantic Ocean, although stronger in the Pine Barrens than further inland, is not responsible for the distinctiveness of the vegetation. (Oak forests occur on uplands between the Pine Barrens and the Atlantic Ocean.) Communities whose climates are subject to strong maritime influence often are dominated strongly by evergreen species, whereas those of continental climates are dominated by deciduous species. Many of the major Pine Barrens plants, including all the oaks and many of the heaths, are deciduous.

Interactions among Relief, Soil, and Fire

The predominantly sandy soils, in interaction with the effects of low relief and of fire, and not climate, determine the distinctive characteristics of Pine Barrens vegetation. In humid climates, sandy soils tend to be drier or more xeric than clay soils because of their free drainage and poor water-retaining properties, whereas in arid climates sandy soils tend to be less xeric than clay because of the greater penetration and retention of water in the former (Walter, 1973). In the humid climate of the Pine Barrens, the sandy soils are responsible for the widespread occurrence of xeric sites supporting the fire- and drought-adapted pine communities. The sandy soils probably intensify the contrast in moisture conditions between lower (and hydric) and upper (and xeric) sites that are so evident despite the low topographical relief of the area. The area has high topographical beta diversity, i.e., relative contrast in communities, consequent on species turnover and change in community composition along the moisture gradient (cf. Whittaker, 1960, 1972; Marks and Harcombe, 1975).

The fires to which almost all the vegetation of the Barrens is subject have profound effects on the plant communities. These effects differ, however, not only with fire frequency but also with soil factors that affect fire frequency (by means of the duration and intensity of the drought to which the vegetation is exposed) and the species composition upon which the fire acts. Soil and fire frequency, then, in determining the structure and species composition of Pine Barrens plant communities, act partly independently and partly in concert, since soil influences frequency. Fire frequency is offered much too easily as a "cause" of the Barrens pattern and as a reason for seeking no further understanding. Without soil research, the particular soil–vegetation relationships suggested here are frankly inference and hypothesis. The Long Island work supports the significance of soil factors, however; fire frequency alone should not be thought of as a sufficient interpretation of the vegetation pattern and the extensive occurrence of different plant communities that are in contact or intergrade with one another without fire barriers.

Some major effects of fires may operate through the soil and its nutrients. The sandy soil has poor nutrient-, as well as water-retaining, properties. When the stock of inorganic nutrients in the vegetation is converted by fire into ash, the nutrients can be carried downward rapidly through a coarse soil by percolating rainwater and thereby lost from the plant community (Foster and Morrison, 1976). Thus leached of their nutrients, the Pine Barrens soils predominantly are acid and infertile. Nutrient stocks in the soil, in the soil surface litter, and in the plant communities themselves are low, as compared with those in oak forests such as occur on other soils in the area (Woodwell and Whittaker, 1968; Woodwell *et al.,* 1975; Woodwell, Chapter 19, this volume; Olsvig *et al.,* Chapter 15, this volume). The open, xeric character of much of the vegetation is adapted to soil nutrient limitations as well as to drought and fire.

Heaths and Pines

The world over, heaths are adapted predominantly to acid and infertile soils. The term "heath" denotes plants of the heath family, the Ericaceae, which are so conspicuous in the shrub strata of the Pine Barrens. It is ecologically appropriate to treat "heaths" more broadly as members of the heath order, Ericales, which includes families often separated from the Ericaceae, namely, Empetraceae (*Empetrum, Corema*), Vacciniaceae (*Vaccinium, Gaylussacia*), Clethraceae (*Clethra*), and

Pyrolaceae. With these plants, I also would group some other North American genera that are ecological, but not taxonomic, heaths, namely, *Myrica* and *Comptonia* (Myricaceae), and *Hudsonia* (Cistaceae). Species of *Ilex* (Aquifoliaceae) also often occur with heaths. "Heathlands" are shrub communities in which heaths are dominant or important; heath forests (e.g., pine heath, oak heath) are forests in which heaths dominate or are important in the understory. A simple characterization of the prevailing vegetation of the Pine Barrens thus is pine–oak heath. *Pinus rigida* and other pines, like the heaths, are adapted to acid and infertile soils and to fires (Monk, 1966; Mutch, 1970; Klötzli, 1975), although pines are not limited to such soils.

Pine Plains

Soil characteristics, fire adaptation, and pine and heath dominance reach their extreme for the area in the dwarf Pine Plains. These, as shrublands 1–2 m tall with a strong heath component, are heathlands. Generalizing about the Pine Plains may be precarious, for the Pine Plains of New Jersey and Long Island differ from each other and from the Shawangunk Mountain plains described below. The work of Olsvig *et al.* (Chapter 15, this volume) suggests, however, that the Long Island pine plains differ from pine–oak forests in: (1) their more coarsely sandy soils, with low water- and nutrient-holding capacity, that (b) subject the community to more severe drought in summer and consequently to more frequent and more severe fire, and (c) permit nutrient loss to low levels that support (d) a shrub community that has limited above-ground height growth and that forms a shrub canopy susceptible to the next fire. The shrubby ecotype of *Pinus rigida* in the Plains, with its root-sprouting habit, low and contorted growth, and early produced serotinous cones, is adapted to this regime, as are the shrub oaks and the heaths (cf. Ledig and Fryer, 1972; Good and Good, 1975). In New Jersey, soil texture may not be coarser in the Pine Plains than in the nearby pine–oak forests, but soil drought resulting from the combination of relatively coarse texture with somewhat higher elevations above the water table may be responsible for the location of the dwarf Pine Plains. In an earlier time influenced by the ideas of Clements (1936) concerning the determination of climax vegetation solely by climate, the dwarf Pine Plains seemed out of place and were likely to be regarded as a consequence only of frequent fire. I suggest that, far from being simply fire successional, the Pine Plains are a distinctively adapted ecosystem, an edaphic climax, and are a key to the understanding of the broader pattern of the Pine Barrens. The Pine Plains illustrate in the extreme those characteristics of soil texture, drought, and nutrient poverty, lowering of community stature and coverage, fire adaptation, and pine and heath dominance that apply to so much of the Pine Barrens vegetation.

RELATIONS TO OTHER AREAS

Northwestern Europe

By the concepts of heath and pine heath, the Barrens may be related to other vegetation. The classic source of the concepts was northern Germany, especially in the work of Graebner (1901). Heath (German *Heide*) there refers to the dwarf-shrub heathlands dominated by heather (*Calluna vulgaris*) and, by extension, to similar dwarf-shrub communities dominated by *Erica* and *Empetrum* species. "By the term *heath,* so far as it concerns northern Europe, is meant a treeless tract that is mainly occupied by evergreen, small-leaved, dwarf-shrubs and creeping shrubs that are largely Ericaceae" (Warming, 1909, p. 210). Variations in the German usage of the term are discussed by Krausch (1969). Scots pine (*Pinus silvestris*) forms with heath undergrowth a pine heath (German *Kiefernheide*), and removal of the pines by fire or cutting may leave a heathland to which the return of pines is long delayed by fire and grazing, and possibly in some cases allelopathic effects of *Calluna* and *Erica* (Brian, 1949; Harley, 1952; Ballester *et al.*, 1977). Vegetational relationships of the western European lowland heaths, which occur from southern Norway and Sweden through Denmark, northern Germany, and the British Isles to western France and coastal Spain and Portugal, are summarized by Gimingham (1961, 1969, 1972), Ellenberg (1963), and Walter (1968). Related dwarf-shrub heaths occur widely in European mountains. The European heathlands are similar to the North American heathlands in that they occur in humid climates on acid soils, but are unlike many North American heathlands in their evergreen character (appropriate to the maritime climates of western Europe), small leaves (leptophyll, less than 25 mm² in area), and low growth (sometimes above 30 cm, but often only 10–20 cm).

Eastern North America

Erica and *Calluna* are not native to North America; *Empetrum* occurs in the north, and *Empetrum, Corema, Leiophyllum,* and *Hudsonia* include smallleaf evergreen dwarf-shrubs in certain North American heathlands. Some features of the North American heathlands are summarized elsewhere (Whittaker, 1979). These heathlands are dominated primarily by taller shrubs (0.5 to 3 m in height) with larger leaves (microphyll, 2–20 cm² or larger). The North American heaths may be said to bracket the continent, extending from the Pine Barrens and other communities of the Atlantic Coast northward to the maritime provinces of Canada, westward across the continent in the shrub belts of bogs and the shrub communities of the lower alpine and arctic zones to the Pacific Coast of Canada, and southward to California. Many of the North American heaths are deciduous; and the genus *Vaccinium,* of which most species are deciduous, is distributed most widely.

Well-developed dwarf pine plains communities are known from the New Jersey Pine Barrens and Long Island (Olsvig *et al.*, Chapter 15, this volume) and also occur on the summits of the Shawangunk Mountains, New York (McIntosh, 1959). The Shawangunk Pine Plains are dominated by shrubby *P. rigida* with *Gaylussacia baccata* and *Vaccinium vacillans.* Oaks are lacking, despite the occurrence of *Q. ilicifolia* and other species in the Shawangunk Mountains. The environment is extreme in a different way from the coastal plains: A resistant quartzite caps the range and strongly limits soil development and fertility. Related, less stunted pine–oak types are described for the Kittatinny Mountains of New Jersey by Niering (1953). Shrublands of oaks (*Q.*

ilicifolia, Q. prinoides) occur from New Jersey and Long Island to Nantucket Island, Massachusetts (Harshberger, 1916, 1918) and inland to the summits of some mountains of eastern New York. Wet shrublands including pond pine (*P. serotina*) occur south of New Jersey on the coastal plain from Virginia to Florida (Christensen, 1979). The evergreen shrub bogs or pocosins are dominated by tall shrubs of *Cyrilla racemiflora* and the heaths *Zenobia pulverulenta* and *Lyonia lucida*, and contain *Clethra alnifolia, Ilex coriacea*, and *I. glabra, Persea borbonia*, and others. *Pinus serotina* occurs either as an emergent or in a stunted form as part of the shrub layer. In areas of sand ridges, the shrub bogs in depressions alternate with sandhill pine forests or pine scrub communities (Wells and Shunk, 1931; Laessle, 1958).

Disturbance in the Long Island Pine Plains produces a heathland dominated by lower deciduous shrubs (*Gaylussacia baccata, Vaccinium vacillans*, and *V. angustifolium*); similar shrub communities can be traced northward through Nantucket Island, Massachusetts (Harshberger, 1918) to Nova Scotia and Newfoundland, where they apparently form long-persistent shrub communities following removal of coniferous trees (Osvald, 1954; Strang, 1970; Damman, 1971), and to the summits of the Mahoosuc Mountains in Maine (Fahey, 1976), where they form the northernmost of the Appalachian heath balds. The balds are mostly taller (1–3 m), closed heath communities capping exposed ridges and extending down southerly and westerly slopes in the Appalachian Mountains. The Appalachian heath balds have been studied primarily in the Great Smoky Mountains of Tennessee (Cain, 1930; Whittaker, 1956, 1963, 1979). In the denser ericaceous canopies of most of their areas, the heath balds of the Smokies differ from any of the communities of the Pine Barrens. The regions are linked floristically, however, by some shared species (*Kalmia latifolia, Gaylussacia baccata, Clethra alnifolia, Vaccinium vacillans, Gaultheria procumbens, Epigaea repens*) and genera, notably the two endemics of the genus *Leiophyllum, L. buxifolium* in the Pine Barrens and *L. lyoni* on open summits of the heath balds. Down the mountain slopes from the heath balds, the shrubs continue under tree cover to form forest heaths, i.e., pine heath, spruce heath, or oak heath. The oak heath communities, although related in composition to the New Jersey oak heaths, e.g., those of the Navesink Highlands (Robichaud and Buell, 1973, p. 210), differ in structure from the latter, for the steep slope oak–chestnut heaths of the Smokies have a very dense, tall (3–4 m) heath stratum (Whittaker, 1956).

Pine heaths occur more widely in the eastern United States and intergrade with pine forests with few heaths. Pine heaths extend northward from New Jersey through Long Island to Cape Cod, Massachusetts and inland and southward in the Appalachian Mountains to the Great Smoky Mountains and beyond. Middle elevations in these mountains have pine heaths that are related in composition and structure to those of the Pine Barrens, that is, dominance by *P. rigida* (or *P. pungens*), with oaks (*Q. coccinea, Q. prinus*, but no shrub oak) and a heath shrub stratum (*Kalmia latifolia, Gaylussacia baccata, Vaccinium vacillans, Rhododendron catawbiense, R. maximum*) and an herb stratum with ground heaths (*Gaultheria procumbens, Epigaea repens*, and *Galax aphylla* of the Diapensiaceae) (Whittaker, 1956). Open pine (*P. echinata*) stands occur also on the mid-Appalachian shale barrens (Platt, 1951), but the heaths in these are limited to the sparse occurrence of *Vaccinium vacillans* and *V. stamineum*. Other pine-heath and pine-oak communities occur inland to Wisconsin and Minnesota and the bluffs of the Mississippi River, southward to Georgia and Florida, and then westward to eastern Texas. The Wisconsin pine barrens are described by Curtis (1959) and Vogl (1970), *Pinus banksiana* and *P. resinosa* occur with *Quercus ellipsoidalis, Gaylussacia baccata, Vaccinium angustifolium, Comptonia peregrina, Ceanothus ovatus, Andropogon scoparius,* etc. The Texas "Lost Pines" areas, on sandy soils in areas of oak woodland and prairie on other soils, are dominated by loblolly pine (*P. taeda*) and by *Quercus stellata* and *Q. marilandica,* the two oaks most characteristic of New Jersey Pine Barrens. The heath element is limited to *Vaccinium arboreum* and (in more mesic sites) *Myrica cerifera,* and grasses are more prominent than in the New Jersey and Long Island Pine Barrens.

The heaths as a family are concentrated in cool-humid and especially maritime climates; their prominence decreases inland toward drier and more continental climates and also may decrease toward the south. Although the heaths are not characteristic of dry environments in general, many of them are characteristic of the leached soils of the driest sites within areas of humid climate.

Western North America

Pine heaths occur in the Pacific Coast states, for example, *Pinus contorta* with *Gaultheria shallon* and other evergreen shrubs along the coast of Washington and Oregon, *Pinus attenuata* with *Arctostaphylos* species on serpentine soils from the Siskiyou Mountains of Oregon (Whittaker, 1960) to the Santa Ana Mountains of California (Vogl, 1973; Vogl et al., 1977), *P. muricata* with a tall heath of *Rhododendron macrophyllum* and *Myrica californica* in Medocino County, California (Westman, 1975), and *P. jeffreyi* with *Arctostaphylos* species in the Sierra Nevada and San Jacinto Mountains of California. *Arctostaphylos* species occur in the California chaparral and dominate some chaparral communities to form heathlands (Vogl and Schorr, 1972). A very dense, tall (1–3 m) evergreen heathland dominated by *Gaultheria shallon* and *Vaccinium ovatum* occurs in a narrow belt between heath forest and the beaches along the coast of Washington and northern Oregon (Heusser, 1960; Franklin and Dyrness, 1969).

Perhaps the most interesting of the western heathlands in relation to the Pine Barrens, however, are the pygmy cypress forests of Mendocino County, California (McMillan, 1956; Jenny *et al.,* 1969; Westman, 1975; Westman and Whittaker, 1975). On some of the level sites of coastal terraces, diminutive trees (1–2 m tall) of cypress (*Cupressus pygmaea*) and Bolander pine (*P. contorta* ssp. *bolanderi*) form an open canopy above a heath stratum dominated by a low evergreen blueberry (*Vaccinium ovatum*), which here is less than 0.5 m tall, an endemic dwarf manzanita (*Arctostaphylos nummularia*), and *Gaultheria shallon,* which here also is reduced to a dwarf-shrub. Like the dwarf Pine Plains, the pygmy cypress barrens suggest a miniature forest in which the tree stratum is reduced to shrub stature, and the shrub stratum to dwarf-shrubs. As in the Pine Plains, the Bolander pine and the cypress have serotinous cones, but neither the pine nor the cypress root-sprouts in the manner of the shrub ecotype of *P. rigida*. Whereas the Pine Plains include many deciduous species, the pygmy cypress forest is almost entirely evergreen as a combined adaptation both to a strongly maritime climate and to highly infertile soils. The soils of the pygmy cypress forests are intensely leached, acid podzols (spodosols) with white, flourlike silica over a hardpan (Jenny *et al.*, 1969; Westman, 1975). Like the Pine Plains, the pygmy cypress forests are the extreme of a soil and community gradient (Westman, 1975). In Mendocino County, this gradient extends from redwood forests (*Sequoia sempervirens*) and mixed evergreen forest (*Pseudotsuga menziesii* with a lower canopy of *Lithocarpus densiflora* and other evergreen–sclerophyll trees) through pine heath (*P. muricata* with *Rhododendron macrophyllum* and *Myrica californica*) and a pine heath transition (*P. muricata* with *P. contorta* spp. *bolanderi*) to the pygmy cypress forests. The latter, like the pine plains, are affected by fires; but the whole vegetation pattern from redwood forest to pygmy forest, like that of the Pine Barrens, is subject to fire. As in the Pine Barrens, heaths are prominent in the undergrowth of all of the communities of the pattern but increase in importance toward the extreme sites to share dominance with conifers in the pygmy cypress forest.

Southern Hemisphere Heaths

Forests with heathlike characteristics and podzol soils formed from sands occur in the humid tropics. Heathlands also occur in the temperate southern hemisphere, notably in the Cape Province of South Africa, southern and especially coastal Australia, and as the *Empetrum* heathlands in southernmost South America. In the South African and Australian heathlands, the family Ericaceae is joined by the allied family Epacridaceae, distinctive plants of the family Restionaceae related to the grasses, and by members of the Proteaceae and other southern hemisphere families. These southern heaths are so rich in families, genera, and species as to make the North American and Eurasian heathlands seem peripheral, simplified derivatives among the heathlands of the world. These southern heaths are predominantly evergreen and, like most of the heathlands of the world, they are fire-adapted. South African heaths (fynbos) occur with widely different species composition on both acid and limestone soils, and the Australian heaths are on diverse soils including coastal sands, limestones, and fossil laterites. On all of these, however, the communities are true heathlands, in their adaptation to present soil sterility and prevalence of smallleaf (leptophyll and nanophyll) shrubs. Heath woodlands and heath forests are formed by *Protea arborea* in South Africa and by species of *Banksia, Eucalyptus,* and *Casuarina* in Australia. Although they are angiosperms, some of the Proteaceae have evolved serotinous cones suggestive of those of some northern hemisphere pines. Some of the Australian heaths have a low canopy (0.5–2 m) of *Casuarina* (*C. nana, C. distyla*) corresponding to the dwarf conifers of the northern hemisphere; these Australian communities seem reasonable southern hemisphere analogues of the Pine Plains of New Jersey and the Shawangunk Mountains.

CONCLUSION

The preceding comments on heaths (see also Specht, 1979) are consistent with the themes of the Pine Barrens suggested above. On a coastal plain landscape of sandy soils in a humid climate, a diverse pattern of vegetation has developed in response to relatively subtle gradients of soil moisture and texture. In this pattern, the prevailing communities are xeric for their climate and have adapted to environmental effects which interrelate drought, fire, and soil nutrient impoverishment; throughout this pattern, conifers are largely dominant and heaths are prominent.

Broadleaf deciduous forest is considered the climax formation for most of the eastern United States. In view of the occurrence of pines throughout most of the same area, one may venture another interpretation, namely, the existence of alternate climax formations—deciduous forests on the one hand, and pine forests and heaths on the other—that are largely coextensive with one another and able to replace one another in response to soil–fire relationships in the eastern United States. [Within the eastern forests, of course, are also the *Tsuga canadensis* forests and local, stable grasslands, such as the Hempstead Plains (Conard, 1935) and cedar glades (Quarterman, 1950 a,b).] Deciduous forests prevail on more favorable soils, and especially in the central area of the formation. On soils that are in various ways drier and more sterile, such as on sandy coastal plains and hills, steep south-facing slopes and river bluffs, and on rocky mountain summits, the alternate pine climaxes establish themselves; these apparently are all susceptible to fire. In many areas, pines are successional to deciduous forests in some sites, whether or not they also form fire-adapted edaphic climaxes on other sites. Toward the northern and southern limits of the eastern deciduous forests, the roles of fires and of pines increase. The New Jersey Pine Barrens are remarkable, however, in the occurrence not merely of pine communities but of a whole vegetation pattern (from swamp white cedar and oak forest through pine and pine–oak heaths to the dwarf Pine Plains) that represents an alternate climax pattern to the deciduous forest pattern on other soils to the west of the Barrens. On the sands of southern Long Island and on the Coastal Plain south of New Jersey as well, the secondary, alternate formation appears in vegetation patterns featuring pines and heaths.

A final point, then, is the conception of the Pine Barrens as a pattern, albeit a pattern broken by local discontinuities of soil and disturbance. Much current research on vegetation seeks to interrelate communities along major gradients of environment; such research will not be easy in the Pine Barrens but should be explored. Efforts at conservation are not adequately served by preserving individual pieces that represent types. These preserves, although valuable to save, may be difficult to relate to one another in research, and some of their species may be vulnerable to extinction as isolated small populations. Conservation should seek the preservation of landscapes of communities interrelated by topography and soil gradients, movement of water and soil nutrients, and dispersal of plant and animal populations. The Pine Barrens should be investigated, interpreted, and preserved (McCormick, 1970) as a landscape pattern.

SUMMARY

The vegetation of the Pine Barrens is distinguished by its strong differentiation of plant communities in an area of low relief and by the widespread occurrence of dry pine and heath communities in a humid, forest climate. Major features of the pattern relate to three groups of environmental factors, i.e., a soil moisture gradient (swamp forest to dry pine–oak forest), soil texture and nutrient relations (oak forest through oak–pine and pine–oak forest to the dwarf Pine Plains), and disturbance. Occurrence of pine–oak forests and dwarf pine plains in a deciduous forest climate probably results from: (a) sandy soils with low water- and nutrient-holding capacity that (b) subject the vegetation to periodic drought, and consequently to frequent fire; and (c) permit nutrient loss from the soil to low levels that support regrowth of (d) pine and shrub communities susceptible to another fire. The dwarf Pine Plains are interpreted as a soil-determined climax representing these interactions at their extreme for the area. Because of the importance of heaths, the prevalent communities of the Pine Barrens are pine and pine–oak heaths, and the dwarf pine plains are heathlands. Some relationships to other heathlands and heath forests are summarized; these communities mostly occur on infertile soils in relatively humid climates, are dominated by pines and/or heaths (and other groups in the southern hemisphere), and are subject to fire.

ACKNOWLEDGMENTS

Research was supported by a grant from the National Science Foundation. I thank R. T. T. Forman, S. Little, P. L. Marks, L. S. Olsvig, and F. C. Schlauch for commenting on the manuscript.

REFERENCES

Andresen, J. W. (1959). A study of pseudo-nanism in *Pinus rigida* Mill. *Ecol. Monogr.* **29**, 309–332.

Ballester, A., Albo, J. M., and Vieitez, E. (1977). The allelopathic potential of *Erica scoparia* L. *Oecologia (Berlin)* **30**, 55–61.

Brian, P. W. (1949). The production of antibiotics by micro-organisms in relation to biological equilibrium in soil. *Symp. Soc. Exp. Biol.* **3**, 357–372.

Buell, M. F., and Cantlon, J. E. (1950). A study of two communities of the New Jersey Pine Barrens and a comparison of methods. *Ecology* **31**, 567–586.

Cain, S. A. (1930). An ecological study of the heath balds of the Great Smoky Mountains. *Butler Univ. Bot. Stud.* **1**, 176–208.

Christensen, N. L. (1979). Shrublands of the southeastern United States. *In* "Heathlands and Related Shrublands" (R. L. Specht, ed.), Elsevier, Amsterdam. (in press).

Clements, F. E. (1936). Nature and structure of the climax. *J. Ecol.* **24**, 252–284.

Conard, H. S. (1935). The plant associations of central Long Island. *Am. Midl. Nat.* **16**, 433–516.

Curtis, J. T. (1959). "The Vegetation of Wisconsin: An Ordination of Plant Communities." Univ. of Wisconsin Press, Madison.

Damman, A. W. H. (1971). Effect of vegetation changes on the fertility of a Newfoundland forest site. *Ecol. Monogr.* **41**, 253–270.

Ellenberg, H. (1963). Vegetation Mitteleuropas mit den Alpen in kausaler, dynamischer and historischer Sicht. *In* Walter, H. "Einführung in die Phytologie," Vol. 4, Part 2. Ulmer, Stuttgart.

Fahey, T. J. (1976). The vegetation of a heath bald in Maine. *Bull. Torrey Bot. Club* **103**, 23–29.

Foster, N. W., and Morrison, I. K. (1976). Distribution and cycling of nutrients in a natural *Pinus banksiana* ecosystem. *Ecology* **57**, 110–120.

Franklin, J. F., and Dyrness, C. T. (1969). Vegetation of Oregon and Washington. *U.S. For. Serv., Res. Pap.* PNW-80, 1–216.

Gimingham, C. H. (1961). North European heath communities: A "network of variation." *J. Ecol.* **49**, 655–694.

Gimingham, C. H. (1969). The interpretation of variation in north-European dwarf-shrub heath communities. *Vegetatio* **17**, 89–108.

Gimingham, C. H. (1972). "Ecology of Heathlands." Chapman & Hall, London.

Good, R. E., and Good, N. F. (1975). Growth characteristics of two populations of *Pinus rigida* Mill. from the Pine Barrens of New Jersey. *Ecology* **56**, 1215–1220.

Graebner, P. (1901). Die Heide Norddeutschlands. *Vegetation Erde* **5**, 1–320.

Harley, J. L. (1952). Associations between microorganisms and higher plants (mycorrhiza). *Annu. Rev. Microbiol.* **6**, 367–386.

Harshberger, J. W. (1911). Phytogeographic Survey of North America. *Vegetation Erde* **13**, 1–790.

Harshberger, J. W. (1916). "The Vegetation of the New Jersey Pine Barrens: An Ecologic Investigation." Christopher Sower, Philadelphia, Pennsylvania.

Harshberger, J. W. (1918). American heaths and pine heaths. *Mem. Brooklyn Bot. Garden* **1**, 175–186.

Heusser, C. J. (1960). Late-Pleistocene environments of North Pacific North America. *Am. Geogr. Soc. Spec. Publ.* **35**, 1–308.

Jenny, H., Arkley, R. J., and Schultz, A. M. (1969). The pygmy forest-podsol ecosystem and its dune associates of the Mendocino coast. *Madroño* **20**, 60–74.

Klötzli, F. (1975). Ökologishe Besonderheiten Pinus-reicher Waldgesellschaften. *Schweiz. Z. Forstw.* **126**, 672–710.

Krausch, H-D. (1969). Über die Bezeichnung "Heide" und ihre Verwendung in der Vegetationskunde. *Mitt. Flor-Soz. Arbeitsgem., Rinteln* **14**, 435–457.

Laessle, A. M. (1958). The origin and successional relationships of sandhill vegetation and sand-pine scrub. *Ecol. Monogr.* **28**, 361–387.

Ledig, F. T., and Fryer, J. H. (1972). A pocket of variability in *Pinus rigida*. *Evolution* **26**, 259–266.

Little, S. (1950). Ecology and silviculture in the white cedar and associated hardwoods in southern New Jersey. *Yale Univ. Sch. For. Bull.* **56**, 1–103.

Little, S. (1951). Observations on the minor vegetation of the Pine Barren swamps in southern New Jersey. *Bull. Torrey Bot. Club* **78**, 153–160.

Little, S. (1979). The Pine Barrens of New Jersey. *In* "Heathlands and Related Shrublands" (R. L. Specht, ed.). Elsevier, Amsterdam. In press.

Lutz, H. J. (1934). Ecological relations in the pitch pine plains of southern New Jersey. *Yale Univ. Sch. For. Bull.* **38**, 1–80.

McCormick, J. (1970). The Pine Barrens: A preliminary ecological inventory. *N.J. State Mus., Rep. Res.* **2**, 1–103.

McCormick, J., and Buell, M. F. (1968). The Plains: Pygmy forests of the New Jersey Pine Barrens, a review and annotated bibliography. *Bull. N.J. Acad. Sci.* **13**, 20–34.

McCormick, J., and Jones, L. (1973). The Pine Barrens: Vegetation geography. *N.J. State Mus., Res. Rep.* **3**, 1–71.

McIntosh, R. P. (1959). Presence and cover in pine-oak stands of the Shawangunk Mountains, New York. *Ecology* **40**, 482–485.

McMillan, C. (1956). The edaphic restriction of *Cupressus* and *Pinus* in the Coast Ranges of central California. *Ecol. Monogr.* **26**, 177–212.

Marks, P. L., and Harcombe, P. A. (1975). Community diversity of coastal plain forests in southern east Texas. *Ecology* **56**, 1004–1008.

Monk, C. D. (1966). An ecological significance of evergreenness. *Ecology* **47**, 504–505.

Mutch, R. W. (1970). Wildland fires and ecosystems—a hypothesis. *Ecology* **51**, 1046–1051.

Niering, W. A. (1953). The past and present vegetation of High Point State Park, New Jersey. *Ecol. Monogr.* **23**, 127–148.

Osvald, H. (1954). The vegetation of Argyle Heath in southern Nova Scotia. *Nytt Mag. Bot.* **3**, 171–182.

Platt, R. B. (1951). An ecological study of the mid-Applachian shale barrens and of the plants endemic to them. *Ecol. Monogr.* **21**, 269–300.

Quarterman, E. (1950a). Ecology of cedar glades. I. Distribution of glade flora in Tennessee. *Bull. Torrey Bot. Club* **77**, 1–9.

Quarterman, E. (1950b). Major plant communities of Tennessee cedar glades. *Ecology* **31**, 234–254.

Robichaud, B., and Buell, M. F. (1973). "Vegetation of New Jersey: A Study of Landscape Diversity." Rutgers Univ. Press, New Brunswick, New Jersey.

Specht, R. L., ed. (1979). "Heathlands and Related Shrublands." Elsevier, Amsterdam. In press.

Stone, W. (1911). The plants of southern New Jersey with a special reference to the flora of the Pine Barrens and the geographic distribution of the species. *N.J. State Mus., Annu. Rep.* 1910, pp. 23–828.

Strang, R. M. (1970). The ecology of the rocky heathlands of western Nova Scotia. *Proc. Tall Timbers Fire Ecol. Conf.* **10**, 287–292.

Vogl, R. J. (1970). Fire and the northern Wisconsin pine barrens. *Proc. Tall Timbers Fire Ecol. Conf.* **10**, 175–209.

Vogl, R. J. (1973). Ecology of knobcone pine in the Santa Ana Mountains, California. *Ecol. Monogr.* **43**, 125–143.

Vogl, R. J., and Schorr, P. K. (1972). Fire and manzanita chaparral in the San Jacinto Mountains, California. *Ecology* **53**, 1179–1188.

Vogl, R. J., White, K. L., Armstrong, W. P., and Cole, K. L. (1977). The closed-cone pines and cypress. *In* "Terrestrial Vegetation of California" (M. G. Barbour and J. Major, eds.), pp. 295–358. Wiley, New York.

Walter, H. (1968). "Die Vegetation der Erde in öko-physiologischer Betrachtung. II: Die gemässigten und arktischen Zonen." Fischer, Jena.

Walter, H. (1973). "Vegetation of the Earth in Relation to Climate and the Eco-Physiological Conditions." Springer-Verlag, Berlin and New York.

Warming, E. (1909). "Oecology of Plants: An Introduction to the Study of Plant-Communities." Oxford Univ. Press, London.

Wells, B. W., and Shunk, I. V. (1931). The vegetation and habitat factors of the coarser sands of the North Carolina coastal plain: An ecological study. *Ecol. Monogr.* **1**, 465–521.

Westman, W. E. (1975). Edaphic climax pattern of the pygmy forest region of California. *Ecol. Monogr.* **45**, 109–135.

Westman, W. E., and Whittaker, R. H. (1975). The pygmy forest region of northern California: Studies on biomass and primary productivity. *J. Ecol.* **63**, 493–520.

Whittaker, R. H. (1956). Vegetation of the Great Smoky Mountains. *Ecol. Monogr.* **26**, 1–80.

Whittaker, R. H. (1960). The vegetation of the Siskiyou Mountains, Oregon and California. *Ecol. Monogr.* **30**, 279–338.

Whittaker, R. H. (1963). Net production of heath balds and forest heaths in the Great Smoky Mountains. *Ecology* **44**, 176–182.

Whittaker, R. H. (1972). Evolution and measurement of species diversity. *Taxon* **21**, 213–251.

Whittaker, R. H. (1979). Appalachian balds and other North American heaths. *In* "Heathlands and Related Shrublands" (R. L. Specht, ed.), Elsevier, Amsterdam. (in press).

Whittaker, R. H., and Woodwell, G. M. (1968). Dimension and production relations of trees and shrubs in the Brookhaven Forest, New York. *J. Ecol.* **56**, 1–25.

Whittaker, R. H., and Woodwell, G. M. (1969). Structure, production and diversity of the oak-pine forest at Brookhaven, New York. *J. Ecol.* **57**, 155–174.

Woodwell, G. M., and Rebuck, A. L. (1967). Effects of chronic gamma radiation on the structure and diversity of an oak-pine forest. *Ecol. Monogr.* **37**, 53–69.

Woodwell, G. M., and Whittaker, R. H. (1968). Primary production and the cation budget of the Brookhaven forest. *In* "Symposium on Primary Productivity and Mineral Cycling in Natural Ecosystems" (H. E. Young, ed.), pp. 151–166. Univ. of Maine Press, Orono.

Woodwell, G. M., Whittaker, R. H., and Houghton, R. A. (1975). Nutrient concentrations in plants in the Brookhaven oak-pine forest. *Ecology* **56**, 318–332.

19

Leaky Ecosystems: Nutrient Fluxes and Succession in the Pine Barrens Vegetation

GEORGE M. WOODWELL

INTRODUCTION

The dominant body of theory in ecology is centered on evolution and succession. The theory holds that terrestrial successions are an evolutionary product, and progress from disturbance through a series of well-defined developmental stages toward a climax vegetation that is more nearly stable than any of the earlier stages. This segment of the theory has become enriched in recent years with hypotheses that describe additional changes with succession, such as a putative increase in the diversity as well as the complexity of trophic structure (Margalef, 1963, 1968; Odum, 1969). Basic changes also are expected in the metabolism and nutrient balances of the communities as succession progresses. At climax total respiration is expected to equal gross production, and this relationship is thought to set a limit on the size of the biomass (Woodwell and Whittaker, 1968). The changes extend to include the fluxes in nutrients; as succession progresses toward midstage, nutrients accumulate within the rapidly developing biota, and losses to the groundwater are thought to be low. In late succession losses from an ecosystem are expected to approach inputs and at climax the two should be equal. At this point a large fraction of the total inventory of nutrients available on any site is expected to be recycled within the system (Bormann and Likens, 1967; Woodwell, 1970).

The usefulness of the basic theory has been questioned in recent years. The challenges have been aimed especially at textbook formulations of the theory (Drury and Nisbet, 1971) and have been based heavily on the difficulties of reconciling the theoretical requirement for progression toward stability with the reality that disturbances such as fire play a major role in many vegetations (Botkin and Sobel, 1975) and prevent the type of century-to-century stability that the simpler formulations of theory seem to demand. The forests of the Boundary Waters Canoe Area of northern Minnesota, for instance, are subject to devastating fires with a frequency ranging from decades to centuries, and the burning results in the establishment of a mosaic of successional vegetations (Heinselman, 1973). The jack pine (*Pinus banksiana*) stands of this area are dependent on periodic burning. In the coastal plain of the southeastern United States, almost annual burning is necessary to maintain the savanna vegetation for which the coastal plain is well known (Braun, 1950). The jack pine stands and the savannas are adapted to fire, and are themselves "stable" in the broader context of ecologists' interpretations of stability, although apparently outside the simplest formulations of current theory (Drury and Nisbet, 1971).

Similarly, the vegetation of the northward extension of the coastal plain into New Jersey, Long Island, and southern and eastern New England has been subject to periodic burning, to which it exhibits clear adaptation. The Pine Barrens, developed on unglaciated Tertiary age deposits in New Jersey and on Wisconsin age glacial deposits in New York, are part of this coastal plain complex, maintained by periodic fires and apparently adapted to them (Whittaker, Chapter 18, this volume). In this chapter I examine certain aspects of the nutrient budgets of successional communities of this vegetation and show how our experience of recent years affects the still-evolving theory of ecology.

The uncertainties in the theory hinge heavily on the usefulness of two concepts: first, the notion of the community as a product of evolution with an array of species that are accommodated to one another; second, of succession as developmental change toward stability and progressively better integrated communities. These two concepts are sufficiently elusive that they probably never will be defined in any generally acceptable way. Nonetheless, recent research on nutrient cycling in the pine barrens vegetation of Long Island has yielded some interesting insights that tend to strengthen certain segments of the general theory and has offered useful new insight into the relationships between vegetation, nutrients, and groundwater quality.

THE NUTRIENT BUDGET

The concept of community appears to have been strengthened somewhat by the analyses of the nutrient composition of the Brookhaven oak–pine forest offered by Woodwell *et al*. (1975). These authors suggested that the pool of nutrients available in support of the biota of any site might be divided, either similarly or differentially among the various species of the community. If the pool were divided similarly, the distribution of nutrients on a species-by-species basis would approach the average distribution for the community as a whole. If differentially distributed, the nutrient contents of the species would differ appreciably from the average for the community. The latter circumstance was shown to occur in the late successional oak–pine forest (Fig. 1). While this distribution of nutrients does not prove the existence of a closely integrated community in which the nutrient inventory is apportioned differentially by

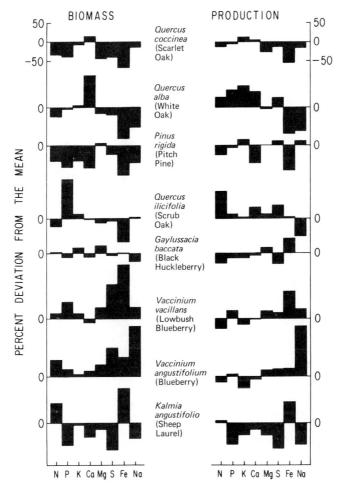

Fig. 1. Average nutrient concentrations in total standing crop (biomass) and in net primary production in the Brookhaven oak–pine (*Quercus–Pinus*) forest, New York expressed as a percent deviation from the average for each element. The three species at the top are trees, and the remainder are shrubs. (Woodwell *et al.,* 1975).

evolutionary design, the pattern is consistent with such a design and gives further strength to the theory that suggests that the nutrient budget of a community or an ecosystem is as much a product of evolution as other characteristics of the community.

The problems surrounding the pattern of nutrient cycling along succession are even more elusive because of the difficulty in stating a simple, general theory of succession. We can avoid, at least momentarily, the more complicated aspects of the problem simply by asking what we observe along seres (sequences of stages in succession). What are the effects of the various ecosystems of a sere on nutrient fluxes into the groundwater? To what extent are these systems net sources or sinks for nutrients? This type of investigation is undertaken in a simple way, based on what is measurable and without special concern for the formation or decay of minerals in the soil.

RECENT RESEARCH ON NUTRIENT CYCLING

We are aided in our examination of this set of questions by another series of studies of the Long Island vegetation (Woodwell *et al.*, 1974, 1978). In this study my colleagues and I, over the course of more than a year, examined the quality of both the groundwater and the percolate under the plant communities of the agriculture-to-forest sere of Central Long Island. This sere normally follows the sequence of plant communities that is similar to those described for other segments of the Eastern Deciduous Forest (Bard, 1952; Blizzard, 1931; Conard, 1935; Keever, 1950; Oosting, 1942; Woodwell and Oosting, 1968). The series of highly variable communities of herbaceous dicots and grasses is followed by communities in which broomsedge *Andropogon virginicus* takes an increasing role. In the absence of fire, the *Andropogon* is displaced by pine and later by oak–pine forest. Burning in late succession favors the oak–pine. Lack of fire favors oak–hickory on most upland sites. For this work we examined stands through the oak–pine stage only, including agriculture, one-year-old abandoned fields, the pine stage, and an oak–pine forest. The study shows an interesting pattern of losses of nutrients into the groundwater and helps clarify our understanding of certain aspects of nutrient cycling and theory in ecology.

The plant communities were located in the section of the Brookhaven National Laboratory site known as "the farm." The agricultural community was a herds–grass stand planted specifically for this purpose in timothy grass (*Phleum pratense*). The field was planted in July 1972 and was treated as a hayfield. It received an annual application of 1680 kilograms of 5–10–10 fertilizer per hectare (1500 pounds per acre). The old-field community was the community of herbaceous plants that developed following the abandonment of agriculture. During the period of this study the old-field community was in the first year following abandonment. The pine stand was a nearly pure stand of *Pinus rigida* that was about 25 years old in 1973, the year of the sampling reported in this paper. The oak–pine stand was a late successional forest dominated by white oak (*Quercus alba*), scarlet oak (*Q. coccinea*), and pitch pine (*Pinus rigida*). The stand was representative of oak–pine stands in central Long Island and had not been burned in recent years.

Data on nutrient losses from the communities along the sere were taken by sampling the percolate with porous-cup lysimeters that extended below the rooting zone and by sampling the upper few centimeters of the groundwater using three tube-type wells in each stand. Samples taken from the upper layers of the groundwater in wells had the same nutrient composition as the percolate from lysimeters. This relationship meant that samples taken from the groundwater alone were perfectly adequate for appraising the quality of the percolate.

Annual precipitation on the Brookhaven National Laboratory site normally is about

143 cm, and percolation is about 75 cm. The estimate of precipitation used here was based on a 15-year record at Brookhaven National Laboratory. The estimate of percolation was derived from a model designed specifically for the purpose by J. Ballard and checked against other models and with field studies of tritium flux as outlined in Woodwell *et al.* (1974).

Three wells were sampled monthly under each community of the sere. Nutrient analyses were carried out at Brookhaven National Laboratory. Variance among samples from the same plant community was small, usually less than 5% of the average.

RESULTS AND DISCUSSION

The total flux of ions to the groundwater along the sere was more than three times higher under the agricultural communities that had been fertilized than under the oak–pine forest (Fig. 2). The flux under the old field was elevated similarly, although it was less than one-half the annual flux of the agricultural field. The ionic content of leachate from the pine forest was slightly higher over the course of the year than that of the oak–pine forest (Fig. 2).

The most abundant anions were nitrate, sulfate, chloride, and bicarbonate. Under both forested communities the abundance of the nitrate ion was reduced to less than 1% of its flux in agriculture.

The most abundant cations (measured in milliequivalents) were calcium, magnesium, and sodium. The sodium flux varied least along the sere, although it was highest in agriculture, as were fluxes of most other ions (Fig. 2). The calcium and potassium fluxes declined systematically as succession progressed; the ammonium ion flux was lowest in the late successional forest but highest in the pine forest (Fig. 2). The magnesium flux of more than 200 mEq was highest in the agricultural field, less than 100 mEq in the oak forest, and about 50 mEq under both the old field and the pine forest.

The ionic inputs to these communities were from three atmospheric sources, namely, deposits including precipitation, impaction, and dry fallout, and, in the case of the agricultural community, residual fertilizer. Nitrogen, of course, may be fixed within the community. The total cation and anion fluxes from precipitation were about 260 and 220 mEq per square meter per year (Fig. 2).

The most abundant anions in precipitation were nitrate, sulfate, and chloride. The cations that dominated in precipitation were hydrogen and sodium, although calcium and magnesium also were abundant. Appraisals of dry fallout suggested that this source of ions was very small. The importance of the removal of particulate matter from the atmosphere through impaction on vegetation could not be appraised, nor could direct measurements be made of nutrient release from decay of primary soil minerals. The objective was a simple comparison of precipitation as an input with losses in percolation.

The largest quantities of nutrients were released into the groundwater by the agricultural field. The source of the nutrients was not simply precipitation; it probably in-

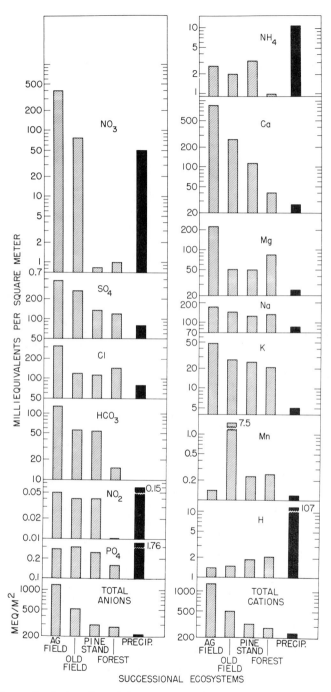

Fig. 2. Fluxes of major ions through the ecosystem of the agriculture-to-forest successional sequence of central Long Island, New York. Fluxes were determined as the product of the ionic concentrations in the upper few centimeters of groundwater and the amount of percolation. Variances are all low enough to be indistinguishable on the logarithmic vertical axis.

cluded both residual fertilizer and the decay of soil humus among other sources. The losses of ions in the percolate exceeded the ions in the precipitation by more than fourfold (Fig. 2) (Woodwell *et al.,* 1976).

If we examine the other end of the sere, the nutrient losses into the groundwater were the least of those observed in this work. In other studies the oak–pine forest has been shown to have a total respiration equal to about 80% of the gross production (Woodwell and Whittaker, 1968). Its net ecosystem production was at the time of this study about 450 g/m²/year.

Nonetheless, despite the accumulation of nutrients in net ecosystem production, the forest was a small net source of ions leached into the groundwater beyond those introduced in precipitation. The forest changed the ion flux appreciably: It absorbed or transformed nitrate and nitrite, absorbed phosphate, and was an appreciable source of sulfate, chloride, and bicarbonate. It was a powerful buffer for pH, a sink for the ammonium ion, and a source of potassium, sodium, calcium, magnesium, and manganese.

The data show clearly that the flux of nutrients into the groundwater is correlated with the vegetation. The highest fluxes occur under the earlier stages of succession, and the lowest fluxes occur under the later stages. While we may question whether the addition of fertilizer to the agricultural communities vitiates the value of the basic knowledge, the fact remains that the plant communities do not retain the nutrients against losses from leaching regardless of the source of the nutrients. The entire sere, in fact, is a net source of nutrients released into the groundwater in excess of the nutrients supplied in precipitation. From this standpoint the entire sere is leaky, but the earlier stages leak more than the later stages. By comparison with the agricultural field and the old field, both forest communities appear "tight."

Neither the sinks along the sere nor their sizes are revealed by this analysis, which shows only that the sinks for nutrients are inadequate to absorb the nutrients available at all stages of succession. The two sinks for nutrients within these ecosystems are the organic matter that accumulates, and chemical immobilization as a part of the soil–plant complex.

The plant and animal communities of the sere and the humus pools are subject to annual changes. The annual increment of change in the total organic pool has been called "net ecosystem production" (Woodwell and Whittaker, 1968). Net ecosystem production is the increment of net primary production that accumulates from one year to the next. It is positive throughout most of the sere. As communities mature consumer populations and organisms of decay become more abundant, and net ecosystem production drops toward zero, a point that is reached at maturity or climax. Net ecosystem production occasionally may become negative when disturbance reduces the organic pool, when net primary production decreases for whatever reason, or when the total respiration of the ecosystem is increased without a parallel increase in net primary production. Vitousek and Reiners (1975) and Vitousek (1977) have drawn on data from New Hampshire forests to suggest the pattern of net ecosystem production after disturbance of a forest. They suggest that the flux of nutrients through the communities of the sere will be dominated by the flow of carbon into net ecosystem production, and that the rapidly growing communities of the sere during the period of rapid successional development will have an appreciable sink for nutrients and will not lose nutrients. As maturity approaches and the net ecosystem production sink diminishes, the communities should appear leakier. The hypothesis is attractive. Can it be tested with these data?

The measurement of net ecosystem production is difficult and detailed data are not available for the entire sere. However, the magnitude of the requirement for ions in support of net primary production in the oak–pine forest can be calculated from data published previously (Whittaker and Woodwell, 1969). The net production along the sere is variable but is commonly lower throughout the earlier stages than that of the oak–pine forest (Woodwell *et al.*, 1978; Woodwell and Oosting, 1965). The annual flux of major ions into the net production is shown in Table I. The total is, of course, large in proportion to the losses of nutrients from the oak–pine forest (Fig. 2). Some of the total is recycled. Some is stored in net ecosystem production. The storage in net ecosystem production probably does not exceed 50% of the net primary production at any point along the sere. Those carbon compounds, moreover, that are accumulated in wood and humus are lower in nutrients than the net primary production. Unfortunately, direct measurements are not available, but the net ecosystem production sink for nutrients is probably substantially less than 50% of the pool held within the net primary production of the oak–pine forest, the most productive community of the sere. This sink is clearly not large in proportion to the nutrients available in the earlier stages of the sere. Whether it dominates the fluxes through later stages remains to be shown.

The chemical transformations in soils along the sere also play a large role in controlling nutrient fluxes. Phosphorus, for instance, is immobilized to a large extent in acid mineral soils and does not move in appreciable quantities into the groundwater under any of the communities of the sere (Fig. 2). Nitrogen is subject to an array of complex microbial transformations in soils, including both fixation and release of molecular N. As humus accumulates along the sere the number and intensity of the exchanges of nutrients that are possible increase, as does the diversity of the number of responses within the plant community to additions of nutrients. These factors, as well as the flux into net ecosystem production, contribute to the apparent tightness of the later successional stages.

The observations offered here are consistent with the theory, at least in the broad context. As succession progresses from agriculture through forest, the losses of nutrients into the groundwater are diminished. The sere develops towards a stage at which

TABLE I   Major Elements in the Net Primary Production of the Oak–Pine Forest of Central Long Island, New York, and the Quantity of Selected Ions to Supply These Elements Annually.[a]

	NO_3^-	PO_4^{3-}	K^+	Ca^{2+}	Mg^{2+}	SO_4^{2-}	Na^+
Ions to supply NPP annually ($mEq/m^2/yr$)	470	84	117	242	88	99.5	5.6

[a] The imbalance indicated between cations and anions is probably corrected by NH_4^+ and H^+.

inputs must approximate outputs. Sources of nutrients include not only those in precipitation but also nutrients in dry fallout, impaction, and retention of small particles in
air on plant parts, and the decay of primary minerals, not considered here.

The series of changes toward equilibrium, however, requires neither succession nor
biological evolution. It would be produced by the mechanisms of leaching without the
complexities of life. If we introduce life, the same processes apply, that is, nutrients that
are sufficiently mobile to be lost by leaching are lost early in succession. Those that are
retained by whatever method, remain. Part of the theory obviously is a tautology; the
later stages of succession are more nearly stable because the changes that were possible
occurred earlier in the succession. Although the tautology does not diminish the usefulness of the concept, it does tend to trick us occasionally in our analyses of ecosystems. We must remember that the conservation of nutrients in ecosystems is not only
the result of a series of evolutionary developments as we assume it to be, but also the
product of differential rates of leaching. Rates of leaching are certain to be higher
immediately after any disturbance and to diminish thereafter. To the extent that a
disturbance causes a loss of the standing crop of organic matter, we obviously can
expect mobilization and loss of some fraction of the nutrient pool, as Vitousek and
Reiners (1975) and Vitousek (1977) suggest. Repeated burning of the Pine Barrens
probably causes such losses, although direct measurements are very difficult.

We can infer some of the changes in flux for this vegetation after burning by
examining the nutrient content of plants of the impoverished communities that develop
following severe and repeated fires (Woodwell and Whittaker, 1967). The data are
crude, but a stand of *Pinus rigida* and scrub oak, *Quercus ilicifolia,* that had a standing
crop equal to that of the late successional oak–pine forest would have a cation content
of about three-fifths that of the oak–pine. The actual standing crop of organic matter of
such stands seldom approaches 50% that of the later-stage communities, and the
nutrient pool held within the impoverished stage is proportionally less. The cause of the
impoverishment is not a single factor, but rather, the combination of fire and nutrient
impoverishment.

The theory of ecology takes no abrupt turn as a result of these recent considerations
of the cycling of nutrients. The concept of community is intact, if not strengthened, by
the observation that nutrients are not distributed equitably among species, but rather,
that the species appear to have divided the nutrient pool differentially. This division, of
course, is what would be expected if nutrients were both in short supply and a cause of
evolutionary divergence among species. We have not shown, of course, that the
divergence among species is complementary, only that the species differ in nutrient
content. The concept of succession as progressive and developmental is strengthened
by the observation that the earlier stages are leaky with respect to nutrients and the later
stages are tight. All stages, of course, were shown to be net sources of most nutrient
ions over the input in precipitation. The pattern of change in flux with succession,
however, is also consistent with what would be expected from leaching following any
disturbance in the absence of a specially adapted system for absorbing nutrients, such
as that suggested for the New England forest by Marks and Bormann (1972). The
evidence presented here shows that no such system exists for the agriculture-to-forest

sere. The evidence also suggests that the concept of net ecosystem production as a major sink for nutrients advanced by Vitousek and Reiners (1975) and Vitousek (1977) is of limited importance for controlling nutrient fluxes to the groundwater in these ecosystems. Other factors, including the chemistry of soils, are of equal and occasionally greater importance. Nonetheless, the usefulness of the basic theory of succession as developmental and augmentive seems clear enough.

The reality of regression in the structure of the vegetation is also apparent in the Pine Barrens. Regression seems to be caused most commonly by severe or repeated burning. The severe burning results in a regression toward dwarfed trees, a scrub oak (*Quercus ilicifolia*) stand, or a blueberry (*Vaccinium*) community. Such communities are indeed impoverished, both in flora and in nutrients, and their development follows a pattern quite apart from the developmental changes associated with succession. The decision of Clements (1928) to consider such circumstances as separate from succession, no matter how common they may be, helps to clarify the basic principles and serves us well in the present attempt to sort the factors controlling nutrient fluxes in nature.

One of the most attractive aspects of research in the Pine Barrens is that, in this well-studied, diminutive, impoverished vegetation, one can find a diversity of opportunities for testing basic concepts in ecology against the facts of nature.

SUMMARY

Evolution and succession are the core of the theory of ecology. Data from a study of an agriculture-to-forest successional sequence of central Long Island, New York have shown that the theory of succession as progressive, developmental change is correct and useful. We must avoid, however, the circularity of thinking that all changes along succession are biotic changes; some may be simply responses to leaching over time. During the earlier stages of succession nutrients were shown to be lost at a high rate; during the later stages nutrients also are released, but at a lower rate. The quality of the groundwater follows this pattern, i.e., higher nutrient content under leakier ecosystems. Fire deflects the succession toward various stages of impoverishment that probably also are leaky, as are the earlier stages of the agriculture-to-forest sequence.

REFERENCES

Bard, G. E. (1952). Secondary succession on the Piedmont of New Jersey. *Ecol. Monogr.* **22**, 195–215.
Blizzard, A. W. (1931). Plant sociology and vegetational change on High Hill, Long Island, N.Y. *Ecology* **12**, 208–231.
Bormann, F. H., and Likens, G. E. (1967). Nutrient cycling. *Science* **155**, 424–429.
Botkin, D. B., and Sobel, M. J. (1975). Stability in time-varying ecosystems. *Am. Nat.* **109**, 625–646.
Braun, E. L. (1950). "Deciduous Forests of Eastern North America." Blakiston, Philadelphia, Pennsylvania.
Clements, F. E. (1928). "Plant Succession and Indicators." H. W. Wilson Co., New York.

Conard, H. S. (1935). The plant associations of central Long Island. *Am. Midl. Nat.* **16**, 433–516.

Drury, W. H., and Nisbet, I. C. T. (1971). Inter-relations between developmental models in geomorphology, plant ecology, and animal ecology. *Gen. Syst.* **16**, 57–68.

Heinselman, M. L. (1973). Fire in the virgin forests of the Boundary Waters Canoe Area, Minnesota. *J. Quat. Res.* **3**, 329–382.

Keever, C. (1950). Causes of succession on old fields of the Piedmont, North Carolina. *Ecol. Monogr.* **20**, 229–250.

Margalef, R. (1963). On certain unifying principles in ecology. *Am. Nat.* **97**, 357–374.

Margalef, R. (1968). ''Perspectives in Ecological Theory.'' Univ. of Chicago Press, Chicago, Illinois.

Marks, P., and Bormann, F. H. (1972). Revegetation following forest cutting; Mechanisms for return to steady-state nutrient cycling. *Science* **176**, 914–915.

Odum, E. P. (1969). The strategy of ecosystem development. *Science* **164**, 262–270.

Oosting, H. J. (1942). An ecological analysis of the plant communities of Piedmont, North Carolina. *Am. Midl. Nat.* **28**, 1–126.

Vitousek, P. M. (1977). The regulation of element concentrations in mountain streams in the Northeastern United States. *Ecol. Monogr.* **47**, 65–87.

Vitousek, P. M., and Reiners, W. A. (1975). Ecosystem succession and nutrient retention: A hypothesis. *BioScience* **25**, 376–381.

Whittaker, R. H., and Woodwell, G. M. (1969). Structure, production and diversity of an oak–pine forest at Brookhaven, N.Y. *J. Ecol.* **57**, 155–174.

Woodwell, G. M. (1970). Effects of pollution on the structure and physiology of ecosystems. *Science* **168**, 429–433.

Woodwell, G. M., and Oosting, J. K. (1965). Effects of chronic gamma irradiation on the development of old field communities. *Radiat. Bot.* **5**, 205–222.

Woodwell, G. M., and Whittaker, R. H. (1967). Primary production and the cation budget of the Brookhaven Forest. *In* ''Primary Productivity and Mineral Cycling in Natural Systems'' (H. E. Young, ed.), Univ. of Maine, Orono.

Woodwell, G. M., and Whittaker, R. H. (1968). Primary production in terrestrial ecosystems. *Am. Zool.* **8**, 19–30.

Woodwell, G. M., Ballard, J. T., Small, M. M., Pecan, E. V., Clinton, J., Wetzel, R., Gorman, F., and Hennessey, J. (1974). ''Experimental Eutrophication of Terrestrial and Aquatic Ecosystems,'' BNL 50420. Brookhaven Natl. Lab., Upton, New York.

Woodwell, G. M., Whittaker, R. H., and Houghton, R. A. (1975). Nutrient concentrations in plants in the Brookhaven oak–pine forest. *Ecology* **56**, 318–332.

Woodwell, G. M., Ballard, J. T., Clinton, J., and Pecan, E. V. (1976). ''Nutrients, Toxins, and Water in Terrestrial and Aquatic Ecosystems Treated with Sewage Plant Effluents,'' BNL 50513. Brookhaven Natl. Lab., Upton, New York.

Woodwell, G. M., Holt, B. R., and Flaccus, E. (1978). Unpublished data.

Part V

PLANTS

20

Pitch Pine (Pinus rigida Mill.): Ecology, Physiology, and Genetics

F. THOMAS LEDIG and SILAS LITTLE

Pitch pine, the characteristic species of the Pine Barrens, grows over a wide geographical range, from central Maine and central New York south to Virginia, southern Ohio, and in the mountains to northern Georgia. Outlying stands occur, such as in southern Quebec and southeastern Ontario. Pitch pine most commonly is found on the sandy soils of the New Jersey Pine Barrens and Cape Cod (Fowells, 1965). In the Barrens, pitch pine is by far the most common pine (Stone, 1911).

Because of the usually poor sites, and especially because of past damage from wildfires, pitch pine often is a scrubby tree. However, in areas where pitch pines started as seedlings or seedling sprouts and have not been damaged by wildfires, the trees often have good form and reach commercially valuable size (Fig. 1). On rare trees in such stands, the first branch stub may be 15 m (50 ft) or more above the ground and may have living branches at a still greater height. Logs from some old-growth trees were sawed into floor boards 60 cm (24 in) wide (Illick and Aughanbaugh, 1930).

HABITAT CONDITIONS

Although climatic conditions within the range of pitch pine vary appreciably (Little, 1959), throughout its range the species usually occurs on relatively infertile soils. Many of the northern stands are on sandy outwash plains of glacial origin. Pitch pine also occupies sandy or gravelly soils of alluvial or marine origin. In the highlands of northern New Jersey, southern New York, Pennsylvania, and south through the mountains, it occurs most commonly on steep slopes, ridges, and plateaus, where soils are shallow (Little, 1959).

Pitch pine usually grows on acid soils having leached A2 horizons. These soils now are included in such orders as entisols, ultisols, and spodosols. In one study of pitch pine in southern New Jersey, the pH of the A and B horizons varied between 3.5 and

347

PINE BARRENS

Fig. 1. An old stand of shortleaf and pitch pines in the Pine Barrens. Pitch pine, indicated with an arrow, may grow tall and straight if stems were started as seedlings and never were damaged by severe fires. The tree indicated has fewer branches along its trunk than the shortleaf pine beside which the man is standing.

5.1 (Lutz, 1934); in a study in northern New Jersey, it varied between 4 and 4.5 (Niering, 1953).

Pitch pine grows in a wide variety of moisture conditions. In the Pine Barrens, it occurs on excessively drained, well drained, imperfectly drained, poorly and very poorly drained sands and gravels, as well as on the muck soils of swamps. Even in the hilly regions, as in Pennsylvania, it occurs both on well or excessively drained slopes and in swamps (Illick and Aughanbaugh, 1930). The characteristics enabling the species to span such a broad moisture gradient are not understood.

At most of the sites where pitch pine is common, the soils are very low in nutrients. In the Pine Barrens, the nitrogen contents of A horizons may be 0.02–0.06% (Burns, 1952) and 0.02% or less in lower horizons (Lutz, 1934). The amount of exchangeable calcium in the A horizons may be 19–146 ppm, potassium 3–15 ppm, and phosphorus even less (Burns, 1952). Nevertheless, in pot culture the growth and productivity of pitch pine increase with fertilization (Ledig and Clark, 1977). It probably is restricted to relatively poor soils by competition from other species.

ASSOCIATED FLORA AND FAUNA

Trees and Shrubs

Pitch pine is a minor component or associate in twelve forest cover types of eastern North America, and in one type it occurs as pure stands of the predominant species (Society of American Foresters, 1954). Because of the wide range in latitude and site, many tree species have been found growing with pitch pine (Little, 1959). Trees and shrubs that grow with pitch pine in the Pine Barrens are described in chapters 13, 14, 15, 16, 18 and 21 of this volume.

Mammals and Birds

Deer (*Odocoileus virginianus*) browse on fresh sprouts and seedlings of pitch pine, particularly those <50 cm (20 in) tall (Little *et al.*, 1958b; Little and Somes, 1949). Cottontail rabbits (*Sylvilagus floridanus*) and meadow mice (*Microtus pennsylvanicus*) also feed on pitch pine seedlings (Illick and Aughanbaugh, 1930). While damage by deer, rabbits, and meadow mice occurs above ground and is easily visible to experienced observers, pine voles (*Pitymys pinetorum*) strip the bark from roots, and their damage often goes unnoticed. However, only an occasional seedling or sapling is stripped so completely that it dies from pine vole damage.

Pitch pine seed is eaten by many species of birds and rodents (Martin *et al.*, 1951; Little, 1959). Chickadees (chiefly *Parus carolinensis*), juncos (*Juncos hyemalis*), and quail (*Colinus virginianus*) may be among the more important birds in the Pine Barrens in their consumption of pine seeds. In areas where pitch pine has serotinous cones and a fire occurs which is hot enough to open these cones, chickadees often appear to feed on the pine seeds while the smoke still is rising. Mice, particularly the white-footed mouse (*Peromyscus leucopus*), feed heavily on pine seeds (Little *et al.*, 1958a). Squirrels shred pine cones in order to reach the seeds; in the Pine Barrens, they create piles of cone scales and cone axes on the ground under favorite branches. Seed predators apparently have created a selection pressure for fewer seeds in serotinous-coned pitch pine, as will be described later.

Fungi and Insects

Several fungi attack pitch pine, but usually none causes serious or extensive damage. Among these are gall rusts (especially *Cronartium quercuum*, *C. comptoniae*, and *C. fusiforme*), which may cause stem or branch swellings, needle casts or needle blights (*Ploioderma lethale*, etc.), pine needle rusts (*Coleosporium asterum*, *C. campanulae*, *C. helianthi*, etc.), and heart rots, chiefly caused by *Fomes pini* (Boyce,

1961; Hepting, 1971). Heart rot does not become important until stands are more than 75 years old.

Many insects feed on pitch pine. The most important are the tip moths (*Rhyacionia frustrana* and *R. rigidana*), the pitch pine looper (*Lambdina athasaria pellucidaria*), the sawflies (chiefly *Neodiprion lecontei, N. pratti paradoxicus, N. pinirigidae*), the southern pine beetle (*Dendroctonus frontalis*), the pine webworm (*Terralopha robustella*), and the pine needle miner (*Exoteleia pinifoliella*) (Craighead, 1950; Baker, 1972). However, damage from insects usually is not a serious problem, or if serious enough to kill a tree, the damage usually affects only scattered stems and not the entire stand.

LIFE HISTORY

Seeding Habits

Flowering and Fruiting

In the Pine Barrens, the male flowers of pitch pine become visible by about mid-April, and female flowers appear somewhat later. Over a three-year period, pollen shedding occurred during the third week of May (Little, 1941), but subsequent observations indicate a greater yearly variability. In rare years, pollen shedding starts in some Barrens stands in late April. Cones reach full size (about 4–8 cm) and mature 16 to 18 months later.

Seed Production

Vigorous, open-grown stems start bearing mature cones at an early age, i.e., sprouts when only three years old or rare seedlings when only four years old. Of 400 planted two-year-old seedlings, two bore a total of three mature cones at the end of their second growing season after planting (Andresen, 1957). However, mature cones usually are not borne on open-grown seedlings until they are 8 to 12 years old (Little, 1959).

Cone production varies greatly with the size of the tree and the characteristics of the crown. Overtopped trees bear few or no cones and intermediate trees a few, whereas the open-grown or dominant trees usually are prolific producers (Little, 1959). However, certain trees produce far more cones than other stems of similar size and crown in the same stand.

Good to excellent crops of cones occur at irregular intervals in southern New Jersey, often four to nine years apart. Poor crops occasionally are borne in two successive years, although a poor crop usually is followed by fair to excellent crops for one to three years (Little, 1959).

Seed Dissemination

Seed dissemination is variable, depending on the length of time after maturity that cones remain closed. There are two extremes of cone behavior: (1) on some trees the cones, like those of most conifers, open soon after maturity; and (2) on other trees the cones are so serotinous that they remain closed for many years, often until the heat of a fire opens them or until the trees have been cut. Cone behavior is believed to be an inherited characteristic, and will be discussed later.

Among the trees on which the cones open soon after maturing, seed dispersal starts by early November and ends in April in the Pine Barrens (Little, 1941). Most of the seeds fall during the first two months, with probably about 90% on the east side of the source, since open cones close during wet weather, and seed dispersal occurs mostly during fair weather when westerly winds predominate (Little, 1959).

Practically all dissemination is by wind, usually short distances, even though the seeds are equipped with large wings. Leeward of one stand, all natural reproduction in an abandoned field was within 91 m (Illick and Aughanbaugh, 1930). Rodents and birds are of minor importance as agents of seed distribution. Rodent hoards are responsible for some occasional dense clumps of seedlings (Little, 1959).

Seed Viability

In one study, the average number of seeds per cone was 74, of which 73% were sound, but the range in seeds per cone varied widely among trees, from 3–151 (Ledig and Fryer, 1974). Seed germination may average about 77%, but varies from 19–99% (U.S. Dep. Agriculture, 1948). The germinative capacity of seeds from serotinous cones declines somewhat with age, at least over the first four years after cones mature (Andresen, 1963).

Illick and Aughanbaugh (1930) report that seeds from trees less than eight years old usually are sterile. However, in the Pine Barrens a cutting test of 200 seeds from three-year-old sprouts showed 94% to be filled (Little, 1959), and 52% of the seeds in two cones from four-year-old seedlings germinated within nine days (Andresen, 1957).

Vegetative Reproduction

Pitch pine is outstanding among eastern conifers in its ability to survive injury. All its foliage may be killed by the heat of a fire, and still the crown will produce new needles. If 60–90 cm of the terminal shoot are killed, a new one often develops. If the entire stem is killed, sprouts frequently start at the base (Little, 1959). Deer may clip a seedling back to 3–5 cm above ground, and still it may live (Little *et al.*, 1958b).

Dormant buds, capable of active growth when properly stimulated, are the key to the recovery of pitch pines from injury. Thick bark, which provides a high degree of protection to the dormant buds and to the cambium, also is an important factor. Both pitch and shortleaf (*Pinus echinata*) pines have dormant buds along the trunk to an age of 60 years or more, but only in pitch pine do the buds at the base retain the potential for growth to such an age. Even in pitch and shortleaf pine seedlings that have not yet developed thick bark, the lowermost buds may be protected by a characteristic basal crook of the stem that brings the buds into or against mineral soil on upland sites (Fig. 2). Because such buds are insulated, they often survive fire and produce new shoots (Little and Somes, 1956; Stone and Stone, 1943, 1954).

Some pitch pine seedlings do not sprout after fires. These include (1) occasional

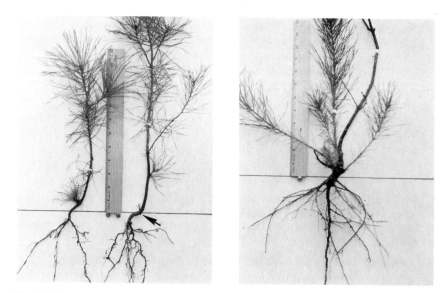

Fig. 2. Dormant basal buds enable many pitch pines to recover from fires that kill the stems. Of the two four-year-old seedlings shown on the left, one has a well developed basal crook. Note the bud (arrow) on the lower side of the stem opposite the short shoot; the bud was below the forest floor (indicated with a line). Right-hand view shows first-year sprouts from such buds. These sprouts are the second set; both the original seedling and the first set of sprouts were killed by fires. Rulers marked in inches (1 in. = 2.5 cm).

seedlings that never develop a basal crook, (2) seedlings that start on *Sphagnum* or the deep humus layer of poorly drained sites and where fire burns below the surface on which seedlings are established, and (3) seedlings too young to have well-developed basal crooks. Although some open-grown seedlings may develop crooks in their first year, shade-grown seedlings may take nine or ten years to develop crooks (Little and Somes, 1956; Little and Mergen, 1966).

Although the sprouting ability of pitch pine is an asset in enabling trees to survive fire or other injuries, it is a liability from the standpoint of wood production. Apparently, the form and growth rate of sprouts decrease markedly with increased age of the expanded root crown (stool) after an age of about 20 years. Where wildfires have occurred at frequent intervals, the stands often are composed mostly of slow-growing sprouts from old stools. In many other stands, the stems have been deformed by past fires, e.g., (1) trunks having many small branches, which developed to replace killed crowns (Fig. 3), (2) trunks having one or more crooks or forks where terminal shoots were killed, or (3) trees having flat tops where no new leader developed after the last one was killed (Little, 1959).

While this recovery is typical of pitch pine, at the same time an erroneous impression is created, namely, that the species never has good form. Actually, uninjured

Fig. 3.   Pitch pines recovering from a severe fire. A wildfire consumed the foliage and killed terminal and branch shoots on these pines, but three trees resprouted from the trunk. The center tree, having the largest crown, may develop a new leader shoot, but the right-hand tree probably will not form a new terminal shoot and its crown may develop a flat top.

stems of seedling or seedling–sprout origin may develop a form similar to shortleaf pine (Fig. 1) (Little, 1959), and straight stems are common in areas where fires are infrequent, such as Ohio (Ledig and Fryer, 1974).

Seedling Establishment and Growth

Establishment

Some pitch pine seeds may remain viable in the forest floor for a year, but evidence of longer viability has not been obtained. In one area, after a July wildfire had opened closed cones, most seeds germinated the following spring, although a few lay dormant until August and then germinated after rains broke a severe dry period (Little, 1959). In an area where 2400 seed spots were sown to pitch pine in late March 1955, delayed germination in the spring of 1956 provided as many as 1.4 seedlings per spot in some treatments (Little *et al.*, 1958a).

Pitch pine seeds are small, e.g., 117,600 per kilogram in one study (Ledig and Fryer, 1974). Because of the small amount of reserve food in the seed, seedlings can develop only a short taproot and hypocotyl, or stem, each about 3 cm long. Hence, for successful establishment of seedlings, adequate moisture must be present near the surface to sustain growth until a sufficiently long taproot can develop (Little, 1959).

Consequently, thick litters are quite unsuitable seedbeds, even on poorly drained sites. In one study, hardly any new seedlings were found in July on the thick litters of unburned sites, whereas on similar areas that had been burned by a severe September fire before seedfall, 16,500–56,300 new seedlings per hectare were found on very poorly to imperfectly drained sites, and 2200 per hectare were found on upland sites (Little and Moore, 1953). The best seedbed for natural establishment of seedlings on upland sites is either mineral soil or a filmlike layer of forest floor (Little and Moore, 1952) where seeds may be lightly covered (Little *et al.*, 1958a).

Droughts kill many pitch pine seedlings, especially those less than 2 years old. A summer drought in 1957 killed 81% of the seedlings from a 1956 direct seeding of plots on Lakewood and Lakehurst soils, while on comparable sites most seedlings that had started in 1955 survived (Little *et al.*, 1958a).

Early Growth

By the end of the first year, shaded seedlings on upland sites usually have attained a height of about 3 cm and produced a taproot 7–10 cm long with few laterals. In contrast, vigorous open-grown one-year seedlings on upland sites have stems 5–10 cm long (maximum of 13 cm), with correspondingly greater root systems. On the moister, poorly drained sites, open-grown one-year stems usually will be 7–15 cm, with a maximum of 20 cm (Little, 1959).

Pitch pine seedlings tend to grow rather slowly for the first three to five years, and then more rapidly. Between six and 17 years in age, some planted stands in Pennsylvania maintained an average height growth of 36–48 cm (Illick and Aughanbaugh, 1930). After a seed-tree cutting in a New Jersey Pine Barrens stand, the average height growth of dominant seedlings among the natural pitch pine seedlings was 46 and 67 cm, respectively, during the third and fourth growing seasons after cutting (Little and Somes, 1951a).

Deer browsing and hardwood competition reduce the growth rate of pitch pine. In one study, pine seedlings uninjured by deer grew 60–120 cm more during a five-year period than those whose leaders had been browsed two or more times (Little *et al.*, 1958b). In another study, cutting back hardwood sprouts twice resulted, after six years, in a 120-cm increase in the height growth of the largest pines (Little and Moore, 1952). Where pine seedlings and sprout hardwoods compete, browsing of the pines handicaps them, sometimes enough to increase the proportion of hardwoods in the next stand (Little and Somes, 1951b).

Sapling Stage to Maturity

Root Development

Root development of the older pitch pines varies with the site. On sandy, well-drained soils, the vertical roots of trees 10 cm and larger in diameter (breast high) may reach depths of 240–270 cm, but on heavier or wetter soils the root systems are more shallow. However, even where the water tables are <30 cm below the surface, the roots of pitch pine may reach depths of 90–150 cm if the soil is sandy. In these sites and in the swamps, pitch pine roots live and grow below the water table, with mycorrhizal fungi occurring on some of the submerged roots (McQuilkin, 1935).

Probably because pitch pine roots penetrate so deeply, the species is relatively windfirm. For example, in Maryland, Virginia pine (*Pinus virginiana*) was much more susceptible to windthrow than pitch pine (Fenton, 1955).

Growth, Yield, and Form

Pitch pine reaches a maximum age of about 200 years, a maximum diameter of 76 cm (30 in), and a maximum height of 30 m (100 ft) in Pennsylvania, but in closed stands is seldom more than 60 cm in diameter or 24 m tall (Illick and Aughanbaugh, 1930). Similar growth patterns occur in the New Jersey Pine Barrens: the tallest pitch pine encountered in the Barrens was 49 cm in diameter at breast height, 31 m tall, and 95 years old.

On the better sites, both in Pennsylvania and in the Pine Barrens, pitch pines of seedling origin and undamaged by wildfires maintain an average annual height growth of 30 cm or more until the trees are 50–60 years old. The rate of height growth then declines, and trees add little to their height after they are 90–100 years old. On the best sites, diameter growth is most rapid in young stands, sometimes being 3 cm in five years at 20 years of age or in eight to ten years at 90 years of age (Illick and Aughanbaugh, 1930; Little, unpublished observations).

Total volumes, especially of sawtimber, reach their maximum in relatively old stands. Fully stocked 90-year-old stands undamaged by wildfires yield 15,000–25,000 board feet per acre or about 270–350 m³ per hectare on the better sites (Illick and Aughanbaugh, 1930; Little, unpublished observations in New Jersey). However, because of sprout origin, low stocking, and wildfire damage, even some of the better stands of pitch pine in the pitch pine–scrub oak type of the Barrens produce only 38–50 m³ of pulpwood in 60 years (Little, 1959).

In closed stands of seedling origin that have not been damaged by fire, pitch pine self-prunes about as well as shortleaf pine. In addition, with increasing size, initial crooks in the stems are overgrown, so that large trees often appear straight and well formed (Fig. 1). However, typical areas of pitch pine have been burned repeatedly so that most of the stands are understocked and most of the trees have suffered fire injury. Consequently, the trees have crooks and either have retained low branches or have developed them from dormant buds along the trunk (Fig. 3).

The productivity of pitch pine is not equal to that of many other conifers. On

Evesboro or heavier soils in the Pine Barrens, loblolly pine (*Pinus taeda*) and white pine (*P. strobus*) outgrow pitch pine, as shown by plantations established in or prior to 1930 in the Lebanon, Green Bank, and Bass River State Forests. In one 29-year-old plantation, the dominant and codominant stems of loblolly pine were 4.9 m, or nearly 40% taller than similar stems of pitch pine (Little *et al.*, 1967). However, loblolly pine and white pine do not sprout after their stems are killed by fire, nor are they able to rebuild crowns after fires kill foliage or branches, so both are far more susceptible to wildfires than pitch and shortleaf pines.

Necessary Management Measures

Pitch pine is intolerant of shade. On swamp sites, it is less tolerant than Atlantic white cedar (*Chamaecyparis thyoides*), and on poorly drained or upland sites it is less tolerant than its common hardwood associates, blackgum (*Nyssa sylvatica*), red maple (*Acer rubrum*), and various oaks and hickories (Little, 1950; Little and Moore, 1949).

Because of its low tolerance of shade and its requirements of mineral soil for seed germination and seedling establishment, pitch pine can be maintained best by management in even-aged stands. Seedbed preparation and some control of competing hardwoods usually are needed to obtain the dominance of an adequate number of pitch pines. Specific measures vary with site, and those that have been successful in establishing seedling stands of pitch pine in the Pine Barrens are described in other publications (Little and Moore, 1950, 1953; Little, 1964).

PHYSIOLOGY

Vegetative Phenology and Shoot Growth

Shoot growth of fast-growing pitch pines in the Pine Barrens is polycyclic, i.e., a winter bud may contain two or three shoots, and under favorable growing conditions there may be a summer shoot (Tepper, 1963). Lateral buds occur at the end of each shoot, but on intermediate shoots these either may remain as buds or may elongate forming a partial whorl of small branches. A major whorl usually occurs only at the terminal shoot. Buds formed at the end of the spring growth may elongate in the same growing season under favorable conditions, resulting in a summer shoot and a second major whorl of branches (Tepper, 1963). Thus, a season's growth for pitch pine differs appreciably from that of such species as white pine, which normally has only one whorl of branches in a season's growth. In the Pine Barrens, the period of height growth for pitch pines that produce summer shoots is 3½–4 months, and 2½ for those that do not (Tepper, 1963). In a nursery study, trees that began growth early tended to cease growth early (Ledig *et al.*, 1976b).

Photosynthesis

The highest rates of net photosynthesis ever recorded for a conifer were observed in highly fertilized 38-day-old seedlings from the Pine Barrens (Ledig and Clark, 1977).

Average rate at 4000 foot candles (ft-c) and 30°C was 46 mg CO_2/hr/g leaf dry weight, and many individuals had substantially higher rates. Measurements of CO_2 exchange in crowns of mature trees in an open woodland indicated maximum rates of about 6.5 mg CO_2/hr/g leaf dry weight, averaged over the entire season from May to November (Botkin *et al.*, 1970). The latter rates suggest that pitch pine is a species of low productivity. The substantially lower rates in mature trees are only partially the product of environmental stress and largely the result of a decrease in photosynthesis with age. In pitch pine, as in most conifers, photosynthesis decreased rapidly during development (Ledig *et al.*, 1976a) as a result of several factors.

Pitch pine seedlings, grown at 2000 ft-c in growth chambers became light saturated at about 2000 ft-c (Ledig *et al.*, 1977), but such values are not absolute, depending on the depth of the seedling crown, temperature, osmotic potential of the leaves, and nutrient regime. The optimum temperature for photosynthesis in seedlings is surprisingly constant at about 25°C (e.g., Ledig *et al.*, 1977). As a result, growth in dry weight of seedlings at 26°/23°C day/night temperature regimes is substantially greater than that at 17°/11°C or 32°/29°C (Good and Good, 1976). The photosynthetic temperature optimum was affected little by light intensity or previous temperature (Ledig *et al.*, 1977).

Respiration

Respiration in pitch pine has been determined for above-ground and below-ground tissues and the amounts for tissue maintenance and tissue construction, or growth, have been distinguished (Ledig *et al.*, 1976a). Maintenance respiration produces the energy to maintain tissue integrity and function and is higher for the above-ground part (85% leaves) than for below ground in first-year seedlings, i.e., 1.15 and 0.29 mg CO_2/hr/g dry weight, respectively. Construction respiration, which provides the energy for tissue synthesis, also is higher in shoots than in roots, 0.47 and 0.19 mg CO_2 to produce each milligram dry weight of new tissue, respectively. However, under growth-chamber conditions, root respiration may expend substantial proportions of daily photosynthate, approaching 70% in six-month-old seedlings.

GENETICS

Genetic variation can be inferred from phenotype patterns observed in nature. Pitch pine is quite variable in growth, form, cone shape, and other characteristics (Ledig and Fryer, 1974). For example, in the Pine Plains it is a dwarf, less than 4 m (13 ft) in height, while only 35 km (22 mi) away it approaches its maximum stature of 30 m (100 ft) on a seasonally wet site near the Great Egg Harbor River. However, genetic effects are confounded with environmental effects. Propagation of clones, families, or populations side by side in uniform environments is necessary to substantiate patterns of genetic variation. Genetic variation can occur at several levels; i.e., among individuals within stands, among stands within regions, and among regions, perhaps as defined by physiography. Differences in wood properties, seed and cone characteristics, growth, reproductive age, isozymes, and DNA content have been related to variation within and among populations. Hybridization complicates variation patterns in pitch pine, and pitch pine hybrids have received special consideration for their potential role in forest management.

Wood Properties

While several southern pines exhibit geographical trends in wood properties such as wood specific gravity and tracheid (wood cell) length, in pitch pine trends are particularly well developed (Ledig *et al.*, 1975). Wood specific gravity adjusted to age 50 decreases from 0.53 in the southwestern corner of the species range to 0.42 at Bar Harbor, Maine in the northeast, and tracheid length decreases from 3.6 to 3.2 mm. These properties are related closely to climatic variables such as average annual snowfall. Pine Barren trees have wood specific gravity in the midpoint of the range, with values of 0.49, but short tracheids, with average length of 3.2 mm. The degree to which these phenotypic trends represent environmental modification or genetic clines (character gradients with respect to geographical or ecological factors) can be determined only by uniform garden plantings. However, breeding in other southern pines (*Pinus* subsect. *Australes* Loud.) has demonstrated that specific gravity is strongly inherited, suggesting that the geographical patterns in pitch pine in part represent genetic trends. Low specific gravity and short tracheids are not necessarily adaptive in northern populations, but may be the by-product of selection for short growing seasons.

Growth

Provenance (i.e., geographical seed source) and progeny testing have been relatively neglected in pitch pine, compared to more economically desirable pines, so comparisons of mature trees in uniform environments are not available. In a small test of four provenances replicated at Green Bank, New Jersey and Petersham, Massachusetts, two provenances from Burlington County, New Jersey outgrew provenances from Cape Cod, Massachusetts and Cornwall, New York (J. Karnig, personal communication). In a recent test, provenances originating throughout the range were grown for two years in the Connecticut State Nursery in the classical "uniform garden" study (Ledig *et al.*, 1976b). By the second year, all variations in height were attributable to differences among areas, and no differences among mother-tree families were observed within stands or between stands within areas. Height growth was related to latitude of origin, and even more closely to average maximum temperatures for April–May at the seed origin. The height of seedlings from the Pine Barrens averaged 52.9 cm, compared to a range of 36.5 cm for seedlings from Maine to 62.5 cm for those from Maryland. In a separate analysis of 15 provenances distributed at close intervals within the coastal plain from Cape Cod through Long Island to the Pine Barrens, second-year height was closely related to latitude of origin (Fig. 4), and even

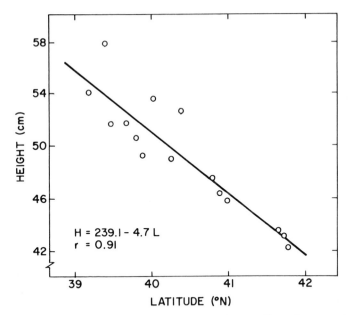

Fig. 4. Second-year height in Connecticut of pitch pine seedlings from populations in coastal Massachusetts, Long Island, and New Jersey as related to latitude of origin. Approximately 50 seedlings per population were measured. From Ledig *et al.* (1976b).

among nine provenances distributed over the narrow north–south range of the Barrens, seedling heights varied. Differences in height were accounted for partly by variation in the dates of growth cessation, with northern provenances tending to cease growth earlier in the summer than southern. Pitch pine is photoperiodically sensitive, and under short photoperiods seedlings from northern populations set bud earlier than seedlings from southern populations (Vaartaja, 1959).

Pine Plains and Pine Barrens

Nanism

The Pine Plains are areas of dwarf forest, covering perhaps 5000 ha (12,500 acres) of total area, in which trees characteristically are less than 3.5 m (12 ft) tall, and are surrounded completely by "tall" forest. Both Lutz (1934) and Andresen (1959) stressed the importance of fires that kill back the stems at about eight-year intervals in creating and maintaining the dwarf stature of the trees. Little and Somes (1964) mentioned coppice (sprout) aging and the intense competition within and between sprout clumps as important factors contributing to the slow growth of sprouts after fire. Seedlings of Plains origin reached heights of 1.4–2.0 m in seven years, so Little and Somes (1964) thought genetics was an unlikely factor in the dwarf characteristic of Plains pitch pines, particularly since the Plains trees must receive pollen from surrounding, relatively tall trees. However, 17 years after treatments to convert the existing sprout stand to seedlings of Plains origin, maximum height of pitch pine was only 4.3 m, compared to 5.5 m for white pines planted six years later in adjoining plots (Little, 1972). Recent data suggest that, in these plots, the pitch pine seedlings may at 50 years reach heights of only 10–11 m, possibly half the height of "normal" pitch pines.

In the uniform garden trial mentioned (p. 358), progeny of six trees from each of the two main Pine Plains areas, the East and West Plains, were compared to 101 progenies distributed among 11 Pine Barrens populations (Ledig *et al.*, 1976b). Barrens and Plains seedlings showed no difference after one growing season, but after two seasons the Plains seedlings on the average were 7.5% shorter than the Barrens seedlings (48.5 cm compared to 52.4 cm). Good and Good (1975) convincingly demonstrated the slower growth of Plains seedlings compared to Barrens seedlings in greenhouse, nursery, and phytotron trials continued for more than five years. Hence, genetics also is a factor in producing Plains-type pitch pine of short stature. Genetically dwarf shoots are known from somatic mutations induced in pitch pine by chronic gamma irradiation (Sparrow, 1966).

Reproductive Strategy

The proportions of growth in leaves, roots, and stems were similar for Barrens and Plains seedlings, but the effort devoted to reproduction was strikingly different (Good and Good, 1975). At 5½ years of age, 22 of 35 Plains trees bore female cones, as compared to only five of 33 Barrens trees. In uniform garden plantations located in Massachusetts and New Jersey, 38% of the Plains seedlings had produced female cones by four years of age (only two years after seedlings were transplanted from the nursery to the field), compared to only 4% of Pine Barrens seedlings (Table I). The number of cones per seedling was 1.9 for Pine Plains seedlings, compared to only 0.05 for the Pine Barrens. Differences in the proportion of trees which had entered the reproductive phase and in number of cones per tree were highly significant, and the relative performance of Plains and Barrens populations was unaffected by climatic differences among plantations.

One is tempted to interpret the differences in growth and reproductive strategy between Barrens and Plains in terms of r- and K-selection (e.g., Pianka, 1970). Historically, fires have been more frequent and have had more serious consequences for the vegetation in the Plains than in the Barrens (Lutz, 1934), so that resources (i.e., light, water, and nutrients or their common correlate, space) were frequently nonlimiting or underutilized. Nonlimiting resources favor selection for rapid rates of reproduction, or r-selection. However, the per capita resource requirement of Plains' trees is also lower than that of Barrens' trees (i.e., carrying capacity, K, is greater for Plains' trees) so the Barrens' population does not exemplify a K-strategy. Therefore, Plains' populations have higher darwinian fitness than Barrens' populations under all resource levels above those required to maintain a stable population. The success of tall forest in most areas of the Barrens lies in the response to limited resources. When population density is so high that per capita resources are below the level required to maintain a

TABLE I   Cone Production by Four-Year-Old Seedlings from Seed of Pine Barrens and Pine Plains Origin.[a]

| | Source of Population | | | | | |
| | Pine Barrens | | | Pine Plains | | |
Test site	Batsto	Great Egg Harbor River	Average	East Plains	West Plains	Average
A. Proportion of seedlings producing female cones in 1976 or earlier						
Clinton, Massachusetts	0.11	0	0.06	0.75	0.45	0.60
Myles Standish State Forest, Massachusetts	—	0	0	0.60	0.43	0.52
Lebanon State Forest, New Jersey	0.08	0	0.04	0.30	0.29	0.30
Average	0.09	0	0.03	0.55	0.39	0.47
B. Number of female cones per tree in 1976						
Clinton, Massachusetts	0.11	0	0.06	3.20	2.45	2.83
Myles Standish State Forest, Massachusetts	—	0	0	3.23	1.48	2.36
Lebanon State Forest, New Jersey	0.08	0	0.04	0.64	0.45	0.55
Average	0.09	0	0.03	2.36	1.46	1.91

[a] Seeds were planted in 1972 and tests were randomized and replicated (Ledig, unpublished observations).

stable population, the longevity and superior height attained by Barrens' trees will enable them to maintain their population number for considerable periods. Mortality will be more rapid in the Plains' trees as they become shaded and as resource levels (particularly light) in their strata fall toward zero. Boyce (1978) has developed a model for the situation that stresses the importance of resource variability during the life cycle and provides a generalized framework within which competition between Barrens' and Plains' populations can be viewed. Resource variability, such as that experienced during the cycle of stand development on newly opened sites, favors competitors with a low rate of population decrease under limiting conditions.

Photosynthesis

Population variation in growth cannot be explained by differences in phtosynthetic rate. Differences in photosynthesis, measured as the rate of CO_2 uptake, while significant, are slight and not related to latitude of origin (Ledig *et al.*, 1976a, 1977). Populations from the northern and southern extremes of the range showed no differences in climatic adaptation as measured by temperature and light response curves. However, differences relative to premeasurement temperature treatment were observed. Northern populations from the most seasonally variable environment maintained nearly the same photosynthetic rate when they were grown at 21°C as at 29°C (Ledig *et al.*, 1977), but rates of southern populations from the least variable environment were reduced substantially after growth at 21°C compared to 29°C. Seedlings from the Pine Barrens, in the central portion of the range, were intermediate in their response to premeasurement temperature. Ability to maintain photosynthesis and therefore productivity, despite seasonal temperature fluctuation, would be of greatest advantage in the more variable northern environments, suggesting that the observed north-south trend is adaptive.

Variation among families within populations was no more striking than variation among populations. Differences between families collected from trees in the Lebanon State Forest and at Clermont, New Jersey were nil, and differences among families within stands were small, ranging from 2–7% of the total variance (Ledig and Clark, 1977). Thus, for photosynthetic characteristics, genetic variance, at least the additive variance utilizable in selection breeding, is low in pitch pine, and differences among families and among populations are smaller than those observed in several other species.

Serotinous Cones

Cone Opening

Cones of some pitch pines are serotinous, i.e., they remain closed for an indefinite number of years after they mature, but open in response to high temperature. The trait is an obvious adaptation to fire, ensuring seed shed at the most opportune time for regeneration—when competing vegetation is eliminated and a mineral seed bed is exposed. Trees whose cones open at maturity under normal autumn temperatures are called "open coned" or nonserotinous. A similar polymorphism exists in jack pine (*Pinus banksiana*), lodgepole pine (*P. contorta* Dougl.), and several other species (e.g., Critchfield, 1957; Rudolph *et al.*, 1957). Some authors have suggested the presence of intermediate types, i.e., trees with both serotinous and nonserotinous cones or trees whose cones open at intermediate temperatures. An obstacle to this hypothesis may exist, however: cryptic insect damage can prevent nonserotinous cones from opening, resulting in apparently mixed collections. Careful study suggests that intermediates are rare or nonexistent. Cones in paper bags placed in a drying rack at room temperature separate trees into two categories, those whose cones open and those whose cones remain closed (Ledig and Prendergast, unpublished data). Cones which remained closed were subjected to increased temperature in 1°C steps. Among trees with serotinous cones, the average temperature required for cone opening ranged from 47° to 75°C. Apparently, opening temperatures were distributed normally, both among cones within trees and among averages for individual trees (Fig. 5). There was no indication of trees with a bimodal distribution, and there were only two modes, namely, trees whose cones open at room temperature, and those with cones requiring elevated temperatures ($> 42°$ C) for opening. In a sample of cones from over 500 trees growing on Long Island and at other locations in New York, F. C. Schlauch (personal

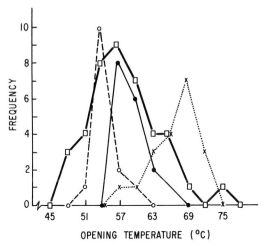

Fig. 5. Opening temperatures for cones. The thick line refers to average cone-opening temperatures for trees with serotinous cones that apparently are distributed normally around 57°C. The other curves are for cones from three serotinous-coned trees. Cones of different trees open at somewhat different temperatures, and within a tree there is variation around the average. However, there are no intermediates between serotinous and open-coned trees (i.e., trees that open at room temperature, about 25°C).

communication) found only three cases with possibly mixed results. In contrast, Frasco and Good (1976) claimed that intermediates were common and required lower temperatures for opening than fully serotinous cones. However, cones of trees which they classed as intermediate opened at a temperature of 45° C, similar to some of the cones classed as serotinous in Fig. 5. Thus, true intermediates, requiring temperatures <42° C but >25° C, do not seem to exist. But within the category of serotinous cones is a broad gradation between the extremes opening at 47° and 75° C. Some cones requiring relatively low temperatures for opening may open in a seemingly erratic fashion over a period of years, depending on micrometeorological influences within the tree crown (Little, 1959).

The physiological/morphological mechanism for cone serotiny and its mode of inheritance is not fully documented. Single gene inheritance has been proposed for the serotinous cone trait in jack pine (Sittman and Tyson, 1971; Teich, 1970), and it probably is the same for pitch pine. A resin bond generally is considered the mechanism responsible for holding scales of serotinous cones closed. However, no resin unique to serotinous cones has been isolated as yet, despite attempts (Lotan, 1970; Ledig *et al.*, unpublished observations).

Geographical Distribution

A geographical pattern exists for cone serotiny. Nearly 100% of the pygmy trees of the Pine Plains have serotinous cones, but with increasing distance from the Plains the frequency drops rapidly (Fig. 6; Ledig and Fryer, 1972). The Pine Plains, termed a

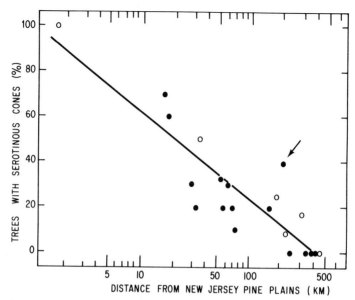

Fig. 6. Decrease in frequency of trees with serotinous cones with distance from the New Jersey Pine Plains. All stands were on the Coastal Plain and New England seaboard. ●, ten-tree stands; ○, combined values for two paired stands of six trees each (Ledig and Fryer, 1972). The stand indicated by an arrow is within several kilometers of the Long Island pine plains, an area with 100% serotinous cones (F. Schlauch, personal communication). Correlation coefficient $r = -0.89$.

pyrotype (i.e., fire ecotype) by Andresen (1963), burn more frequently and severely than the surrounding Barrens, maximizing the selective advantage of serotinous cones. Cone serotiny is almost zero 300 km from the Plains and decreases particularly rapidly away from the coastal plain, where fires are more frequent because of droughty soils. Polymorphic populations near the Plains might be maintained by migration or by temporal heterogeneity, causing cone serotiny to vary in its selective advantage.

F. C. Schlauch (personal communication) collected cones from pygmy forests on Long Island and on Ice Caves Mountain (Ulster County), New York, areas similar in appearance to the New Jersey Pine Plains, and found cone serotiny to be 90–100%. Therefore, the geographical pattern is not as simple as that implied by Ledig and Fryer (1972), who also reported serotinous cones on all six trees sampled in a stand in Clinton County, Pennsylvania. Trees with serotinous cones would be expected to dominate any area with a history of frequent and severe fires, such as along present or former railroads in the Pine Barrens.

Predation Pressure

Serotinous cones constitute a stable resource for squirrels. They are available throughout the year and are a source of seed even in poor seed years. Therefore, selection for characteristics that discourage seed predators, such as heavily armed cones, cones borne in clusters, harder cones, smaller seed, or fewer seeds per cone, would be expected (Smith, 1970). In fact, both Tempel (1976) and Frasco and Good (1976) sampled serotinous and nonserotinous cones from a polymorphic population in the Pine Barrens and found fewer seeds per cone in the serotinous cones, although variability was high in both types. Serotinous cones from the Pine Plains, where squirrel predation was very low, had nearly as many seed per cone as nonserotinous cones from the Pine Barrens, suggesting that the lower seed yield in serotinous cones from the Barrens indeed is a response to predator pressure.

Isozymes and Population Structure

The so-called "endosperm" of conifer seed actually is haploid female gametophyte derived from a single meiotic product. Using electrophoresis, that is, the separation of water-soluble enzymes by differential migration in an electrical field, the female gametophyte can be analyzed for several enzyme systems. If the parental sporophyte was heterozygous for a locus coding for a specific enzyme, its female gametophytes have one of two alternative bands in a 1:1 ratio, indicating genetic segregation of single gene differences (Guries and Ledig, 1978). Recent surveys of isozyme segregation in pitch pine have revealed nine polymorphic genes and eight others with rare variants, more genetic markers than are available in any other tree species (Table II). Some of these genes tend to be inherited together, indicating that they are linked more or less closely on the same chromosome (Guries *et al.,* 1978). Pitch pine is the only forest tree species in which Mendelian genetics have been investigated sufficiently to demonstrate linkage. At this point, pitch pine is an incipient *"Drosophila* tree" for forest genetics research.

In several populations in the Pine Barrens, all of the trees within a plot of 25-m radius have been analyzed for isozyme genotypes to determine whether adjacent individuals are related more closely than those further apart. In fact, no such tendency exists, a finding which suggests that populations up to a size of about 70 individuals are mating on a truly random basis, and that seed dispersal is adequate to distribute progeny randomly within the "stand" (Guries and Ledig, 1977).

Cytogenetics

Chromosome morphology and number in pitch pine are similar to those of other pines in the same subsection (Kim, 1963; Yim, 1963). There are 11 pairs of chromosomes with median centromeres and one pair, the shortest, with a submedian centromere. Secondary constrictions occur in some pairs of homologous chromosomes, but not consistently (Yim, 1963; Ledig, unpublished observations).

Natural and Controlled Hybrids

Hybridization must provide a source of variation important to the adaptability and future evolution of pitch pine. In Cape May, New Jersey and on the Delmarva Penin-

TABLE II   Polymorphic Genes in 1:1 Segregation in Female Megagametophytes and Apparently Monomorphic Genes for Isozymes of Pitch Pine from the East and West Pine Plains, New Jersey[a]

| Enzyme | Gene | No. of alleles | Freq. of most common allele | | Observed segregation ratio[b] |
			East Plains	West Plains	Fast: Slow Migrating allele bonds
A. Polymorphic genes (frequency of most common allele ≤ .95)					
Aconitase	ACO	3	0.68	0.73	42:49
Glutamate oxalate transaminase	GOT-1	3	0.95	0.92	60:78
Glutamate oxalate transaminase	GOT-2	2	0.97	0.93	74:64
Glucose phosphate isomerase	GPI-2	3	0.95	0.97	76:62
Isocitrate dehydrogenase	IDH	2	0.85	0.92	50:53
Leucine aminopeptidase	LAP-1	3	0.86	0.91	68:67
Malate dehydrogenase	MDH-2	3	0.77	0.74	46:46
6-Phosphogluconate dehydrogenase	6PGD-1	4	0.81	0.72	59:44
6-Phosphogluconate dehydrogenase	6PGD-2	4	0.67	0.75	46:57
B. Genes with occasional rare alleles (frequency of most common allele > .95)					
Acid phosphatase	AcPO₄	2	0.97	0.96	
Aldolase	ALD-1	2	0.97	0.98	
Aldolase	ALD-2	2	0.99	0.99	
Fumarase	FUM	2	0.99	0.99	
Glucose phosphate isomerase	GPI-1	2	0.99	0.99	
Malate dehydrogenase	MDH-1	3	0.99	0.97	
Phosphoglucomutase	PGM-1	2	0.98	0.96	
Phosphoglucomutase	PGM-2	2	0.97	0.99	
C. Monomorphic genes					
Glucose-6-phosphate dehydrogenase	G-6-PD	1	1.00	1.00	
Glutamate dehydrogenase	GDH	1	1.00	1.00	

[a] From Guries and Ledig (1978).
[b] Values do not differ significantly from hypothetical 1:1 according to chi-square.

sula of Delaware, Maryland, and Virginia, the ranges of pitch pine and pond pine (historically, *P. serotina* Michx.) meet, and the taxa hybridize. Based on morphological analysis of extensive samples, Smouse (1972) and Smouse and Saylor (1973a,b) considered the area of overlap a zone of secondary intergradation, or hybridization between formerly distinct taxa. Populations in the area of overlap are morphologically transitional, causing Smouse and Saylor (1973a) to propose subspecific status for pitch and pond pine [*P. rigida* Mill. subsp. *rigida* and *P. rigida* subsp. *serotina* (Michx.) Clausen] following Clausen (1939).

The pitch–pond transitional type hybridizes with loblolly pine in the Delmarva Peninsula, further complicating relationships (Little *et al.*, 1967). Near old plantations of loblolly pine in the Pine Barrens, young trees with intermediate characteristics between pitch and loblolly are found (Little *et al.*, 1967). In the Piedmont and mountains, hybrids of pitch pine with shortleaf pine generally are acknowledged (Austin, 1929; Illick and Aughanbaugh, 1930; Little, 1959). Hybrids with Table Mountain pine (*P. pungens* Lamb.) also are suspected (Zobel, 1969; P. E. Smouse, personal communication). Based on a statistical technique known as discriminant analysis, morphological affinities were computed for each pair of taxa in the pitch, pond, loblolly, and shortleaf complex (Smouse, 1972). Results clearly demonstrated the presence of intermediates and illustrated the affinity of pitch and pond pine, which were more similar than any other pair of taxa.

Based on experimental evidence, there is little barrier to crossing between pitch pine, on the one hand, and pond, loblolly, or shortleaf, on the other (Smouse, 1971). These taxa form a particularly crossable subgroup of the eastern Australes, based on hybridizations carried out over several years at the Institute of Forest Genetics, Placerville, California (Critchfield, 1963). No substantial phenological barrier exists between pitch pine and any of the other four species with which hybridization is suspected. Where they grow in the same area, all have maximum pollen shedding and female receptivity in May, but the extent of overlap varies greatly from year to year (Little, 1941).

Meiosis in various hybrids, including those with pond, shortleaf, and loblolly pines, and for the double cross of (shortleaf × loblolly) × (pitch × loblolly) was observed by Saylor and Smith (1966). One pitch × pond hybrid showed a high frequency of lagging chromosomes at telophase II. On the average, the hybrids had slightly higher pollen abortion and meiotic irregularity than the parental species, indicating only slight cytological barriers to hybridization. Obviously, chromosome structure has not changed greatly during evolution of the pines.

Controlled hybrids have been produced between pitch and loblolly, pitch and pond, pitch and shortleaf (Critchfield, 1963), and pitch and Table Mountain pines (P. E. Smouse, personal communication). In 1945 test plantings of pitch × shortleaf pine hybrids in the Pine Barrens and in eastern Maryland, some hybrids had a prostrate form, and none had growth superior to the parent species. In the same plantings, pitch × loblolly hybrids, from crosses made by the U.S. Forest Service in California, grew somewhat better than pitch × shortleaf, but still had a growth rate and form similar to pitch (Little and Somes, 1951c; Little *et al.*, 1967). Pitch × loblolly hybrids have been produced on a large scale in Korea for reforestation and have proved very useful (Hyun and Ahn, 1959). In recent years, careful selection of parent trees and large numbers of controlled crosses have produced some pitch × loblolly hybrids that grow as rapidly as loblolly on Evesboro soils of the Barrens, but are coldhardy like pitch pine, and at three to five years are 50–100% taller than pitch pine controls (Little and Trew, 1976, 1977). Pitch pine breeding programs were reviewed by Ledig and Fryer (1974).

SUMMARY

Pitch pine is a hardy species which is adapted to poor soils with a severe fire history. Its adaptations to fire are its most striking characteristics, namely, the production of dormant buds that permit sprouting from the root crown, trunk and branches, the development of a basal crook and of thick bark to protect buds from fire, and the production of serotinous cones. Other characteristics make it a common invader of cleared sites and enable it to thrive on both droughty and wet sites. Its physiology, however, is not well understood. Although its seedlings are capable of the highest photosynthetic rates on record for conifers, its photosynthesis and productivity in the forest are not outstanding.

Geographical variation is slight for both physiological characteristics and gene frequency in several enzyme systems. However, perhaps in relation to photoperiodic response, populations differ substantially in growth in uniform garden culture. There also are geographical trends in wood properties and other characteristics, but the only distinct ecotype is the dwarf tree pyrotype of the Pine Plains, a tree which may reach only one-half the height of "normal" pitch pine at 50 years. Pitch pine readily hybridizes with related species. Based on the presence of nine polymorphic genes and eight others with rare variants, plus knowledge of its Mendelian genetics and the demonstration of linkage, pitch pine is suggested as an incipient "*Drosophila* tree" for forest genetics research.

ACKNOWLEDGMENTS

Some of the studies reported here were initiated under Michaux Fund Grants 30 and 38 of the American Philosophical Society. Previously unpublished data were gathered and the manuscript prepared with the aid of National Science Foundation Grant DEB 74-11794. The support of the Society and the Foundation is acknowledged gratefully.

REFERENCES

Andresen, J. W. (1957). Precocity of *Pinus rigida* Mill. *Castanea* 22, 130–134.

Andresen, J. W. (1959). A study of pseudo-nanism in *Pinus rigida* Mill. *Ecol. Monogr.* 29, 309–332.

Andresen, J. W. (1963). Germination characteristics of *Pinus rigida* seed borne in serotinous cones. *Broteria Ser. Cienc. Nat.* 32, 151–178.

Austin, L. (1929). The Eddy Tree Breeding Station. *Madroño* 1, 203–212.

Baker, W. L. (1972). Eastern forest insects. U.S. Dept. Agric. Misc. Pub. No. 1175.

Botkin, D. B., Woodwell, G. M., and Tempel, N. (1970). Forest productivity estimated from carbon dioxide uptake. *Ecology* 51, 1057–1060.

Boyce, J. S. (1961). "Forest Pathology", 3rd ed. McGraw-Hill, New York.

Boyce, M. S. (1978). Seasonality and pattern of natural selection for life histories. *Am. Natur.* 112, (in press).

Burns, P. Y. (1952). Effect of fire on forest soils in the Pine Barrens region of New Jersey. *Yale Univ. Sch. For. Bull.* No. 57.

Clausen, R. T. (1939). Contributions to the flora of New Jersey. *Torreya* 39, 125–133.

Craighead, F. C. (1950). Insect enemies of eastern forests. *U.S. Dept. Agric. Misc. Pub. No.* 657.

Critchfield, W. B. (1957). "Geographic variation in *Pinus Contorta,*" Maria Moors Cabot Found. Publ. No. 3. Harvard Univ., Cambridge, Massachusetts.

Critchfield, W. B. (1963). "Hybridization of the southern pines in California." *Proc. For. Genet. Workshop,* Macon, Ga. pp. 40-48.

Fenton, R. H. (1955). Windthrow a hazard in Virginia pine strip cuttings. *U.S. For. Serv., Northeast. For. Exp. Stn., For. Res. Note,* No. 53.

Fowells, H. A. (1965). Silvics of forest trees of the United States. *U.S. Dep. Agric., Agric. Handb.* No. 271.

Frasco, B. R., and Good, R. E. (1976). Cone, seed, and germination characteristics of pitch pine (*Pinus rigida* Mill.) from the Pine Barrens of New Jersey. *Bartonia* **44,** 50-57.

Good, R. E., and Good, N. F. (1975). Growth characteristics of two populations of *Pinus rigida* Mill. from the Pine Barrens of New Jersey. *Ecology* **56,** 1215-1220.

Good, R. E., and Good, N. F. (1976). Growth analysis of pitch pine seedlings under three temperature regimes. *For. Sci.* **22,** 445-448.

Guries, R. P., and Ledig, F. T. (1977). Analysis of population structure from allozyme frequencies. *Proc. South. For. Tree Improv. Conf.,* Gainesville, Fl., pp. 246-253.

Guries, R. P., and Ledig, F. T. (1978). Inheritance of some polymorphic isoenzymes in pitch pine (*Pinus rigida* Mill.). *Heredity* **40,** 27-32.

Guries, R. P., Friedman, S. T., and Ledig. F. T. (1978). A megagametophyte analysis of genetic linkage in pitch pine (*Pinus rigida* Mill.). *Heredity* **40,** 309-314.

Hepting, G. H. (1971). Diseases of forest and shade trees of the United States. *U.S. Dep. Agric., Agric. Handb.* No. 386.

Hyun, S. K., and Ahn, K. Y. (1959). Mass production of pitch-loblolly hybrid pine (× *Pinus rigitaeda*) seed. *Inst. For. Genet. Res. Rep. (Suwon, Korea)* No. 1, 11-24.

Illick, J. S., and Aughanbaugh, J. E. (1930). Pitch pine in Pennsylvania. *Pa. Dep. For. Waters, Res. Bull.* No. 2.

Kim, C. S. (1963). The karyotype analysis in *Pinus rigida* Mill., *Pinus taeda* L. and their F$_1$ hybrid. *Inst. For. Genet. Res. Rep. (Suwon, Korea)* No. 3, 21-28.

Ledig, F. T., and Clark, J. G. (1977). Photosynthesis in a half-sib family experiment in pitch pine. *Can. J. For. Res.* **7,** 510-514.

Ledig, F. T., Clark, J. G., and Drew, A. P. (1977). The effects of temperature treatment on photosynthesis of pitch pine from northern and southern latitudes. *Bot. Gaz.* **138,** 7-12.

Ledig, F. T., and Fryer, J. H. (1972). A pocket of variability in *Pinus rigida. Evolution* **26,** 259-266.

Ledig, F. T., and Fryer, J. H. (1974). Genetics of pitch pine. *U.S. For. Serv., Res. Pap.* WO-27.

Ledig, F. T., Zobel, B. J., and Matthias, M. F. (1975). Geoclimatic patterns in specific gravity and tracheid length in wood of pitch pine. *Can. J. For. Res.* **5,** 318-329.

Ledig, F. T., Drew, A. P., and Clark, J. G. (1976a). Maintenance and constructive respiration, photosynthesis, and net assimilation rate in seedlings of pitch pine. *Ann. Bot.* **40,** 289-300.

Ledig, F. T., Lambeth, C. C., and Linzer, D. I. H. (1976b). Nursery evaluation of a pitch pine provenance trial. *Proc. Northeast. For. Tree Improv. Conf., 23rd, New Brunswick, N.J.* pp. 93-108.

Little, E. L., Jr., Little, S., and Doolittle, W. T. (1967). Natural hybrids among pond, loblolly, and pitch pines. *U.S. For. Serv., Northeast. For. Exp. Stn., Res. Pap.* NE-67.

Little, S. (1941). Calendar of seasonal aspects for New Jersey forest trees. *Pa. For. Leaves* **31**(4), 1-2, 13-14.

Little, S. (1950). Ecology and silviculture of whitecedar and associated hardwoods in southern New Jersey. *Yale Univ. Sch. For. Bull.* No. **56,** 1-103.

Little, S. (1959). Silvical characteristics of pitch pine. *U.S. For. Serv., Northeast. For. Exp. Stn., Stn. Pap.* No. 119.

Little, S. (1964). Fire ecology and forest management in the New Jersey pine region. *Proc. Tall Timbers Fire Ecol. Conf.* **3,** 34-59.

Little, S. (1972). Growth of planted white pines and pitch seedlings in a South Jersey Plains area. *Bull. N.J. Acad. Sci.* **17,** 18-23.

Little, S., and Mergen, F. (1966). External and internal changes associated with basal-crook formation in pitch and shortleaf pines. *For. Sci.* **12**, 268–275.

Little, S., and Moore, E. B. (1949). The ecological role of prescribed burns in the pine–oak forests of southern New Jersey. *Ecology* **30**, 223–233.

Little, S., and Moore, E. B. (1950). Effect of prescribed burns and shelterwood cutting on reproduction of shortleaf and pitch pine. *U.S. For. Serv., Northeast. For. Exp. Stn., Stn. Pap.* No. 35.

Little, S., and Moore, E. B. (1952). Mechanical preparation of seedbeds for converting oak–pine stands to pine. *J. For.* **50**, 840–844.

Little, S., and Moore, E. B. (1953). Severe burning treatment tested on lowland pine sites. *U.S. For. Serv., Northeast. For. Exp. Stn., Stn. Pap.* No. 64.

Little, S., and Somes, H. A. (1949). Slash disposal in oak–pine stands of southern New Jersey. *U.S. For. Serv., Northeast. For. Exp. Stn., Stn. Pap.* No. 31.

Little, S., and Somes, H. A. (1951a). Age, origin, and crown injuries affect growth of South Jersey pines. *U.S. For. Serv., Northeast. For. Exp. Stn., Res. Note* No. 8.

Little, S., and Somes, H. A. (1951b). Deer browsing in New Jersey handicap pine seedlings. *U.S. For. Serv., Northeast. For. Exp. Stn., Res. Note* No. 2.

Little, S., and Somes, H. A. (1951c). No exceptional vigor found in hybrid pines tested. *U.S. For. Serv., Northeast. For. Exp. Stn., Res. Note* No. 10.

Little, S., and Somes, H. A. (1956). Buds enable pitch and shortleaf pines to recover from injury. *U.S. For. Serv., Northeast. For. Exp. Stn., Stn. Pap.* No. 81.

Little, S., and Somes, H. A. (1964). Releasing pitch pine sprouts from old stools ineffective. *J. For.* **62**, 23–26.

Little, S., and Trew, I. F. (1976). Breeding and testing pitch × loblolly pine hybrids for the Northeast. *Proc. Northeast. For. Tree Improv. Conf., 23rd,* New Brunswick, N.J. pp. 71–85.

Little, S., and Trew, I. F. (1977). Progress report on testing pitch × loblolly pine hybrids and on providing hybrid seed for mass planting. *Proc. Northeast. For. Tree Improv. Conf., 24th,* College Park, Md. pp. 14–28.

Little, S., Cramer, C. B., and Somes, H. A. (1958a). Direct seedling of pitch pine in southern New Jersey—a progress report. *U.S. For. Serv., Northeast. For. Exp. Stn., Stn. Pap.* No. 111.

Little, S., Moorhead, G. R., and Somes, H. A. (1958b). Forestry and deer in the Pine Region of New Jersey. *U.S. For. Serv., Northeast. For. Exp. Stn., Stn. Pap.* No. 109.

Lotan, J. E. (1970). Cone serotiny in *Pinus contorta.* Ph.D. Thesis, Univ. of Michigan, Ann Arbor.

Lutz, H. J. (1934). Ecological relations in the pitch pine plains of southern New Jersey. *Yale Univ. Sch. For. Bull.* No. **38**, 1–80.

McQuilkin, W. E. (1935). Root development of pitch pine, with some comparative observations on shortleaf pine. *J. Agric. Res.* **51**, 983–1016.

Martin, A. C., Zim, H. S., and Nelson, A. L. (1951). "American Wildlife and Plants." McGraw-Hill, New York.

Niering, W. A. (1953). The past and present vegetation of High Point State Park, New Jersey. *Ecol. Monogr.* **23**, 127–148.

Pianka, E. R. (1970). On r- and K-selection. *Am. Natur.* **104**, 592–597.

Rudolph, R. D., Libby, W. J., and Pauley, S. S. (1957). Jack pine variation and distribution in Minnesota. *Minn. For. Notes* No. 58.

Saylor, L. C., and Smith, B. W. (1966). Meiotic irregularity in species and interspecific hybrids of *Pinus. Am. J. Bot.* **53**, 453–468.

Sittman, K., and Tyson, H. (1971). Estimates of inbreeding in *Pinus banksiana. Can. J. Bot.* **49**, 1241–1245.

Smith, C. C. (1970). The coevolution of pine squirrels (*Tamiasciurus*) and conifers. *Ecol. Monogr.* **40**, 349–371.

Smouse, P. E. (1971). Population studies in the genus *Pinus* L. Ph.D. Thesis, North Carolina State Univ., Raleigh.

Smouse, P. E. (1972). The canonical analysis of multiple species hybridization. *Biometrics* **28**, 361–371.

Smouse, P. E., and Saylor, L. C. (1973a). Studies of the *Pinus rigida–serotina* complex. I. A study of geographic variation. *Ann. Mo. Bot. Gard.* **60,** 174–191.

Smouse, P. E., and Saylor, L. C. (1973b). Studies of the *Pinus rigida–serotina* complex. II. Natural hybridization among the *Pinus rigida–serotina* complex, *P. taeda* and *P. echinata. Ann. Mo. Bot. Gard.* **60,** 192–203.

Society of American Foresters, Committee on Forest Types (1954). "Forest Cover Types of North America (Exclusive of Mexico)." Soc. Am. For., Washington, D.C.

Sparrow, A. H. (1966). Research uses of the gamma field and related radiation facilities at Brookhaven National Laboratory. *Radiat. Bot.* **6,** 377–405.

Stone, E. L., Jr., and Stone, M. H. (1943). Dormant buds in certain species of *Pinus. Am. J. Bot.* **30,** 346–351.

Stone, E. L., Jr., and Stone, M. H. (1954). Root collar sprouts in pine. *J. For.* **52,** 487–491.

Stone, W. (1911). The plants of southern New Jersey with special reference to the flora of the Pine Barrens and the geographic distribution of the species. *N.J. State Mus., Annu. Rept.* 1910, pp. 21–828.

Teich, A. H. (1970). Cone serotiny and inbreeding in natural populations of *Pinus banksiana* and *Pinus contorta. Can. J. Bot.* **48,** 1805–1809.

Tempel, A. S. (1976). Racial differences in cone characteristics in *Pinus rigida* in relation to seed predation by the red squirrel (*Tamiasciurus hudsonicus*). M. S. Thesis, Rutgers Univ., New Brunswick, New Jersey.

Tepper, H. B. (1963). Leader growth of young pitch and shortleaf pines. *For. Sci.* **9,** 344–353.

United States Department of Agriculture (1948). Woody-plant seed manual. *U.S. Dept. Agric., Misc. Publ.* No. 654.

Vaartaja, O. (1959). Evidence of photoperiodic ecotypes in trees. *Ecol. Monogr.* **29,** 91–111.

Yim, K. B. (1963). Karyotype analysis of *Pinus rigida. Hereditas* **49,** 274–276.

Zobel, D. B. (1969). Factors affecting the distribution of *Pinus pungens,* an Appalachian endemic. *Ecol. Monogr.* **39,** 303–333.

21

Common Vascular Plants of the Pine Barrens

WAYNE R. FERREN, JR., JOHN W. BRAXTON,
and LOUIS HAND

INTRODUCTION

In 1911, Witmer E. Stone reported 565 vascular plant species for the Pine Barrens of New Jersey. Subtracting plants which he considered "obvious intrusions from other districts," he numbered the native Pine Barrens flora at 386 species, that is, about 15 trees, 50 shrubs, and 320 herbaceous plants. McCormick (1970) suggested that introductions and new discoveries have increased the total number of vascular plant species, varieties, and forms to more than 800. This chapter is a guide to the identification of selected vascular plant species of the Pine Barrens, including both widespread Coastal Plain plants and Pine Barrens endemics. Most trees and shrubs listed by Stone are included, but only a few of the herbaceous plants could be mentioned.

This chapter contains two sections: keys, which include additional descriptive information, and figures. The keys are artificial, that is, genera and species are not necessarily grouped according to evolutionary relationships. The format of the descriptions is as follows: general appearance of the plants; habitat conditions; and characteristics of the bark, twig, bud, leaf, leaf scar, and vascular bundle scar, flower, and fruit. All of this information, however, is not provided for each species. Unless otherwise indicated, measurements refer to height of plant (1 m = 3.3 ft) or length of leaves, petals, etc. (1 cm = 0.4 in). Tree heights refer to the maximum heights attained by the species, but often are considerably greater than heights attained in the Pine Barrens. Habitat conditions given here are general. Wet thickets, for example, include margins of bogs, ponds, and streams and other shrubby areas with wet soil conditions. Bark characteristics refer to mature bark. Dates refer to flowering times, unless indicated as the time of ripened fruit. The following abbreviations are used: spp. (species); Fam. (Family); P. B. (Pine Barrens).

Several frequently used terms are defined as follows: (a) capsule—a dry, dehiscent fruit composed of more than one carpel or seed-bearing portion of the flower; (b) catkin—a dry spike of small, unisexual flowers each in the axil of a bract; (c) nutlet—a small, hard, indehiscent, one-seeded fruit; (d) berry—a fleshy fruit with immersed

373

seeds; (e) drupe—a fleshy fruit with a hard or stony inner portion of the ovary wall; (f) persistent—remaining on the plant through the winter.

Illustrations of members of the heath family (Ericaceae) are grouped together for convenient comparison, since this family includes the largest number of woody species in the Pine Barrens. However, the sedge family (Cyperaceae), grass family (Poaceae or Gramineae), and aster or composite family (Asteraceae or Compositae), re pectively, are represented by the most species. Descriptions of these and other herbaceous plants are not included.

In developing the keys and descriptions, we have consulted Fernald (1950), Gleason (1952), Gleason and Cronquist (1963), Grimm (1962, 1966), Graves (1956), and Stone (1911). The reader also may find Fairbrothers *et al.* (1965), Harlow (1957, 1959), Harshberger (1916), Peterson and McKenny (1968), and Symonds (1958, 1963) helpful. The nomenclature follows Fernald (1950).

KEYS TO THE TREES, SHRUBS, AND HERBACEOUS PLANTS

I. PERENNIAL WOODY PLANTS USUALLY WITH SINGLE STEMS REACHING A HEIGHT OF 4 METERS AT MATURITY: Trees, Key I

II. PERENNIAL WOODY PLANTS WHICH ARE SMALLER THAN TREES AND USUALLY WITH SEVERAL STEMS: Shrubs and sub-shrubs, Key II

III. PLANTS WITH NO PERSISTENT WOODY STEM ABOVE THE GROUND: Herbaceous plants, Key III

Trees—Key I

A. LEAVES PERSISTENT AND GREEN IN WINTER . . . B

A. LEAVES NOT PERSISTENT AND NOT GREEN IN WINTER . . . H

  B. LEAVES SCALE-LIKE OR NEEDLE-SHAPED . . . C

  B. LEAVES BROAD, NOT SCALE-LIKE OR NEEDLE-SHAPED . . . G

C. LEAVES NEEDLE-SHAPED, IN CLUSTERS OF TWO OR THREE, >3.5 CM LONG . . . D (pines: *Pinus* spp.)

C. LEAVES SCALE-LIKE OR NEEDLE-SHAPED, NOT IN CLUSTERS, <6 MM LONG . . . F

  D. LEAVES STIFF, IN CLUSTERS OF THREE, 3.5–14 CM LONG; YOUNG TWIGS WITHOUT WHITE COVERING: tree to 25 m (<20 m in P.B.); most common tree of the pinelands and Pine Plains; bark reddish-brown, deeply furrowed; buds pointed, resin-coated; leaves dark green, often sprouting from trunk; May; open cones ovoid, flat at base, 3–7 cm . . . . Pitch pine, *Pinus rigida* (Pine Fam.) (Fig. 1a)

  D. LEAVES FIRM, IN CLUSTERS OF TWO OR SOMETIMES THREE; YOUNG TWIGS WITH WHITE COVERING . . . E

E. LEAVES 3–6(–8) CM LONG, IN CLUSTERS OF TWO; CONES WITH FIRM PRICKLES >2 MM LONG: tree <12 m, often straggling; fringe areas; bark dark brown; shallowly fissured into scaly plates; buds resinous; leaves gray-green, often twisted; Apr.–May; cones ovoid, round at base, 4–8 cm . . . . Virginia, Jersey, or Scrub pine, *Pinus virginiana* (Pine Fam.)

E. LEAVES (3–)5–11(–13) CM LONG, IN CLUSTERS OF TWO OR SOMETIMES THREE; CONES WITH SOFT PRICKLES <1 MM LONG: tree to 40 m, straight; bark reddish-brown, thick, with large scaly plates; buds scarcely resinous; leaves dark green; May; cones oblong, 4–6 cm . . . . Shortleaf pine, *Pinus echinata* (Pine Fam.) (Fig. 1b)

  F. LEAVES ALL SCALE-LIKE, NONE NEEDLE-SHAPED; CONES 6–9 MM IN DIAMETER, SOMEWHAT WOODY; SEEDS SLIGHTLY WINGED: tree to 25 m, base of trunk swollen; swamps; bark reddish-brown, scaly; Apr. . . . . Atlantic white cedar or White cedar, *Chamaecyparis thyoides* (Pine Fam.) (Fig. 1c)

  F. LEAVES NEEDLE-SHAPED ON YOUNG VIGOROUS BRANCHES, SCALE-LIKE ON OLDER BRANCHES; CONES 5–6 MM IN DIAMETER, FLESHY, BLUISH; SEEDS WINGLESS: tree to 30 m; dry open disturbed areas; bark fibrous, peeling lengthwise; Mar.–Apr. . . . . Red cedar, *Juniperus virginiana* (Pine Fam.) (Fig. 1d)

G. LEAVES WITH SMOOTH MARGINS; FRUIT CONE-LIKE: tree to 10 m; swamps; bark thin, smooth, gray; leaves with white coating below; twigs aromatic when broken; leaf buds silky; flowers fragrant, petals 3–5 cm; May–July; fruits 3–5 cm; seeds 8–10 mm . . . . Sweet bay, *Magnolia virginiana* (Magnolia Fam.) (Fig. 1e)

G. LEAVES WITH SHARP SPINES; FRUIT A BERRY-LIKE DRUPE: tree to 30 m; moist soil along streams; bark light gray with small bumps; leaves oval, leathery; male and female flowers on different plants, May–June; drupe red, 7–10 mm, persistent . . . . . . American holly, *Ilex opaca* (Holly Fam.) (Fig. 1f)

H. LEAVES SMOOTH-MARGINED OR FINE-TOOTHED, NOT LOBED OR LARGE-TOOTHED . . . I

H. LEAVES LOBED OR HAVING MARGINS WITH LARGE TEETH, NOT FINE-TOOTHED . . . N

I. LEAVES WITH SMOOTH MARGINS . . . J

I. LEAVES WITH TOOTHED MARGINS . . . K

   J. LEAVES BROADEST BELOW MIDPOINT, TIP ROUNDED, HALF-EVERGREEN, SPICY–AROMATIC WHEN CRUSHED, 8–15 CM LONG; FRUIT CONE-LIKE . . . . .Sweet bay, *Magnolia virginiana;* see G above

   J. LEAVES BROADEST ABOVE MIDPOINT, TIP WITH SHORT ABRUPT POINT, DECIDUOUS, NOT AROMATIC WHEN CRUSHED, 3–10 CM LONG; FRUIT A BERRY-LIKE DRUPE IN CLUSTERS: tree to 35 m; base of trunk often swollen; wet soil or swamps; bark dark brown, rough; leaves turning crimson early; May–June; drupe 1 cm . . . . .Black gum,
Nyssa sylvatica (Dogwood Fam.) (Fig. 1g)

K. LEAVES TRIANGULAR OR INVERSELY TRIANGULAR; FLOWERS IN CATKINS . . . L

K. LEAVES OVAL OR ELLIPTICAL; FLOWERS NOT IN CATKINS . . . M

   L. BARK CHALKY, WHITE AND SMOOTH; LEAVES TRIANGULAR: tree or shrub with one to several trunks to 10 m; bark not peeling; branchlets with resin dots; leaves 5–9 cm, pointed; catkins 1–2.5 cm, Apr.–May . . . . .Gray
or White birch, *Betula populifolia* (Birch Fam.) (Fig. 1h)

   L. BARK BLACK, DEEPLY RIDGED; LEAVES INVERSELY TRIANGULAR . .Blackjack oak, *Quercus marilandica;* see T below

M. INNER BARK OF TWIGS AROMATIC; TREE WITH SINGLE TRUNK TO 30 M: LONGEST STEMS OF FRUIT >1 CM LONG; FRUIT BLACKISH, ONE-SEEDED; FLOWERS WITH ONE STYLE: disturbed areas; bark rough, flaky; branchlets with prominent lenticels (corky spots); leaves tapered to a point, ovate, 3.5 cm; May–June . . . . .Black cherry, *Prunus serotina* (Rose Fam.)

M. INNER BARK OF TWIGS NOT AROMATIC; TALL SHRUB TO 8 M, USUALLY WITH SEVERAL CLUMPED TRUNKS; FRUIT APPLE-LIKE, TEN-SEEDED; FLOWERS WITH FIVE STYLES . . . . .Juneberry
or Serviceberry, *Amelanchier canadensis;* see o' in Key II, Shrubs

   N. LEAVES AND TWIGS OPPOSITE; FRUIT WINGED: tree to 30 m; moist soil or swamps; bark dark gray; branchlets red; leaves with 3–5 toothed lobes, 4–8 cm; flowers small, red, opening before the leaves . . . . .Red maple,
Acer rubrum (Maple Fam.) (Fig. 1j)

   N. LEAVES AND TWIGS ALTERNATE; FRUIT NOT WINGED . . . O

O. LEAVES AND TWIGS AROMATIC, LEAVES USUALLY MITTEN-SHAPED OR THREE-LOBED; FRUIT A DRUPE; BUDS USUALLY SOLITARY; TWIGS GREEN: tree or colonial shrub to 20 m; woods and thickets, Pine Plains; bark red-brown, furrowed, mature twigs dark gray; leaves ovate or 2–3 lobed, 8–15 cm; flowers greenish-yellow, Apr.–May . . . . .Sassafras,
Sassafras albidum (Laurel Fam.) (Fig. 1i)

O. LEAVES AND TWIGS NOT AROMATIC; FRUIT AN ACORN; BUDS CLUSTERED AT TIP OF DARK TWIG . . . P (Oaks: *Quercus* spp.).

   P. LEAVES LARGE-TOOTHED, NOT LOBED . . . Q

   P. LEAVES LOBED . . . R

Q. LEAVES 5–12 CM LONG; LENGTH OF LEAF MORE THAN TWICE WIDTH; 3–7 TEETH ON EACH MARGIN; SHRUB OR SMALL TREE, RARELY ABOVE 4 M; BARK LIGHT BROWN, SCALY . . . . .Dwarf chestnut oak,
Quercus prinoides; see h in Key II, Shrubs

Q. LEAVES 12–20 CM LONG; LENGTH OF LEAF LESS THAN TWICE WIDTH; 10–16 TEETH ON EACH MARGIN; TREE TO 30 M; BARK DARK WITH GROOVES V-SHAPED IN CROSS-SECTION . . . . . . .Chestnut oak, *Quercus prinus* (Beech Fam.) (Fig. 1k)

   R. LOBES ROUNDED, NOT BRISTLE-POINTED; BARK ON MATURE TREES PALE, OFTEN FLAKY; ACORNS MATURING IN ONE YEAR . . . S (White oaks)

   R. LOBES NOT ROUNDED, BRISTLE-POINTED; BARK ON MATURE TREES DARK, FURROWED, NOT FLAKY; ACORNS MATURING OVER TWO YEARS . . . T (Black oaks)

S. TWIGS AND MATURE LEAVES HAIRLESS; LOBES OF LEAVES SLANTING AT ACUTE ANGLES TO LEAF MIDRIB: tree to 50 m; dry pinelands; leaves inversely egg-shaped, white beneath when mature, 10–25 cm; May; acorn 2–3 cm, cup- or bowl-shaped . . . . .White oak, *Quercus alba* (Beech Fam.) (Fig. 1l)

S. TWIGS HAIRY; LEAVES HAIRY BENEATH; MIDDLE PAIR OF LEAF LOBES LONGER THAN THE OTHERS AND NEARLY PERPENDICULAR TO THE MIDRIB, GIVING THE WHOLE LEAF A SHAPE LIKE A LATIN CROSS: tree or tall shrub rarely beyond 20 m; dry pinelands; bark red- to gray-brown, scaly and ridged; leaves leathery, rough above due to star-like hairs, 9–20 cm; May; acorns stalkless, ovoid, 1–2 cm . . . . .Post oak, *Quercus stellata* (Beech Fam.) (Fig. 1m)

   T. LEAVES NOT DEEPLY LOBED, SHAPED LIKE A BROAD INVERTED TRIANGLE: tree to 15 m, usually to 7 m in pinelands, shrubby in Pine Plains; leaves yellow-green, hairy beneath, rounded at base, 10–25 cm; May; acorns on short stems, ovoid, 1–2 cm, cup conical . . . . .Blackjack oak, *Quercus marilandica* (Beech Fam.) (Fig. 1n)

   T. LEAVES DEEPLY LOBED, NOT SHAPED LIKE A BROAD INVERTED TRIANGLE . . . U

U. UNDERSIDE OF LEAVES GRAYISH-WHITE AND DENSELY HAIRY; LEAF LOBES SHORT-TRIANGULAR; SHRUB OR SMALL TREE TO 6 M . . . . .Scrub oak or bear oak, *Quercus ilicifolia;* see a in Key II, Shrubs

U. UNDERSIDE OF LEAVES GREEN OR YELLOWISH-BROWN, HAIRY, OR HAIRLESS; LEAF LOBES USUALLY TAPERING TO NARROW POINTS; LARGE TREES . . . V

   V. UNDERSIDE OF MATURE LEAVES GREEN AND HAIRLESS (SOMETIMES WITH HAIR TUFTS AT FORKS OF VEINS BENEATH); LENGTH OF LONGEST LOBES 2–6 TIMES THE WIDTH OF THE NARROWEST PART OF THE CENTRAL PORTION OF LEAF: tree to 25 m; dry pinelands; bark light brown, finely fissured, inner bark red; leaves very shiny, green above, scarlet in fall, elliptical or oblong–ovate, deeply divided, 7–15 cm; buds smooth, or woolly only above middle; May; acorn ovoid, 2.5 cm . . . . .Scarlet oak, *Quercus coccinea* (Beech Fam.) (Fig. 1o)

   V. UNDERSIDE OF LEAVES EITHER YELLOW-BROWN AND HAIRY OR GREEN AND HAIRLESS; LENGTH OF LONGEST LOBES LESS THAN TWICE THE WIDTH OF THE NARROWEST PART OF THE CENTRAL PORTION OF LEAF: tree to 30 m; dry pinelands; bark rough, inner bark yellow-orange; leaves dark green above, oblong to ovate, often shallowly divided, 10–25 cm; densely woolly, grayish; May; acorn ovoid, 2.5 cm . . . . . . .Black oak, *Quercus velutina* (Beech Fam.) (Fig. 1p)

Shrubs—Key II

A. PROSTRATE OR TRAILING SHRUBS, SUB-SHRUBS OR SHRUBS LESS THAN 30 CM HIGH . . . B

A. ERECT OR CLIMBING SHRUBS USUALLY MORE THAN 30 CM HIGH . . . O

    B. STEMS FLESHY AND JOINTED; LEAVES SMALL, SCALE-LIKE AND DECIDUOUS, BEARING IN THEIR AXILS CLUSTERS OF SMALL BARBED HAIRS: a cactus; dry open sand; flowers yellow, 5 cm wide, June–July; berries inversely egg-shaped, red, or purple, 2.5–5 cm, Aug.–Oct. . . . . .Prickly pear, *Opuntia humifusa* (Cactus Fam.)

    B. STEMS NEITHER FLESHY NOR JOINTED; LEAVES WITHOUT BARBED HAIRS IN THEIR AXILS . . . C

C. LEAVES FLATTENED, SCALE-LIKE OR AWL-LIKE BUT NOT OVER 3 MM WIDE . . . D

C. LEAVES BROADER, USUALLY OVER 3 MM WIDE . . . F

    D. LEAVES FLATTENED, ALTERNATE OR IN THREES, BLUNT; FLOWERS SMALL, PURPLISH IN HEADS AT TIPS OF BRANCHES; FRUIT BERRY-LIKE: diffusely branched, evergreen shrub; Pine Plains; flowers small in the axils of scaly bracts, in terminal heads, Mar.–May; drupe small, brown . . . . .Broom crowberry, *Corema conradii* (Crowberry Fam.)

    D. LEAVES SCALE-LIKE OR AWL-LIKE; FLOWERS YELLOW, WHITE, OR ROSE, SOLITARY; FRUIT A CAPSULE . . . E

E. LOW AND BUSHY; LEAVES SCALE-LIKE, HAIRY; FLOWERS YELLOW; FRUIT A CAPSULE ENCLOSED IN THE CALYX . . . E′ (*Hudsonia* spp.).

    E′. LEAVES HAIRY BUT GREENISH, PROLONGED, AND POINTED; FLOWERS SOLITARY ON HAIRY STALKS: dry open sands; leaves 6 mm; flowers May–July; capsules small . . .Golden heather, *Hudsonia ericoides* (Rockrose Fam.) (Fig. 2a)

    E′. LEAVES WOOLLY, GRAYISH, NOT PROJECTING FROM THE STEM; FLOWERS STALKLESS: dry open sands, more frequently along the coast . . . . .Beach heather, *Hudsonia tomentosa* (Rockrose Fam.)

E. PROSTRATE AND CREEPING; LEAVES AWL-LIKE, SMALL; FLOWERS WHITE OR ROSE; FRUIT A VISIBLE CAPSULE, TRANSVERSELY OPENING: dry open sand, leaves sharply acute, evergreen, 3–8 mm; flowers solitary, numerous, 5–8 mm wide, Apr.–May; capsule nearly spherical, 2 mm long . . . . .Pyxie moss, *Pyxidanthera barbulata* (Diapensia Fam.) (Fig. 2b)

    F. LEAVES COMPOUND (3–5 FOLIATE); FRUITS ARE COMPACT CLUSTERS OF SMALL, ONE-SEEDED DRUPELETS ARRANGED ON A DISC; STEMS WITH BRISTLES: trailing evergreen shrub; swampy ground; stems bristly, glandular, rooting at the tips; leaves bluntly toothed; flowers 5–9 mm, June–July; drupelets July–Aug. . . . . .Swamp dewberry, *Rubus hispidus* (Rose Fam.) (Fig. 2c)

    F. LEAVES SIMPLE; FRUITS NOT ARRANGED ON A DISC; STEMS WITHOUT BRISTLES . . . G

G. LEAVES, LEAF SCARS AND BUDS OPPOSITE OR SOMETIMES IN THREES . . . H

G. LEAVES, LEAF SCARS AND BUDS ALTERNATE . . . I

    H. FLOWERS LIGHT YELLOW, ENCLOSED IN A PAIR OF LARGE, HEART-SHAPED SEPALS; STEMS WITH TWO WING-LIKE RIDGES . . . H′ (*Ascyrum* spp.).

    H′. LEAVES BROADLY OBLONG, THE UPPER CLASPING: pale green shrub; moist or dry open sands; flowers solitary, terminal, July–Sept. . . . . .St. Peter's Wort, *Ascyrum stans* (St. John's Wort Fam.) (Fig. 2d)

    H′. LEAVES LINEAR TO OBLONG, NARROWED TO BASE: a similar shrub of dry open sand . . . . .St. Andrew's Wort, *Ascyrum hypericoides* (St. John's Wort Fam.)

    H. FLOWERS WHITE OR PINK, NOT ENCLOSED IN A PAIR OF SEPALS; STEMS NOT TWO-WINGED: evergreen shrub to 1 m; dry or damp open sand; leaves crowded, ovate, 6–12 mm; flowers small, numerous in terminal clusters, May–June; capsule 2–3-celled . . . . .Sand myrtle, *Leiophyllum buxifolium* (Heath Fam.) (Fig. 3e)

I. LARGEST LEAVES USUALLY <2.5 CM LONG . . . J

I. LARGEST LEAVES USUALLY >2.5 CM LONG . . . K

    J. TRAILING SHRUB OF DRY SANDY SOIL: evergreen; flexible branches; leaves inversely egg-shaped, shiny, untoothed, 0.9–3 cm; flowers white or pink, 5 mm, in terminal clusters, Apr.–May; drupe dull red, persistent . . . . .Bearberry, *Arctostaphylos uva-ursi* (Heath Fam.) (Fig. 3a)

    J. TRAILING SHRUB OF WET PEATY OR SANDY SOIL: evergreen; bogs, swamps, shores; stems elongate and much branched; leaves oblong–elliptical, 16–17 mm; flowers solitary, pink, 2–6 per branch, June–July; berry red, 1–2 cm wide, persistent . . . . .Cranberry, *Vaccinium macrocarpon* (Heath Fam.) (Fig. 3g)

K. ERECT, BRANCHING SHRUBS, LEAVES DECIDUOUS . . . L

K. PROSTRATE OR TRAILING SHRUBS OR SUB-SHRUBS; LEAVES EVERGREEN . . . M

    L. LEAVES RESIN-DOTTED; FRUIT A DRUPE WITH TEN NUTLETS: buds of two sizes, scales of the smaller buds not longpointed; leaves untoothed; leaf scars with one bundle scar; flowers tubular, purple-tinged, May–June; drupe berry-like, July–Sept. . . . L′ (*Gaylussacia* spp.).

    L′. TWIGS HAIRY AND RESIN-DOTTED; LEAVES THICK, DARK GREEN ABOVE; DRUPE HAIRY AND RESIN-DOTTED: height to 0.5 m, colonial; dry pinelands; flower clusters with persistent, leaf-like bracts . . . . .Dwarf huckleberry, *Gaylussacia dumosa* (Heath Fam.) (Fig. 3j)

    L′. TWIGS SMOOTH; LEAVES THIN, DULL WHITE BENEATH; DRUPE DARK BLUE WITH WHITE COATING: height to 2 m; dry woods and clearings; flowers 3–4.5 mm in lax, open clusters with small, deciduous bracts . . . . .Dangleberry, *Gaylussacia frondosa* (Heath Fam.)

    L′. TWIGS SLIGHTLY HAIRY TO SMOOTH; LEAVES RESIN-DOTTED ON BOTH SURFACES; DRUPE BLACK WITHOUT WHITE COATING: dry or moist woods, thickets and clearings; flowers resin-dotted in short, stalkless clusters with small, deciduous bracts . . . . .Black huckleberry, *Gaylussacia baccata* (Heath Fam.)

L. LEAVES NOT RESIN-DOTTED; FRUIT A MANY-SEEDED BERRY: colonial to 0.5 m; dry woods, clearings; twigs smooth or hairy; scales of the smaller buds with long-pointed tips; leaves oval, dull, white beneath, smooth or hairy, untoothed or finely toothed, 1.5–5 cm; flowers white or greenish, often pink-tinged, 4–6 mm, May; berry dark blue with a white coating, June–July . . . . .Low blueberry or Lowbush blueberry, *Vaccinium vacillans* (Heath Fam.) (Fig. 3h)

M. FRUIT FLESHY, RED; PLANT AROMATIC, WINTERGREEN: colonial sub-shrub 5–15 cm; dry or moist woods, thickets; leaves elliptical, obtusely toothed, 1.5–5 cm; flowers cylindrical, few, nodding, white, June–Aug.; capsule surrounded by a fleshy calyx, persistent . . . . .Wintergreen, *Gaultheria procumbens* (Heath Fam.) (Fig. 3b)
M. FRUIT DRY, BROWN; PLANT NOT STRONGLY AROMATIC . . . N
    N. STEMS NEARLY HERBACEOUS, ASCENDING; LEAVES SMOOTH, VARIEGATED WITH WHITE; FLOWERS AND CAPSULES 1–5 IN ERECT TERMINAL CLUSTERS: colonial sub-shrub, 5–20 cm; dry woods; leaves remotely toothed, 3–7 cm; flowers white, 2 cm wide, June–July; capsule five-celled with flattened summit . . . . .Spotted wintergreen,
                      Chimaphila maculata (Wintergreen Fam.) (Fig. 3c)
    N. STEMS SLIGHTLY WOODY, PROSTRATE OR TRAILING; LEAVES STIFF-HAIRY AND NOT VARIEGATED; FLOWERS AND CAPSULES IN SMALL AXILLARY OR TERMINAL CLUSTERS: evergreen; dry sand or loam; leaves oval, clasping; flowers rose to white, 8–15 mm, Apr.–May; capsule five-celled with flattened summit . . . . .Trailing arbutus,
                      Epigaea repens (Heath Fam.) (Fig. 3d)
O. SHRUBS WITH COMPOUND LEAVES (THREE OR MORE LEAFLETS) . . . P
O. SHRUBS WITH SIMPLE LEAVES . . . Q
    P. STEMS AND PETIOLES BRISTLY OR PRICKLY; LEAFLETS 3(-5); FLOWERS USUALLY SHOWY, WHITE; FRUITS ARE COMPACT CLUSTERS OF SMALL, ONE-SEEDED DRUPELETS ARRANGED ON A DISC: colonial; dry sands; stems erect or arching to 1 m; leaves woolly beneath; flowers 1–3 per cluster, May–July; drupelets dry, July–Aug. . . . . .Sand blackberry,
                      Rubus cuneifolius (Rose Fam.)
    P. STEMS AND PETIOLES SMOOTH OR FINELY DOWNY; LEAFLETS 9(-21); FLOWERS SMALL, YELLOW-GREEN; FRUITS SMALL, HAIRY, DRY, AND DRUPE-LIKE IN ERECT, TERMINAL CLUSTERS: colonial shrub or small tree; disturbed areas; twigs stout with a large pith; leaflets shiny, leaf axis with wings; leaf scar with five bundle scars; flowers numerous in terminal clusters, July–Sept.; drupes red, Sept.–Oct. . . . . .Dwarf sumac, *Rhus copallina* (Sumac Fam.)
Q. SHRUBS WITH OPPOSITE OR WHORLED LEAVES, LEAF SCARS AND BUDS . . . R
Q. SHRUBS WITH ALTERNATE LEAVES, LEAF SCARS AND BUDS . . . X
    R. LEAVES LEATHERY IN TEXTURE, EVERGREEN . . . S
    R. LEAVES VERY SLIGHTLY (IF AT ALL) LEATHERY, DECIDUOUS . . . T
S. LEAVES OPPOSITE, USUALLY <1.25 CM LONG; FLOWERS WHITISH; FRUITS 2–3-CELLED, EGG-SHAPED CAPSULES IN DENSE, TERMINAL CLUSTERS . . . . .Sand myrtle, *Leiophyllum buxifolium.* See H. in Key II.
S. LEAVES OFTEN IN WHORLS OF THREE AND LARGER, BUT MOSTLY <5 CM LONG; FLOWERS DEEP PINK; FRUITS FIVE-CELLED, GLOBE-SHAPED, LONG-STALKED CAPSULES IN CLUSTERS ALONG THE TWIGS OF THE PREVIOUS YEAR: height to 1 m; wet or dry sandy soil; leaves thin, elliptical, 3–5 cm; flowers on glandular stems, 8–13 mm wide, May–June . . .Sheep laurel, *Kalmia angustifolia* (Heath Fam.) (Fig. 3k)
    T. LEAVES COMMONLY CONTAIN CLUSTERS OF SMALLER LEAVES IN THEIR AXILS . . . U
    T. LEAVES USUALLY WITHOUT CLUSTERS OF SMALLER LEAVES IN THEIR AXILS . . . V
U. FLOWERS YELLOW AND FOUR-PETALLED; CAPSULES ENCLOSED IN A PAIR OF HEART-SHAPED SEPALS; STEMS WITH TWO WING-LIKE RIDGES BELOW LEAF SCARS . . . . .St. Peters wort, *Ascyrum stans,* and
                      St. Andrew's wort, *A. hypericoides.* See H' in Key II, Shrubs.
U. FLOWERS YELLOW AND FIVE-PETALLED; CAPSULES WITH FIVE SEPALS AT BASE; STEMS TWO-EDGED BELOW LEAF SCARS: much-branched shrub 0.5–2 m; wet open areas; leaves narrow; flowers numerous in branched, terminal clusters, July–Sept.; capsule slender-conical . . . . .Bushy St.John's wort, *Hypericum densiflorum* (St. John's Wort Fam.)
    V. LEAVES ALWAYS OPPOSITE; FLOWERS ARRANGED IN FLAT-TOPPED, TERMINAL CLUSTERS; FRUIT A DRUPE . . . V'
    (*Viburnum* spp.)
        V'. BUDS YELLOW-BROWN; TWIGS DULL; LEAVES DULL ABOVE AND SHALLOWLY TOOTHED: height 1–4 m; wet woods and thickets, swamps; buds with one pair of visible scales; twigs with a terminal bud; leaves 2.5–15 cm; leaf scars with three bundle scars; flowers ill-scented, May–June; drupes changing from whitish-yellow to pink to blue-black, Aug.–Sept. . . . . .Northern withered, *Viburnum cassinoides* (Honeysuckle Fam.) (Fig. 2e)
        V'. BUDS RED-BROWN; TWIGS SHINY; LEAVES SHINY ABOVE; LEAF MARGIN RECURVED, APPEARING UNTOOTHED: a similar shrub or small tree . . . . .Southern withered, *Viburnum nudum* (Honeysuckle Fam.)
    V. LEAVES OFTEN ARRANGED IN THREES; FLOWERS NOT ARRANGED IN FLAT-TOPPED CLUSTERS; FRUIT NOT A DRUPE . . . W
W. LEAVES LANCE-SHAPED; FRUIT AN URN-SHAPED CAPSULE IN THE LEAF AXILS; PLANT CHIEFLY WOODY TOWARD THE BASE; FLOATING BRANCHES WITH CORKY THICKENINGS: soft-wooded shrub; swamps, pond, and stream margins; stem angled, arching, rooting at tips; flowers purple in axillary clusters, July–Sept. . . . . .Swamp loosestrife,
                      Decodon verticillatus (Loosestrife Fam.) (Fig. 2f)
W. LEAVES OVAL OR ELLIPTICAL; FLOWERS AND FRUITS IN LONG-STALKED, DENSE, BALL-SHAPED HEADS; PLANT WITH-OUT FLOATING BRANCHES: height 1–3 m; swamps, pond, and stream margins; buds buried in bark and not visible; leaves smooth, 8–15 cm; leaf scars with one bundle scar; flowers small, tubular, four-parted, July–Aug.; fruit a small nutlet . . . .
                      Buttonbush, *Cephalanthus occidentalis* (Madder Fam.) (Fig. 2g)
    X. PLANTS CLIMBING BY MEANS OF TENDRILS; STEMS WITH THORNS: prickly vines; leaves broad, ribbed; flowers greenish in axillary umbels; fruit a berry . . . X' (*Smilax* spp.).
        X'. LEAVES ROUNDED; BERRIES RED: swamps, wet thickets; flowers May–June; fruit in autumn, persistent . . . .
                      Walter's greenbrier, *Smilax walteri* (Lily Fam.)
        X'. LEAVES ROUNDED; BERRIES BLUE: wet thickets; flowers May–June; fruit in autumn, persistent . . . .
                      Greenbrier, *Smilax rotundifolia* (Lily Fam.)
        X'. LEAVES OBLONG; BERRIES BLACK: evergreen; swamps; flowers Aug.–Sept.; fruit in autumn of second season, persistent . . . . .Laurel-leaved greenbrier, *Smilax laurifolia* (Lily Fam.)

X'. LEAVES TRIANGULAR–OVATE; BERRIES BLUE-BLACK: moist sandy ground; stems herbaceous; flowers June–July; fruit in autumn, persistent . . . . .Halbert-leaved Smilax, *Smilax pseudo-china* (Lily Fam.)

X'. LEAVES ELLIPTICAL OR OVATE, WHITE BENEATH; BERRIES BLUE: dry sandy soil; flowers May–June; fruit in autumn, persistent . . . . .Glaucous-leaved greenbrier, *Smilax glauca* (Lily Fam.)

X. PLANTS NOT CLIMBING; STEMS WITHOUT THORNS . . . Y

Y. LEAVES VERY NARROW, MORE OR LESS STIFF, <3 MM WIDE: . . . . .Broom crowberry, *Corema conradii.* See D in Key II, Shrubs

Y. LEAVES WITH BROADER BLADES, >3 MM WIDE . . . Z

Z. LEAVES LOBED, OR TOOTHED AND LOBED . . . a

Z. LEAVES NOT LOBED, THE MARGINS EITHER TOOTHED OR UNTOOTHED . . . c

a. LEAVES NOT ESPECIALLY AROMATIC WHEN CRUSHED; FRUIT AN ACORN; BUDS USUALLY CLUSTERED AT THE TIP OF TWIGS: shrub or small tree to 6 m, often to only 1.5 m in pinelands and Pine Plains; bark dark brown, smooth, thin; leaves shiny, dark green above, white-felted beneath, variable in shape, 5–12 cm; leaf scars with five or more bundle scars; May; acorns borne in pairs, short-stalked, 1 cm . . . . .Scrub oak or bear oak, *Quercus ilicifolia* (Beech Fam.) (Fig. 2i)

a. LEAVES AROMATIC WHEN CRUSHED; FRUIT NOT AN ACORN; BUDS USUALLY NOT CLUSTERED AT THE TIPS OF TWIGS . . . b

b. LEAVES LONG AND NARROW WITH DEEP, ROUNDED LOBES ON EACH SIDE OF MIDRIB; LEAF SCARS WITH THREE BUNDLE SCARS: shrub to 1.5 m, less in dry open areas; male catkins clustered, cylindrical, nodding; female catkins nearly spherical, Apr.–May; nutlets ellipsoid in a burr 1.2 cm thick. . . . . .Sweet fern, *Comptonia peregrina* (Bayberry Fam.) (Fig. 2h)

b. LEAVES BROAD, USUALLY MITTEN-SHAPED OR THREE-LOBED; LEAF SCARS WITH A SINGLE BUNDLE SCAR . . . . Sassafras, *Sassafras albidum.* See O in Key I, Trees.

c. LEAF MARGINS TOOTHED . . . d

c. LEAF MARGINS UNTOOTHED . . . r

d. LEAVES WITH MINUTE YELLOW RESIN DOTS AT LEAST ON THE LOWER SURFACE, AROMATIC WHEN CRUSHED: evergreen shrub, rarely small tree; wet (-dry) thickets, woods; twigs blackish; leaves shiny, oblong; catkins May–June; nuts wax-covered, persistent, 3.5–4.5 mm . . . . .Wax myrtle, *Myrica heterophylla* (Bayberry Fam.)

d. LEAVES NOT RESIN-DOTTED . . . e

e. LEAVES LEATHERY IN TEXTURE, USUALLY EVERGREEN . . . f

e. LEAVES NOT LEATHERY, MOSTLY DECIDUOUS . . . g

f. PLANTS LOW AND MUCH BRANCHED; LEAF MARGINS WITH A FEW SMALL TEETH OR UNTOOTHED; LEAVES WITH MINUTE RUSTY AND SILVERY SCALES; FRUIT A MANY-SEEDED, FLATTENED CAPSULE: height to 1.5 m; swamps, bog, pond, and stream margins; leaves elliptical, 1.5–5 cm; flowers white, 6–7 mm in a one-sided, leafy cluster, Apr.–May; capsule five-celled with flattened or nearly round summit . . . . .Leatherleaf, *Chamaedaphne calyculata* (Heath Fam.) (Fig. 3f)

f. TALLER, ERECT SHRUB; LEAF MARGINS USUALLY WITH SOME LOW OR BLUNTISH TEETH ABOVE THE MIDDLE; LEAVES DARK GREEN AND SHINY ABOVE, PALER WITH BLACK SPOTS BENEATH; FRUIT A DRUPE, DRY, BLACK: height 1–3 m; wet woods and thickets, swamps, leaves 1.5–5 cm; male flowers several and female solitary in the leaf axils on different plants, June–July; drupe persistent . . . . .Inkberry, *Ilex glabra* (Holly Fam.) (Fig. 2k)

g. TWIGS BEARING CATKINS . . . h

g. TWIGS NEVER BEARING CATKINS . . . i

h. LEAF MARGINS WITH COARSE TEETH; LEAF SCARS WITH FIVE OR MORE BUNDLE SCARS; FRUIT AN ACORN; BUDS USUALLY CLUSTERED AT THE TIPS OF TWIGS; PLANTS OF DRY PINELANDS: shrubs rarely above 4 m; leaves gray-downy beneath, bright green above; May; acorns borne in pairs, short stalked, 1 cm . . . . .Dwarf chestnut oak, *Quercus prinoides* (Beech Fam.) (Fig. 2j)

h. LEAF MARGINS WITH FINE, SHARP TEETH; LEAF SCARS WITH THREE BUNDLE SCARS; FRUITS ARE SMALL NUTLETS BORNE IN PERSISTENT, WOODY CONE-LIKE STRUCTURES; PLANTS OF WET WOODS AND SWAMPS: tall shrub or small tree; leaves elliptical to inversely egg-shaped; male catkins pendulous, clustered; female catkins short, ovoid, Mar.–Apr. . . . . .Common alder, *Alnus serrulata* (Birch Fam.)

i. FLOWERS AND FRUITS ARRANGED IN ELONGATE, ONE-SIDED CLUSTERS AT THE TIPS OF BRANCHES: height 1–4 m; wet thickets; leaves finely toothed, 3–8 cm; leaf scars with one bundle scar; flowers white or pinkish, May–June; capsule ovoid . . . . .Fetterbush, *Leucothoe racemosa* (Heath Fam.) (Fig. 3n)

i. FLOWERS AND FRUITS NOT ARRANGED IN ONE-SIDED CLUSTERS . . . j

j. UPPER LEAF SURFACES WITH DARK GLANDS ALONG THE MIDRIB; FRUIT LIKE A BERRY-SIZED APPLE: colonial shrub 0.3–4 m; low woods, swamps, wet thickets; leaves elliptical to inversely egg-shaped, 3–7 cm; leaf margin with a gland between each incurved tooth; flowers white in flattish, terminal clusters, Apr.–May . . . j' (*Pyrus* spp.)

j'. TWIGS HAIRY; LEAVES WOOLLY BENEATH; FRUIT RED, SEPT.-OCT. . . . . . . , ...Red chokeberry, *Pyrus arbutifolia* (Rose Fam.) (Fig. 2m)

j'. TWIGS AND LEAVES SMOOTH; FRUIT BLACK, JULY–AUG. . . . . .Black chokeberry, *Pyrus melanocarpa* (Rose Fam.)

j. UPPER LEAF SURFACES WITHOUT SUCH GLANDS . . . k

k. LEAF MARGINS DOUBLY TOOTHED; height 1–3 m; wet thickets, swamps; twigs ending in a terminal bud; outer bud scales falling off early, inner scales hairy; leaves inversely egg-shaped, untoothed in lower half, straight-veined, 3.5–7 cm; leaf scars with one bundle scar; flowers white, fragrant in erect, cylindrical, terminal clusters, July–Aug.; capsule rounded, three-celled . . . . .Sweet pepperbush, *Clethra alnifolia* (Sweet Pepperbush Fam.) (Fig. 2n)

k. LEAF MARGINS WITH REGULARLY-SPACED SINGLE TEETH, OR TEETH RATHER OBSCURE . . . l
  l. LEAVES MORE OR LESS CLUSTERED NEAR THE TIPS OF THE BRANCHES: height 1–2 m; wet woods and thickets, swamps; twigs hairy; terminal bud usually much larger than lateral buds; leaves inversely egg-shaped, margins hairy, 3–6 cm; leaf scars with one bundle scar; flowers fragrant, white, 2–3 cm wide, tube 2–3 cm long, in terminal clusters, June–July; capsule glandular–hairy, cylindrical, 1–2 cm . . . . .Swamp azalea, *Rhododendron viscosum* (Heath Fam.) (Fig. 3m)
  l. LEAVES WELL SPACED ALONG THE BRANCHES . . . m
m. TWIGS SHOWING PARTITIONS IN THE PITH WHEN CUT LENGTHWISE; CAPSULE TWO-CELLED: height to 3 m; swamps, wet thickets; buds pointed outward from the twig; leaves oblong, pointed, 3–8 cm; leaf scars with three bundle scars; petals white, not united, 5–6 mm; flowers in loose, open, terminal clusters, 4–15 cm, June . . . . .Virginia willow,
                                                          Itea virginica (Saxifrage Fam.) (Fig. 2o)
m. TWIGS SHOWING A CONTINUOUS PITH WHEN CUT LENGTHWISE; IF FRUIT IS A CAPSULE, FIVE-CELLED . . . n
  n. LEAFSTALKS SLENDER, USUALLY 6 MM OR MORE LONG . . . o
  n. LEAFSTALKS MODERATE OR STOUT, <6 MM LONG . . . p
o. FRUIT JUICY, APPLE-LIKE WITH ABOUT TEN SMALL SEEDS; BUDS NARROW, SEVERAL TIMES LONGER THAN WIDE; BUD SCALES DARK-TIPPED; LEAF SCARS WITH THREE BUNDLE SCARS . . . o′ (*Amelanchier* spp.)
  o′. COLONIAL SHRUB 0.2–1.5 M; DRY OPEN AREAS, THICKETS, LOW WOODS: leaves unexpanded at flowering, woolly beneath when young, oblong to elliptical, 3–5 cm; leaf scars with three bundle scars; petals 6–7 mm; flowers in dense, erect clusters, Apr.–May; fruit purple-black, 6–8 mm, June–July . . . . .Coastal Juneberry,
                                      Shadbush, *Amelanchier obovalis* (Rose Fam.)
  o′. SHRUB OR SMALL TREE WITH SEVERAL TRUNKS TO 8 M; WET SOIL AND SWAMPS: leaves half grown at flowering, woolly beneath when young, oblong to elliptical, 3–6 cm; leaf scars with three bundle scars; petals 7–10 mm; Apr.–May; fruit blackish, June–July . . . . .Juneberry, Serviceberry, *Amelanchier canadensis* (Rose Fam.) (Fig. 2p)
o. FRUIT A BERRY-LIKE DRUPE WITH LARGE SEED-LIKE NUTLETS; BUDS SHORT, NOT MUCH LONGER THAN WIDE; BUD SCALES NOT DARK-TIPPED; LEAF SCARS WITH ONE BUNDLE SCAR . . . o″ (*Ilex* spp.)
  o″. LEAVES DULL ABOVE, SPARSELY HAIRY BENEATH; CALYX SEGMENTS HAIRY: height 1–4 m; swamps, stream and pond margins; leaves lanceolate, toothed; male flowers several per cluster, female solitary but grouped, axillary on different plants, June–July; drupe bright red, 5–7 mm, persistent . . . . .Winterberry, *Ilex verticillata* (Holly Fam.) (Fig. 2l)
  o″. LEAVES SHINY ABOVE, SMOOTH BENEATH; CALYX SEGMENTS SMOOTH: similar shrub; flowers May–June; drupe scarlet, 7–10 mm . . . . .Smooth winterberry, *Ilex laevigata* (Holly Fam.)
p. TWIGS MINUTELY WARTY-DOTTED, GREEN OR REDDISH, SMOOTH OR HAIRY, WITH BUDS OF TWO SIZES . . . . .p′
(*Vaccinium* spp., blueberries). Also see L in Key II, Shrubs, for Low blueberry, *Vaccinium vacillans*.
  p′. LEAVES UNTOOTHED OR TOOTHED, HAIRY ALONG THE VEINS OR SMOOTH: shrub to 4 m; swamps, peaty thickets, low woods; scales of the smaller buds with long-pointed tips; leaves 4–8 cm; flowers white or pink-tinged, tubular, ovoid, 6–13 mm, May; berry blue or blue-black with a white coating, 6–12 mm wide, July–Aug. . . . . .Highbush
                           blueberry, *Vaccinium corymbosum* (Heath Fam.)
  p′. LEAVES UNTOOTHED, SMOOTH, WHITE BENEATH: similar shrub; flowers dull white, 4–6 mm; berry 5–8 mm . . . . . .New
                            Jersey blueberry, *Vaccinium caesariense* (Heath Fam.)
  p′. LEAVES UNTOOTHED, WOOLLY BENEATH: similar shrub; flowers greenish or yellowish-white, often pink-tinged, Apr. –May; berry dull black, 5–8 mm .Black highbush blueberry, *Vaccinium atrococcum* (Heath Fam.)
p. TWIGS NOT WARTY-DOTTED AND WITH BUDS MORE OR LESS ALIKE . . . q
  q. LEAF MARGINS WITH SMALL AND RATHER OBSCURE TEETH; TWIGS WITHOUT A TERMINAL BUD; TIPS DYING BACK TO A LATERAL BUD; FRUIT A SMALL ROUNDISH CAPSULE: height to 4 m; swamps, wet thickets; buds with two visible scales and closely pressed against the twig; leaves inversely egg-shaped; leaf scars with one bundle scar; flowers numerous, white, nearly spherical, 3–5 mm in branched, terminal clusters, June–July; capsule 2.5–3 mm, persistent . . . .
                               Maleberry, *Lyonia ligustrina* (Heath Fam.) (Fig. 3o)
  q. LEAF MARGINS WITH SHARP AND QUITE CONSPICUOUS TEETH; TWIGS ENDING IN A TERMINAL BUD; FRUITS BERRY-LIKE BUT WITH LARGE SEED-LIKE NUTLETS: Winterberry, *Ilex verticillata,* and Smooth winterberry, *I. laevigata.* See O in Key II, Shrubs.
r. LEAVES MORE OR LESS LEATHERY; EVERGREEN OR DECIDUOUS . . . s
r. LEAVES NOT LEATHERY, DECIDUOUS . . . u
  s. LEAVES WHITENED BENEATH, SPICY-AROMATIC WHEN CRUSHED; FLOWERS LARGE AND SOLITARY; TALL SHRUB OR SMALL TREE . . . . .Sweet bay, *Magnolia virginiana*. See G in Key I, Trees.
  s. LEAVES NEITHER WHITENED BENEATH NOR SPICY-AROMATIC WHEN CRUSHED; FLOWERS SMALLER AND IN AXILS OF BRACTS OR IN TERMINAL CLUSTERS . . . t
t. LOW SHRUB OF BOGS AND STREAM MARGINS; LEAVES 2.5–7.5 CM LONG WITH MINUTE SILVERY SCALES; FLOWERS WHITE, BELL-SHAPED IN AXILS OF LEAF-LIKE BRACTS . . . . . . .Leatherleaf, *Chamaedaphne calyculata*. See f in Key II, Shrubs.
t. SHRUB OR SMALL TREE GROWING IN SANDY WOODS; LEAVES 5–9 CM LONG, SMOOTH AND LUSTROUS ABOVE; FLOWERS WHITE TO DEEP PINK, SAUCER-SHAPED IN FLATTENED TERMINAL CLUSTERS: height usually 2–3 m; moist or dry sandy woods or clearings, swamps; leaves thick, elliptical, 5–10 cm; flowers glandular, 1.5–3 cm, May–June; fruit a flattened capsule, 5–7 mm wide . . . . .Mountain laurel, *Kalmia latifolia* (Heath Fam.) (Fig. 3l)
  u. LEAVES WITH YELLOW RESIN DOTS AT LEAST ON THE LOWER SURFACE; FRUIT A BERRY-LIKE DRUPE . . . .
                              Gaylussacia spp. See L in Key II, Shrubs.
  u. LEAVES NOT RESIN-DOTTED . . . v
v. LEAVES WITH MINUTE BLACK DOTS ON THE LOWER SURFACE; FRUIT A PYRAMID-SHAPED CAPSULE: height to 2 m; low

woods and thickets, swamps; buds with three or more visible scales and not closely pressed against the twig; leaves elliptical, hairy on veins beneath, 2–6 cm; leaf scars with one bundle scar; flowers white, urn-shaped, 0.8–1.3 cm, nodding in terminal clusters, May–June; capsules persistent on erect stems . . . . .Staggerbush, *Lyonia mariana* (Heath Fam.) (Fig. 3p)

    v. LEAVES NOT BLACK-DOTTED BENEATH; FRUIT A BERRY OR GLOBE-SHAPED CAPSULE . . . w

        w. TWIGS MINUTELY WARTY-DOTTED, OTHERWISE SMOOTH OR HAIRY, USUALLY GREENISH OR REDDISH; BUDS OF TWO SIZES, THE LARGER WITH SEVERAL SCALES, THE SMALLER USUALLY WITH TWO VISIBLE SCALES; FRUIT A BERRY . . . . .Blueberries,˜*Vaccinium* spp. See P in Key II, Shrubs.

        w. TWIGS NOT WARTY-DOTTED, OTHERWISE SMOOTH OR MINUTELY DOWNY, YELLOWISH-BROWN TO ASHY-GRAY; ALL BUDS MORE OR LESS ALIKE; FRUIT A SMALL GLOBE-SHAPED CAPSULE . . . . .Maleberry, *Lyonia ligustrina.* See Q in Key II, Shrubs.

Herbaceous Plants—Key III

A. FERN-LIKE OR MOSS-LIKE PLANTS WITHOUT TRUE FLOWERS; REPRODUCTION BY SPORES . . . B

A. PLANTS WITH TRUE FLOWERS; REPRODUCTION TYPICALLY BY SEEDS . . . E

    B. LEAVES SMALL, VERY NUMEROUS, AND OVERLAPPING; PLANTS TRAILING . . . . .Club moss, *Lycopodium* spp. (Club moss Fam.); three spp. occur in P.B. bogs; *L. alopecuroides* (Fig. 4a), spores Sept.–Oct.

    B. FRONDS (LEAVES) LARGE AND NOT CLOSELY OVERLAPPING, BUT COMPOUND AND WITH ERECT FROND STEM . . . C (Ferns; about ten spp. occur in the P.B.)

        C. PLANTS OF SANDY, USUALLY DRY, OPEN AREAS . . . . .Bracken, *Pteridium aquilinum* (Fern Fam.) (Fig. 4b), colonial fern of the pinelands, spores July–Aug.

        C. PLANTS OF WET HABITATS . . . D

            D. STERILE FRONDS CLUSTERED AROUND THE REDDISH-BROWN FERTILE FRONDS; BASE OF STEM WOOLLY . . . . Cinnamon fern, *Osmunda cinnamomea* (Flowering Fern Fam.) (Fig. 4c), one of two spp. which occur in swamps and other wet habitats.

            D. STERILE AND FERTILE FRONDS ARRANGED ALONG UNDERGROUND STEMS; EITHER ALIKE, OR THE FERTILE FROND WITH NARROW SUB-DIVISIONS . . . . .Chain fern, *Woodwardia* spp. (Fern Fam.); two spp. occur in wet thickets and swamps.

    E. PLANTS GRASS-LIKE OR RUSH-LIKE; LEAVES GENERALLY DIVIDED INTO OBVIOUS SHEATH AND BLADE; FLOWERS NOT CONSPICUOUSLY COLORED . . . F

    E. PLANTS NEITHER GRASS-LIKE NOR RUSH-LIKE, OR IF SO, THEN THE FLOWERS CONSPICUOUSLY COLORED; LEAVES GENERALLY WITH BLADES ONLY OR BLADES HAVING SHEATHING BASES . . . N

        F. FLOWERS NOT IN AXILS OF DRY BRACTS BUT ARRANGED IN OPEN OR DENSE TERMINAL CLUSTERS; FRUIT A THREE-CELLED CAPSULE . . . . .Rush, *Juncus* spp. (Rush Fam.); about 12 spp. of Rush occur in various habitats; *J. militaris* (Fig. 4d), streams, fruit July–Aug.

        F. FLOWERS IN THE AXILS OF DRY, OVERLAPPING BRACTS FORMING SPIKELETS; FRUIT A GRAIN OR GRAIN-LIKE . . . G

            G. LEAVES IN TWO ROWS ON THE STEM, THEIR LOWER PARTS FORMING SHEATHS AROUND THE STEM BUT THEIR MARGINS NOT UNITED UP TO THEIR SUMMITS TO FORM TUBES; STEMS OFTEN HOLLOW AT THE NODES, NOT TRIANGULAR; TWO BRACTS TO EACH FLOWER . . . H (Poaceae or Gramineae; about 70 spp. belonging to the Grass Fam. occur in the P.B.)

            G. LEAVES, WHEN PRESENT, IN THREE ROWS ON THE STEM, THEIR LOWER PARTS FORMING TUBES AROUND THE STEM; STEMS SOLID AND USUALLY TRIANGULAR; ONE BRACT TO EACH FLOWER . . . J (Cyperaceae; about 75 spp. belonging to the Sedge Fam. occur in the P.B.)

                H. FLOWERS ONE PER SPIKELET; SPIKELETS USUALLY SCATTERED IN A DIFFUSELY-BRANCHED CLUSTER . . . . Panic grass, *Panicum* spp. (Grass Fam.); about 30 spp. occur in various habitats.

                H. FLOWERS TWO TO MANY PER SPIKELET; SPIKELETS NOT IN A DIFFUSELY-BRANCHED CLUSTER . . . I

    I. FLOWERS TWO PER SPIKELET, ONE OF WHICH IS STERILE AND STALKED; SPIKELETS ARRANGED IN LATERAL AND TERMINAL, LONG-HAIRY CLUSTERS WHICH PROTRUDE FROM SHEATHING LEAVES; MARGINS OF SHEATHS NOT UNITED . . . . .Beard grass, *Andropogon* spp. (Grass Fam.); three spp. and one variety occur in the P.B.; Broom sedge, *A. virginicus* (Fig. 4e), dry sands, or wet open ground in var. *abbreviatus,* Aug.–Sept.

    I. FLOWERS SEVERAL TO MANY PER SPIKELET; SPIKELETS ARRANGED IN NARROW, DENSE, TERMINAL CLUSTERS WHICH LACK LONG HAIRS AND SHEATHING LEAVES; LEAF SHEATHS UNITED NEARLY TO THEIR SUMMITS . . . . .Blunt manna-grass, *Glyceria obtusa* (Grass Fam.) (Fig. 4f); stream and pond margins, July–Aug.

            J. FLOWERS PERFECT (MALE AND FEMALE STRUCTURES PRESENT); SPIKELETS ALIKE . .˙. K

            J. FLOWERS UNISEXUAL, MALE AND FEMALE FLOWERS IN DIFFERENT SPIKES; SPIKELETS OF TWO KINDS . . . . Sedge, *Carex* spp. (Sedge Fam.); about 25 spp. occur in various habitats; *C. pensylvanica* (Fig. 4g), dry open sands, pinelands, fruit May–June.

K. SPIKELETS MANY-FLOWERED; FRUIT WITH OR WITHOUT A TUBERCLE (ENLARGED BASE OF STYLE) AND BRISTLES . . . L

K. SPIKELETS 1–2 FLOWERED; FRUIT WITH A TUBERCLE; BRISTLES USUALLY PRESENT . . . . Beak-rush, *Rhynchospora* spp. (Sedge Fam.); about 12 spp. occur in various wet habitats, fruit usually July–Sept.

    L. STEMS WITH A BASAL SHEATH AND NO LEAF BLADES, TERMINATED BY A SINGLE SPIKELET; FRUIT WITH A TUBERCLE AND USUALLY WITH BRISTLES . . . . .Spike-rush, *Eleocharis* spp. (Sedge Fam.); about eight spp. occur in various wet habitats; *E. olivacea* (Fig. 4h), bogs and other moist open ground, fruit July–Oct.

    L. STEMS USUALLY LEAFY; SPIKELETS TWO TO MANY; FRUIT WITHOUT A TUBERCLE . . . M

M. BRISTLES FEW OR NONE FROM BASE OF FRUIT; ONE SPIKELET, APPEARING TERMINAL . . . . .Water club rush, *Scirpus subterminalis* (Sedge Fam.) (Fig. 4i); stream beds, fruit July–Aug.; four additional spp. occur in the P.B.

M. BRISTLES NUMEROUS, ELONGATE, AND SILKY; SPIKELETS IN COTTONY CLUSTERS WITH LEAFY BRACTS . . . .
Cotton-grass, *Eriophorum* spp. (Sedge Fam.); two spp. occur in the P.B.; *E. virginicum* (Fig. 4j), bogs, fruit Aug.–Sept.
N. FLOWERS IN HEADS AND BORNE ON A DISC, SURROUNDED BY BRACTS . . . O
N. FLOWERS NOT BORNE ON A DISC AND NOT SURROUNDED BY BRACTS . . . T
O. LEAVES BASAL, GRASS-LIKE; HEADS SOLITARY ON LEAFLESS STEM, WHITE . . . . .Pipewort, *Eriocaulon* spp.
(Pipewort Fam.); three spp. occur in various wet habitats; *E. septangulare* (Fig. 4k), bogs and ponds, July–Oct.
O. LEAVES NEITHER ALL BASAL NOR GRASS-LIKE; HEADS USUALLY GROUPED TOGETHER ON BRANCHING, LEAFY STEMS,
VARIOUSLY COLORED . . . P (Asteraceae or Compositae; about 60 spp. belonging to the Aster or Composite Fam. occur in the
P.B.)
P. FLOWERS OF EACH HEAD ALIKE: EITHER ALL TUBULAR OR ALL LIGULATE˜(BEARING A FLATTENED, SPREADING
LIMB) . . . Q
P. FLOWERS OF EACH HEAD DIFFERENT: INNER TUBULAR, OUTER LIGULATE . . . R
Q. FLOWERS ALL TUBULAR, WHITE; FRUITS WITH A ROW OF BRISTLES AT THE SUMMIT; FLOWER CLUSTERS BRANCHED
AND FLAT-TOPPED; LEAVES UNTOOTHED OR TOOTHED, OPPOSITE OR WHORLED . . . . .Thoroughwort, *Eupatorium*
spp. (Aster Fam.); eight spp. occur in the P.B.; White boneset, *E. album* (Fig. 4l), dry sandy open areas, Aug.–Sept.
Q. FLOWERS ALL LIGULATE, GOLDEN-YELLOW; FRUIT WITH TWO ROWS OF SCALES AND BRISTLES AT SUMMIT; FLOWER
CLUSTERS FEW-BRANCHED; STEMS GROUPED; LEAVES MOSTLY BASAL . . . . .Dwarf dandelion,
Krigia virginica (Aster Fam.), dry open sands, roadsides.
R. LIGULATE OR OUTER FLOWERS WHITE, BLUE, OR PINK . . . . .Aster, *Aster* spp. (Aster Fam.);
ten spp. occur in various habitats; Showy aster, *A. spectabilis* (Fig. 4m), dry sandy open areas, July–Sept.
R. LIGULATE OR OUTER FLOWERS YELLOW . . . S
S. INNER FRUITS BEARING TWO ROWS OF BRISTLES AT THEIR SUMMITS . . . . .Golden aster,
Chrysopsis spp. (Aster Fam.); two spp. occur in dry sandy open areas of the P.B., Aug.–Sept.
S. INNER FRUITS BEARING ONE ROW OF BRISTLES AT THEIR SUMMITS . . . . .Goldenrod, *Solidago* spp.
(Aster Fam.); 13 spp. occur in various habitats; Fragrant goldenrod, *S. odora* (Fig. 4n), dry sandy open areas, July–Aug.
T. PLANTS OF WET HABITATS . . . U
T. PLANTS OF SANDY, USUALLY DRY HABITATS . . . k
U. LEAVES SUBMERSED OR FLOATING; FLOWERS EMERGENT . . . V
U. LEAVES, STEMS, AND FLOWERS USUALLY EMERGENT AND ASCENDING IN SHALLOW WATER OR NOT IN WATER . . . X
V. LEAVES DISSECTED OR WITH VERY FINE LEAVES BEARING TRAPS OR BLADDERS; FLOWERS BILATERALLY SYMMET-
RICAL ON EMERGENT STEMS; PLANTS USUALLY SUBMERSED OR ROOTED IN MUD .Bladderwort,
Utricularia spp. (Bladderwort Fam.); 11 spp. occur in wet habitats; *U. fibrosa* (Fig. 4o), bogs and ponds, June–Aug.
V. LEAVES BROAD, HEART-SHAPED, AND FLOATING; FLOWERS RADIALLY SYMMETRICAL, TERMINATING LEAFLESS
STEM; PLANTS ALSO WITH UNDERGROUND STEMS . . . W
W. FLOWERS WIDELY EXPANDING, PETALS WHITE OR PINK, SHOWY . . . . .Water lily,
Nymphaea odorata (Water lily Fam.), ponds and open water of bogs, June–Sept.
W. FLOWERS NEARLY SPHERICAL, PETALS SMALL, SEPALS YELLOW, RED- OR GREEN-TINGED . . . . .Spatterdock,
Nuphar variegatum (Water lily Fam.), ponds and streams, May–Sept.
X. LEAVES EMERGENT AND ASCENDING OR FLOATING, OBLONG TO ELLIPTICAL AND WITHOUT DISTINCT MIDVEIN;
FLOWERS YELLOW AND IN A SPIKE . . . . .Golden club,
Orontium aquaticum (Arum Fam.) (Fig. 4p), bogs, ponds, and streams, Apr.–May
X. LEAVES OTHERWISE; FLOWERS NOT IN A SPIKE . . . Y
Y. LEAVES PARALLEL-VEINED; FLOWER PARTS MOSTLY IN THREE'S . . . Z
Y. LEAVES NET-VEINED; FLOWER PARTS MOSTLY IN FOUR'S OR FIVE'S . . . e
Z. LEAVES ARROWHEAD- OR LANCE-SHAPED; FLOWERS WHITE . . . . .Arrowhead, *Sagittaria* spp.
(Arrowhead Fam.); three spp. occur in the P.B.; *S. engelmannii* (Fig. 5a), bogs and stream and pond margins, June–Sept.
Z. LEAVES GRASS-LIKE; FLOWERS WHITE, YELLOW, OR BLUE . . . a
a. FLOWERS BILATERALLY SYMMETRICAL, WHITE AND IN ELONGATED, TERMINAL CLUSTERS . . . . .White-fringed orchid,
Habenaria blephariglottis (Orchid Fam.) (Fig. 5b), bogs, July–Aug.; 17 additional spp. of orchids occur in the P.B.
a. FLOWERS RADIALLY SYMMETRICAL, NOT WHITE . . . b
b. FLOWERS BLUE ON STEMS PROTRUDING FROM A SHEATHING LEAF-LIKE BRACT . . . . .Blue-eyed grass,
Sisyrinchium spp. (Iris Fam.); four spp. occur in the P.B.; *S. atlanticum* (Fig. 5c), bogs and other wet open areas, May–June
b. FLOWERS YELLOW, NOT PROTRUDING FROM A LEAF-LIKE BRACT . . . c
c. STEM AND FLOWERS WOOLLY; FLOWERS SOLITARY ON SHORT STEMS IN A BRANCHED TERMINAL CLUSTER . . . d
c. STEM WITHOUT HAIRS; FLOWERS NUMEROUS IN A SOLITARY HEAD-LIKE CLUSTER CONTAINING STIFF BROWN
BRACTS . . . . .Yellow-eyed grass, *Xyris* spp. (Yellow-eyed grass Fam.);
five spp. occur in the P.B.; *X. caroliniana* (Fig. 5d), wet peaty or sandy areas, July–Sept.
d. UPPER STEM AND FLOWER CLUSTER DENSELY WHITE-WOOLLY . . . . .Golden crest,
Lophiola americana (Amaryllis Fam.), bogs and swamps, June–July
d. UPPER STEM AND FLOWER CLUSTER RUST-COLORED AND WOOLLY . . . . .Redroot, *Lachnanthes tinctoria*
(Redroot Fam.), swamps and bogs, frequently in abandoned cranberry bogs, July–Aug.
e. LEAVES MODIFIED INTO PITCHER-SHAPED STRUCTURES OR WITH STALKED GLANDS, INSECTIVOROUS . . . f
e. LEAVES NOT MODIFIED FOR INSECT CATCHING . . . g
f. LEAVES PITCHER-SHAPED, CAPABLE OF HOLDING WATER; FLOWER SOLITARY FROM A LEAFLESS STEM . . . .
Pitcher plant, *Sarracenia purpurea* (Pitcher plant Fam.) (Fig. 5e), bogs and White cedar swamps, Mar.–June

f. LEAVES LINEAR, SPATULATE, OR ROUNDED AND COVERED WITH STALKED GLANDS; FLOWERS SEVERAL TO MANY ALONG A LEAFLESS STEM . . . . .Sundew, *Drosera* spp. (Sundew Fam.);
three spp. occur in the P.B.; *D. intermedia* (Fig. 5f), bogs, swamps and open wet areas July–Aug.

g. LEAVES PROMINENTLY THREE-VEINED; LEAF MARGINS TOOTHED; FLOWERS BRIGHT PURPLE . . . . . . .Meadow beauty, *Rhexia* spp. (Melastoma Fam.); three spp. occur in the P.B.; *R. virginica* (Fig. 5g), bogs and swamps, July–Sept.

g. LEAVES NOT PROMINENTLY THREE-VEINED; LEAF MARGINS NOT TOOTHED . . . h

    h. LEAVES OPPOSITE . . . i

    h. LEAVES ALTERNATE . . . j

i. LEAVES USUALLY GLANDULAR- OR BLACK-DOTTED; FLOWERS YELLOW OR PINK . . . .
St. John's wort, *Hypericum* spp. (St. John's wort Fam.); five spp. occur in bogs, swamps and other wet or moist habitats

i. LEAVES NOT GLANDULAR- OR BLACK-DOTTED; FLOWERS WHITE . . . . .Lance-leaved
Sabatia, *Sabatia difformis* (Gentian Fam.) (Fig. 5h), bogs and swamps, July–Aug.

j. FLOWERS ORANGE-YELLOW IN DENSE TERMINAL CLUSTERS . . . . .Orange milkwort, *Polygala lutea* (Milkwort Fam.) (Fig. 5i), moist sandy areas, June–Oct.; seven additional milkworts occur in the P.B.

j. FLOWERS BLUE, WELL SPACED ALONG THE STEM . . . . .Nuttall's lobelia, *Lobelia nuttallii*
(Bluebell Fam.) (Fig. 5j), moist sandy areas, July–Sept.; two additional Lobelias occur in the P.B.

k. LEAVES GRASS-LIKE AND TUFTED; FLOWERS MANY IN A LARGE, DENSE, ELONGATE CLUSTER FROM STEM WITH NUMEROUS BRACT-LIKE LEAVES . . . . .Turkeybeard,
Xerophyllum asphodeloides (Lily Fam.) (Fig. 5k), open sandy areas, May–July

k. LEAVES NEITHER GRASS-LIKE NOR TUFTED; FLOWERS NEITHER WHITE NOR IN LARGE ELONGATE CLUSTERS . . . l

    l. FLOWERS BILATERALLY SYMMETRICAL . . . m

    l. FLOWERS RADIALLY SYMMETRICAL . . . p

m. LEAVES COMPOUND (THREE OR MORE LEAFLETS) . . . n

m. LEAVES SIMPLE . . . o

    n. LEAVES TRI-FOLIATE; FLOWERS BRIGHT YELLOW; PODS NEARLY SPHERICAL, PURPLE; PLANTS SMOOTH . . . .
Wild indigo, *Baptisia tinctoria* (Pea Fam.) (Fig. 5l), open sandy soil, pinelands, Pine Plains, clearings, June–July

    n. LEAVES MANY-FOLIATE; FLOWERS YELLOWISH-WHITE, MARKED WITH PURPLE; PODS LINEAR AND FLAT; PLANTS VERY HAIRY . . . . .Goat's rue,
Tephrosia virginica (Pea Fam.) (Fig. 5m), open sandy soil, pinelands and Pine Plains, June–July

o. FLOWERS YELLOW, SLIGHTLY BILATERALLY SYMMETRICAL, SHOWY; LEAVES DEEPLY LOBED; PLANTS GLANDULAR . . . . .Fern-leaved false foxglove, *Gerardia pedicularia* (Figwort Fam.), pinelands, Aug.–Sept.

o. FLOWERS WHITISH, SMALL, TWO-LIPPED; LEAF MARGINS UNTOOTHED, BUT FLOWER BRACTS TOOTHED; PLANTS SLIGHTLY HAIRY . . . . .Cow-wheat,
Melampyrum lineare (Figwort Fam.) (Fig. 5n), open sandy soil, pinelands and Pine Plains, May–Aug.

p. PLANTS WITH MILKY JUICE; FLOWERS WITHOUT PETALS, BUT HAVING FIVE STALKLESS, GREEN GLANDS . . . .
Wild ipecac, *Euphorbia ipecacuanhae* (Spurge Fam.) (Fig. 5o), open sands, Apr.–May

p. PLANTS WITHOUT MILK JUICE; FLOWERS EITHER WITH PETALS, OR LACKING PETALS IN SMALL FLOWERS . . . q

q. LEAVES AWL-SHAPED, BRACT-LIKE; ALL FLOWERS WITH PETALS . . . r

q. LEAVES OVATE, ELLIPTICAL, OR OBLONG; SOME SMALL FLOWERS LACKING PETALS . . . s

    r. LEAVES DENSE AND OVERLAPPING, UPPER DISTANT, OPPOSITE; FLOWERS WHITE, FEW ON ERECT STEMS FROM A SEMI-WOODY BASE . . . . .Pine Barren sandwort, *Arenaria caroliniana* (Pink Fam.) (Fig. 5p), open sands, June–July

    r. LEAVES ALL DISTANT, OPPOSITE; FLOWERS YELLOW-ORANGE, MANY TERMINATING BRANCHES OF A SINGLE AN-NUAL STEM . . . . .Pineweed or Orange grass,
Hypericum gentianoides (St. John's wort Fam.), open sands, disturbed areas, July–Sept.

s. PETALS FIVE, YELLOW, SHOWY, AND EASILY DECIDUOUS, OR SMALL AND WITHOUT PETALS . . . . .Frostweed, *Helianthemum canadense* (Rockrose Fam.), sandy soil, pinelands, May–July

s. PETALS THREE, GREENISH OR PURPLISH, SMALL, AND PERSISTENT . . . . .Pinweed, *Lechea* spp. (Rockrose Fam.); five spp. occur in sandy soil, pinelands, fruit July–Oct.

SUMMARY

The common trees (19 species), shrubs (53 species), and some herbaceous plants (44 genera) of the Pine Barrens of New Jersey have been identified with the aid of keys. Additional descriptive information was provided for trees and shrubs (Figs. 1–5).

ACKNOWLEDGMENTS

We would like to thank the New York Botanical Garden for permitting us to reproduce illustrations from Britton and Brown (1897). We also would like to thank William Carey Grimm for allowing us to adapt portions of the shrub key in Grimm (1966) and to reproduce two illustrations from Grimm (1962).

REFERENCES

Britton, N. L., and Brown, A. (1897). "An Illustrated Flora of the Northern United States, Canada and the British Possessions," 3 vols. Scribner's, New York.

Fairbrothers, D. E., Moul, E. T., Effbach, A. R., Riemer, D. N., and Schallock, D. A. (1965). Aquatic vegetation of New Jersey. *N.J. Agric. Exp. Stn., Ext. Bull.* No. 382, 1–107.

Fernald, M. L. (1950). "Gray's Manual of Botany," 8th Ed. Am. Book Co., New York.

Gleason, H. A. (1952). "The New Britton and Brown Illustrated Flora of the Northeastern United States and Adjacent Canada," 3 vols. N.Y. Bot. Gard., Bronx, New York.

Gleason, H. A., and Cronquist, A. (1963). "Manual of Vascular Plants of Northeastern United States and Adjacent Canada." Van Nostrand, Princeton, New Jersey.

Graves, A. H. (1956). "Illustrated Guide to Trees and Shrubs. A Handbook of the Woody Plants of the Northeastern United States and Adjacent Regions." Harper, New York.

Grimm, W. C. (1962). "The Book of Trees." Stackpole, Harrisburg, Pennsylvania.

Grimm, W. C. (1966). "How to Recognize Shrubs." Stackpole, Harrisburg, Pennsylvania.

Harlow, W. M. (1957). "Trees of Eastern and Central United States and Canada." Dover, New York.

Harlow, W. M. (1959). "Fruit Key and Twig Key to Trees and Shrubs." Dover, New York.

Harshberger, J. W. (1916). "The Vegetation of the New Jersey Pine Barrens. An Ecologic Investigation." Christopher Sower Co., Philadelphia, Pennsylvania.

McCormick, J. (1970). The Pine Barrens. A preliminary ecological inventory. *N.J. State Mus., Res. Rep.* No. 2.

Peterson, R. T., and McKenny, M. (1968). "A Field Guide to Wildflowers (Northeastern and Northcentral North America)." Houghton Mifflin, Boston, Massachusetts.

Stone, W. (1911). The plants of southern New Jersey with especial reference to the flora of the Pine Barrens and the geographic distribution of the species. N.J. State Mus., Annu. Rep. 1910, pp. 21–828.

Symonds, G. W. D. (1958). "The Tree Identification Book." Morrow, New York.

Symonds, G. W. D. (1963). "The Shrub Identification Book." Morrow, New York.

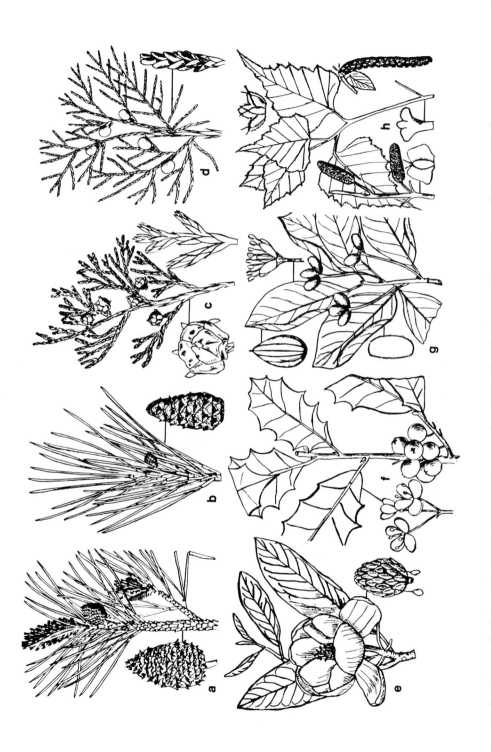

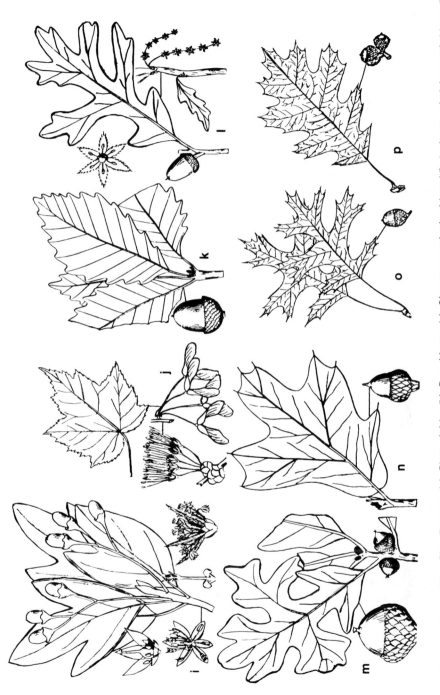

Fig. 1. Common trees of the Pine Barrens. (a) *Pinus rigida*; (b) *P. echinata*; (c) *Chamaecyparis thyoides*; (d) *Juniperus virginiana*; (e) *Magnolia virginiana*; (f) *Ilex opaca*; (g) *Nyssa sylvatica*; (h) *Betula populifolia*; (i) *Sassafras albidum*; (j) *Acer rubrum*; (k) *Quercus prinus*; (l) *Q. alba*; (m) *Q. stellata*; (n) *Q. marilandica*; (o) *Q. coccinea*; (p) *Q. velutina*. Drawings differ in scale.

385

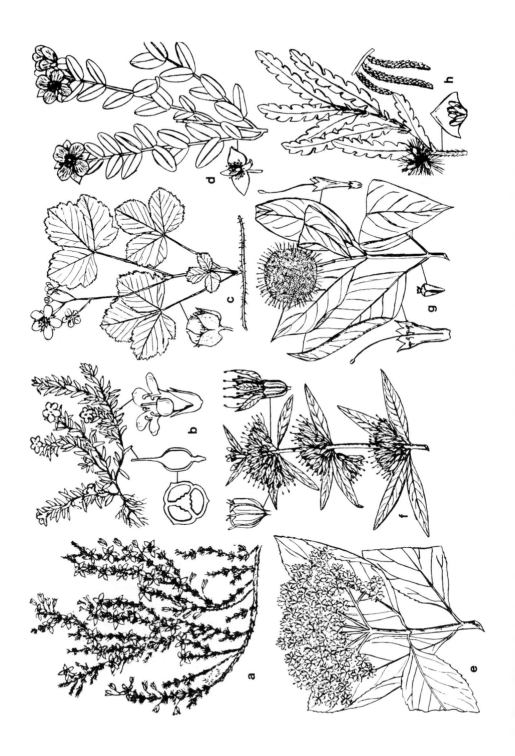

Fig. 2. Common shrubs of the Pine Barrens I. (a) *Hudsonia ericoides*; (b) *Pyxidanthera barbulata*; (c) *Rubus hispidus*; (d) *Ascyrum stans*; (e) *Viburnum cassinoides*; (f) *Decodon verticillatus*; (g) *Cephalanthus occidentalis*; (h) *Comptonia peregrina*; (i) *Quercus ilicifolia*; (j) *Q. prinoides*; (k) *Ilex glabra*; (l) *I. verticillata*; (m) *Pyrus arbutifolia*; (n) *Clethra alnifolia*; (o) *Itea virginica*; (p) *Amelanchier canadensis*. Drawings differ in scale.

Fig. 3. Common shrubs (Heath and Wintergreen Families) of the Pine Barrens II. (a) *Arctostaphylos uva-ursi;* (b) *Gaultheria procumbens;* (c) *Chimaphila maculata;* (d) *Epigaea repens;* (e) *Leiophyllum buxifolium;* (f) *Chamaedaphne calyculata;* (g) *Vaccinium macrocarpon;* (h) *V. vacillans;* (i) *V. corymbosum;* (j) *Gaylussacia dumosa;* (k) *Kalmia angustifolia;* (l) *K. latifolia;* (m) *Rhododendron visosum;* (n) *Leucothoe racemosa;* (o) *Lyonia ligustrina;* (p) *L. mariana.* Drawings differ in scale.

389

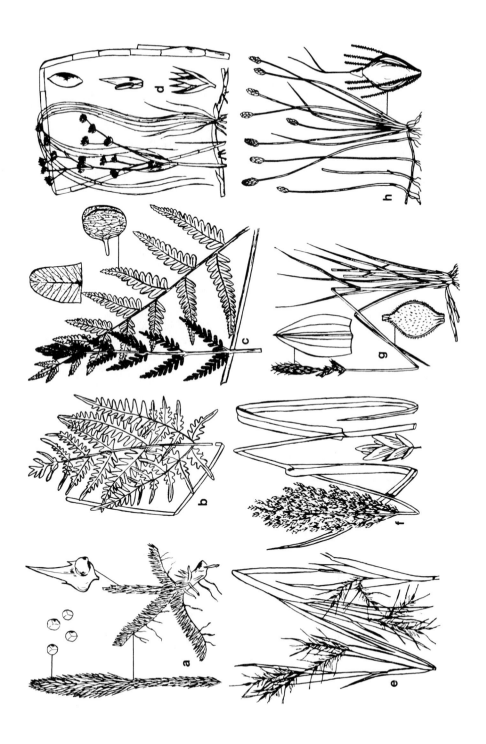

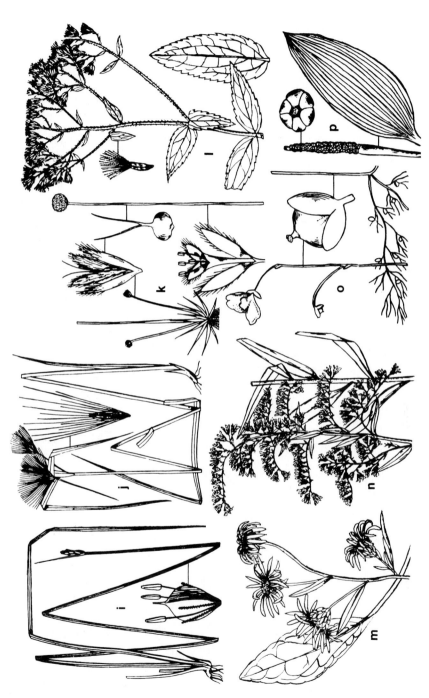

Fig. 4. Common herbaceous plants of the Pine Barrens I. (a) *Lycopodium alopecuroides*; (b) *Pteridium aquilinum*; (c) *Osmunda cinnamomea*; (d) *Juncus militaris*; (e) *Andropogon virginicus*; (f) *Glyceria obtusa*; (g) *Carex pensylvanica*; (h) *Eleocharis olivacea*; (i) *Scirpus subterminalis*; (j) *Eriophorum virginicum*; (k) *Eriocaulon septangulare*; (l) *Eupatorium album*; (m) *Aster spectabilis*; (n) *Solidago odora*; (o) *Utricularia fibrosa*; (p) *Orontium aquaticum*. Drawings differ in scale.

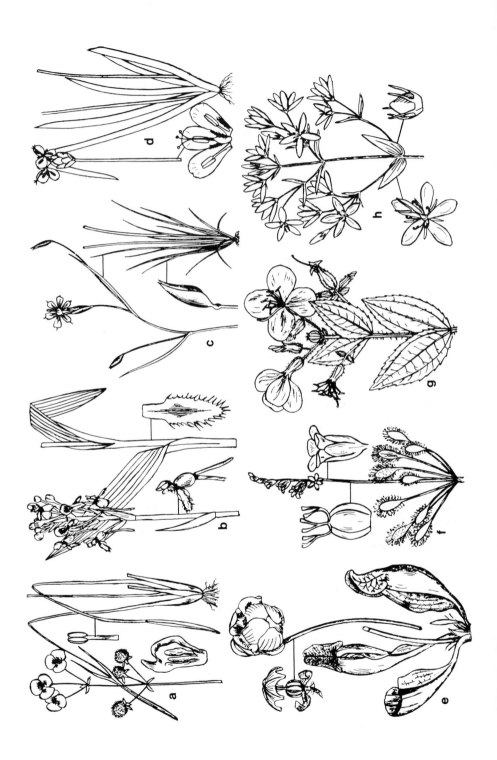

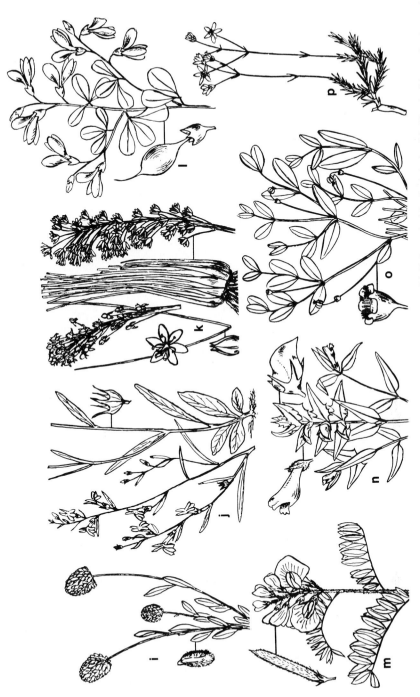

Fig. 5. Common herbaceous plants of the Pine Barrens II. (a) *Sagittaria engelmannii*; (b) *Habenaria blephariglottis*; (c) *Sisyrinchium atlanticum*; (d) *Xyris caroliniana*; (e) *Sarracenia purpurea*; (f) *Drosera intermedia*; (g) *Rhexia virginica*; (h) *Sabatia difformis*; (i) *Polygala lutea*; (j) *Lobelia nuttallii*; (k) *Xerophyllum asphodeloides*; (l) *Baptisia tinctoria*; (m) *Tephrosia virginiana*; (n) *Melampyrum lineare*; (o) *Euphorbia ipecachuanae*; (p) *Arenaria caroliniana*.

22

Endangered, Threatened, and Rare Vascular Plants of the Pine Barrens and Their Biogeography

DAVID E. FAIRBROTHERS

INTRODUCTION

Urgency in preventing the destruction of the flora and vegetation of the United States has fluctuated over several decades. Meanwhile, some species have been depleted to the extent that they are threatened with extinction. As well, some critical areas containing the rarest of plants have been altered seriously, and still others have been destroyed.

Serious consideration of the problems of endangered plant species has greatly lagged, as compared to the interest in preserving endangered animals, particularly mammals and birds (Smith, 1976). Of the approximately 300,000 plant species in the world, over 20,000 are estimated either to be or likely to be endangered or vulnerable and threatened with extinction at the start of the twenty-first century, only 21 years from the present (Smithsonian Institution, 1975).

Worldwide concern for endangered species is channeled largely through the International Union for the Conservation of Nature and Natural Resources. More data are essential, and must be obtained in a relatively short time in order to determine what has happened and what is happening to both rare animals and plants. With such information, biologists may help to make important decisions with regard to the conservation of these organisms.

By the Endangered Species Act of 1973, the Smithsonian Institution was directed to prepare a list of endangered and threatened plant species and to provide recommendations to the United States Congress. This was the first acknowledgment by the United States government that the loss of plant species leads to a loss of the diversity necessary to maintain an ecologically stable globe or biosphere. The 1973 Act also focused on the conservation of ecosystems upon which endangered and threatened species depend.

PINE BARRENS

A 1975 Smithsonian Institution report to the United States Congress provided lists of endangered, threatened, recently extinct, and exploited species of plants native to the United States. In the continental United States, this list comprised approximately 10% of the flora, or 2099 species, citing 100 species as recently extinct or possibly extinct, 761 species as endangered, and 1238 species as threatened. In 1975 and 1976, updated lists of endangered and threatened plants issued by the U.S. Department of the Interior, Fish and Wildlife Service were published in the Federal Register. The Smithsonian Institution revision (1978) indicated 2140 species in jeopardy. These four sources comprise the national lists and are used here for evaluating in part the Pine Barrens flora (Table 1).

The purpose of this chapter is twofold. The endangered, threatened, and rare vascular plants of the New Jersey Pine Barrens will be identified and their major biogeographical patterns and relationships will be briefly discussed.

HISTORY

Since New Jersey is the most densely populated state in the nation, ever-increasing demands have been made upon its natural areas. Before organisms in the state could be preserved in a meaningful way, it was essential to determine which ones were rare, endangered, and threatened. Fairbrothers and Hough (1973) and Fairbrothers (1975) indicated that 200 plant species belonging to 136 genera and 55 families, or 8% of the vascular plants (2400 species) in New Jersey, were rare and/or endangered.

Botanical explorations in New Jersey (Nova Caesarea) date from the early 1700's, with the earliest major recorded collections being those of the Swedish botanist, Peter Kalm (1753–1761, 1772). Kalm collected largely from southwestern New Jersey, although he also collected Pine Barrens plants. New species described from the American colonies by Linnaeus included the diversified flora sent by collectors from colonial New Jersey. Two hundred and thirty years of botanical interest in New Jersey provides an opportunity to follow some changes in the flora of the state. Bassett (1897) and Fables (1962) warned about threatened and endangered species, although mainly in the Pine Barrens of New Jersey. Carnivorous (insectivorous) plants have been of scientific and of much public interest, a focus of several misconceptions, and subject to considerable commercial exploitation. Schnell (1976) indicated that the many acid bogs, swamps, old lakes, slow streams, and sluggish habitats in the Pine Barrens frequently contain various species of pitcher plants, sundew, and bladderworts (*Sarracenia, Drosera,* and *Utricularia*). Several of these carnivorous plants sent from the New Jersey Pine Barrens by Mary Treat contributed to the long and detailed series of investigations that culminated in Charles Darwin's (1875) important book, "Insectivorous Plants." The sundew (*Drosera filiformis*) from the Pine Barrens was one of the most important species used by Darwin (Heslop-Harrison, 1976).

Since 1750, approximately 685 publications by approximately 295 authors have concerned the plants of New Jersey (Fairbrothers, 1964a,b, 1966). However, a complete flora or manual for the entire state never has been published. John Torrey's (1819) early catalog listed plants growing within 48 km (30 mi) of New York City. Knieskern (1856) published an important early paper about a portion of the Pine Barrens flora, and O. R. Willis' (1874, 1878) catalog included a relatively large portion of the state. In 1881, N. L. Britton prepared a preliminary listing of the plants for all of New Jersey and in 1889 presented a revised catalog (annotated listing) containing 2000 species of vascular plants for the state (Britton, 1881, 1889). Stone (1911) published a report, essentially a manual, on the plants of southern New Jersey, paying special reference to the flora of the Pine Barrens. This was followed by Harshberger's (1916) ecological investigations of the vegetation of the New Jersey Pine Barrens. A recent ecological inventory of the Pine Barrens was published by McCormick (1970). Taylor's (1915) "Plants of the Vicinity of New York" included a large portion of the state, while a fern book by Chrysler and Edwards (1947) included the club mosses, ferns, horsetails, quillworts, and spike mosses for the whole state.

Herbarium specimens in the Chrysler Herbarium, Department of Botany, Rutgers University, The Academy of Natural Sciences of Philadelphia, and The New York Botanical Garden provide documentation of the past and present flora of New Jersey. Such stored information is indispensable in helping to understand and evaluate the human impacts and the present distribution of plants in the Pine Barrens and in the state as a whole.

SPECIES IN JEOPARDY

The first publication describing the rare and endangered vascular plants of a state was published for New Jersey in November 1973 (Fairbrothers and Hough, 1973). This preceded the 1973 Federal Endangered Species Act, which helped to stimulate the publication of booklets from 1975–1979 in several states. A 1975 revised edition of the New Jersey publication included 200 species, 136 genera, and 55 families, or 8.0% of the vascular plants in the state.

The following three concepts were used by Fairbrothers and Hough (1973), and have been included in this article to aid in making direct comparisons.

1. *Endangered.* An endangered species is one whose survival in New Jersey is in jeopardy. Its peril may result from the destruction of habitat, change in habitat, over-exploitation by people, predation, adverse interspecific competition, disease, or because New Jersey is at the edge of its geographical range. An endangered species must receive protection, or extinction probably will ensue.

2. *Rare.* A rare species, while currently not threatened with extinction, is one which occurs in such small numbers in New Jersey that it may become endangered if its environment deteriorates or other limiting factors are altered. Continued observation of its status is essential.

3. *Undetermined.* A species known to be either rare or endangered in New Jersey is

considered undetermined if currently available information is inadequate to determine its status accurately. Additional information is required to determine if the species presently exists in dangerously low numbers in New Jersey.

Since the status of rarity and endangerment as defined in the Endangered Species Act of 1973 applied primarily to animals, the definitions were modified for plants in the Smithsonian Institution report (1975) and Federal Register (U.S. Department of Interior, 1975, 1976). The following terms indicate those used in United States government reports (national lists) and are included here for comparison.

1. *Endangered.* Species of plants that are in danger of extinction throughout all or a significant portion of their ranges. Existence may be endangered because of the destruction, drastic modification, or severe curtailment of habitat, or because of overexploitation, disease, predation, or even unknown reasons. Plant taxa from very limited areas, e.g., the type localities only, or from restricted fragile habitats usually are considered endangered.

2. *Threatened.* Species of plants that are likely to become endangered within the foreseeable future throughout all or a significant portion of their ranges. This includes species categorized as rare, very rare, or depleted.

3. *Recently extinct or possibly extinct.* Species of plants no longer known to exist after repeated search of the type localities and other known or likely habitats.

The above definitions define the status categories, but the Smithsonian Report was concerned initially with rarity. The Committee considered a *rare species* as one having a small population in its range. Such a species may be found in a restricted geographical region, or it may occur sparsely over a wider area. Most state publications have used the status categories of rare and endangered or rare and threatened.

Seventy-one vascular plant species native to the Pine Barrens are in jeopardy. These species, belonging to 23 families, and are classified in one of the four precarious species categories (rare, endangered, threatened, or undetermined) (Table I). Two of the species are ferns (Schizaeaceae), 37 species are monocot flowering plants (Cyperaceae, Gramineae, Juncaceae, Liliaceae, Najadaceae, Orchidaceae, Xyridaceae families), and 32 species are dicot flowering plants (Asclepiadaceae, Compositae, Convolvulaceae, Empetraceae, Euphorbiaceae, Gentianaceae, Leguminosae, Lentibulariaceae, Lobeliaceae, Loranthaceae, Lythraceae, Melastomataceae, Onagraceae, Polygalaceae, Scrophulariaceae). The sedge family (Cyperaceae) has the largest number of species (12), and the composite family (Compositae), grass family (Gramineae) and orchid family (Orchidaceae) have eight species each. The bladderwort family (Lentibulariaceae) and lily family (Liliaceae) have four species each, and the other 17 families have one to three species each in jeopardy.

The 71 species in jeopardy represent 12% of the 580 native Pine Barrens species. The largest percentage of the species in jeopardy (55%) has southern geographical affinities, while 6% has northern affinities, and 39% extends north and south and/or west of the Pine Barrens and New Jersey. The national lists indicate that nine of the

TABLE I Rare, Endangered, Threatened, and Undetermined Native Pine Barrens Plants, with Their Geographical Affinities[a]

Asclepias rubra L.
  Red milkweed R–S
Asclepias variegata L.
  White milkweed E–N/S
Asclepias verticillata L.
  Whorled milkweed R–N/S
Aster concolor L.
  Silvery aster R–S
Breweria pickeringii (M.A. Curtis) Gray
  = *Bonamia pickeringii* (Torr.) Gray
  Pickering's morning glory R–S
Calamovilfa brevipilis (Torr.) Scribn.
  Pine Barrens reedgrass R, T–S
Carex barrattii Schwein. & Torr.
  Barratt's sedge R–S
Chrysopsis falcata (Pursh) Ell.
  Sickle-leaved golden aster R–N
Cleistes divaricata (L.) Ames
  Spreading pogonia E–S
Clitoria mariana L.
  Butterfly Pea U–N/S
Corema conradii Torr.
  Broom crowberry E–N
Coreopsis rosea Nutt.
  Rose-colored tickseed R–N
Crotonopsis elliptica Willd.
  Rushfoil E–N/S
Cuscuta cephalanthii Engelm.
  Buttonbush dodder R–N/S
Desmodium strictum (Pursh) DC.
  Stiff tick trefoil R–S
Eleocharis equisetoides (Ell.) Torr.
  Knotted spike rush E–N/S
Eupatorium resinosum Torr.
  Resinous boneset R–S
Eriophorum tenellum Nutt.
  Few-nerved cotton grass U–N/S
Gentiana autumnalis L.
  = *Gentiana porphyrio* Gmel.
  Pine Barrens gentian E–S
Gymnopogon ambiguus (Michx.) BSP.
  Broad-leaved beardgrass U–N/S
Habenaria ciliaris (L.) R.Br.
  Yellow-fringed orchid E–N/S
Habenaria integra (Nutt.) Spreng.
  = *Platanthera integra*
  Southern yellow orchid E, EN–S
Juncus caesariensis Coville
  New Jersey rush T–S

Liparis lilifolia (L.) Richard
  Lily-leaved twayblade R, T–N/S
Liparis loeselii (L.) Richard
  Loesel's twayblade R–N/S
Listera australis Lindl.
  Southern twayblade R–N/S
Lobelia boykinii Torr. & Gray
  Boykin's lobelia E–S
Lobelia canbyi Gray
  Canby's lobelia R–S
Ludwigia hirtella Raf.
  Hairy ludwigia R–S
Ludwigia linearis Walt.
  Linear-leaved lugwigia U–S
Lygodium palmatum (Bernh.) Sw.
  Climbing fern E–N/S
Muhlenbergia torreyana (Schult.) Hitchc.
  Torrey's muhly T–S
Narthecium americanum Ker.
  Yellow asphodel R–S
Nymphoides cordata (Ell.) Fern.
  Floating heart R–N/S
Panicum cryptanthum Ashe
  Sheathed panic grass R–S
Panicum hemitomon Schultes
  Narrow panic grass R–S
Panicum hirstii Swallen
  Hirst's panic grass E, EN–S
Panicum oligosanthes Schultes
  Few-fruited panic grass R–N/S
Panicum scabriusculum Ell.
  Sheathed panic grass U–S
Phoradendron flavescens (Pursh) Nutt.
  American mistletoe R–N/S
Polygala mariana Miller
  Maryland milkwort R–S
Potamogeton confervoides Reichenb.
  Alga-like pondweed R–N/S
Potamogeton oakesianus Robbins
  Oake's pondweed U–N/S
Prenanthes autumnalis Walt.
  Slender rattlesnake root E–S
Rhexia aristosa Britt.
  Awned meadow beauty E–S
Rhynchospora cephalantha Gray
  Capitate beakrush R–S
Rhynchospora filifolia Gray
  Thread-leaved beaked rush R–S

Rhynchospora inundata (Oakes) Fern.
  Slender beaked rush R–S
Rhynchospora knieskernii Carey
  Knieskern's beaked rush R, EN–S
Rhynchospora microcephala Britt.
  Small-headed beaked rush U–S
Rhynchospora oligantha Gray
  Few-flowered beaked rush U–S
Rotala ramosior (L.) Kochne
  Tooth cup R–N/S
Schizaea pusilla Pursh
  Curly grass fern T–N
Schwalbea americana L.
  Chaffseed E, T–S
Scirpus longii Fern.
  Long's bulrush T–N
Scleria minor (Britt.) Stone
  Slender nut rush R–S
Scleria reticularis Michx.
  Reticulated nut rush R–N/S
Sclerolepis uniflora (Walt.) BSP.
  Sclerolepis R–N/S
Solidago elliottii T. & G.
  Elliott's goldenrod R–N/S
Solidago stricta Ait.
  Wand-like goldenrod E–S
Spiranthes tuberosa Raf.
  Little ladies tresses R–N/S
Tipularia discolor (Pursh) Nutt.
  Crane-fly orchid R–N/S
Tofieldia racemosa (Walt.) BSP.
  False asphodel R–S
Utricularia gibba L.
  Humped bladderwort R–N/S
Utricularia olivacea Wright ex. Griseb.
  White-flowered bladderwort R–S
Utricularia purpurea Walt.
  Purple bladderwort R–N/S
Utricularia resupinata B.D. Greene
  Reclined bladderwort R–N/S
Uvularia pudica (Walt.) Fern.
  Pine Barren bellwort R–S
Xyris fimbriata Ell.
  Fringed yellow-eyed grass U–S
Xyris flexuosa Muhl.
  Yellow-eyed grass R–S
Zigadenus leimanthoides Gray
  Coastal zygadine U–S

[a] R, rare; E, endangered; U, undetermined; EN, endangered on national lists (see text); T, threatened on national lists; S, southern geographical affinity; N, northern geographical affinity; N/S, extending both north and south, and/or west of New Jersey.
  Totals (71 species): 41 rare; 16 endangered; 10 undetermined; 3 endangered on national lists; 7 threatened on national lists; 39 southern; 5 northern; 28 extending both north and south, and/or west of New Jersey.

species also are in jeopardy in other parts of the United States.* The percentage of species in jeopardy in the Pine Barrens (12%) exceeds both the national percentage (10%) and the New Jersey percentage (8%). Thus, the New Jersey Pine Barrens is a significant region in terms of the number of species discovered to be in jeopardy.

WHY DO SOME SPECIES BECOME RARE?

Species become rare in the Pine Barrens as a result of both natural events and human activities. Slow geological and climatic changes have resulted in the development of new species, changes in the distribution or abundance of species, and the extinction of other species. Some major natural phenomena that affected plant distributions in New Jersey were sea level rise, flooding, glaciation, fire, eutrophication, and warm dry (xerothermic) periods. Natural biotic factors which affect the distribution and abundance of plants are plant diseases, overgrazing, insect damage, and destruction of seeds and/or fruits.

The destruction or modification of natural habitats, as well as the destruction of plants through human activities, have contributed to the growing number of endangered and threatened species in the Pine Barrens. Some construction practices have led to indiscriminate cutting and clearing, and the drainage or filling of low-lying areas. The development of highways, the growth of industry, the construction of housing projects, timber removal, the dumping of wastes, and specific missions on federally owned property also have altered areas within the Pine Barrens. European human influence on the vegetation in the Pine Barrens can be traced to the late 1600's, with the advent of colonial industries such as tar making, bog iron production, glass making, brick making, charcoal production, and lumbering, all of which had an impact on the flora. Cranberry and blueberry culture also have modified various portions of the lowlands during the last 50–100 years.

Some land use practices and disturbances also have provided habitats for the establishment or expansion of rare plants (Little, 1974). For example, some bogs in the Pine Barrens have been altered by the past removal of iron ore, and of turf for logging road construction and cranberry production. Several orchid species now are found in these human modified bogs. The highly prized *Schizaea pusilla* (curly grass fern) frequently is found growing on exposed moist white cedar stumps which may have resulted from logging or fire (Givnish, 1971; Little, 1974). Discarded upper foliage (slash) provides

*According to the national lists: (1) Pine Barrens reedgrass (*Calamovilfa brevipilis*) is threatened in North Carolina and Virginia; (2) southern yellow orchid (*Habenaria integra*) is threatened in Alabama, Florida, Georgia, Louisiana, Mississippi, North Carolina, South Carolina, Tennessee, and Texas; (3) New Jersey rush (*Juncus caesariensis*) is threatened in Maryland and Virginia; (4) Torrey's muhly (*Muhlenbergia torreyana*) is threatened in Delaware, Georgia, Kentucky, and Tennessee; (5) Hirst's panic grass (*Panicum hirstii*) is endangered in Georgia; (6) Knieskern's beaked rush (*Rhynchospora knieskernii*) is endangered in Delaware; (7) Long's bulrush (*Scirpus longii*) is threatened in Connecticut, Massachusetts, Maine, North Carolina, New York, and Vermont; (8) Curly grass fern (*Schizaea pusilla*) is threatened in New York; (9) Chaffseed (*Schwalbea americana*) is threatened in Connecticut, Delaware, Kentucky, Louisiana, Maryland, Massachusetts, Mississippi, New York, Tennessee, and South Carolina.

suitable sites for the establishment of some endangered and rare species, such as meadow beauty, orchids, milkworts, beaked rushes, spike rushes, and certain other sedges (Little, 1974; Kantor and Pillsbury, 1976).

Therefore, knowledge of individual requirements of species and habitat maintenance clearly is essential to assure the continued existence of the endangered and threatened plant species in the Pine Barrens. However, the habitat of endangered species must be protected even before we can comprehend fully the ecosystem of which they are a part. The accumulation of data alone is insufficient; saving the plants depends upon the application of such data.

The abundance of rare plants in the Pine Barrens is well known internationally. For example, in a Bicentennial commemorative international symposium entitled "Threatened and Endangered Species of Plants in the Americas and Their Significance in Ecosystems and in the Future," held in 1976 at the New York Botanical Garden, the New Jersey Pine Barrens was chosen as the major natural area to visit for the participants hailing from 15 countries and 24 states.

BIOGEOGRAPHY

Frequent differences in interpreting plant and animal distributions are related to major unknowns in the geological and biogeographical history of the Pine Barrens region, e.g., the frequency of coverage of the area by sea water during interglacial times, the environmental conditions during the Pleistocene ice age and subsequent warm period, the character of the vegetation during the Pleistocene, and thus the antiquity of the flora. A vegetation island during the late Pleistocene (Wisconsin) ice age was postulated by Taylor (1912) and Harshberger (1916), but Salisbury and Knapp (1917) rejected such an interpretation. Lutz (1934) and Richards (1960) demonstrated the Pine Barrens to be the region of greatest antiquity in the middle Atlantic coastal area of North America. Some plant geographers believe the Pine Barrens vegetation during the last ice age was similar to the present, and consider the region to have been a refugium from which species moved northward as the glacier retreated (McCormick, 1970).

The status of the vegetation in precolonial and colonial periods is also in dispute. For example, questions often asked include: (1) Did frequent burning by the Indians affect the forest? (2) Did fires increase or decrease after the arrival of Europeans? (3) Did cutting during colonial times change the abundance of oaks? The diversity of vegetation found in the modern Pine Barrens may or may not reflect different fire histories and the resistance to fires of various tree species (McCormick, 1970).

However, the Pine Barrens do represent a region of drier and less fertile sandy soil partially surrounded by more moist and fertile uplands, and these characteristics are reflected in the current vegetation (Robichaud and Buell, 1973).

The bogs located in the Pine Barrens do not owe their origin to glaciers, as do those in northern New Jersey. In the Pine Barrens, the groundwater rises to the surface in shallow stream valleys. Poor drainage plus acid water result in the accumulation of peat, and as a result bogs have developed in some of these shallow stream valleys.

Stone (1911) included slightly less than 1400 species of vascular plants in his manual of plants for southern New Jersey. He indicated that, exclusive of introduced weeds, approximately 565 species grew in the Pine Barrens. The comparable figure today would be approximately 580 species. However, the total Pine Barrens flora, approximately 850 species, currently would be higher, due to introduced species, many of which now are weeds. Thus, approximately 30–35% of the present flora is represented by introduced species. Stone (1911) also indicated that 55 species growing in the Pine Barrens did not grow elsewhere in New Jersey.

The most common species which form most of the vegetation of both the state and the Pine Barrens also extend geographically to the north, south, and/or west of New Jersey. However, many species, including both common and rare plants, reach the northern or southern limits of their geographical range in the Pine Barrens (Stone, 1911; Harshberger, 1916; McCormick, 1970). Because taxa of northern (14) and southern (109) affinities reach their geographical coastal plain limits in the Pine Barrens, the area provides an unusual natural laboratory. Even though the number of taxa with southern affinities greatly exceeds those with northern affinities, two unique species, broom crowberry (*Corema conradii*) and curly grass fern (*Schizaea pusilla*), attain their southernmost limits in the Pine Barrens.

As a result of various natural phenomena, the present flora contains endemics, relicts, habitat-restricted, peripheral, and disjunct species. *Endemic* species are those restricted to very small geographical areas and are examples of geographical isolation and range limitation (Taylor, 1916). Endemic species may be restricted to a very few states, one state, the Pine Barrens, or a small area such as a swamp, sand dune, bog, or other very specific habitat. *Relict* species are those species occurring as remnants of formerly widespread species which are now restricted to relatively small areas. *Habitat-restricted* species often are widespread, yet may be local in occurrence within an area, depending upon the distribution and abundance of their required habitat. *Peripheral* species are those which reach their geographical range limit within the boundaries of the state, while their main distribution is south, north, or west of New Jersey. Some of these species may be classified as *disjuncts* if they are outliers from the main distribution. While it is easy to define the above terms, it may be difficult to determine the proper status for a particular species.

Examples of endemic species found in the Pine Barrens are: Pickerings morning glory (*Breweria pickeringii* var. *caesariensis*), New Jersey rush (*Juncus caesariensis*), blazing star (*Liatris graminifolia* var. *lasia*), sand myrtle (*Leiophyllum buxifolium* var. *buxifolium*), and Knieskern's beakrush (*Rhynchospora knieskernii*).

Some botanists have considered broom crowberry (*Corema conradii*) and curly grass fern (*Schizaea pusilla*) to be relict species. Both are examples of northern species reaching their southern limits in the Pine Barrens.

Two examples of habitat-restricted species are the grasses, Pine Barrens reedgrass (*Calamovilfa brevipilis*) and Hirst's panic grass (*Panicum hirstii*). Both are restricted to bogs located in the Pine Barrens.

Turkeybeard (*Xerophyllum asphodeloides*) is a peripheral southern species which reaches its northern limit in the sandy habitats of the Pine Barrens, yet it grows along the Appalachian Mountains in Virginia, North Carolina, Tennessee, and Georgia. It also can be classified as a disjunct species. False asphodel (*Tofieldia racemosa*) is another peripheral and disjunct southern species; however, this species reaches its northern limit in the bogs of the Pine Barrens, and it grows on the Coastal Plain south to Florida and west to Texas. Pyxie moss (*Pyxidanthera barbulata*) is similar in distribution to *Tofieldia*, except it grows in the dry sandy habitats in the Pine Barrens, southeastern Virginia, North Carolina, and South Carolina. *Xerophyllum, Pyxidanthera,* and *Tofieldia* reveal the two migration routes of southern species into the Pine Barrens, i.e., via the Coastal Plain or via the mountains and then onto the Coastal Plain in New Jersey and Delaware.

Sickle-leaved golden aster (*Chrysopsis falcata*) and rosecolored tickseed (*Coreopsis rosea*) are two peripheral northern coastal species which reach their southern limits in the Pine Barrens. *Chrysopsis* grows in dry sandy soil, while *Coreopsis* grows in damp sandy or peaty shores and depressions. Examples of two northern and western peripheral species are illustrated by the orchid species *Liparis lilifolia* and *L. loeselii,* which grow in the upland regions of New Jersey but also have migrated onto the Coastal Plain and into the Pine Barrens. As they continue south and west of New Jersey, these species remain in the Piedmont and in the mountains. These also are examples of disjunct species in the Pine Barrens.

These selected species are examples illustrating endemic, relict, habitat-restricted, peripheral, disjunct northern and southern species within the Pine Barrens, and indicate that the flora has arrived from several migration routes, with the southern Coastal Plain and southern mountain routes predominating. This region contains valuable research species for the plant geographer to study and trace migration routes.

The Pine Barrens have produced several species new to science; 24 taxa first were described from specimens originally discovered growing in the Pine Barrens: (1) *Amphicarpum purshii;* (2) *Breweria pickeringii* var. *caesariensis;* (3) *Calamovilfa brevipilis;* (4) *Chrysopsis falcata;* (5) *Corema conradii;* (6) *Desmodium strictum;* (7) *Eupatorium resinosum;* (8) *Habenaria integra;* (9) *Juncus caesariensis;* (10) *Leiophyllum buxifolium;* (11) *Lespedeza hirta* var. *longifolia;* (12) *Lobelia canbyi;* (13) *Lophiola americana;* (14) *Muhlenbergia torreyana;* (15) *Narthecium americanum;* (16) *Panicum hirstii;* (17) *Polygala brevifolia;* (18) *Rhexia aristosa;* (19) *Rhynchospora gracilenta;* (20) *Rhynchospora knieskernii;* (21) *Schizaea pusilla;* (22) *Scleria minor;* (23) *Scirpus longii;* and (24) *Spiranthes laciniata.*

The unique characteristics of the total environment of the Pine Barrens are reflected in the flora. The repeated fires, plus dry and sterile soils and interwoven bogs and swamps, have selected the characteristic Pine Barrens species and sifted out those not capable of survival in this remarkable natural, wildland tract in southern New Jersey.

SUMMARY

Botanical explorations made over the course of 230 years in New Jersey and the Pine Barrens provide an excellent opportunity to trace floristic changes, including introductions, rare species, and species threatened with extinction. Species have become rare in the Pine Barrens as a result of both natural events and human activities. Approximately 580 native species and 270 introduced species grow within the region; thus, one-third of the present flora has been introduced. Five species are endemic to the Pine Barrens. Seventy-one of the 580 native species are classified as rare, endangered, threatened, or undetermined. Thus, 12% are in jeopardy, in contrast to 10% for the United States and 8% for all of New Jersey. Of the species in jeopardy, 55% have southern geographical affinities. Thus, the Pine Barrens is a significant region within both the state and the nation, with respect to the number of species in danger of extinction.

ACKNOWLEDGMENT

I express my sincere appreciation to M. Y. Hough for her assistance and comments.

REFERENCES

Ayensu, E. S., and R. A. De Filipps. (1978). "Endangered and Threatened Plants of the United States." Smithsonian Institution and World Wildlife Fund, Inc., Washington, D.C.

Bassett, F. L. (1897). Some rare New Jersey plants. *Gard. For.* **10,** 68.

Britton, N. L. (1881). A preliminary catalogue of the flora of New Jersey. *Annu. Rep. State Geol.,* pp. 1–233. New Brunswick, N.J.

Britton, N. L. (1889). Catalogue of plants found in New Jersey. *Geol. Surv. of N.J., Final Rep. State Geol.,* Vol. 2, Sec. 2, 25–619.

Chrysler, M. A., and Edwards, J. L. (1947). "The Ferns of New Jersey." Rutgers Univ. Press, New Brunswick, New Jersey.

Darwin, C. (1875). "Insectivorous Plants." John Murray, London, England.

Fables, D. (1962). 20 "Lost" plants. *Bartonia* **31,** 7–10.

Fairbrothers, D. E. (1964a). An annotated bibliography of the floristic publications of New Jersey from 1753–1961. *Bull. Torrey Bot. Club* **91,** 47–56.

Fairbrothers, D. E. (1964b). An annotated bibliography of the floristic publications of New Jersey from 1753–1961. *Bull. Torrey Bot. Club* **91,** 141–151.

Fairbrothers, D. E. (1966). An annotated bibliography of the floristic publications of New Jersey from 1962–1965. *Bull. Torrey Bot. Club* **93,** 352–356.

Fairbrothers, D. E. (1975). Rare and endangered plants. *BioScience* **25,** 590.

Fairbrothers, D. E., and Hough, M. Y. (1973). Rare and endangered vascular plants of New Jersey. *N.J. State Mus., Sci. Notes* No. 14. (Reprinted with corrections and additions, 1975.)

Givnish, T. (1971). "A Study of New Jersey Pine Barrens Cedar Swamps." 1971 Report of the Princeton N.S.F. Cedar Swamp study group. Princeton Univ., Princeton, New Jersey.

Harshberger, J. W. (1916). "The Vegetation of the New Jersey Pine-Barrens. An Ecologic Investigation." Christopher Sower Co., Philadelphia, Pennsylvania.

Heslop-Harrison, Y. (1976). Carnivorous plants a century after Darwin. *Endeavour* **35,** 114–122.

Kalm, P. (1753–1761). "En Resa till Norra America," 3 vols. Kongl. Svenska Vetenskops Academiens Stockholm.

Kalm, P. (1772). "Travels into North America." (J. Reinjold Forster, transl.), 2nd Ed., 2 vols. London.

Kantor, R. A., and Pillsbury, M. K. (1976). "Upland Living Resources Endangered and Rare Vegetation. A Staff Working Paper." N.J. Dept. Environ. Prot., Trenton, New Jersey.

Knieskern, P. D. (1856). A catalogue of plants growing without cultivation in the counties of Monmouth and Ocean. *N.J. Geol. Surv. Annu. Rep.*, Trenton, New Jersey.

Little, S. (1974). Wildflowers of the Pine Barrens and their niche requirements. *N.J. Outdoors* **1**, 16–18.

Lutz, H. J. (1934). Concerning a geologic explanation of the origin and present distribution of the New Jersey Pine Barren vegetation. *Ecology* **15**, 399–406.

McCormick, J. (1970). The Pine Barrens—a preliminary ecological inventory. *N.J. State Mus. Res. Rep.* No. 2, 1–103.

Richards, H. G. (1960). The geologic history of the New Jersey Pine Barrens. *N.J. Nat. News* **15**, 146–151.

Robichaud, B., and Buell, M. F. (1973). "Vegetation of New Jersey. A Study in Landscape Diversity." Rutgers Univ. Press, New Brunswick, New Jersey.

Salisbury, R. D., and Knapp, G. N. (1917). The quaternary formations of southern New Jersey. *N.J. Geol. Surv., Final Rep. State Geol.* No. 8, 1–128.

Schnell, D. E. (1976). "Carnivorous Plants of the United States and Canada." John F. Blair, Winston-Salem, North Carolina.

Smith, R. L. (1976). Ecological genesis of endangered species: The philosophy of preservation. *Annu. Rev. Ecol. Syst.* **7**, 33–55.

Smithsonian Institution (1975). "Report on Endangered and Threatened Plant Species of the United States," House Document No. 94-51, Serial No. 94-A. Washington, D.C. Govt. Printing Office.

Stone, W. (1911). The plants of southern New Jersey, with especial reference to the flora of the Pine Barrens and the geographic distribution of the species. *N.J. State Mus., Annu. Rep.* 1910, pp. 23–828.

Taylor, N. (1912). On the origin and present distribution of the Pine Barrens of New Jersey. *Torreya* **12**, 229–242.

Taylor, N. (1915). Flora of the vicinity of New York. *Mem. N.Y. Bot. Gard.* **5**, 1–683.

Taylor, N. (1916). Endemisn in the flora of the vicinity of New York. *Torreya* **16**, 18–27.

Torrey, J. (1819). "A Catalogue of the Plants Growing Spontaneously within Thirty Miles of the City of New York." Lyceum Nat. Hist., New York.

U.S. Department of Interior, Fish and Wildlife Service (1975). Threatened or endangered fauna or flora: Review of status of vascular plants and determination of "critical habitat." *Fed. Regist.* **40**(127), 27823–27924.

U.S. Department of Interior, Fish and Wildlife Service (1976). Endangered and threatened species: Plants. *Fed. Regist.* **41**(117), 24524–24572.

Willis, O. R. (1874). "Catalogue of Plants Growing without Cultivation in the State of New Jersey." J. W. Schermerhorn and Co., New York. (Revised, 1877.)

Willis, O. R. (1878). Flora of New Jersey. *Bull. Torrey Bot. Club* **6**, 252.

23

Common Bryophytes and Lichens of the New Jersey Pine Barrens

RICHARD T. T. FORMAN

INTRODUCTION

It is difficult to walk in the Pine Barrens without stepping on bryophytes and lichens. Virtually all terrestrial habitats contain the organisms in abundance, from wet peat bogs and swamps with extensive *Sphagnum* moss mats, to dry burned pine woods with extensive moss and *Cladonia* lichen mats. Despite their abundance, their roles in the ecological systems in general are poorly understood and remain a challenge for study.

Pine Barrens bryology and lichenology began with the preparation of species lists containing brief ecological descriptions by C. F. Austin (Britton, 1889), who listed 274 moss and 78 liverwort (hepatic) species from New Jersey. E. A. Rau (Britton, 1889) described 19 species of *Sphagnum* mosses, and 279 lichens were named by E. Tuckerman, with the list revised by J. W. Eckfelt (Britton, 1889). Evans (1935, 1938, 1940), Torrey (1933, 1935), and Thomson (1967) elucidated the taxonomic and biogeographical relationships of *Cladonia,* by far the dominant lichen in the Pine Barrens. Species names follow Crum (1976), Schuster (1953), and Hale (1969), except where another source is cited.

Bryophyte and lichen ecology in the Pine Barrens began with Little (1951), who studied 16 Atlantic white cedar (*Chamaecyparis thyoides*) and hardwood swamps. Liverworts were most characteristic of mature, relatively wet, cedar swamps, *Sphagnum* mainly on wet and open areas irrespective of tree composition, and other mosses in small patches most commonly in hardwoods. Lichen diversity was greatest in hardwood or mixed stands. McCormick (1955) found bryophyte diversity higher in cedar swamps than hardwood swamps and pine lowlands, the last having mainly *Sphagnum.* Average percent cover ranged from 62% for cedar swamps to 57% for hardwood swamps and 11% for pine lowlands.

Of eight upland forest types, McCormick (1955) recorded bryophyte and lichen cover of 34% in chestnut oak (*Quercus prinus*) woods, very much higher than other

407

woods. Cover was slightly higher in pine–blackjack oak and oak–pine–scrub oak than the remaining forest types. However, species diversity of both common bryophytes and common lichens was approximately constant among the forest types. Bernard (1960, 1963) found considerable variability in percent cover of mosses by forest type, that is, highest in chestnut oak and pine–blackjack oak–scrub oak (*Pinus rigida, Quercus marilandica, Q. ilicifolia*) woods, and lowest in pine–black oak (*Q. velutina*), pine–black oak–scrub oak, and scarlet oak–shortleaf pine (*Q. coccinea, Pinus echinata*) woods.

Fires appeared to cause an increase in bryophyte and lichen cover, from <10% in upland woods burned at intervals of ten or more years, to 30–40% in woods burned at one- to three-year intervals with light winter fires (Buell and Cantlon, 1953). Moul and Buell (1955) reported upland moss cover of 9% and lichen cover of 8% in a plot burned annually, while a plot burned at three-year intervals had higher moss (29%) and lichen (19%) cover.

Well-developed upland moss mats may absorb about 1.5 cm of water from a rain, and *Cladonia* lichen mats about half that (Moul and Buell, 1955; Stephenson, 1965). Bernard (1960, 1963) estimated that bryophytes and lichens in frequently burned sites may intercept about one-third to one-half the water intercepted by a litter layer in forests unburned for many years. Forman and Dowden (1977) and Reiners (Chapter 32, this volume) also suggest some lichens may play roles in controlling patchiness of the forest floor.

Brodo's (1968) treatise of Long Island, New York lichens includes a wealth of ecological information, although caution in extrapolating to the Pine Barrens is suggested, due to important geological, soil, atmospheric, and biogeographical differences. Bryophyte communities of the Pine Barrens are quite different from those of the New Jersey Piedmont to the north (Bard, 1965; Hamilton, 1953), a loblolly pine (*Pinus taeda*) forest to the south in North Carolina (Bliss and Linn, 1966), or a sandy jack pine (*P. banksiana*) forest in Minnesota (Stern and Buell, 1951; Seim *et al.*, 1955).

Bryophyte distributions within the Pine Barrens are virtually unknown, although different oak combinations in different sectors of the Pine Barrens (Stone, 1911; McCormick, Chapter 13, this volume) suggest that bryophyte studies here might be rewarding. For example, the northern moss, *Tetraphis pellucida*, which extends south in the Coastal Plain to the Pine Barrens and down the southern Appalachian Mountains (Forman, 1963), apparently is limited mainly to swamps in the southwestern half of the Pine Barrens, for reasons that are unclear (Forman, 1964).

Boerner and Forman (1975) compared coastal dune populations of the mosses *Ceratodon purpureus, Aulacomnium palustre,* and *Polytrichum commune* with populations from the Pine Barrens and northern New Jersey for tolerance to chronic salt spray. They found only *Ceratodon* tolerant to salt spray, but no difference in response among populations for any of the three species, suggesting that, at least for salt spray, the Pine Barrens populations were not different ecotypically from coastal dune and northern New Jersey moss populations.

The relative dearth of information about bryophyte and lichen ecology is due at least partially to unfamiliarity with the species. Yet, most common species in the Pine Barrens are just as easy to recognize as trees, shrubs, or birds.

The objectives of this chapter therefore are (1) to determine the most common species of bryophytes and lichens in Pine Barrens habitats and describe some of these species and groups to facilitate their recognition in the field, and (2) to determine the relationships of bryophyte communities along gradients of fire frequency and soil moisture, two major environmental controls in the Pine Barrens.

COMMON BRYOPHYTES OF THE PINE BARRENS

To aid in field recognition, the overall most common bryophyte species of the lowlands and uplands are illustrated (Figs. 1 and 2), with encapsulated descriptions emphasizing characteristics useful for the naked eye or a 10-power lens. One unusual moss, *Buxbaumia aphylla,* also is included (Hancock and Brassard, 1974; Crum, 1976; Grout, 1928–1941).

Two major morphological groups of mosses (excluding *Sphagnum*) are readily recognizable in the Pine Barrens. Acrocarpous mosses have upright, mainly unbranched stems, with the stalk of the spore-bearing capsule emanating from the stem tip. Pleurocarpous mosses have prostrate, much-branched stems, with the stalk of the capsule appearing to originate along the stem. Large acrocarpous species generally have stems averaging >4 cm (1.5 in) in length and small species <2 cm (0.75 in), but exceptions are common in very dry or wet sites.

The several widespread species other than those shown in Figs. 1 and 2 are discussed below.

1. Pleurocarpous mosses on trees. *Platygyrium repens* (small; shiny to dark; appressed to substrate; some shoot tips with clustered elongate reproductive bodies); *Hypnum pallescens* (small; leaves sickle shaped, pointing in same direction); *Thelia asprella* (medium sized; whitish to bluish; leaves triangular, concave; shoots cylindrical in appearance; dense thick mat at tree base; mainly uplands); *Thelia hirtella* (similar to previous species except plant whitish to greenish, mat thinner, more appressed to substrate, often drier woods); *Campylium hispidulum* (small; tiny leaves bent back halfway out their length so that leaf tips are at right angles to stem; tree bases).

2. Pleurocarpous mosses on the ground. *Rhynchostegium* (or *Eurhynchium*) *serrulatum* (medium sized; leaves flattened on stem; leaf tip finely toothed, midvein present; capsule short, brownish, thick, at about 45° angle from stalk); *Plagiothecium denticulatum* (similar to previous except midvein absent; capsule yellowish, cylindrical, nearly upright; mainly lowlands); *Heterophyllium haldanianum* (medium sized; leaves often slightly flattened on stem, midvein absent; some leaf tips curved, pointing in same direction; capsule brown, cylindrical, nearly upright); *Hypnum imponens* medium sized; leaves sickle shaped, pointing in same direction; most stems red).

3. Acrocarpous mosses on trees. *Ulota crispa* (small, greenish black; short stem; leaves lance shaped; capsule on very short stalk; usually forming small rounded tufts);

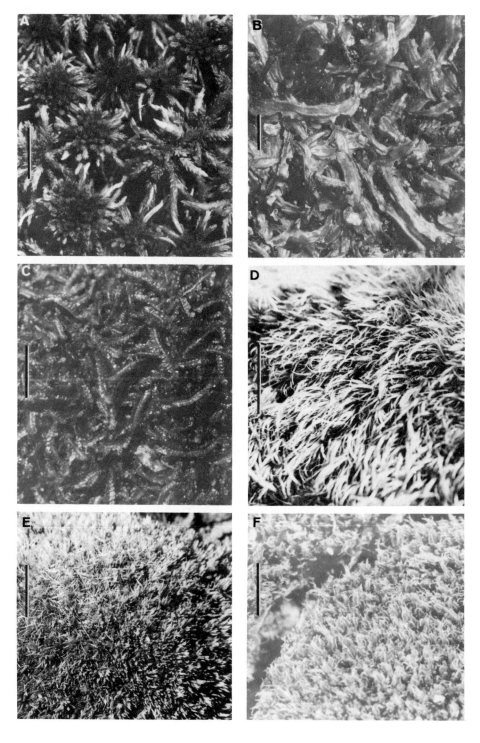

Orthotrichum spp. (similar to previous species, except leaves oblong, capsule appearing stalkless, mainly uplands).

4. Liverworts on trees. *Frullania inflata* and allied species (small; brown to blackish green; round leaves, somewhat far apart, on opposite sides of stem; appears as distinctive dark patches of closely appressed plants on bark).

Several useful references for the identification of Pine Barrens mosses are available: Crum (1976), Conard (1956), Grout (1903, 1923, 1928–1941), Breen (1963), and Moul (1952). References for liverworts include Conard (1956), Schuster (1953, 1966–1974), and Evans and Nichols (1908). Major reference collections are in the herbaria of the New York Botanical Garden and the Academy of Natural Sciences of Philadelphia, with additional specimens in the Chrysler Herbarium of Rutgers University.

Fig. 1. Common bryophytes of the Pine Barrens. Lines on photos are 1 cm (± ⅜ in) long. (A) *Sphagnum* spp. (*Sphagnum* or peat moss): large moss; stems upright, relatively far apart; cluster of branches at tip giving a "star-shaped" appearance, commonly whitish, although varying amounts of green and red may be present; leaves short, wide, concave, with numerous large, empty, leaf cells which hold water; spore-bearing capsules uncommon, blackish, small, spherical, on a short stalk; common in lowlands, especially wetter areas. *S. magellanicum* most common, but >20 species present. (Photo by R. K. Frye).
(B) *Pallavicinia lyellii:* large thallose liverwort; stems like prostrate ribbons, with a prominent thickened midvein, and branching, rounded tips; common in lowlands on wet organic soil or tree bases. (Photo by R. K. Frye).
(C) *Odontoschisma prostratum:* medium-sized leafy liverwort; stems prostrate, branching; leaves nearly round, in 2 symmetrical rows on opposite sides of stem, giving a horizontal flattened appearance when moist, a vertical flattened appearance when dry; leaf cells large, rounded; capsule uncommon, small spherical, on a whitish stalk; common in lowlands on moist organic soil. (Photo by R. K. Frye.)
(D) *Dicranum scoparium* (broom moss): large acrocarpous moss; stems close together; leaves wide at base but like long green hairs for most of length, generally curved and pointing in the same direction so plant appears "wind swept"; leaf tips toothed; capsules relatively common, cylindrical, slightly unsymmetrical from a tall stalk; common in uplands, forming rounded clumps or extensive mats; common in lowlands as rounded clumps. (Photo by R. E. Good.)
(E) *Leucobryum albidum:* medium-sized acrocarpous moss; stems close together; leaves distinctly whitish, greener when wet or young, many detached and lying horizontally on upper plant surface, somewhat thick (several cell layers thick), relatively wide, somewhat keel-shaped; capsules uncommon, relatively short and fat, inclined but not horizontal, dark when dry; common in uplands as rounded "pin cushions" or flatter mats on soil; common in some lowlands. *L. glaucum* (pin cushion moss) is large; stems longer, more separate from one another; leaves longer; detached leaves uncommon on upper plant surface; capsules uncommon, with longer stalk; common in the lowlands as clumps, but rarely mats. (Photo by R. K. Frye.)
(F) *Dicranum flagellare:* small or medium-sized acrocarpous moss; stems close together; leaves moderately wide, somewhat tubular, and moderately pointed, closely appressed or slightly curled and twisted when dry; mats occasionally have numerous upright, nearly leafless branchlets projecting slightly above the leaves; capsules uncommon, thin, cylindrical, upright, symmetrical; common in uplands as mats on soil with some humus, or clumps on moist decaying logs, occasionally common in lowlands. (Photo by R. K. Frye.)

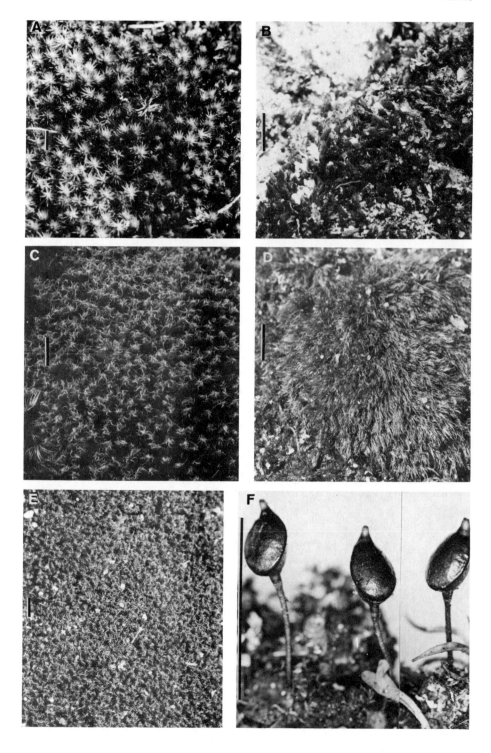

A few quantitative studies give an indication of the most abundant species in different habitats, mostly in the Lebanon State Forest area. In plots within 16 swamps, Little (1951) recorded one thallose liverwort (*Pallavicinia lyellii*), four leafy liverworts (leading dominants, *Odontoschisma prostratum, Microlepidozia sylvatica, Calypogeia trichomanis*), four species of *Sphagnum*, and 14 other mosses with *Dicranum flagellare* and *Leucobryum glaucum* cited as most common. McCormick (1955) sampled bryophyte communities in many lowland forest stands and cited the following dominants: cedar and hardwood swamps, *Sphagnum* spp. and *Plectocolea crenuliformis*; pine lowlands, *Sphagnum* spp.

In the uplands, McCormick found chestnut oak woods dominated by *Dicranum scoparium, Ceratodon purpureus,* and *Polytrichum juniperinum,* and other forest types overall dominated by *Polytrichum juniperinum* and *Ceratodon purpureus*. Olsson (Chapter 15, this volume) reported the following abundant species: (a) pine–scrub oak

Fig. 2. Common bryophytes of the Pine Barrens. Lines on photos are 1 cm ($\pm \frac{3}{8}$ in) long.
(A) *Polytrichum juniperinum* (haircap moss): large acrocarpous moss; stems relatively far apart; leaves long, wide, appearing to be tubular and many cell layers thick, with a usually brown hairlike point, straight and upright when dry, small in lower part of stem; spore-bearing capsule on tall stalk, common, square to hexagonal in cross section, commonly with a whitish hairy cap; common in uplands, often forming extensive mats on sand in woods. *P. ohioense* with a nontubular leaf and a toothed leaf margin, and *P. piliferum* with a white hair tip on leaf are widespread in uplands. (Photo by R. E. Good).
(B) *Pohlia nutans:* small acrocarpous moss; stems relatively far apart; leaves wide, relatively blunt tipped, small in lower part of stem, upright and often slightly twisted when dry; leaf cells wide and somewhat rectangular; capsules relatively uncommon, pear-shaped, and drooping; common in uplands on soil containing humus, and around tree bases. *Bryum capillare* has a very short stem; short wide, concave leaves; short wide leaf cells; a distinct leaf border of elongated cells; occasionally common in similar upland sites. (Photo by R. K. Frye.)
(C) *Dicranum condensatum* (or *sabuletorum*): medium-sized acrocarpous moss; stems somewhat far apart; leaves relatively wide with a long point, much of leaf length strikingly curled and twisted when dry; capsules uncommon, similar to *D. scoparium;* common in frequently burned uplands including the Pine Plains; forms mats on sand. (Photo by R. K. Frye.)
(D) *Dicranella heteromalla:* small acrocarpous moss; stems short, somewhat far apart; leaves very narrow, appearing as green hairs, generally curved and pointing in the same direction, so plants appear "wind swept"; edge of mat sometimes has green filaments matted on soil with scattered small upright shoots; capsules common, on short yellow stalks, relatively short and fat, with red around the teeth at upper end, somewhat unsymmetrical; common in uplands on soil with higher clay and lower humus content or around base of fallen trees. (Photo by R. K. Frye.)
(E) *Ceratodon purpureus:* small acrocarpous moss; stems close together; leaves of equal width through most of their length, relatively short-tipped, margins of leaf slightly curved back from leaf surface; leaf tips curled and twisted when dry; capsules common, inclined to nearly horizontal, prominent lengthwise ridges and valleys in capsule wall when dry; common in uplands, covering sandy areas. (Photo by R. K. Frye.)
(F) *Buxbaumia aphylla:* very small acrocarpous moss; "leafy plant" a green filamentous film on soil surface with scattered, nearly stemless tiny clusters of leaves, rarely seen; capsule is large, inclined at about 45° from the stalk, oddly shaped, about 1–1.5 cm (0.5 in) high; possibly widespread, but uncommon in uplands on soil, unknown in lowlands; usually found on "hands and knees." (Photo by G. R. Brassard.)

woods, *Polytrichum juniperinum,* (b) white oak–chestnut oak–black oak woods, *Dicranum scoparium, Leucobryum glaucum,* and *Polytrichum juniperinum,* (c) scarlet oak stands in the eastern and central Pine Barrens, *Thelia hirtella,* (d) asphalt road edge, *Ceratodon purpureus,* and (e) many wet communities discussed later.

The following section provides further quantitative perspectives on abundant species, as well as other characteristics of bryophyte communities.

BRYOPHYTE COMMUNITY PATTERNS ALONG FIRE FREQUENCY AND SOIL MOISTURE GRADIENTS

Soil moisture and fire are two overriding factors which shape Pine Barrens vegetation. The objective here is to determine whether bryophyte cover and species diversity change significantly with changes in soil moisture and fire frequency and the attendant vascular plant communities. Soil moisture includes the interrelated effects of average height and variability of the water table and the length of time the soil surface is inundated. Fire frequency includes fire intensity differences, and most importantly, the length of time since the last burn. Bryophyte communities, however, are affected not only by these environmental factors but also by differences in the vascular plant community.

The soil moisture gradient was analyzed from dry to moist in representative sites of upland old burns, pine lowlands, hardwood swamps, and cedar swamps. The entire Pine Barrens region burns occasionally; thus, upland forests without evidence of a surface or canopy fire for 20–45 years were chosen. These old woods were dominated by pitch pine, white oak, and black oak with abundant shrubs and saplings. Pine lowlands were dominated by pitch pine with an extremely dense shrub layer composed mainly of leatherleaf and sheep laurel (*Chamaedaphne calyculata, Kalmia angustifolia*). Hardwood swamps were dominated by red maple, black gum, and sweet bay (*Acer rubrum, Nyssa sylvatica, Magnolia virginiana*) with many shrubs and saplings. Cedar swamps were dominated by Atlantic white cedar with considerable undergrowth. Estimated depth of the water table varied from a few meters in upland old burns to 0–20 cm in cedar swamps (Rhodehamel, chapter 9, this volume), where much of the soil surface is inundated at least a short time each year.

The fire frequency gradient was analyzed in representative stands of upland old burn, three-year burn, and annual burn. The three-year burn had had light winter surface fires approximately eight or nine times in 21 years, and had last burned three years previously. The annual burn had burned with light winter surface fires almost every year for many years, one site going back to the 1920's. Our measurements were made in October through December 1976 following the fire of the previous winter. All sites were upland, and included woods of pitch pine, white oak–black oak–pitch pine, and chestnut oak–black oak–white oak. Shrub and sapling cover decreased with increasing fire frequency, and herb cover was sparse in all sites except annual burns. No stones and very few logs with bryophytes were encountered.

Three representative stands of each vegetation type were chosen in and near Lebanon State Forest. In a representative portion of each stand, three regularly distributed 1 ×30 m transects were sampled for cover of each bryophyte species in square centimeters. Cover is the area of a bryophyte clump or mat and is related to biomass and energy (Forman, 1968, 1969). Reproductive status (Forman, 1965) was not recorded, although differences may be present. A timed reconnaissance for additional species in each site lasted until two investigators each only located new species after five to ten minutes of searching. Sites and methods are described more fully by Forman and Kodama (1979). Soil arthropod communities also were studied in these sites (Dindal, Chapter 30, this volume).

Fire Frequency Effects

Bryophyte cover increased with increasing fire frequency (Fig. 3). The annual burn, with an average 0.76 m² per 30 m² sampled, had 2.5% ground cover, four times the cover of the old burn. The annual burn had significantly more cover than the other burn conditions and also the lowest variability from woods to woods.

The most abundant species also changed notably along the fire gradient (Fig. 3). *Leucobryum albidum* and *Dicranum flagellare* dominated the old burns, while in the annual burns *Polytrichum juniperinum, Dicranum scoparium, D. condensatum* (= *D. sabuletorum*), *D. flagellare, Leucobryum albidum,* and *Dicranella heteromalla* were dominant.

Diversity of common species, as measured in the transects, increased with increasing fire frequency (Fig. 3). In contrast, total diversity of common and uncommon species, as measured with both transects and reconnaissance, decreased in the annual burn (Fig. 3). This was due to a major decrease in tree trunk bryophytes, while soil bryophyte diversity remained approximately constant. Rare species, which grow in only a few locations in the Pine Barrens, were not measured with the methods employed. These probably would accentuate this latter pattern, since most would be expected in old burn sites.

All but one of the soil bryophyte species in the transects increased in cover with increasing fire frequency. *Dicranum condensatum* increased the most. Only *Leucobryum albidum* remained approximately constant along the fire gradient.

Profound bryophyte community changes thus are seen with increasing fire frequency. Cover increases fourfold, diversity of common species increases, total diversity decreases, and species composition changes. Indeed, the bryophyte communities are very different and appear at least as different as the vascular plant communities, which change in cover of various strata, and to a lesser extent, species composition and diversity. The increase in cover of soil bryophytes is related to the burning of litter and to the subsequent increased availability of mineral soil for bryophyte growth. With subsequent deposition of leaf litter, bryophyte mats die and cover decreases. The loss in tree trunk bryophyte diversity is due to killing by the heat of fire, since most such species are around tree bases and few grow above 2 m height. Fires remove log microhabitats, literate nutrients, and favor pines (which have few trunk species) over oaks, but these effects here are considered minor.

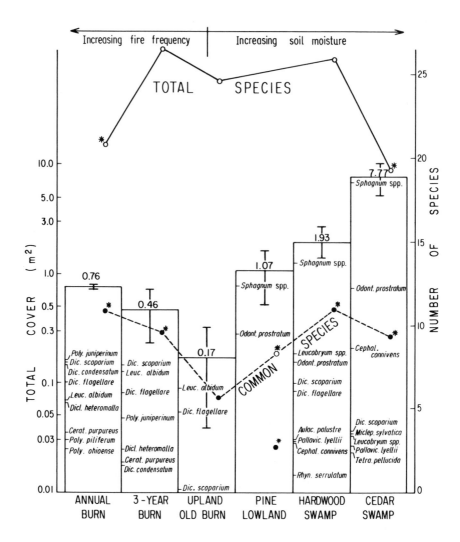

Fig. 3. Bryophyte cover and diversity along fire frequency and soil moisture gradients. Total cover (histograms) is the average bryophyte cover in 30 m², based on sampling three 1 × 30 m transects in each of three stands per vegetation type. Confidence intervals are ±1 standard error. Numbers of species (graphed) is the average of three sites for each vegetation condition. Common species are those recorded in three 1 × 30 m transects at each site. Total species include both those in the transects and in reconnaissance. Pine lowland forest has thick shrub and litter cover; see text. Points indicated with an asterisk differ significantly (p < .05) from the upland old burn. Poly., *Polytrichum*; Dic., *Dicranum*; Leuc., *Leucobryum*; Dicl., *Dicranella*; Cerat., *Ceratodon*; Odont., *Odontoschisma*; Aulac., *Aulacomnium*; Pallavic., *Pallavicinia*; Cephal., *Cephalozia*; Rhyn., *Rhynchostegium*; Miclep., *Microlepidozia*; Tetra., *Tetraphis*. *Leucobyum* spp. includes *L. albidum* and *L. glaucum*, with the former considerably more abundant.

These results for cover are consistent with those of Buell and Cantlon (1953), who compared old burns and one- to three-year burns. However, the much lower cover present in the nine stands studied and the significantly higher cover in the annual burn over the three-year burns contrast with results of Buell and Cantlon (1953) and Moul and Buell (1955). It should be noted that the one- to three-year fires are a product of human management, and that fire intervals of eight to over 40 years are typical in the Pine Barrens (Lutz, 1934; Little, Chapter 17, this volume).

Soil Moisture Effects

Bryophyte cover increased dramatically with increasing soil moisture (Fig. 3). Cedar swamps, with an average 7.8 m^2 per 30 m^2 sampled, had 26% cover, about 45 times the cover in upland old burns. Cedar swamps were significantly higher in cover than hardwoods swamps and pine lowlands, which were significantly higher than upland old burns.

Sphagnum composed at least two-thirds of the bryophyte cover in the three wettest forest types. The leafy liverwort *Odontoschisma prostratum* was the only other species abundant in these wet sites. Two other leafy liverworts were common in the two wettest sites, *Cephalozia connivens* and *Microlepidozia sylvatica,* and one thallose liverwort, *Pallavicinia lyellii.* The most abundant species of the upland old burns, *Leucobryum albidum* and *Dicranum flagellare,* also were present in the wet sites.

Diversity of common species, as measured in the transects, increased with higher soil moisture (Fig. 3). The pattern for total diversity was more complex. Pine lowlands were lowest in diversity, since pitch pine was virtually the only tree present and the shrub layer was very dense. If we omit the rather different pine lowlands, the pattern suggests a slight or no decrease in total diversity, which results from a decrease in tree trunk bryophyte diversity, yet an increase in soil bryophyte diversity. Note however that *Sphagnum* species were not differentiated. Rare species are expected in all types except pine lowlands, and might not change the pattern significantly.

Again for increasing soil moisture, major bryophyte community differences are seen. Cover increases 45-fold, diversity of common species increases, total diversity is variable but appears to decrease, pine lowlands are significantly lower in diversity, and species composition changes, particularly with the increase in *Sphagnum.*

The vascular plant communities along this gradient are extremely different in terms of the most abundant species, but data on diversity and dominance are unavailable. The bryophyte communities may change only slightly less than the vascular plant communities. A major increase in bryophyte cover seems largely a direct result of increased moisture. Similarly, an increase in diversity of soil bryophytes appears related to moisture, since this diversity is evident in two very different wet communities, the hardwoods and cedar swamps. However, a decrease in tree trunk bryophytes appears related to the vascular plants. A moderate diversity of rough-barked trees in the upland old burns contrasts with a slightly lower diversity of mainly smooth-barked trees in the hardwood swamps, and a still lower tree diversity in the cedar swamp, where virtually all trunks have peeling cedar bark.

PINE PLAINS BRYOPHYTES

The same methods were utilized to sample two widely separated sites in the west Pine Plains and one site in the east Pine Plains. These sites were dominated by a low woodland of pitch pine, blackjack oak, and scrub oak about 1–3 m high, with scattered patches of heath shrubs and few herbs.

Dicranum condensatum was encountered in transects in two of the three sites, averaging overall 447 cm² per 30 m² area, or about 0.15% cover, far lower bryophyte cover than any other vegetation condition studied. In reconnaissance, only soil species were found, including *D. condensatum* in the third site. *Polytrichum juniperinum*, *Pohlia nutans,* and *Dicranella heteromalla* were present in two out of three sites, and *Ceratodon purpureus, Leucobryum albidum, Bryum* sp. and *Polytrichum piliferum* in one out of three sites. These species are all common in other Pine Barrens areas. Lutz (1934) noted two *Dicranum* species and *Polytrichum juniperinum* in the Pine Plains, indicating they were more common than in the surrounding Pine Barrens. Thus, no evidence exists for rare or endemic bryophyte species in the Pine Plains. However, the most abundant species, *Dicranum condensatum*, is the species most favored by fire (Fig. 3). Outside the Pine Plains, this *Dicranum,* which was uncommon in old burn areas, became a leading dominant in areas burned annually.

COMMON *SPHAGNUM* MOSSES

Information on the abundance of *Sphagnum* species comes from three studies. Little (1951) found *S. magellanicum* and *S. recurvum* to be most common in cedar and hardwoods swamps. McCormick (1955) recorded *S. papillosum, S. recurvum,* and *S. magellanicum* as most common in cedar swamps, *S. recurvum* in hardwood swamps, and *S. tenerum* and *S. magellanicum* in pine lowlands.

Olsson (Chapter 14, this volume) recognized many additional plant communities and found the following most abundant species of *Sphagnum:* (a) cedar swamps: *S. fallax, S. magellanicum, S. palustre, S. flavicomans, S. pulchrum;* (b) hardwood swamps: *S. fallax, S. palustre;* (c) shrub thickets: *S. capillaceum;** (d) spongy leatherleaf thickets: *S. cuspidatum, S. fallax, S. magellanicum, S. subnitens;* (e) marshy areas: *S. magellanicum, S. pulchrum, S. papillosum;* (f) *Narthecium* marshes: *S. portoricensis;* (g) *Carex* marshes: *S. flavicomans;* (h) *Lachnanthes* marshes: *S. cuspidatum, S. tenellum;* (i) *Rhexia* marshes: *S. pylaesii;* (j) *Polygala–Leiophyllum– Kalmia* marshes: *S. capillaceum,* * *S. compactum;* (k) wet haul roads: *S. capillaceum,* * *S. compactum;* and (1) pond margins: *S. torreyanum, S. teres.* Waksman *et al.* (1943) described the distribution and utilization of peat, but as yet little is published on *Sphagnum* in the Pine Barrens.

---

*[= *S. capillifolium* (Ehrh.) Hedw.].

COMMON LICHENS

The lichen list for New Jersey published by Britton (1889) included 152 crustose species (plant body flattened with lower portion penetrating the substrate, and no lower surface or hairlike attachment structures visible), 86 foliose species (plant body flattened against substrate with lower surface usually containing hairlike attachment structures), and 41 fruticose species (plant body composed of upright or pendant stems which are rounded, hollow and often much branched). The last group included 21 *Cladonia* species, some from the Pine Barrens. Useful references for identifying lichens are by Hale (1969), Thomson (1963, 1967), Fink (1935) and Nearing (1947). Major reference collections for Pine Barrens lichens are in herbaria of the New York Botanical Garden, the Academy of Natural Sciences, and Harvard University, with some specimens in the Chrysler Herbarium of Rutgers University.

Six major species or morphological types of lichens are illustrated (Fig. 4) with encapsulated descriptions.

The most common lichens in the cedar and hardwoods swamps (Little, 1951; Evans, 1935, 1938, 1940; Olsson, Chapter 14, this volume) are: *Cladonia calycantha, C. bacillaris, C. incrassata, C. santensis, C. squamosa, C. cristatella,* and *C. coniocraea. Cladonia incrassata, C. calycantha,* and *C. santensis* are more characteristic of cedar swamps, and *C. bacillaris, C. squamosa,* and *C. cristatella* of hardwood swamps (Little, 1951). *C. incrassata* is common on logs and tree bases (Little, 1951; Olsson, Chapter 14, in this volume), and *C. santensis* on rotting logs in New Jersey swamps (Brodo, 1968). McCormick (1955) cited *C. uncialis* as most common in pine lowlands. Brodo (1968) gives the following species as characteristic of Atlantic white cedar swamps of Long Island, New York: *Bryoria furcellata (Alectoria nidulifera), Cetraria viridis, C. ciliaris, Usnea trichodea, Cladonia incrassata, Hypogymnia physodes,* and *Cladonia bacillaris.* He lists the following for Long Island red maple swamps: *Cetraria ciliaris, Parmelia perforata, Usnea trichodea, Cladonia incrassata, Parmelia saxatilis, P. rudecta,* and *Lecanora caessiorubella.*

In the drier upland Pine Barrens of New Jersey, little is known except about the species of *Cladonia* (Evans, 1935, 1938, 1940; Lutz, 1934; McCormick, 1957; Olsson, Chapter 14, this volume), the most common of which are: (a) much-branched stems (Cladoniae group), *Cladonia squamosa, C. uncialis, C. subtenuis, C. sylvatica, C. caroliniana;* (b) little or unbranched stems (Clausae group), *C. cristatella, C. grayi, C. atlantica, C. chlorophaea, C. clavulifera.*

McCormick (1955) found *Cladonia sylvatica* and *C. grayi* to be the most abundant in chestnut oak woods of the Pine Barrens. Total upland lichen cover was highest in these woods and lowest in pine–black oak woods. Olsson (Chapter 14, this volume) observed *C. cristatella, C. atlantica,* and *C. squamosa* to be particularly abundant in regularly burned areas of pine-scrub oak woods. White oak–chestnut oak–black oak woods had abundant *C. grayi* and *C. squamosa* on the soil, and *C. coniocraea* and *Parmelia rudecta* on tree bases. Olsson recorded *C. squamosa* common in shrub thickets; *C. floridana, C. squamosa,* and *C. submitis* in moist shrub meadows; *C.*

caroliniana and *Pyonothelia papillaria* in old fields; and *C. caroliniana* and *C. strepsilis* in the Pine Plains.

Characteristic lichens of the upland Long Island pine barrens (Brodo, 1968) are: *Bacidia chlorococca, Cladonia atlantica, Lecidea uliginosa, L. scalaris, Cladonia subtenuis, Lecidea anthracophila, Parmelia galbina, Pertusaria trachythallina, Physcia stellaris, Parmeliopsis placorodia, Cladonia clavulifera, C. cristatella, C. chlorophaea, C. bacillaris, Parmelia sulcata, Physcia aipolia, Physcia millegrana, Lecanora caesiorubella,* and *Parmelia caperata.*

CONCLUSION

Thus, in the Pine Barrens we see bryophyte and lichen communities with generally higher cover, lower diversity, and different species composition than are found in surrounding regions. Fire frequency and soil moisture differences produce major effects on the communities. Challenges for the future are manifold. Bryophytes and

---

Fig. 4. Common lichens of the Pine Barrens. Lines on photos are 1 cm (±⅜ in) long.

(A) Fruticose lichen (*Cladonia uncialis,* of Cladoniae group): large; stems upright, much branched, hollow, with holes in many branches; common in uplands, forms extensive mats on sandy soil, especially on frequently burned sites; also common in lowlands where it forms smaller clumps; many species present with upright, much branched stems; yellow-gray species contain usnic acid, gray species do not. (Photo by R. K. Frye.)

(B) Fruticose lichen (*Cladonia cristatella,* British soldiers, of Clausae group): medium sized; stem upright, few or no branches, hollow, bright red tips; common in uplands and lowlands, usually as small patches on logs and on soil with humus. Many other species present, having variously sculptured and colored upright stems with few branches. (Photo by R. K. Frye.)

(C) Foliose lichen (*Parmelia rudecta*): large; central portion of upper surface appears rough with tiny asexual reproductive structures; outer portion of upper surface with white dots; lobes at edge of plant body relatively large; common in uplands on deciduous trees. *P. caperata* is similar except yellow-gray in color, and no or few white dots. Many other *Parmelia* species are present. (Photo by R. E. Good.)

(D) Foliose lichen *(Physcia stellaris* and *P. millegrana*): medium sized; similar to *Parmelia rudecta* except lobes at edge of plant body very small and white dots generally absent. Many species of *Physcia* are present. Small, colored, flattened discs are fungus spore-producing structures found on most lichen species. (Photo by R. K. Frye.)

(E) Squamulose lichen (*Cladonia apodocarpa*): medium sized; composed of numerous tiny plant bodies (squamules) with white lower surfaces and no hairlike attachment structures. Such squamules are the juvenile stage of *Cladonia* species which bear taller upright reproductive structures. The common *Cladonia squamosa* has more finely divided squamules than *C. apodocarpa.* The yellower finely divided squamules of *C. incrassata* are common on Atlantic white cedar trunks. Squamules of many other *Cladonia* species are present. (Photo by R. K. Frye.)

(F) Crustose lichen (*Ochrolechia parella*): medium sized; common in uplands on deciduous trees; small, colored, flattened discs are fungus spore-producing structures. The similar common *Ochrolechia parella* has smaller spores and different organic acids. On upland sandy soil, *Lecidea uliginosa* and allied species (as black, tarlike patches) and the grayish-green *Lecidea granulosa* are common. Many other species are present, particularly on deciduous trees. (Photo by R. K. Frye.)

lichens may be used as unique systems for testing biological ideas. We have little knowledge of the roles of the organisms within the ecosystem, for example, nutrient retention and cycling, productivity, interactions with animals (Gerson, 1969), and control of seed germination, mycorrhizal fungi and vascular plant distributions. Indeed, understanding the ecology of bryophytes and lichens themselves is needed, such as distributions within the region (ecological data are nearly absent beyond the Lebanon State Forest area), rare species, possible hybridization, competition patterns, and community structure and function.

SUMMARY

Bryophytes and lichens are exceptionally prominent in Pine Barrens ecosystems, yet ecologically are little known, with even dominant species rarely recognized. Eight of the most common mosses, three liverworts, and six lichens are illustrated and briefly described to aid in field recognition. Common species in cedar and hardwood swamps are several *Sphagnum* species, *Odontoschisma prostratum*, *Leucobryum* spp., *Dicranum flagellare*, *D. scoparium*, *Pallavicinia lyellii*, *Cladonia calycantha C. bacillaris*, *C. incrassata*, *C. santensis*, *C. squamosa*, *C. cristatella*, and *C. coniocraea*. In the pine and oak uplands, common species are: *Polytrichum juniperinum*, *Dicranum scoparium*, *D. flagellare*, *Leucobryum albidum*, *Ceratodon purpureus*, *Cladonia squamosa*, *C. cristatella*, *C. grayi*, *C. uncialis*, *C. subtenuis*, *C. atlantica*, *C. sylvatica*, *C. chlorophaea*, *C. clavulifera*, *C. caroliniana*, *Parmelia rudecta*, and other foliose and crustose lichens.

With increasing fire frequency, bryophyte communities increased in cover and in diversity of common species, but decreased in total diversity. With increasing soil moisture, the same patterns were observed, although with a spectacular increase in cover and more variability in diversity. Species composition changes also were marked, and overall bryophyte and vascular plant communities appear to change differently but equivalently along environmental gradients. The bryophyte community of the dwarf Pine Plains woodland is the most depauperate, although the dominant species, *Dicranum condensatum*, is the species most favored by fire.

ACKNOWLEDGMENTS

I am deeply grateful to Douglas R. Kodama, whose care in sampling and species identifications was exemplary. I also thank Richard K. Frye, Ralph E. Good, and Guy R. Brassard for photographing specimens, Jack McCormick for providing useful data, Silas Little for information on field sites, Lebanon State Forest personnel for aid, William L. Culberson for suggesting references, John W. Thomson for lichen identification aid, and William C. Steere, Lewis E. Anderson, and David W. Lee for reviewing the manuscript.

REFERENCES

Bard, G. E. (1965). Terrestrial bryophytes in secondary succession in the Piedmont of New Jersey. *Bryologist* **68,** 201–208.

Bernard, J. M. (1960). The forest floor of the New Jersey pine barrens and its role in the hydrologic cycle. M.S. Thesis, Rutgers Univ., New Brunswick, New Jersey.

Bernard, J. M. (1963). Forest floor moisture capacity of the New Jersey pine barrens. *Ecology* **44,** 574–576.

Bliss, L. C., and Linn, R. L. (1966). Bryophyte community changes along a successional gradient in the Piedmont of North Carolina. *Bryologist* **69,** 215–225.

Boerner, R. E., and Forman, R. T. T. (1975). Salt spray and coastal dune mosses. *Bryologist* **78,** 57–63.

Breen, R. S. (1963). "Mosses of Florida, An Illustrated Manual." Univ. of Florida Press, Gainesville.

Britton, N. L. (1889). Catalogue of plants found in New Jersey. *N.J. Geol. Surv., Final Rep. State Geol.* No. 2, 27–649.

Brodo, I. M. (1968). "The Lichens of Long Island, New York. A Vegetational and Floristic Analysis." N.Y. State Mus. Sci. Serv., Albany, New York.

Buell, M. F., and Cantlon, J. E. (1953). Effects of prescribed burning on ground cover in the New Jersey pine region. *Ecology* **34,** 520–528.

Conard, H. S. (1956). "How to Know the Mosses and Liverworts." W. C. Brown, Dubuque, Iowa.

Crum, H. (1976). "Mosses of the Great Lakes Forest," Rev. Ed. Publ. Univ. of Michigan Herbarium, Ann Arbor.

Evans, A. W. (1935). The Cladoniae of New Jersey. *Torreya* **35,** 81–109.

Evans, A. W. (1938). The Cladoniae of New Jersey—supplement. *Torreya* **38,** 137–149.

Evans, A. W. (1940). The Cladoniae of New Jersey—second supplement. *Torreya* **40,** 141–165.

Evans, A. W., and Nichols, G. E. (1908). The bryophytes of Connecticut. *Conn. State Geol. Nat. Hist. Surv., Bull.* No. 11, 1–203.

Fink, B. (1935). "The Lichen Flora of the United States." Univ. of Michigan Press, Ann Arbor.

Forman, R. T. T. (1963). The family Tetraphidaceae in North America: Continental distribution and ecology. *Bryologist* **65,** 280–285.

Forman, R. T. T. (1964). Growth under controlled conditions to explain the hierarchical distributions of a moss, *Tetraphis pellucida. Ecol. Monogr.* **34,** 1–25.

Forman, R. T. T. (1965). A system of studying moss phenology. *Bryologist* **68,** 289–300.

Forman, R. T. T. (1968). Caloric values of bryophytes. *Bryologist* **71,** 344–347.

Forman, R. T. T. (1969). Comparison of coverage, biomass, and energy as measures of standing crop of bryophytes in various ecosystems. *Bull. Torrey Bot. Club* **96,** 582–591.

Forman, R. T. T., and Dowden, D. L. (1977). Nitrogen-fixing lichen roles from desert to alpine in the Sangre de Cristo Mountains, New Mexico. *Bryologist* **80,** 561–570.

Forman, R. T. T., and Kodama, D. R. (1979). Bryophyte diversity and cover along fire frequency and soil moisture gradients in the New Jersey Pine Barrens. *Ecology* **60,** (in review).

Gerson, U. (1969). Moss-arthropod associations. *Bryologist* **72,** 495–500.

Grout, A. J. (1903). "Mosses with Hand-Lens and Microscope." Publ. by Author, New York.

Grout, A. J. (1923). "Moss with a Hand-Lens." Publ. by Author, Newfane, Vermont.

Grout, A. J. (1928–1941). "Moss Flora of North America North of Mexico," 3 vols. Publ. by Author, Newfane, Vermont.

Hale, M. E., Jr. (1969). "How to Know the Lichens." W. C. Brown, Dubuque, Iowa.

Hamilton, E. S. (1953). Bryophyte life forms on slopes of contrasting exposures in central New Jersey. *Bull. Torrey Bot. Club* **80,** 264–272.

Hancock, J. A., and Brassard, G. R. (1974). Phenology, sporophyte production, and life history of *Buxbaumia aphylla* in Newfoundland, Canada. *Bryologist* **77,** 501–513.

Little, S. (1951). Observations on the minor vegetation of the pine barren swamps in southern New Jersey. *Bull. Torrey Bot. Club* **78,** 153–160.

Lutz, H. J. (1934). Ecological relations in the pitch pine plains of southern New Jersey. *Yale Univ. Sch. For. Bull.* **38,** 1–80.

McCormick, J. (1955). A vegetation inventory of two watersheds in the New Jersey Pine Barrens. Ph.D. Thesis, Rutgers Univ., New Brunswick, New Jersey.

Moul, E. T. (1952). Taxonomic and distributional studies of mosses of central and eastern Pennsylvania. *Farlowia* **4**, 139–233.

Moul, E. T., and Buell, M. F. (1955). Moss cover and rainfall interception in frequently burned sites in the New Jersey pine barrens. *Bull. Torrey Bot. Club* **82**, 155–162.

Nearing, G. G. (1947). ''The Lichen Book.'' Eric Lundberg, Ashton, Maryland.

Schuster, R. M. (1953). Boreal hepaticae, a manual of the liverworts of Minnesota and adjacent regions. *Am. Midl. Nat.* **49**, 257–684.

Schuster, R. M. (1966–1974). ''The Hepaticae and Anthocerotae of North America East of the Hundredth Meridian,'' 3 vols. Columbia Univ. Press, New York.

Seim, A. L., Buell, M. F., and Evans, R. I. (1955). Bryophyte growth forms and cover in a jack pine stand, Itasca Park, Minnesota. *Bryologist* **58**, 326–329.

Stephenson, S. N. (1965). Structure and development of the upland heath synusia in the New Jersey Pine Barrens. Ph.D. Thesis, Rutgers Univ., New Brunswick, New Jersey.

Stern, W. L., and Buell, M. F. (1951). Life-form spectra of New Jersey pine barrens forest and Minnesota jack pine forest. *Bull. Torrey Bot. Club* **78**, 61–65.

Stone, W. (1911). The plants of southern New Jersey with special reference to the flora of the Pine Barrens and the geographic distribution of the species. *N.J. State Mus., Annu. Rep.* 1910, pp. 21–828.

Thomson, J. W. (1963). The lichen genus *Physcia* in North America. *Beih. Nova Hedwigia* **7**, 1–172.

Thomson, J. W. (1967). ''The Lichen Genus *Cladonia* in North America.'' Univ. of Toronto Press, Toronto.

Torrey, R. H. (1933). Cladoniae in the range of the Torrey Botanical Club. *Torreya* **33**, 109–129.

Torrey, R. H. (1935). Lichens as relict species of the northward migration of plants since the close of the last glacial period. *Bryologist* **38**, 3–8.

Waksman, S. A., Schulhoff, H., Hickman, C. A., Cordon, T. C., and Stevens, S. C. (1943). The peats of New Jersey and their utilization. *N.J. Dep. Conserv. Dev., Geol. Ser. Bull.* **55**, Part B, 1–278.

24
Algae of the Pine Barrens

EDWIN T. MOUL and HELEN FOOT BUELL

The first reference to the algae of the New Jersey Pine Barrens seems to have been made by Wood (1872), who collected in the "Pines" 16–64 km (10–40 mi) east of Camden and found "some very curious and interesting forms, which are apparently peculiar," but he neither named them nor specified localities. In the following decade, Wolle (1880, 1881a,b, 1882, 1883, 1884, 1885, 1887, 1892) reported on the freshwater algae of the United States, with particular emphasis on desmids, chiefly non-filamentous green algae. He collected in the Pine Barrens region, but rarely indicated sites. Stokes (1885, 1886a,b) published on North American microscopic organisms, and included a few new taxa of Chrysophyceae algae from shallow water and *Sphagnum* of central New Jersey. He gave no information on specific localities.

Boyer (1916) and Patrick (1958, 1964) recorded diatom species from many sites in the Pine Barrens. Grönblad (1956) listed a few desmids present in a collection by E. T. Moul, and three algal genera were noted by Fikslin and Montgomery (1971). We know of no other published records of algae of the Pine Barrens.

The purpose of this chapter is to describe the known flora, habitats, and distributions of Pine Barrens algae. Their ecology also will be analyzed briefly.

HABITATS AND ECOLOGY

The habitats available for algal growth in the Pine Barrens are largely dependent on the region's predominant topography, a low coastal plain with gentle undulations (Tedrow, Chapter 4, this volume). Swiftly moving water is rare, found only in locations such as dams at cranberry bog outlets, temporary dams formed by fallen trees, and sluiceways at stream gauging stations. In general, however, the streams are shallow and slow moving, with flow impeded by emergent plants along their margins. Submerged plant stems or other submerged objects and pebbles are sites for attached algae. Bordering trees and shrubs reduce the light intensity.

Most streams are fringed with nearly level areas, ranging in width from a few meters to a mile (1600 m) or more (McCormick, 1970). These are flooded during the winter and early spring and are saturated most of the year, except during prolonged droughts, when even the residual pools dry up.

Dense, dark stands of Atlantic white cedar (*Chamaecyparis thyoides*) border many streams. Here, the forest floor is uneven, hummocks covered with *Sphagnum* moss being interspersed with small pools. The algal flora is sparse. Openings produced by windthrow, burns, cutting, or mining (S. Little, personal communication) permit light to reach the forest floor. In places, the surface between logs or hummocks is a black organic muck that is oozy even in the driest seasons. These openings and oozy spots may support a varied algal flora.

In lowland areas, bodies of open water, mostly human-made, include permanent ponds or lakes fed by streams, temporary impoundments, ponds in depressions with interior drainage, and savannas or wet meadows flooded during wet periods. All provide habitats for floating (planktonic) algae and organisms attached to the bottom or to vascular plants. In dry seasons, basins with interior drainage may be covered with mats of dry algae and *Sphagnum*. Active cranberry bogs might be classed as temporary ponds; inactive cranberry bogs eventually are covered by *Sphagnum* and lowland shrubs and trees (McCormick, 1970; McCormick and Rhodehamel, 1978).

Sphagnum mosses are abundant in lowland areas of the Pine Barrens. They form a sparse ground cover in dense cedar forests but blanket the ground in many dry-pond bogs and some lake margins, forming what we have designated as *Sphagnum* bogs. In these bogs, shrubs such as leatherleaf (*Chamaedaphne calyculata*) may form a nearly continuous higher stratum. Pools within *Sphagnum* areas frequently are productive collecting sites. Except during droughts, the *Sphagnum* moss provides adequate moisture for many algae, e.g., certain Saccoderm desmids and species of *Eunotia* diatoms.

Water chemistry is a prime factor in determining the algal flora of an area (Smith, 1950). Pine Barrens soils are low in nutrients and calcium and high in silicon (Tedrow, Chapter 4, this volume). The waters of the region are low in nutrients and calcium (Tedrow, Chapter 4, this volume), but little is known of their silicon content (Tedrow, personal communication). The tea-colored waters are highly acid, usually registering a pH of 4–4.5 in our measurements. A particularly low pH is associated with *Sphagnum*, whereas the film of water that covers ooze sometimes has a pH up to 6.

Low nutrients and high acidity are conducive to the growth of diatoms and desmids, but low calcium is restrictive to some algae, such as *Chara* and most blue-green algae (Smith, 1950). Thus, water chemistry strongly determines which of the general groups of algae can be present in the Barrens. Any pollutant that changed the pH to neutral or alkaline probably would eliminate most of the existing flora. Some few ubiquitous species would be exceptions, among them the diatoms *Tabellaria fenestrata* and *T. flocculosa*.

Locally within Pine Barrens habitats, algal distribution is governed primarily by the availability of light. For example, dense cedar swamps have very low light (McCormick and Rhodehamel, 1978) and contain few algae, except for the very productive openings. Some cases of supposed temperature dependence actually may be light dependence (Whitford, 1960).

Some algae are found throughout the year, even under ice cover. Others are primarily cold-water forms, such as species of *Ulothrix* and many of the Chrysophyta. In the cedar swamp of Helmetta, Middlesex County, where most of our water temperature measurements were taken, the small, slow stream had a fairly constant temperature seasonally. In a bordering saturated area was a slow upwelling of water, which in hot weather was cooler than the stream. Daily temperatures fluctuated widely in black muck areas exposed to the sun in small blowdowns. The range of temperatures may be illustrated by our records of June 8, 1965: upwelling, 18°C; stream, 20°C; shady pool, 25°C; sunny pool, 29°C; and the drying, greenish-black gelatinous film on the oozy surface of muck areas in full sun for several hours, 38.5°C. Thus, a wide range of water temperature is available in hot weather. This may explain why some members of the desmid genus *Closterium,* which reach their greatest abundance in spring, nevertheless persist in considerable number into summer. However, it should be noted that many of the same species may be found under ice in January and in drying ooze in July, apparently in good condition.

Algal seasonality and abundance are illustrated (Fig. 1) with five desmid species (*Closterium gracile, Cosmarium pyramidatum, Euastrum crassum, Micrasterias denticulata,* and *Staurastrum alternans*) representing the genera which, in our Pine Barrens records, show the largest number of species. The first four also represent the genera with the greatest biomass. The curves are similar to those for other common members of these genera in the Pine Barrens. *Hyalotheca dissiliens* is included in Fig. 1 as a representative of the three filamentous genera of desmids found in our collections. This species, along with two other filamentous species, *H. mucosa* and *Desmidium grevillii,* sometimes develop locally in great abundance. Figure 1 shows that (a) at least one species is common or abundant at any time except in late fall, (b)

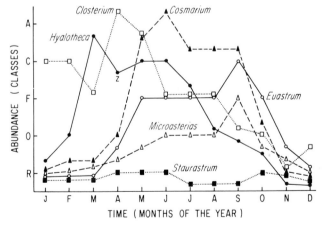

Fig. 1. Abundance of six common algae (desmid species) throughout the year. Algae are *Closterium gracile, Euastrum crassum, Hyalotheca dissiliens* (z, presence of zygotes), *Cosmarium pyramidatum, Micrasterias denticulata,* and *Staurastrum alternans.* Estimated abundance classes: A, abundant; C, common; F, frequent; O, occasional; R, rare. Curves are based on records of the authors over approximately 20 years, with a minimum of 22 collections per month, except for five in December; the maximum was 97 in April.

species generally have broad peaks, i.e., maintain their high abundance for several months, (c) the timing of peak abundance differs among species, and (d) these species are present throughout the year.

Estimates of diversity (Fig. 2) were made by counting the number of taxa (species and varieties) in systematic monthly collections during 1965 in a small opening in the Helmetta cedar swamp. Although no collections were made in July and December, these limited data are considered more reliable than those based on our cumulative collections, which were not spaced evenly throughout the year. The seasonality and abundance curves for this area are similar to those for the Pine Barrens region (Fig. 1).

The genus *Closterium* reached its highest diversity in April and its lowest in September, but it is remarkably uniform compared with the other four genera (Fig. 2). The low September diversity is 58% of the high for April. Its contribution to total diversity ranged from 44% (March) to 20% (September). Its highest diversity is reached in April, the same month as its greatest biomass (cf. Fig. 1), but after May biomass and diversity cannot be correlated. The species of *Closterium* were found in greatest biomass during the earlier months of the year in water at least a few centimeters deep; during hot weather, they were found in shady places or flowing water but never in sunlit ooze.

In contrast to *Closterium,* the other four genera had a much wider range of diversity (Fig. 2); that is, the low diversity figures of February and March ranged from 13 to 22% of the highs of later months. Masses of *Cosmarium* during the period of May

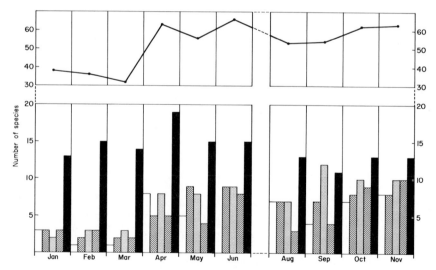

Fig. 2. Diversity of desmids throughout the year in an opening in the Helmetta cedar swamp. The upper curve shows diversity of all desmid species and varieties found during each month of Jan.–June and Aug.–Nov. 1965. The bars below show diversity of each of the five genera with the largest number of species and varieties: ■*Closterium;* ▨*Cosmarium;* ▥*Euastrum;* ▧*Micrasterias;* and □*Staurastrum.* With the exception of *Staurastrum,* these genera also have the greatest biomass.

through September (Fig. 1) were composed of *C. pyramidatum* and *C. ovale*. The high diversity of October and November (Fig. 2) was due to a few individuals of other species, all of small size. The situation is less clear-cut for *Euastrum* and *Micrasterias*, although much of the higher diversity of *Euastrum* in the late fall was due to minute forms. These three genera developed their greatest biomass in very shallow water or ooze with good exposure to the sun. The *Staurastrum* species, all small, never were encountered in abundance; their distribution was spotty.

The number of species found and their abundance depend to a considerable extent on collecting in the right place. Among the desmids we collected in the Pine Barrens, only *Hyalotheca dissiliens* and *Closterium rostratum* were found with zygotes. Thus, most species must persist throughout the year in the vegetative condition, and presumably by sufficient searching virtually all species of an area could be found during all seasons.

Whitford's (1960) theory of ''micro-habitats in time and space'' is illustrated by our collections of *Cosmarium pyramidatum*. This species, present throughout the year, occurred from May through August or September of three successive years as a green film on the same small patch of ooze in an opening in Helmetta cedar swamp. (A dead leaf lying on the patch covered a more varied flora.) A fallen cedar tree a few centimeters in diameter formed a barrier beyond which the *Cosmarium* was present in small numbers. On the opposite side of the *Cosmarium* site, *Desmidium grevillii* was found against the base of a cedar tree in nearly pure masses of coarse green filaments. This species was found in abundance only against the base and over the roots of the cedar tree.

Algae are important as a basis of many food chains in the streams and lakes of the Pine Barrens. Some blue-green algae fix nitrogen, but the blue-greens are not an important part of the flora. Those species present are not primarily members of the nitrogen-fixing group.

Characteristic Algae

Collections of algae by the authors, faculty, and graduate students of Rutgers University were made on many trips to the Pine Barrens during every month of the year. The Pine Barrens outlier at Helmetta, Middlesex County, was visited more regularly. Our field notes indicate that many species are present during every month of the year. Since the majority of algae may be considered cosmopolitan, possible geographical affinities of the flora are not considered. However, algal distributions are closely controlled by habitat conditions, and the following three general habitats are recognized in the Pine Barrens: (1) streams; (2) *Sphagnum* bogs, cedar swamps, and cranberry bogs; and (3) ponds, lakes, and impoundments.

Streams

The slow-moving, brown-water streams of the Pine Barrens have an algal flora typical of that associated with acid waters. Smith (1950) has designated the plankton portion of this type of flora the "Caledonian Flora"—rich in species, especially desmids and diatoms, but low in species of blue-green algae. Most of our stream collections were made over the course of several years at a site adjacent to a gauging station at McDonalds Branch in Lebanon State Forest. Certain genera and species seem to occur regularly. Several species of the red algal genus *Batrachospermum* and its chantrasia stage were present on all collecting days, and in most cases reproductive stages were present. The diatom *Actinella punctata* (Chrysophyta) probably is the most characteristic species, and its absence from the record for one collection date is attributed to an oversight. Species of the genera *Frustulia, Fragilaria, Eunotia,* and *Pinnularia* are characteristic of acid waters and usually were present. *Tabellaria fenestrata,* a ubiquitous diatom species that occurs in waters from pH 4–8, always was present, on many occasions entangled in the branches of *Batrachospermum.*

Among the Chlorophyta, the Zygnemataceae were well represented by the genera *Mougeotia, Zygogonium, Zygnema,* and *Spirogyra,* which were found in most collections. Many desmids were represented, comprising almost a roll call of all the known genera. *Microspora* species were present on each collection date. These attached or entangled algae in many cases occur as long, stringy masses undulating in the slow current, yellowish in bright sun, dark green in shaded portions, or a dirty green color with entrapped soil particles. *Lagynion triangulare,* a Chrysophyte species, was found growing on *Microspora* and *Zygogonium* on several occasions. Blue-green algae were rare in this habitat. A *Calothrix* species occurred on *Batrachospermum,* and *Symploca muralis* formed a scum on a clay bank by the gauging station at McDonalds Branch.

Sporadic collections were made in other streams, such as Webbs Mill Branch of Cedar Creek, Forked River, Oyster Creek, and Rancocas Creek. All samplings showed this acid-type flora, representing the same genera and species mentioned above for McDonalds Branch.

Sphagnum Bogs, Cedar Swamps, and Cranberry Bogs

After reviewing the species present, we find the composition of the flora to show little variation among cedar swamps, *Spagnum* bogs, and cranberry bogs. Many of the species found in the streams are present in these habitats. The blue-green algae are slightly more prominent. *Chroococcus turgidus* was very common in shallow pools surrounded by *Sphagnum,* both in the Helmetta Pine Barrens site and at the McDonalds Branch and South Branch cedar swamps in Lebanon Forest. *Scytonema tolypothrichoides* and *Merismopedia punctata* were collected between hummocks on the black organic ooze in cedar swamps, and *Oscillatoria* species occasionally were common.

Tabellaria fenestrata and *Actinella punctata* were the most common diatoms. Other genera present in abundance were *Stauroneis, Pinnularia, Fragilaria, Surirella, Frustulia,* and *Eunotia. Eunotia curvata* was abundant in water squeezed from *Sphagnum* moss. The Euglenophytes *Euglena mutabilis* and *Trachelomonas volvocina* were found in almost every collection, but never were very common. Aside from the diatoms, the most common Chrysophyte was *Synura ulvella.* The Pyrrophyta were represented by *Gymnodinium* spp. and by the immobile dinoflagellate *Cystodinium bataviense* in water of cedar swamps. *Cryptomonas* species also were present. *Batrachospermum* may occur in spots where there is a slight current.

A green alga found frequently on the floating mat at Helmetta and in cedar swamps in Lebanon Forest was the beautiful *Eremosphaera viridis*, characteristic of acid waters. The same genera of Zygnemataceae found in the streams were present here. The dominant group of algae, however, is the desmids; most known genera were present at one time or another. The filamentous species *Desmidium grevillii* and *Hyalotheca dissiliens* were universally common.

Ponds, Lakes, and Impoundments

The many ponds, lakes, and artificial impoundments in the Barrens are fringed with aquatic vegetation in the shallow water along the shore. Attached algae and planktonic forms are abundant in this zone. The list of species here repeats the flora of the habitats described above, adding a number of species and some genera.

Here, *Oedogonium* species are found growing on the submerged stems of the emergent plants. *Oedogonium undulatum* was observed from March through May in an impoundment near Manahawkin. *Aphanochaete repens* was common on *Oedogonium*. In some of these bodies of water, *Ulothrix zonata* was recorded in the spring. The desmids were not as abundant as in the other habitats.

Phacus species and *Trachelomonas* species represented the Euglenophytes. Chrysophyte species included *Botryococcus braunii*, frequently common in the plankton and entangled in the filamentous species. *Lagynion* species were common on *Oedogonium*. Stokes (1886a) originally described several species of *Lagynion* from central New Jersey as *Chrysopyxis*. *Cyclonexis annularis*, also described by Stokes from this area, occurs in the plankton of these ponds, usually over a bed of submerged *Sphagnum*. Stokes (1885, 1886a,b) identified no specific collecting area for these taxa described from central New Jersey. *Gonyostomum semen*, a green flagellated form, appeared as green patches on the surface of water in protected spots surrounded by emergent vegetation.

THE FLORA

The following list of taxa is based on collections made by the authors and others in the Pine Barrens proper and the outlying Pine Barren at Helmetta. In many cases, time and inadequate material did not allow identification to species. In addition, since many algae cannot be identified to species unless in reproductive condition, the genera observed are included. We have not investigated terrestrial algae, nor have we found such studies by others. This is not intended as a definitive list of the Pine Barrens algae. We hope that scientists may find this useful as a basis for undertaking a more thorough survey in the future.

The arrangement follows that of Smith (1950), except for *Bacillariophyceae* (diatoms), which follows the format of Patrick and Reimer (1966, 1975), and *Ac-*

tinotaenium (Desmidiaceae), which follows that of Teiling (1954). We have omitted the names of families, except in the order Zygnematales to distinguish the desmids (Mesotaeniaceae and Desmidiaceae). We have omitted the names of classes, except in the order Chrysophyta to distinguish the diatoms. For the reader wishing to identify algae, the most useful general works probably are those by Smith (1950) and Prescott (1962), both of which contain numerous references.

The material following the name of a plant in the list below gives some ecological information, to the extent that records are available. Capital letters immediately following the epithet indicate collecting site (see list below). The next series of letters indicates habitat (see list below). Numbers following habitat are months of collection, if records are available; "all" indicates collected throughout the year. The final letter shows our subjective estimate of abundance (see list below). Parenthetical numbers are months of peak abundance, if noticeable, while (c) is peak abundance in cooler months.

For example, for the first taxon in the list, "*Chlamydomonas* spp.—Ats, Ham, Helm, McD; bog, ced, cran, pond, squez; (c)" indicates that more than one species of *Chlamydomonas* was found; collected at Atsion, Hammonton, Helmetta, and McDonalds Branch; in *Sphagnum* bogs, cedar swamps, cranberry bogs, ponds, and squeezings of *Sphagnum* or aquatic mosses; most common in the cooler months of the year.

Collection Sites

The following is a key to abbreviations used in the list of taxa:

Abs, Absecon; Ats, Atsion; Bass, Bass River; BM, Browns Mills; Den, Dennisville; EggR, Egg Harbor River; Fork, Forked River; Fox, Fox River; Ham, Hammonton; Helm, Helmetta; Hor, Horricon Lake; Mal, Malaga; Man, Manahawkin; Manch, Manchester; Mays, Mays Landing; McD, McDonalds Branch; Med, Medford Lakes; Moor, Moorestown; MtM, Mount Misery; Nfd, Newfield; OcC, Ocean County; OswR, Oswego River; Oyst, Oyster Creek; Pak, Pakim Pond; PB, Pine Barrens region; PM, Pleasant Mills; Ran, Rancocas Creek; SB, South Branch; Silv, Silverton Bog; Toms, Toms River; Vine, Vineland; Webb, Webbs Mill Branch, Cedar Creek; West, Westechunk Creek.

Authors

A dash and capital letter immediately following the collection site indicate records by other authors: -B, Boyer (1916); -F, Fikslin and Montgomery (1971); -G, Grönblad (1956); -P, Patrick (1958, 1964); -S, Stokes (1885, 1886a,b); -W, Wolle (1880, 1881a,b, 1882, 1883, 1884, 1885).

An asterisk (*) indicates the location of a type collection (for species from the Pine Barrens named new to science).

Habitats

The following is a Key to the abbreviations used for habitats in the list of taxa:

att, attached; bog, *Sphagnum* bog; ced, cedar swamp; cran, cranberry bog; dit, ditch; ent, entangled with other plants; epi, epiphyte; imp, impoundment; ooze, fine, organic muck with no measurable water over it; plank, plankton; squez, squeezings of *Sphagnum* and aquatic mosses; str, stream. Pond and pool are not abbreviated.

Abundance

The Key to abbreviations of abundance are the following:

R, rare; Oc, occasional; F, frequent; C, common; A, abundant.

KEY TO TAXA

Division Chlorophyta (Green Algae)

Order VOLVOCALES
Chlamydomonas spp.—Ats, Ham, Helm, McD; bog, ced, cran, pond, squez; (c)
Gonium sociale (Duj.) Warm.—Helm; pond; 9

Order TETRASPORALES
Gloeocystis sp.—Helm; pond
Asterococcus limneticus G. M. Smith—Helm, Webb; pond, str; 12
Tetraspora spp.—Ham, McD; cran, str; 2, 3, 6

Order ULOTRICHACEAE
Ulothrix zonata (Weber and Mohr) Kutz.—McD; pond, str; spring
Ulothrix spp.—Ats, Crowfoot bog at Berlin, Ham, OswR; -F; SB; ced, cran, str; 2, 4, 6
Microspora loefgrenii (Nordst.) Lag.—Webb; str; 10, 12
M. quadrata Hazen—McD; str; 4
M. turnidula Hazen—Helm, McD; ced, str; 1, 3
M. willeana Lag.—Helm; pond; 11
Microspora spp.—Fork, Ham, Helm, Man, McD, Oyst, Ranc; bog, ced, dit, imp, pond, str; all
Cylindrocapsa sp.—Helm; pond
Stigeoclonium spp.—Helm; pond, squez, str
Microthamnion strictissimus Rab.—Helm; pond; 3
Microthamnion sp.—Helm; bog; 1
Aphanochaete repens A. Br.—Man; epi, imp; 3–10
Coleochaete irregularis Pringsh.—Helm; epi, pond; spermocarps present
C. pulvinata A. Br.—Helm; epi, pond; 11; spermocarps present

Order OEDOGONIALES
Oedogonium polymorphus Wittr. and Lund.—BM; -W
O. ciliatum (Hass.) Pringsh.—At, -W; pond
O. undulatum A. Br.—Man; imp; 5–10; reproducing
Oedogonium spp.—Man, McD; ced, imp, pond; 5, 6, 10
Bulbochaete brebissonii Kütz.—Ham; -W; pond
Bulbochaete spp.—Helm, Man; imp, pond; 5

Order CLADOPHORALES
Cladophora spp.—Helm, Man; ced, imp

Order CHLOROCOCCALES
Dictyosphaerium ehrenbergianum Näg.—Helm; pond; 1
Pediastrum integrum Näg.—Helm; ced; 9
Coelastrum cambricum Arch.—Helm; ced, str; 4, 9
Coelastrum sp.—Helm; ced; 9
Ankistrodesmus sp.—Helm; ced, pond
Eremosphaera viridis DeBary—Helm, McD; ced, str; 1, 4–7, 9–11

Order ZYGNEMATALES
Family ZYGNEMATACEAE
Mougeotia spp.—Ats, Crowfoot bog at Berlin, Ham, Helm, Man, McD, SB, Webb; bog, ced, cran, dit, imp, pond, str; all
Debarya sp.—OswR; -F
Zygnema spp.—Helm; McD, Webb; ced, pond, str; all
Zygogonium ericetorum Kütz.—Helm, McD, Webb; bog, ent, ooze, pond; 5, 9, 10, 12
Pleurodiscus purpureus (Wolle) Lag.—Helm, McD, Webb; bog, ooze, pond, str; (c)
Spirogyra buchetii Kütz.—Man; dit; 10

S. parvispora Wood—PB; -W
S. punctata Cleve—PM; -W
Spirogyra spp.—Ats, Helm, Man, McD, Silv, Vine, Webb; bog, ced, imp, pond, str; all
Sirogonium sp.—Helm; pond

Family MESOTAENIACEAE (Saccoderm desmids)
Mesotaenium endlicherianum Näg.—Helm; ooze, pool; 1, 4; R
M. mirificum Arch.—McD; squez; 4; R
Gonatozygon brebissonii De Bary—Helm; ent, pond, pool, 1, 4; R
G. monotaenium De Bary—Helm; pond; 4, 10
Cylindrocystis brebissonii Men.—Helm, McD; ced, ent, squez; all; C
Cylindrocystis spp.—Helm, McD; ent, squez; all; C
Netrium digitus (Ehr.) Itz. and Rothe—Helm; ent, ooze, pond, pool, squez; 4–12; Oc
N. interruptum (Bréb.) Lütk.—Helm; ooze, pond, squez; 11; R
N. oblongum (De Bary) Lütk. var. *cylindricum* West and West—Helm; pond, squez; 2–4, 8, 10, 11; F
Netrium spp.—Helm; SB; ced; R
Spirotaenia condensata Bréb.—Helm; ced, ooze, pool; 2, 6, 11; Oc
S. obscura Ralfs—Helm; pool; 3; R

Family DESMIDIACEAE (Placoderm desmids)
Closterium acutum (Lyngb.) Bréb.—Helm; squez; 2, 9, 12; R
C. angustatum Kütz.—Helm; ced, pool; 1–5, 7, 9, 12; C
C. angustatum var. *clavatum* Hast.—Helm; ced, pool; all; C
C. baillyanum Bréb.—Helm; ced; 9–11; C
C. braunii Reinsch—Helm; bog, pond; 11; R
C. costatum Corda—Helm; dit, pond; 4; R
C. costatum var. *angustum* Graff.—Helm; pond; 2; R
C. cynthia De Not.—Helm; ced; all; Oc
C. decorum Bréb.—Ats; -W; pond
C. dianae Ehr.—Helm; ced, pond; 12; R
C. dianae var. *arcuatum* (Bréb.) Rab.—Helm; ced; 12; R
C. didymotocum (Corda) Ralfs—Helm; ced, squez, str; 2, 4, 5; R
C. ehrenbergii Men.—Helm; dit; 2, 5, 9; R
C. gracile Bréb.—Helm; ced, pond, pool, squez; all; A (1–5)
C. gracile var. *elongatum* West and West; Helm; -G; squez; 5; R
C. idiosporum West and West—Helm; ced, pool; 1, 2, 4, 10, 11; Oc
C. intermedium Ralfs—Helm; ced, pool, str; all; Oc
C. juncidum Ralfs—Helm; ced, pool, str; all; C (4)
C. libellula Focke—Helm; ced; 1, 8, 11; R
C. libellula var. *intermedium* (Roy and Biss.) G. S. West—Helm; ced, pool, str; 1–6, 8–11; F (4–5)
C. libellula var. *interruptum* (West and West) Donat—Helm; ced, pool, str; 2, 3, 5, 6, 8–11; Oc
C. lineatum Ehr.—Helm; bog, ced, pool, 1, 2, 4–6; R
C. lunula Ehr.—Helm; ced, dit, squez, str; all; Oc
C. macilentum Bréb.—Helm; ced, dit, pond, squez; 1, 2, 4, 5, 12; Oc
C. moniliferum (Bory) Ehr.—Helm; ced, pond, pool, squez; 1–5, 12; Oc
C. moniliferum var. *concavum* Klebs—Helm; pool; 11; R
C. navicula (Bréb.) Lütk.—Helm; ced, pond, pool; 1, 5, 6, 8–11
C. pritchardianum Arch.—Helm; ced; 3, 7, 8; F (8)
C. pseudodianae Roy—Helm; ced, pond, squez; 1, 2–4, 8, 11; Oc
C. ralfsii Bréb.—Ats; -W; pond
C. ralfsii var. *hybridum* Rab.—Helm; ced, pond, pool, str; 1–8; A (5)
C. regulare Bréb.—Helm; pool, str; all
C. rostratum Ehr.—Helm; pond, pool, squez, str; 1–6, 11, 12; A (1–3), zygotes (4, 11)
C. setaceum Ehr.—Helm; bog, pond; 4, 11, 12; F (4)
C. striolatum Ehr.—Helm; dit, pond, pool, squez, str; all; C (4–5)
C. turgidum Ehr.—Helm; ced; 9; R
C. ulna Focke—Helm; pool, squez, str; all; A (3–4)
C. venus Kütz.—Helm; ent, pond, squez; 2, 3, 12; R
Closterium spp.—Helm, Man; bog, ced, imp, pond, ooze, str
Penium clevei Lund.—BM; -W
P. cylindrus (Ehr.) Bréb.—Helm; pool, ooze; 1–11; Oc
P. spirostriolatum Bark.—Helm; McD; dit, ooze, pool, squez; all; Oc
Penium spp.—Helm; Med
Pleurotaenium constrictum (Bail.) Wood—Helm; pool; 2; R
P. ehrenbergii (Bréb.) De Bary—Helm; ced, dit, ooze, pond, pool, squez; all; Oc
P. minutum (Ralfs) Delp.—Helm; pond, pool; all; Oc
P. minutum var. *latum* Kais.—Helm; ced, pool; squez; all; Oc

P. nodosum (Bail.) Lund. var. *latum* Irénée-Marie—Helm, Vine; ced, pond, pool; 1, 2; R
P. trabecula (Ehr.) Näg.—Helm; bog, ced, pond, pool, squez; 2-4, 7-12; Oc
P. truncatum (Bréb.) Näg.—Helm; ced, ooze, squez; 5, 8; R
Pleurotaenium sp.—Helm; SB; ced, pool; 6
Docidium dilatatum Cleve—BM; -W
D. spinulosum Wolle—(*) Den; -W
D. tridentulum Wolle—(*) BM; -W
D. undulatum Bail.—Helm; pond; 6; R
Triploceras gracile Bail.—Med; pond; 6; R
T. verticillatum Bail.—Helm; pond, squez; 2; R
Tetmemorus brebissonii (Men.) Ralfs—Helm, McD; dit, pond, squez; 2-5, 9, 12; Oc
T. brebissonii var. *minor* De Bary—Helm; pond, squez; 3, 9; R
T. laevis (Kütz.) Ralfs—Helm, McD; ced, pond, pool, squez, str; 4-6, 9, 10; Oc
T. laevis var. *borgei* Först.—Helm; ced, pond; 7, 9; R
T. granulatus (Bréb.) Ralfs—Helm; ced, pond, pool, ooze, squez; 4-9, 12; Oc
Tetmemorus spp.—Helm, SB; bog, ced, str; 6, 9
Euastrum affine Ralfs—Helm; -G; squez; 5; R
E. allenii Cushm.—McD; pool; 5; R
E. bidentatum Näg.—Helm; dit, pond, pool, squez; all; Oc
E. binale (Turp.) Ehr. and vars.—Helm; dit, ooze, pool, squez; all; Oc
E. crassum (Bréb.) Kütz.—Helm; ooze, pool, str; all; C (5-10)
E. crassum var. *scrobiculatum* Lund.—Helm, Mal; -W; McD; pond, pool; 2, 9; R
E. cuspidatum Wolle—(*)Abs; -W; pond
E. denticulatum (Kirchn.) Gay—Helm; pool; 2, 4, 5, 10, 11; R
E. didelta (Turp.) Ralfs—Helm; ooze, pool, str; 2-11; Oc
E. formosum Wolle—(*)Toms; -W; pond
E. giganteum (Wood) Nordst.—Helm, McD; 1, 4-11; Oc
E. humerosum Ralfs—Helm; ced, dit, ooze, pond, pool, squez; all; F (5-10)
E. inerme Lund. var. *depressum* Wolle—(*)Mal; -W; pond
E. insigne Hass.—Helm; pond, pool, str; 1-6, 9-12; Oc
E. insulare (Wittr.) Roy—Helm; pool; 4-6, 9; Oc
E. intermedium Cleve—Den; -W
E. lapponicum Schmid.—Helm; pond; R
E. magnificum Wolle—(*) Mal; -W; Manch; -W
E. montanum West and West—Helm; pool; 5, 9; R
E. purum Wolle—(*) BM; -W
E. validum West and West—Helm, McD; pool, squez, str; 4, 5; R
E. ventricosum Lund.—Helm; pool; 1, 8-12; Oc
E. wollei Lag. var. *pearlingtonense* Presc. and Scott—McD; pool; 11; R
Euastrum spp.
Actinotaenium cucurbita (Bréb.) Teil.—Helm; ced, pond, pool, squez; 3, 5, 6, 9, 10; R
A. cucurbitinum (Biss.) Teil. var. *majellanicum* (Borge) Teil.—Helm; ced, pond, pool, squez; 1; R
A. diplosporum (Lund.) Teil. var. *americanum* (West and West) Teil—Helm; ced, pool, squez; 10, 11; R
Cosmarium abruptum Lund.—Helm; pond; 4; R
C. amoenum Bréb. var. *mediolaeve* Nordst.—Helm; pond, pool, squez; 2, 5, 8, 11, 12; Oc
C. angulosum Bréb.—Helm; pond; 2; R
C. impressulum Elfv.—Helm; pool; 4, 8, 11; R
C. incertum Schmid. forma *consociatum* Croasd. (?)—Helm; pool; 11; R
C. isthmium West—Helm; ced, pool; 11; R
C. kitchellii Wolle—(*) Ham; -W; pond
C. margaritatum (Lund.) Roy and Biss.—Helm; pond; 4, 11; R
C. moniliforme (Turp.) Ralfs—Helm; pond, squez; 2, 12; R
C. norimbergense Reinsch forma *depressa* West and West—Helm; squez; 5; R
C. novae-terrae Taylor—Helm; pond; R
C. ornatum Ralfs—Helm; ced, pond; 4, 11; R
C. orthostichum Lund.—Helm; ent, pond, str; 4, 8, 10, 11; R
C. ovale Ralfs—Helm; ced, ooze, pool; all; A (8)
C. portianum Arch.—Helm; ced, ooze, pond, str; 4, 6, 9-11; Oc
C. pseudoconnatum Nordst.—Helm; ced, ent, pond, ooze; 1, 4-6, 8, 11; Oc
C. pseudoprotuberans Kirchn.—Helm; squez; 11; R
C. pseudopyramidatum Lund.—Helm; pond, squez; 1, 5; R
C. pseudotoxichondron Nordst.—(*) BM; -W
C. punctulatum Bréb.—Helm; ced, pool; 1, 2, 4, 6, 8, 10, 12; R
C. pyramidatum Bréb. and var. *convexum* Krieg. and Gerl.—Helm; ced, dit, ooze, pond, pool, squez; all; A (5-9)
C. rectangulare Grun.—Helm; ooze, pool; 4, 8, 12; R
C. reniforme (Ralfs) Arch.—Helm; ced, ooze, pool; 1, 2, 4, 6, 10; R

C. sejunctum Wolle—(*) Mal; -W; pond
C. subcucumis Schmid.—Helm; pond, squez; 6–8, 11; R
C. subdepressum West and West—Helm; squez; 11; R
C. subtumidum Nordst.—Helm; pond, pool; 3, 4, 12; R
C. tinctum Ralfs—Helm; pond; 4; R
C. trilobulatum Reinsch—Helm; ooze, pool, str; 4, 5, 8; R
Cosmarium spp.—Helm; bog, pond, pool, str
Micrasterias americana (Ehr.) Ralfs—Helm; ooze, pool; 1, 4, 5, 8, 10, 11; R
M. denticulata Bréb.—Helm; ced, ooze, pool, str; all; F (9)
M. depauperata Nordst. var. *kitchelii* (Wolle) West and West—Helm; ced, ooze, pool; all; F
M. dichotoma Wolle—(*) Mal; -W; pond
M. expansa Bail.—McD; str; 6; R
M. fimbriata Ralfs var. *apiculata* Men.—Ats; -W
M. fimbriata var. *spinosa* Biss.—Helm; pond; 4; R
M. foliacea Bail.—Den; -W; pond
M. jenneri Ralfs—Den; -W; pond; Helm; pool; 2, 9, 11; R
M. laticeps Nordst.—Den; -W; pond; Helm; pond; 4; Oc
M. mahabuleshwarensis Hobs. var. *ringens* (Bail.) Krieg.—McD; ced; 10; R
M. muricata (Bail.) Ralfs—Den; -W; pond; Helm; pool; 5, 6, 11; Oc
M. oscitans Ralfs—Helm; pond, pool; 5, 6, 9; Oc
M. papillifera Bréb.—Ats; -W
M. papillifera var. *glabra* Nordst.—Helm; ced, pool; 5, 6, 9–11; Oc
M. papillifera var. *speciosa* Krieg.—Helm; pond; 9; R
M. pinnatifida (Kütz.) Ralfs var. *pseudoscitans* Grönbl.—Helm; pool; 6; R
M. piquata Salisb. var. *lata* Presc. and Scott—Helm; ced, ooze, pool; all; F
M. radiosa Ralfs—Helm, McD; bog, ced, ooze, pond, pool; 4–6, 8, 10–12; R
M. rotata (Grev.) Ralfs—Helm; ooze, pool; 3–10; R
M. triangularis Wolle—Helm; ooze, pool; 5–10; Oc
M. truncata (Corda) Bréb.—Helm; dit, ooze, pond, pool; all; F
Micrasterias spp.—Helm, Silv; bog, pool
Xanthidium antilopaeum Kütz.—Helm; pond, pool; 1–4, 11, 12; R
X. antilopaeum var. *minneapoliense* Wolle—Helm; pond, pool; all; F
X. armatum (Bréb.) Rab.—Helm, Silv; bog, ced, pond, pool; all; F
X. columbianum Wolle—(*) Hor; -W
Xanthidium spp.—Helm, SB; ced, pond, squez
Staurastrum alternans Bréb.—Helm; dit, pond, pool, squez; all; Oc
S. ankyroides Wolle—(*) Mal; -W; pond
S. aspinosum Wolle—(*) BM; -W
S. bienneanum Rab. var. *ellipticum* Wolle—Helm; pond; 4; R
S. brebissonii Arch.—Helm; pond; R
S. botrophilum Wolle—Helm; -G; squez; 5; R
S. calyxoides Wolle—(*) Manch; -W
S. cerastes Lund.—Helm; pond, pool; 1, 4, 5, 10, 11; R
S. coronatum Wolle—(*) Den; -W; pond
S. cyrtocerum Bréb.—Helm; dit, pond, pool, squez; 1, 4–6, 11; Oc
S. dilatatum Ehr.—Helm; pond, pool; 2, 4, 8, 10, 11; Oc
S. divaricatum Wolle—(*) Ham; -W
S. elongatum Bark. var. *tetragonum* Wolle—(*) BM; -W
S. forficatulatum Lund.—BM; -W
S. gracile Ralfs—Helm; pond; 4; R
S. hystrix Ralfs—Helm; squez; 4, 5; R
S. inconspicuum Nordst.—BM; -W; pond
S. leptacanthum Nordst. var. *tetrocterum* Wolle—(*) Mal; -W; pond
S. muricatum Bréb.—Helm; pond, pool, squez; 1, 5, 7, 8; R
S. ophiura Lund. forma—Helm; pond, pool; 1, 4–6, 8–10, 12; Oc
S. orbiculare Ralfs—Helm; ced, pool; 1, 3–6, 8, 9, 12; Oc (4–6)
S. pilosum (Näg.) Arch.—Helm; pool, str; 1, 11; R
S. polytrichum (Perty) Rab.—Helm; 4; R
S. pulchrum Wolle—(*) BM; -W; pond
S. punctulatum Bréb.—Helm; pool; 3–6; R
S. quaternum Wolle—(*) Manch; -W; pond
S. rugulosum Bréb.—Ats, Ham, Helm, Man; bog, cran, imp, pond, squez, str; 3, 4, 9, 11; Oc
S. rugulosum var. *angulare* Grönbl.—Helm; dit, pool, squez; 2, 4, 5; R
S. simonyi Heim.—Helm; pond, squez; 2, 5; R
S. teliferum Ralfs—Helm; pond, pool, squez; 2–6, 8, 9, 11; Oc

S. turgescens De Not.—Helm; squez; 5; R
S. vestitum Ralfs—Helm; pool; 11; R
Staurastrum spp. —PB
Arthrodesmus crassus West and West—Helm; squez; 5; R
A. fragilis Wolle—(*) Ham; -W; pond
A. incus (Bréb.) Hass.—Helm; pool; 2; R
A. rauii Wolle—(*) Nfd; pond
A. subulatus Kütz. var. *subaequalis* West and West—Helm; pool; 8; R
A. triangularis Lag. var. *subtriangularis* (Borge) West and West—Helm; pond; 4; R
Hyalotheca dissiliens (Smith) Bréb.—Ats, Ham, Helm, SB, Silv; bog, ced, cran, ooze, pool, squez, str, A (3–6), zygotes A (4)
H. mucosa (Mert.) Ehr.—Helm; pool, str; all; A (9–11)
Phymatodocis nordstedtiana Wolle—(*) BM; -W; pond
Desmidium aptogonum Bréb.—Helm; ced, pool; 1, 9; R
D. baileyi (Ralfs) Nordst.—Man; pond; 10; R
D. elongatum Wolle—(*) BM; -W
D. grevillii (Kütz.) De Bary—Helm; ooze, pond, str; 2, 4, 9, 11, 12; A
D. quadratum Nordst.—BM; -W; Helm; bog; 3; R
D. swartzii Ag.—Helm; ced, ooze, pond, str; 5, 6, 8, 9, 10, 12; F (5–6)
Bambusina brebissonii Kütz. (*Gymnozygon*)—Ham, Helm, McD, SB, Silv; bog, ced, cran, pool, squez, str; 1–6, 8, 9; Oc
B. delicatissima Wolle—(*) BM; -W; pond

Division Euglenophyta (Euglenoids)

Order EUGLENALES
Euglena acus Ehr.—Helm; pond, str; 9, 10
E. elongata Schewiakoff—Helm; bog, pond; 11
E. gracilis Klebs—Helm; bog; 3
E. mutabilis Schmitz—Helm; near Magnolia; bog, ced, pond, squez; 2–4, 9, 11
E. spirogyra Ehr.—Helm; pond; 9, 11
Euglena spp.—Helm; ced, pond; 2, 9, 11
Phacus crenulata Presc.—Helm; str; 9
P. longicauda (Ehr.) Duj.—Helm; bog, pond; 5, 11
P. pleuronectes (O.F.Müll.) Duj.—Helm, Man; pond, squez, str; 3, 4, 11
P. pyrum (Ehr.) Stein—Helm; pond, str; 4, 9
Phacus spp.—Helm, Man; bog, ced, imp, pond; 9
Trachelomonas armata (Ehr.) Stein—Helm; pond; 4, 11
T. horrida Palm. —PB
T. lacustris Drezepolski—Helm; pond
T. superba (Swir.) Defl.—Helm; pond
T. volvocina Ehr.—Helm, Pak; bog, ced, pond, squez, str; (c)
Trachelomonas spp.—Helm, Man; bog, ced, imp; (c)
Entosiphon sulcatum (Duj.) Stein—Med; str; 10
Peranema trichophorum (Ehr.) Stein—Helm; pond, squez

Division Chrysophyta (Yellow-Green Algae)

Class XANTHOPHYCEAE
Order HETEROCOCCALES
Characiopsis sp.—Helm; bog
Harpochytrium sp.—Helm, McD; bog, ced, epi, pond, str; 3
Ophiocytium capitatum Wolle—Helm; pond; 2, 4
O. parvulum (Perty) A. Br.—Helm, Man; bog, imp, pond; 5, 12
Ophiocytium sp.—Helm; bog, pond
Botryococcus braunii Kütz.—Helm, Man; imp, pond, squez; 5

Class CHRYSOPHYCEAE
Order CHRYSOMONADALES
Chrysococcus sp.—Helm; pond
Derepyxis amphora Stokes—Helm; pond: (*)central New Jersey
Derepyxis sp.—Helm; pond
Synura ulvella Ehr.—Ham, Helm, Vine; bog, ced, cran, pond, str; (c)
Uroglena volvox Ehr.—Bass Lake; pond

Cyclonexis annularis Stokes—Helm; pond, squez, centrifuged; (c); (*)central New Jersey
Dinobryon sertularia Ehr.—Ham, Helm, Med; bog, ced, cran, pond, str; (c)
D. stipitatum Stein—Helm; pond; 11
Epipyxis sp.—Helm; bog

Order RHIZOCHRYSIDALES
Chrysopyxis bipes Stein—McD, SB; ced, epi, str; 3, 6
Lagynion scherffelii Pasch.—Helm, Man; bog, epi, imp; 5
L. triangulare (Stokes) Pasch.—McD, Webb; epi, str; 3, 12; (*)central New Jersey

Class BACILLARIOPHYCEAE (Diatoms)
Order CENTRALES
Melosira sp.—Helm, Silv; bog, pond; 9

Order PENNALES
Tabellaria fenestrata (Lyngb.) Kütz.—Ats, Berlin, Fork, Ham, Helm, Man, McD, MtM, OswR, Oyst, Silv, Webb; bog, ced, cran, pond, str; all
T. flocculosa (Roth) Kütz.—Helm, Man, PB; -B; Vine, West; ced, pond, str; 2, 4, 9
Fragilaria crotonensis Kitt.—Man; imp; 4
F. virescens Ralfs—Ats, Ham, Pb; -B; Webb; cran, pond, str; 2–5, 12
F. virescens var. *capitata* Østr.—EggR; -P
Fragilaria spp.—Ham, Helm, Man, Webb; bog, ced, cran, dit, str; (c)
Synedra spp.—Helm, Man, McD, Webb; ced, imp, str; (c)
Asterionella formosa Hass.—Ats, Ham, Magnolia, McD, SB, Sil, Webb; bog, ced, cran, pond, str; (c)
Semiorbis hemicyclus (Ehr.) Patr.—Ham; -B; pond
Eunotia bactriana Ehr.—Toms; -B
E. bidentula Wm. Sm.—Mays; -B
E. curvata (Kütz.) Lagerst.—Helm, Man, McD; bog, ced, imp, pond, squez, str; (c)
E. flexuosa Bréb. ex Kütz.—Helm; pond, squez; 4
E. incisa W. Sm. ex Greg. var. *incisa* Patr.—Mays; -B
E. pectinalis (O. F. Müll) Rab. var. *minor* (Kütz.) Rab.—EggR; -P
E. pectinalis var. *undulata* (Ralfs) Rab.—ced; -B
E. pectinalis var. *ventralis* (Ehr.) Hust.—EggR; -P
E. serra Ehr. var. *serra* Patr.—Ham, Helm, Helm; -P Man, MtM, Ran, Toms; bog, ced, pond, squez; all
E. soleirolii (Kütz.) Rab.—Moor; -B; Moor; -P
E. sudetica O. Müll.—EggR; -P
E. tenella (Grun.) Hust. *in* Pascher—EggR; -P
Eunotia spp.—Ham, Helm, McD, SB, Webb; bog, ced, cran, pond, squez, str; (c)
Actinella punctata Lewis—Fork, Ham, Helm, Mays, Mays; -B; McD, Silv, Toms; -B; Webb; bog, ced, cran, ent, epi, str; all
Navicula oblongata Kütz.—Helm; ced
Navicula spp.—Helm, McD, Med; bog, ced, pond, str; 1, 6, 9–11
Pinnularia gibba Ehr.—Helm; pond
P. legumen Ehr.—Mays; -B
P. maior (Kütz.) Rab. var. *pulchella* Boyer—Ham; pond; -B
P. nobilis (Ehr.) Ehr.—Helm; pond
P. parvula (Ralfs) Cl. Eul. var. *parvula* Patr.—Atco
Pinnularia spp.—Ats, Crowfoot Bog at Berlin, Ham, Helm, Man, McD, SB, Silv; bog, ced, cran, dit, pond, squez; all
Anomoeoneis serians (Bréb.) Cl.—Mays; -B
Stauroneis anceps Ehr.—Helm; ced
S. phoenicenteron (Nitzsch) Ehr.—Helm; ced, pond; all
Stauroneis spp.—Helm, McD; ced; (c)
Frustulia rhomboides (Ehr.) DeT.—Helm, McD, Webb; squez, str; 3, 4, 8, 12
Frustulia spp.—Helm, McD, Webb; bog, ced, pond, squez, str; (c)
Cymbella gracilis (Rab.) Cl.—Ham; pond; -B
Cymbella spp.—Helm; ced; 3
Nitzschia sigmatella Greg.—Ham; pond; Mays; -B
Nitzschia spp.—Helm; bog, ced; 1, 4, 5, 9
Surirella anceps Lewis—Ham; pond; Mays; -B
S. arctissima A.S.—Mays; -B
S. linearis W. Sm.—Helm; pond
Surirella spp.—Helm, Silv; bog, ced; 1, 4, 9, 11
Stenopterobia intermedia Lewis—Helm; ced; 2

Division PYRROPHYTA (Dinoflagellates)
Order GYMNODINIALES
Gymnodinium spp.—Helm, Man, Webb; ced, imp, pond, str; 2, 9, 10

Order PERIDINIALES
Peridinium sp.—Helm; pond; 9

Order DINOCOCCALES
Cystodinium bataviense Klebs—Helm; ced; 10

Division CYANOPHYTA (Blue-green algae)

Order CHROOCOCCALES
Chroococcus turgida (Kütz.) Näg. [*Anacystis dimidiata* (Kütz.) Dr. and Dailey]—Helm, Silv, Webb; bog, ced, str; all
Aphanocapsa sp.—Helm; pond; 2
Eucapsis alpina Clem. and Shantz—PB
Merismopedia punctata Meyen—Helm, SB, Silv; bog, ced, pond; 1, 6, 11

Order OSCILLATORIALES
Oscillatoria princeps Vauch.—PB
O. tenuis Ag.—PB
Oscillatoria spp.—Helm, Man, Med; ced, dit, imp, pond; 6, 9
Symploca muralis Kütz.—McD; mud; 9
Anabaena spp.—Helm; pond, squez; 2, 3, 12
Cylindrospermum sp.—Helm; pond, squez
Scytonema tolypothrichoides Borr. and Flah.—McD; ced, ooze; 9
Stigonema turfaceum (Bréb.) Cooke—Helm; pond; 11
Hapalosiphon sp.—Helm; pond; heterocysts
Rivularia sp.—Helm; pond, squez; heterocysts
Calothrix sp.—Webb; ent, str; 12

Division RHODOPHYTA (Red Algae)

Order NEMALIONALES
Batrachospermum brugiense Sirod.—Fox, McD, Webb; str; 3, 4, 10. Chantrasia stages present. Reproducing.
B. coerulescens Sirod.—OswR; str; 10
Batrachospermum spp.—Colliers Mills, Fork, Helm, Jesse Creek, McD, OswR; -F; Oyst, Webb; ced, pond, str; all. Chantrasia stages 10
Audouinella violacea (Kütz.) Hamel—McD; str; 12. Reproducing.

Groups of UNCERTAIN POSITION

Order CHLOROMONADALES
Gonyostomum semen (Ehr.) Diesing—Helm; bog, pond, squez; 4, 9–12

Order CRYPTOMONADALES
Cryptomonas spp.—Helm; Man, McD; bog, ced, imp, pond, squez; (c)

SUMMARY

The composition of the algal flora is strongly linked to the acid waters of three major habitat types present in the New Jersey Pine Barrens, i.e., slowly moving streams, ponds and lakes with dams, and poorly drained lowlands with *Sphagnum* moss present. Green algae are common and well represented by an abundance of desmids, plus other members of the Zygnematales. Yellow-green algae, particularly diatoms, are abundant. Euglenoids are common, and of the red algae, *Batrachospermum* species and *Audouinella* are present. In species number and biomass, blue-green algae are unimportant. A list of all of the 360 known algal taxa is given, together with available information on sites of collections, habitats, seasonality, and abundance of each species.

ACKNOWLEDGMENT

The authors thank the Rutgers University Research Council for financial assistance.

REFERENCES

Boyer, C. S. (1916). "The Diatomaceae of Philadelphia and Vicinity." Lippincott, Philadelphia, Pennsylvania.

Fikslin, T. J., and Montgomery, J. D. (1971). An ecological survey of a stream in the New Jersey Pine Barrens. *Bull. N.J. Acad. Sci.* **16,** 8–13.

Grönblad, R. (1956). Desmids from the United States collected in 1947–49 by Dr. Hannah Croasdale and Dr. Edwin T. Moul. *Commentat. Biol., Soc. Sci. Fenn.* **15**(12), 3–38.

McCormick, J. (1970). The Pine Barrens: A preliminary ecological inventory. *N.J. State Mus., Spec. Res. Rep.* No. 2.

McCormick, J., and Rhodehamel, E. C. (1979). Water, vegetation, fire, and man in the Pine Barrens: Development of the pine region hydrological research project and physical description of the experimental watersheds. *U.S. Geol. Surv., Prof. Pap.* **563-A** (in press).

Patrick, R. (1958). Some nomenclatural problems and a new species and a variety in the genus *Eunotia* (Bacillariophyceae). *Not. Nat. Acad. Nat. Sci. Philadelphia* No. 312.

Patrick, R. (1964). A discussion of natural and abnormal diatom communities. *In* "Algae and Man" (D. F. Jackson, ed.), pp. 185–204. Plenum, New York.

Patrick, R., and Reimer, C. W. (1966). "The Diatoms of the United States," Vol. 1, Monogr. No. 13. Acad. Nat. Sci. Philadelphia, Philadelphia, Pennsylvania.

Patrick, R., and Reimer, C. W. (1975). "The Diatoms of the United States," Vol. 2, Monogr. 13. Acad. Nat. Sci. Philadelphia, Philadelphia, Pennsylvania.

Prescott, G. W. (1962). "Algae of the Western Great Lakes Area." W. C. Brown, Dubuque, Iowa.

Smith, G. M. (1950). "The Fresh-Water Algae of the United States." McGraw-Hill, New York.

Stokes, A. C. (1885). Notes on some apparently undescribed forms of fresh-water infusoria, No. 2. *Am. J. Sci., Ser. 3* **29,** 313–328.

Stokes, A. C. (1886a). Some new infusoria from American fresh waters. *Ann. Mag. Nat. Hist.* **17,** 98–112.

Stokes, A. C. (1886b). Notices of new fresh-water infusoria. *Proc. Am. Philos. Soc.* **23,** 562–568.

Teiling, E. (1954). *Actinotaenium:* Genus desmidiacearum resuscitatum. *Bot. Not.* pp. 376–426.

Whitford, L. A. (1960). Ecological distribution of fresh-water algae. *In* "The Ecology of Algae" (C. A. Tryon, Jr. and R. T. Hartman, eds.), Spec. Publ. No. 2, pp. 2–10. Pymatuning Lab. Field Biol., Univ. of Pittsburgh, Pittsburgh, Pennsylvania.

Wolle, F. (1880). Fresh water algae. IV. *Bull. Torrey Bot. Club* **7,** 43–48, 91.

Wolle, F. (1881a). American fresh-water algae. Species and varieties of desmids new to science. *Bull. Torrey Bot. Club* **8,** 32–40.

Wolle, F. (1881b). Fresh-water algae. V. *Bull. Torrey. Bot. Club* **8,** 1–4.

Wolle, F. (1882). Fresh-water algae. VI. *Bull. Torrey Bot. Club* **9,** 25–30.

Wolle, F. (1883). Fresh-water algae. VII. *Bull. Torrey Bot. Club* **10,** 13–21.

Wolle, F. (1884). Fresh-water algae. VIII. *Bull. Torrey Bot. Club* **11,** 13–17.

Wolle, F. (1885). Fresh-water algae. IX. *Bull. Torrey Bot. Club* **12,** 1–6.

Wolle, F. (1887). "Fresh-Water Algae of the United States (Exclusive of the Diatomaceae) Complemental to Desmids of the United States," 2 vols. Comenius Press, Bethlehem, Pennsylvania.

Wolle, F. (1892). "Desmids of the United States and List of American Pediastrums." Comenius Press, Bethlehem, Pennsylvania.

Wood, H. C. (1872). A contribution to the history of the freshwater algae of North America. *Smithson. Contrib. Knowl.* **19**(241), 1–262.

Part VI

ANIMALS AND ANIMAL COMMUNITIES

25

Mammals of the New Jersey Pine Barrens

LEONARD J. WOLGAST

INTRODUCTION

Mammals differ from other vertebrates by possessing mammary glands, which enable the female to provide the young with milk, and hair (present at lest during the early stages of development). Unique internal characteristics include the structure of the jaw and circulatory system. More than 40 species of land-dwelling mammals reside in New Jersey (Shoemaker, 1963; Applegate, 1974), and more than 30 of these live in the Pine Barrens (McCormick, 1970; Wolgast *et al.*, 1972; Applegate, 1974). This chapter describes the species present, and information will be given on their relative abundance, breeding, and generalized diets expected in this area.

Abbot (1868) first listed the mammals of New Jersey, with a revision following by Nelson (1890). Rhoads (1903) reported on the mammals of Pennsylvania and New Jersey, and Stone (1908) published a treatise on the mammals of New Jersey. More recently, Connor (1953) provided information on the habitat preferences of small mammals in the Pine Barrens. McCormick (1970), providing estimates of relative abundance, listed the mammals of the Pine Barrens, and Applegate (1974) provided a more detailed list, including abundance estimates, for all habitats of New Jersey including the Pine Barrens.

Some information also is available concerning the effects of various habitat perturbations on mammals, as well as the effects of mammals on Pine Barrens vegetation. White (1961) found no association between burning with light winter surface fires and population size of the white-footed mouse (*Peromyscus leucopus*) in upland and lowland pine–cedar habitats. Hall (1976) concluded that these light winter fires have no easily measured impacts on mammal populations, but that white-tailed deer (*Odocoileus virginianus*) and eastern cottontail rabbits (*Sylvilagus floridanus*) utilize areas where the fires remove both the litter and the understory.

Little *et al.* (1958) found that, in the uplands during the dormant season, deer browsed heavily on small Virginia pines (*Pinus virginiana*), shortleaf pines (*P. echinata*), and pitch pines (*P. rigida*). However, once the height of these species exceeds 30 cm (1 ft), they no longer are utilized by deer. Deer also browse sprouts of

443

tree and scrub oaks (*Quercus* spp.) during the first three years following logging or fire. However, lowland sites provide most of the food for deer, as well as protective cover in the winter. Atlantic white cedar (*Chamaecyparis thyoides*) is the preferred browse of deer in the Pine Barrens. As a result of intense browsing pressure from deer, many stands of white cedar are unable to regenerate after logging or fire and are replaced by hardwood trees and shrubs.

During the fall, the acorns of bear or scrub oak (*Quercus ilicifolia*) provide a highly concentrated source of food for deer and other mammals (Wolgast, 1974). Antler development and reproductive rate of deer are linked closely to the acorn crop. Frost or high humidity at the time of flowering (early May) significantly reduces acorn yields (Wolgast and Stout, 1977a). Bear oak acorn production generally starts on three-year-old sprouts, peaks at five to seven years, and then declines (Wolgast, 1973a,b). Various treatments, such as fertilization, cutting, and applying herbicides, may increase acorn productivity (Wolgast and Stout, 1977b).

McCormick and Andresen (1960) noted that the most conspicuous and important effect of deer on Pine Barrens vegetation results from browsing. However, they also reported effects of deer bedding, antler rubbing, and deer urine on vegetation. Tunneling by eastern moles (*Scalopus aquaticus*) and pine mice (*Pitymys pinetorum*) form ridges of exposed soil on the surface that are excellent sites for the haircap moss (*Polytrichum juniperinum*) and pine seedlings.

Wolf and black bear populations have been reduced to extinction in the Pine Barrens. Heintzelman (1971) listed the southern bog lemming (*Synaptomys cooperi*) as rare, the river otter (*Lutra canadensis*) as endangered, and the rice rat (*Oryzomys palustris*) as status undetermined. However, a recent unpublished list of the New Jersey Division of Fish, Game and Shellfisheries considers no current Pine Barrens mammal species in jeopardy.

The large mammals (adult body length >1 m or 3.3 ft) residing in the Pine Barrens include the white-tailed deer and man (*Homo sapiens,* discussed elsewhere in this book). The intermediate-sized mammals (adult body length, excluding tail, of 26–76 cm or 10–30 in) include the opossum, eastern cottontail, woodchuck, beaver, muskrat, red fox, gray fox, raccoon, mink, striped skunk, and river otter. The body lengths of the remaining small mammal species excluding tail, are <26 cm (10 in) and generally are considerably smaller. Species in the following orders of mammals are described: pouched mammals (marsupials), insect eaters (insectivores), bats, rabbits, rodents, flesh eaters (carnivores), and even-toed hoofed mammals. Diets and breeding characteristics are general for the species and may be expected to apply in the Pine Barrens.

ORDER MARSUPIALIA: POUCHED MAMMALS

Opossum (*Didelphis virginiana*)

The opossum is gray, with a white face and thin black ears, often tipped in white; its body length, including head, is 38–51 cm (15–20 in). The tail is naked and prehensile, and 23–51 cm long; it has an opposable, clawless thumb on its hindfoot; five toes facilitate the identification of opossum tracks; it is occasional (McCormick, 1970) or common (Applegate, 1974).

Opossums nest in hollow trees, in burrows of other animals, or under buildings. The young are born in March or April, 12–13 days after mating. The tiny young crawl into the female's pouch and attach to a teat, where they remain for two months. At one year of age, they are capable of breeding. This species is omnivorous, feeding on fruits, insects, mice, birds' eggs, young birds, and carrion. Opossums occasionally are consumed by people. Although their fur is of some value, their trapping usually is incidental to the intentional trapping of other species.

ORDER INSECTIVORA: INSECT EATERS

Masked Shrew (*Sorex cinereus*)

The masked shrew is grayish brown, with pale underparts and a bicolored tail; its body length, 5–6 cm (2–2.5 in), is smaller than a mouse; its tail measures 3–5 cm; its ears are nearly concealed by fur, and it is uncommon (Applegate, 1974). The animal is found in most Pine Barrens habitats, but reaches its greatest density in ecotones between uplands and open sedge bogs (Connor, 1953).

Masked shrews are noted for their daily consumption of approximately their own body weight in food, usually insects but also other small animals. They reach sexual maturity at four to five months and produce litters of two to ten young.

Least Shrew (*Cryptotis parva*)

The least shrew has a cinnamon-colored body smaller than that of a mouse; its tail measures 1–2 cm; it has short, fur-covered ears, and its abundance is undetermined (Applegate, 1974) or occasional (McCormick, 1970), with the animal found primarily in tidal river meadows. One, however, was captured in an ecotone between a pitch pine woods and a field (Connor, 1953).

Least shrews eat insects and other small animals in daily amounts nearly equaling their own body weight. Sites for nesting are under debris or below ground. More than one litter is produced annually, and each consists of three to six young.

Short-Tailed Shrew (*Blarina brevicauda*)

This shrew has a lead-colored body measuring 8–10 cm (3–4 in) in length; its tail is 2–3 cm long; it has very small and inconspicuous external ears; its small eyes hardly are discernible; it is common (Applegate, 1974), captured in most major habitats except in the Pine Plains (Connor, 1953).

Short-tailed shrews construct tunnels and feed on insects and other small animals. Nests are constructed beneath logs, stumps, rocks, or other protective cover, and litters of five to eight young are produced two to three times per year.

Eastern Mole (*Scalopus aquaticus*)

The eastern mole is slate colored; with a body 11–17 cm (4.5–6.5 in) long; its naked tail measures 2.5–4 cm; it is subterranean, and easily recognized by its broad feet with outward-turned palms. The animal has a pointed snout, naked on the end with upward-opening nostrils; its ears are evident only as small openings beneath the fur, and its eyes are pinhead sized; it is common throughout the uplands, except in the Pine Plains.

Eastern moles feed primarily on insects and other invertebrates, although some vegetation is consumed. Breeding occurs at one year of age, and four to five young are produced in a single litter each year.

Star-Nosed Mole (*Condybura cristata*)

The star-nosed mole is dark brown or black; its body is 11–13 cm (4.5–5 in) long; its hairy tail measures 8–9 cm; its front feet are as long as they are wide; it has a star composed of 22 fingerlike projections on the end of the nose; the animal is rare to occasional in lowland habitats (McCormick, 1970) or not listed as present in the Pine Barrens (Applegate, 1974).

Star-nosed moles sometimes are observed above ground or in the water. Aquatic and terrestrial insects form a major portion of its diet. One litter per year numbering three to seven young is produced when the animal is at least one year of age.

ORDER CHIROPTERA: BATS

Little Brown Myotis (*Myotis lucifugus*)

The upper parts of the little brown myotis are cinnamon buff to dark brown, and underparts are buff to pale gray; hairs are long and shiny at the tips, giving an almost metallic sheen; its body is 4–5 cm (1.6–2.1 in) long; when laid forward, the ear reaches approximately to the nostril; the tragus, a leaflike structure in the ear, is half as high as the ear; the animal is common (Applegate, 1974).

This species feeds on insects captured while flying. Hollow trees or buildings serve as roosting areas, and in winter this bat hibernates in caves or other similar habitats. One young is produced in late spring or early summer.

Big Brown Bat (*Eptesicus fuscus*)

Upper parts of the big brown bat usually are dark brown; underparts are somewhat paler; its body measures approximately 7 cm (2.8 in) in length; it possesses a blunt tragus; it is uncommon (Applegate, 1974).

Hollow trees and buildings are the preferred roosting sites of the big brown bat, which hibernates in caves in the northern part of its range. Insects are its primary food. In May or June, usually two young per litter are born.

Eastern Pipistrelle (*Pipistrellus subflavus*)

The eastern pipistrelle is yellowish to drab brown. It is the smallest bat present, possesses a blunt tragus, and is uncommon (Applegate, 1974).

Eastern pipistrelles are entirely insectivorous, feeding at dusk and throughout the night. In the North, this species hibernates. Two young are produced in early summer.

Other Species

Four other bat species also can be found in the Pine Barrens, at least during migration. These include Keen's bat (*Myotis keenii*), red bat (*Lasiurus borealis*), hoary bat (*Lasiurus cinereus*), and silver-haired bat (*Lasionycteris noctivagens*). The red bat is common in late summer and fall, especially around ponds and streams.

ORDER LAGOMORPHA: RABBITS

Eastern Cottontail (*Sylvilagus floridanus*)

The eastern cottontail is brown to gray, with a cottony white tail and rusty patch generally present on the nape; its body measures 36–43 cm (14–17 in) in length, and its ears are 6–8 cm long; it is found in all habitats, occurring with the highest densities in recently burned areas, around cedar swamps, and at the edges of farmland.

A wide variety of herbaceous and woody plants is eaten by the cottontail. Young are born from March to September in litters of four to five young. Young born early in the breeding season may produce young of their own toward the end of the season. This species is the most popular small-game mammal in the Pine Barrens, where it is hunted with hounds and shotguns. This hunting pressure has had very little impact on the population stability of this prolific species.

ORDER RODENTIA: RODENTS

Eastern Chipmunk (*Tamias striatus*)

The face and sides of the eastern chipmunk are striped, with the side stripes terminating at a reddish rump; the head and body are 13–15 cm (5–6 in) long, and its bushy tail, carried straight up, measures 8–10 cm in length. The animal is uncommon.

Seeds, nuts, and fruits are the main foods of the chipmunk, although some animal matter also is eaten. These animals dig their own burrows, in which they construct a large nest of plant materials. Breeding occurs during the first year, and two litters are produced each year during the spring and summer.

Woodchuck (*Marmota monax*)

The woodchuck is reddish or brownish, and its feet are dark brown to black, with the only white appearing around the nose; its body measures 41–51 cm (16–20 in) in length, and its tail is 10–18 cm long; it has short legs, and may be rare (McCormick, 1970) or common (Applegate, 1974), with highest densities in cultivated areas or near towns.

This species is active during the day and feeds on fleshy herbaceous plants. Its extensive burrows, up to 9 m (30 ft) long, have at least two openings. Hibernation occurs in late fall and winter. Woodchucks breed in early spring at one year of age and produce litters of two to six young. Although woodchucks are hunted for food and recreation, population densities are influenced very little by sport hunting. Woodchuck burrows provide escape cover for several other mammals.

Gray Squirrel (*Sciurus carolinensis*)

The gray squirrel is gray, with a bushy tail bordered by white-tipped hairs; its body measures 20–25 cm (8–10 in) in length, and its tail is 20–25 cm long; it is arboreal, using its tail as a rudder as it leaps from tree to tree; the animal is occasional (McCormick, 1970) or common (Applegate, 1974), and oak-dominated forests are the preferred habitat.

The primary food includes acorns, other seeds, and fruits, but mushrooms, buds, and the cambium layer of woody plants also are eaten. Gray squirrels store acorns singly in holes or crevices, and some unrecovered nuts later germinate and produce oak trees. Nests are of two types, holes in partially hollow trees or leaf nests in branches. Two litters of three to five young are produced annually, in late winter and early summer. Gray squirrels are hunted for food and sport. The fur is of minor value, although hair from the tail is prized by those who construct fishing lures.

Red Squirrel (*Tamiasciurus hudsonicus*)

The upperparts of the red squirrel are rusty red, somewhat paler on the back; its underparts are whitish, sometimes tinged with yellow; a black line is present on the sides in summer; its bushy, rufous tail sometimes is washed with black, white, or fulvous-tipped hairs; its body measures 18–20 cm (7–8 in) in length, and its tail is 10–15 cm long; the animal is arboreal and common throughout the region.

Red squirrels feed on the seeds of oaks, pines, and associated species. Accumulations of opened pine cones are found at the bases of favored feeding trees or stumps. Nests are constructed of leaves, twigs, and bark in hollow trees or in tree branches near the trunk. Two litters of two to seven young are produced annually, in early spring and early summer.

Southern Flying Squirrel (*Glaucomys volans*)

The southern flying squirrel is olive brown with white underparts; its body measures 9–11 cm (3.5–4.5 in) in length, and its tail is as long as its body; a folded layer of loose skin joins the animal's fore- and hindlegs, providing an "airfoil" to support the animal as it glides from tree to tree; it is common (McCormick, 1970) or uncommon (Applegate, 1974) but rarely seen because the species is nocturnal.

The diet of flying squirrels consists of acorns, other seeds, insects, birds' eggs, and animal material. Some food is stored in the nest chamber, which may be in a hollow portion of a tree, in a building, or in a leaf-and-twig nest. Litters of two to six young are born in late spring and late summer.

Beaver (*Castor canadensis*)

The beaver has dense brown fur. Its head and body measure 64–76 cm (25–30 in) in length, and its tail is 23–25 cm long; it is aquatic, with a naked, scaly, paddlelike tail and webbed feet. Beavers were extirpated from the Pine Barrens, but have been reintroduced in all suitable habitats, and trapping is regulated.

Beavers impound water with dams constructed of sticks, mud, and rocks. Within the impoundment, they build dome-shaped lodges of sticks and mud, with underwater entrances below the ice level. Several families may occupy a lodge, and lodges often are grouped into colonies. Rather than constructing lodges, some beavers may use burrows in stream banks. The cambium layer of several tree species is the primary food of this mammal.

Rice Rat (*Oryzomys palustris*)

The rice rat is grayish brown, with gray to fulvous underparts and whitish feet; its body measures 12–14 cm (4.8–5.5 in) in length. The status of this species in New Jersey is undetermined, although it probably occurs in marshes along several rivers (Connor, 1953; Applegate, 1974).

The semiaquatic rice rat is chiefly nocturnal, feeds on herbaceous vegetation and seeds, and nests under debris or in woven nests in vegetation 30 cm or more above water level in marshy areas. Several litters of three to four individuals are produced annually.

White-Footed Mouse (*Peromyscus leucopus*)

The white-footed mouse is reddish brown, with white feet and underparts, its body measures 9–11 cm (3.6–4.5 in) in length, and its tail, which is brownish above and whitish below, 6–10 cm long. Connor (1953) trapped this species in all habitats except cedar swamps.

Stomach content analyses (Connor, 1953) indicated that principal summer foods of the white-footed mouse are blueberries (*Vaccinium* spp.), black huckleberry (*Gaylussacia baccata*), seeds, and arthropods. Acorns are important in late summer and fall. This species nests in artificial nest boxes, old bird nests, under logs, or in a variety of other sheltered spots. Females breed at 10–11 weeks, producing several litters of two to six young per year.

Red-Backed Vole (*Clethrinonomys gapperi*)

The red-backed vole has a reddish back and gray sides; its body measures 9–12 cm (3.7–4.7 in) in length, and its tail is 3–5 cm long; the animal is common (Applegate, 1974). Connor (1953) indicated that, although this species is common in damp areas from cedar swamps to open *Sphagnum* bogs, none were trapped in the same localities as the white-footed mouse.

Stomach content analyses (Connor, 1953) indicated that fruit was a major constituent of the red-backed vole's diet; blueberries and cranberries were most common, followed by unidentified seeds, blackberries, and fungi. He also indicated these rodents were known to be consumed by rattlesnakes (*Crotalus horridus*) and raccoons (*Procyon lotor*). The nest, a simple platform, usually is placed under roots or logs. Two or more litters of four to six young are produced annually.

Meadow Vole (*Microtus pennsylvanicus*)

The meadow vole has brown upperparts and gray underparts; its body measures 9–13 cm (3.5–5 in) in length, and its bicolored tail is 3.5–7 cm long; it is common (Applegate, 1974). Connor (1953) captured this species in bogs and river meadows; it is occasional to common in lowland areas, and it may be a pest in cranberry bogs in some years (McCormick, 1970).

Meadow voles feed on grasses, sedges, seeds, bark, and insects. Nests may be constructed above or below ground, and typically this vole produces several litters of three to five young per year.

Pine Vole (*Pitymys pinetorum*)

The pine vole is russet brown to chestnut in color; its body measures 7–11 cm (2.8–4.2 in) in length, and its tail is 1.5–2.5 cm long. It has small ears and a short tail, and is very abundant in open pine and oak woods, but absent from the Pine Plains (Connor, 1953).

The presence of pine voles often is indicated by tunnels in the soil or litter, close to the surface. Root bark, bulbs, and seeds are the favored foods. Logs or stumps are utilized as nesting cover.

Muskrat (*Ondatra zibethicus*)

The muskrat's dense fur ranges from rich brown to nearly black on the upperparts to silvery on the belly; its body is 25–36 cm (10–14 in) long, and its long, naked, black, scaly, and laterally compressed tail measures 20–28 cm in length. Although primarily inhabitants of tidal meadows, during severe storms muskrats may move upstream to cranberry bogs (Conner, 1953). The muskrat usually is rare in the interior Pine Barrens.

Muskrats construct conical houses of marsh vegetation, although mud bank dens are utilized in some areas. Its primary foods are various species of aquatic vegetation, but animal material also is taken. Two to three litters of five to six young are produced annually. Economically, muskrats are the most important furbearers in New Jersey.

Southern Bog Lemming (*Synaptomys cooperi*)

The upperparts of the southern bog lemming are brownish gray, and the underparts are gray; its body is 9–11 cm (3.4–4.4 in) long, and its short tail measures 1.5–2.2 cm. Its ears are nearly concealed; there is a shallow groove along the outer edge of the upper incisors. The lemming's preferred habitat is open, treeless bogs characterized by *Sphagnum,* leatherleaf, huckleberry, and sedges, areas where it often is the dominant small mammal (Connor, 1959).

Leaves and other vegetative parts of sedges comprise the principal food, although fruits of blueberry also are consumed. This mammal nests just under the vegetative surface in the tops of hummocks of *Sphagnum.* The nests are formed from shredded sedge or grass. Breeding peaks in the spring but continues into the fall (Connor, 1959). Typically, three to four young are produced in each of two to three litters. Several large snake species, the long-tailed weasel (*Mustela frenata*), and the gray fox (*Urocyon cinereoargenteus*) are reported to be significant predators of the southern bog lemming in the Pine Barrens (Connor, 1959).

Norway Rat (*Rattus norvegicus*)

The Norway rat is grayish brown above with a grayish belly; its body measures 18–25 cm (7–10 in) in length, and its scaly tail is 13–20 cm long; it is an introduced species found in close association with humans, near farms or human habitation.

Norway rats breed when three to four months old and produce litters of six to 22 young. They eat most forms of animal or vegetable matter.

House Mouse (*Mus musculus*)

The house mouse is grayish brown above with a gray belly; its head and body measure 8–9 cm (3.2–3.4 in) in length, and its scaly tail is 7–10 cm long; it is an introduced rodent usually found in close association with humans.

House mice are extremely prolific. They may breed at 35 days of age and produce litters of up to 12 young.

Meadow Jumping Mouse (*Zapus hudsonius*)

The meadow jumping mouse is olive yellow to brown on the back, with paler sides, and white to yellowish white below; its head and body measure 7.5–8.5 cm (3–3.3 in) in length, and its tail is 10–12 cm long; it has large hind feet and a long, sparsely-haired tail; it is common (Applegate, 1974), most abundant in open bogs and near streams, although one was seen on the edge of a dry, sandy field; they also have been observed hibernating in the dikes of cranberry bogs (Connor, 1953).

Seeds, insects, and fruits are eaten. Nesting sites are beneath logs, stumps, or brush, and two litters of four to five young are produced annually. Hibernation sites are 60–90 cm beneath the ground surface.

ORDER CARNIVORA: FLESH EATERS

Red Fox (*Vulpes fulva*)

The red fox is reddish yellow with black legs and feet, black upper surface of ears, and tail tipped in white; its body measures 56–64 cm (22–25 in) in length, and its tail is 36–41 cm long; it is common (Applegate, 1974) or rare in the central Pine Barrens but found along some of the tidal rivers (Connor, 1953).

Bounties still are paid by several counties for killing foxes, a wasteful practice, since hunters or trappers rarely influence fox populations significantly. The fur of the red fox is very valuable, and the species is hunted with hounds or predator calls for sport. Red foxes are omnivorous, feeding on a variety of animal and plant foods, including insects, amphibians, reptiles, birds, small mammals, acorns, and a variety of fruits. A single litter of four to nine pups is produced in early spring. These pups remain in the den until five weeks old.

Gray Fox (*Urocyon cinereoargenteus*)

The gray fox is predominantly gray, grading to rust colored on the belly; it has a gray face with white throat. Its body is 53–74 cm (21–29 in) long, and its long, bushy tail, with a median black stripe down its total length and tipped in black, measures 28–41 cm; it is common throughout the Pine Barrens (Connor, 1953; Applegate, 1974).

Gray foxes are omnivorous and eat a wide variety of vegetable and animal materials, e.g., small mammals, insects, fruit, acorns, birds, and eggs. This mammal is hunted and trapped for sport and for its fur, with little impact on the abundance of the species.

Raccoon (*Procyon lotor*)

The raccoon is gray to blackish, suffused with rust or buff; it has a black mask over the eyes, and alternating rings of yellowish white and black on the tail; its body measures 46–71 cm (18–28 in) in length, and its tail is 20–30 cm long; it is a common predator (Connor, 1953).

The raccoon is a nocturnal, omnivorous species which eats fruits, nuts, acorns, insects, frogs, crayfish, ducklings, and a wide variety of other foods. Analyses of feces in the pine region indicated crayfish, insects, and fruit were present in decreasing order of importance (Connor, 1953). The raccoon generally lives close to water. Hollow logs or trees often are used as den sites. Activity decreases during very cold weather, but hibernation does not occur. Litter size ranges from two to seven, with young born in April or May. This mammal is a highly prized game species as well as an important furbearer. It is hunted at night with hounds, and the meat is considered a delicacy by some hunters. Raccoons also are trapped for their pelts, which have shown a marked increase in value in recent years.

Long-Tailed Weasel (*Mustela frenata*)

Upperparts of the long-tailed weasel are brown, and underparts lighter colored, tinged with buff or yellow; its slender body is 20–27 cm (8–10.5 in) long, and its black-tipped tail is 2/5–7/10 the length of the head and body; it is uncommon (Applegate, 1974), found most commonly around water courses and bogs (Connor, 1953).

Long-tailed weasels are predators feeding mostly on small mammals, but also on insects, amphibians, reptiles, and birds. Nesting sites are in wood piles, stumps, hollow logs, or the burrows of other animals. Females mate when three to four months old, but males are not sexually mature until almost a year old. Mating occurs in July or August, and one litter per year of four to eight young is produced in April or May. This species has some value as a furbearer.

Mink (*Mustela vison*)

The mink is dark brown, often with white spots present somewhere on the underparts; its head and slender body measure 30–43 cm (12–17 in) in length, and its tail is 14–23 cm long; females, on the average, are 10% or more smaller than males and weigh half as much; the mink generally is found near water, occasionally along Pine Barrens streams (Connor, 1953).

The mink is an excellent swimmer, and is capable of catching fish, an important component of its diet, along with small mammals, birds, eggs, reptiles, and amphibians. Dens are often in abandoned muskrat burrows. Females bear one litter per year of two to six young, which are born in April or May. This species is a valuable furbearer and is trapped for its pelt.

Striped Skunk (*Mephitis mephitis*)

The striped skunk is black, with white on top of its head and neck extending posteriorly and often separating into two stripes; its body is 33–46 cm (13–18 in) long; it is rare (Connor, 1953; McCormick, 1970).

The striped skunk feeds on a wide variety of vegetable and animal foods, primarily insects and fruit in summer, and small mammals and carrion in winter. Burrows are often under buildings or in hollow logs. Each year, one litter of four to seven young is produced in May. The pelt of this species has some value in the fur market.

River Otter (*Lutra canadensis*)

The river otter is rich brown above with paler underparts; it is aquatic, having webbed feet; its relatively large body measures 66–76 cm (26–30 in) in length, and its tail, which is thick at the base and tapering toward the tip, is 30–43 cm long. It is occasional (McCormick, 1970) or not uncommon along the streams (Connor, 1953).

Fish, frogs, crayfish, and other aquatic invertebrates are important components of the river otter's diet. Bank dens with underwater entrances are utilized for cover, and litters of one to five young are produced in April or May. Although the river otter is a valuable furbearing animal, relatively low population densities preclude trapping of this species in New Jersey.

ORDER ARTIODACTYLA: EVEN-TOED HOOFED MAMMALS

White-Tailed Deer (*Odocoileus virginianus*)

The white-tailed deer is reddish in summer and grayish in winter, and the undersurface of the tail is white; young are spotted for as long as they nurse; body height at the shoulder measures 91–107 cm (3–3.5 ft); adult males have antlers which are shed each year, with antler size a reflection of habitat quality. The white-tailed deer is common throughout the Pine Barrens, with populations often exceeding the carrying capacity of the range.

Woody browse, acorns, and herbaceous plants are seasonally valuable foods. White-tailed deer breed in November, and young are born in late May and June. Well-nourished adult deer are capable of producing twins annually. In most areas hunting has been restricted to male deer only, resulting in some poorly nourished animals with lower than normal reproductive rates and poor antler development. Winter starvation of deer is not uncommon. A carefully regulated annual harvest of female deer probably would bring the deer density down to the carrying capacity of the range in the Pine Barrens.

SUMMARY

Thirty-four species of mammals reside in the New Jersey Pine Barrens, and four additional species of bats are found during migration. The fauna includes the large mammal, the white-tailed deer, 11 intermediate-sized mammals ranging in size from the river otter to the muskrat, and 22 small mammals, the smallest of which is the masked shrew, measuring about 5 cm (2 in) in length. Two species are introduced and associated with human habitation, and all species range widely beyond the Pine Barrens. Several species are restricted to very specific Pine Barrens habitats, but none presently is considered to be threatened or endangered. In general, diets are relatively broad. A number of species are valuable game and/or furbearers. Deer browsing is the most important of several effects of mammals on Pine Barrens vegetation.

REFERENCES

Abbot, C. C. (1868). Catalogue of vertebrate animals of New Jersey. *In* "Geology of New Jersey," Appendix E. George H. Cook, Newark, New Jersey.

Applegate, J. E. (1974). The wildlife resources of New Jersey. *In* "New Jersey Trends" (T. P. Norman, ed.), pp. 243–266. Inst. Environ. Stud., Rutgers Univ., New Brunswick, New Jersey.

Connor, P. F. (1953). Notes on the mammals of a New Jersey pine barrens area. *J. Mammal.* **34,** 227–235.

Connor, P. F. (1959). The bog lemming, *Synaptomys cooperi,* in southern New Jersey. *Publ. Mus. Mich. State Univ., Biol. Ser.* **1**(5), 165–248.

Hall, R. B. (1976). "A Study of Controlled Burning and its Effect on South Jersey Game Habitat," Job V-B, Pittman-Robertson Rep., Proj. No. W-52-R-4. N.J. Dep. Environ. Prot., Trenton, New Jersey.

Heintzelman, D. S., ed. (1971). Rare or endangered fish and wildlife of New Jersey. *N.J. State Mus., Sci. Notes* No. 4.

Little, S., Moorhead, G. R., and Somes, H. A. (1958). Forestry and deer in the pine region of New Jersey. *U.S. For. Serv., Northeast. For. Exp. Stn., Stn. Pap.* No. 109.

McCormick, J. (1970). The Pine Barrens. A preliminary ecological inventory. *N.J. State Mus., Res. Rep.* No. 2.

McCormick, J., and Andresen, J. W. (1960). Some effects of animals on the vegetation of the New Jersey Pine Barrens. *Bull. Torrey Bot. Club* **87,** 375–385.

Nelson, J. (1890). "Descriptive Catalogue of the Vertebrates of New Jersey," Final Rep. State Zool., Vol. 2, Part 2. Trenton, New Jersey.

Rhoads, S. N. (1903). "The Mammals of Pennsylvania and New Jersey." Philadelphia, Pennsylvania.

Shoemaker, L. M. (1963). Mammals of New Jersey. *N.J. State Mus., Bull.* No. 8.

Stone, W. S. (1908). The mammals of New Jersey. *N.J. State Mus., Annu. Rep.*

White, J. E. (1961). The effect of control burning on small mammals of the New Jersey pine barrens. Ph.D. Thesis, Rutgers Univ., New Brunswick, New Jersey.

Wolgast, L. J. (1973a). Genetic and ecological factors influencing acorn yields in scrub oak. *Trans. Northeast. Sect. Wildl. Soc.* **30,** 231–255.

Wolgast, L. J. (1973b). Mast production in scrub oak on the coastal plain in New Jersey. Ph.D. Thesis, Rutgers Univ., New Brunswick, New Jersey.

Wolgast, L. J. (1974). Bear oak. *U.S. For. Serv., Gen. Tech. Rep. NE* **NE-9,** 108–110.

Wolgast, L. J., and Stout, B. B. (1977a). The effects of relative humidity at the time of flowering on fruit set in bear oak. *Am. J. Bot.* **64,** 159–160.

Wolgast, L. J., and Stout, B. B. (1977b). Effects of age, stand density, and fertilizer application on reproduction in bear oak. *J. Wildl. Manag.* **41,** 685–691.

Wolgast, L. J., Rogers, R., and Clark, W. R. (1972). Predicted environmental impact of salt drift from a proposed cooling tower on land dwelling vertebrates on the outer coastal plain of New Jersey. *Trans. Northeast. Sect. Wildl. Soc.* **29,** 113–123.

26
Birds of the Pine Barrens

CHARLES F. LECK

Despite considerable study by ornithologists and birdwatchers along the coast and in forests north of the Pine Barrens, very little about the birdlife of the Pine Barrens has been published. The reports of the early 1900's generally are limited to brief comments on distributions and nesting of individual species (e.g. Hunt 1908). Recently, Fables (1962), McCormick (1970), and Leck (1975) have provided overviews of the entire avifauna, although they were restricted severely by the field data available. This chapter will introduce the common birds of the region, examine population trends in both breeding and winter bird communities, and discuss the effects of habitats and fire on bird communities.

THE BREEDING BIRD COMMUNITY

Although all breeding birds show preferences for particular habitats within the Pine Barrens (Fig. 1), many species are widespread in the upland habitats. For example, two birds of prey, the turkey vulture and sparrow hawk (*Cathartes aura, Falco sparverius*), are particularly common. The vulture soars effortlessly in thermals above the pines, searching for carrion. While the bird is seen commonly, its nest site on the ground is so well hidden and remote from areas of human activity that few observers find breeding birds. In contrast, the sparrow hawk is a conspicuous nester, even along roadsides, and is an active predator of insects and rodents.

The upland game birds include the ruffed grouse and bobwhite (*Bonasa umbrellus, Colinus virginianus*). I most frequently note the grouse foraging on buds, berries, and seeds along grassy borders of pineland roads. Bobwhites are heard calling from upland fields. Although hunting laws protect the mourning dove (*Zenaidura macroura*), it often has been considered for addition to the game list of New Jersey.

Whip-poor-wills and common nighthawks (*Caprimulgus vociferus, Chordeiles minor*) are the most abundant nocturnal birds in the Barrens. Their night flights for insects and their continuous calls are well known to local residents. Also widespread are both the common and fish crows (*Corvus brachyrhynus, C. ossifragus*), although the latter favors the coastal perimeter. These omnivores have very diverse diets, which include carrion. Several southern birds also are conspicuous in the uplands, including

457

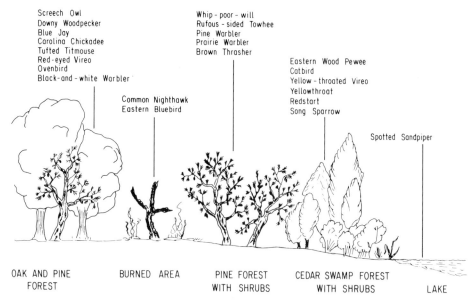

Screech Owl
Downy Woodpecker
Blue Jay
Carolina Chickadee
Tufted Titmouse
Red-eyed Vireo
Ovenbird
Black-and-white Warbler

Whip-poor-will
Rufous-sided Towhee
Pine Warbler
Prairie Warbler
Brown Thrasher

Eastern Wood Pewee
Catbird
Yellow-throated Vireo
Yellowthroat
Redstart
Song Sparrow

Common Nighthawk
Eastern Bluebird

Spotted Sandpiper

OAK AND PINE
FOREST

BURNED AREA

PINE FOREST
WITH SHRUBS

CEDAR SWAMP FOREST
WITH SHRUBS

LAKE

Fig. 1. Major preferred habitats of the most common breeding birds.

the Carolina chickadee, Carolina wren, and mockingbird (*Parus carolinensis, Thryothorus ludovicianus, Mimus polyglottus*). The mild winter climate of the Barrens probably results in higher survival of these species than would be possible in northern New Jersey. In winter, their diets may shift from insects to a wide variety of berries and fruits. Foremost among the widespread species, however, is a large member of the sparrow family, the rufous-sided towhee (*Pipilo erythrophthalmus*). This species is common in all upland sites and may outnumber all other species combined, at least in areas with scrubby undergrowth.

The upland species, more limited in distribution, require the presence of deciduous trees. For example, the broad-winged hawk (*Buteo platypterus*) prefers nesting in tall oaks and would be unlikely to nest in pure pine forest. Other birds that prefer mixed oak–pine forest include the predators, screech owl and great horned owl (*Otus asio, Bubo virginianus*). Similarly, several woodpeckers, namely, the yellow-shafted flicker, hairy woodpecker, and downy woodpecker (*Colaptes auratus, Dendrocopus villosus, D. pubescens*), often prefer deciduous trees for nesting. These insect eaters build tree trunk nesting cavities in a variety of hardwoods (the resinous wood of live pines is too sticky). Thus, other birds that use old woodpecker cavities for nesting also breed more commonly in mixed woodlands than in pure pine forest. For blue jays (*Cyanocitta cristata*), mature oaks provide acorns, an important addition to the diet, and these noisy birds are common and widespread during all seasons.

Oak–pine woodlands are probably also richer in insects than pure pine stands, so insectivorous vireos and flycatchers are more common where oaks are prevalent. For example, the red-eyed vireo (*Vireo olivaceus*) is a summer resident among young oaks.

Warblers such as the black-and-white warbler and the ovenbird (*Mniotilta varia, Seiurus aurocapillus*) also are associated with oaks, since both species are dependent upon leaf litter for nest construction. Pine and prairie warblers (*Dendroica pinus, D. discolor*) nest in areas of mixed pine–oak, especially where tall pines (pine warbler) or shrub undergrowth (prairie warbler) are found. Hunt (1905) reported brown thrashers (*Toxostoma rufum*) to be attracted to both forest and the Pine Plains. Few bird species show a preference for the short vegetation of the Pine Plains.

Other species are more common near areas of human development. These include the robin, starling, chipping sparrow, rock dove, and house or English sparrow (*Turdus migratorius, Sturnus vulgaris, Spizella passerina, Columba livia, Passer domesticus*).

Shallow lakes, rivers, and cedar swamps attract a rich assortment of birds that greatly enhance the otherwise limited diversity of the region. Summer wading birds include the green heron and great egret (*Butorides virescens, Casmerodius albus*), both fish-eating species that nest in taller trees of riparian habitats. Wood ducks and spotted sandpipers (*Aix sponsa, Actitus macularia*) nest by lakes. The ducks require tall dead trees for nesting cavities, although human-constructed nest boxes are accepted readily. The sandpipers prefer undisturbed lake edges, particularly on predator-free islets. Belted kingfishers (*Megaceryle alcyon*) also fish the cedar lakes and nest in local sand or gravel quarries. Insectivorous birds that regularly forage over the waterways include the tree swallow and purple martin (*Iridoprocne bicolor, Progne subis*); both species accept bird boxes for nesting. Where cattails and other emergent vegetation are available, red-winged blackbirds (*Agelaius phoeniceus*) invade the lake edges and swamps with blueberry bushes.

Within the cedar swamps, breeding species are primarily insectivores: i.e., eastern wood pewee, catbird, wood thrush, white-eyed vireo, parula warbler, yellow warbler, yellowthroat, redstart, and song sparrow (*Contopus virens, Dumetella carolinensis, Hylocichla mustilina, Vireo griseus, Parula americana, Dendroica petechia, Geothlypis trichas, Setophaga ruticilla, Melospiza melodia*). Most of these species are present only in summer. The parula warbler uses old-man's beard (*Usnea*) lichens as nesting material (Wilde, 1905), e.g., *Usnea barbata* in the Pine Barrens (Stone, 1894), and may fly great distances to obtain it (Parmelee, 1973). The hooded warbler (*Wilsonia citrina*) has been reported to be a common summer resident in cedar swamp forests (McCormick, 1970), but I believe it is uncommon to rare in most areas. Also found along swamp borders is the ruby-throated hummingbird (*Archilochus colubris*), whose diet includes nectar of the local azaleas and spiders delicately plucked from their webs.

BIRDLIFE IN THE NONBREEDING SEASONS

Even though midwinter may be cold and wet, 60–70 species may be recorded by "Christmas Count" observers in a single day. However, only a few species seem consistently numerous; that is, starling, slate-colored junco (*Junco hyemalis*), mourning dove, Carolina chickadee, house sparrow, and blue jay (Table I). The first three species are abundant in fields and other open areas, and the chickadee and jay are associated primarily with mixed woods. All six are frequent visitors to any available feeding stations.

Some less common species that nevertheless are found consistently throughout the winter include the rock dove, downy woodpecker, tufted titmouse (*Parus bicolor*), white-breasted nuthatch (*Sitta carolinensis*), American robin, northern mockingbird (in recent years), tree sparrow (*Spizella arborea*), and white-throated sparrow (*Zonotrichia albicollis*).

Finally, some wintering species vary in abundance from year to year, being common one year and scarce or absent the next. Waterfowl show great annual fluctuations depending upon the amount of freezing weather and open water. The three most numerous waterfowl are the mallard, black duck, and Canada goose (*Anas platyrhynchos, A. rubripes, Branta canadensis*). The black duck historically has dominated winter flocks, but the mallard has increased dramatically in recent years. Marked annual changes in sparrow hawk and bobwhite populations may reflect changes in prey abundance and hunting pressures, respectively. Blackbirds such as the common grackle (*Quiscalus quiscula*) also vary greatly in winter abundance, apparently as they

TABLE I Winter Bird Abundance in the Pine Barrens.[a]

Species	Total number in census		
	1973–1974	1974–1975	1975–1976
Starling	1116	770	957
Dark-eyed junco	269	649	946
Mourning dove	258	769	927
Carolina chickadee	222	482	472
American robin	74	159	471
House sparrow	454	410	443
Red-wing blackbird	85	45	327
Blue jay	284	293	317
Mallard	127	287	310
Evening grosbeak	33	206	246
Canada goose	1	15	176
Golden-crowned kinglet	31	38	159
Common crow	81	133	152
Whistling swan	91	183	137
Field sparrow	5	42	130
Tufted titmouse	84	201	125
Song sparrow	13	37	119
Brown-headed cowbird	5	42	113
American goldfinch	76	48	102
Bobwhite	36	119	101

[a] The most common species on "Christmas Count" censuses on "Pine Lands" at Indian Mills, New Jersey, 1973–1976. Source: Am. Birds **28,** 248; **29,** 271; **30,** 278.

move farther south when weather is severe. Cold weather, however, increases the number of horned larks (*Eremophila alpestris*) which often move ahead of advancing snow storms. "Northern finches," such as the evening grosbeak and pine siskin, (*Hesperiphona vespertina, Spinus pinus*), invade the Barrens when seed crops of more northerly conifers are depleted. A poor cone year in Canadian forests may produce an abundance of these boreal birds in New Jersey.

Migrations in the Pine Barrens generally are less impressive than along the coast or in richer woodlands to the north. The few habitats of simple structure seem only minimally attractive to the >180 species that must pass through or over this part of New Jersey on migratory flights. Nevertheless, transients do become evident during the periods August–October and March–May for landbirds and October–November and March–April for waterbirds. During waterfowl flights, several species may be common, even a few species such as the whistling swan (*Olor colombianus*), which are scarce elsewhere in New Jersey. Landbird movements include impressive flights of hawks, especially the sharp-shinned hawk (*Accipiter striatus*), and large numbers of warblers, thrushes, and sparrows. The most abundant of the small landbirds are the transient yellow-rumped or myrtle warbler (*Dendroica caronata*) and the white-throated sparrow.

POPULATION STUDIES

In reviewing our knowledge of breeding bird populations, Fables (1962) termed the Pine Barrens a *terra incognita*. Whereas few quantitative studies of the common breeding birds existed, the occasional nesting of rare species sometimes had been recorded. Fables (1947–1954) conductd annual breeding bird censuses in a 30-hectare (75-acre) plot at Pine Lake Park, about 5 km (3 mi) south of Lakehurst. The study area was 95% pitch pine barrens and 5% cedar bog, and he included valuable comments on habitat changes and increases or decreases in avian populations. Five of the last sample years (Table II) overwhelmingly show the rufous-sided towhee to be the most abundant species, sometimes equal to all other species combined. The 30-hectare plot had a relatively constant diversity during the five sample years, averaging 35.6 species (Table II). Similarly, the average 91.6 territorial males were relatively constant, and equivalent to 121.6 territorial males per 40 ha (100 acres).

However, over the 17-year period of study there were some noteworthy changes in Pine Barrens birds. Increases included the ovenbird (as a breeding species), American robin, blue jay, and blackbirds, including the red-winged blackbird, brown-headed cowbird (*Molothurs ater*), and common grackle. At least two species declined drastically, the eastern bluebird (*Sialia sialis*) and common nighthawk. Fables believed decline of the nighthawks to be a result of decreases in burned-over areas, which are crucial for the birds' nest sites. The bluebird has shown a serious decline throughout the entire northeastern United States.

Swinebroad and Sussman (1964) provide the first ranking of abundances for breeding birds from mist-netting studies. Their list, in decreasing order of abundance is the

TABLE II Breeding Bird Surveys in the Pine Barrens[a]

Species	Number of territorial males in 30-hectare plot				
	1949	1950	1952	1953	1954
Rufous-sided towhee	37	32	20	26	23
Redwing blackbird	4	1	8	3	1
Great-crested flycatcher	1	1	6	2	3
Prairie warbler	13	5	5	5	3
Yellowthroat[b]	0	6	4	5	4
Song sparrow	1	2	4	2	0
Whip-poor-will	4	3	3	2	2
Catbird[b]	0	4	3	2	3
Black-and-white warbler	1	1	3	0	2
Eastern wood pewee	3	3	2	3	3
Tree swallow	0	0	2	0	3
Purple martin	0	4	2	3	3
American robin	3	3	2	4	2
Purple grackle[b]	3	1	2	1	0
Chipping sparrow	3	2	1	2	3
Mourning dove	3	2	1	3	3
Yellow-shafted flicker[b]	1	3	1	3	1
Carolina chickadee	1	1	1	3	2
Total no. species	35	40	35	32	36
No. of territorial males (all species)	89	103	88	90	88
Estimated no. territorial males/ 40 ha	118	137	117	120	116

[a] Common birds of a 30 ha (75 acre) plot containing 95% pine barrens and 5% cedar swamp, 1949–1950 and 1952–1954. From Fables (1949–54); see text for notes on location, habitat, and additional years.

[b] Current names: common yellowthroat, gray catbird, common grackle, common flicker.

following: catbird, rufous-sided towhee, wood thrush, Carolina chickadee, blue jay, red-eyed vireo, tufted titmouse, ovenbird, black-and-white warbler, and pine warbler. The sampling was apparently within mixed oak–pine forest and would not be descriptive of drier upland sites where pines are uniformly dominant. For example, the catbird, which is listed as the most abundant species of the Pine Barrens, is dependent upon low-lying wet areas. The rufous-sided towhee usually dominates in dry uplands.

The red-eyed vireo, the sixth most abundant bird of the Swinebroad and Sussman report, would be far down the list today. The species has declined in some northeastern states in the last decade.

McCormick's (1970) inventory includes a summary of the entire avifauna, both breeding and nonbreeding species of the region. For each of the 144 species, he offers brief comments on status, and often a habitat note (e.g., "common in cedar swamps").

This annotated list is quite useful for relative abundances and distributions, although a few changes in status of species might be noted. The red crossbill (*Loxia curvirostra*) has been recorded as nesting in some years, and the red-headed woodpecker (*Melanerpes erythrocephalus*) nests and remains throughout the summer. Many species may be added to the list as transients, including swans, a variety of ducks, and the common snipe (*Capella gallinago*). A good review of bird populations in the pine barrens of eastern Long Island was recently published (Salzman 1977); it shows numerous avian population trends that are shared with the New Jersey Pine Barrens.

THE EFFECTS OF FIRE ON PINE BARREN BIRDLIFE

Surprisingly little is known of the effects of fire on the avifauna in this fire-maintained regional habitat. Charles Urner's (1926) breeding bird survey of Ocean County after severe fires is brief but useful. In areas of strong burn, he found decreases in the abundance of rufous-sided towhees and brown thrashers but increases in several other species, including the eastern bluebird and common nighthawk. I also have noted this association of nesting bluebirds with fire areas in the pinelands, and Fables (1962) mentioned the increase in nighthawks on burned land. Urner also indicated that the chipping sparrow may increase after fires, but not dramatically. A variety of birds, including woodpeckers, catbird, and the two common warblers, pine and prairie warblers, remained essentially stable in numbers after burns. Such population stability usually is not expected with severe habitat disturbance, and this subjective listing of several "constant" species at best should be considered tentative. In fact, Fables (1962) presented conflicting data for the prairie warbler, as he noted a 50% increase in populations in years following severe Lakewood fires of the 1940's.

Fire may be expected also to affect avian populations in the winter. For example, northern finches that feed on pine seeds might be attracted to burned areas. In the spring of 1976, for example, J. Terborgh (personal communication) reported red crossbills in fire areas where cones had opened and had become an easy food source.

CONSERVATION

The gallinaceous game birds of the Pine Barrens have diverse histories and are an important group for conservationists. The native turkey (Fig. 2) probably was common throughout the State during the 17th and 18th centuries but subsequently was extirpated by excessive hunting. Apparently none remained at the turn of this century (Stone, 1909). In recent years, the species occasionally reappears along the Kittatinny Ridge in northwestern New Jersey, and repeated attempts have been made to reestablish native turkeys in the Pine Barrens with stock releases. Most recently, hunting clubs have been involved in the release program, but success or failure remains uncertain. The small numbers of introduced birds have not been reproducing as yet. Both bobwhite and

Fig. 2. The native turkey, reduced to extinction in the Pine Barrens, has been reintroduced in recent years. This game species (*Meleagris gallopavo*) is one of the most majestic birds of New Jersey. (Photo by the author.)

ring-necked pheasants are among the locally stocked game species, and often are established successfully by releases. Fields of seed grasses for food greatly increase the yields of the game birds, but field management is difficult.

The ruffed grouse (*Bonasa umbellus*) is native to the Barrens and remains a permanent resident and popular game bird. One lost native is another grouse, the extinct heath hen (*Tympanuchus cupido cupido*). This eastern race of the prairie chicken (*Tympanuchus cupido*) was limited to northeastern United States; in New Jersey it once was abundant in the "plains" of Burlington and Ocean Counties (Fables, 1955). Old New Jersey hunting stories from the 1830's give a fascinating but sad glimpse of the history of this bird (Stone, 1965). Its sensitivity to recurrent fires and hunting led to regional extinction by 1870. Subsequent attempts to introduce a western race of the species failed before the turn of the century (Bull, 1964). Other western species have been introduced with similarly poor results, e.g., the recently released Chukar partridges (*Alectoris graeca*).

However, introductions of nonnative species should be considered only after extensive research. Some introduced birds have become established all too well, and we now see a variety of European birds among the dominants of the avifauna, namely, the starling, rock dove, and house or English sparrow. Each of these is particularly prolific in areas of human habitation, and they may be unable to invade undisturbed areas of the Pine Barrens.

Conservationists also are interested in rare species, and, as with plants, the Pine Barrens avifauna includes a variety of noteworthy species. Some of the rarer New Jersey birds have southern geographical affinities and maintain sparse populations in the Barrens, e.g., the prothonotary warbler (*Protonotaria citrea*), hooded warbler, chuck-will's-widow, and Swainson's warbler (*Limnothlypis swainsonii*). The chuck-will's-widow was being reported regularly in Cape May County by 1930, although the first nest was not found until 1952 (Bull, 1964). Apparently, it now is well established and even may be expanding to the pinelands of Long Island. The prothonotary warbler is scarce in New Jersey and is dependent upon dead trees or stumps for a nesting cavity. Mixed cedar–maple–gum forests are said to be its optimal habitat in the Pine Barrens (McCormick, 1970). Swainson's warblers rarely are reported in the more southern cedar swamps, but birds singing during the summer months suggest possible nesting. The hooded warbler was abundant in Cape May cedar swamps before the turn of the century (Stone, 1894), but I believe it no longer is common.

The Pine Barrens also have a complement of ''northern'' species that breed irregularly. The red crossbill nested at least several years between 1935 and 1942 (Fables, 1955), and as recently as 1963 (B. Murray, personal communication). The rarer white-winged crossbill (*Loxia leucoptera*) probably nested in Ocean County in 1936. The small saw-whet owl (*Aegolius acadicus*) and brown creeper (*Certhia familiaris*) are other irregular winter visitors that have remained to nest in the Barrens. McCormick (1970) gives one definite breeding record for the owl (1961 at Lebanon State Forest) and several for the brown creeper (1950's at Browns Mills and Quaker Bridge). The northern raven (*Corvus corax*) formerly nested along the New Jersey coast and in the southern cedar swamps (Stone, 1894), but the last definite records for its breeding in the region are pre-1890 (Bull, 1964).

Two endangered species of the state, the bald eagle (*Haliacetus leucocephallus*) and the eastern bluebird, also are present in the Pine Barrens. The continued decline of the bluebird has been mentioned earlier, but since some nesting still is successful (Leck, 1976 unpublished observations), hope remains. The bald eagle had an even more marked decline and generally remains unsuccessful in local nesting attempts. Bull (1964) discusses the New Jersey history of our national bird; today, only a few pairs at most are nesting in the state and these are in the Pine Barrens.

FUTURE RESEARCH

The most critical need is for studies of bird populations in cedar swamps, especially during the breeding season, when a variety of rare ''northern'' and ''southern'' species nest; indeed, many uncertainties remain. For example, the current status of the hooded warbler is questionable, and the Swainson's warbler has yet to be verified as nesting in New Jersey. Possible annual breeding of rarer birds, such as the saw-whet owl, also should be examined. The effects of fire on avian populations, both in winter and the breeding season, warrant study. Avian community studies also are needed for cedar swamps (which are threatened by human developments in some areas), upland habitats, and human-modified habitats. Conservational research must pay particular attention to the protection of some large natural swamps, as well as lakes.

SUMMARY

   Throughout the year, the avifauna of the New Jersey Pine Barrens is remarkably simple. Common breeding birds are presented with some diet and habitat preferences, the rufous-sided towhee being overwhelmingly the most abundant nesting species in the uplands. In wetter areas, the catbird and other scrub species increase in importance. In winter, flocking species, such as junco, mourning dove, Carolina chickadee, starling, and house sparrow, are most common. Severe winters usually mean fewer waterfowl but more horned larks and "northern finches." Fires appear to favor the eastern bluebird and common nighthawk, but over recent decades these two species have declined markedly. Rare species of both southern and northern affinities breed in the Pine Barrens, and two species, the bald eagle and eastern bluebird, are endangered in the state. The native turkey, which became extinct in the region, has been reintroduced with uncertain success. Large cedar and hardwood swamps, which may be centers of rarer species, warrant study and protection.

REFERENCES

Bull, J. (1964). "Birds of the New York Area." Harper, New York.

Fables, D. G. (1947–1954). Pine Barrens and cedar bog. *Audubon Field Notes* **1**, 223–224; **3**, 255–256; **4**, 301; **6**, 315; **7**, 353; **8**, 374–375.

Fables, D. G. (1955). "Annotated List of New Jersey Birds," pp. 1–95. Urner Ornithol. Club, Newark, New Jersey.

Fables, D. G. (1962). Breeding birds of the New Jersey Pine Barrens. *N.J. Nat. News* **17**, 60–64.

Hunt, C. J. (1905). A-birding among the New Jersey pines. *Wilson Bull.* **17**, 105–107.

Hunt, C. J. (1908). The Kentucky Warbler in southern New Jersey. *Auk* **25**, 87.

Leck, C. F. (1975). "The Birds of New Jersey." Rutgers Univ. Press, New Brunswick, New Jersey.

McCormick, J. (1970). The Pine Barrens: A preliminary ecological inventory. *N.J. State Mus., Res. Rep.* No. 2.

Parmelee, D. F. (1973). The nest of the northern Parula. *Living Bird* **12**, 197–198.

Salzman, E. (1977). Some notes on breeding birds in the eastern Long Island Pine Barrens. *Linnaean News-Letter,* **31**: no. 2–4.

Stone, W. (1965). "Bird studies on Old Cape May." Vol. I. Dover Publications, New York.

Stone, W. (1894). Summer birds of the Pine Barrens of New Jersey. *Auk* **11**, 133–140.

Stone, W. (1909). The birds of New Jersey. *N.J. State Mus., Annu. Rep.* 1908, pp. 11–347.

Swinebroad, J., and Sussman, O. (1964). Breeding bird populations in New Jersey. *N.J. Nat. News* **19**, 102–110.

Urner, C. A. (1926). Effect of fires on Pine Barren bird life. *Auk* **43**, 558–559.

Wilde, M. L. C. (1905). Breeding habits of the Parula Warbler (*Composothylypis americana usneae*) in New Jersey. *Wilson Bull.* **17**, 4–8.

27

A Zoogeographical Review of the Amphibians and Reptiles of Southern New Jersey, with Emphasis on the Pine Barrens

ROGER CONANT

INTRODUCTION

The herpetofauna of southern New Jersey is varied, relatively large for such a northern region, and unique in some respects. Fifty-eight species occur naturally within its borders, including 11 salamanders, 14 frogs and toads, 11 turtles, three lizards, and 19 snakes. In addition, a treefrog and a turtle have been introduced by man during the twentieth century. This chapter will review this array of species and indicate which occur only in the Pine Barrens, which enter that area and survive under special conditions, which range broadly across southern New Jersey, etc.

Distribution maps (Figs. 1–4), based primarily on amphibians and reptiles I personally examined, were selected from among work maps kept for all species. A great many specimens were examined incidental to my own fieldwork; others were brought to my home at Taunton Lake (in the Barrens) or to the Philadelphia Zoological Garden, with which I was associated for 38 years. I also have studied the New Jersey collections of many natural history museums. Hearsay records have not been accepted, but many from the literature or correspondence that were recorded by competent investigators have been used for mapping, but with a different symbol (see Fig. 1).

In this paper, southern New Jersey is defined as the area extending northward to include all of Mercer County and that part of Middlesex County which lies south of the Raritan River. The criterion for acceptance of a species as native or established in southern New Jersey is evidence that reproduction is or has been taking place.

467

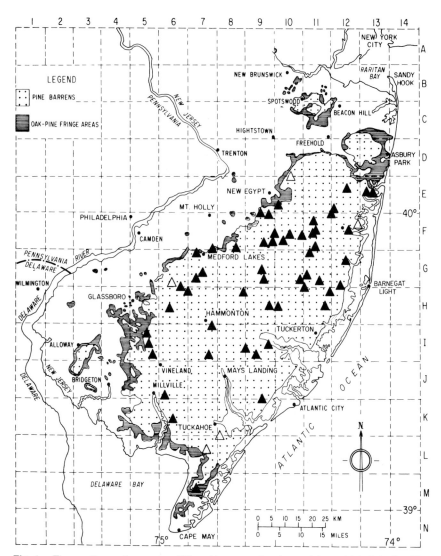

Fig. 1. The northern pine snake (*Pituophis m. melanoleucus*) is restricted to the Pine Barrens. Localities have been plotted on the maps as accurately as possible. Most museum specimens and the large majority of those collected by other persons lack precise habitat data, and are stated simply as distance and direction from the nearest town. Solid triangles on all maps represent localities from which the author has seen specimens; hollow triangles indicate localities from other sources that are presumed to be reliable.

Before zoogeographical interpretations are attempted, it must be understood that these animals, like most organisms, are not distributed evenly throughout their ranges. Common snapping turtles (*Chelydra serpentina*) and northern water snakes (*Natrix sipedon*) probably live in virtually every sizable permanent body of freshwater in southern New Jersey, or at least they did before pollution and persecution partially restricted their ranges. In contrast, many species exhibit spotty distributional patterns. Some appear only where habitat conditions meet their special requirements; others occur in isolated colonies without apparent correlation with soil, vegetative, or moisture conditions. For some species, there are scores of locality records, whereas for others there are few.

The increased popularity of amphibians and reptiles as pets during the past few decades inevitably has resulted in many specimens escaping or being liberated intentionally. Boa constrictors, pythons, and other species have turned up in localities where they obviously do not belong. For example, a Blanding's turtle (*Emydoidea blandingi*) was found at Taunton Lake on October 3, 1971. An out-of-place specimen from an earlier period is a large American toad (*Bufo americanus*) in the collectin of the Academy of Natural Sciences of Philadelphia that was caught at Penns Grove, Salem County, on September 21, 1909. This is the only specimen extant from southern New Jersey, where the widespread and abundant representative of the genus is Fowler's toad (*Bufo woodhousei*). The American toad once was widespread in and near marshes on the Pennsylvania side of the Delaware River, and it still survives where pollution and disturbance of habitat have not been too severe. It is reasonable to assume that the Academy specimen was transported across the river in produce or a balled tree root or in some other accidental manner.

Verbal reports of copperheads (*Agkistrodon contortrix*) and cottonmouths (*Agkistrodon piscivorus*) are heard frequently but no evidence indicates that either occurs in the area. During my long tenure as Curator of Reptiles at the Philadelphia Zoo, more than 100 alleged copperheads, many from southern New Jersey, were brought to me for identification. Only two actually were copperheads, and both were from Pennsylvania. The others were nonpoisonous water snakes, milk snakes (*Lampropeltis triangulum*), and hognose snakes (*Heterodon platyrhinos*). Presumed "water moccasins" invariably were water snakes.

HABITAT DESTRUCTION

New Jersey has been altered greatly since precolonial days. The intensive agriculture that gave it the nickname "Garden State" has been responsible for the destruction of original habitats over vast areas. Before settlement, most of the state was forested, but forest-adapted animals now either have disappeared, or they survive only in the Pine Barrens or a few refugia in the midst of cultivated regions, such as state parks or the tenuous, often swampy, areas bordering streams. In contrast, clearing of the land and subsequent human activities have been favorable for certain species, notably some amphibians that use ditches, borrow pits (e.g., sand and gravel removal), the perimeters of impoundments, and similar areas as breeding sites.

The urbanization in recent years that continues at an accelerating pace is even more destructive. Industrialization, particularly along the Delaware River, also has made sizable tracts of land uninhabitable for the vast majority of native animals and plants.

In contrast, the Pine Barrens, which include large, relatively undisturbed areas, have provided a huge refugium for many species extirpated or severely restricted in other parts of southern New Jersey. For example, there are numerous records of the four-toed salamander (*Hemidactylium scutatum*) in the Barrens, but also in a number of isolated localities outside the Barrens. It usually is associated with areas of *Sphagnum* moss, habitats which rapidly disappear when water tables and surface drainages are manipulated for agriculture. One may assume that the four-toed salamander originally was much more widespread, and that it has survived in the Pine Barrens while largely vanishing elsewhere. The water is so close to the surface in its optimal habitats in the Barrens that it is little affected by the wildfires that periodically sweep across the area.

ZOOGEOGRAPHICAL COMMENTS

The bulk of the species of amphibians and reptiles of southern New Jersey are wide ranging over broad areas of the eastern and northeastern United States. Many others, however, are at the extremes of their ranges. Among the latter, the most important are southern Coastal Plain species which contribute substantially to the large size of the herpetofauna of the region (Table I).

A few species have northern or upland affinities, however, notably the red-bellied snake (*Storeria occipitomaculata*). The late Emmett R. Dunn, an active fieldworker in southern New Jersey, believed (personal communication) that this species, the timber rattlesnake (*Crotalus horridus*), and the wood turtle (*Clemmys insculpta*) invaded what is now the Pine Barrens region by following stream valleys seaward from the northwest. The Schuylkill River flows southeastward and so, in part, does the Delaware River. In presumably the same general direction, one or more ancient rivers transported sand and gravel from the highlands to form the surface mantle of the Barrens.

Kauffeld (unpublished observations), on the basis of a small series of specimens, thought the rattlesnakes of the Pine Barrens showed relationships with the southern subspecies, the canebrake rattlesnake (*Crotalus horridus atricaudatus*). Gloyd (1940) was inclined to agree, but provisionally placed these snakes with the northern race, *Crotalus horridus horridus*. I recently examined a sizable sample of specimens, and am convinced that the Pine Barrens population is morphologically intermediate between the two races in several respects. The Pine Barrens population may have been derived from two sources: (1) from snakes with southern affinities that survived in the Pine Barrens, as other southern Coastal Plain organisms have done; and (2) from contributions from gene pools of rattlesnakes which may have invaded the region from the northwest, in conformance with Dunn's hypothesis.

TABLE I   Distribution and Status of Amphibians and Reptiles in Southern New Jersey, with Special Reference to the Pine Barrens[a]

Common Name	Scientific Name	Status in the Pine Barrens	Status in southern New Jersey	Approximate Range in United States and Canada
SALAMANDERS				
Spotted salamander	Ambystoma maculatum	Uncertain	WR?, rare	Widespread: so. Canada to Gulf of Mex.; W to Wis. and Tex.
Marbled salamander	Ambystoma opacum	REL, locally common	Locally common	Widespread: so. New Engl. to Gulf of Mexico; W to Mo. and Tex.
Eastern tiger salamander	Ambystoma tigrinum tigrinum	BOR, endangered	Scattered records; endangered	Widespread: chiefly Coastal Plain, Long Island to Fla.; W to Minn. and Tex.
Red-spotted newt	Notophthalmus viridescens viridescens	REL, few records	Scattered records	Widespread: so. Canada to Ga. and Ala.; W to Mich. and Miss.
Northern dusky salamander	Desmognathus fuscus fuscus	BOR, rare	Locally common	Widespread: New Brunswick to N.C. and Ky.
Red-backed salamander	Plethodon cinereus cinereus	Abundant	WR, abundant	Widespread: Canad. Maritime Provs. to Minn., Mo., and N.C.
Slimy salamander	Plethodon glutinosus glutinosus	Uncertain	WR?, uncertain	Widespread: New Engl. to Fla. and Tex.
Four-toed salamander	Hemidactylium scutatum	REL, numerous records	Scattered records	Widespread: Nova Scotia to Gulf of Mex.; W to Wis. and Okla.
Eastern mud salamander	Pseudotriton montanus montanus	Uncertain	WR?, rare	Southern: so. N.J. to S.C. and Ga.
Northern red salamander	Pseudotriton ruber ruber	Abundant	WR, abundant	Widespread: SE N.Y. to N.C. and Ala.
Northern two-lined salamander	Eurycea bislineata bislineata	BOR, rare	Locally common	Widespread: New Brunswick and so. Quebec to Ill. and Ala.
TOADS AND FROGS				
Eastern spadefoot	Scaphiopus holbrooki holbrooki	Locally common	WR, locally common	Widespread: so. New Engl. to Fla.; W to Mo. and Miss.
Fowler's toad	Bufo woodhousei fowleri	Abundant	WR, abundant	Widespread: so. New Engl. to Gulf of Mex.; W to Mich., Mo., and Miss.
Northern cricket frog	Acris crepitans crepitans	BOR, scattered records	WR, locally common	Widespread: extreme so. N.Y. and Long Island to Tex. and Fla.

(continued)

TABLE I (*continued*)

Common Name	Scientific Name	Status in the Pine Barrens	Status in southern New Jersey	Approximate Range in United States and Canada
Pine barrens treefrog	*Hyla andersoni*	PBO, declining	Threatened by any drop in water table level	Southern: isolated populations in so. N.J., N.C., S.C., Ga., and w. Fla.
Cope's gray treefrog	*Hyla chrysoscelis*	PER, not present	Uncertain	Widespread: extreme so. N.J. to Fla.; W to Minn. and Tex.
Northern spring peeper	*Hyla crucifer crucifer*	Abundant	WR, abundant	Widespread: Canad. Maritime Provs. to James Bay and Manitoba; S to Gulf of Mexico
Barking treefrog	*Hyla gratiosa*	INT, possibly extirpated	Possibly extirpated	Southern: SE Va. to so. Fla.; W to La.
Gray treefrog	*Hyla versicolor*	BOR, scattered records	WR, locally common	Widespread: New Brunswick to Manitoba; S to S.C.; W to Okla. and Tex.
New Jersey chorus frog	*Pseudacris triseriata kalmi*	BOR, numerous records	Abundant	Local: N.J. and east of Chesapeake Bay in Del., Md., and Va.
Bullfrog	*Rana catesbeiana*	BOR, scattered records	Abundant	Widespread: Canad. Maritime Provs. to Fla. and Rocky Mts.
Green frog	*Rana clamitans melanota*	Abundant	WR, abundant	Widespread: Canad. Maritime Provs. to Manitoba; S to Ga., Ala., and Okla.
Pickerel frog	*Rana palustris*	BOR, few records	WR, locally common	Widespread: Canad. Maritime Provs. to Wis.; S to S.C. and Tex.
Wood frog	*Rana sylvatica*	BOR, few records	WR, locally common	Northern: Labrador to Alaska; S to Ga.
Southern leopard frog	*Rana utricularia*	Abundant	WR, abundant	Southern: extreme so. N.Y. and L.I. to Fla.; W to Okla. and Tex.
Carpenter frog	*Rana virgatipes*	PBO, common	Common in Pine Barrens	Southern: so. N.J. S through Coastal Plain to Fla.
TURTLES				
Common snapping turtle	*Chelydra serpentina serpentina*	Common	WR, common	Widespread: Atlantic coast to Rocky Mts.; so. Canada to Gulf of Mex.
Stinkpot	*Sternotherus odoratus*	Abundant	WR, abundant	Widespread: New Engl. and so. Ontario to Gulf of Mex.; W to Wis., Kan., and Tex.
Eastern mud turtle	*Kinosternon subrubrum subrubrum*	Numerous records	WR, common	Chiefly southern: extreme SW Conn. and L.I. to Fla.; W to Ill. and Miss.
Spotted turtle	*Clemmys guttata*	Abundant records but declining	WR, declining	Widespread: so. Quebec to Fla.; W to Mich. and Ill.

472

Common name	Scientific name			Distribution
Wood turtle	*Clemmys insculpta*	BOR, few records, threatened	Threatened	Northern: Nova Scotia to Minn.; S to ea. W. Va.
Bog turtle	*Clemmys muhlenbergi*	BOR, endangered	Endangered	Widespread but disjunct: N.Y. and so. New Engl. to w. N.C.
Eastern box turtle	*Terrapene carolina carolina*	Numerous records but declining	WR, declining	Widespread: New Engl. to Fla.; W to Ill. and Miss.
Northern diamondback terrapin	*Malaclemys terrapin terrapin*	PER, not present	Abundant along coasts	Coastal: Cape Cod, Mass. to Cape Hatteras, N.C.
Map turtle	*Graptemys geographica*	PER, not present	Delaware River, Trenton and above	Western: Vt. to Minn., Kan., and Ala.; Susquehanna and Delaware R. basins
Eastern painted turtle	*Chrysemys picta picta*	Abundant	WR, abundant	Eastern: Nova Scotia and S New Engl. to Ala.
Red-bellied turtle	*Chrysemys rubriventris*	Common	WR, common	Eastern: ea. Mass.; so. N.J. to e. N.C.
Eastern spiny softshell	*Trionyx spiniferus spiniferus*	INT, at western edge only	One river system only; Salem County	Western: N.Y. to Wis.; S to Ala.
LIZARDS				
Northern fence lizard	*Sceloporus undulatus hyacinthinus*	Abundant	WR, locally abundant	Southern: so. N.Y. to S.C.; W to Okla. and Tex.
Ground skink	*Scincella lateralis*	PBO, uncommon	Uncommon	Southern: so. N.J. to Fla.; W to Kan. and Tex.
Five-lined skink	*Eumeces fasciatus*	REL, few records	Uncertain	Widespread: New Engl. to Fla.; W to Minn., Kan., and Tex.
SNAKES				
Queen snake	*Natrix septemvittata*	PER, not present	Uncertain	Western: so. Ontario and SE Pa. and adjacent N.J. to w. Fla.; W to Ill. and Ark.
Northern water snake	*Natrix sipedon sipedon*	Abundant	WR, abundant	Widespread: Me. to N.C.; W to Colo.
Northern brown snake	*Storeria dekayi dekayi*	Scattered records	WR, locally common	Widespread: so. Quebec and New Engl. to N.C.; W to Ohio
Northern red-bellied snake	*Storeria occipitomaculata occipitomaculata*	PBO, numerous records	Local in Pine Barrens	Widespread: Canad. Maritime Provs. to Ga.; W to Saskatchewan and Tex.
Eastern ribbon snake	*Thamnophis sauritus sauritus*	Numerous records but uncommon	WR, widespread but uncommon	Widespread: New Engl. to S.C. and Fla.; W to Ill. and La.
Eastern garter snake	*Thamnophis sirtalis sirtalis*	Numerous records	WR, locally common	Widespread: Canad. Maritime Provs. and James Bay to Fla.; W to w. Ontario, Ark., and Tex.
Eastern earth snake	*Virginia valeriae valeriae*	Uncertain	WR?, rare	Chiefly southern: N.J. to Fla.; W to Ohio and Ala.

(continued)

473

TABLE I (continued)

Common Name	Scientific Name	Status in the Pine Barrens	Status in southern New Jersey	Approximate Range in United States and Canada
Eastern hognose snake	*Heterodon platyrhinos*	Locally common but declining	WR, locally common	Widespread: so. New Engl. to Fla.; W to Minn., Kan., and Tex.
Northern–southern ringneck snake (intergrading population)	*Diadophis punctatus punctatus × edwardsi*	Scattered	WR, spotty distribution	Parent pops. widespread: Northern from Canad. Maritime Provs. to Wis. and Ala.; Southern to Fla. and Ala.
Eastern worm snake	*Carphophis amoenus amoenus*	REL, common	Common in Pine Barrens	Widespread: so. New Engl. to S.C.; W to Ky. and Ala.
Northern black racer	*Coluber constrictor constrictor*	Locally common but declining	WR, locally common but declining	Widespread: New Engl. to S.C.; W to Tenn. and Ala.
Rough green snake	*Opheodrys aestivus*	PBO, common	Common in Pine Barrens	Southern: so. N.J. to Fla.; W to Kan., Tex. and Mexico
Corn snake	*Elaphe guttata guttata*	PBO, scattered records	Occasional in Pine Barrens	Southern: so. N.J. to Fla.; W to Ky. and La.
Black rat snake	*Elaphe obsoleta obsoleta*	Locally common	WR, locally common	Widespread: so. New Engl. to Ga.; W to Neb., Okla., and Tex.
Northern pine snake	*Pituophis melanoleucus melanoleucus*	PBO, locally common	Local in Pine Barrens	Southern: so. N.J.; SW Va. to W cent. Tenn. and cent. Ala.; E to SE N.C.
Eastern kingsnake	*Lampropeltis getulus getulus*	PBO, locally common	Local in Pine Barrens	Southern: so. N.J. to Fla.; W into Appalachians and Ala.
Eastern milk snake–scarlet kingsnake (intergrading population)	*Lampropeltis triangulum triangulum × elapsoides*	Numerous records	WR, locally common	Parent pops. widespread: eastern milk from New Engl. to Minn. and Tenn.; scarlet king S to Gulf of Mex.
Northern scarlet snake	*Cemophora coccinea copei*	PBO, scattered records	Secretive; probably common in Pine Barrens	Southern: so. N.J. to Fla.; W to Mo., Okla., and Tex.
Timber–canebrake rattlesnake (intergrading population)	*Crotalus horridus horridus × atricaudatus*	PBO, threatened	Threatened	Parent pops. widespread: timber from New Engl. to Minn., Tex., and Ga.; Canebrake in Coastal Plain, SE Va. to Fla. and Tex.

^a PBO, Pine Barrens only; WR, wide ranging; BOR, border entrant; REL, relict in Pine Barrens; PER, peripheral to Pine Barrens; INT, introduced.
Totals of 60 species: 10 Pine Barrens only; 28 wide ranging; 11 border entrants; 5 relicts in Pine Barrens; 4 peripheral to Pine Barrens; 2 introduced.

Two other species, the milk snake and the ringneck snake (*Diadophis punctatus*), have populations in southern New Jersey that are intermediate between two related subspecies, one southern and the other northern and upland. Individual variation in markings and pattern characteristics is extensive, and the populations must be designated as *Lampropeltis triangulum triangulum* × *elapsoides* and *Diadophis punctatus punctatus* × *edwardsi* (Conant, 1943, 1946).

Two members of the southern New Jersey herpetofauna, the map turtle (*Graptemys geographica*) and the queen snake (*Natrix septemvittata*), have ranges that otherwise are chiefly western. These species barely enter the state.

On the basis of geographical distribution, the amphibians and reptiles of southern New Jersey can be sorted into six general categories (Table I). Each of these is defined and annotated below.

SPECIES CONFINED TO THE PINE BARRENS

Eight species in southern New Jersey occur only within the borders of the Pine Barrens. Two others included here, the rough green snake (*Opheodrys aestivus*) and the eastern kingsnake (*Lampropeltis getulus*), are confined chiefly to the Barrens, but also are known from a few localities in or very close to oak–pine fringe areas that border the Barrens in Cape May, Cumberland, and Salem counties.

Among the ten species in this category (Plate 1), eight are distributed widely throughout the Atlantic Coastal Plain, and some, including the green snake, the king-snake, and the corn snake (*Elaphe guttata*), have ranges more or less continuous to and throughout most of Florida. Others, such as the pine barrens treefrog (*Hyla andersoni*) and the northern pine snake (*Pituophis melanoleucus*), exhibit broad gaps (see maps in Conant, 1975), but the pattern indicates that their distributions formerly were widespread through the southern Coastal Plain. The sandy soils and pine forests of the more southern parts of the Coastal Plain offer habitats that are similar in many respects to those of the Pine Barrens even though they differ in numerous components. As an example, pitch pine (*Pinus rigida*), which is so abundant in the Barrens, is replaced by other pine species farther south (Little, 1971).

The northern scarlet snake (*Cemophora coccinea*), the pine snake (Fig. 1), and to a lesser extent the corn snake, are semifossorial, and the sandy substrate of the Pine Barrens offers a suitable medium for burrowing. The pine barrens treefrog and the carpenter frog (*Rana virgatipes*) are highly tolerant of the acid waters of the Barrens (Gosner and Black, 1957).

Of the remaining Pine Barrens forms, the red-bellied snake is essentially a northern and upland species and the rattlesnake population, as suggested above, may have been derived in part from northern sources.

WIDE-RANGING SPECIES

More than half of the native species of the Pine Barrens range widely across southern New Jersey (Plate 2; see also Fig. 2). Most are also widespread throughout a

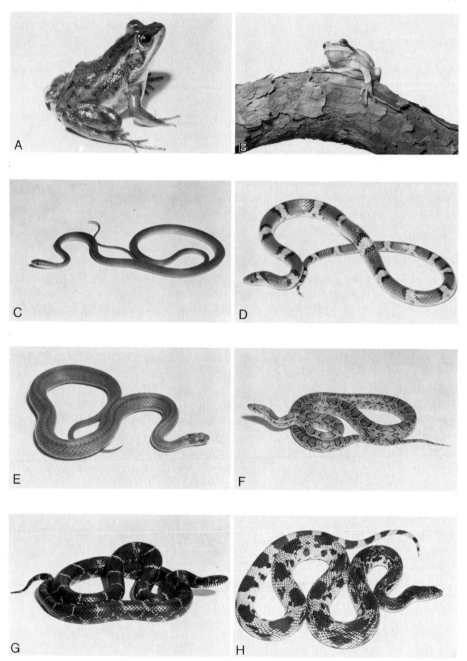

Plate 1. Pine Barrens species. (A) carpenter frog; (B) pine barrens treefrog; (C) rough green snake; (D) northern scarlet snake; (E) northern red-bellied snake; (F) corn snake; (G) eastern kingsnake; (H) northern pine snake.

Plate 2. Species that are wide ranging in southern New Jersey. (A) Fowler's toad; (B) southern leopard frog; (C) northern water snake; (D) eastern ribbon snake; (E) eastern hognose snake; (F) spotted turtle; (G) common snapping turtle; (H) red-bellied turtle.

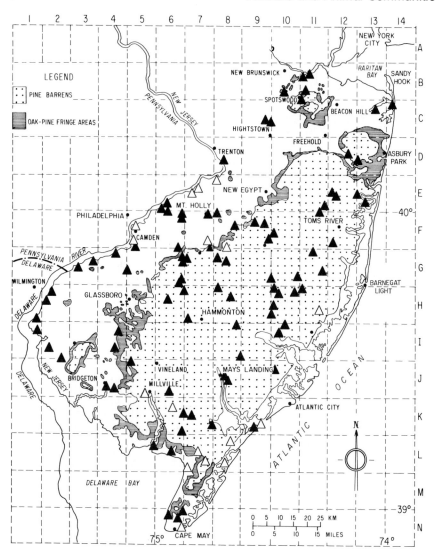

Fig. 2. Distribution of the southern leopard frog (*Rana utricularia*). This species ranges widely across southern New Jersey, and is abundant in many localities outside as well as within the Pine Barrens.

large part of eastern North America (Table I). Two are noteworthy in that their ranges terminate relatively short distances north of southern New Jersey. The southern leopard frog (*Rana utricularia*) occurs on Staten Island and Long Island and in extreme southern mainland New York (Pace, 1974). The eastern mud turtle (*Kinosternon subrubrum*) has a similar northward distribution, but is also known from extreme southwestern Connecticut. In a third species, the red-bellied turtle (*Chrysemys rub-*

riventris), the continuous northward range ends in southern New Jersey, but disjunct, relict colonies are found in eastern Massachusetts.

Several species distributions are poorly known (indicated by "WR?" in Table I). Among these, the spotted salamander (*Ambystoma maculatum*), the eastern mud salamander (*Pseudotriton montanus*), and the eastern earth snake (*Virginia valeriae*) are rarities in southern New Jersey. Although the few records for each suggest that they may be wide ranging, the evidence is meager. For example, the only two records currently available for the mud salamander are from opposite sides of the Pine Barrens in eastern Atlantic and western Burlington Counties, but, judging from habitats that the species occupies in Delaware, it is likely to be found in localities outside the Barrens.

The slimy salamander (*Plethodon glutinosus*) is a relatively common amphibian of forested northern New Jersey, but its presence in the Pine Barrens is surprising. The American Museum of Natural History, however, has seven specimens from Ocean County (collected at Lakewood, Lakehurst, and near Toms River) that were obtained by several reliable naturalists over a period extending from 1905 to 1942. Unfortunately, no habitat data are available for any of these specimens. Elsewhere in southern New Jersey, the species is known from Mercer County.

BORDER ENTRANTS: SPECIES ENTERING THE PINE BARRENS UNDER EXCEPTIONAL CONDITIONS

These species (Plate 3), mostly amphibians, barely enter the Barrens or maintain themselves within them only where habitats have been disturbed by mankind or where conditions are especially suitable for survival. Most are widely distributed outside the Barrens (Table I).

Several species of frogs may invade the Pine Barrens and survive for a year or more, but if and when breeding occurs the tadpoles may fail to develop in the acid waters of the region (Gosner and Black, 1957). I reported on such a colony of the gray treefrog (*Hyla versicolor*) that utilized a small pond at Taunton, Burlington County (Conant, 1962). Additional comments now can be made on two other species that moved into the Pine Barrens in the same general vicinity. The chorus frog (*Pseudacris triseriata*) became established in roadside ditches near an active cranberry bog, and the colony survived for many years, presumably aided by spring rains that made the acidity of the water tolerable during the period when tadpoles were developing. Three times (in 1962, 1969 and 1970) during the quarter-century that I lived on the shore of Taunton Lake, a single calling male bullfrog (*Rana catesbeiana*) was heard for a few days in late spring in marshy areas near the upper end of the impoundment. The animal that called during 1969 may have survived to call again in 1970, but it is likely that the 1962 male was a different individual. No vocalization by this species was noticed during the intervening years.

The late James D. Anderson (unpublished observations) commented on the inability of the eastern tiger salamander (*Ambystoma tigrinum*) to maintain itself in the Pine Barrens, even though the species enters the area in a few places along its perimeter.

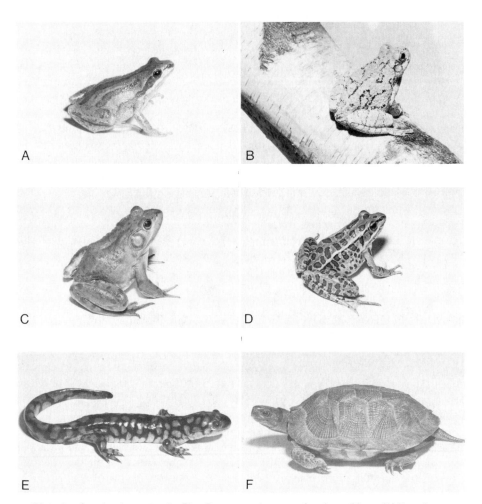

Plate 3. Species that enter the Pine Barrens under exceptional conditions. (A) New Jersey chorus frog; (B) northern gray treefrog; (C) bullfrog; (D) pickerel frog; (E) eastern tiger salamander; (F) wood turtle.

Some species that ordinarily do not occur in the Barrens are established where there has been much habitat disturbance, where the mantle of sand is thin, or where there has been protection from wildfires and the pines have been largely crowded out by mature deciduous trees. The northern cricket frog (*Acris crepitans*) near Hammonton is a case in point. Lakewood and Lakehurst, from which several border entrant species have been reported, also belong in this category, and so does the forest near the dam site at Taunton Lake, where the gray treefrog was active for a time, and where it probably would have survived if its habitat had not been ravaged in the name of mosquito control procedures.

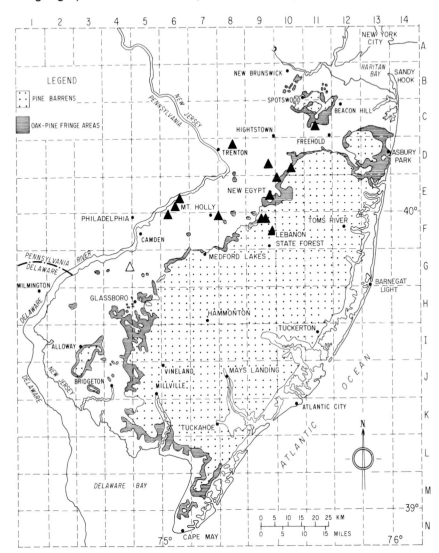

Fig. 3. Distribution of the wood turtle (*Clemmys insculpta*), a species of northern affinities. This enters the Pine Barrens in a few localiities, chiefly along streams, some of which it may have followed headward from outside the area.

The wood turtle (Fig. 3) and the bog turtle (*Clemmys muhlenbergi*) may belong in this category. The wood turtle now is a rarity in the Barrens, although in the past it often was found in or near some of the larger streams in the northern part of the area, notably along Rancocas Creek. It may have penetrated the Barrens by moving up-stream from the Inner Coastal Plain. The bog turtle enters the Pine Barrens in several places, and Conant and Bailey (1936) reported a thriving colony in sluggish ditches along the Manasquan River near Allaire, Monmouth County. The recent discovery of this species in southern Burlington County well within the Pine Barrens (K. A. Hawthorne, unpublished observations) was unexpected (perhaps a human introduction?), but the species is not generally distributed throughout the Barrens.

RELICTS IN THE BARRENS

Five species probably once were wide ranging across southern New Jersey, but their habitats have been decimated and they now are restricted largely to the Barrens (Fig. 4; Table I). Among them, the four-toed salamander has been mentioned. The marbled salamander (*Ambystoma opacum*) and the eastern worm snake (*Carphophis amoenus*) are not rare within the Pine Barrens and also are known from a few outside localities. The marbled salamander, for example, is fairly common in Cape May County, where it occurs with the tiger salamander in such artificial habitats as borrow pits. The red-spotted newt (*Notophthalmus viridescens*) is placed here tentatively, although there are too few records for definite conclusions to be drawn. The known localities from southern New Jersey for the five-lined skink (*Eumeces fasciatus*) are all from within the Barrens, but the species is likely to be found in refugia outside them. This lizard occupies a wide variety of usually moist habitats in other parts of its range, including northern New Jersey. It, too, is included tentatively.

PERIPHERAL SPECIES

Four species barely enter southern New Jersey or are restricted to the perimeter of the area and are not known from the Pine Barrens (Table I). Among these, the map turtle is confined to the Delaware River but only as far south as the immediate vicinity of Trenton, Mercer County (Raymond J. Stein, unpublished observations). The northern diamondback terrapin (*Malaclemys terrapin*) occupies salt or brackish-water environments along the coasts.

The queen snake is known with certainty only from near the mouths of creeks emptying into the Delaware River. Cope's gray treefrog (*Hyla chrysoscelis*) which only recently has been recognized as a cryptic species of the *Hyla versicolor* complex, has been recorded from southern Cape May County and westward paralleling Delaware Bay into adjacent Cumberland County. This amphibian is recognized most readily by its call and eventually may be found within the Barrens.

THE INTRODUCTIONS

Two species, the eastern spiny softshell (*Trionyx spiniferus*) and the barking treefrog (*Hyla gratiosa*), have been introduced in southern New Jersey during the present century (Table I).

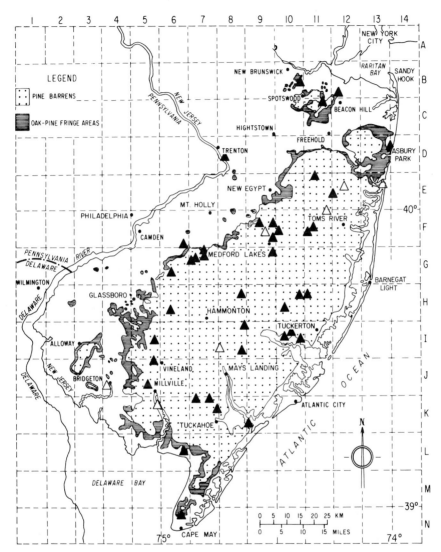

Fig. 4. Distribution of the eastern worm snake (*Carphophis a. amoenus*). This species presumably at one time was widespread across southern New Jersey, but now is restricted largely to the Pine Barrens and to scattered refugia outside that area.

The arrival of the softshell turtle is well documented (Conant, 1961). Four specimens from near Marion, Indiana, and "each about the size of a small plate," were liberated intentionally in Keans Lake at Elmer, Salem County, approximately in June 1910. The species is now well established at several localities along Muddy Run, at least in impoundments along its course, such as Keans Lake.

The origin of the introduction of the barking treefrog from the South is obscure. Its presence was unsuspected until Black and Gosner (1958) reported tadpoles and breeding adults from the vicinity of Bennett, Cape May County. The Bennett area, and especially the Bennett bogs, have been visited by generations of naturalists and, if the species had been present, especially giving voice to its distinctive call, it surely would have been reported. The duration of the colony may have been ephemeral, since no one in recent years has found additional specimens.

GEOGRAPHICAL ORIGIN OF THE HERPETOFAUNA

Because of the meager fossil record, comments on the origins of the present distributions of amphibians and reptiles in southern New Jersey fall largely into the realm of speculation, although plausible inferences may be drawn from information available on other organisms and from the general directions from which certain species may have entered the area.

Probably all, or virtually all, species were absent from the region during the glacial maxima. The close proximity of the ice sheets in northern New Jersey (Flint, 1971) probably had a profound effect on the cold-blooded vertebrates previously present. Braun (1951, 1955) and Thomas (1951) presented arguments that many plants and animals may have survived close to the ice front, but more recent studies, at least for plants (see summary in Whitehead, 1965), suggest that this was unlikely.

A sequence of three major post-Pleistocene climatic periods which profoundly influenced the distributions of many organisms has been documented by pollen profiles accumulated by palynologists and by the findings of zoogeographers and phytogeographers. In brief, these were a cool moist period followed by a warm period and then a return to the cool moist conditions that have continued to the present.

Most members of the herpetofauna that range widely throughout northeastern North America and which constitute the bulk of the species now living in southern New Jersey probably entered the area during the first cool moist period soon after suitable habitats were provided for them by the reestablishment of the forest, streams, and ponds. Some of these species, after becoming established in more upland areas to the west, may have followed stream basins southeastward into the Coastal Plain. The Coastal Plain elements (species that are more or less confined to the Pine Barrens, plus a few others) presumably moved northward, in some cases as far as New England, during the early part of the warm period, when the coastline was far to the east and a broad avenue was provided for their northward dispersal. The warm period, especially during its xerothermic subdivision (see below), also contributed to the melting and recession of the continental glaciers and to the resultant rise in sea level that moved the coastline westward.

A novel pathway for the entry of one of the frogs has been suggested. Smith (1965) pointed out that the warm climatic period consisted of two phases, the climatic optimum, a warm moist phase, which was followed by the xerothermic interval, a warm dry phase. Both lasted about 20 centuries. The desiccation during the xerothermic was of sufficient duration and severity to permit the development of a tongue of prairie (the

Prairie Peninsula) that extended eastward to the Atlantic coast. Smith (1957) suggested that the chorus frog (*Pseudacris triseriata*), a western prairie form, made its way through this peninsula into New Jersey and then southward into the Delmarva Peninsula. The subsequent return to cool, moist conditions truncated the range to the north, leaving a relict population that since has differentiated subspecifically into the race *kalmi*.

COMMENTARY

Herpetological fieldwork in the Pine Barrens is often disappointing and unproductive. A few species almost always are in evidence during warm weather, e.g., frogs calling during their respective breeding seasons, turtles basking except when temperatures are high, and the abundant northern fence lizard (*Sceloporus undulatus*) climbing upward on tree trunks when approached. Most other amphibians and reptiles are secretive, and hiding places are so extraordinarily numerous that finding specimens often is the result of sheer luck. Under these circumstances, it is not surprising that the northern scarlet snake (*Cemophora coccinea*) was not discovered in New Jersey until 1934 (Kauffeld, 1935) and the eastern mud salamander (*Pseudotriton montanus*) until 1953 (Conant, 1957). Even the common and widespread carpenter frog was unknown until it was described by Cope in 1891. The sophisticated techniques (chromosomes, size of red blood cells, and analysis of calls) for distinguishing the two gray treefrogs have been developed only recently, and the presence of Cope's gray treefrog (*Hyla chrysoscelis*) in New Jersey was not demonstrated until then.

Additions to the known native herpetofauna of southern New Jersey are still possible, and the chances of making them would be improved by the preservation of large tracts of the Pine Barrens under the aegis of the National Park Service or the New Jersey State Park System. The amphibians and reptiles of the region contribute strongly to the uniqueness of the area, and their populations, which through long isolation have developed gene pools that differ from related populations occurring elsewhere, are eminently worthy of being safeguarded. Many of the species are highly vulnerable to pollution, alterations in water table levels, mass destruction of habitats, and other human-induced assaults upon the Barrens. Prominent among them would be the small but beautiful pine barrens treefrog, which, although it is known from a number of sites in the southern states, has its headquarters in the Pine Barrens of southern New Jersey.

The Barrens annually are overrun by large numbers of amateur and commercial collectors whose impact on the herpetological fauna is difficult to evaluate. Specimens, especially snakes, that are found in the open or under such easily moved shelters as logs, boards, and the rubbish along sandy roadsides, are heavily collected. On the other hand, the fossorial habits of several of the more desirable species assure that large fractions of their populations are inaccessible at any given time. Limited areas can be decimated quickly, however. Soon after Kauffeld (1957), in a popular book, extolled the virtues of collecting at Crossley, Ocean County, hordes of snake hunters descended on that locality and literally tore its surface apart in their eagerness to find specimens.

It also is difficult to assess the results of transplant activities by well-meaning persons who move specimens from vulnerable localities to others considered safer from indiscriminate collecting. Whereas such activities theoretically may be favorable to the survival of some species, no data are available on potential damage to gene pools or the carrying capacities at the locales of such introductions. The numbers of liberated animals are relatively large in some instances, especially when snakes bearing eggs or young are kept in captivity, and their offspring are fed and retained until they have grown large enough presumably to survive.

Further useful information on the amphibians and reptiles of southern New Jersey is available in the publications of Abbott (1868), Nelson (1890), Fowler (1905, 1907, 1908, 1909), Noble and Noble (1923), Burger (1934), Trapido (1937), Kauffeld and Trapido (1944), and Kauffeld (1966, 1967).

SUMMARY

Distributional patterns of the 58 native and two introduced species of amphibians and reptiles known to occur in southern New Jersey are analyzed, and comments are presented on the probable geographical origins of and human impacts upon this fauna. Six categories of species are recognized, those which are: (a) confined to the Pine Barrens; (b) wide ranging across southern New Jersey; (c) known from a relatively few localities within the borders of the Pine Barrens; (d) relict in the Pine Barrens; (e) restricted to areas outside the Pine Barrens; and (f) present because of introductions by people. Species that range broadly across eastern North America may have invaded the region shortly after the last glacial period, whereas many Coastal Plain species at or near the northern extremes of their ranges may have arrived at the onset of a more recent warm period. Major injurious effects on the herpetological fauna are evident as the result of intensive agriculture, urbanization, and industrialization and the activities of amateur and commercial collectors. In the midst of the region, however, the Pine Barrens serve as a huge, immensely valuable refugium for amphibians and reptiles.

ACKNOWLEDGMENTS

Literally hundreds of persons have aided in the accumulation of the data on which this chapter is based, and I thank all of them for their contributions, both large and small. For help in critically reviewing the manuscript, I am indebted to J. Kevin Bowler, William G. Degenhardt, the late Howard K. Gloyd, Kathryn J. Gloyd, Keith A. Hawthorne, James S. Jacob, Frederick C. Schlauch, and Philip W. Smith. The photographs were taken by the late Isabelle Hunt Conant.

REFERENCES

Abbott, C. C. (1868). Catalogue of vertebrate animals of New Jersey. *In* "Geology of New Jersey" (for Reptiles and Amphibians), pp. 799–805. George H. Cook, Newark, New Jersey.

Black, I. H., and Gosner, K. L. (1958). The barking treefrog, *Hyla gratiosa* in New Jersey. *Herpetologica* **13**, 254–255.

Braun, E. L. (1951). Plant distribution in relation to the glacial boundary. *Ohio J. Sci.* **51**, 139–146.

Braun, E. L. (1955). The phytogeography of unglaciated eastern United States and its interpretation. *Bot. Rev.* **21**, 297–375.

Burger, J. W. (1934). The hibernation habits of the rattlesnake of the New Jersey pine barrens. *Copeia* 1934, p. 142.

Conant, R. (1943). The milk snakes of the Atlantic coastal plain. *Proc. New Engl. Zool. Club* **22**, 3–24.

Conant, R. (1946). Intergradation among ring-necked snakes from southern New Jersey and the Del-Mar-Va peninsula. *Bull. Chicago Acad. Sci.* **7**, 473–482.

Conant, R. (1957). The eastern mud salamander, *Pseudotriton montanus montanus:* A new state record for New Jersey. *Copeia* 1957, pp. 152–153.

Conant, R. (1961). The softshell turtle, *Trionyx spinifer,* introduced and established in New Jersey. *Copeia* 1961, pp. 355–356.

Conant, R. (1962). Notes on the distribution of reptiles and amphibians in the pine barrens of southern New Jersey. *N.J. Nat. News* **17**, 16–21.

Conant, R. (1975). "A Field Guide to Reptiles and Amphibians of Eastern and Central North America," 2nd Ed. Houghton, Boston, Massachusetts.

Conant, R., and Bailey, R. M. (1936). Some herpetological records from Monmouth and Ocean counties, New Jersey. *Occas. Pap. Mus. Zool. Univ. Mich.* **328**, 1–10.

Cope, E. D. (1891). A new species of frog from New Jersey. *Am. Nat.* **25**, 1017–1019.

Flint, R. F. (1971). "Glacial and Quaternary Geology." Wiley, New York.

Fowler, H. W. (1905). The sphagnum frog of New Jersey—*Rana virgatipes* Cope. *Proc. Acad. Nat. Sci. Philadelphia* **57**, 662–664.

Fowler, H. W. (1907). The amphibians and reptiles of New Jersey. *N.J. State Mus., Rep.* pp. 23–250.

Fowler, H. W. (1908). A supplementary account of New Jersey amphibians and reptiles. *N.J. State Mus., Rep.* pp. 190–202.

Fowler, H. W. (1909). Notes on New Jersey amphibians and reptiles. *N.J. State Mus., Rep.* pp. 393–408.

Gloyd, H. K. (1940). The rattlesnakes, genera *Sistrurus* and *Crotalus. Chicago Acad. Sci. Spec. Publ.* **4**, 1–270.

Gosner, K. L., and Black, I. H. (1957). The effects of acidity on the development and hatching of New Jersey frogs. *Ecology* **38**, 256–262.

Kauffeld, C. F. (1935). The scarlet snake, *Cemophora coccinea,* in southern New Jersey. *Copeia* 1935, p. 191.

Kauffeld, C. F. (1957). "Snakes and Snake Hunting." Hanover House, Garden City, New York.

Kauffeld, C. F. (1966). The history of the corn snake *Elaphe guttata guttata* in southern New Jersey. *HERP.* **3**(2), 6–9.

Kauffeld, C. F. (1967). The history of the scarlet snake, *Cemophora coccinea,* in southern New Jersey. *HERP.* **3**(5), 7–9.

Kauffeld, C. F., and Trapido, H. (1944). Additional records of the scarlet snake in New Jersey. *Copeia* 1944, pp. 62–63.

Little, E. L., Jr. (1971). Atlas of United States trees: Vol. 1. Conifers and important hardwoods. *U.S. Dep. Agric., Misc. Publ.* No. 1146.

Nelson, J. (1890). Descriptive catalogue of the vertebrates of New Jersey. (A revision of Dr. Abbott's catalogue of 1868.) *Final Rep. State Geol.* No. 2, 637–657, 772.

Noble, G. K., and Noble, R. C. (1923). The Anderson tree frog (*Hyla andersonii* Baird): Observations on its habits and life history. *Zoologica (N.Y.)* **2**, 413–455.

Pace, A. E. (1974). Systematic and biological studies of the leopard frogs (*Rana pipiens* complex) of the United States. *Misc. Publ. Mus. Zool. Univ. Mich.* **148**, 1–140.

Smith, P. W. (1957). An analysis of post-Wisconsin biogeography of the Prairie Peninsula region based on distributional phenomena among terrestrial vertebrate populations. *Ecology* **38**, 205–218.

Smith, P. W. (1965). Recent adjustments in animal ranges. *In* "Quaternary of the United States" (H. E. Wright, Jr. and D. G. Frey, eds.), pp. 633–642. Princeton Univ. Press, Princeton, New Jersey.

Thomas, E. S. (1951). Distribution of Ohio animals. *Ohio J. Sci.* **51,** 153–167.

Trapido, H. (1937). "The Snakes of New Jersey: A guide," Newark Museum Publ., pp. 1–60. Newark, New Jersey.

Whitehead, D. R. (1965). Palynology and Pleistocene phytogeography of unglaciated eastern North America. *In* "Quaternary of the United States" (H. E. Wright, Jr., and D. G. Frey, eds.), pp. 417–432. Princeton Univ. Press, Princeton, New Jersey.

28
Fish of the Pine Barrens

ROBERT W. HASTINGS

This chapter will introduce the species present in each of the major categories of Pine Barrens fish. In addition, the fish species will be examined in relation to their habitat characteristics and biogeographical affinities.

HABITAT CHARACTERISTICS OF PINE BARRENS STREAMS

The waters of the New Jersey Pine Barrens generally are low in nutrients, hardness, turbidity, and dissolved solids. In contrast, acidity and dissolved iron tend to be high, and most waters are dark tea colored (Rhodehamel, 1970, 1973). In southern New Jersey lakes and streams, pH values usually range from 4.0–7.0, with those in the Pine Barrens generally <6.0 (Smith, 1953). Such water conditions significantly limit the fish fauna present, either directly, by affecting the egg and larval development of some species, or by affecting the distribution of invertebrates which provide their food. Productivity of phytoplankton also is quite low (Smith, 1960).

Streams generally are shallow and slow moving since relief is low. For example, Fikslin and Montgomery (1971) recorded a maximum surface current of 0.6 m/sec in the Oswego River. Runoff also is low because of the porous sandy soils. Temperatures usually range from slightly above 0°C during the winter to about 25°C in summer, with average annual water temperature about 12°C (54°F) (Rhodehamel, 1973).

Substrates in the Pine Barrens usually are sandy, but gravel bottoms occur in places and most streams have extensive deposits of decaying organic material. Many typical fish of the Pine Barrens are rather sedentary species associated with vegetation. Extensive beds of such aquatic plants as *Utricularia, Myriophyllum, Eleocharis, Sagittaria, Xyris, Sphagnum, Nymphaea, Juncus,* and *Sparganium* form important habitats for fish.

Most streams of the Pine Barrens are relatively free of the pollution characteristic of northeastern United States waterways. The most significant human influence has been the extensive damming to form mill ponds, lakes, or cranberry bogs. Natural lakes are virtually absent from the Pine Barrens, but man-made lakes represent a significant aquatic habitat today. In agricultural areas, such as Hammonton and Vineland, extensive deforestation apparently has had a profound effect upon certain streams and lakes, and hence, on their aquatic fauna. Average temperatures, turbidity, and pH probably have increased in such streams due to increased insolation, runoff, and the leaching of fertilizers. Direct application of hydrated lime, $Ca(OH)_2$, and limestone, $CaCO_3$, to increase pH also has been attempted in some Pine Barrens lakes (Smith, 1952, 1957; Stewart, 1972).

GENERAL NATURE OF THE PINE BARRENS FISH FAUNA

Fish are extremely adaptable animals, and some are present in virtually all aquatic habitats. However, the total number of species occurring in the Pine Barrens is low. Some 70 species of native freshwater fish have been reported for New Jersey, but only 24 species, including two introduced species, were listed by McCormick (1970) as occurring in the Pine Barrens. The list is even shorter, 16 species, if peripheral and introduced species are excluded. Thus, these waters represent a somewhat unique habitat for fish that only a few species can occupy. Certain species, however, are common in the Pine Barrens, even though rare in other areas.

Collette (1962) recognized three groups of New Jersey freshwater fish: (1) species limited to the sluggish, brown-stained, acid lowland ponds and streams (the Pine Barrens); (2) species of upland, clear, alkaline bodies of water, and (3) species found throughout the state in both types of situations. Such divisions are not always clear-cut, but they indicate the general composition of the Pine Barrens fish fauna. Members of the second group are absent from the Pine Barrens, although some occur in lowland streams in central and western New Jersey. Conversely, although the fish of the first group tend to be most characteristic of the Pine Barrens, no species is limited strictly to acid waters. The third group includes two subgroups; some fishes are about equally common throughout the state, including the Pine Barrens, whereas others occur only in the less acid fringe areas of the Pine Barrens. Two additional groups of Pine Barrens fish are present: (a) anadromous marine fish which spawn in the freshwaters of the state; and (b) introduced or exotic species, which originally were brought into the Pine Barrens by people. Thus, four groups are presented; (1) characteristic species of the Pine Barrens; (2) peripheral species; (3) anadromous species; and (4) introduced species.

CHARACTERISTIC SPECIES OF THE PINE BARRENS

No fish species is restricted to Pine Barrens habitats, but several species are so common that they may be considered characteristic of the area. Probably the most characteristic is the blackbanded sunfish (*Enneacanthus chaetodon*). This small fish, with striking black and white bands, is common in most lakes and streams of the area, especially in dense vegetation, but also is found in some non-Pine Barrens locations in the central part of the state (Fig. 1). The Pine Barrens are well known as a source for this popular aquarium fish (Quinn, 1967a,b; see Breder and Rosen, 1966, for

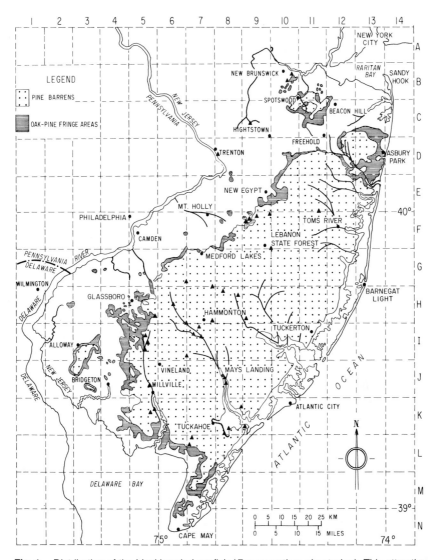

Fig. 1. Distribution of the blackbanded sunfish (*Enneacanthus chaetodon*). This attractive black- and white-banded fish at the northern limit of its Florida-to-New Jersey range is a characteristic species of the Pine Barrens, and is found in southern and central New Jersey, north to and including Mercer and Middlesex counties. Localities based upon collections taken by personnel of Rutgers University (Camden) and the New Jersey Division of Fish, Game and Shellfisheries (unpublished electrofishing survey data), State Lakes and Ponds Surveys (N.J. Div. Fish and Game, 1951; Smith, 1953, 1957; Stewart, 1971), and catalogued collections in the Academy of Natural Sciences of Philadelphia.

additional references). The species has an unusual disjunct distribution pattern, with populations in New Jersey, Maryland (Schwartz, 1961), North and South Carolina, southern Georgia, and northern Florida (Sweeney, 1972). Breder and Rosen (1966) emphasized the association of the blackbanded sunfish with strongly acid waters and stated that it "apparently does not thrive in waters of different and less acid content." The importance of acid waters to the species has not been demonstrated adequately, and it does occur in substantial numbers in some nonacid habitats, e.g., Smithville Pond, Maryland with pH 7.1 (Schwartz, 1961). Smith (1957) speculated that this and other small sunfish are excluded from many nonacid habitats by competition from introduced sunfish, which have been stocked widely in New Jersey waters but are unable to tolerate the acid waters of the Pine Barrens. Smith (1953) also indicated that blackbanded sunfish could survive at pH levels as low as 3.7–4.0.

Two other species of *Enneacanthus* are common in the Pine Barrens, the banded or *Sphagnum* sunfish (*E. obesus*) and the bluespotted sunfish (*E. gloriosus*). Primarily restricted to the Pine Barrens, the banded sunfish is similar in distribution to the blackbanded sunfish in New Jersey, but it ranges continuously in the Atlantic Coast region from New Hampshire to western Florida (Sweeney, 1972). In contrast, the bluespotted sunfish, ranging continuously from southern New York to western Florida (Sweeney, 1972), is distributed more widely in New Jersey, and may be more common in the neutral or slightly alkaline waters of northern and central New Jersey than in the Pine Barrens (Smith, 1957). The species generally occupies sluggish water habitats with dense vegetation, although it is less numerous in the Pine Barrens than other species of *Enneacanthus*.

The mud sunfish (*Acantharchus pomotis*) also is common in Pine Barrens streams, although present in a few lakes and streams of the Raritan and Musconetcong drainages of northern New Jersey (Smith, 1957). It is similar in habits to the species of *Enneacanthus*, but attains a larger size with a larger mouth and apparently is a more voracious predator. The four species are similar in being the only sunfish with rounded caudal fins, a characteristic apparently correlated with their occupation of thick vegetation and with the need to swim "carefully and at low speeds" (Gosline, 1971).

Other important species generally recognized as being characteristic of the "cedar water" habitats of the Pine Barrens are the yellow bullhead (*Ictalurus natalis*), pirate perch (*Aphredoderus sayanus*), ironcolor shiner (*Notropis chalybaeus*), and swamp darter (*Etheostoma fusiforme*). The first two species are distributed widely throughout much of eastern North America. Although both are characteristic of sluggish streams or standing water with dense vegetation, they are not restricted to acid water. Hubbs and Lagler (1958) suggested that the yellow bullhead was more common than other bullheads in clean waters and vegetation. It has been collected at a number of locations in northern New Jersey but is considerably more numerous in the Pine Barrens (Fig. 2). In contrast, the brown bullhead (*Ictalurus nebulosus*) is distributed widely throughout the state, but seems to be replaced at least partially by the yellow bullhead in the Pine Barrens. Here again, competition may be important in determining the distribution of the two species in the state (Smith, 1953), but this possibility has not been studied adequately. Water chemistry also is important, since the brown bullhead is more

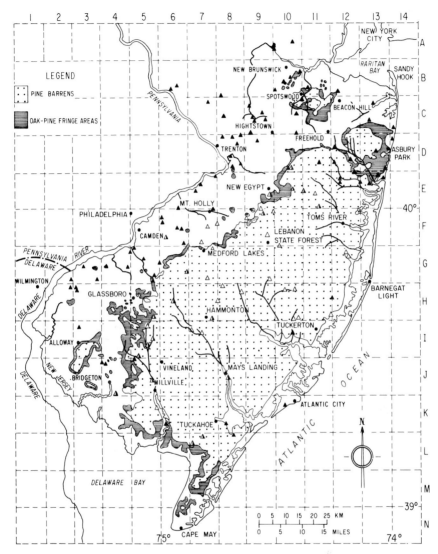

Fig. 2. Distribution of the yellow bullhead (*Ictalurus natalis*, △) and brown bullhead *I. nebulosus*, ▲. Both species, ▲. These characteristic species of the Pine Barrens may be limited by competition and (or) water chemistry. See legend to Fig. 1.

tolerant of polluted waters and the yellow bullhead is more tolerant of acid waters.

The pirate perch has not been collected in northern New Jersey but does occur on the Atlantic slope in New York (Moore, 1968). In southern New Jersey, it is most numerous in the Pine Barrens region, but also has been collected at sites outside the Pines. The ironcolored shiner is quite similar in distribution to the pirate perch, occurring from New Jersey to Florida, Texas, and the Great Lakes region (Hubbs and Lagler,

1958). The two species occur together in New Jersey, although they occupy quite different habitats. The ironcolor shiner is a typical minnow (family Cyprinidae), living in open-water habitats where it feeds on crustaceans and insects (Marshall, 1947). It apparently is rare in most of New Jersey, but it once occurred in substantial numbers at some localities. Most collections are from outside the Pine Barrens, and Smith (1957) suggested that it was typical of waters not excessively acid (Fig. 3). However, Fowler

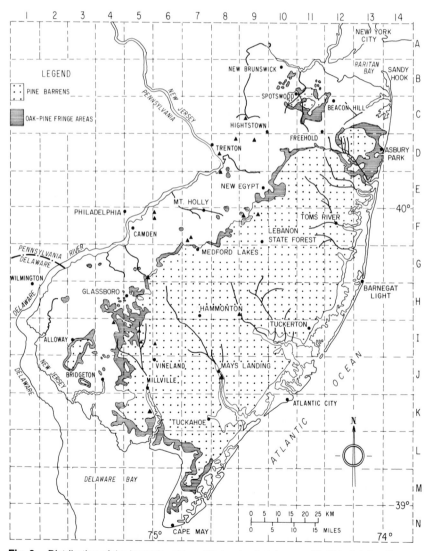

Fig. 3.   Distribution of the ironcolor shiner (*Notropis chalybaeus,* ▲). This fish is rather rare at the northern limit of its range along the eastern seaboard. See legend to Fig. 1.

(1906) considered this fish (his race *Notropis chalybaeus abboti*; Fowler, 1904) to be closely associated with the *Sphagnum* bank streams of the Pine Barrens. The absence of planktonic food sources in most Pine Barrens streams (Smith, 1960) may be a limiting factor for this species. Since New Jersey is the northern limit of its range, low winter temperatures may also be a significant limiting factor.

Collette (1962) concluded that, although the swamp darter (*Etheostoma fusiforme*)

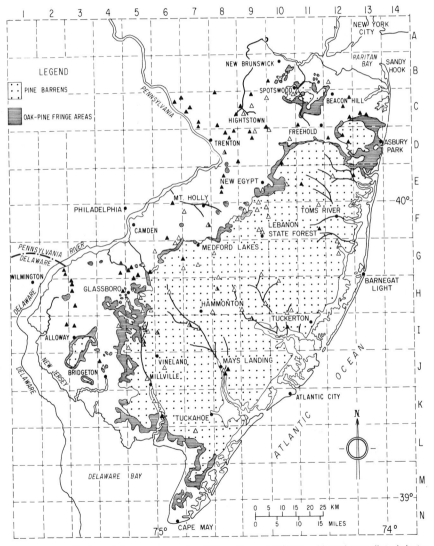

Fig. 4. Distribution of the swamp darter (*Etheostoma fusiforme,* △) and tessellated darter (*E. olmstedi,* ▲ Both species, ▲. Diverse factors have been suggested as limiting the two Pine Barrens darters. See legend to Fig. 1.

is not limited in New Jersey (Fig. 4) to acid, brown-stained waters it usually is found in such habitats for two reasons: (1) it is found primarily in slow waters, and many of these on the Coastal Plain are acid, brown-stained waters; and (2) it avoids competition from other species which are poorly adapted to this type of habitat. The only other darter to occur in the Pine Barrens, the tessellated darter (*E. olmstedi*), is more characteristic of streams in western and northern New Jersey and is much less common in the Pines than the swamp darter (Fig. 4). Where the two occur together, the

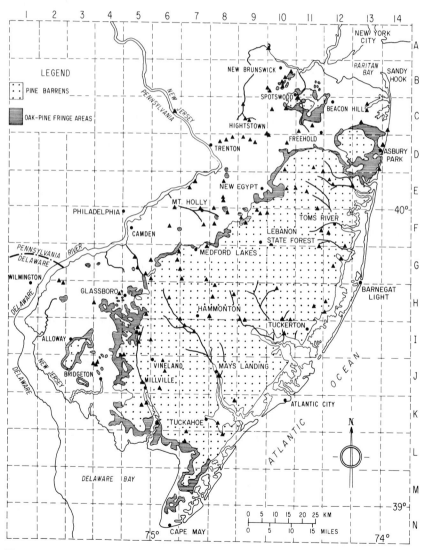

Fig. 5. Distribution of the chain pickerel (*Esox niger*, ▲). This species, found throughout New Jersey, is the only large native game fish in the Pine Barrens. See legend to Fig. 1.

tessellated darter occurs over open sand, usually in the central part of the stream, and the swamp darter occurs over mud or organic matter in the weedy backwater areas. In the absence of the tessellated darter, the swamp darter may be abundant over open sand. Collette (1962) further suggested that the artificial mill ponds and cranberry bogs of the Pine Barrens provide an ideal habitat for the swamp darter.

The eastern mudminnow (*Umbra pygmaea*), although restricted somewhat in distribution and primarily a coastal lowland inhabitant, in New Jersey is also common to the north, including the Raritan, Musconetcong, Pequest, and Paulins Kill drainages. In the Pine Barrens, the mudminnow is abundant and occupies a variety of habitats, but almost always is associated with vegetation. It has the ability to survive in stagnant, low-oxygen waters, since it also may breathe air (Black, 1945).

The chain pickerel (*Esox niger*) is found throughout New Jersey (Fig. 5), but is distinctive in the Pine Barrens as the only large native game fish. Although other game species have been introduced, they are not established in the typically acid Pine Barrens waters, and the chain pickerel remains a popular quarry for the sportsman. The smaller redfin (grass) pickerel (*Esox americanus*) also is common in the Pine Barrens but less so than the chain pickerel. The absence of other fish-eating fish may be due largely to their inability to survive or reproduce in acid waters, but the absence of some typical food species also may be a factor. Smith (1957) found that chain pickerel in the Pine Barrens fed primarily upon organisms utilized less in nonacid habitats, e.g., dragonfly larvae, crayfish, chubsuckers, and darters.

Other widely distributed species in New Jersey (including the Pine Barrens) are the American eel (*Anguilla rostrata*), the tadpole madtom (*Noturus gyrinus*), and the creek chubsucker (*Erimyzon oblongus*). The American eel may be more common outside the Pine Barrens, but it has been collected in substantial numbers at some localities in the Pines. The tadpole madtom is characteristic of dense vegetation and is present in relatively large numbers in the Pine Barrens, where aquatic plants are present in a slow-to-moderate current. This and several other "secretive" species of the Pine Barrens, such as bullheads and pirate perch, are nocturnal. The creek chubsucker is one of the few open-water, free-swimming fish in the Pine Barrens and as such is a major source of food for the chain pickerel (Smith, 1957). In contrast, the chubsucker is abundant in some northern New Jersey lakes, yet rarely is utilized by pickerel when other forage fishes are present.

PERIPHERAL SPECIES

Although virtually all waters are acid as they leave the Pine Barrens, soon after, they are buffered and become almost neutral or even slightly alkaline. Several fish widely distributed in New Jersey are relatively intolerant of acid waters and consequently are absent from typical Pine Barrens waters. However, some of these are common in the moderately acid or nonacid waters at the periphery of the Pine Barrens or in lakes or streams within the Pines where environmental modifications, such as agriculture, have reduced acidity. Important species are the golden shiner (*Notemigonus crysoleucas*), white sucker (*Catostomus commersoni*, Fig. 6), banded killifish (*Fundulus diaphanus*), mummichog (*Fundulus heteroclitus*), white perch (*Morone americana*), redbreast sunfish (*Lepomis auritus*), pumpkinseed (*Lepomis gibbosus*), and yellow perch (*Perca flavescens*), although several other species might be included. White perch are especially common in the tidal portion of larger rivers draining the Pine Barrens, such as the Mullica, Great Egg Harbor, and Maurice Rivers. This habitat also is important for

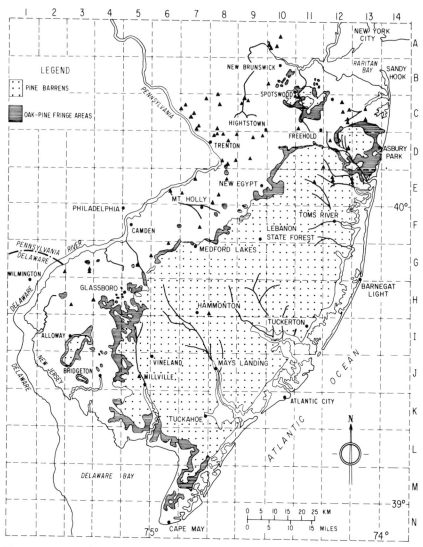

Fig. 6. Distribution of the white sucker (*Catostomus commersoni*, ▲). This species, characteristic of the periphery of the Pine Barrens, apparently does not feed at the low acidities typical of the Pine Barrens. See legend to Fig. 1.

several non-Pine Barrens fish, such as the white catfish (*Ictalurus catus*) and marine species that move into tidal freshwaters. Important species taken in the upper Great Egg Harbor River estuary are Atlantic menhaden (*Brevoortia tyrranus*), bay anchovy (*Anchoa mitchilli*), and hogchoker (*Trinectes maculatus*) (McClain, 1972). In addition, a number of small, brackish-water fishes are abundant in coastal salt marshes on the south and east and occasionally stray into freshwater streams draining the Pines, especially if tidal.

White perch, pumpkinseed, and yellow perch were stocked extensively in New Jersey waters prior to 1950, and their abundance in some Pine Barrens lakes may be related to this early stocking. However, in most acid-water lakes, these stockings were unsuccessful, and the species are not established, e.g., Horicon Lake, New Brooklyn Lake, and Oswego Lake (Smith, 1957). Attempts to neutralize the acidity of Nummy Lake during 1952 resulted in some pumpkinseed spawning that year, but during subsequent years the lake returned to its original acidity and further spawning of pumpkinseed was unsuccessful (Smith, 1957). Golden shiners also have been stocked as forage in some lakes and numerous individuals probably have been introduced as escaped "bait." The two species of *Fundulus* also are used commonly as bait in southern New Jersey and are dispersed in this way.

White suckers are common throughout New Jersey except for the Pine Barrens (Fig. 6). The species ceases to feed at pH <5.0 (Beamish, 1972), and thus is excluded from typical Pine Barrens waters.

The mosquitofish (*Gambusia affinis*) apparently is native to the extreme southern portion of New Jersey, but its widespread introduction for mosquito control renders this speculative (Gerberich, 1946). Collections from Cape May County in the Academy of Natural Sciences of Philadelphia were taken as early as 1907. Since New Jersey is the northern limit of its range, the mosquitofish may be excluded from most of the state, including the Pine Barrens, by low winter temperatures. However, it does not seem to thrive in extremely acid waters and may be limited further by acidity. The use of this fish in mosquito control in New Jersey probably is futile in view of the history of the species in the state. The desirability of using native species for such projects whenever possible bears emphasis. For example, Moore (1922) noted the importance of *Umbra pygmaea*, *Fundulus heteroclitus,* and *Lepomis gibbosus* in mosquito control. The availability of such native fishes should obviate introductions of nonnative species.

The brook trout (*Salvelinus fontinalis*) might be regarded as a peripheral Pine Barrens species, since it is indigenous to the state and may have occurred naturally in some streams draining the Pines. It is tolerant of quite low pH values (e.g., 4.3; Pyle, 1957), but requires low temperatures. Today, it is maintained in southern New Jersey primarily, if not exclusively, by stocking.

A number of other southern New Jersey fish occur occasionally in peripheral Pine Barrens waters, but generally are restricted to nonacid waters and are rare in the Pine Barrens. Examples are American brook lamprey (*Lampetra lamottei*), gizzard shad (*Dorosoma cepedianum*), silvery minnow (*Hybognathus nuchalis*), comely shiner (*Notropis amoenus*), satinfin shiner (*N. analostanus*), bridled shiner (*N. bifrenatus*), common shiner (*N. cornutus*), spottail shiner (*N. hudsonius*), swallowtail shiner (*N. procne*), bluntnose minnow (*Pimephales notatus*), blacknose dace (*Rhinichthys atratulus*), creek chub (*Semotilus atromaculatus*), fallfish (*Semotilus corporalis*), and margined madtom (*Noturus insignis*).

ANADROMOUS SPECIES

Several anadromous marine fish occur in coastal waters of New Jersey and move upstream into Pine Barrens rivers to spawn. Examples are the blueback herring (*Alosa aestivalis*), alewife (*A. pseudoharengus*), American shad (*A. sapidissima*), and striped bass (*Morone saxatilis*). Most probably are confined to the tidal portion of larger rivers and may never enter the higher acid streams. However, confirmed spawning runs of alewife have been reported for many Pine Barrens locations on the Maurice, Tuckahoe, Great Egg Harbor, Mullica, Toms, Manasquan, and Metedeconk River drainages, as well as some of the smaller drainages (unpublished report, New Jersey Division of Fish, Game and Shellfisheries). Such movements upstream may have been more extensive prior to construction of dams, which block virtually all of the streams leaving the Pine Barrens. Some Pine Barrens lakes were stocked with striped bass and alewife. Union Lake at Millville has yielded adult striped bass to fishermen, but there apparently has been no spawning in the lake (New Jersey Division of Fish and Game, 1951). Alewife were stocked in Batsto Lake during 1970 and 1971 (Pyle, 1971), but the present status of this population is unknown. The sea lamprey (*Petromyzon marinus*) also may spawn in Pine Barrens rivers, but there appear to be no records.

INTRODUCED SPECIES

Some 20–30 species of freshwater fish have been introduced into New Jersey waters. At least nine of these nonnative or exotic species have become naturalized and now are recognized as characteristic members of the state fauna. Important species which are well established as reproducing populations in the state are brown trout (*Salmo trutta*), goldfish (*Carassius auratus*), carp (*Cyprinus carpio*), rock bass (*Ambloplites rupestris*), bluegill sunfish (*Lepomis macrochirus*), smallmouth bass (*Micropterus dolomieui*), largemouth bass (*Micropterus salmoides*), white crappie (*Pomoxis annularis*), and black crappie (*Pomoxis nigromaculatus*). Of these, the rock bass, smallmouth bass, and white crappie apparently are absent from southern New Jersey except for some upland streams in Mercer, Middlesex, and Monmouth counties north of the Pine Barrens. The remaining six species are common in some peripheral locations in the Pine Barrens, but apparently are intolerant of the typical acid Pine Barrens waters.

Smallmouth bass was listed as occurring in the Pine Barrens (McCormick, 1970), but this apparently was based upon misidentifications of largemouth bass. Prior to 1950, however, both species of *Micropterus* were stocked in almost all lakes within the state. In most Pine Barrens lakes, these fish never were seen again and never were successful in spawning. The relatively high summer temperatures of shallow Pine

Barrens lakes may be as much a limiting factor for smallmouth bass as the high acidity (Scott and Crossman, 1973).

In contrast, the largemouth bass has become well established in most southern New Jersey lakes, except for the more acid waters of the Pine Barrens. Calabrese (1969) found that young largemouth bass could survive at acidities of pH 4.0, which would include most Pine Barrens lakes, but the species apparently is unable to reproduce successfully in such acid waters. The neutralization experiments on Nummy Lake in 1952 allowed some largemouth bass spawning during that year, but not in subsequent years, as the water gradually returned to its original acidity (Smith, 1957). Similar experiments elsewhere in the Pine Barrens have resulted in successful bass spawning (Stewart, 1972). The state has continued to stock this species on a limited scale at selected sites in southern New Jersey.

The bluegill sunfish and black crappie also are well established in most neutral or low-acid lakes at the periphery of the Pine Barrens. Both species were stocked extensively prior to 1950, and in recent years farm and park ponds have been stocked with bluegills in combination with largemouth bass.

Goldfish and carp have been present in the state since the late 1800's and are tolerant of a wide range of environmental conditions. However, since neither species appears to be tolerant of acid waters, they have not become established in most Pine Barrens lakes.

Three salmonid species are maintained in peripheral Pine Barrens locations by stocking and occasionally may spawn in some of the cooler streams of Middlesex, Monmouth, and Ocean counties. These are the brook trout (*Salvelinus fontinalis*), the brown trout (*Salmo trutta*), and the rainbow trout (*Salmo gairdneri*). The brook trout is a native New Jersey fish, but the brown trout was introduced from Europe and the rainbow trout from western North America. The three species are used almost exclusively in southern New Jersey for "put and take" fishing. Few probably survive past the year of their release. In general, the Pine Barrens waters that receive these fishes are town park ponds and lakes in the southern part of the state and streams of the Toms, Metedeconk, Manasquan, Shark, and South River drainages of Ocean, Monmouth, and Middlesex counties (New Jersey Division of Fish, Game and Shellfisheries, 1976).

Other species have been introduced in southern New Jersey at sites in the Pine Barrens, but most have been unsuccessful or only marginally successful. The state Division of Fish, Game and Shellfisheries presently stocks the fathead minnow (*Pimephales promelas*) as a forage fish and large numbers of channel catfish (*Ictalurus punctatus*) in some parts of southern New Jersey (New Jersey Division of Fish, Game and Shellfisheries, 1976).

ZOOGEOGRAPHY OF PINE BARRENS FISHES

The characteristic Pine Barrens fish are primarily Atlantic Coastal Plain species that reach their northern limit in New Jersey or only slightly farther north. Other common Pine Barrens fish are distributed widely throughout eastern North America in a variety of habitats but generally are characteristic of sluggish streams with dense vegetation. These correspond to the two groups noted by Smith (1960) as characteristic of acidotrophic waters: the first group is highly specialized and restricted to Coastal Plain waters; the second group is very adaptable and capable of living in many types of waters. In contrast, peripheral species tend to be more characteristic of upland streams and intolerant of acid water.

The affinities of the Pine Barrens fish fauna are with the warm, temperate, lowland Coastal Plain region of southeastern North America and represent a northward extension of this region. It is easy to visualize a northward dispersal of these fish along the Coastal Plain as glacial periods ended and the climate of New Jersey warmed from one which supported boreal forests or tundra (Buell, 1970). No significant physical barriers that might have prevented such northward movement appear to exist. Physical barriers preventing dispersal of common species throughout New Jersey also are lacking, and it seems that the present distribution patterns are determined primarily by chemical and biological factors rather than physical forces (Smith, 1953), although climatic factors also may be important. The lack of physical barriers is demonstrated further by the distribution of many coastal species north of New Jersey. Lowland coastal plain habitat is poorly represented north of New Jersey, however, so most of these species occur only sporadically to the north.

Three major factors apparently affect the distribution of the characteristic Pine Barrens fishes: (1) requirement for sluggish streams or standing water with dense vegetation; (2) competition from similar or related species; and (3) tolerance of highly acid waters. The first is especially important, since these are slow-swimming, secretive fishes not adapted to living in currents. The second factor may be important, since the typical Pine Barrens fish tend to be retiring and unobtrusive, and could be affected adversely by more active species with similar nesting or feeding habits. The third factor is important, since the Pine Barrens acid waters serve as a refugium for acid-tolerant species which would be out-competed in less acid waters by other species, which in turn cannot survive in the acidity of the Pine Barrens.

SUMMARY

The Pine Barrens fish fauna is depauperate, with four major groups containing approximately 36 species, and only 16 species indigenous to the typical acid waters. These 16 species are either (a) characteristic of sluggish lowland Coastal Plain streams or (b) widely distributed in many habitats in eastern North America. These fish are noted for their tolerance of high acidities; however, slow-moving water, food availability, and reduced competition also may be important factors. About ten other species common in southern New Jersey occur in less acid, peripheral Pine Barrens locations. Six introduced species are established in peripheral Pine Barrens locations. Four anadromous marine fish spawn in Pine Barrens streams. The Pine Barrens fish fauna is primarily a northward extension of the warm temperate Coastal Plain fish fauna of southeastern North America.

ACKNOWLEDGMENTS

I thank the following individuals who contributed to this article: John Graham, who made available his extensive notes on Pine Barrens centrarchids; Walter S. Murawski, who provided valuable unpublished data from the State Freshwater Fisheries Laboratory; James E. Böhlke who made available fish collections and catalogs of the Academy of Natural Sciences of Philadelphia for plotting distribution maps; and the many Rutgers University students who have assisted in my fish-collecting in New Jersey.

REFERENCES

Beamish, R. J. (1972). Lethal pH for the white sucker *Catostomus commersoni* (Lacépédé). *Trans. Am. Fish. Soc.* **101**(2), 355–358.

Black, V. S. (1945). Gas exchange in the swimbladder of the mudminnow. *Proc. Nova Scotian Inst. Sci.* **21**(1-2), 1–22.

Breder, C. M., Jr., and Rosen, D. E. (1966). "Modes of Reproduction in Fishes." Nat. Hist. Press, Garden City, New York.

Buell, M. F. (1970). Time of origin of New Jersey Pine Barrens bogs. *Bull. Torrey Bot. Club* **97**, 105–108.

Calabrese, A. (1969). Effect of acids and alkalies on survival of bluegills and largemouth bass. *U.S. Bur. Sport Fish. Wildl., Tech. Pap.* No. 42, 1–10.

Collette, B. B. (1962). The swamp darters of the subgenus *Hololepis* (Pisces, Percidae). *Tulane Stud. Zool.* **9**(4), 115–211.

Fikslin, R. J., and Montgomery, J. D. (1971). An ecological survey of a stream in the New Jersey Pine Barrens. *Bull. N.J. Acad. Sci.* **16**(1-2), 8–13.

Fowler, H. W. (1904). Description of a new race of *Notropis chalybaeus* from New Jersey. *Proc. Acad. Nat. Sci. Philadelphia* **56**, 239–240.

Fowler, H. W. (1906). The fishes of New Jersey. *N.J. State Mus., Annu. Rep.* 1905, Part II, pp. 34–477.

Gerberich, J. B. (1946). An annotated bibliography of papers relating to the control of mosquitoes by the use of fish. *Am. Midl. Nat.* **36**, 87–131.

Gosline, W. A. (1971). "Functional Morphology and Classification of Teleostean Fishes." Univ. Press of Hawaii, Honolulu.

Hubbs, C. L., and Lagler, K. F. (1958). "Fishes of the Great Lakes Region." Univ. of Michigan Press, Ann Arbor.

McClain, J. F., Jr. (1972). Fish studies. *In* "Studies of the Great Egg Harbor River and Bay." *N.J. Dep. Environ. Prot., Div. Fish, Game Shellfish., Misc. Rep.* No. 8M, pp. 1–54.

McCormick, J. (1970). The Pine Barrens. A preliminary ecological inventory. *N.J. State Mus., Res. Rep.* No. 2.

Marshall, N. (1947). Studies on the life history and ecology of *Notropis chalybaeus* (Cope). *Q. J. Fla. Acad. Sci.* **9**(3-4), 163–188.

Moore, G. A. (1968). Fishes. *In* "Vertebrates of the United States" (W. F. Blair, A. P. Blair, P. Brodkorb, F. R. Cagle, and G. A. Moore, eds.), 2nd Ed., pp. 21–165. McGraw-Hill, New York.

Moore, J. P. (1922). Use of fishes for control of mosquitoes in northern fresh waters of the United States. *Rep. U.S. Comm. Fish. 1922 (Appendix IV), U.S. Dep. Commer., Bur. Fish., Doc.* No. 923.

New Jersey Division of Fish and Game (1951). "Lakes and Ponds," Fish. Surv. Rep. No. 1. N.J. Dep. Conserv. Econ. Dev., Trenton, New Jersey.

New Jersey Division of Fish, Game and Shellfisheries (1976). "List of Waters Stocked." N.J. Dep. Environ. Prot., Trenton, New Jersey.

Pyle, A. B. (1957). Preliminary report of studies on the ability of trout to withstand various acidities in New Jersey streams. *N.J. Dep. Environ. Prot., Div. Fish, Game Shellfish., Misc. Rep.* No. 20.

Pyle, A. B. (1971). "Annual Report." Freshwater Res. Dev. Sec., Bur. Fish., Div. Fish, Game Shellfish., N.J. Dep. Environ. Prot., Trenton, New Jersey.

Quinn, J. P. (1967a). The strange and beautiful fishes of the Pine Barrens. *Trop. Fish Hobbyist* **16**(3), 26–27, 29, 37, 41, 45.

Quinn, J. P. (1976b). The exotic native. *Aquarium (Farmingdale, N.Y.)* **1**(2), 4–5, 44–45, 64.

Rhodehamel, E. C. (1970). A hydrologic analysis of the New Jersey Pine Barrens region. *N.J. Div. Water Policy Supply, Water Resour. Circ.* No. 22.

Rhodehamel, E. C. (1973). Geology and water resources of the Wharton Tract and the Mullica River Basin in southern New Jersey. *N.J. Div. Water Resour., Spec. Rep.* No. 36.

Schwartz, F. J. (1961). Food, age, growth and morphology of the blackbanded sunfish, *Enneacanthus c. chaetodon,* in Smithville Pond, Maryland, *Chesapeake Sci.* **2**(1-2), 82–88.

Scott, W. B., and Crossman, E. J. (1973). "Freshwater Fishes of Canada." Fish. Res. Board Can., Ottawa.

Smith, R. F. (1952). Neutralization experiments in certain acid ponds in New Jersey. *Proc. Annu. Conf. Natl. Lime Assoc., 50th* pp. 89–95.

Smith, R. F. (1953). Some observations on the distribution of fishes in New Jersey. *In* "Lakes and Ponds," Fish. Surv. Rep. No. 2, pp. 165–174. N.J. Dep. Conserv. Econ. Dev., Div. Fish Game, Trenton, New Jersey.

Smith, R. F. (1957). "Lakes and Ponds," Fish. Surv. Rep. No. 3. N.J. Dep. Conserv. Econ. Dev., Div. Fish Game, Trenton, New Jersey.

Smith, R. F. (1960). An ecological study of an acid pond in the New Jersey Coastal Plain. Ph.D. Thesis, Rutgers Univ., New Brunswick, New Jersey.

Stewart, R. W. (1971). Studies on standing crops of fish in New Jersey Lakes and Ponds. *N.J. Dep. Environ. Prot., Div. Fish, Game Shellfish., Misc. Rep.* No. 34.

Stewart, R. W. (1972). Neutralization experiments. *N.J. Dep. Environ. Prot., Div. Fish, Game Shellfish., Misc. Rep.* No. 35.

Sweeney, E. F. (1972). The systematics and distribution of the centrarchid fish tribe Enneacanthini. *Diss. Abstr. Int. B* **33**(4), 1408.

29

Arthropods of the Pine Barrens

HOWARD P. BOYD AND PHILIP E. MARUCCI

INTRODUCTION

Arthropods are animals which have an external skeleton, bodies usually divided into two or three regions, and paired, jointed appendages. Insects are arthropods further characterized by having three distinct body regions (head, thorax, abdomen), one pair of compound eyes, a pair of antennae, three pairs of segmented legs, and usually one or two pairs of wings.

Smith (1910) referred to the insect fauna of the Pine Barrens as "rich" in species, but it may be characterized more appropriately as unique. The richness designation is quite appropriate for groups such as moths, whose larvae (caterpillars) feed on the abundant pine and oak trees; for gall wasps, which lay their eggs in the many species of oaks; and for antlions, tiger beetles, and velvet ants, which inhabit open sandy areas.

On the other hand, since half of all insect species are dependent upon plants for food (Brues, 1972), the somewhat modest flowering plant diversity in the Barrens limits other insect groups. For example, in over 50 years of collecting aphids in New Jersey, 242 species were found on 313 different plants in the state, but in the Pine Barrens only 40 species were recorded (Leonard, 1972, 1974).

Another limiting factor is the high acidity of Pine Barrens soils, cedar and *Sphagnum* bogs, and surface waters of ponds and streams. Of 55 species of mosquitoes found in New Jersey, only 19 breed in the Barrens (L. E. Hagmann, personal communication). This acid environment, in combination with a scarcity of shell-building calcium and the low levels of magnesium and potash in the soils, may be responsible for the virtual absence of earthworms and snails (McCormick, 1970). Thus, certain predaceous insects, such as snail-eating beetles (*Scaphinotus* spp.), may be expected to be either rare or entirely absent.

Some species are considered characteristic of the region. Although present elsewhere, these rarely reach the abundance of Pine Barrens populations. Included among these characteristic species are several underwing moths (*Catocala herodias gerhardi* B. and B., *C. gracilis* f. *lemmeri* Mayfield, and *C. sordida* f. *engelhardti* Lemmer): a noctuid moth [*Lithophane (Graptolitha) lemmeri* B. and B.]; the buck moth, [*Hemileuca*

505

maia (Drury)] and the silkworm moth (*Citheronia sepulchralis* G. and R.) (J. W. Cadbury, personal communication). Several small hairstreak, elfin, copper, and dusky wing butterflies and skippers also are characteristic and are listed later in this chapter.

The original descriptions of many species were based on collections in Pine Barrens locations, which thus are type localities for the species. In one family of plant bugs (Miridae), at least 15 species have been described from the area (A. G. Wheeler, personal communication).

A few insects seem to be restricted to the Pine Barrens and, so far as presently known, are found nowhere else. Two such endemic species are the moths *Agrotis buchholzi* B. and B. and *Crambus daeckellus* Haimbach. (J. G. Franclemont, A. B. Klots, and D. F. Schweitzer, personal communication).

Although "the species on the whole resemble those of more southern states" (Smith, 1910), many species reach either the northern or southern limits of their ranges in the Barrens. Probably more species reach their northern than their southern limits here. One reaching its northern limit is the leaf-cutting ant [*Trachymyrmex septentrionalis* (McC.)]. At least eight species of tabanid flies (Diptera) also reach their northern limits here, while two tabanids with northern ranges reach their southern limits of coastal distribution here (L. L. Pechuman, personal communication).

The Pine Barrens have long been a favorite collecting area for entomologists, especially those from New York City and Philadelphia. In the early 1900's, railroads took New York collectors to Lakewood, Lakehurst, and stations down the line and Philadelphia collectors into locations in the southern parts of the Barrens, such as DaCosta. Few places in North America have been collected as thoroughly as Lakehurst.

Despite this, there is a dearth of literature specifically treating the insects of the Pine Barrens. The only study published on the overall subject (Weiss and West, 1924) is based on March–October insect collections in a four-hectare (ten-acre) dry woods and an adjoining 1.6-ha (four-acre) open area near Lakehurst (Table I). Approximately 85% of all species were captured in flight, on the ground, or by sweeping vegetation, and about half of these were Hymenoptera and Coleoptera. Considering the differences in the areas sampled, the total diversity of species and families and the number of species in most orders were rather alike in the woods and the open area. Plant eaters were most abundant in both habitats (Table II). The percentages of plant-eating, predatory, and parasitic insects were nearly the same for both woods and open areas, although more pollinators were found in open areas where flowers were more abundant. The only other references that specifically refer to Pine Barrens insects are Boyd, 1973; Darlington, 1952; Leng, 1902; Leonard, 1974; McCormick, 1970; and McCormick and Andresen, 1960.

Arthropods are by far the most abundant fauna in the Pine Barrens, and a mere listing of species would take volumes. Thus, we review here only a very few species, considered in groups under the following headings: (I) arthropods other than insects; (II) insects found on vegetation in pine and oak woods; (III) insects found in shrub and semiopen areas with scattered vegetation; (IV) insects of open, sandy areas; (V) insects more often heard than seen; (VI) insects found under bark and in dead trees and old

ABLE I   Insect Diversity and Microhabitats in a Woods and an Open Area[a]

Insect order[b]	On flowers		Taken flying or sweeping		Other microhabitats		Total no. families		Total no. species	
	Woods	Open	Woods	Open[d]	Woods	Open	Woods	Open	Woods	Open
Odonata	—	—	3	6	—	—	1	2	3	6
Orthoptera	—	—	21	18	1[e]	—	4	3	22	18
Isoptera	—	—	—	—	1[e]	—	1	—	1	—
Psocoptera[c]	—	—	2	—	—	—	1	—	2	—
Thysanoptera	—	—	1	—	1[f]	—	1	—	2	—
Hemiptera	2	1	21	19	1[e]	—	5	7	24	20
Homoptera	—	—	31	22	—	—	7	6	31	22
Neuroptera	—	—	4	1	—	—	3	1	4	1
Coleoptera	4	7	96	43	20[g]	—	28	15	120	50
Lepidoptera	—	2	34	19	—	—	16	10	34	21
Diptera	4	15	37	21	—	—	20	12	41	36
Hymenoptera	6	14	87	60	6[h]	—	21	25	99	74
Totals	16	39	337	209	30	—	108	81	383	248

[a] Woods sampled are ten acres of dry wood, (⅔ pitch pine; ⅓ mixed oak; scrub oak abundant) including a emi–wooded section; open area of shrubs and herbs is an adjoining tour acres. Near Lakehurst, March–October 1922 (Weiss and West, 1924). Number of species is given except as otherwise noted.

[b] Odonata: dragonflies and damselflies; Orthoptera: grasshoppers, crickets, cockroaches, walking sticks, tc.; Isoptera: termites; Psocoptera: psocids; Thysanoptera: thrips; Hemiptera: true bugs; Homoptera: cicadas, oppers, aphids, etc.; Neuroptera: antlions, lacewings, etc.; Coleoptera: beetles; Lepidoptera: moths and utterflies; Diptera: flies and mosquitoes; Hymenoptera: ants, wasps, bees, etc.

[c] Corrodentia of Weiss and West (1924).

[d] Includes species collected on the ground.

[e] In dead stumps, under bark.

[f] In fungi.

[g] Thirteen in dead stumps, under bark and seven in fungi.

[h] One in dead stumps, under bark and five as a result of sifting.

TABLE II   Food Habits of Insects in the Pine Barrens[a]

		Plant eaters	Scaven- gers	Pred- ators	Para- sites	Polli- nators	Totals
Woods	No. insect species	171	79	69	53	8	381
	Percentage (%)	45	21	18	14	2	100
Open area	No. insect species	102	25	59	43	17	246
	Percentage (%)	41	10	24	18	7	100

[a] From Weiss and West (1924). See Table I footnotes.

stumps; and (VII) insects found in aquatic and semiaquatic habitats. The characteristics of habitat, habit, presence, and abundance given below refer to the Pine Barrens.

ARTHROPODS OTHER THAN INSECTS

Wood Ticks (Acarina: Ixodidae)

Wood ticks are pests of reptiles, birds, and mammals. The most common species is the American dog tick [*Dermacentor variabilis* (Say)]. It is small (10–12 mm), oval, and hard bodied, having eight legs and a protruding head. It is reddish brown with whitish markings and is most common during spring and early summer. People walking through low-growing shrubs or other vegetation, especially along deer trails, may find one or more ticks on their clothes or their body. Usually they can be picked off easily. A small percentage of ticks in the Barrens may transmit Rocky Mountain spotted fever.

Harvest Mites, Chiggers, or Redbugs (Acarina: Trombiculidae)

These reddish mites also are pests of various vertebrates but are so small that they seldom are seen. During immature stages, they crawl on vegetation from which they attach themselves to any passing host. On humans, they seem to prefer areas where clothing is tight and their bites cause considerable irritation. The common chigger is *Eutrombicula alfreddugesi* (Oudemans).

Spiders (Araneida)

Spiders have bodies that are separated into two distinct regions. Wolf spiders (Lycosidae) are hunters that chase their prey and commonly run over the ground. Most are dark brown and can be recognized by the arrangement of the eyes; that is, four small eyes in a frontal row, two very large eyes behind these, and two medium-sized eyes in a third row. The female carries her egg sac beneath her abdomen until the young spiderlings emerge and climb on her back.

The black widow spider [*Latrodectus mactans* Fab. (Oxyopodae)] rarely is found in the open woods but may be found under boards, in woodpiles, or around piles of cranberry-picking boxes. The female, which often eats the male after mating, thus becoming a "widow," is shiny coal black, 12–13 mm long, and bears a conspicuous red hourglass-shaped spot on the underside of the body. The male is much smaller, with variously shaped red or yellow spots on the abdomen. Although poisonous, it is not aggressive and will bite only in self defense.

Harvestment or Daddy-Long-Legs (Phalangida)

Often mistakenly called spiders, daddy-long-legs are easily recognized by their single, compact, oval body and their extremely long, thin legs. They are common on vegetation and feed on plant juices and dead insects, but some may feed on living insects.

Sowbugs and Pillbugs (Isopoda)

These arthropods are small, measuring up to 10 mm in length, are light gray to slate colored, soft bodied and distinctly segmented, and have seven pairs of legs. They are found hiding in dark, protected places, such as about the bases of plants and under boards, bark, and rotting logs.

Millipedes and Centipedes

These arthropods are found under bark and in and under old logs and forest litter. Millipedes (Diplopoda) are elongate, and wormlike in form, with many body segments, each having two pairs of short legs. They move with a slow, flowing motion and often curl up when disturbed. Centipedes (Chilopoda) have elongated, flattened bodies with many segments, each with one pair of long legs. They move rapidly and usually scurry away when uncovered. Millipedes feed entirely on decaying vegetation and aid in the breakdown of decaying wood into humus. Centipedes are predaceous and feed on small insects and other animals.

INSECTS FOUND ON VEGETATION IN PINE AND OAK WOODS

Grasshoppers (Orthoptera: Acrididae)

Grasshoppers have enlarged hindlegs and two pairs of wings with antennae usually shorter than the body. The forewings usually are long, narrow, and somewhat thickened. The membranous hindwings used in flight often are brightly colored and are folded fanwise under the front wings when at rest. Grasshoppers are plant feeders with chewing mouthparts.

The post oak locust (*Dendrotettix quercus* Packard) has an unusual life history. First known in Texas, it was discovered in the New Jersey Pine Barrens in 1907 (Davis, 1912; Rehn and Rehn, 1938), its only currently known location along the Atlantic seaboard. It occurs in limited areas during June–August, but at irregular intervals the normal population has undergone several massive population explosions (Rehn and Rehn, 1938; Rehn, 1946), the last record of which was in 1954 (McCormick and Andresen, 1960). This gaily colored insect is grayish with a prominent broad, horizontal, black stripe on the sides of its midbody (pronotum). The enlarged jumping segment (femur) of its leg is bright orange to reddish in color. The knee of the leg is black, and there is a narrow pale band between the reddish shank and the knee. Although normally a winged insect, during population explosions only about 20% of the adults have fully developed wings while 80% have short, stubby nonfunctional wings less than one-quarter the normal length (Rehn and Rehn, 1938). During outbreaks, the insects climb the trunks of trees, mainly oaks, in great numbers and feed on foliage so extensively that they literally strip the forest canopy. During the year following some of these outbreaks, however, scarcely an individual can be found.

Walking Sticks (Orthoptera: Phasmatidae)

Walking sticks are slender, elongate, sticklike insects with very long antennae. All six legs also are long and slender. Our only species, *Diapheromera femorata* (Say), is wingless and measures 50 mm or more in length. It is pale green when immature, becoming dark green, brown, or gray when adult. These odd, slow-moving creatures usually are found in trees and shrubs and bear a striking resemblance to twigs, a form of mimicry which probably has protective value. Walking sticks may occur in abundance in our oak–pine woods feeding on the foliage of many plants, especially oaks.

Long-Horned Beetles (Coleoptera: Cerambycidae)

Long-horned beetles are elongate, cylindrical insects with hard wing covers and antennae which sometimes are twice as long as the body. Although plant feeders as adults, most larvae are wood borers, many of which are a food source for woodpeckers. A common species is *Prionus laticollis* (Drury), a very large (up to 50 mm), stout, jet black beetle found walking along the ground or attracted to lights at night. Their larvae bore and feed in roots of oak, pine, and blueberry. Another conspicuous prionid is the light brown *Orthosoma brunneus* (Forst.), which is 25–50 mm long. The round-headed borers of the sawyer beetles (*Monochamus* spp.) work in the inner bark and heartwood of dead and dying pines (Baker, 1972). Adult beetles are brownish to black speckled with grayish markings and attain lengths up to 30 mm, with an additional 30 mm of antennae.

Weevils or Snout Beetles (Coleoptera: Curculionidae)

Weevils usually have well-developed beaks with antennae arising about midway on the snout. The beaks of nut and acorn weevils (*Curculio* spp.) are decurved, slender, and very long, sometimes longer than the body. Adults use these beaks to bore holes in acorns, which serve both as food and as cavities into which females lay their eggs. Several species are common on the various oaks. Two other common weevils in the area are the blueberry blossom weevil (*Anthonomus musculus* Say) and the plum curculio [*Conotrachelus nenuphar* (Hbst.)].

Moths (Lepidoptera)

Most moths are readily recognized by the scales on their wings, body, and legs that come off like dust on one's fingers when handling the insect. Antennae of moths either are thread-, or comblike, or feathery, but never clubbed or knobbed on the end. Moths usually rest with their wings folded over their back or outstretched in a horizontal position. Mouthparts arise from beneath the head and form a tube for sucking liquid food. This tube is coiled up when not in use. Most moths are night flyers and may be attracted to lights or by sugaring. Caterpillars of moths, an immature (larval) stage in their development, have chewing mouthparts, and most are plant feeders. Many of these caterpillars are a major source of food for birds, especially during the nesting season.

Several very beautiful moths are characteristic of the Pine Barrens. Underwing moths (Noctuidae) are so named because the hindwings in many species are brilliantly colored in reds, oranges, or yellows. A few have black wings. Forewings are usually in shades of gray, black, brown, and white, often closely resembling the bark of trees. Of the underwings, perhaps the best known among lepidopterists is *Catocala herodias gerhardi* B. and B., with brilliant crimson on hindwings banded with jet black. Its forewings are marked in a way that resembles dead pine needles, with a broad whitish streak along the leading edge. It occurs in July and has a wingspread of 55–65 mm (J. W. Cadbury, personal communication). A medium-sized (30–35 mm) noctuid moth that closely resembles the *Catocala* underwings is *Drasteria graphica atlantica* B. and McD. It is gray with forewings marked with black and hindwings light orange with two black bands. It is a characteristic Pine Barrens species and sometimes may be flushed during the day in sandy areas during May and June.

Giant silkworm and royal moths (Saturniidae) are the largest (up to 150 mm) moths, and most are conspicuously colored and many have transparent eyespots in the wings. The next three species are characteristic of the Pines. The buck moth, [*Hemileuca maia* (Drury)], is a day-flying moth, a habit which is unusual. It flies on sunny days in October and early November when leaves are falling. It is grayish black with a white band crossing the central portion of all four wings and has an eye spot in the white band of each wing. The male has a brick red tuft at the tip of the abdomen. The wingspread is 40–70 mm. Masses of larvae often are seen feeding on oak branches during May and June. The pine devil moth (*Citheronia sepulchralis* Gr. and Rob.) is colored a dark ash gray brown, but the hindwings are flushed with rose pink toward the base. Adults occur in June and July. It is called the pine devil because of the menacing appearance of its horned larva. It feeds on various species of pine. The orange-striped oakworm [*Anisota senatoria* (Smith and Abb.)] periodically denudes large areas of both shrub and white oak. The mature caterpillar (up to 60 mm) is black with eight orange-yellow stripes running parallel along the body and is densely covered with spines. Other large saturniids are the cecropia [*Platysamia cecropia* (L.)], promethea [*Callosamia promethea* (Drury)], polyphemus [*Antheraea polyphemus* (Cram.)], luna [*Actias luna* (L.)], io [*Automeris io* (Fab.)], and imperial [*Eacles imperialis* (Drury)].

Gypsy moth [*Porthetria dispar* (L.)] (Liparidae) is an introduced pest in oak woods. Males are smaller than females, are brownish, and fly readily. Females measure up to 60 mm, are white with black markings, and are too heavy to fly. Females lay their eggs on tree trunks and in other protected places. The egg masses may be recognized by their hairy, light brownish covering and are easily destroyed. In spring, the blue- and red-spotted, hairy caterpillars emerge and often defoliate trees completely.

Cankerworms, measuring worms, or inchworms (Geometridae) are looping caterpillars that feed on oaks and other trees and shrubs. The spring cankerworm [*Paleacrita vernata* (Peck)] is a brown- to black-colored worm with a single yellow stripe on each side of the body. The fall cankerworm [*Alsophila pometaria* (Harris)], is light green, gray, or brownish black with one yellow and three white stripes on each side. These caterpillars, which reach a size of about 25 mm and occur every year, periodically become very abundant, feeding on trees over large acreages. In such outbreaks, large predaceous ground beetles (Coleoptera: Carabidae) often climb the trees to feed on the caterpillars, an excellent example of natural control. Two species of these caterpillar hunters are *Calosoma scrutator* (Fab.), which is 28–30 mm long, and *C. wilcoxi* LeC., measuring 18 mm. The wing covers (elytra) of both are metallic green with reddish margins.

A small (18-mm) leafroller, *Exentera spoliana* (Clem.) (Tortricidae), has gray wings with strong whitish contrasts and two small blackish areas. It is abundant just before the leaves appear, sometimes flying in multitudes at every step and settling on bare twigs and brush (Weiss and West, 1924). Leafrollers are so named because the caterpillars roll the edges of leaves to form enclosures in which they rest and from which they emerge to feed.

The greenish-golden larvae of the gold-striped leaftier (*Machimia tentoriferella* Clem.) (Oecophoridae) often are as common on oak leaves as oak galls and are easy to find. The wormlike larva makes a web on the underside of a leaf along the midrib and then folds the edge of the leaf over to form a tubular shelter in which it feeds (Schaffner, 1959).

The saddleback caterpillar [*Sibine stimulea* (Clem.)] (Limacodidae), is a very striking larva which has a large green patch on its back resembling a saddle cloth and an oval purple brown spot in the center that looks like a saddle. The sides of the body are densely covered with sharp, pointed spines, which, if touched, break off in one's skin and produce irritating reactions. It feeds on oaks and other deciduous trees and shrubs.

Pine Sawflies (Hymenoptera: Diprionidae)

These are small (12 mm or less), stout-bodied, wasp-like insects whose abdomens are broadly joined to the midbody (thorax). Their larvae look like those of Lepidoptera, but have more pro-(false) legs. The larva of the European pine sawfly [*Neodiprion sertifer* (Geoff.)] has a shiny black head, and its body is light green with two longitudinal stripes of dark gray. Larvae of both this species and the redheaded pine sawfly [*N. lecontei* (Fitch)] feed on the needles of pines, often clustering near the ends of the branches (Boyd, 1953; Soraci, 1941).

Gall Wasps (Hymenoptera: Cynipidae)

Gall wasps are small insects, mostly black in color, with a shiny, compressed abdomen. These are largely parasitic upon plants. The insects themselves are not as noticeable as the various plant galls they cause on vegetation. Most galls are abnormal plant growths produced by chemicals associated with a gall wasp's egg inserted into the plant and the minute larva which develops from that egg. Each gall wasp species lays its egg on a particular part of a specific host plant and causes the development of a distinctively shaped gall that encloses the egg and developing larva. Oak trees are favored host plants for gall wasps, and since several oak species are common in the Barrens, gall wasps and their more evident gall growths are abundant. The large (up to 50 mm) oak apple [*Amphibolips confluenta* (Harr.)] is one of the most conspicuous of the leaf galls (H. V. Cornell, personal communication).

INSECTS FOUND IN SHRUB AND SEMI-OPEN AREAS WITH SCATTERED VEGETATION

Grasshoppers (Orthoptera: Acrididae)

Included in this group are several species common in open areas. One of the most conspicuous is the Carolina grasshopper [*Dissosteira carolina* (L.)]. Its hindwings are black with a pale yellow border, and it makes a crackling sound with its wings when in flight.

Plant, Leaf, and Stink Bugs (Hemiptera)

These are small, soft-bodied, oval, or slightly elongate insects that are somewhat flattened above. Many people refer to all insects and some other arthropods as "bugs," but the only true bugs are those whose membranous wing tips overlap, and whose feeding is accomplished by piercing with a beak that arises from under the front of the head and extends back between the legs. Usually colored in mottled greens and browns, some may be strikingly marked with red, orange, and black bands and spots. Plant bugs (Miridae) are abundant on vegetation in both woods and open areas, and a common species is *Lygus pratensis* (L.). Stink bugs (Pentatomidae) are noted for the pungent odor they emit when disturbed. A common species is the bright green *Acrosternum bilare* (Say).

Leafhoppers (Homoptera: Cicadelidae)

Leafhoppers are small (usually less than 13 mm), elongate insects that usually taper toward the back. The head is short, blunt, and more or less crescent shaped. They feed by piercing plant tissues with a beak arising from under the back of the head, its tip projecting between the front legs. Antennae are short and bristlelike. Hindlegs are long, adapted for jumping, and have one or more rows of small spines on the lower leg (tibia). They are variously marked, many with a beautiful color pattern like that of the red-banded leafhopper [*Graphocephala coccinea* (Forst.)], which has reddish wings striped with bright green. Other common Pine Barrens species are *Scaphytopius magdalensis* (Prov.), *Gyponana octolineata* Say, and *Macrosteles divisus* (Uhler).

Leafhoppers are common on all types of vegetation, including trees, shrubs, grasses, flowers, and herbaceous plants. They feed on juices which they suck from the leaves of food plants. Some species cause damage to vegetation and a few are vectors of viral plant diseases.

Froghoppers or Spittlebugs (Homoptera: Cercopidae)

Froghoppers are small, hopping insects similar to leafhoppers, but have only one or two stout spines on their hind tibia. They usually are brown or gray in color. Immature spittlebugs surround themselves with protective masses of frothy bubbles in the axils of leaves and on blades of grass. The adult pine spittlebug [*Aphrophora parallela* (Say)] has sloped wings with white bands bordered by parallel black bands on each side. The nymphs within the spittles have scarlet-colored eyes and a salmon orange body color. This sap sucker is one of the most common insects on pines (Spears, 1941).

Ladybird Beetles (Coleoptera: Coccinellidae)

These are small (10 mm or less), oval, and convex insects that have the hard wing covers (elytra) typical of beetles. They are often brightly colored, either red or yellow with black spots or black with red or yellow spots. Most ladybird beetles are predaceous, both as larvae and as adults. They feed chiefly on aphids, plant lice, and scale insects, and thus most are regarded as economically beneficial insects. Some common ladybird beetles are the convergent *Hippodamia convergens* Guer, the nine-spotted *Coccinella novemnotata* Hbst., the fifteen-spotted *Anatis quindecimpunctata* (Oliv.), and the two-spotted *Adalia bipunctata* (L.).

Leaf Beetles (Coleoptera: Chrysomelidae)

This is a large group of small (usually under 13 mm), oval beetles with hard wing covers. Their antennae are rarely as long as the body, and the segments of the antennae usually become gradually stouter and larger toward the tip. Many are brightly colored. Leaf beetles always are found on vegetation and usually feed on foliage and flowers. They are common in both woods and open areas. Two common species are the metallic green dogbane beetle [*Chrysochus auratus* (Fab.)] and the blueberry flea beetle (*Altica sylvia* Malloch).

Butterflies (Lepidoptera)

Like moths, butterflies are covered with scales. Their mouthparts also are similar to the moths' but butterflies differ in that their antennae are threadlike and clubbed or knobbed at the end. Butterflies are day fliers and at rest usually hold their wings together in a vertical position. The first three butterflies presented are conspicuous, beautiful, and widespread both inside and outside the Barrens. The wings of the mourning cloak [*Nymphalis antiopa* (L.)] (Nymphalidae) are a rich, deep maroon with a straw-colored border and a submarginal row of blue spots. It usually is the first butterfly to occur in the spring freshly emerged from hibernation, and often is seen with its wings expanded in sunny spots on tree trunks or on leaves of the forest floor. It has a wingspread of 65–75 mm. Swallowtail butterflies (Papilionidae) are named for the taillike projections on their hindwings. The large yellow and black tiger swallowtail (*Papilio glaucus* L.), with a wingspread of 75–125 mm, is one of our most familiar and conspicuous butterflies. It has a strong sailing flight, is attracted to flowers, and inhabits both woods and open areas. The spicebush swallowtail (*P. troilus* L.) is blackish, with a row of small yellowish spots along the margins of the frontwings and extensive blue-gray areas in the rear half of the hindwings. It has a wingspread of 100–125 mm and inhabits both wooded and open areas. Its caterpillar (up to 50 mm long) is green, and behind the head there is a pair of large, orange, black-centered eyespots, behind which is another, smaller pair. It has chewing mouthparts and feeds on spicebush (*Lindera benzoin*) and sassafras (*Sassafras albidum*).

Other beautiful but smaller butterflies that are particularly characteristic of the Pine Barrens are Hessel's hairstreak (*Mitoura hesseli* R. and Z.), brown elfin (*Incisalia augustinus* Westwood), hoary elfin (*I. polios* C. and W.), Henry's elfin (*I. henrici* G. and R.), frosted elfin (*I. irus* Godart), pine elfin (*I. niphon* Hubner) and bog copper (*Lycaena epixanthe* B. and LeC.). Characteristic skippers (Hesperiidae) are Horace's dusky wing [*Erynnis horatius* (S. and B.)], sleepy dusky wing (*E. brizo* B. and LeC.), cobweb skipper (*Hesperia metea* Scudder) and dusted skipper (*Atrytonopsis hianna* (Scudder). (Comstock, 1940; Shapiro, 1966; R. Dirig and D. Schweitzer, personal communication).

Ichneumons (Hymenoptera: Ichneumonidae)

This group varies in size, form, and coloration, but most members resemble small wasps, except that they have longer antennae and usually do not sting. In many species, the taillike appendage (ovipositor) is quite long, sometimes longer than the body, arises before the tip of the abdomen, and is permanently outside the body. All ichneumons are parasites of other insects or invertebrates and, because of their abundance, most are important in keeping the population of other arthropods in balance. A common species is *Ophion bilineatus* Say. It is light brown, has a compressed abdomen, and is parasitic upon caterpillars.

Leaf-Cutting Ant (Hymenoptera: Formicidae)

As an adult, the leaf-cutting ant looks like any other small (3–4 mm), leaf brown-colored ant, but its colony hill sites can be identified by their crescent rather than circular shape. These ants, *Trachymyrmex septentrionalis* (McCook), cut off sections of pine needles and other leaves and carry them underground to their nest sites, where they use the leaves as a culture medium for the fungi on which they feed (McCook, 1880; Weber, 1956).

Social Wasps (Hymenoptera: Vespidae)

This group includes (a) the familiar black- and yellow-banded yellow jackets [*Vespula maculifrons* (Buy.)] and other species that often fly around, walk over, and feed on foods at picnic tables, (b) the reddish-brown and yellow-banded paper wasps (*Polistes fuscatus pallipes* Lep.) and (c) the bald-faced or white-faced hornet [*Vespula maculata* (L.)], which is primarily black with yellowish-white markings. All are recognized as wasps by the narrow waist between the midbody (thorax) and the abdomen, by the longitudinally folded forewings when at rest, and by the ovipositor and sting which emerge from the tip of the abdomen. They are pugnacious, resent interference, and can inflict powerful stings. All are common in open areas, live in colonies, and build nests of paper made by masticating plant materials. Yellow jackets build nests in cavities in the ground. Paper wasps build circular horizontal combs, suspended by slender stalks, often from the eaves of buildings or inside roofs of open shelters. Bald-faced hornets build large gray paper nests in trees and other exposed places.

Carpenter Bees (Hymenoptera: Xylocopidae)

These are large (18–20 mm), robust, black bees that look like large bumble bees except that the back of their abdomen is mostly bare and shining. The most common species is *Xylocopa virginica* (L.), which is common around old buildings, open sheds, and pavilions, where it makes its nest cavities by boring holes and tunnels about 1.3 cm in diameter in boards and beams.

Bumble Bees (Hymenoptera: Apidae)

Bumble bees are recognized by their robust shape, large size (20 mm or more), dense covering of hairs, and black and yellow coloration. Several species, including *Bombus pennsylvanicus* (DeGeer) and *B. vagans* Smith, are common. Most bumble bees nest in colonies in cavities in the ground and are important pollinators of certain varieties of cultivated blueberries (Marucci, 1967).

Honey Bees (Hymenoptera: Apidae)

These are the common, golden-brown domesticated bees that are the most important insects in the pollination of plants. Our only species is *Apis mellifera* L. These social insects live in colonies which are kept in hives for fertilization and to produce honey. Occasionally, some escape in swarms and nest in hollow cavities in trees and other protected places. Throughout the season, these bees work on the flowers of herbaceous plants, shrubs, and trees in both open areas and in the woods. These insects are valuable in pollinating cranberry and cultivated blueberry blossoms, and hives are moved into blueberry fields during blossoming periods for this purpose. However, the colonies cannot maintain themselves throughout the year without human assistance, probably due to the scarcity of plants in flower and the high incidence of foul brood, a bacterial disease.

INSECTS OF OPEN, SANDY AREAS

Antlions (Neuroptera: Myrmeleontidae)

These are delicate insects resembling damselflies. Adults have two pairs of long, narrow, membranous, many-veined wings. They are very soft bodied, have a long, slender abdomen and short, clubbed antennae, are weak fliers, and seldom are noticed. Their odd-looking predaceous larvae, often called doodlebugs, are short (16–18 mm), stout, and have long sicklelike jaws. Our species have the habit of concealing themselves at the bases of small, cone-shaped pits which they dig in the sand. There, they wait for ants and other small arthropods to fall into their traps so they can seize them in their ·jaws and feed on them. These pits, which are 2.5–5 cm deep and up to 5 cm across, usually are dug in dry, protected areas near the bases of trees, under tufts of grass, and under the eaves of buildings. A common species is *Hesperoleon (Brachynemurus) abdominalis* (Say).

Tiger Beetles (Coleoptera: Cicindelidae)

Tiger beetles are small (10–18 mm), long-legged, active beetles that run along the ground and fly readily when disturbed. Somewhat slender and elongate, they often are brightly colored, sometimes in metallic and iridescent hues. Their wing covers (elytra) usually are marked with distinctive color patterns. The head is large compared to the body size and is equipped with strong, sickle-shaped, and toothed jaws (mandibles) which are used to capture and feed on ants and other small arthropods. Open, sunny, and sandy areas throughout the Pine Barrens are ideal habitats for these insects. Fifteen of the nineteen species of *Cicindela* known to occur in the state occur in the Barrens (Boyd, 1973). Larvae live in vertical burrows in the ground, and both adults and larvae are predaceous. A common Pine Barrens species is *C. tranquebarica* Herbst., which is black with white bands on the wing covers. Other common species are *C. repanda* Dej., *C. formosa generosa* Dej., *C. scutellaris rugifrons* Dej., and *C. punctulata* Oliv.

Robber Flies (Diptera: Asilidae)

These are flies in the true sense, because they have only one pair of wings, which are membranous. The head is prominent and very hairy, the face more or less bearded, and the top of the head hollowed out between the eyes. The antennae are short, and the proboscis, or beak, which extends down from under the head, is short, stout, and formed for piercing. The midbody (thorax) is stout, the abdomen long and tapering, and the legs long, strong, and spiny. A common species is *Stichopogon trifasciatus* (Say), which is gray with blackish markings. This insect attacks a variety of other arthropods by pouncing upon them, and piercing and sucking juices from them while holding them between their legs. It is common in open areas and on bare stretches of sand.

Velvet Ants (Hymenoptera: Mutillidae)

Velvet ants are really wasps that are densely clothed with hair in contrasting bands of black and orange. A common species is *Dasymutilla occidentalis* (L.). Females are wingless and antlike, run along the ground in open sandy areas, and can inflict a painful sting. Males are winged and occur on flowers but seldom are noticed. Many velvet ants are external parasites of the larvae and pupae of various wasps and bees.

INSECTS MORE OFTEN HEARD THAN SEEN

Northern True Katydid (Orthoptera: Tettigoniidae)

This insect sings a "katy did–katy didn't" song from treetops on summer evenings from late July until frost. The insect, *Pterophylla camellifolia* (Fab.), is large (38–42 mm) and green, with hindlegs somewhat enlarged for jumping. It has two pairs of wings, and the fore or outer pair seems to wrap around the insect in a bulblike fashion. The hairlike antennae are long, usually longer than the wings. Katydids have chewing mouthparts and are plant feeders. The insect itself, however, seldom is seen, for it spends most of its time feeding and singing at night in the topmost foliage of deciduous trees in the woods.

Crickets (Orthoptera: Gryllidae)

Crickets also are insect musicians. Adult field crickets, *Gryllus assimilis luctuosus* Serv. and *G. pennsylvanicus* Burm., are dark brown to blackish, 20–25 mm long, with stout hindlegs and antennae longer than the body. Females have a long, spearlike blade (ovipositor) that extends from the tip of the abdomen, and is almost as long as the rest of the body. These crickets hide in vegetative litter during the day and come out on cloudy days and at night to sing and feed on both living and decaying vegetable matter. Tree crickets are slender, pale green insects, 15–18 mm long, which occur on trees, shrubs, and tall weeds. The snowy tree cricket (*Oecanthus fultoni* Walker), also known as the temperature cricket, stridulates throughout the night, in unison with others of its species, at a rate dependent upon the temperature.

Dog-Day Cicadas or Harvestflies (Homoptera: Cicadidae)

Often erroneously called "locusts," cicadas are medium to large (25–50 mm) insects with membranous wings which are held rooflike over the body when at rest. Their antennae are very short and bristlelike. They usually are black with greenish body markings and wing veins, and often are coated underneath with a chalky white, powdery down. Usually, these insects first are noticed making a high-pitched, shrill sound during the day from some nearby shrub or tree. Produced by the males, this song or call is loud and piercing and different for each species. If one tries to approach a cicada, it usually will stop singing and fly off to a nearby tree before renewing its song.

Adult cicadas feed very little or not at all. Their immature larvae live underground sucking on the juices of tree and other plant roots, but they grow so slowly that they do not affect the growth or health of their hosts. Three common species found in pine woods during June and July are *Tibicen auletes* (Germ.), *T. canicularis* (Harr.) and *Cicada hieroglyphica* Say, our smallest species.

INSECTS FOUND UNDER BARK AND IN DEAD TREES AND OLD STUMPS

Wood Cockroaches (Orthoptera: Blattellidae)

Wood roaches are medium-sized (15–30 mm), oval, flattened, and soft-bodied insects. The head is concealed under a forward-projecting sheath (pronotum), the antennae are hairlike and very long, and the long legs are spiny and adapted for running. Adults have two pairs of brown wings which lie flat over the body. Two common species found under the bark of dying and dead trees in pine woods are *Parcoblatta pennsylvanica* (DeG.) and *P. uhleriana* (Sauss.).

Termites (Isoptera: Rhinotermitidae)

These are small, light-colored insects that live in colonies in standing tree trunks, old stumps, buried wood, fallen trees, and logs throughout the woods. Several different forms (castes) are present in a colony. Most often seen are the workers, which are small (5–6 mm), whitish insects with large heads and small bodies. Often, termites erroneously are called "white ants," but they differ from ants in several ways. Termites are soft bodied and usually light colored, while ants are hard bodied and darker colored. Termite wings, in the reproductive caste, are similar in size and are held flat over the body. Hindwings of ants are smaller than the forewings, and all wings are held together vertically over the body. The abdomen in termites is broadly joined to the midbody (thorax). In ants, it is narrowly joined by a slender petiole. Finally, antennae of termites are bead- or threadlike, while those of ants usually are elbowed (Borror *et al.*, 1976). This eastern subterranean termite, *Reticulitermes flavipes* (Kollar), is a destructive insect in wooden houses, but in the woods, by digesting the cellulose in woody plants, it is a major factor in the breakdown process converting dead trees to humus.

Click Beetles (Coleoptera: Elateridae)

These are small to medium-sized, elongate, and hard-bodied insects which have the hind angles of their midbody (pronotum) extended back to form sharp points. Most species are uniformly colored in dull browns or blacks. When placed on their back, the beetles spring up into the air, accompanied by a clicking sound, a procedure they will repeat until they land rightside up. Our most conspicuous species is the eyed elater [*Alaus oculatus* (L.)], a large (36–40 mm), shining, black beetle mottled with white spots and having two large, black eyelike spots on the pronotum. Click beetles are common under the bark of trees and in decaying wood, where they also hibernate. Occasionally, smaller species are found on flowers and vegetation.

Darkling or Bark Beetles (Coleoptera: Tenebrionidae)

Bark beetles are medium- to large-sized, oval or oblong, hard-bodied, brownish or black insects with beadlike antennae. Many species have a peculiar, loosely jointed appearance when they walk, due to long, rather clumsy, and awkward legs. The front and middle feet (tarsi) are five segmented, an important identification character that is easily seen on these insects. These beetles are common in wooded areas under the bark of dead trees, old stumps, and fallen logs, often hibernating there. A common black species, measuring 20–23 mm in length, is *Alobates pennsylvanica* (DeG.).

Ants (Hymenoptera: Formicidae)

These insects are very common. Their most distinguishing structural feature is the presence of one or two lobes on the slender petiole which connects the abdomen to the midbody (thorax), and the usually elbowed antennae, the first segment of which often is very long. All ants are social insects that live in colonies, usually with three or more forms (castes) in a colony. Wingless female workers, which make up the bulk of a colony, are observed most frequently. Reproductive females and males are winged.

Many ant species live in both wooded and open areas, and their colonies vary greatly in size and form. Many species live in dead and dying trees, old logs, and rotting wood, while others have underground colonies below mounds. Different species feed on different types of food and, in turn, ants are a major source of food for various predaceous arthropods. In addition to the leaf-cutting ant previously described, the carpenter ant [*Camponotus pennsylvanicus* (DeG.)] and *Formica fusca* L. are two common, conspicuous species. The carpenter ant, with a black abdomen and a dusky red head and thorax, is the largest (10–14 mm) ant. It excavates a series of galleries and chambers in old stumps and logs for its nest but does not actually feed on the wood, as termites do. *Formica fusca,* slightly smaller than the carpenter ant, is entirely black, but a dense pubescence gives the abdomen a silver luster. It nests in the ground, sometimes under but not inside logs. When these ants are observed climbing on trees and shrubs, this usually indicates the presence of aphids, which the ants protect in exchange for their "honeydew" excretions. Other common species are *Tapinoma sessile* (Say) and *Monomorium minimum* (Buckley).

INSECTS FOUND IN AQUATIC AND SEMIAQUATIC HABITATS

Sphagnum bogs, abandoned cranberry bogs, white cedar swamps, and hardwood swamps are included here, along with stream and lake habitats. All of these areas contain acid water.

Pitcher Plant Insects

Many insects die upon or within the leaves of sundews (*Drosera* spp.) and pitcher plants (*Sarracenia purpurea* L.), in bogs and other damp habitats. However, several insects also live within the hollow leaves or other tissues of the pitcher plants. These include: (a) Lepidoptera: the larvae of a species of a small noctuid moth (*Exyra rolandiana* Grt.) feed upon the tissues of the pitcher-shaped leaves. Another noctuid caterpillar (*Papaipema appassionata* Harv.) feeds on the roots of the plant, constructing upright tubes above the surface of the ground, probably for air; (b) Diptera: several scavenger fly larvae, including several flesh flies (*Sarcophaga sarraceniae* Riley) and other species, live within the leaves of pitcher plants, feeding on the dead insects trapped there. A mosquito [(*Wyeomyia smithii* (Coq.)] flies into the open pitchers and lays its eggs, and the wriggling larvae develop in the small pools of water; and (c) Hymenoptera: the hollow stems of pitcher plants sometimes are used as nesting sites by hunting wasps (*Isodontia* spp.). Finally, a species of acrobatic ant, (*Crematogaster pilosa* Emery) often nests in pitcher plant leaves (Hutchins, 1966).

Dragonflies and Damselflies (Odonata)

These are medium to large insects with four elongate, membranous, and many-veined wings. The compound eyes are so large that they often occupy much of the head. Antennae are small and bristlelike. The midbody (thorax) is relatively small, and the abdomen is long and slender. The two groups are readily distinguished from each other, because dragonflies (Anisoptera) usually are rather robust, strong flyers, and hold their wings nearly horizontal when at rest. One of the largest species (80–85 mm) is *Epiaeschna heros* (Fab.), which is dark brown with greenish markings and is found around ponds in early summer. Damselflies (Zygoptera) are more slender, are weak flyers, and hold their wings together vertically above the body when at rest. The light, powdery blue, bluet damselflies that alight on grasses just above the water surface of small ponds are several species of *Enallagma*.

Immature stages of dragonflies and damselflies are completely aquatic, and adults are common around cedar bogs, small ponds, streams, and the edges of lakes. Females often fly just above the surface of the water, laying their eggs (ovipositing) under the water surface by dipping their abdomens into the water. Sometimes males fly in tandem with them and provide additional flight power. All stages are predaceous and feed on insects and other organisms. Both dragonflies and damselflies are an important food source for flycatchers and other nesting birds. Adult dragonflies neither bite nor sting and are completely harmless to humans.

Water Boatmen, Backswimmers, Water Bugs, Waterscorpions, and Water Striders (All Hemiptera)

These are aquatic true bugs that range up to 50 mm in size. All may be recognized as true bugs by the overlapping membranous tips of the forewings and by the beak. Water boatmen (Corixidae) are small, oval to elongate, and somewhat flattened in shape.

They swim by using their legs as oars. Backswimmers (Notonectidae) are shaped similarly, but swim upside down on their backs, which are keeled. Most larger (8–17 mm) species belong to the genus *Notonecta*. Creeping water bugs (Naucoridae) are 10–12 mm long and are broadly oval and flattened in shape. Their forelegs are greatly thickened and adapted for grasping. They swim or slowly creep through submerged vegetation and can inflict a painful sting when handled. Only one species, *Pelocoris femoratus* (Pal. Beauv.), is present. Giant water bugs (Belostomatidae) are brownish, oval, and flattened, and some species are as large as 50 mm, the largest belonging to the genus *Lethocerus*. All have a short powerful beak, the underparts of their bodies are keellike, and their enlarged forelegs are fitted for grasping. They are common in ponds and lakes and can inflict a painful sting if handled carelessly. Waterscorpions (Nepidae) are narrow, long legged, and look something like walking sticks crawling about aquatic vegetation. Their front legs are armed with stout spines, that can be closed about a prey. They also have a pair of long taillike appendages which form an air-breathing tube. Most species belong to the genus *Ranatra*. Water striders (Gerridae) have long legs and can walk on top of the water. Their bodies are narrow and elongate and are covered with a velvety pile underneath to repel and shed water. All these Hemiptera are common in aquatic habitats, and most are predaceous, feeding on other arthropods as well as on snails, tadpoles, and small fish.

Predaceous Diving Beetles, Water Scavenger Beetles, and Whirligig Beetles (All Coleoptera)

These are aquatic beetles ranging up to 38 mm in size. All are recognized as beetles by their hard wing covers. Both the predaceous diving beetles (Dytiscidae) and the water scavenger beetles (Hydrophilidae) inhabit ponds and quiet streams. Both are oval-shaped, smooth, shining black beetles that can be distinguished by their antennae, which in the diving beetles are long and threadlike, but short, clubbed, and usually partially concealed under the sides of the head in the scavenger beetles. A large (35–40 mm) common, shining black species of scavenger beetle is *Hydrophilus triangularis* Say. Whirligig beetles (Gyrinidae) swim on the surface of ponds and quiet streams and habitually swim very rapidly in endless gyrations or gather in large rafts of resting individuals. Whirligig beetles are unusual, because they have two pairs of compound eyes, one pair above and one pair below the surface of the water, which enable the beetles to locate food more easily and to avoid predators. Most larger (10–15 mm) species belong to the genus *Dineutus*. Both the diving beetles and the whirligig beetles are predaceous on a variety of small aquatic animal life, while the water scavenger beetles, as their name implies, are scavengers. All three groups are common in aquatic habitats.

Mosquitoes (Diptera: Culicidae)

Having only one pair of wings, mosquitoes really are flies, but are distinguished from other biting flies by their slender body, long slender legs, and long slender beak or proboscis. Mosquito larvae, or wrigglers, are aquatic and occur in a variety of situations, usually distinctive for each species. Many species "bite" humans, and several serve as vectors in the transmission of diseases. As in similar groups, only female mosquitoes feed on blood.

Mosquitoes are common in aquatic habitats as well as throughout both pine woods and open areas. A very common species is the banded-leg salt marsh mosquito [*Aedes sollicitans* (Walker)], which flies in from nearby salt marshes. Weiss and West (1924) reported it as "being present in numbers far exceeding those of any other species" in their study near Lakehurst. A mosquito that breeds in our cedar bogs is *Culiseta melanura* (Coq.), a vector in the avian cycle of eastern encephalitis (L. E. Hagmann, personal communication). Another common species is the house mosquito, *Culex pipiens* L., found around human habitation everywhere. It prefers polluted water and will breed in any container with water. Effluent from sewage treatment plants often becomes heavily infested by this species, and it has been implicated in the transmission of viral encephalitis. One of the dangers of encroaching residential developments in the Pine Barrens is the creation of conditions whereby this species will become more abundant and threatening to health (L. E. Hagmann, personal communication).

Not all mosquito species feed on blood. The larvae of *Toxorhynchites rutilus septentrionalis* (D. and K.) feed on wrigglers of other mosquitoes breeding in tree holes, and the large and brilliantly colored adults feed entirely on plant juices (L. Blaustein, personal communication).

Black Flies (Diptera: Simuliidae)

Black flies are small, blood-sucking flies that persistently annoy humans. These flies are aquatic in the larval stages and usually live in flowing streams. Adults, often referred to as "gnats" by natives, are short (3–5 mm), stout, black flies with the thorax region behind the head arched markedly, giving the fly a hump-backed appearance. *Prosimulium fuscum* S. and D. is one of the most common species in the Pine Barrens (W. J. Crans, personal communication).

Horse Flies (Diptera: Tabanidae)

Horse flies are large, biting, and blood-sucking flies. The largest is the mourning horse fly (*Tabanus atratus* Fab.), measuring about 24 mm in length. It has black wings and a black body with a bluish tinge. When horse flies are trapped inside buildings or cars, they make a loud buzzing noise until they escape.

Deer Flies (Diptera: Tabanidae)

These are small (7–9 mm), brownish, biting flies, slightly larger than house flies. They have short, broad heads, very large bright green and gold eyes, flattened abdomens, and short antennae. Usually, their single pair of wings has darker designs or smoky patches, the size and shape of which aid in identification. Female deer flies buzz persistently around one's head and hair, often alighting to "bite" with their piercing mouthparts. They usually inhabit streams and marshes but also occur in wooded areas far from water. Some species, such as *Chrysops delicatulus* O.S., are particularly abundant, and the region is the type locality for five species (L. L. Pechuman, personal communication).

SUMMARY

Over 125 arthropods found in the Pine Barrens of New Jersey are presented and briefly described. These are considered to be either the most common and representative of each major habitat type, or the most significant ecologically, economically, or aesthetically. Notes on ecological relationships and behavioral patterns often are included. The Diptera (flies, etc.) probably are present in the greatest numbers; the Coleoptera (beetles) and Hymenoptera (bees, wasps, ants, etc.) have the greatest diversity; and the Lepidoptera (moths and butterflies) include many characteristic Pine Barrens species.

ACKNOWLEDGMENTS

The authors gratefully acknowledge the data provided by Leon Blaustein, John W. Cadbury, III, Howard V. Cornell, Wayne J. Crans, Robert Dirig, John G. Franclemont, Lyle E. Hagmann, Alexander B. Klots, Daniel Otte, L. L. Pechuman, Dale F. Schweitzer, and Alfred G. Wheeler, Jr. Special appreciation is expressed to John Cadbury, who also reviewed this article and made many helpful suggestions.

REFERENCES

Baker, W. L. (1972). Eastern forest insects. *U.S. Dep. Agric., Misc. Pub.* No. 1175.
Borror, D. J., DeLong, D. M., and Triplehorn, C. A. (1976). "An Introduction to the Study of Insects," 4th Ed. Holt, New York.
Boyd, H. P. (1973). Collecting tiger beetles in the Pine Barrens of New Jersey. *Cicindela* 5(1), 1-12.
Boyd, W. M. (1953). Insects of importance in New Jersey nurseries. *N.J. Dep. Agric., Circ.* No. 390.
Brues, C. T. (1972). "Insects, Food and Ecology." Dover, New York. (Formerly "Insect Dietary." Harvard Univ. Press, Cambridge, Massachusetts, 1946.)
Comstock, W. P. (1940). Butterflies of New Jersey. *J. N.Y. Entomol. Soc.* **48,** 47-84.
Darlington, E. P. (1952). Notes on blueberry Lepidoptera in New Jersey. *Trans. Am. Entomol. Soc.* **78,** 33-57.
Davis, W. T. (1912). An injurious grasshopper at Ridgeway, New Jersey. *Entomol. News* **23,** 2-3.
Hutchins, R. E. (1966). "Insects." Prentice-Hall, Englewood Cliffs, New Jersey.
Leng, C. W. (1902). Notes on the Cicindelidae of the Pine Barrens of New Jersey. *J. N.Y. Entomol. Soc.* **10,** 236-240.
Leonard, M. D. (1972). Aphids of New Jersey, a few more records. *J. N.Y. Entomol. Soc.* **80,** 182-194.
Leonard, M. D. (1974). Aphids in the Pine Barrens of New Jersey. *Coop. Econ. Insect Rep., U.S. Dep. Agric.* **24**(28), 530-534.
McCook, H. C. (1880). Note on a new Northern Cutting Ant, *Atta septentrionalis. Proc. Acad. Nat. Sci. Philadelphia* **32,** 359-363.

McCormick, J. (1970). The Pine Barrens: A preliminary ecological inventory. *N.J. State Mus., Res. Rep.* No. 2.

McCormick, J., and Andresen, J. W. (1960). Some effects of animals on the vegetation of the New Jersey Pine Barrens. *Bull. Torrey Bot. Club.* **87**, 375–385.

Marucci, P. E. (1967). Blueberry pollination. *Proc. Int. Soc. Hort. Sci. Symp., Venlo, Neth.* pp. 155–159.

Rehn, J. A. G. (1946). The Post-Oak Locust at Mt. Misery, N.J., in 1944. *Entomol. News* **57**, 147–148.

Rehn, J. A. G., and Rehn, J. W. H. (1938). The Post-Oak Locust in the Eastern U.S., with notes on macropterism in the species. *Trans. Am. Entomol. Soc.* **64**, 79–95.

Schaffner, J. V. (1959). Microlepidoptera and their parasites reared from field collections in the northeastern U.S. *U.S. Dep. Agric., Misc. Publ.* No. 767.

Shapiro, A. M. (1966). Butterflies of the Delaware Valley. *Am. Entomol. Soc.*, pp. 1–79.

Smith, J. B. (1910). The insects of New Jersey. *N.J. State Mus., Annu. Rep.* 1909.

Soraci, F. (1941). Insects of importance in New Jersey nurseries. *N.J. Dep. Agric., Circ.* No. 326.

Spears, C. F. (1941). The pine spittle bug. *N.Y. State Coll. For., Tech. Bull.* No. 54.

Weber, N. A. (1956). Fungus growing ants and their fungi: *Trachymyrmex septentrionalis. Ecology* **37**, 150–161.

Weiss, H. B., and West, E. (1924). Insects and plants of a dry woods in the Pine Barrens of New Jersey. *Ecology* **5**, 241–253.

30

Soil Arthropod Microcommunities of the Pine Barrens

DANIEL L. DINDAL

INTRODUCTION

Soil invertebrate microcommunities are present in virtually all soils. The cosmopolitan occurrence of soil invertebrates is determined generally by the colonizing ability of the species, adequate soil moisture, and available food sources. In addition to the detritivores, which obtain energy from all sorts of decomposing organic matter, many soil invertebrates graze on fungi, algae, and bacteria associated with most decomposing plant and animal tissue. Invertebrate predators prey in turn upon the fungus grazers, upon the detritivores, and upon one another. Thus, all soil organisms are organized into intricate food web systems.

The total ecological impact of soil invertebrates is very subtle and significant. In part, this is due to the minute size and cryptic behavior of the animals. Part is due to a very small horizontal "home range" and the limited vertical distribution exhibited by soil organisms. However, the microcommunities exhibit a structure and function very similar to those of a macrocommunity (Dindal, 1973), serving the following several purposes: organic matter decomposition by comminution (reducing to fine particles); incorporation of organic matter into the mineral soil; enhancement of soil structure; release and accumulation of nutrients bound in organic debris; and population control and distribution of soil microflora throughout organic microhabitats.

Even though soil invertebrates are common, they are little known in the soils of the New Jersey Pine Barrens. Therefore, the objectives of this chapter are to analyze: (1) community patterns of microarthropods* with new data from several Pine Barrens vegetation conditions; (2) community patterns of macroarthropods* mainly based on published literature; and (3) the effects of fire on Pine Barrens soil arthropod communities.

*As used here, microarthropods = <5 mm length; macroarthropods = >5 mm length.

527

Methods

No published data were available on ecological characteristics of microarthropods of the Pine Barrens. Accordingly, collections were taken in order to explore relationships.

The vegetative communities investigated were the same as those used by Forman (Chapter 23, this volume) for his study of bryophyte communities. Briefly, the characteristics of each site are the following: (a) cedar swamps are dominated (~95%) by Atlantic white cedar (*Chamaecyparis thyoides*), with an abundance of *Sphagnum* moss growing in a saturated muck soil; (b) hardwood swamps are composed of several tree species, including red maple (*Acer rubrum*) and black gum (*Nyssa sylvatica*), and are associated with *Sphagnum* in a very wet substrate; (c) pine lowlands are almost pure stands of small pitch pine (*Pinus rigida*) with a dense heath layer growing in a damp sandy soil; (d) upland old burns are oak–pine forests with a relatively continuous layer of oak litter over a well-drained sandy soil, and sites have not burned for an estimated 20–40 years; (e) annual burns are oak–pine woods characterized by the presence of extensive bryophytes and lichens, a meager cover of herbs, shrubs, and small trees, and patches of litter and bare sandy soil; (f) Pine Plains are dwarf woodlands dominated by abundant pitch pine and oak sprouts resulting from high fire frequency; their soils are well-drained sands with a mosaic of litter, ground cover, and bare soil. All sites were in the Lebanon State Forest except that of the Pine Plains, located several kilometers to the southeast. Thus, sites of a particular vegetative community generally were a few kilometers apart.

Sixty core samples (6.5 cm diameter × 6.5 cm depth) were collected on December 22, 1976 with the temperature about 0°–5°C. Four samples were taken from each of three cedar swamps, three upland old-burn sites, three Pine Plains sites, two hardwood swamps sites, two pine lowlands sites, and two annual-burn sites. Representative locations within sites were selected such that one sample was from a drier than average spot, one from a moister than average spot, and two from approximately average spots. Studies in Sweden (Tarras-Wahlberg, 1961) and temperate regions of Europe and North America (Wallwork, 1967) indicate that soil samples taken during the autumn and winter seasons express the maximum microarthropod density for a given site. Using modified Tullgren funnels, invertebrates from the soil cores were extracted, sorted, and identified to order or suborder. All related tables and figures are based on the 60 soil samples.

Several quantitative techniques were used to analyze and compare the community structure of the soil organisms. These methods included a measure of the richness of groups or taxa (order or suborder) present, using the formula of Margalef (1958). Richness is defined as the total number of taxa present in a given community and is estimated here by the index $r = (s-1)/\ln N$, where $s =$ the number of taxa and $N =$ the total number of individuals present. Shannon–Wiener group diversity and evenness also were calculated for each microcommunity following the methods described by Shannon and Weaver (1963) and Pielou (1969), respectively. The pattern of diversity values was very similar to that of richness, and evenness values showed no evident pattern. Only richness is discussed further in this chapter.

Each soil sample was dried at 100°C for 24 hours, and the dry weight of soil and litter plus the percent of soil moisture were determined using the following formula (Gardner, 1965):

$$\text{Percentage of soil moisture} = \frac{\text{Wet weight of soil} - \text{Dry weight of soil}}{\text{Dry weight of soil}} \times 100$$

Results

In an equal volume of soil, swamp sites are almost entirely water, while annual burn and Pine Plains sites are almost all soil (Fig. 1). Profound effects on microarthropod communities can be expected from these major environmental differences.

A total of 9057 individual microarthropods were encountered in this study, with an average of >150 individuals per core. The number of microarthropods per gram of soil was highest in the cedar swamp, and decreased progressively to the Pine Plains (Fig. 2). The number per square meter of soil surface, however, did not show a consistent change among the vegetation conditions, although the Pine Plains again was lowest.

Comparison of Figs. 1 and 2 shows an interesting direct relationship between soil moisture and number of organisms per gram of soil. Conversely, more soil means fewer organisms per gram. The upland old burn and pine lowland with intermediate moisture conditions had the highest density of microarthropods per soil surface area, but even the hardwood swamp had 32,000/m² and the cedar swamp 50,000/m².

"Variability polygons" were constructed (Fig. 3) showing the variation of total microarthropod numbers among the four samples taken at a site. The following standard statistical formula for coefficient of variability (*CV*) was used (Sokal and Rohlf, 1969):

$$CV = (\text{standard deviation/average}) \times 100$$

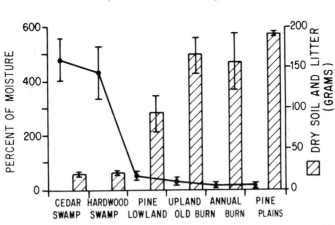

Fig. 1. Moisture and dry weight of soil samples under different vegetation conditions. Based on four 6.5-cm diameter × 6.5-cm depth cores in each of either two or three stands for each vegetation condition. Soil and litter dried at 100°C for 24 hours. Confidence intervals are ±1 standard error of the mean.

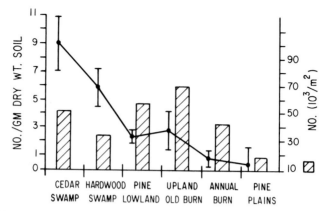

Fig. 2. Numbers of microarthropods associated with Pine Barrens soils. Organisms were extracted with a modified Tullgren funnel from four cores in each of either two or three sites for each vegetation condition. Dry weight of soil and litter from Fig. 1. Confidence intervals are ±1 standard error of the mean.

Coefficients of variation were plotted as vertical lines in order of increasing variability. Polygons then can be defined by connecting the ends of those CV lines for a particular vegetative community. Therefore, the degree of fluctuation between individual sites, as well as between specific vegetative communities, can be compared graphically.

Microarthropod numbers in the pine lowlands exhibited the least fluctuation, and the annual-burn sites showed the greatest variation, although the cedar swamp and upland old burn also were high (Fig. 3). Sites such as the pine lowland with lower spatial variability suggest a more stable community organization than those with a high degree of fluctuation.

The index of microarthropod richness was highest in the pine lowlands and hardwood swamps and lowest in annual-burn sites (Fig. 4). Richness does not seem

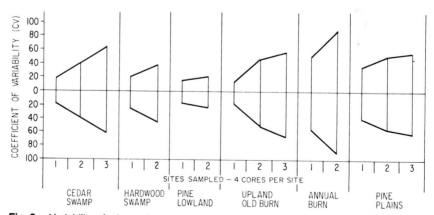

Fig. 3. Variability of microarthropod numbers among samples from different Pine Barrens soils. See Fig. 2 legend; see also text.

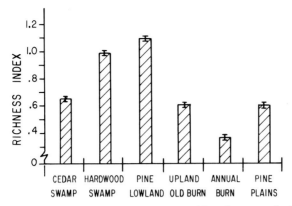

Fig. 4. Community richness index of microarthropods of Pine Barrens soils. Richness index $r = (s+1)/\ln N$; see Fig. 2 legend; also see text.

related either to the amount of soil moisture (Fig. 1) or to the number of microarthropods per gram or per square meter (Fig. 2). However, the index of richness does appear to be correlated inversely with the coefficient of variability (Fig. 3) such that the greater the richness, the less the variability.

Discussion

Feeding or trophic levels of the invertebrate decomposers are well developed in Pine Barren soils and litter. Oribatid mites, springtails (Collembola), and some prostigmatid mites are the predominant grazers of the fungi associated with decomposition. Although prostigmatid mite populations are very abundant in soils of old-field, conifer, and hardwood sites (Dindal *et al.,* 1975a,b), little is known about the ecology of soil representatives of this suborder (Wallwork, 1967). While the feeding roles of this group are characterized overall as heterogeneous, most forms of the Pine Barrens prostigmatid mites feed on fungi, and a few are predaceous.

Although present in all sites, the predatory component of the microarthropod community varied in the proportions of organism types. Predatory mesostigmatid mites were found in all sites. Where their numbers were low, predatory prostigmatid populations were high, or, alternatively, larger microarthropods such as pseudoscorpions often dominated the predatory niche.

In describing the horizontal distribution of pseudoscorpions in coastal sands of North Carolina, Weygoldt (1969) found nine species specific to microhabitats ranging from the intertidal zone through dune grass stands into pine–oak communities. Five species were predators within pine–oak stands. The pine–oak stands of North Carolina are relatively comparable to the upland Pine Barrens sites in this study.

Where populations of microarthropod predators were low, beetle larvae and ants were present as potential macroarthropod predators of the smaller oribatid mites, springtails, prostigmatid mites, and mesostigmatid mites.

Loots and Ryke (1967) showed that specific oribatid/prostigmatid mite ratios exist relative to differences in soil composition. For organic soils, the ratio is >1, while <1 in mineral soils. The authors cite several reasons for this pattern: (a) For food, oribatid mites prefer fungi and algae, both of which are associated with high percentages of organic matter in the soil; (b) Oribatid mites are relatively large in size and cannot move through pore spaces as small as those which allow passage of prostigmatids; (c) Prostigmatid mites are thought to feed upon microorganisms such as soil protozoa and bacteria inhabiting thin water films in smaller pore spaces common in mineral soils. The oribatid/prostigmatid mite ratios reported by Loots and Ryke for three sandy soils ranged from 0.023 to 0.185. Pine Barren soils, with the exception of the cedar and hardwood swamps, were all very sandy, but ratios (Table I) were much greater than those of Loots and Ryke. In the Pine Barrens, the cedar and hardwood swamps have almost identical ratios, reflecting the similarly high organic matter concentrations of the two areas. Even though the sandy mineral component of the other Pine Barren soils is high, organic matter concentration evidently is sufficient to support a relatively high number of oribatid mites. The upland old-burn and annual-burn sites having the highest ratios may be an expression of either a positive selection pressure of fire on the prostigmatid mites or a negative selection pressure on oribatid mites.

Comparing Figures 1 and 3, one finds microarthropod variation to be lowest in the pine lowland, where the percent of soil moisture and the amount of soil present were at intermediate levels. This suggests that in pine lowlands, near optimal conditions exist in terms of soil moisture, relative amount of dry soil present, and vegetative input from the dense shrub growth and pure stand of pitch pine. Low moisture levels and some history of fire seem to be related to the greater CV values of the Pine Plains, upland old-burn, and annual-burn sites. It also is interesting that the index of richness parallels closely the variability for microarthropods from the cedar swamp, upland old-burn, and Pine Plains sites. Perhaps all three sites possess similar potential stress conditions for microarthropods. The cedar swamp, with many characteristics of a *Sphagnum* bog, has a more rigorous environment than other sites for microarthropods, e.g., low oxygen conditions, low pH, high percentage of soil moisture, and possibly more phenolic

TABLE I   **Mites (Acari) and Springtails (Collembola) of Pine Barrens Soils[a]**

Vegetation	Oribatid mites (no./m²)	Prostigmatid mites (no./m²)	Oribatid/ prostigmatid ratio	Springtail/ mite ratio
Cedar swamp	40,034	7559	5.297	1:8.9
Hardwood swamp	28,255	5274	5.367	1:12.0
Pine lowland	39,671	11,717	3.386	1:10.0
Upland old burn	50,131	6832	7.343	1:4.5
Annual burn	35,864	3165	11.333	1:55.5
Pine Plains	11,654	5124	2.274	1:30.7

[a] See legend Fig. 2.

compounds originating from cedar litter. Old-burn and Pine Plains sites provide different stresses, since both have a very low percent of soil moisture and a history of frequent fire.

MACROARTHROPODS

This group of larger soil invertebrates is very important as the feeding link between the minute, microscopic creatures of soil and litter and the terrestrial vertebrates, such as shrews (*Blarina* spp.), white-footed mice (*Peromyscus* spp.), and many species of ground-feeding birds.

The best overview of the soil macroarthropods of the Pine Barrens was presented by Buffington (1967), who sampled sites throughout Lebanon State Forest, excluding cedar swamps and prescribed-burn areas (Little, Chapter 17 this volume). Buffington found a total of 42 families of soil macroarthropods. In areas unburned for many years, he recorded 43 species out of 888 individuals collected (Table II).

Nineteen percent of the families were herbivores, 31% decomposers, and 50% carnivores. Twenty-six percent of the families were spiders, which comprised about half of the predators of the litter and soil. Spiders prey on other litter-inhabiting micro- and macroarthropods.

The family represented by the most species was the Formicidae, the ants. Thirty-four ant species are suggested as inhabitants of the Pine Barrens, although only 29 have been observed (Table III). Eleven of these, plus three others, also are known from a pine barrens area on Long Island, New York (Table III).

Ants are both scavengers of organic debris and seeds and predators of almost all soil fauna, including invertebrates and some vertebrates. Ants also extensively mix soil materials and incorporate masses of organic substances within the sand matrix that forms the perimeter of their burrows and colonies. Talbot (1953, 1954) showed that some ants (*Aphaenogaster treatae, Lasius niger neoniger* Emery, *Myrmica americana* Weber, *Formica neogagates* Emery, *Formica rubicunda* Emery) also are important in causing the degeneration of herbaceous successional stages back to denuded pioneer vegetational communities, thus maintaining early developmental vegetative condi-

TABLE II   **Soil Macroarthropods of Burned and Unburned Pine Barrens Areas.**[a]

	Total arthropods		Ants		Spiders	
	Burned	Unburned	Burned	Unburned	Burned	Unburned
Number of individuals	348	888	334	827	2	17
Number of species	27	43	16	14	2	9

[a] From Buffington (1967).

TABLE III Ants in the Pine Barrens of New Jersey and New York[a]

Subfamily and species	New Jersey	New York	Subfamily and species	New Jersey	New York
Ponerinae			Dorymyrmex (Conomyra) pyramicus (Roger)	*	
Ponera pennsylvanica Buckley	B		Dorymyrmex sp.	C	C
Myrmicinae			Tapinoma sessile (Say)	B	
Myrmica emeryana Wheeler	B		Formicinae		
M. pinetorum Wheeler	*		Brachymyrmex depilis Emery	B	C
Aphaenogaster rudis Mayr	B		Camponotus pennsylvanicus ferruginea (Fabricius)	B,C,*	C
A. treatae Forel	B	C	C. (Myrmentoma) nearcticus Emery	C,*	C
Pheidole davisi Wheeler		C	C. pennsylvanicus (DeGeer)	B	
P. morrisi Forel	C	C	C. subbarbatus Emery	*	
Pheidole spp.	*		Paratrechina arenivaga (Wheeler)		
Crematogaster lineolata (Say)	B		P. (Nylanderia) melanderi (Wheeler)		C
C. pilosa Emery	B		P. parvula (Mayr)	B	
Monomorium viridium (W.L. Brown)	C,*		Prenolepis imparis (Say)	C	C
Solenopsis molesta (Say)	B	C	Lasius flavus (Fabricius)	B	
S. texana Emery		C	Formica fusca Linne	B	
Leptothorax ambiguus Emery	B	C	F. pallidefulva Lat.	B	
L. curvispinosus Mayr	B		F. (Neoformica) schaufussi Mayr	C	
L. pergandei Emery	B		F. subintegra Emery	B,C	
L. taxanus Wheeler	B	C			
Trachymyrmex septentrionalis McCook	C,*	C			
Dolichoderinae					
Dolichoderus (Hypoclinea) pustulatus (Mayr)	B				
D. (H.) taschenbergi Mayr	B				

[a] B, species reported present by Buffington (1967); (*), species listed by Brown (as cited in Buffington, 1967) as probably occurring in such sandy soils; C, collected by Stefan Cover (personal communication). New York collections are from near Selden, Long Island.

TABLE IV   **Ecological Roles of Scarabaeidae Beetles of the Pine Barrens**[a]

Dung decomposers (coprophages)
  Dialytes striatulus (Say): specific for deer dung
  Copris minutus (Drury): make food balls from dung
  Onthophagus cribricollis Horn: associated with rabbit pellets

Vertebrate nest and burrow inhabitants [All are associated with rodents (some dung decomposers) and found in open sandy areas, sand dunes, and herbaceous communities]
  Aphodius campestris Blatch.
  A. crassulus Horn
  A. erraticus (Linne)
  A. haemorrhoidalis (Linne)
  A. lentus Horn
  A. prodromus (Brahm)
  A. serval (Say)
  A. stupidus Horn

Fungus feeders (All are associated with fungi in sandy soils. The first two are found in pine and pine–oak communities, the last two in old-field and other herbaceous communities)
  Odontaeus (Bolboceras) darlingtoni Wallis
  O. liebecki Wallis
  O. simi Wallis
  Bolbocerosoma tumefactum (Beauv.)

Plant feeders (phytophages)
  Anomala nigropicta Csy.: under leaf litter; feed on maples and Rosaceae
  Serica carolina Daws: sandy beach drift lines and sandy soils
  S. lecontei Daws.
  S. opposita Daws: feed on oak leaves at dusk
  Phyllophaga diffinis (Blatch.): under leaf litter during day; feed on oak leaves at night

---

[a] Compiled from Sim (1930), Buffington (1967), and Arnett (1968).

tions. One of these ant species is present in both the New Jersey and New York pine barrens.

The Scarabaeidae, one of the largest families of beetles, includes several or all stages of the life cycle in soil or litter. Smith (1910) reported 163 species of this family common to New Jersey, many in the Pine Barrens region. Sim (1930), working mainly in the southern Coastal Plain of New Jersey, found 22 additional species. Some are specific in decomposing different types of dung, carcasses, or litter (Table IV). Others are associated with insects such as ants and horned passalus beetles [*Odontotaenius* (=*Popilius*) *disjunctus* (Illiger)], which are decomposers in decaying oak logs. Some live commonly within the nests or burrows of vertebrates. In all of these microhabitats, organic debris is fed upon, comminuted, and eventually combined with mineral soil as fine organic complexes. Comminution results from burrowing, feeding, and the ultimate formation of fecal pellets by the beetle. These processes cause an increase in surface area, which, in turn, provides a more optimal substrate for further decomposition by soil microorganisms.

FIRE AS A SELECTION PRESSURE ON SOIL ARTHROPODS

Responses of Microarthropods

Because of differences in fire intensity and frequency and nature of fuel, naturally occurring fires, wildfires, and prescribed burns (Little, Chapter 17, this volume) affect the community structure and populations of microarthropods in different ways. Fire is considered a selection pressure (Dindal and Metz, 1977) to which microarthropod populations respond positively or negatively over time.

Differences between upland old-burn and annual-burned sites were pronounced. The index of richness in the upland old burn was twice that of the annual burn (Fig. 4). Indeed, richness in the Pine Plains, an area with a history of frequent fire, equalled that of the annual burn. The "variability polygon" was largest for the annual-burn samples (Fig. 3), and again upland old-burn and Pine Plains samples were equally variable.

Working in a loblolly pine (*Pinus taeda*) stand in the sandy Coastal Plain of South Carolina, Metz and Farrier (1973) stated that total microarthropod populations were reduced by both periodic and annual burns. In the Pine Barrens, the present author observed the oribatid/prostigmatid mite ratio to be 7:1 in the upland old-burn site and 11:1 in the annual-burn area (Table I). The ratio between springtails (Collembola) and mites (Acari) was reduced even more drastically by frequent fire; the old-burn site ratio was 1:5, whereas annual-burn areas were 1:56 (Table I). The mite component of these ratios was 90% and 87% oribatid mites, respectively. Compared to springtails, oribatid mites as a group appear capable of either withstanding or responding positively to the direct and indirect selection pressures associated with fire. Karppinen (1958) also found that, after a prescribed burn within a forest, the oribatid community changed little.

Similar springtail–fire relationships were found (Metz and Dindal, 1975; Dindal and Metz, 1977) in three sites within a coastal loblolly pine plantation of South Carolina. One was unburned, one periodically burned, and one burned annually. The latter two loblolly pine sites correspond closely in fire frequency and treatment to the Pine Barrens upland old-burn and annual-burn sites, respectively.

Even though the numbers of springtails in the loblolly pine periodic burn decreased from a control site, the community structure appeared to be improved, as evidenced by the increase in species diversity (Metz and Dindal, 1975). Considering springtail/mite ratios on all Pine Barrens sites studied (Table I), the highest number of springtails relative to mites was in the upland old burn. The lowest springtail numbers were on annual-burn areas.

Apparently, periodic burning exerts few adverse effects on most microarthropods. However, conditions associated with annual burns inflict a negative selection pressure, greatly reducing the stability of both the population and community structure of microarthropods as a whole.

Responses of Macroarthropods

Buffington (1967) found that unburned sites usually had a richer macroarthropod fauna than burned areas, both in number of taxa and individuals. This supports previous results (Pearse, 1943) indicating a reduction in macroarthropods by fire in loblolly pine forests of North Carolina.

Focusing on ant–fire interactions, Buffington reported that most species given in Table III were selected against by fire. However, two species, *Formica fusca* and *Leptothorax pergandei,* responded positively to the selection pressure of fire evidently by colonizing burned sites in small numbers. Two additional species, *Lasius flavus* and *Solenopsis molesta,* increased in number, thus showing a positive response to conditions caused by fire. A dry, open, wooded area is the optimal habitat of *Lasius flavus,* and *Solenopsis molesta* is adapted best to arid conditions. Talbot (1953) also reported *S. molesta* to be common in pioneer old-field communities. Periodic burning thus directly or indirectly produces better habitat conditions for these four species.

The spider fauna was reduced by burning from nine to two species (Buffington, 1967). The two species remaining after fire included a crab spider (Thomisidae) [*Misumenops oblongus* (Keyserling)] and a jumping spider (Salticidae) [*Habrocestum pulex* (Hentz)]. Huhta (1971) also observed that burning in coniferous forests destroyed the community of ground-dwelling spiders almost completely. This was due largely to the extreme heat produced by fire, but additionally to the permanence of unfavorable microenvironmental conditions caused by burning. Furthermore, Huhta noted that the species richness and number of individuals remained at a very low level for 7–13 years until recovery began following the fire.

It thus can be concluded that, in general, populations and communities of soil macroarthropods are reduced drastically by both periodic and annual fires.

SUMMARY

The community structure of soil microarthropods is compared under six vegetative conditions of the New Jersey Pine Barrens. Microarthropod density ranged from 9000/m² in the Pine Plains to 69,000/m² in upland old-burn sites. The decomposer food web was well developed in microsites with abundant organic matter. Microarthropod richness was highest in pine lowlands and lowest in annually burned soils. Oribatid mites, the major decomposer organisms, dominated the microarthropod community on all sites, whereas predatory arthropods were diverse. The microarthropod community in pine lowland soil appeared exceedingly stable, based on high richness and low spatial variability. Published data on larger soil arthropods indicate that predatory litter-dwelling spiders and ants are prevalent. Many species of scarab beetles, mostly decomposers, are reported in the Pine Barrens.

Periodic burns have enhanced the richness of microarthropods, and oribatid mites have been affected less than springtail (Collembola) decomposers by fires. Periodic burns selected against spiders and most ants. However, two new ant species colonized, and two others increased in abundance after periodic fires. Annual burning was very detrimental to the richness and population dynamics of all soil arthropod groups.

ACKNOWLEDGMENTS

I would like to thank Richard T. T. Forman for collecting the samples for this study. Appreciation is extended to Stefan Cover for use of unpublished data.

REFERENCES

Arnett, R. H. (1968). "The Beetles of the U.S." Am. Entomol. Inst., Ann Arbor, Michigan.

Buffington, J. D. (1967). Soil arthropod populations of the New Jersey pine barrens as affected by fire. *Ann. Entomol. Soc. Am.* **60**, 530–535.

Dindal, D. L. (1973). Microcommunities defined. *In* "Soil Microcommunities I" (D. L. Dindal, ed.), pp. 2–6. USAEC, Natl. Tech. Inf. Serv., U.S. Dep. Commer., Springfield, Virginia.

Dindal, D. L., and Metz, L. J. (1977). Community structure of Collembola affected by fire frequency. *In* "The Role of Arthropods in Forest Ecosystems" (W. J. Mattson, ed.), pp. 88–95. Springer-Verlag, Berlin and New York.

Dindal, D. L., Folts, D. D., and Norton, R. A. (1975a). Effects of DDT on community structure of soil microarthropods in an old field. *In* "Progress in Soil Zoology" (J. Vanek, ed.), pp. 505–513. Junk, The Hague; Academia, Prague.

Dindal, D. L., Schwert, D. P., and Norton, R. A. (1975b). Effects of sewage effluent disposal on community structure of soil invertebrates. *In* "Progress in Soil Zoology" (J. Vanek, ed.), pp. 419–427. Junk, The Hague; Academia, Prague.

Gardner, W. W. (1965). Water content. *In* "Methods of Soil Analysis, Part I" (C. A. Black, ed.), pp. 82–127. Am. Soc. Agron. Publ., Madison, Wisconsin.

Huhta, V. (1971). Succession in the spider communities of the forest floor after clear-cutting and prescribed burning. *Ann. Zool. Fenn.* **8**, 483–542.

Karppinen, E. (1958). Über die Oribatiden (Acari) der finnischen Waldböden. *Ann. zool. Soc. Zool. Bot. Fenn. Vanamo* **19**, 1–43.

Loots, G. C., and Ryke, P. A. J. (1967). The ratio Oribatei:Trombidiformes with reference to organic matter content in soils. *Pedobiologia* **7**, 121–124.

Margalef, R. (1958). Information theory in ecology. *Gen. Syst.* **3**, 36–71.

Metz, L. J., and Dindal, D. L. (1975). Collembola populations and prescribed burning. *Environ. Entomol.* **4**, 583–587.

Metz, L. J., and Farrier, M. H. (1973). Prescribed burning and populations of soil mesofauna. *Environ. Entomol.* **2**, 433–440.

Pearse, A. S. (1943). Effects of burning over and raking off litter on certain soil animals in the Duke Forest. *Am. Midl. Nat.* **29**, 406–424.

Pielou, E. C. (1969). "An Introduction to Mathematical Ecology." Wiley (Interscience), New York.

Shannon, C. E., and Weaver, W. (1963). "The Mathematical Theory of Communication." Univ. of Illinois Press, Urbana.

Sim, R. J. (1930). Scarabidae Coleoptera: Observations on species unrecorded or little known in New Jersey. *J. N.Y. Entomol. Soc.* **38**, 139–147.

Smith, J. B. (1910). The insects of New Jersey. *N.J. State Mus., Annu. Rep.* 1909, pp. 15–188.

Sokal, R. R., and Rohlf, F. J. (1969). "Biometry." Freeman, San Francisco, California.

Talbot, M. (1953). Ants of an old-field community on the Edwin S. George Reserve, Livingston Co., Mich. *Contrib. Lab. Vertebr. Biol. Univ. Mich.* No. 63, 1–13.

Talbot, M. (1954). Populations of the ant *Aphaenogaster (Attomyrma) treatae* Forel on abandoned fields on the Edwin S. George Reserve. *Contrib. Lab. Vertebr. Biol. Univ. Mich.* No. 69, 1-9.

Tarras-Wahlberg, N. (1961). The Oribatei of a central Swedish bog and their environment. *Oikos* **13,** Suppl. 4, 1-56.

Wallwork, J. A. (1967). Acari. *In* "Soil Biology" (A. Burges and F. Raw, eds.), pp. 365-395. Academic Press, New York.

Weygoldt, P. (1969). "The Biology of Pseudoscorpions." Harvard Univ. Press, Cambridge, Massachusetts.

31

Animal Communities of the New Jersey Pine Barrens

EDMUND W. STILES

INTRODUCTION

Studies of animal communities in the New Jersey Pine Barrens only recently have developed beyond the stage of compilation of species lists. The underutilization of the Pine Barrens as a natural laboratory for animal community study is surprising. First, this large, relatively undisturbed natural area is readily accessible to a large scientific community. Second, the plant associations that so strongly affect the structure of animal communities are low in species diversity and are relatively simple structurally. Thus, a major problem in the interpretation of animal community studies, i.e., the high level of environmental (physical and biological) complexity, is minimized in the Pine Barrens. Third, environmental patches are relatively homogeneous and distinct, thus minimizing the problems of interpreting environmental gradients to make effective statements about animal communities. Fourth, the discreteness and diversity of vegetation types, based primarily on distribution of water and recurrence of fire, provide an arena for comparative studies of animal communities, as well as habitats with similar characteristics in which studies may be replicated. In short, many questions concerning animal communities may be asked and answered relatively simply in the Pine Barrens.

In this chapter, I will review briefly the literature concerning animals in the Pine Barrens and then consider how various physical and biological factors affect resource availability for animals and how this affects the structure of communities.

TYPES OF ANIMAL STUDIES

Studies of animals in the Pine Barrens have been of two basic types. Most have asked questions about the occurrence of individual species (reptiles and amphibians: Conant, 1943, 1946, 1962; Conant and Bailey, 1936; Engelhart, 1916; Reed, 1957;

Fowler, 1905; Kauffeld, 1935; mammals: Connor, 1959; Storer, 1940; insects: McCormick and Andresen, 1961). These studies will be explored in chapters in this volume dealing with individual groups of organisms. The incorporation of individual species studies into an integrated community analysis usually is not feasible due to variations in methods of data collection. The second major type of study has been the compilation of lists of organisms (fish: Cope, 1883; Fowler, 1952; snakes: Trapido, 1937; mammals: Connor, 1953; spiders: Stone, 1890; insects: Boyd, 1973; Comstock, 1940; Comegys and Schmitt, 1966; Leonard, 1956; Weiss and West, 1924). These lists are a first step toward understanding animal communities. However, even these lists are incomplete, and adequate information is available only for fish, amphibians, reptiles, birds, mammals, and a few groups of insects, such as butterflies and tiger beetles. For example, the bat fauna is little known.

Two other major foci are evident in the Pine Barrens animal literature. One group of studies concerns unusual species in the region (Barbour, 1916; Burger, 1934; Davis, 1907), including the Pine Barrens treefrog (*Hyla andersoni*), the carpenter frog (*Rana virgatipes*), and the timber rattlesnake (*Crotalus horridus*). Second, and more important for community studies, are studies of economically important groups. The two most important groups under the latter heading are the insects that influence the production of blueberries and cranberries (Marucci, 1947, 1966; Marucci and Moulter, 1963, 1971; Tomlinson, 1948, 1961, 1968; Beckwith, 1943; Darlington, 1952), and game species (Applegate, 1974; Wolgast, 1973; Little and Somes, 1951), including primarily the white-tailed deer (*Odocoileus virginianus*) and the ruffed grouse (*Bonasa umbellus*). The questions posed in most cases deal with the impact of these groups on local and regional economies rather than questions involving their effect on the remainder of the animal community.

Amphibians and reptiles have received special attention in the Pine Barrens. The sandy soil provides an excellent substrate for burrowing snakes, and the region has long been recognized as excellent for finding snakes, with sixteen species present. Amphibians also have been the focus of attention, but for different reasons. The region's acid waters provide severe conditions for developing amphibian eggs and larvae. The adaptations that have enabled some species to inhabit this area, also have resulted in notably restricted ranges and habitats of species such as the Pine Barrens treefrog and the carpenter frog.

FACTORS AFFECTING RESOURCE AVAILABILITY

Water

Animal communities in the Pine Barrens are affected by the availability of resources in different habitat types. Many factors are involved in influencing this availability, but few have been studied adequately. One factor is water, a determinant of major vegetation types in the Pine Barrens that is influential in the structure of animal communities. The reduced availability of water in the uplands restricts desiccation-prone amphibians and invertebrates to lowland areas, such as cedar and hardwood swamps. Acid conditions affect amphibians (Gosner and Black, 1957), fish, and invertebrates. In a less direct fashion, water affects the vegetation available for herbivores, and hence, the food items available for higher feeding or trophic levels. In addition, water affects the vegetation structure, which in turn influences the nature of the interactions or organisms in higher trophic levels, and hence, the animal communities. Thus, by directly affecting animals and by controlling plant species composition and productivity, water and nutrients, are important factors affecting animal community structure.

Fire

The plant and animal communities of the Pine Barrens have evolved under the selective pressure of recurrent fires. Animal communities are affected by fire in a short-term sense, in that animal population densities may be reduced by death due to fire. More importantly, fire causes changes in the composition and structure of the vegetation, and animal communities respond to these changes.

Although several explanations are possible, the oak forests appear to out-compete the pines in the absence of severe fire (McCormick, 1970). This change in canopy vegetation strongly influences the communities of animals (primarily herbivorous insects) that feed on oaks versus those which feed on pines, as well as the insectivorous animals that forage in these trees. Gula (1977) examined the number of individuals and the biomass of arthropods in pine and oak forest plots and found marked differences in abundance and biomass in the different sites throughout the summer (Fig. 1). A large early peak of arthropod numbers and biomass in the oak woods was due primarily to lepidopteran (moth and butterfly) larvae feeding on young oak leaves. An early peak was not evident in the pine woods, although both woods showed increases in arthropod

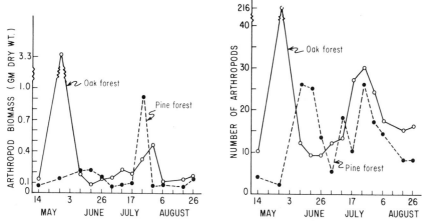

Fig. 1. Total biomass and number of arthropods on pine forest and oak forest branches. One hundred 0.3 m-length branches (30 m total branch length) were sampled in each forest at 1–2 week intervals from May 14–August 26, 1975. From Gula (1977).

abundance and biomass in late July. These different patterns influence the foraging behavior of insect-feeding animals in the communities by changing the rates of encountering prey. Such differences may be important in the timing of reproductive periods in the two habitats.

Fires which reduce understory vegetation but do not kill canopy trees result in different changes in animal communities. After such surface fires Urner (1926) noted: (1) increases in bird species which forage in open areas, such as eastern bluebirds, chipping sparrows, and common nighthawks; (2) decreases in species which forage in dense scrub, such as brown thrashers and rufous-sided towhees; and (3) little change in pine warblers, prairie warblers, woodpeckers, and gray catbirds, species which forage in areas that are not changed greatly by surface fires.

Frequent, low-intensity (prescribed) burning greatly reduces the litter and the cover of the two primary species of huckleberry (*Gaylussacia baccata* and *G. frondosa*) (Buell and Cantlon, 1953). This reduces the availability of huckleberry pollen, nectar, leaves, and berries, as well as litter cover for animals. White (1961) found, however, that upland small mammal populations consisting primarily of white-footed mice were not affected significantly by this burning. Over a three year period, mouse populations fluctuated greatly, but no increases or decreases in population density could be associated with these surface fires.

Seasonality

Temporal availability of plant productivity for animals affects community structure. Many plant species are deciduous, and the available food for animals thus drops in winter, accompanied by changes in animal community composition. As for most of the north temperate zone, seasonal changes in animal communities are marked. In the Pine Barrens, over 60% of the breeding, perching birds (Passeriformes) migrate south in the winter, and the number of remaining resident species is approximately doubled by winter visitors migrating to the Pine Barrens from the North. As in other temperate environments, most insects, reptiles, and amphibians and some mammals become dormant or hibernate during the winter, leaving communities very different from those of the summer months. The precise nature of these changes has not been studied.

Plant–Herbivore Interactions

Another set of factors becoming more evident in studies of animal community structure is the effects of physical and chemical deterrents on herbivory in plants. Although little direct evidence is available from the Pine Barrens, terpenes in pines, tannins in oak leaves, and many noxious chemicals in heath shrubs hold much promise as areas for future research in terms of their effects on animal populations. Feeny (1968, 1969, 1970) demonstrated the importance of oak tannins in reducing herbivory by the winter moth in Europe and in the temporal synchrony that had evolved between the spring feeding of the winter moth larvae and the availability of nutrients in oak leaves. The moth larvae grew faster eating the leaves prior to the production of tannins,

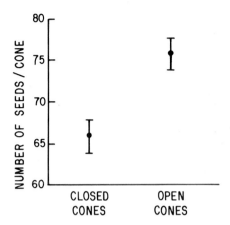

Fig. 2. Average number of seeds per pitch pine cone from Pine Plains and Pine Barrens. Closed (or serotinous) cones from the Pine Plains open at high temperatures; open cones from the surrounding Pine Barrens open at maturity. Averages adjusted for total number of seeds through analysis of covariance. Intervals are 95% LSI's based on error mean squares. From Tempel (1976).

which inhibit certain enzymes of the caterpillars. Gula's (1977) data for insects feeding on oaks in the Pine Barrens (Fig. 1) also show an early peak in insect abundance on oak which might be a similar response to that demonstrated by Feeny. Pine forest insects did not show this trend.

Tempel (1976) demonstrated differences in the relationship between sterile seeds (seed wings) and nonsterile seeds in closed and open cones of pitch pine (*Pinus rigida*) (Fig. 2). Closed cones are serotinous, i.e., open at high temperatures such as with fire, while open cones normally open at maturity. She hypothesized that the observed differences were in part an evolutionary response to the intensity of seed predation by the red squirrel (*Tamiasciurus hudsonicus*). The differences result in lower seed density per cone in serotinous cones. The seeds in these cones are exposed to a higher level of squirrel predation, since they are retained on the tree for longer periods. In addition, there is a greater physical deterrent to squirrels for each seed of the serotinous cones that they eat, since each of these cones contains fewer seeds than the same-sized open cone.

Resource Predictability

Environmental predictability also influences animal communities in the Pine Barrens. The predictability of the recurrence of fire in many Pine Barrens areas has selected for well-known adaptations in plants, such as stump sprouting, closed (serotinous) pine cones, and needles growing from the trunk in pitch pine. Similar adaptations to fire in animals, such as increased burrowing behavior in Pine Barrens populations relative to populations of the same species outside the Pine Barrens, or a correlation of breeding in herbivores with new growth of vegetation following fires,

TABLE I Foraging Height of Birds in Structurally Similar Pine Forests of Central America and the Pine Barrens[a]

Pine forests	Niche breadth (for foraging height)	
	$\bar{H}$	$\bar{H}/H_{\max}$
Belice, Central America	0.776	0.618
Pine Barrens, New Jersey	0.907	0.722

[a] Birds studied (the gleaning guild) forage for insects among pine needles and branches. Foraging height is expressed as niche breadth, a measure of the vertical interval used in foraging by individuals of the species present. Niche breadths are calculated in two ways: (1) from the information theory index of diversity, the average niche breadth $\bar{H} = -\Sigma p_i \log p_i$ = the proportion of observations in the ith height category, and (2) $\bar{H}/H_{\max}$, the average niche breadth divided by the maximum possible niche breadth. From Stiles and Orians (unpublished observations).

may be present in life-history strategies of animal populations; however, to my knowledge no studies have approached this question directly.

Climatic variance and predictability vary latitudinally. Stiles and Orians (unpublished observations) examined the response of bird community structure to different degrees of climatic predictability in the Pine Barrens and a pine forest in Belice, Central America.

In the Central American pine forest, whose vegetation structure was similar to that of the Pine Barrens, the diversity of methods and locations used for foraging by birds was lower (Table I). These differences probably are a result of the lower level of predictability of resources for the New Jersey birds. This has selected for the more general foraging methods that have evolved in the Pine Barrens community. Birds which forage for food primarily among the pine needles (foliage-gleaning guild) were utilized in this analysis because they respond to this structurally similar component in the forests and are directly affected by the availability of insects on foliage. Foliage insects are strongly affected by weather conditions, and the predictability of a set of weather conditions at a given time of year is less in New Jersey than in Belice, Central America. Although other factors, such as plant species composition, may influence bird foraging behavior, we suggest that Pine Barrens foliage-gleaning birds are more diverse in their foraging methods due to the greater unpredictability of their food.

Resource Distribution

The Pine Barrens provide a diversity of resource distributions for animals. These distributions may be appreciated through an examination of different environmental scales. An important scale is that of habitat-type distribution, easily seen by driving through the Pine Barrens. One passes through pine–oak and oak–pine forests and through pine lowlands and across streams surrounded by cedar swamps; the habitat discontinuities often are quite marked. A broader picture of the patchy nature of the Pine Barrens is apparent in the habitat-mapping of McCormick and Jones (1973) on U.S. Geological Survey topographical maps. Three major forces have created this

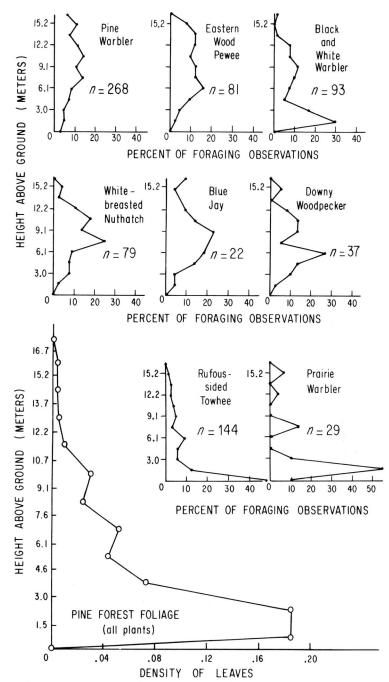

Fig. 3. Foliage height profile for a pitch pine forest and foraging heights of eight common bird species. In Lebanon State Forest; n = number of times the species was observed foraging. Foliage height profiles constructed using the method of MacArthur and Horn (1969). Foliage density is expressed as the average number of leaves above a point in a height interval. From Gula (1977).

TABLE II Distribution and Abundance of Small Mammals in Pine Barrens Habitats[a]

Species	Upland	Swamp[b]	Upland	Cedar swamp	Pine Plains
A. Number of captures per 100 trap nights					
Short-tailed shrew, *Blarina brevicauda*	0.12	0.43	0	0	0
Masked shrew, *Sorex cinereus*	0	1.44	0	0	0
White-footed mouse, *Peromyscus leucopus*	6.09	0.43	1.79	0.43	6.11
Boreal redback vole, *Clethrionomys gapperi*	0	2.76	0	1.57	0
Pine vole, *Pitymys pinetorum*	0.05	0.18	0	0	0
House mouse, *Mus musculus*	0.004	0	0	0	0.11
Woodland jumping mouse, *Napaeozapus insignis*	0	0.025	0	0	0
Source of data	White	White	McManus	McManus	McManus
Number of trap nights	24,000	3950	1400	700	1800

Species	Upland	Upland	Upland	Upland	Cedar swamp	Pine Plains
B. Estimated number of animals per hectare.						
White-footed mouse	1.0	0.22	1.93	4.75	[c]	11.2
Boreal redback vole	[c]	[c]	[c]	[c]	53.9	[c]
Source of data	White[d]	White[d]	White[d]	McManus	McManus	McManus
Year of study	1957	1958	1959	1969	1968	1969

[a] Data from White (1961) and McManus (1969).
[b] Low pine–cedar swamp.
[c] No estimate made.
[d] Average of five sites.

patchiness, that is, water, fire, and human disturbance. The patterns, in the sizes, shapes, and interconnections of habitat types, provide an excellent laboratory for the study of terrestrial islands, much as Forman and others have done in the Piedmont of New Jersey (Forman and Elfstrom, 1975; Galli *et al.,* 1976).

Vertical, within-habitat vegetation structure has been explored briefly as a predictor of animal community structure. Bird species in forests of pitch pine with oak understory used different foraging heights (Fig. 3) and different foraging methods (Stiles, unpublished observations) to exploit the resources of these areas. For example, the pine warbler, which gleans primarily from pine foliage, utilized the full range of the canopy. The white-breasted nuthatch, which forages from trunks and large branches, utilized primarily the middle heights in the forest, and the rufous-sided towhee, which often forages by digging with its feet, utilized primarily the ground layer but also foraged into the canopy. A diversity of types of vertical vegetation structure in the Pine Barrens offers many opportunities for study.

Community structure variations in response to horizontal habitat structure, or differences in habitat type, are poorly known. White (1961) and McManus (1969) studied small-mammal populations in various Pine Barrens habitats and found a distinct change in dominance from the white-footed mouse (*Peromyscus leucopus*) in the dry uplands to the boreal redback vole (*Clethrionomys gapperi*) in wet areas (Table II). The estimated mouse density in the upland varied from 0.2–4.8 per hectare, possibly due to differences in winter food availability. In addition, a high white-footed mouse density of 11 per hectare in the Pine Plains is striking. The resource utilization patterns that affect these distributions, the importance of rare species, and factors affecting spatial and temporal changes in density are poorly understood.

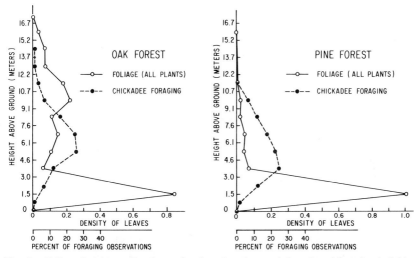

Fig. 4. Foliage height profiles for a pine forest and an oak forest and foraging heights of Carolina chickadees. Near Lebanon State Forest. Number of chickadee foraging observations: oak forest = 264; pine forest = 222. See legend to Fig. 3. From Gula (1977).

TABLE III Wasp Nesting in Habitats of Different Shape and Type[a]

Habitat type	Linear habitat patches		Large continuous patches	
	Total no. of com-pleted trap nests	Minimum distance (m)	Total no. of com-pleted trap nests	Minimum distance (m)
Oak–pine forest	6	135	19	715
Pine–oak forest (Site 1)	8	110	17	1230
Pine–oak forest (Site 2)	—	—	17	1100
Pine lowland forest	4	55	7	425
Cedar swamp forest (Site 1)	3	50	1	190
Cedar swamp forest (Site 2)	4	98	—	—
Hardwood swamp forest	0	70	5	210
Pine Plains	—	—	3	1320

[a] Sixteen sticks with holes bored in them were placed at each site in narrow-linear habitat patches and large continuous patches. Every 2 weeks from June 14 to November 1, 1974 completed wasp "trap nests" were removed and replaced by new sticks. Minimum distance is the distance to the nearest patch of different habitat.

Differences in the behavior of individual species responding to habitat differences probably are marked in these animal communities. For example, the foraging behavior of Carolina chickadees differed significantly between pine and oak forests of the Pine Barrens (Gula, 1977) (Fig. 4). Chickadees foraged higher in the oak foliage, and the difference primarily resulted from foraging height differences in late summer.

An effect of spatial distribution of forest habitat for wasp nesting is suggested in Table III. Sticks of wood with holes drilled in them were placed in several Pine Barren forest types, which either were narrow linear in shape or contained large continuous patches, and the number of wasp nests in the holes was recorded (Krombein, 1967). More nests were produced in the large continuous forest patches than in the narrow linear patches. The wasp nesting rates varied among the different habitat types.

CONCLUSION

Interpreting patterns in animal communities is difficult in any habitat due to the complexity and unpredictability of the environment. The New Jersey Pine Barrens offer a mosaic of environments which are relatively simple in vegetation structure and animal communities. In light of this important factor and the accessibility of the area, which presently receives relatively light human disturbance, the Pine Barrens should be a promising area for future study of animal communities.

SUMMARY

A rich literature on animal species in the Pine Barrens contrasts with the few, but useful, studies of animal communities. Water, fire, seasonality, plant–herbivore interaction, resource distribution, and resource predictability are suggested as the major controls on the nature of the animal communities. Fire brings about increases, decreases, or constancy in bird species, depending on foraging habits, while the absence of fire results in variations among foliage insect communities as tree species change. Temporal differences are illustrated by a late spring peak in caterpillars in oak forest not evident in pine forest. Spatial differences are seen as avian communities change vertically in the forest, and small mammal communities change horizontally with habitat differences. The relatively simple and homogeneous vegetation structure in the Pine Barrens is particularly useful for the study of animal communities.

REFERENCES

Applegate, J. E. (1974). The wildlife resources of New Jersey. *In* ''New Jersey Trends'' (T. P. Norman, ed.), pp. 243–266. Inst. Environ. Stud., Rutgers Univ., New Brunswick, New Jersey.
Barbour, T. (1916). A note on two interesting New Jersey amphibians. *Copeia* **26,** 5–7.
Beckwith, C. S. (1943). Insects attacking blueberry fruit. *N.J. Agric. Exp. Stn., Circ.* No. 472.

Boyd, H. P. (1973). Collecting tiger beetles in the Pine Barrens of New Jersey. *Cicindela* **5**(1), 1–12.

Buell, M. F., and Cantlon, J. E. (1953). Effects of prescribed burning on ground cover in the New Jersey pine region. *Ecology* **34**, 520–528.

Burger, J. W. (1934). The hibernation habits of the rattlesnake in the New Jersey Pine Barrens. *Copeia* **3**, 142.

Comegys, G. R., and Schmitt, J. B. (1966). A list of the Thysanoptera or thrips of New Jersey. *J. N.Y. Entomol. Soc.* **73**, 195–222.

Comstock, W. P. (1940). Butterflies of New Jersey: List of the Lepidoptera, suborder Rhopalacera occurring in the state of New Jersey giving time of flight, food plants, records of capture with locality and data. *J. N.Y. Entomol. Soc.* **48**, 47–84.

Conant, R. (1943). The milk snakes of the Atlantic coastal plain. *Proc. N. Engl. Zool. Club* **22**, 3–24.

Conant, R. (1946). Intergradations among ring-necked snakes from southern New Jersey and the Del-Mar-Va peninsula. *Bull. Chicago Acad. Sci.* **7**, 473–482.

Conant, R. (1962). Notes on the distribution of reptiles and amphibians in the Pine Barrens of southern New Jersey. *N.J. Nat. News* **17**, 16–21.

Conant, R., and Bailey, R. M. (1936). Some herpetological records from Monmouth and Ocean Counties, New Jersey. *Occas. Pap. Mus. Zool. Univ. Mich.* **328**, 1–10.

Connor, P. F. (1953). Notes on the mammals of a New Jersey Pine Barrens area. *J. Mammal.* **34**, 227–235.

Connor, P. F. (1959). The boglemming, *Synaptomys cooperi,* in southern New Jersey. *Publ. Mus., Mich. State Univ., Biol. Ser.* **1**, 165–248.

Cope, E. D. (1883). The fishes of the Batsto River, N.J. *Proc. Acad. Nat. Sci. Philadelphia* **35**, 132–133.

Darlington, E. T. (1952). Notes on blueberry Lepidoptera in New Jersey. *Trans. Am. Entomol. Soc.* **78**, 33–57.

Davis, W. T. (1907). Additional observation of *Hyla andersoni* and *Rana virgatipes* in New Jersey. *Am. Nat.* **41**, 49–51.

Engelhardt, G. P. (1916). An unusually large pine snake from New Jersey. *Copeia* **26**, 7–8.

Feeny, P. P. (1968). Effects of oak leaf tannins on larval growth of the winter moth *Operophtera brumata.* *J. Insect Physiol.* **14**, 805–817.

Feeny, P. P. (1969). Inhibitory effect of oak leaf tannins on the hydrolysis of proteins by trypsin. *Phytochemistry* **8**, 2119–2126.

Feeny, P. P. (1970). Seasonal changes in oak leaf tannins and nutrients as a cause of spring feeding by winter moth caterpillars. *Ecology* **51**, 565–581.

Forman, R. T. T., and Elfstrom, B. A. (1975). Forest structure comparison of Hutcheson Memorial Forest and eight old woods on the New Jersey Piedmont. *William L. Hutcheson Mem. For. Bull.* **3**, 44–51.

Fowler, H. W. (1905). The sphagnum frog of New Jersey—*Rana virgatipes* Cope. *Proc. Acad. Nat. Sci. Philadelphia* **57**, 662–664.

Fowler, H. W. (1952). A list of the fishes of New Jersey with offshore species. *Proc. Acad. Nat. Sci. Philadelphia* **104**, 89–151.

Galli, A. E., Leck, C. F., and Forman, R. T. T. (1976). Avian distribution patterns in forest islands of different sizes in central New Jersey. *Auk* **93**, 356–364.

Gosner, K. L., and Black, I. H. (1957). The effects of acidity on the development and hatching of New Jersey frogs. *Ecology* **38**, 256–262.

Gula, T. M. (1977). Foraging patterns of the Carolina chickadee (*Parus carolinensis*) compared in oak and pine forests of the New Jersey Pine Barrens. M.S. Thesis, Rutgers Univ., New Brunswick, New Jersey.

Kauffeld, C. F. (1935). The scarlet snake, *Cemophora coccinea,* in southern New Jersey. *Copeia* **4**, 191.

Krombein, K. V. (1967). "Trap-Nesting Wasps and Bees: Life Histories, Nests and Associates." Smithson. Press, Washington, D.C.

Leonard, M. D. (1956). A preliminary list of the aphids of New Jersey. *J. N.Y. Entomol. Soc.* **64**, 99–124.

Little, S., and Somes, H. A. (1951). Deer browsing in New Jersey handicaps pine seedlings. *U.S. For. Serv., Northeast. For. Exp. Stn., Res. Note* No. 2, 3–4.

MacArthur, R. H., and Horn, H. S. (1969). Foliage profile by vertical measurements. *Ecology* **50**, 802–804.

McCormick, J. (1970). The Pine Barrens: A preliminary ecological inventory. *N.J. State Mus., Res. Rep.* No. 2.

McCormick, J., and Andresen, J. W. (1961). Infestation of pitch and shortleaf pines by the red pine sawfly in southern New Jersey. *Am. Mus. Novit.* No. 2032, 1-6.

McCormick, J., and Jones, L. (1973). The Pine Barrens: Vegetation geography. *N.J. State Mus., Res. Rep.* No. 3.

McManus, J. J. (1969). Small mammal studies report for spring and summer 1969. Fairleigh-Dickinson Univ., Madison, New Jersey. (Unpublished report.)

Marucci, P. E. (1947). A leaf hopper survey in blueberry fields. *Proc. Annu. Blueberry Open House* 16, 3-5.

Marucci, P. E. (1966). Blueberry insects and their control. *In* "Blueberry Culture" (P. Eck and N. Childers, eds.), pp. 199-235. Rutgers Univ. Press, New Brunswick, New Jersey.

Marucci, P. E., and Moulter, H. J. (1963). Biological and integrated control of cranberry insects. *Cranberries* 35, 8-12.

Marucci, P. E., and Moulter, H. J. (1971). Oxygen deficiency kills cranberry insects. *Cranberries* 35, 13-15.

Reed, C. F. (1957). *Rana virgatipes* in southern Maryland, with notes upon its home range from New Jersey to Georgia. *Herpetologica* 13, 137-138.

Root, R. B. (1967). The niche exploitation pattern of the blue-gray gnatcatcher. *Ecol. Monogr.* 37, 317-350.

Stone, W. (1890). Pennsylvania and New Jersey spiders of the family Lycosidae. *Proc. Acad. Nat. Sci. Philadelphia* 42(3), 420-434.

Storer, R. W. (1940). The hoary bat in New Jersey. *J. Mammal.* 21, 354-355.

Tempel, A. S. (1976). Racial differences in cone characteristics of *Pinus rigida* in relation to seed predation by the red squirrel (*Tamiasciurus hudsonicus*). M.S. Thesis, Rutgers Univ., New Brunswick, New Jersey.

Tomlinson, W. E., Jr. (1948). Seven important blueberry insects. *Proc. Annu. Blueberry Open House* 17, 10-13.

Tomlinson, W. E., Jr. (1961). Berry fruitworm (*Acrobusis vaccinnii*) and its control. *Cranberries* 25, 12-13.

Tomlinson, W. E., Jr. (1968). A new cranberry cutworm and other insects of 1967. *Cranberries* 32, 15-16.

Trapido, H. (1937). "The snakes of New Jersey: A guide." Newark Mus. Publ., Newark, New Jersey.

Urner, C. A. (1926). Effect of fires on Pine Barrens bird life. *Auk* 43, 558-559.

Weiss, H. B., and West, E. (1924). Insects and plants of a dry woods in the Pine Barrens of New Jersey. *Ecology* 5, 241-253.

White, J. E. (1961). The effect of control burning on small mammal populations of the New Jersey Pine Barrens. Ph.D. Thesis, Rutgers Univ., New Brunswick, New Jersey.

Wolgast, L. J. (1973). Mast production in scrub oak on the coastal plain in New Jersey. Ph.D. Thesis, Rutgers Univ., New Brunswick, New Jersey.

Part VII

CONCLUSION

32

Ecological Research Opportunities in the New Jersey Pine Barrens

WILLIAM A. REINERS

The purpose of this chapter is to outline areas of research for which the Pine Barrens are appropriate that have not been performed or previously suggested by my fellow authors. I make no special claims for insight or prescience; omissions will be obvious to any thoughtful reader. The base of ideas presented has been broadened by the assistance of Richard T. T. Forman and a number of Murray F. Buell's students and associates, who at some time have done research in the Pine Barrens. Unless otherwise noted, reference to the ideas of these contributors, who are listed at the end of this article, is from personal communication. Where no credit is given, responsibility for the research suggestion lies with the author.

IDEAS FOR HISTORICAL ANALYSIS OF THE PINE BARRENS

Biogeographical and paleoecological questions are particularly intriguing for this region. Unfortunately, the lack of natural lakes and their sediments makes satisfactory historical analyses of the Pine Barrens difficult, particularly with regard to conditions during the Pleistocene ice age. Heusser (Chapter 12, this volume) suggests, however, where we might best look for more information on some critical questions of paleoecology.

Historical interpretation of the New Jersey Coastal Plain still is open to refinement. For example, some geologists suspect that Cohansey sand, a dominant geological surface formation in the area, actually is a deposit whose origin is much younger than Tertiary. If this were true, it would have profound implications for the historical interpretation of the geology, soils, and biota of the region.

Several suggestions concern human history in the Pine Barrens. Levin suggested that careful analysis of land ownership and land use since colonial times would be valuable in interpreting historical factors underlying today's modified ecosystems. Forman noted many references to an agriculture much more widespread than today's. Cattle-grazing in savannalike areas apparently was common. Were these savannas relics of precolonial fire patterns, or were they responses to agricultural management? To what degree did present forests regenerate from "old field" succession, rather than from cutting and burning episodes? Some careful historical studies of land use, well dispersed throughout the Pine Barrens, might provide us with new insights on such questions.

Laycock suggested the value of a social anthropological study of the "Pineys," natives who have developed a somewhat unique subculture in the Pine Barrens. A study of the reciprocal effects of a population and a special environment could be of wide interest.

IDEAS FOR THE STUDY OF POPULATIONS

Genetics

Quinn asked whether ecotypic variation might be found within species of the adjacent Inner and Outer Coastal Plains, and whether such differentiation might exist between uplands and lowlands or between high-frequency, and low-frequency-burn areas. If such differentiation exists, then the Pine Barrens has a much wider genetic diversity than vegetation data suggest and a higher degree of evolutionary "fine-tuning" than we realize.

Similarly, we might ask whether Pine Barrens trees are genetically selected for smaller size, shorter life span, greater sprouting capacity, and greater sexual precocity than populations of the same species in neighboring, less fire-prone environments. In other words, the same conclusions drawn by Good and Good (1975) for differences between Pine Plains and Pine Barrens' populations can be extended hypothetically to differences between the Pine Barrens and the more moist sections of New Jersey and adjacent Pennsylvania. Certainly, frequent fires would select for such characters as sexual precocity. Little and Ledig in this volume present ample evidence for genetic differentiation in pitch pine (*Pinus rigida*). Oak species could be similarly variable. If Pine Barrens populations are relatively limited by genetic factors in duration of maximum growth, maximum size, and life span, then the answer to the perennial question of how productivity is limited in the Pine Barrens may not revolve around water or nutrients directly, but around the genetic characteristics controlling growth that are selected by frequent fire. This hypothesis is testable by the approach of Good and Good (1975; see also Good *et al.*, Chapter 16, this volume).

Levin suggested that, since European settlement, cutting, agriculture, and other disturbances probably have altered the gene pools of sexually reproducing species, and that introgressive hybridization of oaks in 300 years may have exacerbated the confusing picture in that genus. In a related concern, Schlauch indicated that introductions of nonindigenous plants and animals by governmental forestry and conservation agencies may have adverse effects upon the integrity of local gene pools and community structures. Forman noted that interbreeding of introduced species with a native species may lead to extinction of the native species in its native genetic form, even though the species may continue in a modified genetic form.

Life History and Evolutionary Strategies

Several consultants cited the value of detailed studies of individual species. For example, Cantlon wrote:

> In terms of herbaceous plants the hemi-parasites, especially *Melampyrum lineare* remain of interest. We did some work on growing the various races of this species and found that the New Jersey/Long Island pine barrens populations show substantial differences from Northern Michigan, New England and Southern Appalachian populations. I've wondered whether the striking, long internodes and high anthocyanin that marked these New Jersey plants were associated with major ecological adaptive traits. Also, we were able to make a pretty good case that Michigan population levels of this annual parasite are in part determined by seed eating insect "predator" levels. I suspect the same is true there and wonder if the structure of the interactive web shows any major differences.
>
> This question is somewhat beyond the 'gee whiz' level of interest in two levels. First, man is altering the remaining natural ecosystems of the earth at an accelerating rate. It becomes of interest to get a better understanding of some of the regulatory mechanisms in the more simple interactive webs of ecosystems which are relatively self-contained, i.e., dependent on recycling of the soil nutrient pools. If we can begin to understand the population dynamics of some of the characteristic species we may get a better fix on what would tend to produce instability and what tends to dampen oscillations. In a word, how much redundancy is there in stability generating mechanisms of simple ecosystems? Or how big is the 'safety factor' resisting system collapse?
>
> At a second level this green plant hemi-parasite is more like a lemming than an autotrophic green plant, i.e., it requires host root systems. Are its population dynamics basically different from autotrophs or not? It is of some interest that most annuals are restricted to disturbed sites in the pine barrens. *Melampyrum* is one of the few annuals which is a common herb in the thick humus-root mat of the stable forest floor. What does this tell us about adaptation and the annual life form?

Bernard urges careful permanent plot studies involving counts and measurements of individuals. He argues that information on seasonal and life history aspects such as the emergence and growth of new shoots, flowering, the death of old shoots aboveground, and the development of roots and rhizomes is of vital importance. Without such information, interpreting strategies of carbon allocation or adaptations to stress is difficult.

While organizing this book, Forman quickly discovered that almost nothing was known about the microbiology of the Pine Barrens. Even fungi, which effect major litter decomposition and play other roles in this acid region, have received scarce attention.

McCormick pointed out that our knowledge of the ecology of rare and endangered species (see, e.g., Fairbrothers, Chapter 22, and other Chapters in this volume), is only superficial, poorly equipping us to aid their survival. In fact, with the exception of *Vaccinium corymbosum* and *Pinus rigida,* very little experimental research has been done on common species. Some may be of horticultural value in the Pine Barrens. *Carex pensylvanica* may be a good lawn species, according to McCormick, and *Gaultheria procumbens* a hardy ground cover species.

Questions regarding strategies of energy acquisition, energy redistribution, and efficiency of water and element use could provide new insights, as seen in studies of Mediterranean-type ecosystems (Di Castri and Mooney, 1973; Miller and Mooney, 1976). What are the energetic costs of leathery, evergreen leaves? What is the physiological basis of the trade-off between evergreen and deciduous growth forms in the Pine Barrens, where, for example, forests with a deciduous canopy and evergreen understory grow adjacent to those with an evergreen canopy and deciduous understory?

IDEAS FOR STUDY OF COMMUNITIES

The following ideas concern plant and animal communities and proceed from specific to general topics.

Cantlon pointed out that old charcoal pits, relics of operations from colonial times to World War I, were easily detectable by the rich shrub cover capping the 18–25-cm layer of ash and charcoal bits. These pits may represent small islands of better soil moisture and fertility conditions and provide insight into limiting factors in a sandy environment. Their distribution and possible role as refugia might warrant study.

Forman has puzzled over the differences and distribution of "oak–pine" versus "pine–oak" vegetation. He raises the old question of the relative importance of successional time, specific fire history, or subtle differences in site quality in determining increase in various oak species. All are involved, but interpretations of spatial pattern rest largely on general observation rather than specific study. Could insight on the historical frequency of fire be gained from an analysis of natural and artificial fire breaks? Could a stochastic model be written to predict the composition of stands based on a combination of these factors?

Olsson and Forman (Chapters 14 and 23) described ground-dwelling, or terrestrial, lichens in this volume. These forms are reminiscent of more extensive mats of fruticose lichens in parts of the boreal forest. Brown and Mikola (1974) presented evidence that organic substances leached from some principal terrestrial lichens of the Finnish boreal forest inhibit mycorrhizal fungi and thus conifer seedlings. These lichens thereby maintain a favorable, open environment for their own growth. *Cladonia*-dominated patches might be investigated for similar interactions in the Pine Barrens.

The reader also will find a rich array of ideas on animal communities, niche theory, the importance of plant chemistry, and other topics in the Chapter by Stiles in this volume (Chapter 31).

A broader comparative approach for Pine Barrens research is overdue. The chapters by Whittaker (Chapter 18) and Olsvig *et al.* (Chapter 15) in this volume represent a genre of studies which raises new questions and insights. The Pine Barrens are part of a continuous Coastal Plain forest extending to Mexico. Variations on the New Jersey pitch pine woods extend south into the Delmarva Peninsula and on exposed ridges of the southern Appalachian Mountains. Variants have been studied in the nearby Appalachians of New Jersey (Niering, 1953) and New York (McIntosh, 1959). Similar, pine–oak and oak–pine forests of Long Island, New York have received considerable ecological study (e.g., Reiners 1965, 1967; Woodwell, 1967; Woodwell and Rebuck, 1967; Whittaker and Woodwell, 1969), and versions are known for the Mohawk Delta around Albany, the upper Hudson River, the Champlain Valley of Vermont, the Merrimac Valley of New Hampshire, coastal Maine, and Cape Cod, Massachusetts. No systematic comparison among these Pine Barrens types is yet available that might give new insights on the New Jersey Barrens. For example, a floristic analysis over this range would indicate whether the New Jersey Barrens are part of a geographical pattern of species change or whether in some quantitative sense they are unique. It might show whether species diversity varies over a continuum, or whether a gap exists between Barrens on glacial outwash deposits to the north and the unglaciated New Jersey Barrens. If the Cohansey sands are of Pleistocene age, as has been suggested (Widmer, personal communication), the impact of glaciation may have been as severe in southern New Jersey as in New England. How do the flora and vegetation differ between the rocky "pine barrens" of the Appalachians and the sand plain Pine Barrens? Many other questions concerning genetic variability, species ecology, fire frequency gradients, soil characteristics, and coevolutionary development may be promising at this scale. From an even broader, global perspective, e.g., as offered in Whittaker's chapter in this volume (Chapter 18), the possibilities for studies of convergent evolution may be imagined.

IDEAS FOR STUDY OF ECOSYSTEMS AND LANDSCAPES

Most suggestions for future research are for terrestrial ecosystems. Such little information on aquatic ecosystems in the Pine Barrens is available that we have only a dim consciousness of the streams and ponds of the region. Thus, one of the primary recommendations for future research is for ecological studies of these Coastal Plain aquatic systems.

With the exception of inferences we may make for the N.J. Pine Barrens from work conducted at Brookhaven National Laboratory, Long Island, New York (e.g., Woodwell, 1967), little is known about succession in the New Jersey Pine Barrens from an ecosystem standpoint. The classical paradigm of succession concluded by a steady state may not be appropriate. Alternatively, the Pine Barrens might be better envisioned as a quasi "pulse–reset" system, with fire being the reset mechanism returning an ecosystem to a ground state. To be meaningful, this reset must occur with high frequency compared to the time required to reach a steady state. Fire may have been, and still may be, so prevalent that all units of the regional landscape are in some stage of biomass accumulation (aggrading), only to be reset in relative flashes of time by fire. Fire need not be totally destructive to effectively act as a reset mechanism. If this model were descriptive of ecosystem dynamics in the Pine Barrens, the region might be fertile ground for other research questions requiring manipulatable, pulse-reset, forest systems.

In this volume, Wacker and Little (Chapters 1 and 17) described the exploitation of saw logs from pitch pines of the Pine Barrens at the time of settlement. This suggests that the Pine Barrens were exposed to light fires so frequently in precolonial times that individual pines may have grown to larger size and older age in less dense stands than are found today. Might such systems have represented steady states more precisely with frequent, but minor, resets by light fires? If so, the exaggerated pulse-reset character of today's Pine Barrens may be an artifact of fire suppression leading to less frequent, but more destructive fires. Has fire thus changed from a chronic stimulus to an infrequent stress?

What is the pattern of net ecosystem production (net accumulation of organic matter) through the history of a typical stand? How do the rates of accumulation over long time sequences compare with other systems such as budworm-afflicted boreal forests, frequently burned chaparral, or lodgepole pine forests? How does the length of the period of net ecosystem production relate to limiting resources or to average fire frequency? The dimensional analysis of woody plants performed at Brookhaven National Laboratory (Whittaker and Woodwell, 1969) provided allometric equations to estimate plant volume, biomass, surface, etc., that could be readily used in the New Jersey Pine Barrens, thereby facilitating related investigations enormously.

Assuming the pulse–reset concept of Pine Barrens ecosystems is appropriate, net ecosystem production should be positive for all units of the upland landscape except at the moment of combustion by fire. According to Vitousek and Reiners' (1975) hypothesis for the balance of nutrient inputs and outputs in such systems, outputs always will be less than inputs except for those brief periods during and immediately after fires. A sequence of stands in the Pine Barrens would be highly amenable to a test of this hypothesis using lysimeters in place of a watershed budget approach. Ballard and Woodwell (1974) performed a similar test with successional stands originating from agricultural abandonment, but the effect of net ecosystem production on the balance of nutrients was partially obscured by residual fertilizer effects. It is conceivable that, with careful characterization of nitrogen inputs and the sampling of deep soil leachates for nitrogen losses, an index of net ecosystem production or of the maturity status of the stand could be derived more easily and accurately than by estimating gross photosynthesis and net community respiration.

Symbiotic nitrogen-fixing plants appear to play prominent roles in early stages of primary succession in virtually all of the cases studied (Stevens and Walker, 1970). This phenomenon is less prominent and less consistent in secondary successions. Walker (1965) suggested that the early burst of symbiotic nitrogen fixation may be phosphorus limited; that is, the nitrogen-fixing systems are dependent on abundant phosphorus, and as the available pool is diminished by incorporation into new biomass and dead organic matter, insufficient phosphorus remains to support the nitrogen-fixing systems. This hypothesis suggests a relationship between phosphorus supply or supply rates and nitrogen supply, and thus with growth rate and possibly with potential maximum biomass. The analogy with eutrophication in lakes is obvious. This hypothesis is eminently testable on sufficiently scarified sites which would effectively represent primary succession.

The Pine Barrens also are suited exceptionally well to large-scale ecological experiments. The breadth of the interstream uplands, the large-scale sweep of fires, and the reasonably homogeneous soils and vegetation all contribute to a potential for large experimental plots, comparable to the agronomic plots of agricultural research stations. The existence of large tracts of public land and a diminutive forest amenable to easy manipulation and sampling also are noteworthy factors. Future research in the Pine Barrens should include the potential for large-scale experiments.

Turning away from questions directly involving succession, Stephenson suggested a test of a hypothesis relating diversity to productivity.

> In nature, plant communities vary widely in the number of species they possess (species richness) and in the proportions in which individual species are represented in the community (evenness). Recent studies suggest that, within a particular community, these organizational properties bear a predictable relationship to primary production (Margalef, 1963; McNaughton, 1968; Reed, 1973; Stephenson, 1973; Kroh, 1975).
>
> It has long been assumed that utilization of an environment by several plant species is more efficient, and therefore more productive, than by a population consisting of a single species (McIntosh, 1970). However, as Harper (1967) has pointed out, most studies have demonstrated just the opposite. Margalef (1963) for example, noted that planktonic communities in high production environments were less diverse than those in low production environments. McNaughton (1968) found the same relationship between primary production and diversity in California annual grassland communities; experimental manipulation of productivity through fertilization (Reed, 1973; Stephenson, 1973) and diversity (Kroh, 1975) also bore out a generally inverse relationship between diversity and productivity within early successional communities in Michigan.
>
> The New Jersey Pine Barrens constitute a natural laboratory for testing the extent and applicability of these observations. Consisting, as they do, of a few dominant taxa distributed over a relatively uniform substrate, the Pine Barrens constitute a single community or association of species dispersed in a mosaic of units differing primarily in the relative proportions of their components. A test of the relationships among functional and structural attributes represented within this vegetational mosaic, independent of the historical factors giving rise to them, would make a unique contribution to the theory of community ecology, as well as providing a basis for understanding the dynamics of this important region.

Several major research questions involve biogeochemical (or nutrient cycling) processes. Little, if anything, is known about the geographical pattern of precipitation chemistry over the Pine Barrens region. To what degree is it affected by the sea? How important are atmospheric inputs to the nutrient budgets of the various ecosystems? How important are aerosol impaction and gas absorption in this region? How severe is the acid precipitation stress in a region already apparently limited by nutrients? Has the rate of nutrient leaching from the canopy increased? Are native organic acids in the forest floor able to buffer the effects of the strong acids in precipitation (Cronan *et al.* 1978)?

Is a measurable amount of nutrients derived from weathering of soil minerals in any of the soil types present? What nitrogen-fixing organisms exist in the Pine Barrens? When might such nitrogen-fixing systems be active through the year or in successional time?

Some evidence suggests that inorganic nutrients other than nitrogen may be critical or limiting to animal populations where energy sources are ample (Schultz, 1964; Aumann and Emlen, 1965; Weir, 1972; Botkin *et al.*, 1973; Arms *et al.*, 1974; Weeks and Kirkpatrick, 1976). Could sodium be limiting to some invertebrates? Might such a limitation vary with proximity to the ocean and its supply of sea salt? Might vertebrates be limited by sodium and calcium? If not, by what mechanisms do they ensure or conserve a supply?

Jordan remarked on the analogy between Pine Barrens forests and wet tropical forests, especially on podzol soils. In each case, litter seems to be the major source of nutrients for plants, while the underlying mineral soil seems to be principally a source of water and physical support. Jordan and his colleagues in Venezuela have produced reasonably convincing evidence for a direct connection between tree mycorrhizal fungi and decomposing leaf litter. While no such direct connections are known in the Pine Barrens, intimate connections might exist between decay fungi and mycorrhizal fungi. Is evergreenness among several Pine Barrens species adaptive for nutrient conservation as much as, or more than, for water relations? Is it possible that other nutrient-conserving mechanisms more obvious in the wet tropics, might, on close inspection, be found operating in the Pine Barrens?

At this point, I shall leave biogeochemical considerations to introduce a more general topic. Until quite recently, ecosystem studies have concentrated on "steady-state" systems (often overlooking the fact that they were not in steady state), and on isolated systems (even though this isolation probably was more a product of wishful thinking or convenient abstraction than fact). In the future, it may be more fruitful for ecologists to consider whether steady state can be considered only for a sufficiently large landscape unit or over a sufficiently long period of time and to study mosaic subunits in all stages of aggradation and degradation. The sum of these changes would equal zero change in mass (Vitousek and Reiners, 1975).

Perhaps it now is time for ecosystem ecologists to take the cue from their biogeography- and population-oriented colleagues, and investigate the significance of landscape spatial–temporal heterogeneity (Giesel, 1976; Hedrick *et al.*, 1976; Wiens, 1976). The more or less repetitive pattern of variation in the Pine Barrens, that is, the change from upland pine woods to lowland swamps, lends itself exceptionally well to investigations on the exchange of energy, mass, and biological information between landscape units. Ballard has demonstrated the reciprocal effects of upland and lowland ecosystems on their thermal and water regimes (Chapter 8, this volume). Litter, leachates, soil water, animals, and propagules of all kinds similarly may move across these boundaries in ways that may be interesting and significant.

One of the most elegant examples of such intersystem transfer is the demonstration by Van Arsdel (1967) of how, in the upper Lake States, descending night air rolls down gentle slopes into swamps of the shallow valleys. The wetter swamps have more residual heat in the peat soils through at least part of the night, so the descending air column is heated, rises, and recirculates back over the upland to descend and cycle again (see also Reiners and Anderson, 1968). The biological significance of this circulation pattern lies in the fact that white pine blister rust spores are carried upward from the *Ribes* plants in the swamps and deposited over the uplands, creating definite zones of blister rust-prone areas. This example simply illustrates one of the many ways that research on relations between heterogeneous areas may provide important new insights on ecosystem structure and function.

A final recommendation for future research is for large-scale analysis of land–water interactions from the watershed divides of the Pine Barrens to the sea. How do rivers arising on the Coastal Plain differ from those arising in the Appalachians or on the Piedmont? Are these differences significant to estuarine ecology at the river mouths? Do the sandy uplands contribute a special hydrological stability and chemistry to Coastal plain rivers that regulate riverine and estuarine processes? Is there a difference, for example, in the frequency and amplitude of flushing events? What is the effect of swamps lying between the uplands and rivers? What role is played by tannins and humic compounds that color the water of the Coastal Plain rivers in controlling light penetration, nutrient availability, and thus plant production in rivers? Does this effect extend into estuaries? The chapter by Durand in this volume (Chapter 11) touches on some of these questions. McCormick asked whether fires influence groundwater and eventually river water chemistry, a question closely related to the earlier discussion on net ecosystem production and the balance between inputs and outputs. What might be the lag time or the attenuation role of swamps in such an effect? Levin suggested that dams in the Pine Barrens withhold a large proportion of sediments that otherwise would feed riverine and estuarine systems. At least preliminary information on such questions is needed before proceeding to an analysis of intensity and spatial patterning of land use in the Pine Barrens region.

SUMMARY

This chapter suggests ideas for ecological study in the Pine Barrens that, for the most part, were not developed in the other chapters of this volume. The author's ideas are supplemented by many important suggestions tendered by the students and associates of Murray F. Buell. Research ideas are categorized into historical analysis, and four levels of ecological study. Several ideas concern gene flow and speciation in Pine Barrens populations while other studies are suggested in which the Pine Barrens are considered in the broader context of continuous biogeographical change, progressing from the coastal plains and dry Appalachian ridges of the South to glacial outwash plains of the North. Finally, ecosystem questions are discussed, particularly those involving biogeochemistry and large-scale manipulative experiments for which the Pine Barrens are especially well suited. Ideas for future research are biased toward ecosystem-level questions, a natural consequence of my personal focus. Another compiler could spin out an entirely different set, the nature of that set depending on his or her perspective on the discipline of ecology. Perhaps this particular selection should be taken only as an indicator of the wealth of questions remaining to be attacked and of the discoveries to be made in the Pine Barrens. In the pursuit of sound environmental management, or simple intellectual curiosity, we have much to do.

ACKNOWLEDGMENTS

Ideas for this paper were contributed by the following ecologists: John M. Bernard (Department of Biology, Ithaca College, Ithaca, New York), John E. Cantlon (Office of the Vice President for Research and Graduate Studies, Michigan State University, East Lansing, Michigan), Richard T. T. Forman (Department of Botany, Rutgers University, New Brunswick, New Jersey), Carl F. Jordan (Instituto Venezolano de Investigaciones Cientificas, Centro de Ecología, Apartado 1827, Caracas 101, Venezuela), William A. Laycock (Agricultural Research Service, Crops Research Laboratory, Colorado State University, Fort Collins, Colorado), Michael H. Levin (Environmental Research Associates, Inc., 61 Cassatt Ave., Berwyn, Pennsylvania 19312), Jack McCormick (Jack McCormick and Associates, WAPORA, Inc., 6900 Wisconsin Ave. NW, Washington, D.C. 20015), James A. Quinn (Department of Botany, Rutgers University, New Brunswick, New Jersey 08903), Frederick C. Schlauch (Department of Zoology and Physiology, Rutgers University, Newark, New Jersey 07102), and Stephen N. Stephenson (Department of Botany, Michigan State University, East Lansing, Michigan 48824).

REFERENCES

Arms, K., Feeny, P., and Lederhouse, R. C. (1974). Sodium: Stimulus for puddling behavior by tiger swallowtail butterflies, *Papilio glaucus. Science* **185**, 372–374.

Aumann, G. C., and Emlen, J. T. (1965). Relation of population density to sodium availability and sodium selection by microtine rodents. *Nature (London)* **208**, 198–199.

Ballard, J., and Woodwell, G. M. (1975). Succession and water quality: The flux of nutrients from natural and sewage eutrophied seral ecosystems. *Bull. Ecol. Soc. Am.* **56**, 37. (Abstr.)

Botkin, D. B., Jordan, P. A., Dominski, A. S., Lowendorf, H. S., and Hutchinson, G. E. (1973). Sodium dynamics in a northern ecosystem. *Proc. Natl. Acad. Sci. U.S.A.* **70**, 2745–2748.

Brown, R. T., and Mikola, P. (1974). The influence of fruticose soil lichens upon the mycorrhizae and seedling growth of forest trees. *Acta For. Fenn.* **151**, 1–22.

Cronan, C. S., W. A. Reiners, R. C. Reynolds, Jr., and Lang, G. E. (1978). Forest floor leaching: contributions from mineral, organic, and carbonic acids in New Hampshire subalpine forests. *Science* **200**, 309–311.

Di Castri, F., and Mooney, H., eds. (1973). "Mediterranean Type Ecosystems." Springer-Verlag, Berlin and New York.

Giesel, J. T. (1976). Reproductive strategies as adaptations to life in temporally heterogeneous environments. *Annu. Rev. Ecol. Syst.* **7**, 57–79.

Good, R. E., and Good, N. F. (1975). Growth characteristics of two populations of *Pinus rigida* Mill. from the pine barrens of New Jersey. *Ecology* **56**, 1215–1220.

Harper, J. L. (1967). A Darwinian approach to plant ecology. *J. Ecol.* **55**, 247–270.

Hedrick, R. W., Ginevan, M. E., and Ewing, E. P. (1976). Genetic polymorphism in heterogeneous environments. *Annu. Rev. Ecol. Syst.* **7**, 1–32.

Kroh, G. C. (1975). The effects of pattern on the relative yields of four first year fallow field species. Ph.D. Thesis, Michigan State Univ., East Lansing.

McIntosh, R. P. (1959). Presence and cover in pitch pine-oak stands of the Shawangunk Mountains, New York. *Ecology* **40**, 482–485.

McIntosh, R. P. (1970). Community, competition and adaptation. *Q. Rev. Biol.* **45**, 259–280.

McNaughton, S. J. (1968). Structure and function in California grasslands. *Ecology* **49**, 962–972.

Margalef, R. (1963). On certain unifying principles in ecology. *Am. Nat.* **97**, 357–374.

Miller, P. C., and Mooney, H. A. (1976). The origin and structure of American arid-zone ecosystems. The producers: Interactions between environment, form, and function. *In* "Critical Evaluation of System Analysis in Ecosystems Research and Management" (C. T. deWit and G. W. Arnold, eds.), Simulation Monographs Series, pp. 38–56. Cent. Agric. Publ. Doc., Wageningen, Netherlands.

Niering, W. A. (1953). The past and present vegetation of High Point State Park, New Jersey. *Ecol. Monogr.* **23**, 127-148.

Reed, F. C. P. (1973). Effects of chronic and single nutrient inputs on first year fallow vegetation in Michigan. Ph.D. Thesis, Michigan State Univ., East Lansing.

Reiners, W. A. (1965). Ecology of a heath-shrub synusia in the pine barrens of Long Island, New York. *Bull. Torrey Bot. Club* **92**, 448-464.

Reiners, W. A. (1967). Relationships between vegetational strata in the pine barrens of central Long Island, New York. *Bull. Torrey Bot. Club* **94**, 87-99.

Reiners, W. A., and Anderson, R. O. (1968). CO_2 concentrations in forests along a topographic gradient. *Am. Midl. Nat.* **80**, 111-117.

Schultz, A. M. (1964). The nutrient-recovery hypothesis for arctic microtine cycles. II. Ecosystem variables in relation to microtine cycles. *In* "Grazing in Terrestrial and Marine Environments" (D. J. Crisp, ed.), pp. 57-68. Blackwell, Oxford.

Stephenson, S. N. (1973). A comparison of productivity and diversity in early and late season old field plant communities. *Mich. Acad. Sci.* **5**, 325-334.

Stevens, P. R., and Walker, T. W. (1970). The chronosequence concept and soil formation. *Q. Rev. Biol.* **45**, 333-350.

Van Arsdel, E. P. (1967). The nocturnal diffusion and transport of spores. *Phytopathology* **57**, 1221-1229.

Vitousek, P. M., and Reiners, W. A. (1975). Ecosystem succession and nutrient retention: A hypothesis. *BioScience* **25**, 376-381.

Walker, T. W. (1965). The significance of phosphorus in pedogenesis. *In* "Experimental Pedology" (E. G. Hallsworth and D. V. Crawford, eds.), pp. 295-315. Butterworth, London.

Weeks, H. P., Jr., and Kirkpatrick, C. M. (1976). Adaptations of white-tailed deer to naturally occurring sodium deficiencies. *J. Wildl. Manage.* **40**, 610-625.

Weir, J. S. (1972). Spatial distribution of elephants in an African national park in relation to environmental sodium. *Oikos* **23**, 1-13.

Whittaker, R. H., and Woodwell, G. M. (1969). Structure, production and diversity of the oak-pine forest at Brookhaven, New York. *J. Ecol.* **57**, 155-174.

Wiens, J. S. (1976). Population responses to patchy environments. *Annu. Rev. Ecol. Syst.* **7**, 81-120.

Woodwell, G. M. (1967). Radiation and the patterns of nature. *Science* **156**, 461-470.

Woodwell, G. M., and Rebuck, A. L. (1967). Effects of chronic gamma radiation on the structure and diversity of an oak-pine forest. *Ecol. Monogr.* **37**, 53-69.

33

The Pine Barrens of New Jersey: An Ecological Mosaic

RICHARD T. T. FORMAN

INTRODUCTION

The authors in this volume devoted to pine barrens have provided a remarkable series of insights and information on both an ecosystem type and a specific landscape. As a conclusion I have chosen to focus on the concepts presented, using information as examples, rather than simply summarizing or synthesizing the information. By so doing, the treatment naturally will be incomplete. Indeed, I have attempted to select particular concepts, which, when viewed together, suggest additional patterns.

The following broad themes are mentioned at the outset. Human activities in the past and in the present are mirrored in today's Pine Barrens ecosystems. The sandy depositions of Tertiary age have been followed by soil alteration and migrations of floras and faunas during and following the Pleistocene glaciation to the north. Frequent wildfire, favoring pine over oak, has molded the vegetation. Water flows through a huge underground reservoir, and out of the Barrens in tea-colored streams and upward in evapotranspiration. Nutrients leached from scarce clay minerals move through the acid region until they affect organisms in the outside estuaries. The patterns in species composition, diversity, genetics, and trophic relationships are remarkable in several cases, but overall are broadly comparable to other temperate forest ecosystems. Vegetational patterns are contrasted in community type, phytosociological classification, and gradient analysis approaches. The New Jersey Pine Barrens show relationships with pine barrens elsewhere in the world, as well as having ecological interactions with surrounding regions.

Many unique and special characteristics of the New Jersey Pine Barrens make the area immensely valuable ecologically. These characteristics developed over varying lengths of time presumably were present before humans exerted a significant environmental effect. None of the characteristics appears dependent on human disturbance; all developed and are maintained by natural causes, including wildfire.

569

It is important that the New Jersey Pine Barrens be viewed as a landscape, that is, as a spatial and dynamic whole. A great deal is known about the vegetation, hydrology, soil, insects, fish, etc., but surprisingly little is understood about the spatial and chronological relationships among these components. The Pine Barrens constitute a mosaic, actually a series of superimposed mosaics, containing isodiametric, rectangular, odd-shaped, and long narrow patches of these components. Species, energy, and nutrients are heterogeneously distributed, and move from patch to patch through the mosaic. Viewing the landscape as an ecological mosaic or ecomosaic helps one to synthesize information, but also suggests a dearth of usable ecological theory.

descriptive portrait of the ecology of pine barrens; (2) to pinpoint and interrelate concepts emanating from diverse pine barrens studies; and (3) to examine the idea of an ecological mosaic in view of our knowledge of pine barrens. These are approached by considering the following: (a) the uniquenesses and special characteristics of the New Jersey Pine Barrens; (b) human impact; (c) time; (d) succession, fire, and stability; (e) water; (f) nutrients; (g) species patterns; (h) vegetational patterns; (i) similar ecosystems; and (j) interactions with surrounding regions. My perspective of the Pine Barrens landscape as an ecological mosaic concludes the chapter.

THE PINE BARRENS OF NEW JERSEY

Uniquenesses and Special Characteristics

The Pine Barrens of southern New Jersey are unique and of global interest. A similar combination of species and ecosystems exists nowhere else. The Pine Barrens are composed essentially of a single extensive contiguous forest. Many tiny separated patches nearby in the vicinity, and two main outliers near Alloway, Salem County) and Spotswood (Middlesex County), bring the total area to about 550,000 hectares (1.4 million acres or 2250 mi^2). Scattered elsewhere across cool temperate portions of North America and other continents are generally relatively small areas on sandy or shallow soils which might be labeled pine barrens, or pine heaths (Whittaker, Chapter 18, this volume). Although all of these areas have crooked pines and heath shrubs, their species compositions differ and generally are less rich than that of the New Jersey Barrens; similarly, a narrower range of ecosystems is encompassed.

The presence of pine barrens in a temperate deciduous forest climate results from the success of low nutrient- and fire-adapted species in invading and maintaining themselves competitively over the last several millennia on sandy unglaciated soils having low water- and nutrient-holding capacity. These soils subject the community to periodic drought and consequently to frequent fire.

The Pine Plains, dwarf woods which generally measure <3.5 m (11 ft) in height, are likewise unique in the world. These, however, are limited in extent to three patches of about 2500, 2400, and 100 hectares (6200, 6000, and 250 acres) located near the center of the Pine Barrens. The dwarf nature of the ecosystem is interpreted as primarily due to the high frequency of fire in past centuries or millennia. However, the reasons for the high fire frequency still are controversial; the consequences of high elevation, coarse soil texture, low soil moisture, and differences in soil ions have been proposed and, along with the simple probability of fire in the center of a wildfire area, suggest the underlying control by a complex of contributing factors. Evolution has provided Pine Plains species with many special morphological, physiological, and genetic characteristics which today help maintain the dwarf appearance of the ecosystem (Ledig and Little, Chapter 20; Good *et al.*, Chapter 16, this volume).

A small pine plains of 350 hectares (875 acres) on Long Island, New York is described. This region's species are of even lower stature, and only one oak species is recorded (Olsvig *et al.*, Chapter 15, this volume).

Many plant and animal species are in jeopardy* in the Pine Barrens. Two ferns, 37 monocotyledonous, and 32 dicotyledonous flowering plants comprise a total of 71 native vascular plant species in jeopardy (Fairbrothers, Chapter 22, this volume). This is 12% of the total native flora and a high percentage compared with the rest of New Jersey and the United States. The causes include both natural and human factors. The largest group of these (55%) has southern biogeographical affinities. Two breeding birds, the bald eagle and eastern bluebird, as well as several amphibians, reptiles, and insects are considered endangered species (Leck, Chapter 26; Conant, Chapter 27; Boyd and Marucci, Chapter 29, all this volume).

Beavers, wild turkeys, heath hens, bears, wolves, wapitis, bobcats, mountain lions, and possibly bison and moose have become extinct in southern New Jersey since the 17th century. Both beavers and wild turkeys have been reintroduced, the former attempt with success, but the latter with success unknown at present. Heath hens are extinct, bears and bobcats live today in northern New Jersey, and the remaining species live farther to the north and west.

Five vascular plant species as well as apparently several insects are endemic (native nowhere else) to the Pine Barrens (Fairbrothers, Chapter 22; Boyd and Marucci, Chapter 29, both this volume). Twenty-four vascular plants, some *Cladonia* lichens, 29 algae, and many insects were named new to science from Pine Barrens specimens (Fairbrothers, Chapter 22; Forman, Chapter 23; Moul and Buell, Chapter 24; Boyd and Marucci, Chapter 29, all in this volume). The area also is known for the large number of plant and animal species whose distributional ranges extend to the Pine Barrens and no farther (McCormick, 1970; see also all chapters on plants and animals in this volume). Most are southern Coastal Plain or mountain species (e.g., 109 vascular plants), although a notable proportion of arctic–alpine species extend south to the Pine Barrens (e.g., 14 vascular plants, McCormick, 1970).

The Pine Barrens also are remarkable hydrologically. The Cohansey–Kirkwood sands (of Miocene age) throughout the entire Pine Barrens region contain a huge aquifer of unpolluted freshwater, one of the largest on the continent. In size, this

---

*Species whose status is variously termed rare, endangered, threatened, undetermined, extinct, or possibly extinct.

underground reservoir is approximately equivalent to a lake measuring 5800 km² (2300 mi²) in area, averaging 12 m (38 ft) deep and containing 80.5 billion m³ (17.7 trillion gallons) of water (Rhodehamel, Chapter 9, this volume).

The levels of water flow from Pine Barrens streams control many characteristics of animal communities in the estuaries below the Pine Barrens (Durand, Chapter 11, this volume). Similarly, phytoplankton blooms and other changes in the estuary are prevented by the low levels of nutrients, including nitrate, in Pine Barrens streams. Finally, the Pine Barrens are the largest, relatively undeveloped "wilderness" located in the Washington-to-Boston megalopolis.

Human Impact

Human impact on the Pine Barrens has been heavy. A relatively small Indian population used the area in the 17th century, and widespread systematic Indian burning has been hypothesized, but the evidence is tenuous. Since European settlement, a sequence of overlapping human exploitations have had a major impact on the environment, in the form of lumber and fuel wood removal; charcoal, iron, and glass making; crop agriculture, real estate, livestock, transportation systems, and human-caused fire (Wacker, Chapter 1, this volume). In general, human population density has remained low. The nearby cities of Philadelphia and New York have affected the area by providing both entrepreneurs and markets.

The extent or boundary of the Pine Barrens appears to have been slightly greater in the 17th century and somewhat smaller in the early 20th century than at present (Wacker, Chapter 1, this volume; Gifford, 1900; Stone, 1911; Harshberger, 1916). These boundary changes appear to be due to varying levels of human impact, especially cutting and human-caused fire. A similar pattern is seen in the average diameters and heights of trees, varying over time from large to small to intermediate (Applegate *et al.*, Chapter 2; Little, Chapter 17; Wacker, Chapter 1, all this volume; Harshberger, 1916). Even the Pine Plains appear less fire-stressed today than 60 years ago (Stone, 1911; Harshberger, 1916; Olsson, Chapter 14; Good *et al.*, Chapter 16; Leck, Chapter 26; this volume). In the last 30 years effective fire control has been introduced.

Management today includes wildlife for hunting, fire control for forestry, provision of water for cranberry fields, and pest control for blueberry and cranberry crops (Applegate *et al.*, Chapter 2; Little, Chapter 17, both this volume). However, numerous other current human impacts are evident. Probably the greatest impacts are exerted by development of the land for housing* and the control of wildfire. Because the area was subjected to enormous impact for two centuries, the total immediate effect of human impacts today probably is less than at any time since the 17th century.

Disturbance of the landscape through human activities increases habitat diversity in the Pine Barrens, and several open habitats with higher species diversity would disappear without disturbance (Olsson, Chapter 14; Olsvig, Chapter 15; Little, Chapter 17,

---

*Note the extreme effect, for example, on the Spotswood (Middlesex County) Pine Barrens outlier, on localized areas in Ocean County, and elsewhere.

all this volume). Indeed, human activities have increased the types of vegetation in the Pine Barrens described by Olsson (Chapter 14) by 50%. Two hundred-seventy vascular plant species, representing one-third of the Pine Barrens flora, are nonnative species that have been introduced since the time of European settlement (Fairbrothers, Chapter 22, this volume). Introduced mammals, birds, a reptile, fish, and insects are common and often associated with human habitation. Species introductions may change the genetic makeup of native populations (Ledig and Little, Chapter 20; Conant, Chapter 27, both this volume) in addition to adding competitors. Introductions of nonnative insects, fish, frogs, herbs, trees, and other organisms continue. Without a change in approach, further human-caused changes in Pine Barrens ecosystems may be expected.

Time

Pollen deposits indicate that both oaks (*Quercus*) and pines (*Pinus*) grew in the present Pine Barrens area during the Cretaceous period, >70 million years ago (Heusser, Chapter 12). Across the western surface of the Pine Barrens, sands of the Kirkwood formation were deposited under marine conditions in mid-Miocene time. Limited pollen studies indicate that oak and hickory (*Carya*) were common nearby at the same time. Later in the Miocene, perhaps 10–20 million years ago, more sands were deposited, including the Cohansey formation, which today forms the surface of most of the Pine Barrens region. These sands probably were deposited in a partly dissected ancient subdelta plain which included stream, fluvial plain, deltaic, estuarine, lagoonal, beach, and nearshore–marine deposits. Oak and pine appear to have been the principal genera, although many of today's eastern deciduous forest genera were present, plus plants such as tree ferns (*Cyathea*) common to tropical or warm temperate areas today. Uplift of the land >5 million years ago has been followed by erosion of an immense amount of material. Some sandy deposits of late Tertiary and limited Quaternary materials remain today, generally as small thin patches, often forming the summits of low hills. Thus, an "inverted topography" is present, with older deposits in lower areas and younger deposits on hilltops.

During the late Pleistocene glaciation (Wisconsin), the ice front of northern New Jersey reached to within 35 km of the main Pine Barrens area. Pollen evidence suggests the primary genera present at that time were pine, spruce (*Picea*), fir (*Abies*), and birch (*Betula*), as in today's boreal forest (Heusser, Chapter 12). Geological evidence suggets the presence of a tundra or arctic climate at the time but soil evidence does not (Rhodehamel, Chapter 3; Tedrow, Chapter 4). Thus widespread tundra vegetation between the glacier and the boreal forest in the Pine Barrens region, sometime during late Pleistocene time, is possible but unknown. Oak, pine, and hemlock (*Tsuga*) were abundant after the glacial melt, followed by oak and pine during the past eight millennia.

A present disjunct distribution pattern of many animal and plant species (i.e., the Coastal Plains of the Pine Barrens, the Carolinas, and Florida) is related to the present distribution of suitable habitats. For certain species with limited dispersability, the pattern also may relate to northward migration during a postglacial warm period, followed by survival of remnant populations in these locations during subsequent cooling. Atlantic white cedar (*Chamaecyparis thyoides*) appears to be a new arrival, appearing in the last four to seven millennia following the thermal maximum of this warm period. An abundance of composite pollen, largely ragweed (*Ambrosia*), beginning within the last millennium suggests the effects of European settlers (or less probably, Indians) on the landscape.

The species of pine and oak present during this sequence are unknown, but they probably included alternating periods of northern and southern species. Also noteworthy is the ready hybridization of pitch pine with four southern species, all of which currently overlap its distribution in New Jersey (Stone, 1911; Ledig and Little, Chapter 20, this volume). With the additional presence of hybrids between three pairs of northern and southern snakes (Conant, Chapter 27), the region may be a significant zone for hybrids in eastern North America.

The Pine Barrens region has been part of a coastal migration route for both northern and southern species; its overall role as a refugium probably has been minor. Virtually all animal and plant groups include two major and one lesser components of species. Respectively, these components include: species widespread throughout the temperate deciduous forest of eastern North America; southern Coastal Plain and mountain species reaching their northern limit in the Pine Barrens; and northern species reaching their southern limit in the Pine Barrens.

Succession, Fire, and Stability

Succession is more rapid in the uplands than in the lowlands. In both cases, however, early herb–shrub stages usually are minimal, and conifers are replaced by hardwoods (Little, Chapter 17, this volume). The change, for example, from pines to oaks, causes sharp changes in many groups, including foliage insects, birds, small mammals, and mosses (Stiles, Chapter 31; Boyd and Marucci, Chapter 29; Leck, Chapter 26; Forman, Chapter 23, all this volume). Succession in an ecosystem may never reach the stage of hardwoods completely replacing conifers, since fire is so frequent and widespread. Succession in the upland leads to oak–hickory forest, but wildfires at perhaps four-decade intervals produce oak–pine forests, and more frequent wildfires produce forests of pitch pine (*Pinus rigida*) and shrub oak (Little, Chapter 17, this volume). Differences in the frequency and intensity of wildfires and the length of time since last burn have played the major direct role in molding the mosaic of upland vegetation. Fire frequency, in turn, is related to soil conditions and human activities.

Climatic conditions generally are most favorable for wildfire in the spring, although fires occur throughout the year (Havens, Chapter 7; Little, Chapter 17, this volume). Regional habitat diversity, particularly open areas, increases with wildfire. Exceptionally high fire frequencies of one- to three-year intervals produce major changes in the litter and in communities of soil arthropods, bryophytes, birds, lichens, shrubs, and trees (Dindal, Chapter 30; Forman, Chapter 23; Stiles, Chapter 31; Little, Chapter 17, all this volume). A high water table in the lowlands decreases the frequency of burning, and the generally long winding swamps of the Pine Barrens are the only natural fire breaks. Cedar swamps may be shrinking and hardwood swamps expanding.

Resistance to fire, the major periodic stress affecting ecosystem stability, is seen in some pine barrens species, e.g., thick bark, large underground root crowns, a basal crook in seedlings which protects buds, and deep root systems (Little, Chapter 17; Ledig and Little, Chapter 20, both this volume). However, recovery following stress is also high, as evidenced by root crown sprouts, stem sprouts, prolific seed production, rapid initial productivity, and few successional stages. Persistence of vegetation in the Pine Barrens, as a different indication of stability, exceeds that in northern New Jersey in the time scale of millennia (Heusser; Chapter 12, this volume). Over centuries, humans have caused extensive changes, although the degree of recovery today is of considerable interest. In the scale of decades and years, patches within the regional mosaic of ecosystems are highly dynamic, commonly undergoing major changes following periodic wildfire, while the total change is minimal for the Pine Barrens as a whole.

Water

Precipitation is relatively constant seasonally and spatially across the Pine Barrens, but varies widely from year to year (Havens, Chapter 17, this volume). Fifty percent of the precipitation input returns directly to the atmosphere as evapotranspiration, and 50% percolates to the groundwater reservoir (Rhodehamel, Chapter 9, this volume). From this reservoir, water either is discharged directly to surface streams or, moving at up to about 50 m (160 ft) per year in the geological strata, is discharged many years later to the downstream portions of major Pine Barrens rivers. Thus, average stream output per unit of land surface area varies by a factor of two, ranging from 36 cm water in the high inland areas to 84 cm water in the low downstream areas. Streamflow varies widely due to heavy rains during all seasons, but floods are of very local extent. The depth of the water table from the soil surface varies greatly, both spatially and seasonally, with the lowest levels recorded in higher areas during the summer.

An annual long-term hydrological budget relating water input and output (Rhodehamel, Chapter 9, this volume) is: Precipitation of 114 cm (45 in) = direct runoff 6 cm + groundwater runoff 51 cm + interception 15 cm + evapotranspiration from undrained depressions 2 cm + evapotranspiration from soil and groundwater 40 cm.

Evapotranspiration from lowlands varies seasonally and is increased significantly by heat energy blown in from the uplands (Ballard, Chapter 8, this volume). Thus, the spatial configuration of swamps or the relative homogeneity of the landscape affects evapotranspiration. The evapotranspiration per unit area in lowland swamps with trees is twice that of lowland shrub areas, which have higher rates than upland areas.

Nutrients

At least sixteen soil varieties or series now are recognized in the Pine Barrens. Most of these are either well to excessively drained or poorly to very poorly drained; relatively few are moderately drained (Tedrow, Markley; Chapters 4 and 5 this volume). The low pH of Pine Barren soils has contributed to mineral alteration in the Pine Barrens, especially in clay-sized material (Douglas and Trela, Chapter 6, this volume). Both the amount and the crystal structure of such minerals in part are dependent on the time since deposition in these sandy, unglaciated, geological deposits.

Nutrients are leached and taken up in different concentrations (Woodwell, Chapter 19) by dominant species with stratified root systems (Harshberger, 1916) and mycorrhizal fungi. Soil texture characteristics and nutrient contents vary somewhat with vegetation type in the upland glacial deposits of the Long Island pine barrens (Olsvig *et al.,* Chapter 15, this volume). Here, nutrient leakiness decreases progressively through the successional sequence without reaching zero. This process may be as much simple physical leaching as a process under biological control (Woodwell, Chapter 19).

Water from the aquifer (underground reservoir) discharging to major rivers may be broadly classified as a sodium–bicarbonate–chloride–sulfate ionic type, with high concentrations of iron, dissolved carbon dioxide, and carbonic acid (Rhodehamel, Chapter 9, this volume). Nutrient concentrations in both the discharge of the aquifer and in stream waters are low, although localized areas may show high levels (Rhodehamel, Chapter 9; Patrick *et al.,* Chapter 10, in this volume). Except in winter, streams are tea colored due to an abundance of organic iron complexes together with some inorganic iron. Bog iron accumulates at the bottom of streams. Both Pine barrens streams, and the estuaries into which they empty, are extremely sensitive to pollutants, including nitrate, from agricultural, urban, or sewage treatment runoff (Patrick *et al.,* Chapter 10; Durand, Chapter 11, this volume). The pollutants cause large algal blooms. Tracing nutrients from the original mineral alteration (plus atmospheric input) through soil, vegetation, lakes, aquifers, streams, estuaries, and estuarine organisms aids in understanding and predicting the role of both physical and biological processes, and the causes and disappearance of nutrient pulses.

Species Patterns

Major vegetation types in the Pine Barrens are striking contrasts in appearance and dominant species, and generally exhibit a high turnover in species from type to type. However, the diversity levels of most plant and animal communities are relatively constant throughout the region. Native amphibian and reptile faunas for the region are relatively large, while bird, mammal, and fish faunas are small. Introduced fish species, however, are widespread.

Plant productivity as the base of the food chain is rather low overall (Little, Chapter 17; Woodwell, Chapter 19 in this volume; Woodwell and Whittaker, 1968; Whittaker and Woodwell, 1969). Many herbivorous mammals largely depleted by hunting today are common and widespread (Applegate *et al.,* Chapter 2, this volume), while herbivorous arthropods are species which feed predominantly on oaks and pines (Boyd and Marucci, Chapter 23, this volume). In all terrestrial Pine Barrens habitats, oribatid mites are the major animal decomposers (Dindal, Chapter 30, this volume), complementing the predominant decomposition by fungi. Predatory arthropods, especially ants and spiders, also are generally abundant. The densities of all major vertebrate groups are relatively low, largely because of fire and the acid (low-nutrient) conditions, but a diversity of amphibians and reptiles suggests a reasonably complex food web. Stiles (Chapter 31, this volume) has suggested that plant–herbivore interactions and resource diversity and predictability are important controls on animal communities.

Mammal species include small insectivores, many rodents, and the large mammals, white-tailed deer and man (Wolgast, Chapter 25, this volume). The most abundant breeding bird is the rufous-sided towhee, with catbirds found in wetter areas and flocking species observed in winter (Leck, Chapter 26, this volume). Although dominated by wide-ranging species, the amphibian and reptile fauna includes two introduced species and ten species not found elsewhere in New Jersey (Conant, Chapter 27, this volume). Sixteen fish species are native to the Pine Barrens. Although tolerant of acid conditions, their success also is related to the sluggish nature of streams, food availability, and reduced competition (Hastings, Chapter 28; Patrick *et al.*, Chapter 10, both this volume). Dragonflies, damselflies, and whirligig beetles are common aquatic insects (Patrick *et al.*, Chapter 10, this volume). All soil arthropod groups, especially predators, decrease in diversity with increasing fire frequency (Dindal, Chapter 30, this volume).

Common stream algae include the red alga *Batrachospermum*, diatoms and other Chrysophyta, Euglenophyta, desmids, and other members of the Zygnematales (Moul and Buell, Chapter 24; Patrick *et al.*; Chapter 10, both this volume). Dominant species peak in different months during the year but, except for a decrease in winter, diversity remains relatively constant. Bryophyte dominants are acrocarpous mosses such as *Dicranum, Polytrichum, Leucobryum,* and *Dicranella;* these species, along with the dominant *Cladonia* lichens, increase in cover following fire, although bryophyte diversity decreases with higher fire frequency (Forman, Chapter 23, this volume). Bryophyte cover in swamps is very high. It consists principally of *Sphagnum,* but also includes many liverworts.

Pitch pine seedlings have produced the highest photosynthetic rates ever recorded for conifers (Ledig and Little, Chapter 20, this volume). Geographical variation in pitch pine is slight for physiological characteristics and for gene frequencies in several enzyme systems. Wood properties and other morphological characteristics vary geographically, but the only distinct ecotype is the low tree of the Pine Plains, distinguished by its cone serotiny (opening at high temperatures), cone production at a young age, stump sprouting, seed germination, and seedling characteristics (Ledig and Little, Chapter 20, this volume). Pitch pine is becoming in genetics a potential "fruit fly (*Drosophila*) of trees."

Vegetational Patterns

Each of three approaches in analyzing vegetation has provided different insights. Upland and lowland communities, controlled by soil moisture differences, were the principal habitat divisions in all three, although biogeographical differences within the

Pine Barrens are present (McCormick, Chapter 13; Olsson, Chapter 14; Olsvig *et al.*, Chapter 15; Conant, Chapter 27; Hastings, Chapter 28; Forman, Chapter 23; all this volume; Stone, 1911).

A community type analysis ascribes major importance to the dominant species, primarily trees, and recognizes few lowland communities and many upland communities (McCormick, Chapter 13, this volume). Pitch pine has an exceptionally wide moisture tolerance, and in the uplands the dominant heath shrub species are widespread. Thus, the major upland community types vary mainly according to the overlapping combinations of eight oak species, producing a mosaic appearance. The northern, southern, and western portions of the Pine Barrens also have different oak combinations. Fire, which often is limited by a high water table in the lowlands, is considered the major environmental factor.

A community classification based on relevés indicates that the Pine Barrens are characterized by six major vegetation types containing 19 community entities and 51 finer separations (Olsson, Chapter 14, this volume). Although the number of communities delineated here is slightly higher, they are extremely different, that is, few upland and many lowland communities. Since all plant species are considered in this classification, herbs, bryophytes, and lichens are relatively more important in determining communities. Human disturbance is essential to many communities, while fire and human disturbance together are considered the major environmental factors producing habitat and community diversity.

A gradient analysis mainly of the upland pine barren region of Long Island indicates a primary gradient from oak–pine forest to pine plains that is associated with a gradual decrease in both soil nutrient content and percentage of silt and clay (Olsvig *et al.*, Chapter 15, this volume). A secondary gradient from pine plains to heaths is associated with disturbance. Species composition and dominance differentiate the relatively few upland communities. Soil texture and nutrients are considered the major environmental factors, with fire and human disturbance as secondary factors.

Similar Ecosystems

Pine Barrens vegetation is distinctive for its strong differentiation of plant communities in an area of low topographical relief. Equally unique is the widespread occurrence of dry pine, pine–oak, and heath communities in a humid forest climate (Whittaker, Chapter 18, in this volume).

The upland Pine Barrens may be considered to be composed of pine heath, pine–oak heath, and heath (Whittaker, Chapter 18, this volume). Pine heaths are present in the humid temperate climate of northwestern Europe, where Scotch pine (*Pinus silvestris*) and heather (*Calluna*), heath (*Erica*), and crowberry (*Empetrum*) usually are major components (Whittaker; Chapter 18; Olsson; chapter 14, both this volume). In North America, pine barrens or pine heaths are distributed widely throughout the cooler moister regions of the United States and Canada; generally, however, they are found on drier sites with leached soils within those regions. Relatively small patches of pine barrens in the Appalachian Mountains and the coastal areas of New York–New England are dominated by pitch pine and some heath species of the New Jersey Pine Barrens, but lack many of the other dominants. Pine barrens or pine heaths elsewhere in North America are dominated by different species, but some Pine Barrens species also are found.

Pine plains may be considered either as an extreme form of the pine–blackjack oak (*Quercus marilandica*) forest (McCormick, Chapter 13, this volume), or a heathland dominated by heath and heathlike plants (Whittaker, Chapter 18, this volume). Heathlands in northwestern Europe and North America are widespread and dominated by many species. Alternatively, the pine plains may be considered as a pygmy pine woodland growing under severely limiting environmental conditions and may be compared to piñon–juniper woodlands in the southwestern United States, krummholz between tundra and coniferous forest, or a Mendocino, California pygmy forest (Good *et al.*, Chapter 16, this volume). The New Jersey Pine Plains remain an ecological keystone and an enigma.

Interactions with Surrounding Areas

The Pine Barrens are surrounded by salt and brackish water habitats to the east and mainly oak forests and farmland to the north, west, and south (Robichaud and Buell, 1973; Braun, 1950; Horn, 1971; Forman and Elfstrom, 1975; Buell *et al.*, 1966). These surrounding regions affect the Pine Barrens ecosystems in diverse fashions. From the east, saltwater fish spawn in Pine Barrens streams, and ocean storms deposit salts on vegetation and soil. Wind, primarily from the southwest in summer and northwest in winter, brings dust, haze, and precipitation, plus seeds, spores, and insects. From the south and north enter flocks of migrating birds, and over geological time, entire faunas and floras.

Conversely, the Pine Barrens exert significant effects on surrounding ecosystems and regions. The levels of water and nutrient in Pine Barrens rivers maintain environmental conditions and strongly affect productivity in the nearby estuaries and possibly the nearshore ocean. Several major streams with headwaters in the Pine Barrens flow westward and southward into the Inner Coastal Plain region of New Jersey and to the Delaware River and Bay. Regional climate is affected by heat and evapotranspiration from the swamps and extensive forests of the Pine Barrens. Birds breed and migrate south. Smoke, seeds, spores, and animals disperse to surrounding regions. In addition, other patches of pine barrens within and outside of New Jersey probably are affected by gene flow from the main Pine Barrens area.

AN ECOLOGICAL MOSAIC

An ecological mosaic, or ecomosaic, is an area containing patches of two or more ecosystems or communities, with a structure based on the spatial distributions of, and the dynamics based on the changes in, the patchily-distributed ecosystems and ecosystem components. The Pine Barrens of New Jersey and the Boundary Waters Canoe Area of Minnesota (Heinselman, 1973) are examples of landscape or regional ecological mosaics. Patchy fields, *Calluna* heaths, and rocky intertidal zones illustrate the ecological mosaic on a far different scale (Watt, 1947; Levin and Paine, 1974; Siccama, 1972; Allen and Forman, 1976).

The theory of island biogeography (MacArthur and Wilson, 1967), a conceptual and mathematical landmark in ecology, has been used to analyze patches in a terrestrial landscape. This theory indicates that species number on an island is in dynamic equilibrium, resulting from species immigration and speciation, less extinction and emigration (Terborgh, 1973). It also maintains that species number on an island is determined strongly by the distance from a species source (isolation), and the size, internal environmental heterogeneity, and age of an island. This theory was developed primarily from oceanic island patterns, and patchy terrestrial landscapes are enriched with the following additional factors that might be incorporated into the theory.

Patches may originate from several causes. Natural (Levin and Paine, 1974) or human disturbance may occur at a spot within an ecosystem, e.g., a small forest clearcut or a burned spot where the plants died. Succession within these "*spot disturbance patches*" normally follows, and the species gain gradually decreases until extinction rates approximate immigration rates, producing an equilibrium species number. A second type of patch, the "*remnant patch*," originates from natural or human disturbance in the matrix (area surrounding a patch), leaving an undisturbed remnant, e.g., a woodlot surrounded by agriculture, an island formed from surrounding inundation, or a patch of vegetation missed by a population explosion of herbivores. Assuming the matrix remains disturbed, evidence from oceanic islands suggests that such biological remnant patches exhibit an initial rapid species loss as extinction exceeds immigration, gradually decreasing until a species equilibrium number is approached (Diamond, 1972; Terborgh, 1974, 1975). A disturbance-free third patch type, the "*environmental resource patch*," results from the natural heterogeneous spatial distribution of environmental resources in landscapes, e.g., a wet spot, hilltop, or glacial erratic. A fourth type, the "*temporal patch*," also is disturbance-free and results from the natural sequence of changes in species distributions over time, e.g., patches of shrubs in old fields during succession, mixed flocks of post-breeding foraging birds in the annual cycle, or, in a diurnal cycle, various animal aggregations feeding at dusk.

Other special characteristics of patchy terrestrial areas include: (1) a generally much higher patch turnover than for islands; (2) a usually heterogeneous matrix surrounding a patch; (3) a wide variability in the relative discreteness of patches, that is, the sharpness of the gradient between patch and matrix (e.g., areas with no distinct patch boundaries, reflecting a series of gradients, may be heterogeneous without being patchy); (4) effects of the matrix on the patch, and thus the importance of differing kinds of matrix; and (5) the use of the matrix for species dispersal such that the matrix often is an ineffective barrier to dispersal, unlike a central characteristic of island biogeographical theory. Finally, in addition to species and species number, spatial distributions and flow of energy, nutrients, and allelochemics may play relatively larger roles in patchy terrestrial landscapes than archipelagos.

In view of the several substantial differences between islands in the sea and patches on land, attempting to modify or extend the classical and useful theory of island biogeography therefore may be undesirable. Indeed, a theory of terrestrial mosaic landscapes would be more satisfying if its basic premises incorporated the major characteristics of those mosaics. Thus, it seems logical to assume that a body of theory with its own somewhat distinct characteristics will develop and be related to several major areas of current ecological thought such as: scale and patchiness (e.g., Erickson, 1945; Watt, 1947; Kershaw, 1963; Greig-Smith, 1964; Forman, 1964; Levins, 1968; MacArthur, 1969; Monk, 1971; Levin and Paine, 1974; Weins, 1976; Whittaker and Levin, 1977); island biogeography (e.g., MacArthur and Wilson, 1967; Simberloff and Wilson, 1970; Diamond, 1972; Terborgh, 1973, 1975; Simberloff, 1976; Galli *et al.*, 1976; Forman *et al.*, 1977), ecosystem structure and function (e.g., Odum, 1971; Woodwell and Whittaker, 1968; Likens *et al.*, 1977), and evolution.

Some traits of ecological mosaics are suggested below, with possible examples from the Pine Barrens cited for most. I visualize the ecomosaic as a spatially based concept, with structure being the amount and distribution of characters at a given point in time, and function the flow and change of characters over time. The mechanisms driving these flows and changes are not developed here; in some cases they await empirical tests and theoretical modeling.

Species, energy, and nutrients are the three categories or groups of characters which are spatially distributed and flow through an ecological mosaic. The species category includes species, subspecies, varieties, ecotypes, races, and genes (and hence, gene flow). The energy category includes energy in biomass and dead organic matter as well as heat energy. The nutrient category includes elements, ions, inorganic molecules, and organic molecules such as allelochemics. In time, it may be useful to consider six conceptual categories, species, genes, organic matter, heat energy, nutrients and al-lelochemics, although the three broader categories probably are more useful at present in working out the spatial relationships. The structural and functional traits of an ecological mosaic suggested below clearly are only a preliminary conceptual framework.

Structure

Ecosystem Types and Components

These include the ecosystem or vegetation types present, with descriptions of their components, the trophic levels and characteristics of the nonbiological environment. Pine Barrens ecosystems such as pine–oak, bog, hardwood swamp, etc., are described in Chapters 13, 14 and 15 and several other chapters in this volume. Similarly, components of the ecosystems, such as geological strata, soil, shrub communities, herbivore communities, water, etc., are described in many Chapters of this volume.

Patch Sizes, Shapes, and Configurations

This subheading includes the number of patches present of different sizes and shapes, plus their spatial relationships to one another, e.g., the degree of clustering or regularity. It refers to both ecosystem types and ecosystem components, since often these are not spatially congruous. Patch sizes, shapes, and configurations are seen for soils, streams, the Pine Plains (Tedrow, Chapter 4; Markley, Chapter 5; Patrick *et al.,* Chapter 10; Good *et al.,* Chapter 16, all this volume) and in greater detail or scale for soil, geological strata, 1957 vegetation, and wasp nesting (see county maps cited by Markley, Chapter 5; Rhodehamel, Chapter 3, this volume; see also McCormick and Jones, 1973; Stiles, Chapter 31, this volume). Similar but limited information on geological formations, depth of the water table, and evapotranspiration also is provided (Rhodehamel, Chapter 9; Ballard, Chapter 8, both this volume).

Component Congruity

This is a measure of the degree to which ecosystem components coincide spatially. No measure of component congruity was made in the Pine Barrens. However, preliminary insight into the degree of congruity among several components may be gained; namely, between soil and vegetation, soil and geological formation, water table and vegetation, fire and vegetation, and among soil arthropods, bryophytes, and vegetation.

Isolation Barriers

Geographical and habitat isolation barriers are known best for gene flow but also apply to species, energy, and nutrient flow. Ledig and Little (Chapter 20, this volume) discuss the genetics and spatial relations of pines in the Pine Barrens, but no clear isolation barriers emerge. Cedar swamps often are effective barriers for stopping the movement of fires from one side of a watershed to another.

Function

Patch–Matrix Interactions

Described under this heading are the flows from a patch to the matrix and from the matrix to a patch. The matrix surrounding a patch varies from relatively homogeneous to extremely heterogeneous or patchy. Thus, patch–matrix interactions commonly may be different in different directions from a patch. Several Pine Barrens examples are suggested, i.e., the effects of uplands on lowland evapotranspiration; aeolian activity; upland fires, deer, and birds entering the lowlands; ground water flow from high topographical areas to peripheral Pine Barrens portions; fire and gene flow between pine barrens and pine plains (Ballard, Chapter 8; Tedrow, Chapter 4; Little, Chapter 17; Rhodehamel, Chapter 9; Good *et al.,* Chapter 16; Ledig and Little, Chapter 20, all this volume).

Patch–Patch Interactions

These refer to the flows between patches of the same ecosystem type, both near and far. These interactions have not been studied directly in the Pine Barrens, although some examples cited under isolation barriers and patch–matrix interactions may be relevant. Birds foraging among patches of a certain vegetation type or gene flow from the main pine barrens area to smaller outliers may be hypothesized as examples.

Patch Changes

These refer to the degree to which patches themselves change. Remnant, spot disturbance, and temporal patches may appear and disappear at various rates. Environmental resource patches usually are relatively permanent. These changes also imply that the matrix surrounding a patch changes, a process which may have important effects on the patch–matrix and patch–patch interactions. In the Pine Barrens, patch changes are seen in foliage insects, bird migration, seasonal fluctuations of water table, evapotranspiration, and algal communities (Stiles, Chapter 31; Leck, Chapter 26; Rhodehamel, Chapter 9; Ballard, Chapter 8; Moul and Buell, Chapter 24, all this volume), or for a longer term, glaciation, effects of nutrient leaching, fire, and human disturbance (Heusser, Chapter 12; Tedrow, Chapter 4; Douglas and Trela, Chapter 6; Wacker, Chapter 1; Little, Chapter 17, this volume).

Ecomosaic Dynamics

This is the total flow and change in the landscape, and integrates the patch–matrix interactions, patch–patch interactions, and patch changes. Glimpses of portions of the total dynamics are provided in the hydrological budget, chemical and biological characteristics of streams and aquifer discharge, geological deposits, soil maps, and the history of fire (Rhodehamel, Chapter 9; Patrick *et al.*, Chapter 10; Little, Chapter 17; Wacker, Chapter 1; Tedrow, Chapter 4; Markley, Chapter 5, all this volume).

CONCLUSION

The authors of this volume have focused on pine barrens and have provided us a feast of ideas. With this richness, the flow of ideas and information meshes into a surprisingly complete portrait of an ecosystem and a landscape. But frontiers are manifest and manifold. A perception of an ecological mosaic emerges, and its resolution is a challenge to scholars of many fields. However, protection of a remarkable area, the Pine Barrens of New Jersey, is a challenge to all.

ACKNOWLEDGMENT

I thank Michel Godron and David W. Lee for comments on the manuscript.

REFERENCES

Allen, E. B., and Forman, R. T. T. (1976). Plant species removals and old-field community structure and stability. *Ecology* **57**, 1233-1243.

Braun, E. L. (1950). "Deciduous Forests of Eastern North America." Blakiston, Philadelphia, Pennsylvania.

Buell, M. F., Langford, A. N., Davidson, D. W., and Ohmann, L. F. (1966). The upland forest continuum in northern New Jersey. *Ecology* **47**, 417-432.

Diamond, J. M. (1972). Biogeographic kinetics: Estimation of relaxation times for avifaunas of southwest Pacific islands. *Proc. Natl. Acad. Sci. U.S.A.* **69**, 3199-3203.

Erickson, R. O. (1945). The *Clematis Fremontii* var. *Riehlii* population in the Ozarks. *Ann. Mo. Bot. Gard.* **32**, 413-460.

Forman, R. T. T. (1964). Growth under controlled conditions to explain the hierarchical distributions of a moss, *Tetraphis pellucida*. *Ecol. Monogr.* **34**, 1-25.

Forman, R. T. T., and Elfstrom, B. A. (1975). Forest structure comparison of Hutcheson Memorial Forest and eight old woods on the New Jersey Piedmont. *William L. Hutcheson Mem. For. Bull.* **3**(2), 44-51.

Forman, R. T. T., Galli, A. E., and Leck, C. F. (1977). Forest size and avian diversity in New Jersey woodlots with some land use implications. *Oecologia* **26**, 1-8.

Galli, A. E., Leck, C. F., and Forman, R. T. T. (1976). Avian distribution patterns within different sized forest islands in central New Jersey. *Auk* **93**, 356-364.

Gifford, J. (1900). State reports on the forestal conditions and silvicultural prospects of the Coastal Plain of New Jersey, with remarks in reference to other regions and kindred subjects. *N.J. Geol. Surv., Annu. Rep. State Geol.* 1899, pp. 233-318.

Greig-Smith, P. (1964). "Quantitative Plant Ecology." Butterworth, London.

Harshberger, J. W. (1916). "The Vegetation of the New Jersey Pine Barrens. An Ecologic Investigation." Christopher Sower Co., Philadelphia, Pennsylvania.

Heinselman, M. L. (1973). Fire in the virgin forests of the Boundary Waters Canoe Area, Minnesota. *J. Quat. Res.* **3**, 329-382.

Horn, H. S. (1971). "The Adaptive Geometry of Trees." Princeton Univ. Press, Princeton, New Jersey.

Kershaw, K. S. (1963). Pattern in vegetation and its causality. *Ecology* **44**, 377-388.

Levin, S. A., and Paine, R. T. (1974). Disturbance, patch formation, and community structure. *Proc. Natl. Acad. Sci. U.S.A.* **71**, 2744-2747.

Levins, R. (1968). "Evolution in Changing Environments." Princeton Univ. Press, Princeton, New Jersey.

Likens, G. E., Bormann, F. H., Pierce, R. S., Eaton, J. S., and Johnson, N. M. (1977). "Biogeochemistry of a Forested Ecosystem." Springer-Verlag, Berlin and New York.

MacArthur, R. H. (1969). Patterns of communities in the tropics. *Biol. J. Linn. Soc.* **1**, 19-30.

MacArthur, R. H., and Wilson, E. O. (1967). "The Theory of Island Biogeography." Princeton Univ. Press, Princeton, New Jersey.

McCormick, J. (1970). The Pine Barrens. A preliminary ecological inventory. *N.J. State Mus., Res. Rep.* No. 2.

McCormick, J., and Jones, L. (1973). The pine barrens vegetation geography. *N.J. State Mus., Res. Rep.* No. 3.

Monk, C. D. (1971). Species and area relationship in the eastern deciduous forest. *J. Elisha Mitchell Sci. Soc.* **87**, 227-230.

Odum, E. P. (1971). "Fundamentals of Ecology," 3rd Ed. Saunders, Philadelphia, Pennsylvania.

Robichaud, B., and Buell, M. F. (1973). "Vegetation of New Jersey. A Study in Landscape Diversity." Rutgers Univ. Press, New Brunswick, New Jersey.

Siccama, T. G. (1972). A computer technique for illustrating three variables in a pictogram. *Ecology* **53**, 177-181.

Simberloff, D. S. (1976). Experimental zoogeography of islands: Effects of island size. *Ecology* **57**, 629-648.

Simberloff, D. S., and Wilson, E. O. (1970). Experimental zoogeography of islands. A two-year record of colonization. *Ecology* **51**, 934-937.

Stone, W. (1911). The plants of southern New Jersey with especial reference to the flora of the Pine Barrens and the geographic distribution of the species. *N.J. State Mus., Annu. Rep.* 1910, pp. 21-828.

Terborgh, J. (1973). On the notion of favorableness in plant ecology. *Am. Nat.* **107**, 481-501.

Terborgh, J. (1974). Preservation of natural diversity: The problem of extinction prone species. *BioScience* **24,** 715–722.

Terborgh, J. (1975). Faunal equilibria and the design of wildlife preserves. *In* ''Tropical Ecological Systems'' (F. B. Golley and E. Medina, eds.), pp. 369–380.

Watt, A. S. (1947). Pattern and process in the plant community. *J. Ecol.* **35,** 1–22.

Weins, J. S. (1976). Population responses to patchy environments. *Annu. Rev. Ecol. Syst.* **7,** 81–120.

Whittaker, R. H., and Levin, S. A. (1977). The role of mosaic phenomena in natural communities. *Theor. Popul. Biol.* **12,** 117–139.

Whittaker, R. H., and Woodwell, G. M. (1969). Structure, production and diversity of the oak–pine forest at Brookhaven, New York. *J. Ecol.* **57,** 155–174.

Woodwell, G. M., and Whittaker, R. H. (1968). Primary production in terrestrial ecosystems. *Am. Zool.* **8,** 19–30.

Index